Great American Vacations

25 Affordable Family Trips
to the USA's Best-Loved Destinations

Fodor's Travel Publications
New York Toronto London Sydney Auckland
www.fodors.com

Fodor's Great American Vacations
Editor: Mary Beth Bohman
Editorial Contributors: Rob Aikins, Anne Dubuisson Anderson, Kristina Brooks, Laura Knowles Callanan, Joanne Cleaver, Robert Fleming, Elizabeth Gehrman, Maureen Graney, Paul Greenberg, Tom Griffith, Carolyn Heller, John A. Kelly, Christina Knight, Jack Kohane, Gary McKechnie, Carrie Miner, Ruth Mitchell, Candy Moulton, Kevin Myatt, Susan Reigler, Judy Sutton Taylor, John Vlahides, Mike Weatherford, CiCi Williamson, Sharron Wood
Editorial Production: David Downing
Maps: David Lindroth, *cartographer*; Bob Blake and Rebecca Baer, *map editors*
Design: Siobhan O'Hare, *art director*; Fabrizio La Rocca, *creative director*; Melanie Marin, *photo editor*
Cover Photograph: Patrick Molnar/The Image Bank/Getty Images
Production/Manufacturing: Angela L. McLean

Copyright

First Edition
ISBN 1-4000-1242-2
ISSN 1543-1061

Special Sales
Fodor's Travel Publications are available at special discounts for bulk purchases for sales promotions or premiums. Special editions, including personalized covers, excerpts of existing guides, and corporate imprints, can be created in large quantities for special needs. For more information, contact your local bookseller or write to Special Markets, Fodor's Travel Publications, 1745 Broadway, New York, NY 10019. Inquiries from Canada should be directed to your local Canadian bookseller or sent to Random House of Canada, Ltd., Marketing Department, 2775 Matheson Blvd. East, Mississauga, Ontario L4W 4P7. Inquiries from the United Kingdom should be sent to Fodor's Travel Publications, 20 Vauxhall Bridge Road, London SW1V 2SA, England.

Important Tip
Although all prices, open times, and other details in this book are based on information supplied to us at press time, changes occur all the time in the travel world, and Fodor's cannot accept responsibility for facts that become outdated or for inadvertent errors or omissions. So **always confirm information when it matters,** especially if you're making a detour to visit a specific place.

PRINTED IN THE UNITED STATES OF AMERICA
10 9 8 7 6 5 4 3 2 1

CONTENTS

v **GREAT AMERICAN VACATIONS**

v **HOW TO USE THIS BOOK**

Map Great American Vacations Overview...viii

1 **BADLANDS NATIONAL PARK, MOUNT RUSHMORE AND THE BLACK HILLS**

Map Badlands National Park...2

Southwest South Dakota...4

14 **BOSTON**

Map Boston...15

33 **CAPE COD**

Map Cape Cod...34

50 **CHICAGO**

Map Chicago...52–53

70 **GETTYSBURG**

Map Gettysburg...71

79 **GRAND CANYON NATIONAL PARK**

Map Grand Canyon National Park...80

92 **GRAND TETON NATIONAL PARK**

Map Grand Teton National Park...93

105 **GREAT SMOKY MOUNTAINS NATIONAL PARK**

Map Great Smoky Mountains National Park...106

116 **HOT SPRINGS AND THE OZARKS**

Map Hot Springs and the Ozarks...117

128 **LAS VEGAS**

Map Las Vegas...129

143 **THE LINCOLN TRAIL**

Map The Lincoln Trail...144

152 **LOS ANGELES**

Map Los Angeles...154–155

177 **MAMMOTH CAVE NATIONAL PARK**

Map Mammoth Cave National Park...178

187 **NEW ORLEANS**

Map New Orleans...188

204 **NEW YORK CITY**

Map New York City...205

225 **NIAGARA FALLS**

Map Niagara Falls...226

239 **PHILADELPHIA AND THE PENNSYLVANIA DUTCH COUNTRY**

Map Philadelphia...240

Pennsylvania Dutch Country...241

260 **SAN DIEGO**

Map San Diego...261

278 **SAN FRANCISCO**

Map San Francisco...279

300 **SHENANDOAH VALLEY AND THE BLUE RIDGE**

Map Shenandoah Valley and the Blue Ridge...301

317 **WALT DISNEY WORLD® RESORT, UNIVERSAL ORLANDO® RESORT, AND THE ORLANDO AREA**

Map Central Florida...318

338 **WASHINGTON, DC**

Map Washington, DC...339

358 **WILLIAMSBURG**

Map Williamsburg...359

370 **YELLOWSTONE NATIONAL PARK**

Map Yellowstone National Park...371

384 **YOSEMITE NATIONAL PARK**

Map Yosemite National Park...385

399 **INDEX**

Great American Vacations

A guide to the USA like no other, *Great American Vacations* is a vacation planner for exploring 25 of the nation's most beloved destinations. Since so many Americans are hitting the road—often with kids, parents, siblings, and sometimes the neighbors' kids in tow—this book pays particular attention to places that are easy to explore and fun for the entire family but that won't empty your wallet.

Inside you'll find all the tools you need to plan a perfect family trip to the nation's top vacation destinations. In the dozens of parks, towns, amusement parks, and cities we describe, you'll find thousands of places to explore. So you'll always know what's around the next bend. And with the practical information we provide, you can easily call to confirm the details that matter and study up on what you'll want to see and do, before you leave home.

Keep *Great American Vacations* on hand for all your travel planning—it's a great source of vacation ideas. Maybe your extended family always spends a week in July on the beach in North Carolina. Why not break up the return drive to Ohio with a few days in the Great Smoky Mountains? Perhaps your college roommate is getting married in San Jose. Take a few extra days to hang out in San Francisco. And there's always next year's trip to consider.

How to Use This Book

Alphabetical organization makes it a snap to navigate through these pages. Still, in putting these vacations together, we've made certain decisions and used certain terms that you need to know about.

ORGANIZATION

Each chapter contains a single, complete vacation. For each vacation, the Exploring section covers things to see and do in alphabetical order. Dining and Lodging follow, with suggestions for convenient, affordable places to stay and eat. Turn to Shopping for an overview of the best shopping areas, as well as for some hints on regional finds (like the speckleware made by Mennonites in the Shenandoah Valley) and original souvenirs (like surf-shop art in San Diego). Arts and Entertainment and Sports and the Outdoors are included depending on their importance to the destination. For instance, the Grand Teton chapter advises you on fishing and hiking, while New York City tells you how to get half-price tickets for Broadway. The Essential Information section provides logistical details—such as when to go and how to get there. Check out the Discounts here for great bargains and money-saving tips.

STARS

Stars (★) denote our editors' top picks for the vacation. Favorites include everything from sights to restaurants and hotels to singular experiences and beyond.

EXPLORING

Admission prices given apply to adults; substantially reduced fees are almost always available for children, students, and senior citizens. The exception is the Orlando chapter, where the admission prices for children are noted.

DINING

Assume that restaurants are open for lunch and dinner unless otherwise noted; we always indicate days closed. Reservations are always a good idea, we don't mention them unless they're essential or are unaccepted.

Prices listed are based on the cost per person for a main course at dinner.

LODGING

The reviews describe the lodgings and detail their facilities (such as hot tubs and refrigerators) and policies (such as seasonal closings and whether pets are allowed). We always list the facilities that are available—but we don't specify whether they cost extra: when pricing accommodations, always ask what's included and what costs extra. Also, be sure to ask about policies for children staying in their parents' room.

Prices listed are for a standard double room, excluding service charges and tax.

CAMPING

You'll learn what each campground has to offer, including facilities such as showers and fire grates, seasonal closings, and how much you will pay for the pleasure of camping out.

Prices listed are for a single site; prices for full and partial hook-ups and cabins are noted where available.

NATIONAL PARKS

National parks protect and preserve the treasures of America's heritage. And they're such popular destinations that no fewer than 9 of our 25 vacations are centered around a national park. If you are visiting more than one park in a year, look into discount passes to save money on park entrance fees. The National Parks Pass ($50) gets you and your companions free admission to all parks for one year. (Camping and parking are extra.) A percentage of the proceeds from sales of the pass will fund national parks projects. Both the Golden Age Passport ($10), for those 62 and older, and the Golden Access Passport (free), for travelers with disabilities, entitle holders to free entry to all national parks, plus 50% off fees for the use of many park facilities and services. You must show proof of age and of U.S. citizenship or permanent residency (such as a U.S. passport, driver's license, or birth certificate) and, if requesting Golden Access, proof of disability. The Golden Age and Golden Access passes are available at all national parks wherever entrance fees are charged. The National Parks Pass is available by mail or through the Internet.

National Park Service | National Park Service/Department of Interior, 1849 C St. NW, Washington, DC 20240 | 202/208–4747 | www.nps.gov.

National Parks Pass | 27540 Mentry Ave., Valencia, CA 91355 | 888/GO–PARKS or 888/467–2757 | www.nationalparks.org.

Bus and Train Information: The availability of train and long-distance bus service to each destination is noted.

Amtrak | 800/872-7245 | www.amtrak.com

Greyhound | 800/231-2222 | www.greyhound.com

Trailways | 800/343-9999 | www.trailways.com

Important Tip

Although all prices, opening times, and other details in this book are based on information supplied to us at press time, changes occur all the time in the travel world, and Fodor's cannot accept responsibility for facts that become outdated or for inadvertent errors or omissions. So always confirm information when it matters, especially if you are making a detour to visit a specific place.

Let Us Hear from You

Keeping a travel guide fresh and up-to-date is a big job, and we welcome any and all comments. We'd love to have your thoughts on places we've listed, and we're interested in hearing about your own special finds. Our guides are thoroughly updated for each new edition, and we're always adding new information, so your feedback is vital. Contact us via e-mail in care of editors@fodors.com (specifying *Great American Vacations* on the subject line) or via snail mail in care of *Great American Vacations*, at Fodor's, 1745 Broadway, New York, NY 10019. We look forward to hearing from you. And in the meantime, have a wonderful trip.

–The Editors

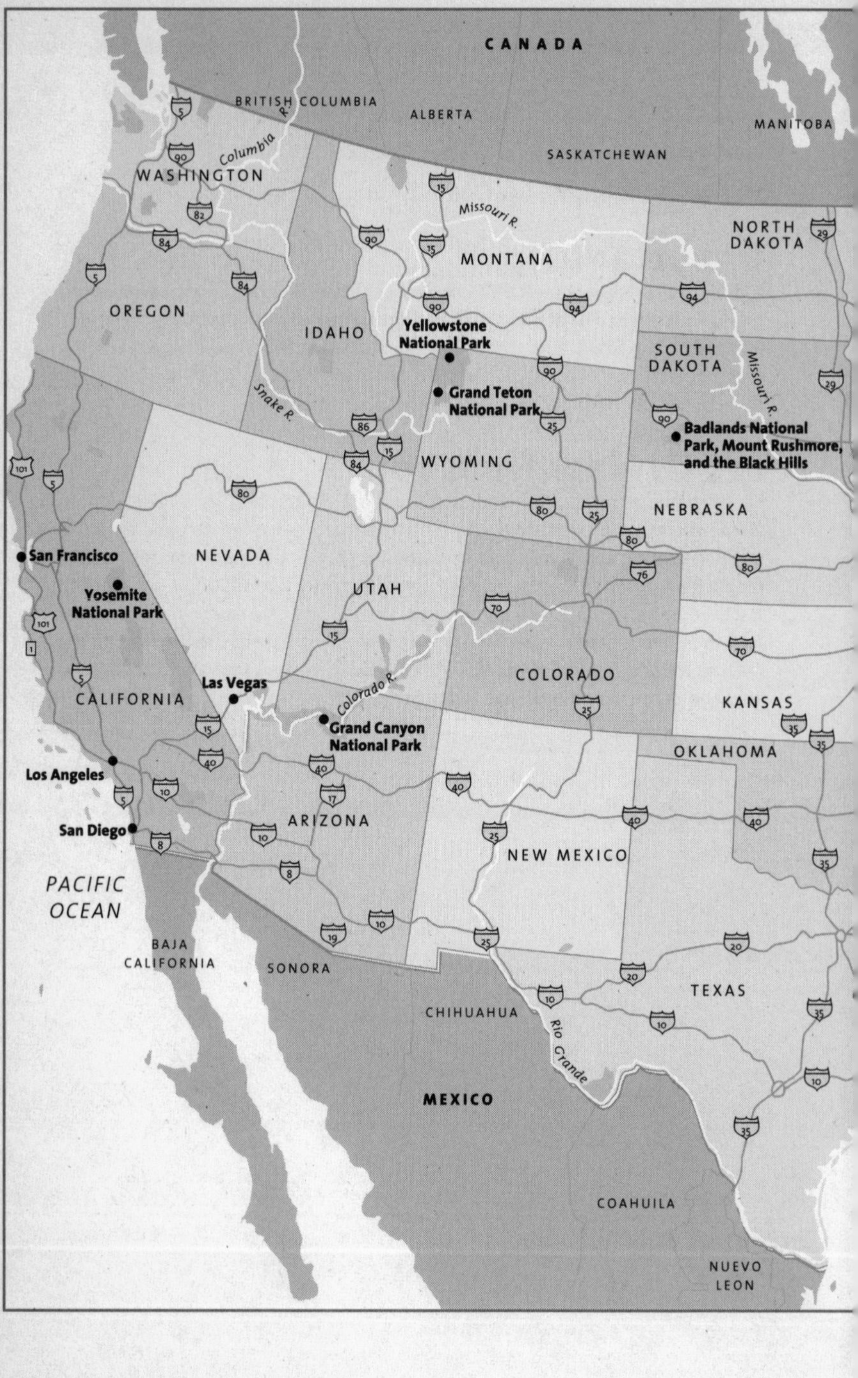
CANADA
BRITISH COLUMBIA
ALBERTA
SASKATCHEWAN
MANITOBA
Columbia R.
WASHINGTON
Missouri R.
MONTANA
NORTH DAKOTA
OREGON
IDAHO
Yellowstone National Park
Grand Teton National Park
SOUTH DAKOTA
Missouri R.
Snake R.
Badlands National Park, Mount Rushmore, and the Black Hills
WYOMING
NEBRASKA
San Francisco
NEVADA
Yosemite National Park
UTAH
COLORADO
KANSAS
Las Vegas
Colorado R.
CALIFORNIA
Grand Canyon National Park
OKLAHOMA
Los Angeles
ARIZONA
San Diego
NEW MEXICO
PACIFIC OCEAN
BAJA CALIFORNIA
SONORA
TEXAS
CHIHUAHUA
Rio Grande
MEXICO
COAHUILA
NUEVO LEON

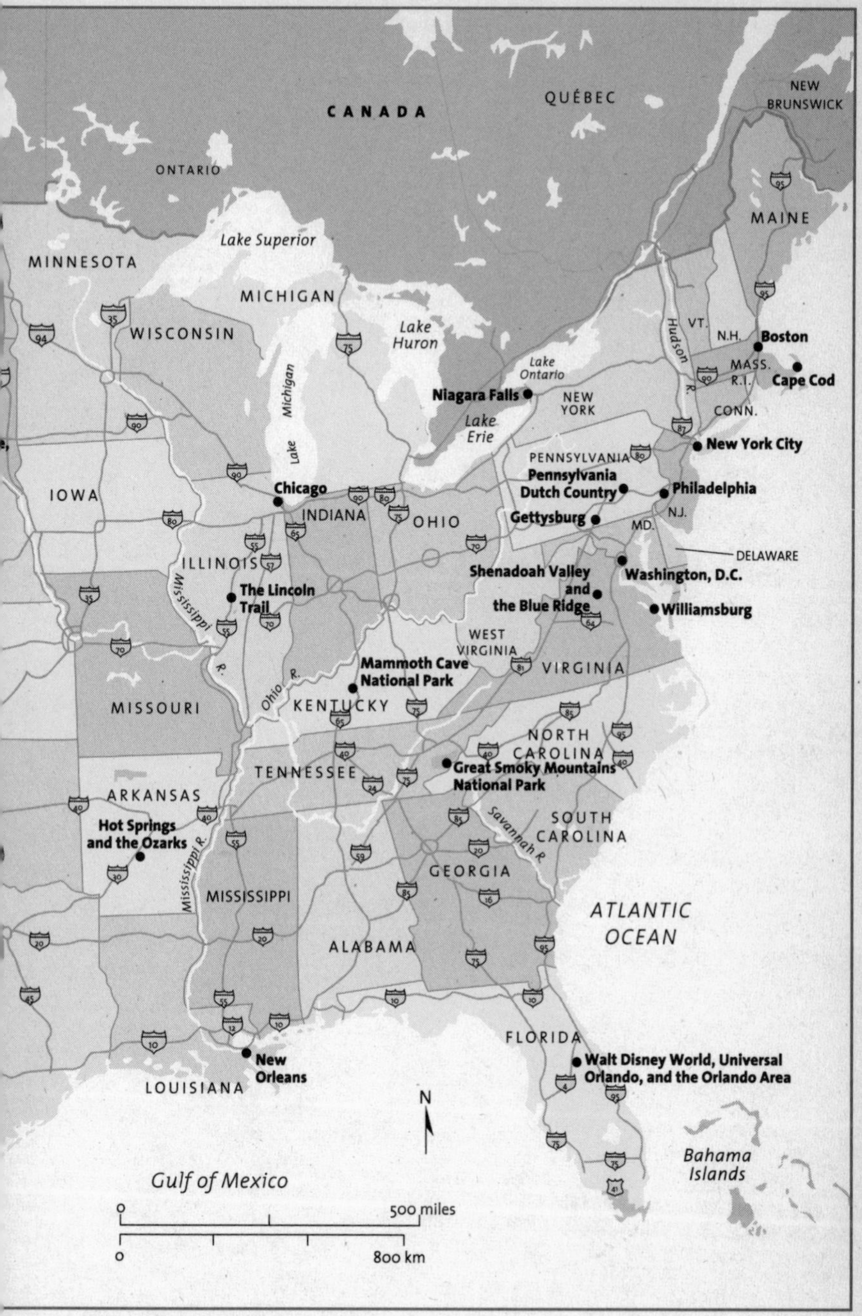
CANADA
QUÉBEC
ONTARIO
NEW BRUNSWICK
MAINE
Lake Superior
MINNESOTA
MICHIGAN
WISCONSIN
Lake Huron
Lake Michigan
Lake Ontario
Niagara Falls
Lake Erie
NEW YORK
VT.
N.H.
Boston
MASS.
R.I.
Cape Cod
CONN.
Hudson R.
New York City
PENNSYLVANIA
Pennsylvania Dutch Country
Philadelphia
N.J.
IOWA
Chicago
INDIANA
OHIO
Gettysburg
MD.
DELAWARE
ILLINOIS
Washington, D.C.
Shenadoah Valley and the Blue Ridge
Williamsburg
The Lincoln Trail
Mississippi R.
WEST VIRGINIA
Mammoth Cave National Park
VIRGINIA
Ohio R.
KENTUCKY
MISSOURI
NORTH CAROLINA
TENNESSEE
Great Smoky Mountains National Park
ARKANSAS
Hot Springs and the Ozarks
SOUTH CAROLINA
Savannah R.
GEORGIA
MISSISSIPPI
ATLANTIC OCEAN
ALABAMA
FLORIDA
New Orleans
Walt Disney World, Universal Orlando, and the Orlando Area
LOUISIANA
N
Bahama Islands
Gulf of Mexico
0
500 miles
0
800 km

Revised and Updated by Tom Griffith

BADLANDS NATIONAL PARK, MOUNT RUSHMORE, AND THE BLACK HILLS

Nature provides a fitting backdrop for the widely recognized Mount Rushmore National Memorial in western South Dakota, where the faces of Presidents George Washington, Thomas Jefferson, Abraham Lincoln, and Theodore Roosevelt are carved into granite cliffs, surrounded by the Black Hills' pine-covered mountains, icy trout streams, and secluded valleys. While the memorial and the facilities immediately surrounding it can become quite crowded during the busy summer season, those seeking serenity can easily retreat to the wilder seclusion of the Black Hills National Forest, covering an area roughly 50 mi wide and 120 mi long.

Just a two-hour drive east, 244,000-acre Badlands National Park offers a sharp contrast in environment. The lush, pine-tree-blanketed high country of the Black Hills is a far cry from this stark, almost lunar landscape marked by sheer cliffs and buttes. Formed over the eons by sedimentary rock deposits from the Black Hills and by ash from the volcanoes at Yellowstone Park, the eerie Badlands are home to fossils from an extinct menagerie of saber-toothed cats, giant pigs, and other unusual creatures.

Exploring

Begin your visit by exploring the stark beauty of the Badlands, and then travel to Rapid City—gateway to the breathtaking scenery of the Black Hills. Experience the exquisitely restored gold-rush town of Deadwood, and then retreat to the vast wildlife preserve of Custer State Park. Along the way, don't miss South Dakota's best-known memorials, Mount Rushmore and Crazy Horse.

Badlands National Park

So stark and isolated are the chiseled spires, ragged ridgelines, and deep ravines of South Dakota's badlands, that Lt. Col. George Custer once described the area as "hell with the fires burned out." While a bit more accessible and host to considerably more life than the depths of the underworld, the landscape of the badlands is easily the strangest in the state. Ruthlessly ravaged over ages by wind and rain, the 380 square

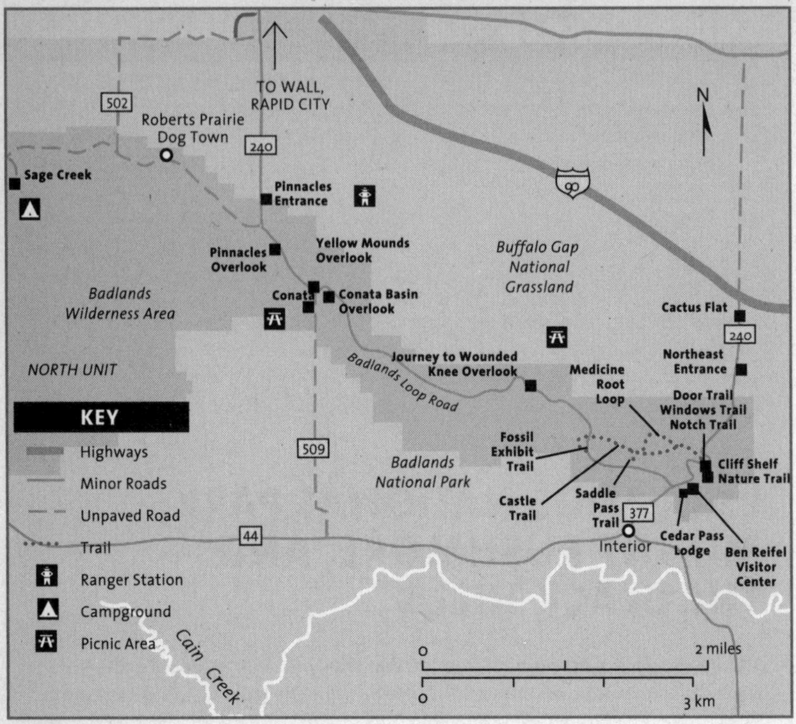

mi of wild terrain continue to erode and evolve, sometimes visibly changing shape in a few days. Despite harsh conditions, a community of prairie creatures, from bison and bald eagles to rattlesnakes and pronghorn antelope, thrive on the untamed territory. Fossil evidence shows that mammals have roamed the area for more than 35 million years. In fact, there are more Oligocene fossil deposits in the badlands than anywhere else in the world. Within the ancient rock formations, paleontologists have detected the evolution of such mammals as horses, cats, sheep, rhinoceroses, and pigs, plus traces of various birds and reptiles.

The park, first established as a national monument in 1939, then designated a national park in 1978, is divided into three units: the North Unit, which includes the Badlands Wilderness Area, and the Stronghold and Palmer units, which are within Pine Ridge Indian Reservation. The National Park Service and the Oglala Sioux Tribe manage the southern units together.

Hours: The park is open 24 hours, seven days a week, year-round.

Fees: Park fees, collected year-round and good for seven days, are \$10 per car or \$5 per person on a motorcycle or on foot. Bus rates are \$25–\$100, depending on the number of passengers aboard.

SCENIC DRIVES

★ **Badlands Loop Road.** The simplest and most popular drive through the badlands is on two-lane Badlands Loop Road (Route 240 outside the park). The drive circles from Exit 110 off I–90 through the park and back to the interstate at Exit 131. Start from either end and make your way around to the various overlooks along the way. Pinnacles Overlook and Yellow Mounds Overlook are outstanding places to examine the sandy pink- and brown-toned ridges and spires distinctive to the badlands. At a certain point the landscape flattens out slightly to the north, revealing spectacular views of mixed-grass prairies. In the rugged Cedar Pass area, the drive takes you past some of the park's best trails.

Sage Creek Rim Drive. This drive follows the road less traveled and covers rougher terrain than Badlands Loop Road. Enter the park via the Pinnacles entrance; then turn west onto unpaved Sage Creek Rim Road. The road is completely negotiable by most vehicles but should be avoided during a thunderstorm, when the sudden rush of water may cause flooding. The road follows the northern border of the park for several miles, passing several overlooks. Only a third of this area is composed of the eroded rocky spires and sharp ridges distinctive to the park. A vast mixed-grass prairie covers the rest. The road continues out of the park and junctions with Route 44 near the town of Scenic. A quick 30-mi drive east will take you through a portion of Buffalo Gap National Grassland and into the Cedar Pass area, while a 50-mi drive west will take you to Rapid City.

SIGHTS TO SEE

Badlands Wilderness Area. This 100-square-mi area is part of the largest prairie wilderness in the United States and takes up about 25% of the park. About two-thirds of the Sage Creek region is mixed-grass prairie, making it the ideal grazing grounds for bison, pronghorn, and many of the park's other native animals. Feel free to hike your own route into the untamed prairie, but remember that any water in this region is unfit for drinking—be sure to pack your own.

Ben Reifel Visitor Center. Although the visitor center is at the extreme eastern edge of the park, in the developed Cedar Pass area, it's a good idea to stop here to pick up park brochures and maps. The lodge, campground, amphitheater, and six trails are less than 2 mi away. | Badlands Loop Rd. (Rte. 240), Interior | 605/433–5361 | Early June–mid-Aug., daily 7–8; mid-Aug.–early Sept., daily 8–6; early Sept.–early June, daily 9–4.

BADLANDS SCENERY AND WILDLIFE

The sharply defined lines and edges of the park's cliffs, canyons, and mesas are all the more impressive when viewed in the morning or late afternoon, when the low-hanging sun catches the rock forms and casts them in deep shadow, highlighting their depth and providing definition to their ethereal structure. The morning is probably the better choice, since the mid- to late-afternoon sun turns the rock walls into an oven. However, those who brave the high temperatures are more than aptly rewarded—a sunset and subsequent moonrise over the badlands are two of the most beautiful experiences the park has to offer.

If you stick around for a badlands sunset, you will be rewarded with a display of animal life few daytime visitors see. Many of the park's creatures are nocturnal and begin their day's activity around sunset, about the same time that the daytime animals start to settle down for the night. For a few brief moments, both the day and night creatures can be seen roving around the park—a rare occurrence that is repeated only at sunrise, when the animal roles are reversed. At these two times of the day, it's not unusual to see herds of pronghorn antelope and mule deer darting across the flat plateaus, coyotes slinking around canyon walls, prairie dogs barking warnings from the safety of their burrows, and sharptail grouse running through the tall grass as golden eagles, turkey vultures, and hawks soar on the rocky region's updrafts.

The Big Pig Dig. In a depression by the Conata Basin picnic area, paleontologists dig for fossils and field questions from curious visitors. This site was named for a large fossil originally thought to be the remainder of a prehistoric pig, though it actually turned out to be from a small, hornless rhinoceros. The dig is open and staffed June through August. | 17 mi northwest of the Ben Reifel visitor center | Early June–late Aug., hrs vary.

Roberts Prairie Dog Town and Overlook. Once a homestead, this site is owned today by the largest colony of black-tailed prairie dogs in the world. | 5 mi west of Badlands Loop Rd. on Sage Creek Rim Rd.

Attractions Nearby

Wall Drug. Visit this South Dakota original, which got its start by offering free ice water to road-weary travelers, just before or after exploring the Badlands. Its four dining rooms seat 520 visitors. The walls are covered with art for sale. A life-size mechanical Cowboy Band and Chuckwagon Quartet greet you in the store. The attached Western Mall has 14 shops selling all kinds of souvenirs, from T-shirts to fudge. | 510 Main St., Wall | 605/279–2175 | www.walldrug.com | Free | Late May–early Sept., daily 6 AM–10 PM; early Sept.–late May, daily 6:30 AM–6 PM.

Mount Rushmore National Memorial

The carving of Mt. Rushmore, one of the nation's most famous attractions, was begun by sculptor Gutzon Borglum in 1927 and finished in 1941. Borglum died in March of that year, leaving his son, Lincoln, to put the finishing touches on the massive mountain memorial and close down the work. The giant, 60-ft-high likenesses of Presidents Washington, Jefferson, Lincoln, and Theodore Roosevelt grace a granite cliff, which, at an elevation of 5,725 ft, towers over the surrounding countryside and faces

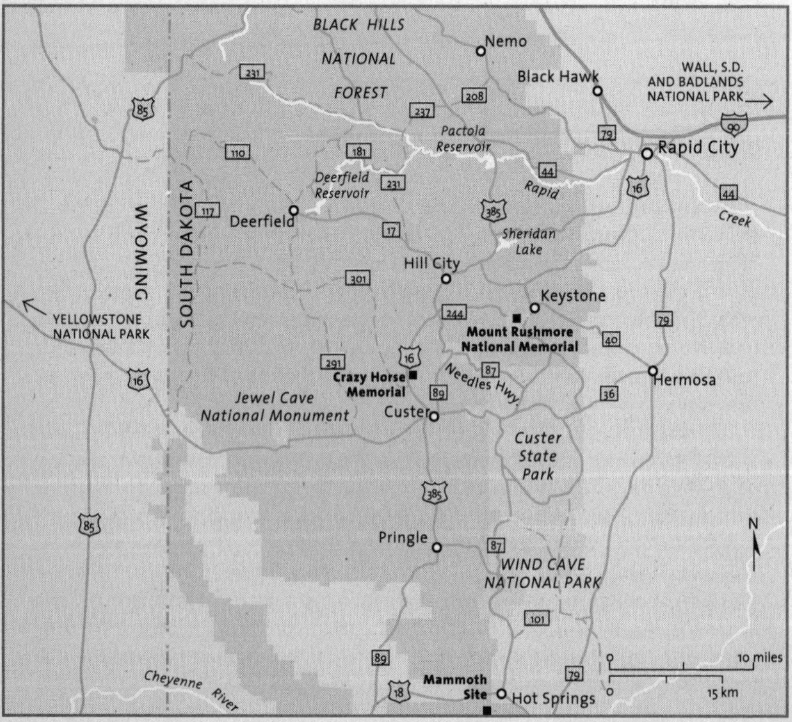

the sun most of the day. The memorial is equally spectacular at night, when a special lighting ceremony (June–mid-September) dramatically illuminates the carving. From Keystone, take Route 244 (Gutzon Borglum Memorial Highway) west 3 mi. | Rte. 244, Keystone | 605/574–2523 | www.nps.gov/moru | Free, parking $5 | Daily.

Attractions Nearby

RAPID CITY

Bear Country U.S.A. Bears, wolves, elk, bighorn, and other North American wildlife roam free on 250 privately owned acres. Bear cubs, wolf pups, and other park offspring are housed in a newly remodeled walk-through area. Allow at least 1½ hours for your visit. | U.S. 16, Rapid City | 605/343–2290 | www.bearcountryusa.com | $9.50 | May–Oct., daily 8–6:30.

Black Hills National Forest. Hundreds of miles of hiking, mountain-biking, and horseback-riding trails crisscross this million-acre forest on the western edge of the state. Entry points include Custer, Deadwood, Hill City, Hot Springs, Lead, Rapid City, Spearfish, and Sturgis. | Visitor center: 803 Soo San Dr., Rapid City | 605/343–8755 | www.fs.fed.us/bhnf | Free | Visitor center mid-May–Sept., daily 8–6.

Storybook Island. Nursery rhymes come to life in animated and real-life scenes at this children's fantasy theme park, which also has children's summer theater. | 1301 Sheridan Lake Rd., Rapid City | 605/342–6357 | Donations accepted | Late May–early Sept., daily 8–8.

DEADWOOD

Broken Boot Gold Mine. Join guides on a journey into an authentic underground gold mine and pan for gold. If nothing else, you'll receive a souvenir stock certificate. | Upper Main St., Hwy. 14A | 605/578–9997 | $4.50, gold panning $4.50 extra | May–Aug., daily 8–5:30; Sept., daily 9–4:30.

Mount Moriah Cemetery. This cemetery is the final resting place for such notables as Wild Bill Hickok, Calamity Jane Canary, and Potato Creek Johnny. You can pick up a walking map with gravesite locations and some interesting tales. This classic "Boot Hill" has the best panoramic view of the town and the gold-filled gulch. | Top of Lincoln St. | 605/578–1087 | $1 | Late May–early Sept., daily 7–8; early Sept.–end of Sept., daily 9–5.

The Shooting of Wild Bill Hickok. A reenactment of one of Deadwood's most infamous events takes place four times a day in the summer months. Step inside the nearby Old Style Saloon No. 10, the only museum in the world with a bar. | On street in front of 657 Main St. | 605/578–3346 | www.saloon10.com | Free | Late May–early Sept. at 1, 3, 5, and 7.

SOUTHERN HILLS

Black Hills Central Railroad. You step back in time when you board this train. The antique steam locomotive takes you through the Black Hills backcountry from Hill City to Keystone. | Hill City Depot, Railroad Ave. | 605/574–2222 | www.1880train.com | $18 | Mid-May–early Oct., four daily departures; call for schedule. Reservations essential.

Crazy Horse Memorial. This colossal mountain carving in progress depicts Lakota leader Crazy Horse atop his steed. At the memorial's base are a restaurant, gift shop, and legendary work by Crazy Horse sculptor Korczak Ziolkowski. From Custer, go 5 mi north on U.S. 385. | U.S. 385, Custer | 605/673–4681 | www.crazyhorse.org | $8 per person, $19 per vehicle | June–Aug., daily 7–8:30; Sept.–May, daily 8–5.

At the base of the memorial, the **Indian Museum of North America** houses one of the most impressive collections of Plains Indian artifacts in the country.

Custer State Park. These 115 square mi of scenic grandeur, granite spires, and pristine mountain lakes are considered the crown jewel of South Dakota's state park system. Take the 18-mi Wildlife Loop Road to see prairies teeming with animals. Here, a buffalo jam is much more likely than a traffic jam. The park's several lodges provide comfortable retreats for road-weary travelers. The 14-mi Needles Highway between the State Game Lodge and Sylvan Lake Resort takes you past immense granite spires towering over the forest floor. Iron Mountain Road, a 17-mi scenic drive from Custer State Park to Keystone, is best known for its three pigtail bridges and three narrow tunnels through which you'll find perfectly framed views of the four presidential faces on Mt. Rushmore. | U.S. 16A, Custer | 605/255–4515 | www.state.sd.us/sdparks | $5 Nov.–Apr., $10 May–Oct. | Daily.

HOT SPRINGS

Black Hills Wild Horse Sanctuary. More than 300 wild horses run free across endless prairies at this wilderness area. | 12 mi south of Hot Springs on Rte. 71 | 605/745–5955 or 800/252–6652 | $20 | Tours May–Sept., Mon.–Sat. at 10, 1, and 3.

Evans Plunge. Get ready to splash in the world's largest natural warm-water indoor swimming pool. Includes indoor-outdoor pools, water slides, pool games, traveling rings, a sauna, a steam room, and a fitness center. | 1145 N. River St. | 605/745–5165 | www.evansplunge.com | $8 | Daily.

Mammoth Site. Discovered in 1974, the site is believed to contain up to 100 mammoths (52 have been unearthed so far) and 35 other species in the sinkhole where the mammoths came to drink some 26,000 years ago. Excavation is in progress. | 1 block north of U.S. 18 Bypass | 605/745–6017 | www.mammothsite.com | $6.50 | Daily.

Dining

Most restaurants in the Badlands and Mount Rushmore National Memorial area are found in the towns outside the parks, but be aware that many establishments close for the winter. Those who are adventurous will want to try the local specialty—buffalo—found on the menus of several regional restaurants (raised on a number of western South Dakota ranches, buffalo tastes similar to beef but contains far less fat and cholesterol).

In Badlands National Park

Cedar Pass Lodge Restaurant. American. Cool off within the comforting confines of dark, knotty-pine walls under an exposed-beam ceiling and enjoy a hearty meal of steak, trout, or Indian tacos and fry bread. | 1 Cedar St. (Rte. 240), Interior | 605/433–5460 | $8–$17 | Closed Nov.–Mar. | AE, D, DC, MC, V.

Picnic Areas: You may picnic wherever your heart desires, but the National Park Service does provide several structured picnic areas. The wind may blow hard enough to make picnicking a challenge, but the views are unrivaled.

A dozen or so covered picnic tables are scattered over the **Conata picnic area,** which rests against a badlands wall ½ mi south of Badlands Loop Road. There's no potable water, but there are bathroom facilities and you can enjoy your lunch in peaceful isolation at the threshold of the Badlands Wilderness Area. The Conata Basin area is to the east, and Sage Creek area is to the west. | 15 mi northwest of Ben Reifel visitor center on Conata Rd.

There are only a handful of tables at **Journey Overlook,** and no water, but the incredible view makes it a lovely spot to have lunch. Rest rooms are available. | 7 mi northwest of Ben Reifel visitor center on Badlands Loop Rd.

Near Badlands National Park and the Black Hills

★ **Botticelli Ristorante Italiano.** Italian. Statues and columns give this northern Italian eatery a classic European appearance. Daily specials, seafood and otherwise, complement the main menu's chicken, veal, and creamy pasta dishes. | 523 Main St., Rapid City | 605/348–0089 | $8–$22 | AE, MC, V.

Buffalo Dining Room. American. With stunning views of Mount Rushmore before you, you won't mind waiting for your meal in this glass-enclosed cafeteria. The menu lists many low-cost choices for breakfast, lunch, and dinner, including standard fare like burgers and pasta, plus the popular buffalo stew. | Rte. 244, Mt. Rushmore | 605/574–2515 | No dinner mid-Oct.–early Mar. | $6–$11 | AE, D, MC, V.

Deadwood Social Club. Italian. You'll find a homey, relaxed setting with historic photos on the walls and one of South Dakota's best wine selections in the cellar. The restaurant is known for Black Angus beef and chicken, seafood, and pasta dishes. Downstairs is the Old Style Saloon No. 10, with nightly live entertainment and the "only museum in the world with a bar." | 657 Main St., Deadwood | 605/578–3346 or 800/952–9398 | $8–$18 | AE, MC, V.

Elkton House Restaurant. American/Casual. This comfortable restaurant with wood paneling and a sunroom has fast service and a terrific hot roast-beef sandwich, served on white bread with gravy and mashed potatoes. | 203 South Blvd., Wall | 605/279–2152 | $7–$15 | D, MC, V.

State Game Lodge and Resort. American. President Calvin Coolidge once frequented the historic Pheasant Dining Room for a tasty meal of meticulously prepared buffalo and pheasant. There's a salad bar and a buffet at lunch. Kids' menu. Take Route 16A 13 mi east of Custer. | Rte. 16A, Custer | 605/255–4541 or 800/658–3530 | Reservations essential | Closed mid-Oct.–mid-May | $15–$23 | AE, D, MC, V.

Sylvan Lake Resort. American/Casual. The Lakota Dining Room has an exceptional view of Sylvan Lake and Harney Peak, the highest point between the Rockies and the Swiss Alps. You can enjoy your cocktail or tea out on the veranda. On the menu are buffalo selections, including steaks. A fine choice is the rainbow trout. Kids' menu. From Hill City, drive south on U.S. 385 past Mount Rushmore to Route 87. The resort is 9 mi south of Hill City. | Rte. 87, Hill City | 605/574–2561 | Reservations essential | Closed Oct.–mid-May | $10–$22 | AE, D, MC, V.

Lodging

In Badlands National Park

★ **Cedar Pass Lodge.** Each small, white cabin has two beds and views of the badlands peaks. The lodge's gallery displays the work of local artists, and the gift shop is well stocked with local crafts, including turquoise and beadwork. Restaurant, picnic areas, hiking, some pets allowed | 1 Cedar St. (Rte. 240), Interior | 605/433–5460 | fax 605/433–5560 | 24 cabins | $55 | Closed Nov.–Mar. | AE, D, DC, MC, V.

Near Badlands National Park and the Black Hills

Badlands Ranch and Resort. This 2,000-acre ranch is just outside the national park. The ranch house and cabins have spectacular views of the park. The grounds and newly remodeled 16-bed lodge are ideal for summer family vacations and reunions. Picnic area, cable TV, pool, fishing, horseback riding | HCR 53, Box 3, Interior | 605/433–5599 | fax 605/433–5598 | www.badlandsranchandresort.com | 4 ranch-house rooms, 7 cabins, 1 lodge, 35 RV hook-ups | $48–$90 | AE, D, MC, V.

Blue Bell Lodge and Resort. This hideaway retreat in Custer State Park is made up of handcrafted log cabins with modern interiors and fireplaces, a lodge, a conference center, and a campground. Hayrides, trail rides, and cookouts are part of the entertainment. From Custer, take Route 16A east in the state park, then Route 87 south about 6 mi. Restaurant, picnic area, some kitchenettes, cable TV, hiking, horseback riding, bar, playground, laundry facilities; no air-conditioning | Rte. 87, Custer | 605/255–4531 or 800/658–3530 | fax 605/255–4752 | 29 cabins | $99–$175 | AE, D, MC, V.

State Game Lodge and Resort. Once the summer White House for President Coolidge, and host to President Eisenhower as well, this stately stone-and-wood lodge has well-appointed rooms and pine-shaded cabins. You can arrange for Jeep safaris into the buffalo herds. Restaurant, picnic area, cable TV, hiking, bar; no A/C in some rooms, no phones in some rooms | Rte. 16A, Custer | 605/255–4541 or 800/658–3530 | fax 605/255–4706 | 7 lodge rooms, 40 motel rooms, 33 cabins | Lodge rooms $81–$243, motel rooms $106–$151, cabins $86–$370 | AE, D, MC, V.

★ **Sylvan Lake Resort.** The spacious stone-and-wood lodge overlooks pristine Sylvan Lake. Rustic cabins, some with fireplaces, are scattered along the cliff and in the forest. Numerous hiking trails make this a great choice for active families. Restaurant, dining room, picnic area, room TVs, lake, beach, boating, hiking, bar; no A/C in some rooms | Custer State Park | 605/574–2561 or 800/658–3530 | fax 605/574–4943 | 35 lodge rooms, 31 cabins | Lodge rooms $95–$150, cabins $120–$250 | AE, D, MC, V.

Camping

In Badlands National Park

Cedar Pass Campground. This campground is the most developed in the park. It's right next door to the Ben Reifel visitor center, Cedar Pass Lodge, and a half-dozen hiking trails. You can buy $1 or $2 bags of ice at the lodge. Flush toilets, pit toilets, dump station, drinking water, public telephone | 96 sites | Rte. 377, ¼ mi south of Badlands Loop Rd. | 605/433–5361 | $10.

Near Badlands National Park and the Black Hills

Badlands KOA. Southeast of Interior, this campground's green, shady sites, spread over 31 acres, are pleasant and cool after a day among the dry rocks of the national park. White River and a small creek border the property on two sides. Flush toilets, full hook-ups, partial hook-ups, dump station, drinking water, showers, fire pits, picnic tables, public telephone, general store, playground, pool | 44 full hook-ups, 38 partial hook-ups, 62 tent sites; 10 cabins | 4 mi south of Interior on Rte. 44 | 605/433–5337 | RV sites $23–$28, tent sites $18–$20, cabins $36–$56 | Closed early Oct.–Apr.

Days of '76 RV Park. On the banks of trout-filled Whitewood Creek, this campground is within walking distance of downtown Deadwood. Flush toilets, full hook-ups, dump station, showers | 40 full hook-ups, unlimited tent sites | 17 Crescent St. Deadwood | 605/578–2872 | Full hook-ups $20, tent sites $15 | Closed Nov.–Apr.

Happy Holiday Campground. Outside of Rapid City on U.S. 16, this campground has the advantage of easy access to Mt. Rushmore and beautiful forest surroundings. It's a favorite for RVs. You get 10% off on gas when you stay here. Flush toilets, full hook-ups, partial hook-ups (electric and water), dump station, drinking water, laundry facilities, showers, fire grates, picnic tables, public telephone, playground, pool | 258 sites | 8990 Rte. 16 S, Rapid City | 605/342–7365 | Full hook-ups $30, partial hook-ups $27, tent sites $22 | D, MC, V.

Shopping

Wall Drug and Keystone's Main St. are souvenir meccas near the Badlands and in the Black Hills. Don't leave without some taffy and a jackalope or bison bank. The

Rushmore Mall in Rapid City houses 120 stores, including department stores, bookstores, and specialty shops.

Sports and Outdoor Activities

Bicycling

In the Badlands bicycles are permitted only on designated roads, which may be paved or unpaved. They are prohibited from closed roads, trails, and the backcountry. Flat-resistant tires are recommended. Nearby, the heart of the Black Hills is open to bicyclists along the 109-mi Mickelson Trail.

Mickelson Trail. The trail follows the historic 109-mi Burlington Northern Rail Line from Deadwood to Edgemont. | Black Hills Trail Office, 11361 Nevada Gulch Rd., Lead.

Sheep Mountain Table Road. In the south unit of the Badlands, on the Pine Ridge Indian Reservation, this 7-mi dirt road, ideal for mountain biking, climbs Sheep Mountain for unique views from a high, flat mesa. The road should only be taken when dry. The terrain is level for the first 3 mi, then climbs the table and levels out again. At the top you can see a great view of the entire Stronghold Unit. | About 14 mi north of White River visitor center on Rte. 27.

Rushmore Bicycles. Based in the central Black Hills, this local outfitter has nearly 50 mountain bikes available to rent by the day or half-day, including comfort cruisers, standard mountain bikes, and high-end demo bikes. You can also rent a bike trailer to tow the bikes 80 mi back to Badlands, or you can have them dropped at your hotel for an extra fee. Inquire about guided bike tours of the Badlands. | 107 Elm St., Hill City | 605/574–3930 | www.rushmorebicycles.com.

Hiking

The isolation and otherworldliness of the Badlands are best appreciated with a walk through them. Take time to examine the dusty rock beneath your feet, look for fossils and animals, and remember, bring at least 1 liter of water per person.

Castle Trail. This easy hike stretches for 5½ mi one-way from the Fossil Exhibit trailhead on Badlands Loop Road to the parking area for the Door and Windows trails; if you choose to use the Medicine Root Loop, which detours off the Castle Trail, you'll add ½ mi to the trek. | 5 mi north of Ben Reifel visitor center.

Door Trail. A ¾-mi round-trip trail leads through a natural opening, or door, in a badlands rock wall. The eerie sandstone formations and passageways beckon, but it's recommended that you stay on the trail. The first 100 yards of the trail are on a boardwalk. | 2 mi east of Ben Reifel visitor center.

Horseback Riding

The Badlands are one of the largest and most beautiful territories in the state in which to ride a horse. Horses are prohibited only on marked trails, roads, and developed areas. The mixed-grass prairie land of the Badlands Wilderness Area is especially popular with riders.

★ **Gunsel Horse Adventures.** A local outfitter since 1968, Gunsel provides multiday pack trips into the badlands and Buffalo Gap National Grassland. The four- to seven-day trips are based in one central campsite and are all-inclusive, with the exception of sleeping bags and personal effects. | Box 1575, Rapid City | 605/343–7608.

Winter Sports

The Black Hills is a wonderland for winter sports enthusiasts. The more than 300 mi of groomed snowmobile trails are consistently ranked among the best in the nation. Cross-country and downhill skiing and ice fishing will round out your winter vacation.

Days Inn at Deadwood Gulch Resort. Enjoy 24-hour gaming, creek-side rooms, a restaurant, and easy access to 330 mi of groomed snowmobile trails. Located on the Mickelson Trail. Snowmobile rentals available. | U.S. 86 S, Deadwood | 605/578–1294 or 800/695–1876.

Deer Mountain Ski Area. Soak in the Black Hills winter scenery while skiing the 45 trails on this mountain with an 850-ft vertical drop. Deer Mountain also offers night skiing, rentals, lessons, a tubing area, and 10 mi of cross-country trails. | Box 622, Lead | 605/584–3230.

Terry Peak Ski Area. The highest lift-served resort east of the Rocky Mountains boasts a 1,100-ft vertical drop, five lifts, and state-of-the-art snowmaking. | Box 774, Lead | 605/584–2165.

Essential Information

When to Go

South Dakota's weather tends to be as diverse as its geography, and its climate ranks as one of the most extreme in the world. Except for hurricanes, the state has witnessed virtually every type of weather condition imaginable, yet, for the most part, its climate is extremely pleasant. Low humidity, brilliant sunshine, and crystal clear skies are the rule. The vast majority of visitors descend on the Black Hills and Badlands National Park between Memorial Day and Labor Day. Fortunately, the area's vast size prevents it from ever being too packed. A possible exception is the first week in August, when hundreds of thousands of motorcycle enthusiasts flock to the Black Hills for the annual Sturgis Motorcycle Rally. On the flip side, it's possible to drive Badlands Loop Road in winter without seeing more than one or two other vehicles.

FESTIVALS AND SEASONAL EVENTS

WINTER

Jan.–Feb.: **Black Hills Stock Show and Rodeo.** Watch world-champion wild horse races, bucking horses, timed sheepdog trials, draft horse competitions, and steer wrestling during this professional rodeo at the Rushmore Plaza Civic Center in Rapid City. The stockman's banquet and ball are not to be missed. | 605/342–8325.

SUMMER

June: **Crazy Horse Volksmarch.** At the Crazy Horse Memorial, near Custer, this 10K hike is the largest event of its kind in the world and also offers a rare opportunity to hike up the mountain carving in progress. | 605/673–4681.

July–Aug.: **Days of '76.** This Black Hills classic, staged in Deadwood, has been around for more than 75 years and has pro rodeos, free street dances, western arts and crafts, and two exquisite 3-mi-long parades that include marching bands, authentic carriages, covered wagons, stagecoaches, Native American dancers, and characters in Old West costume. | 800/999–1876 or 605/578–1876.

Oglala Nation Powwow and Rodeo. This traditional powwow and rodeo is hosted by the Oglala Sioux tribe at the Powwow Grounds on the west side of Pine Ridge. | 605/867–5821.

AUTUMN

Sept.–Oct.: **Custer State Park Buffalo Roundup.** The nation's largest buffalo roundup is also one of South Dakota's most exciting events. Watch as cowboys and park crews saddle up and corral the park's 1,500 head of bison so that they may later be vaccinated. Check out the Buffalo Roundup Arts Festival and Buffalo Wallow Chili Cook-off. | 605/255–4515.

Bargains

All the activities and programs at ☞ **Mount Rushmore National Memorial** are free. In Rapid City, follow Main Street to Jackson Boulevard and turn left to reach **Canyon Lake** (605/394–4175). The city park there has canals and acres of manicured grass and trees. Farther west down Jackson Boulevard is the **Cleghorn Springs Fish Hatchery** (605/394–2397). Several varieties of trout are spawned here by the thousands, and you can inspect the facilities free of charge. Families traveling with young children will love a free visit to ☞ **Storybook Island**.

Black Hills Central Reservations offers real deals on all-inclusive Black Hills vacation packages, including lodging, airline travel, rentals cars, and attraction and special-event ticketing. | 800/529–0101 | www.blackhillsvacations.com.

Nearby Towns

Built against a steep ridge of badland rock, **Wall** was founded in 1907 as a railroad station and today is the town nearest Badlands National Park, 8 mi from the Pinnacles entrance of the North Unit. Wall is home to 834 residents and the world-famous Wall Drug Store, best known for its fabled jackalopes and free ice water. **Rapid City,** on the east slope of the Black Hills, is South Dakota's second-largest city and a good base from which to explore the treasures of the state's southwestern corner, including the Badlands 70 mi to the east, Mt. Rushmore and Wind Cave National Park 25 mi and 50 mi to the south, respectively, and neighboring Black Hills National Forest. **Hot Springs** is the gateway to Wind Cave National Park, 7 mi north of town, and scores of other natural and historical sites, including Evans Plunge, a large, naturally heated indoor-outdoor pool; the Mammoth Site, where more than 50 woolly and Columbian mammoths have been unearthed to date; and the Black Hills Wild Horse Sanctuary. **Custer** is where George Armstrong Custer and his expedition first discovered gold in 1874, leading to the gold rush of 1875–76. Minutes away from Wind Cave, Mount Rushmore, Crazy Horse Memorial, and Custer State Park, Custer is an excellent base for a Black Hills vacation. **Keystone** is the closest town to Mount Rushmore and, therefore, has an abundance of motels, restaurants, and gift shops. A visit to the Borglum Historical Center will enlighten you about Mount Rushmore's sculptor, and a stop at the National Presidential Wax Museum brings you face-to-face with all U.S. presidents in historical settings. If you would rather stay in a small, quiet mountain town, **Hill City,** founded by gold miners in 1876, is one of the most charming communities in the Black Hills. Surrounded by heavy pine forests and imbued with a full logging, mining, and railroad history, the town embodies the essence of the region and hosts an eclectic collection of art galleries. A decade after legalized gambling was brought to the community of **Deadwood,** $150 million has gone into restoring this once infamous gold camp, turning the entire town into a National Historic Landmark. Brick streets, old-fashioned trolleys, period lampposts, original Victorian architecture, and Main Street shoot-outs make Deadwood irresistible.

Tours

Ben Reifel Visitor Center. All Badlands National Park programs and activities are free. Call to confirm daily schedules. | 605/433–5361.

At the **Evening Program,** watch a 40-minute outdoor slide presentation on the wildlife, natural history, paleontology, or another aspect of the badlands. | Cedar Pass campground amphitheater | Mid-June–mid-Aug., daily.

Children ages 7–12 may participate in the 45-minute **Junior Ranger Program,** typically a short hike, game, or other hands-on activity focused on badlands wildlife, geology, or fossils. Parents are welcome. | Cedar Pass Campground Amphitheater | June–Aug., daily at 11:30.

★ **Mysterious Badlands Tour.** Golden Circle Tours schedules eight-hour narrated trips to the badlands, Custer State Park, and to Mt. Rushmore and Crazy Horse memorials in bright yellow-and-white passenger vans. Prices average around $65 per person, depending on how many people are in your group. | 605/673–4349 or 877/811–4349 | www.goldencircletours.com.

Visitor Information

Badlands National Park. | Box 6, Interior, SD 57750 | 605/433–5361 | www.nps.gov/badl. **Black Hills National Forest.** | 25041 N. Hwy. 16, Custer, SD 57730 | 605/673–9200 | fax 605/673–9350 | www.fs.fed.us/bhnf. **Mt. Rushmore National Monument.** | Box 268, Keystone, SD 57751 | 605/574–2523 | www.nps.gov/moru.

Custer Area Chamber of Commerce and Visitors Bureau | 615 Washington St., Custer, SD 57730 | 605/673–2244 or 800/992–9818 | www.custersd.com. **Deadwood Chamber of Commerce** | 735 Main St., Deadwood, SD 57732 | 605/578–1876 or 800/999–1876 | www.deadwood.org. **Hill City Area Chamber of Commerce** | Box 253, Hill City, SD 57745 | 605/574–2368 or 800/888–1798 | www.hillcitysd.com. **Hot Springs Area Chamber of Commerce** | 801 S. 6th St., Hot Springs, SD 57747 | 605/745–4140 or 800/325–6991 | www.hotsprings-sd.com. **Keystone Chamber of Commerce** | 110 Swanzey St., Keystone, SD 57751-0653 | 605/666–4896 or 800/456–3345 | www.keystonechamber.com. **Oglala Sioux Tribe** | Box 570, Kyle, SD 57752 | 605/455–2584. **Rapid City Chamber of Commerce, and Convention and Visitors Bureau** | 444 Mt. Rushmore Rd. N, Rapid City, SD 57701 | 605/343–1744 or 800/333–2072 | www.rapidcitycvb.com. **Wall–Badlands Area Chamber of Commerce** | 501 Main St., Wall, SD 57790 | 605/279–2665 or 888/852–9255 | www.wall-badlands.com.

Arriving and Departing

BY AIR

Airports

Rapid City Regional Airport (RAP). The only commercial airport in the area has several major carriers and daily flights. | 605/394–4195.

Airport Transportation

To see the Black Hills and the Badlands, you'll want to rent a car. Avis, Budget, Hertz, Thrifty, and National all have offices at the airport.

BY BUS

Milo Barber Transportation Center. Jefferson and Powder River Lines serve this depot in downtown Rapid City. Both are regional bus lines, and you can make connections with Greyhound Lines. | 333 6th St., Rapid City | 605/348–3300.

BY CAR

I–90 is the most direct route to the Badlands and the Black Hills. To reach Badlands National Park from I–90, take Exit 110 at Wall or Exit 131 at Cactus Flat. To get to Mount Rushmore from I–90, take Exit 57 in Rapid City and follow U.S. 16 south to U.S. 16A.

Getting Around

BY CAR

Badlands National Park is one of the least-developed places on Earth, and few roads, paved or otherwise, pass within park boundaries. Badlands Loop Road (Route 240) is the most traveled road through the park, and the only one that intersects I–90. It's well maintained and rarely crowded. Portions of Route 44 and Route 27 run at the fringes of the badlands, connecting the visitor centers and Rapid City. Keep an eye on your speed—bison roam the flat, grassy plains these roads cut through, and it's common to come up over the crest of a hill and find one standing on the road. Some roads through the park are unpaved and should be traveled with care when wet. Sheep Mountain Table Road, a 7-mi road carved by homesteaders in the early 20th century, is the only public road into the Stronghold Unit of the park. It is impassable when wet, with deep ruts—sometimes only high-clearance vehicles can get through. Off-road driving is prohibited. There's plenty of free parking at the visitor centers, scenic overlooks, and trailheads.

Massachusetts

Revised and Updated by Elizabeth Gehrman

BOSTON

New England's largest and most important city and the cradle of American independence, Boston is more than 370 years old, far older than the republic its residents helped create. The city's most famous buildings are not merely civic landmarks but national icons, and its local heroes are known to the nation: John and Samuel Adams, Paul Revere, John Hancock, John F. Kennedy, and many more who live at the crossroads of history and myth.

At the same time, Boston is a contemporary center of high finance and high technology, a place of granite and glass towers rising along what once were rutted village lanes. Its many students, artists, academics, and young professionals have made the town a haven for the arts, international cinema, late-night bookstores, ethnic food, alternative music, and unconventional politics.

Best of all, Boston is meant for walking. Most of its historical and architectural attractions are in the compact city core, and its varied and distinctive neighborhoods reveal their character to those who take the time to stroll through them.

Exploring

Beacon Hill and Boston Common

Beacon Hill—bounded by Cambridge Street to the north, Beacon Street to the south, the Charles River Esplanade to the west, and Bowdoin Street to the east—is Boston at its most Bostonian. The redbrick elegance of its narrow, cobbled streets transports you back to the 19th century. From the gold-topped splendor of the State House to the neoclassical panache of its mansions, "the Hill" exudes power, prestige, and a calm yet palpable undercurrent of history.

Black Heritage Trail. Until the end of the 19th century, Beacon Hill's north side was home to many free blacks. The 1½-mi Black Heritage Trail celebrates that community at 14 sites. Free tours guided by National Park Service rangers meet at the Shaw Memorial on the Beacon Street side of the Boston Common; the hours change seasonally. | 617/742–5415.

Boston Common. The oldest public park in the United States—set aside in 1634 as a cattle pasture—is the largest and undoubtedly the most famous of the town com-

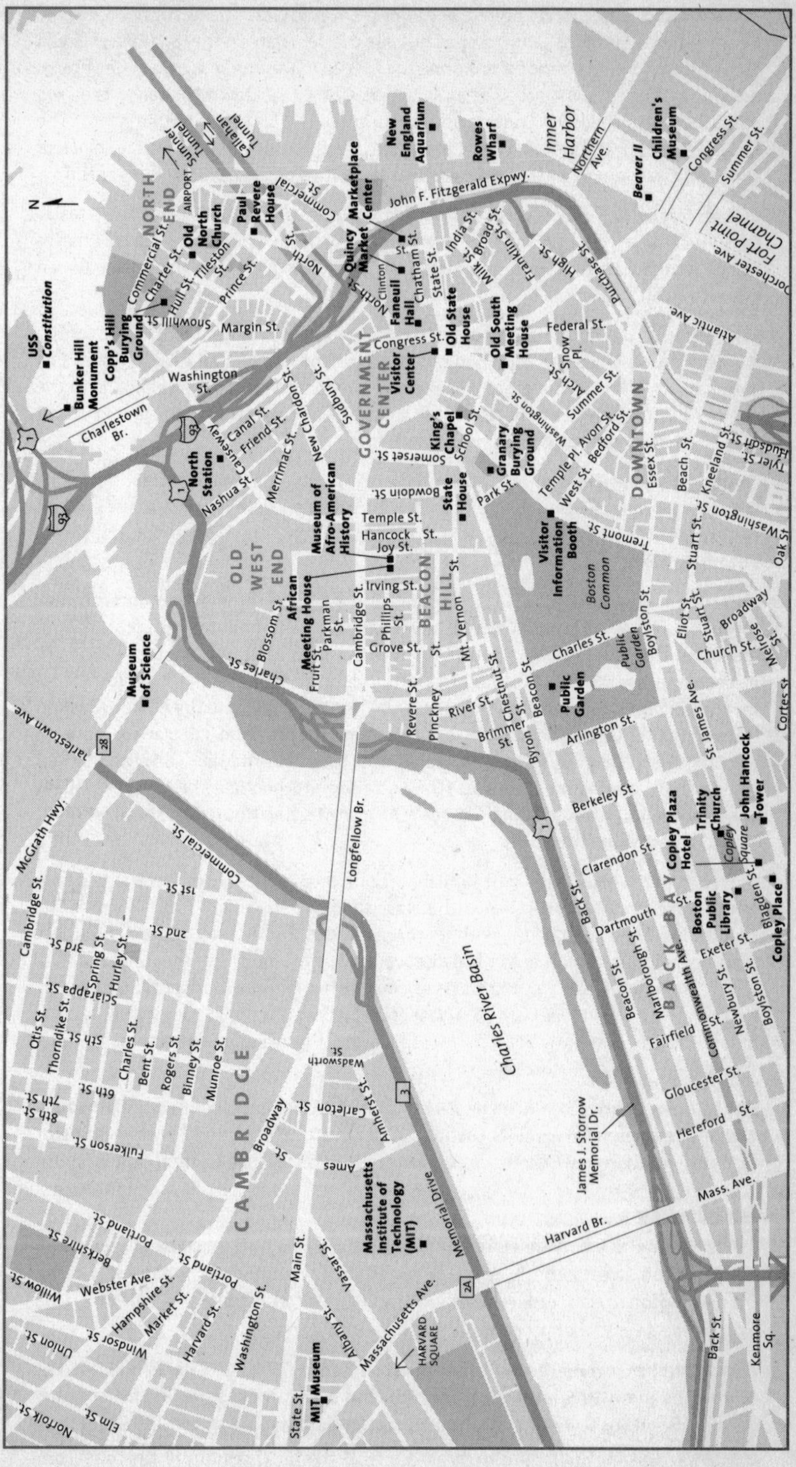

USS Constitution
Bunker Hill Monument
Copp's Hill Burying Ground
Old North Church
Paul Revere House
NORTH END
Quincy Market
Marketplace Center
New England Aquarium
Rowes Wharf
Faneuil Hall
Old State House
Visitor Center
Old South Meeting House
King's Chapel
Granary Burying Ground
State House
Museum of Afro-American History
African Meeting House
Visitor Information Booth
Boston Common
Public Garden
North Station
Museum of Science
GOVERNMENT CENTER
OLD WEST END
BEACON HILL
DOWNTOWN
BACK BAY
Inner Harbor
Fort Point Channel
Beaver II
Children's Museum
Trinity Church
John Hancock Tower
Copley Plaza Hotel
Copley Square
Boston Public Library
Copley Place
Charles River Basin
Longfellow Br.
Harvard Br.
Charlestown Br.
John F. Fitzgerald Expwy.
James J. Storrow Memorial Dr.
Memorial Drive
Massachusetts Institute of Technology (MIT)
MIT Museum
CAMBRIDGE
HARVARD SQUARE
Kenmore Sq.
Mass. Ave.
Massachusetts Ave.
McGrath Hwy.
Sumner Tunnel
Callahan Tunnel
AIRPORT
Northern Ave.
Congress St.
Summer St.
Atlantic Ave.
Washington St.
Tremont St.
Charles St.
Cambridge St.
Beacon St.
Boylston St.
Commonwealth Ave.
Newbury St.
Marlborough St.
Arlington St.
Berkeley St.
Clarendon St.
Dartmouth St.
Exeter St.
Fairfield St.
Gloucester St.
Hereford St.
Main St.
Broadway

mons around which New England settlements were traditionally arranged. On the Beacon Street side of the Common just outside the park gates is the 1897 Robert Gould Shaw 54th Regiment Memorial honoring the first Civil War unit made up of free blacks, whose stirring saga inspired the 1989 movie *Glory.* Just down the hill is the Frog Pond, used as a children's wading pool in summer and for ice skating in winter. The Central Burying Ground, along the Boylston Street side, is the final resting place of Tories and Patriots, as well as many British casualties of the Battle of Bunker Hill.

Charles Street. Antiques shops, bookstores, small restaurants, and flower shops tastefully vie for attention: even the 7-Eleven conforms to the Colonial aesthetic. Charles Street sparkles at dusk with gas-fueled lamps, making it a romantic place for an evening stroll.

Esplanade. At the northern end of Charles Street is one of several footbridges crossing Storrow Drive to the Esplanade, which stretches along the Charles River. The scenic patch of green is a great place to jog, picnic, and watch the sailboats on the river. In summer, hordes of Bostonians haul chairs and blankets to the lawn in front of the Hatch Memorial Shell for free concerts.

Granary Burying Ground. The Old Granary, just to the right of Park Street Church, is the resting place of Samuel Adams, John Hancock, Benjamin Franklin's parents, and Paul Revere. | Entrance on Tremont St. | Dec.–Apr., daily 9–dusk; May–Nov., daily 9–5 | T stop: Park St.

★ **Museum of Afro-American History.** Founded in 1964, this museum promotes the history of African-Americans in Colonial New England. Throughout the 19th century, abolition was the cause célèbre for Boston's intellectual elite, and during that time the black community thrived on Beacon Hill. The museum encompasses the first public school for black children in the United States, the Abiel Smith School, and the African Meeting House, a hotbed of abolitionist fervor. At press time, the museum had plans to renovate the African Meeting House, so call ahead for the latest information. | 8 Smith Ct. | 617/725–0022 | www.afroammuseum.org | Free | Abiel Smith School late May–early Sept., daily 10–4; early Sept.–late May, Mon.–Sat. 10–4. African Meeting House, call ahead for hrs | T stop: Charles/MGH.

Museum of Science. With 15-ft lightning bolts in the Theater of Electricity and a 20-ft-high T-rex model, this is just the place to ignite any child's Jurassic spark. The Charles Hayden Planetarium, with its sophisticated multi-image system, produces exciting programs on astronomical discoveries. The Mugar Omni Theater has a five-story domed screen and 27,000 watts of power driving its 84 loudspeakers. | Science Park at the Charles River Dam | 617/723–2500 | www.mos.org | $11, or with CityPass | Museum early July–early Sept., Sat.–Thurs. 9–7, Fri. 9–9; early Sept.–early July, Sat.–Thurs. 9–5, Fri. 9–9 | T stop: Science Park.

State House. Charles Bulfinch's neoclassical State House is an architectural triumph, with guided tours and exhibits. | Beacon St. between Hancock and Bowdoin Sts. | 617/727–3676 | state.ma.us/sec/trs | Free | Tours weekdays 10–3:30 | T stop: Park St.

Back Bay

In the folklore of American neighborhoods, the Back Bay—flanked by Marlborough and Boylston streets and bisected by eight streets named in alphabetical order, from Arlington to Hereford—stands with New York's Park Avenue and San Francisco's Nob Hill as a symbol of propriety and high social standing.

★ **Boston Public Garden.** The oldest botanical garden in the United States is beloved by Bostonians and visitors alike. The park's pond has been famous since 1877 for its pedal-powered Swan Boats, which make leisurely cruises during warm months. Its statues and charming fountains—including the *Make Way for Ducklings* bronze statue group—are surrounded by old-growth trees and vibrant perennials in the English-garden style. | 617/522–1966 or 617/635–4505 | www.swanboats.com | Swan Boats $2 | Swan Boats mid-Apr.–mid-June, daily 10–4; mid-June–early Sept., daily 10–5; early Sept.–mid-Sept., weekdays noon–4, weekends 10–4 | T stop: Arlington.

Copley Square. The Boston Public Library, the Copley Plaza Hotel, and Trinity Church peacefully coexist here with Copley Place, an upscale glass-and-brass urban mall. The John Hancock Tower looms over all. | T stop: Copley.

First Church of Christ, Scientist. The world headquarters of the Christian Science faith was established here by Mary Baker Eddy in 1879. The stunning complex includes the original granite church, the domed basilica, and the 670-ft reflecting pool, which is a splendid sight on a hot summer day. It's worth visiting for its famed Aeolian-Skinner organ and its Mapparium, a huge stained-glass globe whose 30-ft interior can be traversed on a footbridge. | 175 Huntington Ave. | 617/450–3790 | www.tfccs.com or www.marybakereddylibrary.org | Free church tours Mon.–Sat. 10–4, Sun. 11:30. Sun. services Sept.–June at 10 and 7, Wed. services at noon and 7:30 | T stop: Prudential.

Prudential Center Skywalk. A 50th-floor observatory atop the Prudential Tower, the Skywalk offers panoramic vistas of Boston, Cambridge, and the suburbs to the west and south—on clear days, you can even see Cape Cod. | 800 Boylston St. | 617/236–3114; 617/859–0648 Skywalk | www.prudentialcenter.com | Skywalk $6, or with CityPass | Mon.–Sat. 10–8, Sun. 11–7; Skywalk daily 10–10 | T stop: Prudential.

Trinity Church. The centerpiece of Copley Square, this Episcopal church is Henry Hobson Richardson's 1877 Romanesque Revival masterpiece. | 206 Clarendon St. | 617/536–0944 | www.trinitychurchboston.org | Tours $5, self-guided tours $3 | Daily 8–6. Sun. services at 8, 9, 11:15, and 6; services Mon.–Thurs. at 7:30, 12:10, and 5:30, Fri. at 7:30. Tours weekdays at 1, 2, and 3 (call to confirm) | T stop: Copley.

Government Center and the North End

Government Center—roughly the area between Downtown and Mass General Hospital—is not well loved for its architecture, which includes the treeless expanse of City Hall Plaza, the twin towers of John F. Kennedy Federal Office Building, and the crescent-shape Center Plaza building. But it is enlivened by feisty political rallies, free summer concerts, the occasional festival, and, in winter, the Animatronic Enchanted Village, a Boston children's tradition since the 1940s.

At its northern border is the North End, currently cut into sections by I–93, which will eventually be replaced by an underground highway in a massive construction project known as the Big Dig. Boston's Little Italy, the North End, has narrow, winding streets that are filled with restaurants and—despite recent gentrification—the aromas and sounds of the Old World.

Blackstone Block. The city's oldest commercial block was dominated for decades by butchers, but today it offers a time-machine view of Old Boston. The centerpiece of the block is the Union Oyster House, whose patrons have included Daniel Webster and John F. Kennedy. | Blackstone St., between North and Hanover Sts. | T stop: Government Center.

Copp's Hill Burying Ground. Look for musket-ball pockmarks in the headstones of this Colonial-era cemetery, where British soldiers practiced their skills during the occupation of Boston. | Between Hull and Snowhill Sts. | www.cityofboston.gov/parks/buryinggrounds | Apr.–Nov., daily 9–5; Dec.–Mar., daily 9–dusk | T stop: North Station.

★ **Faneuil Hall Marketplace.** Faneuil—pronounced "*fan*-yuhl"—Hall was erected in 1742 to serve as a meeting hall and public market. After falling into disrepair, the venerable Greek Revival structure was recycled in 1976, along with the three arcade buildings of Quincy Market behind it, into a dining-entertainment-shopping complex that is a stroller's dream. The stores range from chains like Crate & Barrel to one-of-a-kind boutiques and are complemented by kiosks and push-cart vendors. You'll find every kind of food imaginable, from à la carte items heavy on local flavor to sit-down dinners in the market's many café-restaurants—which include an exact replica of *Cheers* bar. Jugglers, magicians, performance artists, and folk singers appear throughout the day. | Between Clinton and Chatham Sts. | 617/338–2323 | www.faneuilhallmarketplace.com | Mon.–Sat. 10–9, Sun. noon–6. Restaurants and bars generally daily 11 AM–2 AM; food stalls open earlier | T stop: Haymarket, Government Center, State St.

For history buffs, the headquarters and museum of the **Ancient and Honorable Artillery Company of Massachusetts,** founded in 1638 and the oldest militia in the Western Hemisphere, occupy the top floors of Faneuil Hall itself. Admission is free, and the museum is open weekdays from 9 to 3:30. | 617/227–1638.

Holocaust Memorial. At night, these six 50-ft-high glass-and-steel towers—etched with 6 million numbers in random sequence symbolizing the Jewish victims of the Nazi horror—glow like ghosts that vow never to forget. | Union St. | T stop: Government Center.

★ **Old North Church.** Also known as Christ Church, Old North is the oldest in Boston (1723). Its steeple is where, on the night of April 18, 1775, two lanterns signaled the departure by water of the British regulars to Lexington and Concord. | 193 Salem St. | 617/523–6676 | www.oldnorth.com | June–Oct., daily 9–6; Nov.–May, daily 9–5. Sun. services at 9, 11, and 5 | T stop: Haymarket, North Station.

Paul Revere House. Built nearly a hundred years before Revere's 1775 midnight ride, the house has special events scheduled throughout the year, many designed with children in mind. | 19 North Sq. | 617/523–2338 | www.paulreverehouse.org | $2.50, $4 with Pierce-Hichborn House | Jan.–Mar., Tues.–Sun. 9:30–4:15; Nov.–Dec. and first 2 wks of Apr., daily 9:30–4:15; mid-Apr.–Oct., daily 9:30–5:15 | T stop: Haymarket, Aquarium, Government Center.

Charlestown

Charlestown was a thriving settlement a year before Colonials headed across the Charles River to found Boston proper. The district holds two of the most visible—and vertical—monuments in Boston's history: the Bunker Hill Monument and the USS *Constitution.*

Bunker Hill Monument. The Patriots eventually lost here in one of the first major confrontations of the Revolutionary War; but their battle strategies and courage made it clear that the British—who sustained heavy losses—could be challenged. It's 294 steps to the top of the monument, but the views from the observatory are worth the arduous climb. | Main St. to Monument St., then straight uphill | 617/242–5641 | Free | Lodge daily 9–5, monument daily 9–4:30 | T stop: Community College.

USS *Constitution.* Better known as "Old Ironsides," the more than two-centuries-old USS *Constitution* is docked at the Charlestown Navy Yard. Launched in 1797, the oldest commissioned ship in the U.S. fleet never lost a battle. | Charlestown Navy Yard, off Water St. | 617/242–5670 | www.ussconstitution.navy.mil or www.ussconstitutionmuseum.org | Free | Daily noon–sunset; continuous tour (last one about 15 mins before sunset). | T stop: Haymarket; then MBTA Bus 92 or 93 to Charlestown City Sq. Or MBTA water shuttle from Long Wharf to Pier 4.

The adjacent **Constitution Museum** has artifacts and hands-on exhibits. It's open May–October, daily 9–6; November–April, daily 10–5. | 617/426–1812.

Downtown Boston

Downtown is a mishmash of neighborhoods, including the Financial District, Chinatown, the Theater District, the New England Medical Center, and the old Leather District, now home to chichi lofts. The 1950s began the decline of the quarter of Downtown bordered on the west by Boston Common and on the south by the "Mass Pike" when shortsighted city officials, in an attempt to contain the spread of vice, created the Lower Washington Street Adult Entertainment District—quickly dubbed "the Combat Zone" by locals. Today, the area is a shadow of its sleazy self, and the Millennium Place commercial complex on Washington Street bordering it promises to seal its coffin. Already open are the new Ritz-Carlton Boston Common, a 19-screen Loews theater, a huge spa–fitness center, three restaurants, extended-stay residences, and luxury condominiums; new retail space is filling quickly.

Boston Tea Party Ship and Museum. An August 2001 lightning strike caused a fire that closed down the *Beaver II,* a replica of one of the ships forcibly boarded and unloaded the night Boston Harbor became a teapot. At press time it was scheduled to reopen in early 2003 with improved exhibits. | Congress St. Bridge | 617/338–1773 | www.bostonteapartyship.com | T stop: South Station.

Children's Museum. Hands-on exhibits at this popular museum include computers, video cameras, the Japanese House, Arthur's World, and Boats Afloat. | 300 Congress St. | 617/426–6500; 617/426–885 recorded information | www.bostonkids.org | $7 | Sat.–Thurs. 10–5, Fri. 10–9 | T stop: South Station.

Chinatown. Not as picturesque as New York's or San Francisco's Chinatown, Boston's nonetheless has a history dating back to the 1870s and is home to the third-largest concentration of Chinese-Americans in the United States. Shops carry Chinese clothing, furniture, and herbs, but the real reason to visit is the large number of pan-Asian eateries. After dinner, stop by a Chinese bakery for a unique sweet. | T stop: Chinatown.

King's Chapel. Somber yet dramatic, the 1754 King's Chapel is a masterpiece of proportion and Georgian calm. The chapel's bell is Paul Revere's largest and, in his judgment, his sweetest-sounding. To the church's right is the King's Chapel Burying Ground, the oldest cemetery in the city; it contains the 1704 gravestone of Elizabeth Pain, the model for Hester Prynne in Hawthorne's *The Scarlet Letter.* | 58 Tremont St., at School St. | 617/227–2155 | www.kings-chapel.org | Mid-Apr.–Nov., Mon. and Fri.–Sat. 10–4; Dec.–mid-Apr., Sat. 10–4. Year-round music program Tues. 12:15–1; services Sun. at 11, Wed. at 12:15 | T stop: Park St., Government Center.

★ **New England Aquarium.** This facility has a café, a gift shop, an outdoor seal tank, and changing exhibits. Inside the main building are more than 2,000 species of marine life from sharks to jellyfish. | Central Wharf (between Central and Milk Sts.) | 617/973–5200 or 617/973–5277 | www.neaq.org | $13, or with CityPass | July–early Sept., Mon.–Tues. and Fri. 9–6, Wed.–Thurs. 9–8, weekends 9–7; early Sept.–June, weekdays 9–5, weekends 9–6 | T stop: Aquarium, State St.

Old South Meeting House. Some of the most fiery pre-Revolutionary town meetings were held at Old South, culminating in the tumultuous gathering of December 16, 1773, convened by Samuel Adams to address the question of dutiable tea that activists wanted returned to England. This was also the congregation of Phillis Wheatley, the first published African-American poet. | 310 Washington St. | 617/482–6439 | www.oldsouthmeetinghouse.org | $3 | Apr.–Oct., daily 9:30–5; Nov.–Mar., daily 10–4 | T stop: State St., Downtown Crossing.

Old State House. This was the seat of the Colonial government from 1713 until the Revolution, and after the evacuation of the British from Boston it served the independent Commonwealth until its replacement on Beacon Hill was completed in 1798. The permanent collection traces Boston's Revolutionary War history. | 206 Washington St., at corner of State St. | 617/720–3290 | www.bostonhistory.org | $3 | Daily 9–5 | T stop: State St.

South End

The South End, a formerly fashionable enclave filled with redbrick bowfront row houses patterned on those of Beacon Hill, was rediscovered a few decades ago, largely by the gay community. It has since become one of the trendiest spots in town, filled with home-decor and gift shops, avant-garde galleries, and restaurants of all descriptions. It has a couple of tree-lined parks, some playgrounds, and a friendly, neighborly feel, but it is decidedly lacking in "sights," per se, for the visitor. If you go for an afternoon stroll, be sure to stop by **Olde Dutch Candy and Antiques** first to fortify yourself with penny candy. | 518 Tremont St. | 617/338–0233.

The Fens and Kenmore Square

The Fens mark the beginning of Boston's Emerald Necklace, a loosely connected chain of parks designed by Frederick Law Olmsted that extends along the Fenway, Riverway, and Jamaicaway to Jamaica Pond, the Arnold Arboretum, and Franklin Park.

Fenway Park. Fenway may be one of the smallest ballparks in the major leagues (capacity 34,000), but it is also one of the most loved. Since its construction in 1912, there has been no shortage of heroics: Babe Ruth pitched here when the place was new, and it's where Ted Williams and Carl Yastrzemski played out their epic careers. | 4 Yawkey Way, between Van Ness and Lansdowne Sts. | 617/267–1700 box office; 617/267–8661 recorded information; 617/236–6666 tours | www.redsox.com/fenway | Tours $5 | Tours May–Sept. weekdays at 10, 11, and noon on day-game days; additional tour at 2 on nongame or night-game days.

★ **Isabella Stewart Gardner Museum.** Named for a spirited young society woman from New York who occupied its top floors until her death in 1924, this Venetian palazzo houses old master paintings, Medici treasures, rooms bought outright from great European houses, and Gothic tapestries. A restaurant overlooks the courtyard, and in the spring and summer tables and chairs spill outside. | 280 The Fenway | 617/566–1401; 617/566–1088 café | www.gardnermuseum.org | $10 | Museum Tues.–Sun. 11–5, café Tues.–Sun. 11:30–4. Weekend concerts at 1:30. | T stop: Museum.

★ **Museum of Fine Arts.** The MFA's holdings of American art—Winslow Homer, John Singer Sargent, Edward Hopper, Georgia O'Keeffe—surpass those of all but two or three other U.S. museums. The museum also has a sublime collection of French Impressionists—including the largest collection of Monet's work outside France—and renowned collections of Asian, Egyptian, and Nubian art. A gift shop, two restaurants, a cafeteria, and the gallery café will keep you from getting museum fatigue. | 465 Huntington Ave. | 617/267–9300 | www.mfa.org | $14, or with CityPass; by donation Wed. 4–9:45 | Museum Mon.–Tues. and weekends 10–5:45, Wed.–Fri. 10–9:45. West Wing only Thurs.–Fri. 5–10. 1-hr tours available weekdays. Garden Apr.–Oct., Tues.–Sun. 10–4 | T stop: Museum.

Cambridge

Known locally as "the People's Republic of Cambridge," this independent city across the Charles has long been a haven for freethinkers, writers, and activists of every stamp. Cambridge is now known for its high-tech and biotechnology firms—and, of course, for two of the country's greatest educational institutions, Harvard University and the Massachusetts Institute of Technology.

Arthur M. Sackler Museum. The richness of the East and artistic treasures of the ancient Greeks, Egyptians, and Romans fill three of the four floors of this modern structure. The changing exhibits are first-rate. The fee for the Sackler gains you entrance to the Fogg Art Museum, the Busch-Reisinger Museum, and the Sert Gallery. | 485 Broadway | 617/495–9400 | www.artmuseums.harvard.edu | $5, free all day Wed. and Sat. 10–noon | Mon.–Sat. 10–5, Sun. 1–5.

★ **Fogg Art Museum.** Harvard's art museum's collection of 80,000 works focuses primarily on European, American, and East Asian works, with notable 19th-century French Impressionist and medieval Italian paintings. Included with Fogg admission is the Arthur M. Sackler Museum. | 32 Quincy St. | 617/495–9400 | www.artmuseums.harvard.edu | $5, free all day Wed. and Sat. 10–noon | Mon.–Sat. 10–5, Sun. 1–5.

The **Sert Gallery,** in the adjacent Carpenter Center for the Visual Arts, hosts changing exhibits of contemporary works and also houses a café.

The **Busch-Reisinger Museum** focuses on German Expressionism.

Harvard Museum of Natural History. Many museums promise something for every member of the family; the Harvard museum complex actually delivers. One fee admits you to all on-site museums, as well as to the Peabody Museum of Archaeology and Ethnology. | 26 Oxford St. | 617/495–3045 | www.hmnh.harvard.edu | $6.50, or with CityPass; free Sun. 9–noon, and Wed. 3–5 (Sept.–May only) | Daily 9–5.

In the **Botanical Museum,** the astonishingly lifelike glass flowers, including 3,000 models of 847 plant species, were meticulously created from 1887 to 1936; everything is, indeed, made of glass.

The **Museum of Comparative Zoology** traces the evolution of animals (including dinosaurs) and humans.

Oversize garnets and crystals are among the holdings of the **Mineralogical and Geological Museum,** which also has an extensive collection of meteorites.

Harvard Square. Gaggles of students, musicians and other street performers, and soapbox speakers make for a nonstop pedestrian flow at this most celebrated of Cambridge crossroads. Surrounded by restaurants and shops, it's the best place in town for free entertainment any night of the week.

The **Cambridge Visitor Information Booth,** just outside the T station entrance, is a volunteer-staffed kiosk with maps and brochures. The booth—open weekdays 9–5, Saturday 10–3, and Sunday 1–5—has maps for historic and literary walking tours of the city and other information. | 617/497–1630 | www.cambridge-usa.org.

Harvard University. In 1636 the Great and General Court of the Massachusetts Bay Colony established the country's first college here. Named in 1639 for John Harvard, a young Charlestown clergyman who died in 1638, leaving the college his entire library and half his estate, Harvard remained the only college in the New World until 1693, by which time it was firmly established as a respected center of learning. | Holyoke Center, 1350 Massachusetts Ave. | 617/495–1000 general information | www.harvard.edu.

Students run the **Harvard University Events and Information Center,** which has maps of the university area and offers a free hour-long walking tour of Harvard Yard. | 617/495–1573.

Longfellow National Historic Site. Henry Wadsworth Longfellow—the poet whose stirring renditions about Hiawatha and Paul Revere's midnight ride thrilled 19th-century America—once lived in this elegant mansion. | 105 Brattle St. | 617/876–4491 | www.nps.gov/long | $3 | May–Oct., Wed.–Sun. 10–4:30; 45-min guided tours at 10:30, 11:30, 1, 2, 3, and 4.

Peabody Museum of Archaeology and Ethnology. The Peabody holds one of the world's most outstanding anthropological collections; exhibits focus on Native American and Central and South American cultures. The admission fee includes entrance to the Harvard Museum of Natural History as well. | 11 Divinity Ave. | 617/496–1027 | www.peabody.harvard.edu | $6.50; free Sun. 9–noon, and Wed. 3–5 (Sept.–May only) | Daily 9–5.

Dining

The main ingredient in Boston's restaurant fare is still the bounty of the North Atlantic, the daily catch of fish and shellfish that appears on virtually every menu. Seafood or no, the choice of dining experience in Boston has expanded to include a variety of ethnic cuisines.

Beacon Hill

Black Goose. American. All things to all members of the family: kid-friendly burgers and fries, parent-friendly veggie wraps and linen napkins. A patio in summer adds to the casual elegance. | 21 Beacon St. | 617/720–4500 | $10–$20 | AE, D, DC, MC, V.

DeLuca's. American. DeLuca's offers an endless variety of gourmet deli food and beverages to be unwrapped beside the Swan Boats or under a willow in the Public Garden. Sandwiches are made to order; there's also a salad bar, wines, and even prepared hot dinners, from chicken breast stuffed with mashed potato to lasagna. | 11 Charles St. | 617/523–4343 | $5–$20 | AE, D, DC, MC, V.

King & I. Pan-Asian. Generic decor doesn't detract from the wide variety of Thai and Pan-Asian dishes, which are well executed (many awards hang in the window) and served by a friendly staff. There's plenty of rice, noodles, tofu, and other classics, but why not go for something more exotic, like Dancing Squids, Seafood Typhoon, or the romantic Shrimp in Love? | 145 Charles St. | 617/227–3320 | $3–$10 | AE, D, MC, V.

★ **Lala Rokh.** Middle Eastern. A beautifully detailed and delicious fantasy of food and art, Lala Rokh's superb, mainly Azerbaijanian food includes both exotically flavored specialties as well as familiar dishes like pilaf and kebabs. | 97 Mt. Vernon St. | 617/720–5511 | $14–$19 | AE, DC, MC, V.

Panificio. American. This cozy neighborhood hangout and old-fashioned Italian café has pizza and beer for lunch and complex, sophisticated tastes for dinner that possess European flair with an occasional South American or Asian twist. Soups and breads are made on the premises. | 144 Charles St. | 617/227–4340 | $8–$23 | AE, DC, MC, V.

21st Amendment. American. If you want to overhear the latest political gossip from newspaper reporters and other State House habitués, this is the place to be at lunchtime. Classic pub food coexists happily with wraps, burritos, and salads ranging from Cajun Chicken to Smoked Applewood Bacon & Blue Cheese. | 148 Bowdoin St. | 617/227–7100 | $4–$9 | AE, MC, V.

Back Bay

Bangkok Blue. Pan-Asian. This small, spare space offers a café in summer, a friendly and helpful staff, and a couple tanks of curious fish to keep you occupied if conversation lags. Dishes like salmon sautéed in a kaffir lime and lemongrass curry are good, but anything with peanut sauce is rapturous; it's so creamy and sweet you'll want to ask for extra on the side. | 651 Boylston St. | 617/266–1010 | $9–$17 | AE, DC, MC, V.

Cottonwood. American. "Creative Southwest cuisine" includes such specialties as Snakebites—fried jalapeños stuffed with shrimp and jack cheese—and salmon Veracruz. Save room for the chocolate nachos, dark and white chocolate mousse topped with fresh fruit and Belgian-chocolate-dipped butter cookies. | 222 Berkeley St. | 617/237–2225 | $14–$24 | AE, D, DC, MC, V.

Fire + Ice. American. There's something for everyone in the family at the two Fire + Ice locations, which are a mix between table service and do-it-yourself all-you-can-eat buffet. Everyone gets a bowl, to be filled at various stations with veggies, meat, seafood, and sauces and then handed to a chef, who grills the individual choices. Jasmine rice and warm tortillas await at the table. | 205 Berkeley St., Back Bay | 617/482–3473 | 50 Church St., Cambridge | 617/547–9007 | $8–$17 | AE, D, DC, MC, V.

Marché Mövenpick. American. The first U.S. location of this European chain has proved to be a great success. It's fun and casual, and if you can't find something you'll eat here, you're just not hungry. You pay by the dish, which you pick up at various stations set up like a town square: grill and rotisserie, seafood, Far East, soup and salad, pasta, pizza, coffee bar, "Fruit Tree," wine and spirits bar, and pastry and ice cream. | The Prudential Center, 800 Boylston St. | 617/578–9700 | $4–$20 | AE, D, DC, MC, V.

Parish Cafe. American. With an outdoor café in nice weather, Parish attracts a big after-work crowd that can sometimes get raucous, but the large tables in back are family-friendly. The menu consists mainly of sandwiches by chefs from around city. Try the best-selling Norma's Zuni Roll: smoked turkey breast with crispy bacon, scallions, dill Havarti cheese, and cranberry chipotle sauce on a flour tortilla. | 361 Boylston St. | 617/247–4777 | $8–$20 | AE, DC, MC, V.

Government Center and the North End

Antico Forno. Italian. Many of the menu choices come from the eponymous wood-burning brick oven, which turns out surprisingly delicate pizzas simply topped with tomato and fresh mozzarella. Don't overlook the handmade pastas; the specialty, gnocchi, is rich and creamy but light. The room is cramped and noisy, but the hubbub is part of the fun. | 93 Salem St. | 617/723–6733 | $14–$20 | AE, MC, V.

Barking Crab Restaurant. Seafood. It's a seaside clam shack plunk in the middle of Boston, with a stunning view of the Downtown skyscrapers. An outdoor lobster tent in summer, in winter it retreats indoors to a warm-hearted version of a waterfront dive, with chestnuts roasting on a cozy wood stove. | 88 Sleeper St. (Northern Ave. Bridge) | 617/426–2722 | $7–$20 | AE, DC, MC, V.

Billy Tse. Pan-Asian. Most people don't think of going to the Italian North End for Chinese, but Billy Tse is probably the best Chinese restaurant in town. It's a calm and relaxed spot, and the moo shu is to die for. | 240 Commercial St. | 617/227–9990 | $8–26 | AE, D, MC, V.

Durgin Park. American. You should be hungry enough to cope with enormous portions, yet not so hungry you can't tolerate a long wait. Durgin Park, founded in 1827, serves hearty New England fare: Indian pudding, baked beans, corned beef and cabbage, and a prime rib that hangs over the edge of the plate. The service is famously brusque bordering on rude bordering on good-natured. | 340 Faneuil Hall Marketplace, North Market Bldg. | 617/227–2038 | $6–$18 | AE, D, DC, MC, V.

Lucia Ristorante. Italian. Though it's a bit off the beaten path at the far end of Hanover Street, Lucia offers real Italian cuisine and homey atmosphere that have earned the loyalty of North End residents. Try the Scallopine Abruzzese—a chicken, broccoli, and pasta dish said to have originated in Lucia's kitchen—while gazing at the Sistine Chapel–replica ceiling and intricately muraled walls. | 415 Hanover St. | 617/367–2353 | $8–$20 | AE, MC, V.

Pizzeria Regina. Italian. If you crave pizza, the North End's most popular spot has a line out the door and around the corner—but it's worth the wait for aficionados of the thin but chewy crust loaded down with tangy tomato sauce and creamy mozzarella. In business for 76 years, this place is obviously doing something right. | 11 Thatcher St | 617/227–0765 | $7–$18 | No credit cards.

Union Oyster House. American. The oldest restaurant in Boston (1826) has had only three owners but plenty of history. John F. Kennedy and Daniel Webster both dined frequently in the eatery, whose fabled semicircular raw bar and five dining rooms are still so popular with Bostonians and visitors alike that on Saturday the wait for a table can be up to two hours. | 41 Union St. | 617/227–2750 | $10–$30 | AE, D, DC, MC, V.

Downtown Boston

Chau Chow City. Chinese. Spread across three floors, this place is large, glitzy, and versatile, with dim sum by day and live-tank seafood by night. Overwhelmed? Order the clams in black-bean sauce, the sautéed pea-pod stems with garlic, or the honey glazed–walnut jumbo shrimp. | 83 Essex St. | 617/338–8158 | $9–$22 | AE, D, MC, V.

Jacob Wirth. American. It's easy to find: just look for the clock that hangs outside. With a huge wood-floor dining room and free live music on Friday and Saturday nights, "Jake's"—in business since 1868—is an institution here and a popular hangout for neighborhood office workers and Tufts medical students. A taste of Europe and a little American ingenuity—specialties like Wiener schnitzel, potato pancakes, and sauerbraten share the menu with cornmeal fried oysters and cranberry barbecued chicken—raise its pub fare far above the norm. | 33–37 Stuart St. | 617/338–8586 | $8–$20 | AE, D, DC, MC, V.

Legal Sea Foods. Seafood. What began as a tiny restaurant upstairs over a Cambridge fish market has grown to important regional status, with more than 20 East Coast locations. The hallmark is the freshest possible seafood, whether you have it wood-grilled, in New England chowder, or accompanied by an Asia-inspired sauce. The smoked-bluefish pâté is delectable. A preferred-seating list allows calls ahead. | 26 Park Sq., Theater District | 617/426–4444 | 255 State St., Financial District | 617/227–3115 | 5 Cambridge Center, Kendall Sq., Cambridge | 617/864–3400 | Logan Airport, Terminal C, East Boston | 617/569–4622 | Reservations not accepted | $6–$25 | AE, D, DC, MC, V.

South End

Baja Mexican Cantina. Mexican. Anything-but-traditional Mexican food is served in this postmodern Southwest spot. All the Cal-Mex food is quite good, with lots of vegetarian options. If you're health-conscious, go for the salads, relatively low-fat burritos, or the lean hamburger on tortilla. | 111 Dartmouth St. | 617/262–7575 | $8–$15 | AE, D, DC, MC, V.

Bob the Chef's. Southern. Boston's home of genteel soul food and jazz attracts a mellow mix of yuppies and neighborhood families. Try the crab cakes, catfish fingers, chitterlings, or "glorifried" chicken; all-you-can-eat Sunday brunch is a surefire way to lift your spirits, especially when there's live gospel music. | 604 Columbus Ave. | 617/536–6204 | Closed Mon. | $11–$15 | AE, D, DC, MC, V.

Cambridge

Cardullo's. American. In the heart of Harvard Square, Cardullo's is a great place to pick up a box meal to unwrap along the waterfront on Memorial Drive or even under a shady tree in Harvard Yard. Four-ounce sandwiches are a meal in themselves, and most everything is made in-house, including the delicious soups like creamy wild rice and pumpkin sweet potato. Finish up with a package of imported Harry Potter sweets. | 6 Brattle St. | 617/491–8888 | $6–$12 | AE, D, MC, V.

La Groceria. Italian. A trattoria before trattorias were cool, this place would do Carmela Soprano proud with its homemade pasta and cannoli. It's a block off Mass Avenue near Central Square. | 853 Main St. | 617/876–4162 | $12–$20 | AE, D, DC, MC, V.

Mr. and Mrs. Bartley's Burger Cottage. American. Tiny tables in a crowded space don't hinder the hoards that come for the variously garnished thick burgers, french fries, and onion rings. (There's also a competent veggie burger.) The nonalcoholic "raspberry lime rickey," made with fresh limes, raspberry juice, sweetener, and soda water, is the must-try classic drink. | 1246 Massachusetts Ave. | 617/354–6559 | Reservations not accepted | Closed Sun. | $6–$14 | No credit cards.

Poppa & Goose. Pan-Asian. If you're down MIT way, this is *the* spot for fast, light, cheap Pan-Asian dishes. The primarily Vietnamese menu offers pad thai, chicken teriyaki, and such specialties as shrimp in buttery green onions over rice vermicelli—all best followed by cognac-drizzled warm mango crepes with vanilla ice cream. | 69 1st St. | 617/497–6772 | $7–$14 | AE, D, DC, MC, V.

Rock Bottom Brewery. Italian. Yes, it's a chain, but there's one conveniently located near Harvard Square. Plus the children's menu pleases kids—with its chicken tenders, grilled cheese sandwich, macaroni and cheese, and root beer float—as well as Mom and Dad, with its kids' entrée price of $3.95. | 50 Church St. | 617/499–2739 | 115 Stuart St., Back Bay | 617/742–2739 | $10–$20 | AE, D, DC, MC, V.

Tanjore. Indian. Tanjore's menu runs the gamut of dishes from so many areas of India that it will be hard to choose. An extra menu of *nashta,* or Indian tapas, adds to the confusion—or the fun, depending on how adventurous you're feeling. The rice dishes, chais, and breads are all excellent; the spicing is on the easy side, so don't be afraid to order "medium." | 18 Elliot St. | 617/868–1900 | Reservations essential | $10–$13 | AE, D, MC, V.

Lodging

Back Bay

Greater Boston YMCA. This is a great summer option for the budget-minded family. The coed facility near the Museum of Fine Arts has single ($45), double ($65), triple ($81), and quad ($96) rooms. You must write in advance to reserve a room, especially if you plan to bring children. Cafeteria, pool, health club, sauna, laundry facilities | 316 Huntington Ave., 02115 | 617/536–7800 | fax 617/267–4653 | 108 rooms, most with shared bath | $45–$96 | Closed early Sept.–late June | AE, D, MC, V.

The Fens and Kenmore Square

Howard Johnson's Kenmore Square. Convenient to Fenway Park and Downtown, this HoJo has many rooms with balcony views of the Charles River. Children under 18 stay free in their parents' room. Restaurant, in-room data ports, pool, lobby lounge, babysitting, free parking, no-smoking rooms. | 575 Commonwealth Ave., 02215 | 617/267–3100 or 800/654–2000 | fax 617/424–1045 | www.hojo.com | 178 rooms, 1 suite | $135–$235 | AE, D, DC, MC, V.

Cambridge

Harding House. It may not be full of period details, but this 1867 inn combines the charm of a B&B with the reliability of a hotel. Halfway between Harvard and MIT, it's just three blocks from funky Central Square and the Red Line. Children under 7 stay free, and those 7–17 stay for $5 each in their parents' room. Kitchenettes and museum passes are available. Free parking; no smoking | 288 Harvard St. | 617/876–2888 or 877/489–2888 | fax 617/497–0953 | www.irvinghouse.com | 11 rooms, 3 suites | $99–$250 | AE, D, DC, MC, V | CP.

Harvard Square Hotel. Casual and family-friendly, this hotel is an affordable option in the heart of Harvard Square. Rooms are simple but clean, desk clerks are helpful, and there's Internet access in the lobby. Children under 16 stay free in their parents' room. Café, in-room data ports, laundry service, car rental, parking (fee); no-smoking rooms. | 110 Mt. Auburn St., 02138 | 617/864–5200 or 800/458–5886 | fax 617/864–2409 | 73 rooms | $159–$229 | AE, D, DC, MC, V.

Irving House. A notch above student living, this no-smoking B&B is still a bargain. On a residential street three blocks from Harvard Square, its two small porches, hardwood floors, and Oriental rugs make it homier than a hotel. Children 7 and under stay free; those 8–17 stay at a discount. Free off-street parking and museum passes are available. Free parking; no smoking | 24 Irving St., | 617/547–4600 or 877/547–4600 |

fax 617/576–2814 | www.irvinghouse.com | 44 rooms, 29 with bath | $89–$250 | AE, D, MC, V | CP.

Boston Outskirts

Beacon Inns. A B&B budget option, these two guest houses in the "streetcar suburb" of Brookline are convenient to several local colleges, restaurants, and the T, which stops just outside and gets you Downtown in 20 minutes. Inexpensive parking is available. In-room data ports, cable TV, parking (fee); no smoking | 1087 Beacon St., Brookline 02446 | 1750 Beacon St., Brookline 02445 | 617/566–0088 or 888/575–0088 | fax 617/278–9736 or 617/264–7948 | 1087: 8 rooms with bath. 1750: 14 rooms with bath | $99–$169 | AE, MC, V.

Best Western Terrace Inn. This well-priced and well-maintained hotel is in a bustling neighborhood in Brookline, with the T less than a block away. Sixty rooms have kitchenettes, and there's a supermarket two blocks away. Children under 18 stay free in their parents' room. Refrigerators, free parking | 1650 Commonwealth Ave., 02135 | 617/566–6260 or 800/242–8377 | fax 617/731–3543 | www.bestwestern.com/terraceinn | 66 rooms, 6 suites | $99–$179 | AE, D, DC, MC, V | CP.

Holiday Inn Express. The neighborhood is more commercial than scenic, but it's a five-minute walk to public transportation into the city; hourly shuttles to the airport (4 mi away) are free. Children under 18 stay free in their parents' room. Gym, laundry service, free parking | 69 Boston St., 02125 | 617/288–3030 or 800/465–4329 | fax 617/265–6543 | 110 rooms, 8 suites | $109–$179 | AE, D, DC, MC, V | CP.

Howard Johnson's Hotel Boston Bayside and the Ramada Inn Boston. Just off I–93, these two hotels are separated by a 90-game arcade room, candlepin bowling, and a candy store. Some rooms have a refrigerator-microwave unit. A free shuttle takes guests to the T, and a Beantown Trolley Tour departs from the complex daily. Children under 18 stay free in their parents' room. 3 restaurants, in-room data ports, refrigerators, cable TV, pool, lounge, piano bar, laundry facilities, free parking, no-smoking rooms | 800–900 Morrissey Blvd., 02122 | 800/886–0056 | fax 617/282–2365 | www.bostonhotel.com | 306 rooms, 3 suites | $99–$209 | AE, D, DC, MC, V | CP.

Arts and Entertainment

BosTix. The city's largest ticket agency is a full-price Ticketmaster outlet, and beginning at 11 AM, it sells half-price tickets for same-day performances; the "menu board" in front of the booth announces the available events. Only cash and traveler's checks are accepted. | Faneuil Hall Marketplace | 617/482–2849 | www.bostix.org | Tues.–Sat. 10–6, Sun. 11–4 | Copley Sq., near corner of Boylston and Dartmouth Sts. | Mon.–Sat. 10–6, Sun. 11–4.

Ticketmaster allows phone charges to major credit cards, weekdays 9 AM–10 PM, weekends 9–8. There are no refunds or exchanges, and you pay a service charge. It also has outlets in local stores; call for the nearest address. | 617/931–2000 or 617/931–2787 | www.ticketmaster.com.

Dance

Boston Ballet. The city's premier dance company performs classical and modern works, primarily at the Wang Center. Its annual *Nutcracker* is a Boston holiday tradition. | 19 Clarendon St., South End | 617/695–6950 or 800/447–7400.

Music

Hatch Memorial Shell. The Boston Pops performs free summer concerts in this jewel of an acoustic shell. | Off Storrow Dr., at the embankment, Beacon Hill | 617/727–9547.

Symphony Hall. One of the world's most perfect acoustical settings is home to the Boston Symphony Orchestra, conducted by Seiji Ozawa, and the Boston Pops, conducted by Keith Lockhart. | 301 Massachusetts Ave., Back Bay | 617/266–1492 or 800/274–8499.

Theater

Charles Playhouse. Two long-running shows include the avant-garde *Blue Man Group* (617/426–6912) and *Shear Madness* (617/426–5225), an audience-participation who-dunit. | 74 Warrenton St., Theater District | 617/426–6912.

Emerson Majestic Theatre. Everything from dance to drama to classical concerts is performed here. | 219 Tremont St., Theater District | 617/824–8000.

Huntington Theatre Company. Affiliated with Boston University, this company performs a mix of established 20th-century plays and classics. | 264 Huntington Ave., Back Bay | 617/266–0800 | www.bu.edu/huntington.

Loeb Drama Center. The acclaimed American Repertory Theater, which produces classic and experimental works, makes its home here. | 64 Brattle St., Harvard Sq., Cambridge | 617/495–2268 or 617/547–8300 | www.amrep.org.

Publick Theatre. It's heavy on the Shakespeare—but who really cares what's playing at an open-air theater set on a hillside on the banks of the Charles? | Christian Herter Park, off Soldiers Field Rd., Cambridge | 617/782–5425 | www.publick.org.

Shopping

The best shopping is in the area bounded by Quincy Market, the Back Bay, Downtown, and Copley Square, where you'll find many of the idiosyncratic boutiques, handcrafts shops, and galleries that remain Boston's strength. Hunt for bargains in Downtown Crossing. There is no state sales tax on clothing. However, there is a 5% luxury tax on clothes priced higher than $175 per item; the tax is levied on the amount in excess of $175.

Boston

Pretty **Charles Street,** one of the oldest streets in the city, is crammed with antiques stores and boutiques, though they're generally a bit pricey, due to their high Beacon Hill rents. **Copley Place** and the **Prudential Center** are Back Bay malls connected by a glass skywalk over Huntington Avenue. Copley packs more wallet-wallop, while "the Pru" contains moderately priced chain stores. In **Downtown Crossing,** entrenched independents coexist with prosaic chains, outlets snuggle against down-market competitors, and pushcarts thrive alongside the city's two largest department stores, Macy's and Filene's (with the famous Filene's Basement beneath it). Historic **Faneuil Hall Marketplace** is an enormous complex that's hugely popular with visitors, perhaps because it successfully combines the familiar with the unique, as such chains as the Gap and Banana Republic provide the backdrop for street performers and one of the area's truly great casual dining experiences. In just eight blocks, **Newbury Street** in the Back Bay goes from New York's 5th Avenue stylish to SoHo funky. The gentrified **South End** has become a retailing force, specializing in offbeat home furnishings and gift shops.

Cambridge

Traveling west along Massachusetts Avenue toward Harvard Square, you will pass through eclectic **Central Square,** which holds a mix of furniture stores, used-record shops, ethnic restaurants, and small, hip performance venues. **Harvard Square** comprises just a few blocks but contains more than 150 stores selling clothes, books and records, furnishings, and specialty items. **Porter Square,** on Massachusetts Avenue, has several distinctive clothing and home furnishings stores, crafts shops, natural food markets, and restaurants.

Sports and Outdoor Activities

Bicycling

Many Bostonians—particularly those who don't like sitting in traffic jams—are passionate about biking. Visitors unused to the unpredictable traffic patterns would do best to stay on the bike paths bordering each side of the Charles. The **Dr. Paul Dudley White Bikeway,** approximately 18 mi long, follows both banks of the Charles River as it winds from Watertown Square to the Museum of Science.

Community Bicycle Supply. Cycles are available for rent from April through September, at rates of $20 for 24 hours or $5 per hour (minimum 2 hours). | 496 Tremont St., at E. Berkeley St., South End | 617/542–8623.

Boating

One of Boston's most iconic and beautiful sights is the white triangles of sail dotting the Charles River on a sunny day. Sailing is practically the official activity of this part of New England, steeped as it is in maritime tradition and avidly enamored with the outdoors.

Community Boating. Near the Charles Street footbridge on the Esplanade, this is America's oldest public sailing program. From April through October, a $75 registration fee—about the cost of renting a boat for the day elsewhere—nets you unlimited use of sailboats, kayaks, or Windsurfers for up to 45 days. | 21 David Mugar Way, Beacon Hill | 617/523–1038 | www.community-boating.org.

In-Line Skating

As in the rest of the country, in-line skating continues to pick up converts in Boston, even as its trend-of-the-moment appeal has worn down. From April through October, **Memorial Drive,** on the Cambridge side of the Charles River, is closed to auto traffic on Sunday 11 AM–7 PM, when the area between the Western Avenue Bridge and Eliot Bridge is transformed into an in-line skater's mecca. The **Esplanade,** on the Boston side of the river, swarms with skaters (and joggers) on weekends.

Beacon Hill Skate Shop. This handy shop rents blades and safety equipment for $8 per hour or $20 for 24 hours. You need a credit card for a deposit. | 135 S. Charles St., off Tremont St., near the Wang Center for the Performing Arts, South End | 617/482–7400.

Essential Information

When to Go

The best times to visit Boston are late spring and early fall. Like other American cities of the Northeast, Boston can be uncomfortably hot and humid (days in the 90° range are not uncommon) in high summer and bitingly cold (25°–30°) in the winter. Autumn in New England brings out scores of "leaf-peepers" enchanted by the combination of blazing foliage, white church steeples, and meandering blue rivers in the suburbs and countryside. Cape Cod and the Islands (Nantucket and Martha's Vineyard) are less crowded in spring and fall, though nearly all the lodging places and restaurants are open; many Bostonians consider "the shoulder season," after most tourists have gone, the ideal time for their seaside vacations.

FESTIVALS AND SEASONAL EVENTS

WINTER

Dec.–Jan.: **First Night Celebration.** Bostonians turn out in force for a full day and night of outdoor and indoor concerts and festivities, culminating in fireworks over Boston Harbor. | 617/542–1399 | www.firstnight.org.

SPRING

Mar.: **Annual Spring New England Flower Show.** The blooms are at the Bayside Expo Center. | 617/933–4900 | www.masshort.org.

St. Patrick's Day Parade. The parade is always a big event in this most Irish of cities. | 888/733–2678.

Apr.: **Patriots' Day.** On the third Monday of the month, celebrants reenact Paul Revere's ride from Hanover Street in Boston's North End to suburban Lexington. On the same day, the Boston Marathon fills the streets from Hopkinton to the Back Bay. | 617/236–1652 | www.bostonmarathon.org.

May: **Duckling Parade.** Everyone "makes way for ducklings" as hundreds of children, many in costume, walk from Beacon Hill to the Public Garden lagoon. | 617/635–4505.

SUMMER

June: ***Boston Globe* Jazz and Blues Festival.** Performances at various venues usually start around Father's Day and last for more than a week. | 617/929–2649 | www.boston.com/jazzfestival.

July: **Harborfest.** Boston's annual weeklong Fourth of July celebration has 200-plus events, from a free Party on the Plaza concert to historical reenactments of Boston's Colonial and maritime past, including the reading of the Declaration of Independence on July 4 at the Old State House. | 888/484–7677 | www.bostonharborfest.com.

Fourth of July Concert. The Boston Pops continues a decades-long tradition with its annual concert and fireworks on the Esplanade. The nationally televised event begins with the "Star-Spangled Banner" and includes such patriotic classics as "America the Beautiful" and "Stars and Stripes Forever" before ending with a bang with Tchaikovsky's 1812 Overture. | 617/227–1528 | www.july4th.org/concert.

AUTUMN

Oct.: **Head of the Charles Regatta.** College crew teams and spectators bearing blankets and beer come from all over for the world's largest two-day rowing event. | 617/868–6200 | www.hocr.org.

Haunted Happenings. Kids love the three weeks of creepy fun in Salem's Halloween festival, which includes haunted houses, street vendors, dramatic productions, and psychic fairs and games. | 978/744–3663 | www.hauntedhappenings.org.

Nov.: **America's Hometown Thanksgiving Celebration.** Spend Thanksgiving Day where it all began. Plymouth parties with reenactments, Indian cultural exhibits, and "Dining with the Pilgrims." | 508/747–7533 or 800/872–1620 | www.visit-plymouth.com.

Bargains

BosTix. Half-price, same-day music, dance, and theater tickets can be purchased from 11 AM to 4 PM daily at these booths in Copley Square and Faneuil Hall Marketplace. For $9, you can also purchase an Arts/Boston coupon book, which offers two-for-one admission to 60 museums, attractions, and tours in and around the city. | 617/482–2849 | www.bostix.org.

CityPass. This reduced-fee combination ticket to six major Boston sights includes the Museum of Science, the New England Aquarium, and the Harvard University Museum of Natural History. The passes cost $30.25 and are available at participating attractions and the Greater Boston Convention and Visitors Bureau information booths. | 888/330–5008 | www.citypass.net.

MBTA Boston Visitor Pass. Passes are available for unlimited travel on subway, local bus, and inner-harbor ferry for one-, three-, and seven-day periods (fares: $6, $11, and $22, respectively). | 877/927–7277 | www.mbta.com.

Tours

BOAT TOURS

Boston Duck Tours. Tour the city's streets and the Charles River in a World War II amphibious vehicle. From April to November, the 80-minute tours leave the Prudential Center's Huntington Avenue entrance every half hour from 9 AM till dark; the fare is about $22. Tickets are sold inside the Prudential Center 9–8 Monday–Saturday and 9–6 Sunday; weekend tours often sell out early. | 617/723–3825.

Boston Harbor Cruises. Harbor tours and other cruises (including whale-watching, sunset, and evening entertainment cruises; prices vary) run from mid-April to October. | 617/227–4321.

The Charles Riverboat Co. Fifty-five-minute narrated tours of the Charles River Basin depart from the CambridgeSide Galleria mall at 10:30 AM and then on the hour from noon to 5 daily from June to August and on weekends in April, May, and September; the fare is $9. | 617/621–3001 | www.charlesriverboat.com.

ORIENTATION TOURS

Beantown Trolleys. The red trolleys make more than 20 stops; get on and off as many times as you like. Cost is $22. Trolleys run every half hour from 9 AM until 4 PM. Tickets are available from hotel concierges, at many attractions, and sometimes on board. | 617/720–6342 or 800/343–1328 | www.brushhilltours.com.

WALKING TOURS

The Black Heritage Trail. This self-guided walk explores Boston's 19th-century black community, passing 14 sites; free guided tours meet at the Shaw Memorial on Beacon Hill, Memorial Day weekend through Labor Day weekend daily at 10 AM, noon, and 2 PM. | 617/742–5415 or 617/725–0022 | www.afroammuseum.org.

Freedom Trail. The 2½-mi red line on the sidewalk leads you past 16 of Boston's most important historic sites. National Park Service Rangers lead tours from mid-April through November, but you can do it on your own with a copy of "The Complete Guide to Boston's Freedom Trail," an 80-page illustrated booklet by local scholar Charles Bahne. It's $5.95 and available at the Convention and Visitors' Bureau on Tremont Street in Boston Common, where the trail begins, and at nearly all Freedom Trail sites with a gift shop. | 617/242–5642 | www.thefreedomtrail.org.

Visitor Information

Greater Boston Convention and Visitors Bureau. The Visitors Bureau runs information centers, where you can pick up brochures. | www.bostonusa.com.

Boston Common | Tremont St. in Boston Common | Daily 9–5.
Prudential Center | 800 Huntington Ave., next to customer service desk | 617/536–4100 or 888/733–2678 | Mon.–Sat. 8:30–6, Sun. 9–6.

National Park Service Visitor Center. In addition to brochures and information, the Park Service Visitor Center offers ranger-led tours of the Freedom Trail mid-April through November. | 15 State St. | 617/242–5642 | www.nps.gov | Daily 9–5.

Arriving and Departing

BY AIR

Airports
Logan International (BOS) | 617/561–1800 | www.massport.com.
Airport Transportation
For recorded information about traveling to and from Logan Airport, as well as parking, contact the ground-transportation hot line at 800/235–6426. The roadways in and around Logan are likely to remain under major construction well into 2003, and due to tough new security measures, curbside parking is forbidden and parking in the Terminal B garage and central garage has been severely restricted. Give serious thought to taking public transportation or a taxi to and from Logan.

Bus: Massport Shuttle. Bus 22 runs between Terminals A and B and the subway. Shuttle Bus 33 goes to the subway from Terminals C, D, and E. | 800/235–6426.

Car: Unless you plan to go out of the city itself, you do not want to have a car in Boston. If you *must* drive from Logan to Downtown, the most direct route is by way of the incessantly jammed Sumner Tunnel ($3 toll inbound; no toll outbound). It takes you into the North End and can also connect you to I–93 and, via 93, the Massachusetts Turnpike.

Public Transit: The MBTA subway, or T, from Airport Station is one of the fastest ways to reach Downtown from the airport. The subway's Blue Line runs from the airport to Downtown Boston in about 20 minutes; from there, you can reach the Red, Green, or Orange Line, or commuter rail.

Taxi: Cabs can be hired outside each terminal. Fares to and from Downtown average about $18, including tip via the most direct route, the Sumner Tunnel, assuming no major traffic jams.

Water Shuttle: Airport Water Shuttle. The shuttle crosses Boston Harbor in about seven minutes, running between Logan Airport and Rowes Wharf (a free shuttle bus operates between the ferry dock and airline terminals). Adult fare is $10 one-way. | 800/235–6426.

BY BUS

South Station. This is the depot for most of the major bus companies that serve Boston. | Atlantic Ave. and Summer St. | 617/345–7551.

BY CAR

Reach Boston from the south via I–93, from the north via I–93 and U.S. 1, and from the west via the Massachusetts Turnpike (I–90, a toll road).

BY TRAIN

Amtrak serves Boston at Back Bay (Atlantic Ave. and Summer St.) and South Stations.

Getting Around

BY CAR

Boston is not an easy city to drive in because of one-way streets, many streets with the same name, streets that abruptly change name in the middle, illogical twists and turns, and kamikazelike Boston drivers. If you must drive, bring a good map, keep to the main thoroughfares, and plan to pay highway-robbery prices to park in lots, since most neighborhoods enforce resident-only parking.

Parking

Major public lots are at Government Center and Quincy Market, beneath Boston Common (entrance on Charles Street), beneath Post Office Square, at the Prudential Center, at Copley Place, off Clarendon Street near the John Hancock Tower, in the Theater District, and at several hotels. Smaller lots are scattered throughout Downtown. Most are expensive (expect to pay $20 just for pulling in). The few city-run garages are a bargain at about $10 per day—but try finding a space in them.

BY PUBLIC TRANSIT

Massachusetts Bay Transportation Authority (MBTA)

The MBTA operates city buses and the "T"—a system of subways, elevated trains and trolleys along four connecting lines. | 617/222–3200 or 800/392–6100; 617/222–5854 TTY | www.mbta.com.

Bus: City buses crisscross the metropolitan area and travel farther into suburbia than subway and trolley lines. They run roughly from 5:30 AM to 12:30 AM; the Night Owl service runs limited routes until 2:30 AM Friday and Saturday nights.

The T: Easy, cheap, and hassle-free, the T can get you quickly from one end of Boston or Cambridge to another on its Red, Orange, Green, and Blue lines, and to outlying towns via commuter rail. Trains operate from about 5:30 AM to about 12:30 AM. The fare is $1 for adults, 50¢ for children ages 5–11, slightly more for distant Red and Green Line stops. Pick up an easy-to-read map at any T station.

BY TAXI

It's not easy to hail a cab on the street; your best bet is a hotel taxi stand or a cab stand, found at Harvard Square, around South Station, near Faneuil Hall Marketplace, and in the Theater District. A cab ride within the city of Boston starts at $1.50, plus 25¢ for the first ¼ mi and 25¢ for each ⅛ mi thereafter.

Boston Cab Association | 617/536–3200. **Cambridge Checker Cab** | Boston | 617/536–7000 | Cambridge | 617/497–1500. **Green Cab Association** | 617/628–0600. **Independent Taxi Operators Association** | 617/426–8700. **Town Taxi** | 617/536–5000.

Massachusetts

Revised and Updated by Carolyn B. Heller

CAPE COD

The peninsula called Cape Cod, separated from the Massachusetts mainland by the 17½-mi Cape Cod Canal, pairs sandy beaches and dunes jutting into the open Atlantic with well-preserved towns dating from Colonial times. Everyone comes for the seaside, yet the crimson cranberry bogs, forests of birch and beech, freshwater ponds, and historic homes that grace the interior are just as splendid.

The Cape is only about 70 mi from end to end; you can make a cursory circuit of it in about two days. But it is really a place for relaxing—for swimming, sunning, fishing, or boating; for sampling simple fresh seafood, creative contemporary cuisine, or most anything in between; or for taking leisurely walks, bike rides, or drives along the country roads. Paved trails wander through nature preserves, which protect the natural beauty of the forests and marshes. Thanks to the establishment of the Cape Cod National Seashore, almost 30 mi of dune-backed Atlantic beach are protected from most traces of human habitation.

Away from the sand, along tree-shaded roads, you'll see traditional saltboxes and Cape Cod–style cottages, their shingles weathered to a silvery gray. You'll also pass village greens and white-steepled churches that epitomize old New England. In striking contrast, Provincetown, at the tip of the Cape, boasts an active gallery scene, plus lively nightlife.

Exploring

Sandwich

The oldest town on Cape Cod, Sandwich was established in 1637 by some of the Plymouth Pilgrims and incorporated in 1638. Today it is a well-preserved, quintessential New England village with a white-columned town hall and streets lined with 18th- and 19th-century homes.

★ **Heritage Plantation.** The fine complex of museum buildings, gardens, and a café sits on 76 acres overlooking Shawme Pond. Exhibits range from historic cars to antique firearms to an extensive Currier & Ives collection. For the kids, there's a working 1912 Coney Island–style carousel and Clue tours, scavenger-hunt games for exploring the grounds. | Grove and Pine Sts. | 508/888–3300 | www.heritageplantation.org | $12 | Mid-May–Oct., Sat.–Wed. 9–6, Thurs.–Fri. 9–8; Nov.–Apr., Tues.–Sun. 10–4.

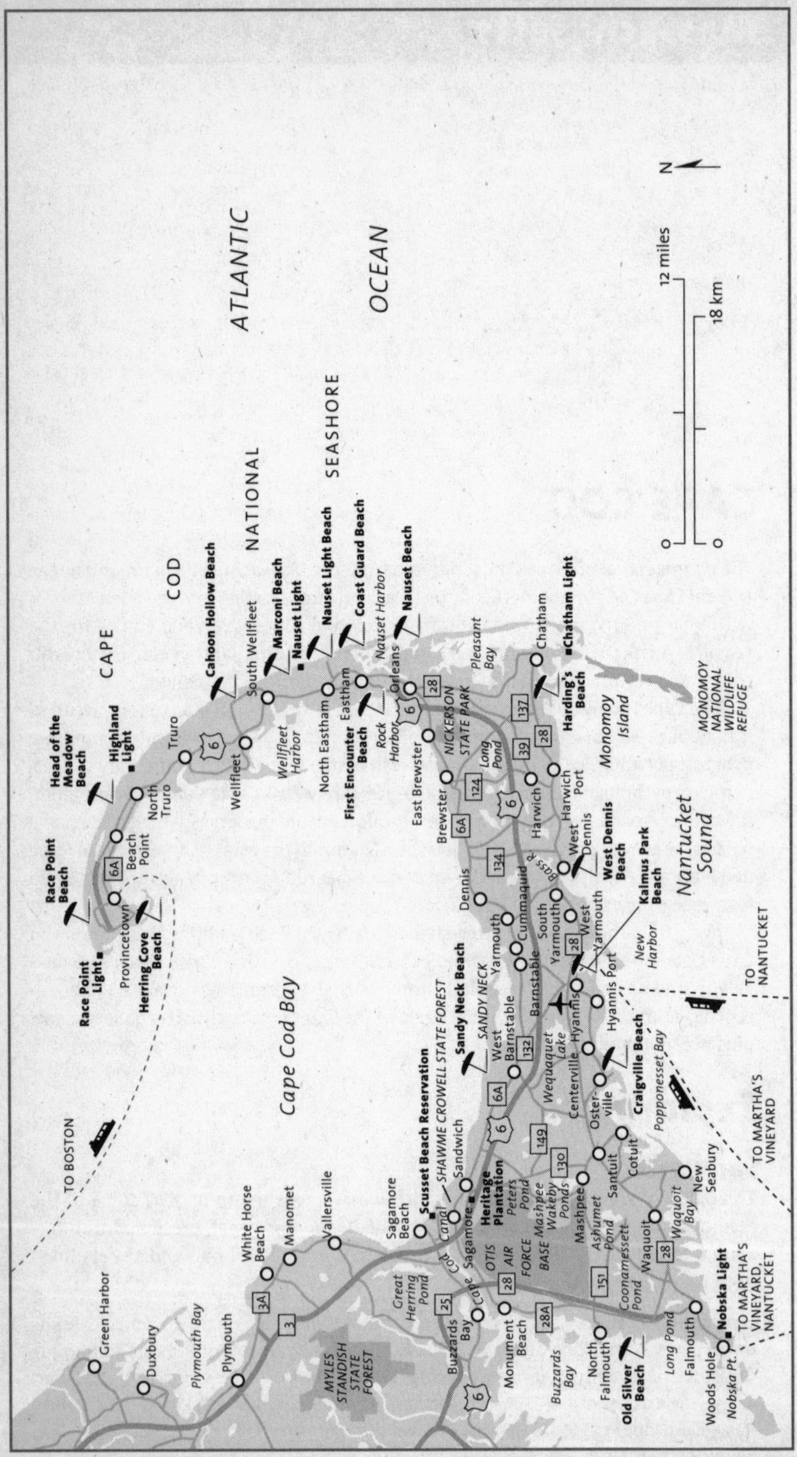
ATLANTIC
OCEAN
CAPE
COD
NATIONAL
SEASHORE
Cape Cod Bay
Nantucket Sound
Buzzards Bay
Plymouth Bay
TO BOSTON
TO MARTHA'S VINEYARD
TO NANTUCKET
TO MARTHA'S VINEYARD, NANTUCKET
Race Point Light
Race Point Beach
Herring Cove Beach
Provincetown
Beach Point
North Truro
Head of the Meadow Beach
Highland Light
Truro
Wellfleet
Cahoon Hollow Beach
South Wellfleet
Marconi Beach
Nauset Light
Nauset Light Beach
Coast Guard Beach
Nauset Harbor
Nauset Beach
Wellfleet Harbor
North Eastham
Eastham
Orleans
First Encounter Beach
Rock Harbor
East Brewster
NICKERSON STATE PARK
Long Pond
Pleasant Bay
Chatham
Chatham Light
Harding's Beach
Monomoy Island
MONOMOY NATIONAL WILDLIFE REFUGE
Brewster
Harwich
Harwich Port
West Dennis
West Dennis Beach
Dennis
Bass R.
Kalmus Park Beach
Yarmouth
Cummaquid
South Yarmouth
West Yarmouth
Yarmouth Port
Barnstable
West Barnstable
SANDY NECK
Sandy Neck Beach
New Harbor
Hyannis
Hyannis Port
Centerville
Wequaquet Lake
Craigville Beach
Osterville
Popponesset Bay
Cotuit
Santuit
New Seabury
Waquoit Bay
Waquoit
Mashpee
Mashpee Wakeby Ponds
Peters Pond
Heritage Plantation
Sandwich
SHAWME CROWELL STATE FOREST
Scusset Beach Reservation
Sagamore Beach
Sagamore
Cape Cod Canal
OTIS AIR FORCE BASE
Ashumet Pond
Coonamessett Pond
Great Herring Pond
Buzzards Bay
Monument Beach
Vallersville
Manomet
White Horse Beach
Plymouth
Duxbury
Green Harbor
MYLES STANDISH STATE FOREST
North Falmouth
Old Silver Beach
Long Pond
Falmouth
Woods Hole
Nobska Pt.
Nobska Light
0
12 miles
0
18 km
N
3
3A
6
6A
25
28
28A
124
130
132
134
137
149
151
39

Sandwich Boardwalk. Built over a salt marsh, a creek, and low dunes, the boardwalk leads to Town Neck Beach. Cape Cod Bay stretches out at the end of the walk, where a platform provides fine views.

Falmouth

Falmouth, the Cape's second-largest town, was settled in 1660. Today, much of Falmouth is suburban, with a large year-round population and a busy Main Street. In the town's more rural North and West Falmouth sections, country lanes lead to secluded coves, sandy beaches, and harbors dotted with sailboats.

BEACH

Old Silver Beach. The long crescent of white sand is especially good for small children because a sandbar keeps it shallow at one end and creates tidal pools full of crabs and minnows. There are lifeguards, rest rooms, showers, and a snack bar. | Off Quaker Rd., North Falmouth | Parking $10 in summer.

Woods Hole

Woods Hole is home to several major scientific institutions: the Woods Hole Oceanographic Institution (WHOI), the Marine Biological Laboratory (MBL), the National Marine Fisheries Service, and the U.S. Geological Survey's Branch of Marine Geology. The town is also the departure point for ferries to Martha's Vineyard.

Woods Hole Oceanographic Institution (WHOI). The WHOI is the largest independent private oceanographic laboratory in the world. Its staff led the successful U.S.-French search for the *Titanic* (found about 400 mi off Newfoundland) in 1985. Although the Oceanographic Institution is not open to the public, you can learn about it at the small WHOI Exhibit Center. | 15 School St. | 508/289–2663 | www.whoi.edu | Suggested donation $2 | Late May–early Sept., Mon.–Sat. 10–4:30, Sun. noon–4:30; call for off-season hrs.

Hyannis

Perhaps best known for its association with the Kennedy clan, Hyannis is the Cape's year-round commercial and transportation hub. Nearby malls have taken their toll on Main Street, but there are plenty of shops and eateries here.

John F. Kennedy Hyannis Museum. Enlarged and annotated photographs document JFK's Cape years (1934–63). | Old Town Hall, 397 Main St. | 508/790–3077 | $5 | Feb.–Dec., Mon.–Sat. 9–5, Sun. noon–5.

Kennedy Compound. Hyannis Port, 1½ mi south of Hyannis, became the summer White House during the Kennedy presidency. The best way to get a glimpse of the compound is on one of the many harbor tours.

Barnstable

Barnstable is the second-oldest town on the Cape (it was founded in 1639), and you'll get a feeling for its age in Barnstable Village, a lovely area of large old homes dominated by the Barnstable County Superior Courthouse.

BEACH

★ **Sandy Neck Beach.** Here at one of the Cape's loveliest beaches, the dunes and sand extend for 6 mi. There are lifeguards, a snack bar, rest rooms, and showers. | Sandy Neck Rd. off Rte. 6A, West Barnstable | 508/362–8300 | Parking $10 late May–early Sept. | Daily 8 AM–9 PM, but staffed only until 5.

Yarmouth and Yarmouth Port

Yarmouth was settled in 1639 by farmers from the Plymouth Bay Colony. By 1829, when Yarmouth Port was incorporated as a separate village, the Cape had begun a thriving maritime industry. Many impressive sea captains' houses—some now B&Bs and museums—still line the streets, and Yarmouth Port has some real old-time stores.

★ **Bass Hole Boardwalk.** One of Yarmouth Port's prettiest spots is Bass Hole, which stretches from Homer's Dock Road to the salt marsh. The boardwalk extends over a marshy creek. The 2½-mi Callery-Darling nature trails meander through salt marshes, vegetated wetlands, and upland woods. Gray's Beach is a little crescent of sand with calm waters. | Trail entrance on Center St. near the Gray's Beach parking lot.

Hallet's. For a peek into the past, stop at this country drugstore preserved as it was when it opened in 1889. | 139 Main St. (Rte. 6A), Yarmouth Port | 508/362–3362 | Free | Call for hrs.

Dennis

Hundreds of sea captains lived in Dennis when fishing, salt making, and shipbuilding were the main industries in this part of the Cape. The elegant houses they constructed still line the streets. The town has conservation areas, nature trails, and numerous ponds for swimming.

★ **Cape Museum of Fine Arts.** The holdings include more than 850 works by Cape-associated artists. The museum hosts film festivals, lectures, and art classes. | 60 Hope La. (on grounds of Cape Playhouse), off Rte. 6A | 508/385–4477 | www.cmfa.org | $7 | Mid-May–mid-Oct., Mon.–Sat. 10–5, Sun. 1–5; mid-Oct.–mid-May, Tues.–Sat. 10–5, Sun. 1–5.

BEACHES

Corporation Beach. On Cape Cod Bay, this attractive stretch of white sand is backed by low dunes; there are lifeguards, showers, rest rooms, and a food stand. | Corporation Rd. | Parking $10 in summer.

West Dennis Beach. This long, wide beach on Nantucket Sound has bathhouses, lifeguards, a playground, and food concessions. | Davis Beach Rd., West Dennis | Parking $10 in summer.

Brewster

Brewster is the perfect place to learn about the natural history of the Cape: the area contains conservation lands, state parks, forests, freshwater ponds, and marshes. When the tide is low in Cape Cod Bay, you can stroll the beaches and explore tidal pools up to 2 mi from the shore on the Brewster flats.

Brewster Store. This local landmark was built in 1852. It's a typical New England general store, providing such essentials as the daily papers, penny candy, and benches out front for conversation. | 1935 Main St. (Rte. 6A), at Rte. 124 | 508/896–3744 | www.brewsterstore.com.

★ **Cape Cod Museum of Natural History.** A visit here is a must for nature enthusiasts. In the museum and on the grounds are nature and marine exhibits, and trails through 80 acres of forest and marshland rich in birds and wildlife. The museum also offers guided canoe and kayak trips and several cruises that explore different Cape waterways. | 869 Main St. (Rte. 6A) | 508/896–3867; 800/479–3867 in Massachusetts | www.ccmnh.org | $5 | Mon.–Sat. 9:30–4:30, Sun. 11–4:30.

Chatham

At the bent elbow of the Cape, Chatham has all the charm of a quiet seaside resort, with relatively little commercialism—just gray-shingle houses with cheerful flower gardens and an attractive Main Street with crafts and antiques stores alongside homey coffee shops.

Chatham Light. At this fine spot to take in the view of the harbor, the sandbars, and the ocean beyond, coin-operated telescopes allow a close look at the famous Chatham Break, the result of a fierce 1987 nor'easter that blasted a channel through a barrier beach just off the coast. | Main St., near Bridge St. | 508/945–0719.

★ **Monomoy National Wildlife Refuge.** The 2,500-acre preserve includes the Monomoy Islands, a fragile, 9-mi-long barrier-beach area south of Chatham. Perfect for bird-watchers, the islands are an important stop along the North Atlantic flyway for migratory waterfowl and shore birds. The Cape Cod Museum of Natural History and the Massachusetts Audubon Society in South Wellfleet conduct island tours.

The **Monomoy National Wildlife Refuge headquarters,** on Morris Island, has a visitor center, open daily 8–4. | Off Morris Island Rd. | 508/945–0594.

Orleans

Incorporated in 1797, Orleans is part quiet seaside village and part bustling commercial center.

BEACHES

Nauset Beach. Not to be confused with Nauset Light Beach at Cape Cod National Seashore, Nauset Beach is a 10-mi-long sweep of sandy ocean beach with low dunes and large waves good for bodysurfing or boardsurfing. There are lifeguards, rest rooms, showers, and a food concession. | Beach Rd. | Parking $8.

Skaket Beach. This sandy stretch on Cape Cod Bay has calm, warm water good for children. There are rest rooms, lifeguards, and a snack bar. | Skaket Beach Rd. | 508/240–3775 | Parking $8.

Eastham

Like many other Cape towns, Eastham (incorporated in 1651) started as a farming community, later turning to the sea for its livelihood. A more atypical industry here was asparagus growing; from the late 1800s through the 1920s, Eastham was known as the Asparagus Capital.

★ **Cape Cod National Seashore.** Along 30 mi of shoreline from Chatham to Provincetown, the 27,000-acre preserve encompasses superb ocean beaches, rolling dunes, wetlands, pitch pine and scrub oak forest, wildlife, and several historic structures. Self-guided nature, hiking, biking, and horse trails lace these landscapes. | www.nps.gov/caco | Free; beach parking $10 per day mid-June–early Sept. or $30 for yearly pass good at all national seashore beaches.

Salt Pond Visitor Center has a museum and offers guided tours, boat trips, and lectures, as well as evening beach walks and campfire talks in summer. | Doane Rd., off U.S. 6 | 508/255–3421 | Mar.–June and Sept.–Dec., daily 9–4:30; July–Aug., daily 9–5; Jan.–Feb., weekends 9–4:30.

BEACHES

Coast Guard Beach. Low grass and heathland back this long beach. It has no parking lot, so park at the Salt Pond Visitor Center and take the free shuttle or walk the 1¾-mi Nauset Trail to the beach. | Off Ocean View Dr. | Parking $10 per day or $30 for an annual national seashore pass.

First Encounter Beach. A bronze marker here commemorates the first encounter between local Indians and passengers from the *Mayflower,* who explored the area for five weeks in late 1620. The beach is also a great spot for watching sunsets over the bay. | Samoset Rd., off U.S. 6 | Parking $5 in summer.

Wellfleet

Tastefully developed Wellfleet attracts many artists and writers because of its fine restaurants, historic houses, and many art galleries.

★ **Massachusetts Audubon Wellfleet Bay Sanctuary.** The 1,000-acre haven for more than 250 species of birds is a superb place for walking, birding, and looking west over the salt marsh and bay at wondrous sunsets. The Audubon Society hosts naturalist-led wildlife tours year-round; reservations are essential. | Off U.S. 6, South Wellfleet | 508/349–2615 | www.wellfleetbay.org | $5 | Nature center late May–mid-Oct., daily 8:30–5; mid-Oct.–late May, Tues.–Sun. 9–4:30. Trails daily 8 AM–dusk.

BEACHES

Cahoon Hollow Beach. This spectacular dune-bordered public beach on the Atlantic side has lifeguards, rest rooms, and a restaurant and music club on the sand. | Cahoon Hollow Rd. | Parking $10 in summer.

Provincetown

Provincetown's shores form a curled fist at the very tip of the Cape. The town was for decades a bustling seaport, with fishing and whaling as its major industries. Fishing is still an important source of income, although the town is now a major whale-watching, rather than hunting, mecca. Provincetown is also the nation's oldest continuous arts colony: painters began coming here in 1899, Eugene O'Neill's first plays were written and produced here, and the Fine Arts Work Center continues to lure notable writers.

In the busy downtown—particularly along Commercial Street, the main thoroughfare—Portuguese-American fishermen mix with painters, poets, whale-watching families, cruise-ship passengers on brief stopovers, and many lesbian and gay residents and visitors, for whom P-town, as it's almost universally known, is one of the most popular East Coast seashore spots.

As you approach Provincetown, **massive dunes** meet the road in places, turning U.S. 6 into a sand-swept highway.

Pilgrim Monument. The monument commemorates the first landing of the Pilgrims in the New World and their signing of the Mayflower Compact, America's first rules of self-governance. Climb the 252-ft-high tower (116 steps and 60 ramps) for a panoramic view—dunes on one side, harbor on the other, and the entire bay side of Cape Cod beyond. At the base is a museum of Lower Cape and Provincetown history. | High Pole Hill | 508/487–1310 | www.pilgrim-monument.org | $6 | Apr.–June and Sept.–Nov., daily 9–5; July–Aug., daily 9–7 (last admission 45 mins before closing).

The **Province Lands,** scattered with ponds, cranberry bogs, and scrub, begin at High Head in Truro and stretch to the tip of Provincetown. Bike and walking trails wind through forests of stunted pines and across desertlike expanses of rolling dunes—these are the "wilds" of the Cape. | Visitor center, Race Point Rd. | 508/487–1256 | Apr.–Nov., daily 9–5.

BEACHES

Race Point Beach. At the end of U.S. 6, this beach has a remote feeling, with a wide swath of sand stretching around the point. | Race Point Rd. | Parking $10 per day or $30 for an annual national seashore pass.

Dining

The Cape offers plenty of fresh fish and shellfish. Each restaurant has its version of New England clam chowder, while other specialties are fried clams, Wellfleet oysters, and buttery-sweet bay scallops. A long history of Portuguese immigration has left a legacy of Portuguese dishes, such as kale soup or *linguiça* (a spicy sausage). Though many Cape restaurants serve traditional Yankee fare in casual settings, a growing number offer more contemporary cuisine.

Sandwich

Aqua Grille. Contemporary. The far-ranging menu and lively atmosphere at this smart-casual bistro by the marina make it a good choice for groups. Fried or grilled seafood, pastas, and steaks are all available. Try the lobster salad, a hearty serving of greens, avocados, baby green beans, and meaty lobster chunks. | 14 Gallo Rd. | 508/888–8889 | www.aquagrille.com | Closed late Oct.–Mar. | $9–$20 | AE, DC, MC, V.

Marshland Restaurant and Bakery. American/Casual. Sandwich's version of down-home is this tiny coffee shop. For breakfast try an Italian omelet, a mix of sausage, fresh vegetables, and cheese. The lunch specials—a grilled chicken club sandwich, lobster salad, a turkey Reuben, and the like—are the best choices midday, and for dinner the prime rib does not quit. | 109 Rte. 6A | 508/888–9824 | No dinner Mon. | $7–$13 | No credit cards.

Falmouth

Betsy's Diner. American/Casual. At this shiny, happy, busy place, a reassuring pink neon sign urges you to EAT HEAVY. The gleaming counter and the booths by the big windows are done in pretty pastel mauve-and-cream tones. A classic diner menu with pancakes, waffles, and omelets is served all day, and typical dinner options are meat loaf and mashed potatoes, knockwurst and sauerkraut, and charbroiled pork chops. | 457 Main St. (Rte. 28) | 508/540–4446 | Reservations not accepted | $6–$14 | MC, V.

The Clam Shack. Seafood. Fried clams—what else?—top the menu at this basic seafood joint on Falmouth Harbor. The clams are crisp and fresh tasting; the meaty lobster roll and the fish-and-chips platter are good choices, too. Place your order at the counter and then take your tray to the picnic tables on the roof deck for the best views. Just don't plan on a late night here—the Shack closes most evenings around 8. | 227 Clinton Ave., Falmouth Harbor | 508/540–7758 | Closed early Sept.–late May | $5–$12 | No credit cards.

Woods Hole

★ **Fishmonger's Café.** Seafood. The ambitious contemporary menu at this restaurant on the sound includes a fried calamari appetizer with a hot-pepper sauce and grilled seafood dishes with tropical fruit sauces. The mango and cilantro sauce over grilled salmon is particularly delectable. | 56 Water St. | 508/540–5376 | Reservations not accepted | Closed Dec.–mid-Feb. and Tues. early Sept.–Mar. | $9–$21 | AE, MC, V.

Hyannis

Baxter's Fish N' Chips. Seafood. The delicious fried clams here are cooked hot to order. The picnic tables outside, some set up on an old floating ferry, allow you to lose no time in the sun while you dine on lobster, fish-and-chips, or delicacies from the excellent raw bar. | Pleasant St. | 508/775–4490 | Reservations not accepted | Closed mid-Oct.–Apr. and weekdays early Sept.–mid-Oct. | $8–$20 | AE, MC, V.

Brazilian Grill. Brazilian. The Cape has a growing Brazilian population, and you'll find many of these residents, plus plenty of satisfied visitors, at this all-you-can-eat *churascurra*, a Brazilian barbecue. Waiters circulate through the dining room offering grilled meat—beef, pork, chicken, sausage, even quail—on long swordlike skewers. You can help yourself to a buffet of salads and side dishes, including *farofa* (a couscouslike dish), rice, and beans. Don't mind the fake bricks and tacky cowboy paintings; just bring a big appetite. | 680 Main St. | 508/771–0109 | $6–$15 | AE, D, DC, MC, V.

Barnstable

★ **Mill Way Fish and Lobster.** Seafood. This seafood market–lunch place on Barnstable Harbor has only a few outside picnic tables, but the fried clams and fish sandwiches are worth the inevitable wait. Try the fat onion rings or the almost-too-big-for-lunch clambake, which comes with chowder, lobster, steamers, and an ear of corn. Mill Way closes at 7 PM. | 275 Mill Way | 508/362–2760 | Closed Oct.–Mar. | $7–$17 | AE, D, MC, V.

Yarmouth and Yarmouth Port

Jack's Outback. American/Casual. Tough to find, tough to forget, this eccentric local hangout lives up to its motto: "Good food, lousy service." Solid breakfasts give way to thick burgers and traditional favorites like Yankee pot roast. Jack's has no liquor license, and you can't BYOB. | 161 Main St. (Rte. 6A), Yarmouth Port | 508/362–6690 | Reservations not accepted | No dinner | $6–$12 | No credit cards.

Dennis

Cap'n Frosty's. Seafood. At this locally acclaimed though very modest fried-seafood-and-ice-cream joint, you order at the counter and take a number written on a french fries box. The staff is young and hard-working, pumping out fresh fried clams and fish-and-chips on paper plates. There's seating inside as well as outside on a shady brick patio. | 219 Main St. (Rte. 6A) | 508/385–8548 | Reservations not accepted | Closed early Sept.–Mar. | $10–$18 | No credit cards.

Red Cottage Restaurant. American/Casual. Up Old Bass River Road just 1/2 mi north of the town hall, this friendly place is indeed a red cottage that serves breakfast and lunch year-round. The breakfasts are better than the lunches, but both are no-nonsense and reliably good. | 36 Old Bass River Rd. | 508/394–2923 | Reservations not accepted | No dinner | $5–$7 | No credit cards.

Brewster

Brewster Inn and Chowder House. American. Traditional New England home cooking is the rule at this casual local institution; you'll find no fancy or fussy fusion recipes here. Look for simple but tasty meat and seafood standards, and don't miss the full-bodied New England clam chowder. The service is friendly, the prices are kind, and you won't leave hungry. | 1993 Rte. 6A | 508/896–7771 | $12–$16 | MC, V.

CHILDREN'S ONBOARD SURVIVAL KITS

Snacks.
Paper towels or wet wipes for messes and spills, in a resealable plastic bag.
Water bottles.
Coloring or activity book, crayons, colored pencils.
Card game.
Small stuffed animal or doll.
Flight or driving map.
Personal CD players, video games, CDs.
Extra batteries.
Pacifiers and blankets for babies.

Orleans

Lobster Claw. Seafood. If you're over 6 ft tall, keep an eye out for the fishnets hanging from the ceiling in this goofy little seafood spot. Tables are lacquered turquoise, portions are huge, and the lobster roll is one of the best. You can get all the Cape basics here: fish and seafood poached, broiled, baked, or fried, along with an assortment of steaks. The children's menu includes seafood and chicken tenders. | Rte. 6A | 508/255–1800 | Reservations not accepted | $10–$18 | AE, D, DC, MC, V.

Sir Cricket's Fish and Chips. Seafood. For a beautifully turned-out fish sandwich, pull off the highway into this tiny local favorite, a hole-in-the-wall attached to the Nauset Lobster Pool. Built mainly for takeout, this no-frills fried-food joint does have three or four tiny tables and a soda machine. Try the fresh oyster roll or go for a full fisherman's platter. Be sure to check out the chair seats—each is an exquisitely rendered mini mural of Orleans history or a personality painted by legendary local artist Dan Joy. | Rte. 6A, near Stop & Shop | 508/255–4453 | Reservations not accepted | $9–$18 | No credit cards.

Eastham

Beach Break Grill and Lounge. American/Casual. Hawaiian surfer is the style at this fun, affordable place, complete with long boards on the ceiling and grassy adornments on the bar. The menu is basic and varied, with seafood (even a raw bar), lots of burgers, fajitas, pasta, and steak. Children under age 10 eat free at dinner. There's an outdoor deck for dining, too. | Main St. Mercantile, off Rte. 6 | 508/240–3100 | $7–$9 | AE, D, DC, MC, V.

Fairway Restaurant and Pizzeria. Italian. The family-run Fairway serves up Italian comfort food in a casual, friendly setting. Attached to the popular Hole in One Donut Shop, the Fairway puts a jar of crayons on every paper-covered table and sells its own brand of root beer. Try the orange tequila shrimp and scallops with a little Cajun heat, eggplant Parmesan, or a well-stuffed calzone. You can order from the extensive breakfast menu from 6:30 to 11:30. | 4295 U.S. 6 | 508/255–3893 | Reservations not accepted | $9–$17 | AE, D, DC, MC, V.

Wellfleet

Captain Higgins. Seafood. Fish is the specialty at this spot across from Wellfleet's town pier. From the deck overlooking the marsh, you can watch the reeds sway in the breeze as you sip an icy Seabreeze and finish a plate of fresh Wellfleet oysters or some marinated calamari. This is a good place to get a big boiled lobster dinner or fresh bluefish with a sweet mustard glaze. A more surprising option is a delicious ostrich burger. Reservations are accepted if you call before 6. | Across from Wellfleet Town Pier | 508/349–6027 | Closed Nov.–Apr. | $11–$13 | MC, V.

Serena's. Italian. A family place that caters to children, Serena's (Italian for "mermaid") offers an assortment of blackboard specials every night. Red sauces prevail on the Italian menu. Try the seafood *fra diavolo*, a bouillabaisse-like stew that can be ordered hot or extremely hot. | U.S. 6, South Wellfleet | 508/349–9370 | No lunch | $9–$10 | AE, D, DC, MC, V.

Provincetown

Lobster Pot. Seafood. Provincetown's Lobster Pot is fit to do battle with all the Lobster Pots anywhere on the Cape. As you enter you'll pass through one of the hardest-working kitchens on the Cape, which consistently turns out fresh New England classics and some of the best chowder around. | 321 Commercial St. | 508/487–0842 | www.ptownlobsterpot.com | Reservations not accepted | Closed Jan. | $9–$26 | AE, D, DC, MC, V.

★ **Mojo's.** American/Casual. At this fast-food institution, the tiniest of kitchens turns out everything from fresh-cut french fries to fried clams, tacos, and tofu burgers. How they crank it out so fast and so good is anybody's guess. | 5 Ryder St. Ext. | 508/487–3140 | Reservations not accepted | Closed mid-Oct.–early May, depending on weather and crowds; call ahead | $5–$15 | No credit cards.

Lodging

With a tourism-based economy, the Cape abounds in lodging choices. A number of appealing (if sometimes pricey) bed-and-breakfasts in old sea captains' houses are located along Route 6A from Sandwich to Brewster, as well as in Falmouth. Route 28, in the very commercial section between Hyannis and Orleans, has many motels in all price ranges.

Families may prefer to rent a vacation home, where you'll have space to spread out and a kitchen for preparing meals. Most Cape Cod rentals run weekly, from Saturday to Saturday.

Commonwealth Associates can assist in finding rentals in the Harwiches. | 551 Main St., Harwich Port 02646 | 508/432–2618 | www.commonwealthrealestate.com.

Donahue Real Estate lists apartments and houses in the Falmouth area. | 850 Main St., Falmouth 02540 | 508/548–5412 | www.falmouthhomes.com.

Vacation Cape Cod lists apartments and houses on the Outer Cape. | Main St. (U.S. 6), Mercantile Unit 19, Eastham 02642 | 508/240–7600 or 800/724–1307 | www.vacationcapecod.com.

Sandwich

Earl of Sandwich Motor Manor. Single-story Tudor-style buildings form a "U" around a duck pond and wooded lawn set with lawn chairs. Rooms in the main building (1966) and the newer buildings (1981–83) are rather somber, with dark paneled walls, quarry-tile floors with Oriental throw rugs, and chenille bedspreads, but they are of good size and have large windows. Refrigerators, cable TV, pool, no-smoking rooms. | 378 Rte. 6A, East Sandwich 02537 | 508/888–1415 or 800/442–3275 | fax 508/833–1039 | www.earlofsandwich.com | 24 rooms | $85–$109 | AE, D, DC, MC, V | CP (Apr.–Nov.).

Spring Garden Inn Motel. From the road the Spring Garden looks like yet another roadside motel, albeit a nice, well-maintained gray-shingle one. Out back, you'll step into another world—a wide green lawn overlooking a broad, peaceful expanse of marsh. Sink into a hammock, an Adirondack chair, or a swing and relax. Grills and picnic tables are available for barbecues. Inside, the simple knotty-pine-wall rooms have two double beds topped with floral comforters. For the best marsh views, choose one of the second-floor rooms with a balcony. Picnic area, refrigerators, cable TV, pool. | 578 Rte. 6A, East Sandwich 02537 | 508/888–0710 or 800/303–1751 | fax 508/833–2849 | www.springgarden.com | 8 rooms, 2 efficiencies, 1 suite | $89–$119 | Closed Dec.–mid-Apr. | AE, D, MC, V | CP.

Falmouth

Cape Wind. If you're traveling with children who need space to run, this motel is a good choice. The rooms face a broad green lawn that slopes down to the bay, where rowboats and pedal boats are available. Rooms are basic, with standard motel furnishings and hand-me-downs; some have been updated more recently than others—so ask before you reserve. Some kitchenettes, microwaves, refrigerators, room TVs, pool, boating; no smoking | 34 Maravista Ext., East Falmouth 02536 | 508/548–3400 or 800/267–3401 | fax 508/495–0316 | www.capewind.com | 31 rooms, 1 apartment | Closed Nov.–Mar. | $115–$150 | D, MC, V.

Hyannis

Sea Breeze Inn. Each room in this comfortable cedar-shingle B&B two blocks from the beach has antique or canopied beds and is simply decorated with quilts or floral comforters and well-chosen antiques. There's also an efficiency unit with a stove and refrigerator. Breakfast is served in the dining room or in the outdoor gazebo, surrounded by winsome gardens. Room TVs; no smoking. | 270 Ocean Ave., at Sea St., 02601 | 508/771–7213 | fax 508/862–0663 | www.seabreezeinn.com | 13 rooms, 1 efficiency | $90–$120 | AE, D, MC, V | CP.

Yarmouth and Yarmouth Port

Americana Holiday Motel. If you want the convenience of staying on Route 28, this family-owned and -operated strip motel is a good choice. The rooms in the rear Pine Grove section overlook serene sea pines and one of the motel's three pools rather than traffic snarls. The two-room suites have a bedroom plus a separate living room with a sleep sofa and VCR. The off-season rates can't be beat. Coffee shop, refrigerators, cable TV, putting green, 3 pools (1 indoor), hot tub, sauna, shuffleboard, playground. | 99 Main St. (Rte. 28), 02673 | 508/775–5511 or 800/445–4497 | fax 508/790–0597 | www.americanaholiday.com | 117 rooms, 19 suites | Closed Nov.–Mar. | $79–$89 | AE, D, DC, MC, V | CP (in off-season only).

Mariner Motor Lodge. Although the rooms at this family-friendly lodging near the Hyannis–West Yarmouth line are standard-issue motel—think basic furnishings like floral bedcovers and carpets that can take a direct hit from a spilled soft drink—the heated outdoor pool is large, and the indoor pool is great for rainy days. Also on site is a miniature golf course and vending machines for snacks. Kids stay free. Coffee shop, refrigerators, cable TV, in-room safes; no-smoking rooms. | 573 Rte. 28, 02673 | 508/771–7887 or 800/445–4050 | fax 508/771–2811 | www.mariner-capecod.com | 100 rooms | $79–$119 | AE, D, MC, V.

Dennis

★ **Scargo Manor.** This 1895 sea captain's home with a big screened porch has a prime location on Scargo Lake, with a private beach and dock. Inside, an eclectic collection of modern art shares space with the Victorian furnishings. Unlike many other upscale B&Bs, this one welcomes kids. Cable TV, beach, boating, bicycles; no room phones, no smoking. | 909 Main St. (Rte. 6A), 02638 | 508/385–5534 or 800/595–0034 | fax 508/385–9791 | www.scargomanor.com | 4 rooms, 2 suites | $115–$155 | AE, D, DC, MC, V | BP.

Brewster

★ **Old Sea Pines Inn.** Fronted by a white-column portico, the Old Sea Pines evokes the summer estates of an earlier time. A sweeping staircase leads to rooms decorated with framed old photographs and antique furnishings. Rooms in a newer building are sparsely but well decorated. The rooms with shared baths are *very* small but a steal in summer. Restaurant, some room TVs; no smoking. | 2553 Main St. (Rte. 6A) 02631, | 508/896–6114 | fax 508/896–7387 | www.oldseapinesinn.com | 24 rooms, 19 with bath; 3 suites; 2 family-size rooms | Closed Jan.–Mar. | $75–$160 | AE, D, DC, MC, V | BP.

Orleans

Sea Breeze Motel. About a mile from Nauset Beach, this motel is also an easy walk to town restaurants and shops. Guest rooms are nothing fancy, but each has either a queen-size or two twin-size beds, wall-to-wall carpeting, and a decent-size tile bathroom. A Continental breakfast is offered for weekend visitors. Picnic area, refrigerators, cable TV | Nauset Beach Rd., 02643 | 508/240–5500 or 877/648–6732 | www.capecodtravel.com/seabreeze | 16 rooms | Closed late Sept.–late May | $85–$100 | MC, V.

Eastham

Cove Bluffs Motel. Nestled among the trees near the Town Cove and several nature trails is this old-fashioned haven for families. Choose from standard motel rooms and fully equipped one- to two-bedroom housekeeping units. Grounds include basketball courts, shuffleboard, swing sets, a playhouse, a sandbox, grills, and swinging hammocks in the shade. Cable TV, pool, basketball, shuffleboard, laundry facilities; no-smoking rooms. | U.S. 6 and Shore Rd., 02642 | 508/240–1616 | www.capecod-orleans.com/covebluffs | 5 rooms, 8 housekeeping units | Closed Nov.–Mar. | $70–$120 | MC, V.

Hostelling International–Mid Cape. On 3 wooded acres near the Cape Cod Rail Trail and a 15-minute walk from the bay, this hostel has cabins that sleep six to eight each; two can be used as family cabins. It has a common area and a kitchen, and there are a number of guest programs. Ping-Pong, volleyball; no room TVs. | 75 Goody Hallet Dr., 02642 | 508/255–2785 | www.usahostels.org | 8 cabins | Closed mid-Sept.–mid-May | $19–$45 | MC, V.

Wellfleet

Even'tide. This longtime favorite motel is set back from the road, surrounded by trees and close to the Cape Cod Rail Trail. A central attraction is the 60-ft indoor pool (although Wellfleet's beaches are not far). Rooms are simple and have queen-size or double beds, two-room family suites, and efficiencies with kitchens. Cottages are also available for stays of a week or longer. Refrigerators, cable TV, indoor pool, playground. | 650 U.S. 6, South Wellfleet 02663 | 508/349–3410 | fax 508/349–7804 | www.eventidemotel.com | 31 units, 10 cottages | 1- or 2-wk minimum for cottages in summer | $98–$145 | MC, V.

Inn at Duck Creek. Set on 5 wooded acres, this inn consists of the circa-1815 main building and two other old houses. Rooms in the main inn (except rustic third-floor rooms) and in the Saltworks house have a simple charm. Typical furnishings include claw-foot tubs, country antiques, lace curtains, and rag rugs. There's formal dining at Sweet Seasons or pub dining with entertainment at the Tavern Room. 2 restaurants; no room phones, no room TVs. | 70 Main St., Wellfleet 02667 | 508/349–9333 | fax 508/349–0234 | www.innatduckcreeke.com | 25 rooms, 17 with bath | 2-night minimum weekends July–Aug. | Closed mid-Oct.–mid-Apr. | $65–$110 | AE, MC, V | CP.

Provincetown

Dexter's Inn. A block from lively Commercial Street, this inn has simple, pretty rooms at some of Provincetown's more reasonable prices. Adorned with colorful quilts or lace bedspreads, beds are backed by wicker or brass headboards. Ceiling fans whir above the decent-size rooms, most of which have views of the Pilgrim Monument. Cable TV | 6 Conwell St. | 508/487–1911 or 888/521–1999 | www.ptowndextersinn.com | 15 rooms, 12 with bath | $75–$115 | MC, V | C.

Camping

Sandwich

Shawme-Crowell State Forest. Less than a mile from the Cape Cod Canal, this 742-acre state forest is a good base for biking, hiking, or swimming at Scusset Beach. Open-air campfires are allowed at the wooded tent and RV (no hook-ups) sites. Heated bathroom and shower facilities are a blessing on chilly mornings. The campground is generally open year-round, but if you're planning a winter trip, call to confirm before visiting. Flush toilets, dump station, showers, fire pits, picnic tables, store. | 285 sites | Rte. 130, 02563 | 508/888–0351; 877/422–6762 reservations | www.reserveamerica.com | $10–$12 | MC, V.

Brewster

★ **Nickerson State Park.** The Cape's largest and most popular campground is on almost 2,000 acres teeming with wildlife, white pine, and spruce forest. The area is jammed with opportunities for trout fishing, walking, or biking along 8 mi of paved trails and for canoeing, sailing, motorboating, and bird-watching. In addition to the basic sites, yurts—which include electricity and water—are available. Flush toilets, dump station, showers, picnic tables, fire pits, public telephone, store, swimming (pond) | 418 sites | 3488 Main St. (Rte. 6A), 02631 | 508/896–3491; 877/422–6762 reservations | fax 508/896–3103 | www.state.ma.us/dem/parks/nick.htm or www.reserveamerica.com | $15–$30 | MC, V | Mid-Apr.–mid-Oct.

Eastham

Atlantic Oaks Campground. This campground in a pine and oak forest is less than a mile north of the Salt Pond Visitor Center and minutes from Cape Cod National Seashore. Primarily an RV camp, it offers limited tenting as well. There are bikes for rent and direct access to the Cape Cod Rail Trail. Movies for children are shown at night. Flush toilets, full hook-ups, laundry facilities, showers, general store, playground. | 100 full hook-ups, 30 tent sites | 3700 U.S. 6, 02642 | 508/255–1437 or 800/332–2267 | www.atlanticoaks.com | $47.50 full hook-ups, $33 tent sites | D, MC, V | Closed Nov.–Apr.

Shopping

Crafts—from exquisite blown glass to earthy pottery and homespun country creations—are a specialty of this area, along with antiques and art. Shoppers can look for antique and new examples of scrimshaw—the art of etching finely detailed designs of sailing ships and sea creatures onto whalebone or teeth (today, a synthetic substitute).

Shopping Districts: Provincetown is the Cape's art center, with galleries showing works by internationally recognized artists. In Wellfleet, you'll find more local art and crafts. Crafts, antiques, and antiquarian bookshops line Route 6A from Sandwich to Brewster.

Hyannis's Main Street includes souvenir-type shops, ice cream and candy stores, and miniature-golf places. Chatham's Main Street is more genteel, with more upscale merchandise in galleries and antiques and clothing stores.

Flea Markets and Farm Stands: The **Wellfleet Drive-In Theatre** is the site of a giant flea market (weekends in spring; Wed., Thurs., and weekends July–fall).| Rte. 6, Eastham–Wellfleet line | 508/349–2520. **Fancy's Farm** sells local and exotic produce, fresh-baked breads and pastries, and more. | 199 Main St., Orleans | 508/255–1949.

Sports and Outdoor Activities

Bicycling

The Cape's premier bike path, the Cape Cod Rail Trail, follows the paved right-of-way of the old Penn Central Railroad. About 25 mi long, the easy-to-moderate trail passes salt marshes, cranberry bogs, ponds, and Nickerson State Park. The trail starts at the parking lot off Route 134 south of U.S. 6, near Theophilus Smith Road in South Dennis, and it ends at the post office in South Wellfleet. If you want to cover only a segment, there are parking lots in Harwich (across from Pleasant Lake Store on Pleasant Lake Avenue) and in Brewster (at Nickerson State Park).

Little Capistrano Bike Shop. | Salt Pond Rd., Eastham | 508/255–6515.

Rail Trail Bike Shop. | 302 Underpass Rd., Brewster | 508/896–8200.

Boating

Jack's Boat Rentals. Jack rents canoes, kayaks, Seacycles, Sunfish, pedal boats, and sailboards. | Nickerson State Park, Flax Pond, Rte. 6A | 508/896–8556.

Fishing

The Cape Cod Chamber of Commerce's *Sportsman's Guide* describes fishing regulations and surf-fishing access locations and contains a map of boat-launching facilities.

The Cape Cod Canal is a good place to fish; the **Army Corps of Engineers** operates a canal-fishing hot line. | 508/759–5991.

Whale-Watching

Several tour operators take whale-watchers out to the feeding grounds at Stellwagen Bank, about 6 mi from Provincetown.

Dolphin Fleet. Scientists from the Center for Coastal Studies in Provincetown accompany the tour. They know many of the whales by name and tell you about their habits and histories. Reservations essential. | Tickets: MacMillan Wharf, Chamber of Commerce building | 508/349–1900 or 800/826–9300 | www.whalewatch.com | $20 (varies with season) | Tours Apr.–Oct.

Essential Information

When to Go

Cape Cod's climate is generally milder than the mainland's, with average minimum and maximum temperatures of 63°–78° in July and 25°–40° from December through February. Although winter sometimes brings dampness and cold winds, and many facilities shut down, cozy country inns and family-friendly motels offer getaways at as much as 50% below summer rates. After a late-arriving unpredictable spring, Memorial Day through Labor Day constitutes the high season, when the weather makes you think nothing but "beach" and everything is open; unfortunately, it is also a time of higher prices, crowds, and traffic. In fall, the moorland turns rich autumn colors and the mild weather and thinned-out crowds make exploring a pleasure.

FESTIVALS AND SEASONAL EVENTS

WINTER

Dec.: **Christmas by the Sea,** the first full weekend of December in Falmouth, includes lighting ceremonies at the Village Green, caroling at Nobska Light in Woods Hole, church fairs, and a parade. | 508/548–8500 or 800/526–8532.

SPRING

Apr.: **Brewster in Bloom.** The weekend-long daffodil fest greets spring with arts-and-crafts shows, a parade, tours of historic homes, a golf tournament, and a giant antiques and collectibles market. | 508/896–3500.

May: **Cape Cod Maritime Week** celebrates the Cape's maritime history with lighthouse tours, guided shorefront walks, and special exhibits Capewide. | 508/362–3828 | www.capecodcommission.org/hdn.

SUMMER

Summer theater, town-band concerts, and **arts-and-crafts fairs** enliven most every Cape town.

June: **The Portuguese Festival** honors Provincetown's Portuguese heritage with a lively weekend of traditional foods, dances, concerts, games, fireworks, and other events, concluding with the Blessing of the Fleet. | 508/487–3424.

July: **The Mashpee Powwow** brings together Wampanoags from North and South America for three days of dance contests, drumming, a fireball game, and a clambake. | 508/477–0208.

AUTUMN

Sept.: **The Harwich Cranberry Festival** includes an arts-and-crafts show, a carnival, fireworks, pancake breakfasts, an antique-car show, and much more. | 508/430–2811 | www.harwichcranberryfestival.com.

Oct.: **Fall foliage.** The leaf season usually peaks around the end of October. Colors might flame a few weeks earlier or later, however, depending on the weather in the preceding months.

Nov.: **Lighting of the Monument** festivities commemorate the Pilgrims' landing, with the lighting of 5,000 white and gold bulbs draped over the Pilgrim Monument in Provincetown. The lighting occurs each night until just after the New Year. A musical performance accompanies the event, and the monument museum holds an open house and tours. | 508/487–1310.

Bargains

Factory outlets are scattered throughout the Cape, a number of them along Route 28 east of Hyannis. The visitor centers of the Cape Cod National Seashore offer free slide shows, exhibits, and free or inexpensive nature-oriented programs and tours. Most of the historical museums throughout the Cape charge only nominal fees. In the off-season especially, weekday lodging prices may be significantly reduced.

Tours

Cape Cod Central Railroad. Two-hour, 42-mi scenic rail tours travel from Hyannis to the Cape Cod Canal and back. Trains run late May–October, generally Tuesday–Sunday, but call for a schedule. There are also dinner trains, including one for families, as well as a lunch train. | 508/771–3800 or 888/797–7245 | www.capetrain.com.

Cape Cod Duck Mobile. Restored U.S. military amphibious vehicles take land-and-sea tours of downtown Hyannis and the harbor. These 45-minute tours roll through downtown, then splash into Lewis Bay to cruise past the Kennedy compound and other sights. | 508/362–1117.

Visitor Information

Cape Cod Chamber of Commerce. | U.S. 6 and Rte. 132, Hyannis | 508/862–0700 or 888/332–2732 | www.capecodchamber.org.

Arriving and Departing

BY AIR

Airports

Logan International Airport (BOS). Major U.S. airlines serve Logan which is in Boston, the nearest gateway city to the Cape. | 617/561–1806 or 800/235–6426 | www.massport.com/logan.

T. F. Green Airport (PVD). PVD, in Providence, Rhode Island, is also served by the major carriers, and it's an easy drive from the Cape; fares to Providence are sometimes lower than fares into Boston. | 401/737–8222 or 888/268–7222 | www.pvd-ri.com.

Barnstable Municipal Airport (HYA). This airport in Hyannis is the most centrally located airport on Cape Cod itself. | 508/775–2020.

Provincetown Municipal Airport (PVC). Provincetown is another option on the Cape. | 508/487–0241.

Airport Transportation

Bus: Bonanza Bus Lines offers service to the Cape from the Boston and Providence airports.

Car: Budget rents cars at the Barnstable and Provincetown airports.

Taxi: From the Barnstable or Provincetown airport, taxis run into Hyannis or P-town, but to travel farther afield, it's more convenient to rent a car.

Cape Cab. | Provincetown | 508/487–2222. **Checker Taxi.** | Hyannis | 508/771–8294.

BY BOAT AND FERRY

Bay State Cruise Company. Express boats run from Boston to Provincetown daily from Memorial Day through September; the trip takes about 90 minutes. The company also operates a slower (three-hour) Boston–Provincetown ferry weekends from Memorial Day to Labor Day. | 617/748–1428 in Boston; 508/487–9284 in Provincetown | www.baystatecruisecompany.com | 90-min express boat $29 one-way, bicycles $5; round-trip $49. 3-hr boat $18 one-way, bicycles $5; round-trip $30.

BY BUS

Bonanza Bus Lines. Buses travel to Bourne, Falmouth, and Woods Hole from Boston and Providence. | 508/548–7588 or 800/556–3815 | www.bonanzabus.com.

Plymouth & Brockton Street Railway. Bus service is available to Provincetown from Boston and Logan Airport, with stops in several Cape towns en route. | 508/746–0378 | www.p-b.com.

BY CAR

From Boston (60 mi), take Route I–93 south to Route 3 south, across the Sagamore Bridge, which becomes U.S. 6, the Cape's main artery. From western Massachusetts, northern Connecticut, and northeastern New York State, take I–84 east to the Massachusetts Turnpike (I–90 east) and take I–495 south and east to the Bourne Bridge. From New York City, and all other points south and west, take I–95 north toward Providence, where you'll pick up I–195 east (toward Fall River/New Bedford) to Route 25 east to the Bourne Bridge.

From the Bourne Bridge, go around the rotary following the signs to U.S. 6 if you're headed for Mid- and Outer-Cape towns, or take Route 28 south for Falmouth and Woods Hole. Beyond Falmouth, Route 28 heading toward Hyannis and Chatham passes through some of the Cape's most overdeveloped areas, full of malls, heavy traffic, and tacky motels; U.S. 6 is a faster west-to-east road. An alternative to U.S. 6, Route 6A winds along the Cape's north shore through scenic towns from Sandwich to Orleans. It's a pretty drive if you're not in a hurry.

Getting Around

BY CAR

The Cape is linked to the mainland by two heavily traveled bridges, where congestion frequently causes delays. On summer weekends, avoid arriving in the late afternoon.

U.S. 6, Route 6A, and Route 28 are heavily congested eastbound on Friday evening, westbound on Sunday afternoon, and in both directions on summer Saturdays.

When approaching one of the Cape's numerous rotaries (traffic circles), keep in mind that vehicles already in the rotary have the right of way.

SmarTraveler. This traffic hot line reports delays throughout the Boston area, on the Sagamore and Bourne bridges, and on U.S. 6. | 617/374–1234 or *1 (from cellular phones) | www.smartraveler.com.

BY PUBLIC TRANSIT

Bus: Cape Cod Regional Transit Authority. Buses operate along Route 28 between Hyannis and Woods Hole and connect in Hyannis with the Plymouth & Brockton line. Another line runs between Hyannis and Orleans along Route 28. The "b-bus" is a fleet of minivans that transports passengers daily door-to-door anywhere on the Cape. You must register in advance to use the b-bus service; phone between 1 and 4 PM on weekdays to sign up. You must also make advance reservations when you want to ride the b-bus. | 508/385–8326; 800/352–7155 in Massachusetts | www.capecodtransit.org.

Revised and Updated by Judy Sutton Taylor

CHICAGO

Chicago has everything for city lovers: culture, commerce, historic buildings, public transportation, ethnic neighborhoods, chic boutiques, and grit and grime. Masterpieces of skyscraper architecture embrace the curving shore of Lake Michigan, creating one of the most spectacular skylines in the world. An elegant system of boulevards and parks encircles the central city.

Home to the blues and the Chicago Symphony, to storefront theaters and the Lyric Opera, to neighborhood murals and the Art Institute, Chicago has come a long way in shedding its rough-and-tumble image as "city of the big shoulders," immortalized in the writings of Theodore Dreiser, Upton Sinclair, and Carl Sandburg. The infamous stockyards have long been closed, and the steel mills to the south lie largely idle. Except for a few bullet holes in the masonry around the Biograph Theater (where John Dillinger was shot), few traces remain of the disreputable 1920s gangster period that made Chicago infamous around the world; the Biograph itself is now run by the Cineplex Odeon chain, and Chicago has become, for better or worse, a hub of finance second only to New York. But Chicagoans remain friendly in the midwestern manner: helpful and generally lacking in pretense.

Long and thin (in many spots less than 10 mi wide), Chicago proper hugs the shore of Lake Michigan. Many of the major attractions are clustered within a mile of the lakefront, either in the Loop (defined by the tracks of the elevated train) or near the Loop, in the Near North Side.

Exploring

With careful planning, you can hit Chicago's high points in three or four days—but it would take weeks to exhaust all of the city's possibilities. The major attractions are concentrated in the Loop and its surrounding downtown neighborhoods, but architecture buffs will want also to tour Hyde Park and the suburb of Oak Park, while shoppers will want to venture beyond the Magnificent Mile to neighborhoods like Bucktown, Wicker Park, and Lake View to sample the different retail flavors. Whether you focus your visit on the downtown must-sees or venture beyond into some of the many exciting neighborhoods, you're sure to find plenty to keep you entertained.

Loop

★ **Art Institute of Chicago.** Some of the world's most famous paintings are housed in this museum, including an incredibly strong collection of Impressionist and post-Impressionist paintings, with seminal works by Monet, Renoir, Gauguin, and van Gogh, among others. The museum also has impressive collections of medieval, Renaissance, and modern art. Less well known are its fine holdings in Asian art and photography. The museum store has an outstanding collection of art books, calendars, and merchandise related to current exhibits, as well as gift items. | 111 S. Michigan Ave. | 312/443–3600 | www.artic.edu | $10, free Tues. | Mon. and Wed.–Fri. 10:30–4:30, Tues. 10:30–8, weekends 10–5.

At the **Kraft Education Center,** your child can choose from an assortment of 25 or so gallery games, some of which come with picture postcards. The delightful and informative games will keep children from becoming hopelessly bored as you tramp through the galleries.

Carson Pirie Scott. Extraordinary cast-iron swirls and curls, as well as flower and leaf motifs, adorn the cylindrical entrance to this large department store. Look for the letters "LHS" in the rotunda ornamentation, initials of Louis H. Sullivan, the architect of the original 1899 building and one of its later expansions. The building is also a prime example of the "Chicago window," typical of the so-called Chicago School of architects: a large, fixed central pane with smaller movable windows on each side. The picture windows let in light, and the small double-hung windows let in the Lake Michigan breeze. | 1 S. State St. | 312/641–7000 | www.carsons.com | Store hrs vary throughout the year.

Chicago Cultural Center. Elegant ornamental details abound in this building, including sparkling mosaic tiles, sculptured ceilings, inscribed literary quotations, and a sweeping white Carrara marble staircase. The Cultural Center houses splendid public spaces, with acclaimed free concerts and performances of all kinds, including live music every weekday at 1 in the Randolph Cafe, exhibitions, and family programming. Building tours are offered Tuesday–Saturday at 1:15 PM. | 78 E. Washington St. | 312/346–3278 | www.cityofchicago.org/Tourism/CulturalCenter | Mon.–Wed. 10–7, Thurs. 10–9, Fri. 10–6, Sat. 10–5, Sun. 11–5.

There's a **Chicago Office of Tourism Visitor Information Center** near the Randolph Street entrance.

The **Museum of Broadcast Communications,** also housed here, displays TV and radio exhibits and has a large archive of programs and commercials.

Daley Center. Named for the late mayor Richard J. Daley, the father of the current holder of the office, this boldly plain high-rise is the headquarters of the Cook County court system. In summer, the building's plaza is the site of concerts, political rallies, dance presentations, and a weekly farmers' market (Thursday); in November, the city's official Christmas tree is erected here. | Bounded by Washington, Randolph, Dearborn, and Clark Sts. | 312/346–3278 | www.ci.chi.il.us/tourism/Picasso.

The Daley Center also draws visitors' attention because of what stands outside: a sculpture by Picasso. Known simply as ***"The Picasso,"*** it provoked an outcry when it was installed in 1967. Speculation about what it is meant to represent (knowledgeable observers say it is the head of a woman, especially when viewed in profile; others have suggested it is an Afghan dog) has diminished but not ended. Still, the sculpture has become a recognized symbol of the city.

Marshall Field's. The original site of Chicago's best-known department store holds some 500 departments to please all shoppers. Designed by D. H. Burnham & Co. and built between 1892 and 1907, the mammoth emporium has a spectacular Tiffany dome in the southwest corner above the cosmetics area near State and Washington streets. Check out the grand Walnut Room on the seventh floor (especially around Christmas) for a rejuvenating meal. Don't miss the landmark clock outside the entrance at State

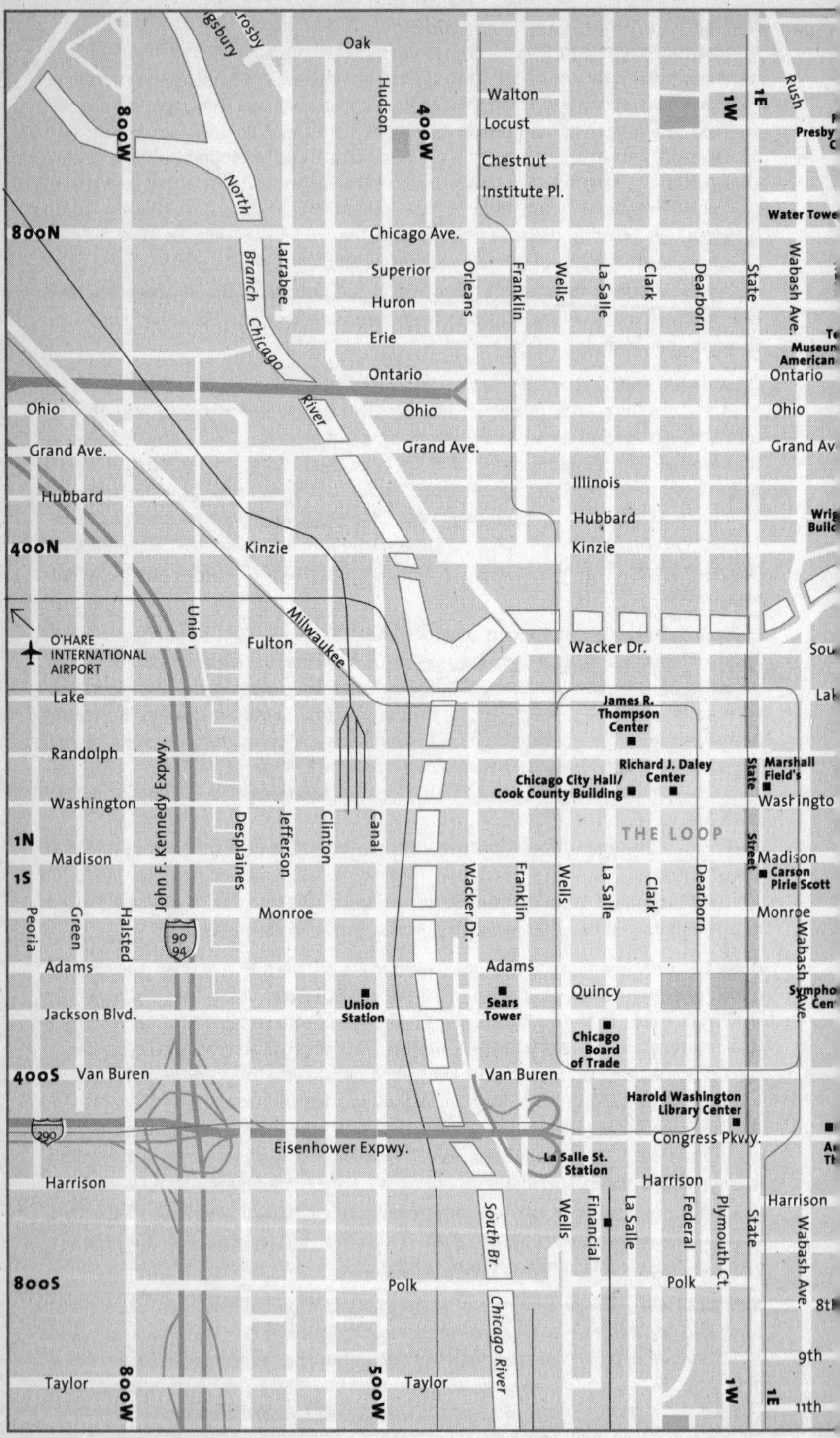
Crosby
Kingsbury
Oak
Hudson
400W
800W
Walton
Locust
Chestnut
Institute Pl.
North
1W
1E
Rush
Presby
Water Tower
800N
Chicago Ave.
Superior
Huron
Erie
Ontario
Ohio
Grand Ave.
Larrabee
Branch Chicago River
Orleans
Franklin
Wells
La Salle
Clark
Dearborn
State
Wabash Ave.
Museum
American
Illinois
Hubbard
Kinzie
400N
Milwaukee
O'HARE INTERNATIONAL AIRPORT
Fulton
Wacker Dr.
Lake
Randolph
Washington
Madison
1N
1S
Union
John F. Kennedy Expwy.
Desplaines
Jefferson
Clinton
Canal
James R. Thompson Center
Richard J. Daley Center
Chicago City Hall/ Cook County Building
Marshall Field's
State Street
THE LOOP
Carson Pirie Scott
Monroe
Peoria
Green
Halsted
90
94
Adams
Quincy
Jackson Blvd.
Union Station
Sears Tower
Chicago Board of Trade
Symphony Center
400S
Van Buren
Harold Washington Library Center
290
Eisenhower Expwy.
Congress Pkwy.
La Salle St. Station
Harrison
Financial
Federal
Plymouth Ct.
South Br. Chicago River
800S
Polk
8th
9th
Taylor
500W
11th

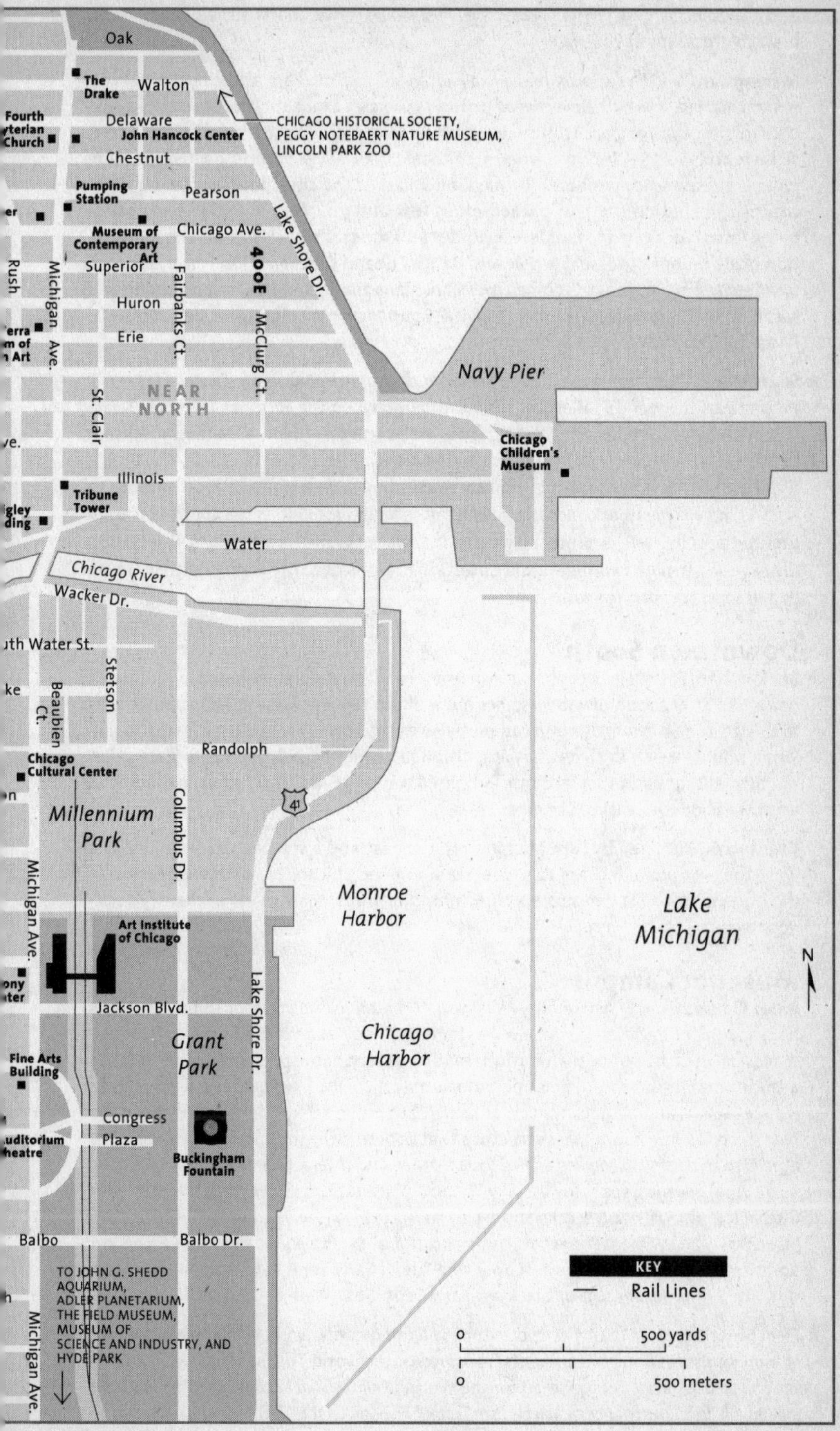
Oak
The Drake
Walton
Fourth
yterian
Church
Delaware
John Hancock Center
CHICAGO HISTORICAL SOCIETY,
PEGGY NOTEBAERT NATURE MUSEUM,
LINCOLN PARK ZOO
Chestnut
Pumping Station
Pearson
Museum of Contemporary Art
Chicago Ave.
Lake Shore Dr.
400E
Rush
Michigan Ave.
Superior
Fairbanks Ct.
Huron
McClurg Ct.
Erie
Navy Pier
NEAR NORTH
St. Clair
Chicago Children's Museum
Illinois
Tribune Tower
Water
Chicago River
Wacker Dr.
Stetson
Beaubien Ct.
Randolph
Chicago Cultural Center
41
Millennium Park
Columbus Dr.
Michigan Ave.
Monroe Harbor
Lake Michigan
Art Institute of Chicago
N
Jackson Blvd.
Grant Park
Lake Shore Dr.
Chicago Harbor
Fine Arts Building
Congress Plaza
Buckingham Fountain
Balbo
Balbo Dr.
KEY
Rail Lines
TO JOHN G. SHEDD AQUARIUM,
ADLER PLANETARIUM,
THE FIELD MUSEUM,
MUSEUM OF SCIENCE AND INDUSTRY, AND
HYDE PARK
0
500 yards
0
500 meters

and Randolph streets. | 111 N. State St. | 312/781–1000 | www.marshallfields.com | Store hrs vary throughout the year.

Millennium Park. The approximately 24½-acre Millennium Park, at the northwest corner of Grant Park, is in the process of turning an eyesore into another of the city's jewels. Only the McCormick Tribune Ice Rink has been completed (admission is free, skate rentals cost $3), but renowned architect Frank Gehry's stunning music pavilion will be the showstopper here. The pavilion will host the city's popular free summer concerts, including the jam-packed blues fest and jazz fest. The high-tech, sand-based lawn is designed to handle the hordes and shed rain quickly. Another good addition is the indoor 1,500-seat Music and Dance Theater Chicago, a long-needed space for midsize performing-arts companies. Park plans also include a 2½-acre garden and a 400-space indoor bicycle parking facility. | Bounded by Michigan Ave., Columbus Dr., Randolph Dr., and Monroe St.

★ **Sears Tower.** This soaring 110-story skyscraper, designed by Skidmore, Owings & Merrill in 1974, was the world's tallest building until 1996 when the Petronas Towers in Kuala Lumpur, Malaysia, claimed the title. | 233 S. Wacker Dr. | 312/875–9696 | www.theskydeck.com | $9.50 | May–Sept., daily 10–10; Oct.–Apr., daily 10–8.

The **Skydeck** is really something to boast about. On a clear day you can see to Michigan, Wisconsin, and Indiana. At the top, interactive exhibits tell about Chicago's dreamers, schemers, architects, musicians, writers, and sports stars. Knee-High Chicago, a 4-ft-high exhibit, should entertain the kids. Security is very tight, so figure in a little extra time for your visit.

Downtown South

★ **Buckingham Fountain.** A centerpiece in Grant Park, this decorative, tiered fountain was patterned after a fountain at Versailles but is about twice as large as its model. Thanks to its size, the 25-ft-tall fountain can propel water 150 ft high and circulate 14,000 gallons a minute. See it in all its glory May through September, when it's elaborately illuminated at night and sprays colorfully lighted waters. | Grant Park between Columbus and Lake Shore Drs. east of Congress Plaza.

Grant Park. Bordered by Lake Michigan to the east and a spectacular skyline to the west, the ever-popular Grant Park, the site where the Chicago Bulls thanked fans during huge rallies after winning six NBA championships, hosts many of the city's outdoor events. | 312/747–1534.

Museum Campus

Adler Planetarium & Astronomy Museum. Interactive and state-of-the-art exhibits hold appeal for traditionalists as well as for technology-savvy kids and adults. Opened in 1930 as the first public planetarium in the western hemisphere, the Adler still has a traditional in-the-round Zeiss planetarium (called the Sky Theater), which shows constellations and planets in the night sky. A $40 million upgrade has resulted in the high-tech Sky Pavilion, a glass structure that contains the interactive StarRider Theater. Also in this building are a telescope terrace and interactive exhibition galleries. Additional charges apply for the Sky Theater planetarium shows and the StarRider interactive shows. | 1300 S. Lake Shore Dr. | 312/922–7827 | www.adlerplanetarium.org | General $5, Sky Theater planetarium additional $5, StarRider interactive theater additional $5; general admission only, free Tues. | Early Sept.–late May, Mon.–Thurs. 9–5, Fri. 9–9, weekends 9–6; late May–early Sept., Sat.–Wed. 9–6, Thurs.–Fri. 9–9.

★ **Field Museum.** More than 6 *acres* of exhibits fill this gigantic world-class museum, which explores cultures and environments from around the world. The museum was founded in 1893 to hold material gathered for the World's Columbian Exposition. Shrink to the size of a bug to burrow beneath the surface of the soil in the Underground Adventure exhibit ($4 extra). As part of Inside Ancient Egypt, the remarkable Mastaba complex includes a working canal and 23 mummies. Don't miss the Life over Time: DNA to Dinosaurs exhibit, which traces the evolution of life on Earth from one-celled organisms to the great reptiles. Kids especially enjoy 65-million-year-old "Sue," the largest and most complete Tyrannosaurus rex fossil ever found. The DinoStore sells a mind-boggling assortment of dinosaur-related merchandise. Be sure to get a map and plan your time here. | 1400 S. Lake Shore Dr. | 312/922–9410 | www.fieldmuseum.org | $8, free Wed. | Weekdays 10–5, weekends 9–5.

John G. Shedd Aquarium. At the world's largest indoor aquarium, which houses more than 8,000 aquatic animals, interactive walk-through environments allow you to travel from the flooded forests of the Amazon to the coral reefs of the Indo-Pacific. You can have a stare-down with one of the knobby-headed beluga whales (they love to people-watch), observe Pacific white-sided dolphins at play, and explore the simulated Pacific Northwest nature trail. An educational dolphin presentation, scheduled daily, shows natural behaviors including vocalizing, breaching, and tail-walking. A special treat on Thursday evening from June through September is live jazz on the Shedd's north terrace, with a great view of the lake and skyline. | 1200 S. Lake Shore Dr. | 312/939–2438 | www.sheddaquarium.org | $15 including Oceanarium, $18 including audio pass; $7 Mon. and Tues. for Oceanarium and Aquarium | Late May–early Sept., Fri.–Wed. 9–6, Thurs. 9 AM–10 PM; early Sept.–late May, weekdays 9–5, weekends 9–6.

Near North

Within this area you'll find the Magnificent Mile, a stretch of Michigan Avenue between the Chicago River and Oak Street, which owes its name to the swanky shops that line both sides of the street—and to its once elegant low-rise profile, which used to contrast sharply with the urban canyons of the Loop.

John Hancock Center. The crisscross braces in this 1,107-ft-tall building help keep it from swaying in the high winds that come off the lake. The 94th floor has an observation deck; you can enjoy the same view while having an exorbitantly priced drink in the bar that adjoins the Signature Room at the 95th restaurant. The Chicago Architecture Foundation has a shop and tour center off the plaza. | 875 N. Michigan Ave. | 312/751–3681 | www.hancock-observatory.com | Observation deck $9.50 | Daily 9 AM–11 PM.

Museum of Contemporary Art. Founded in 1967 by a group of art patrons who felt the great Art Institute was unresponsive to modern work, the MCA's dramatic quarters were designed by Berlin architect Josef Paul Kleihues. About half the museum is dedicated to temporary exhibitions; the other half showcases objects from the MCA's growing 7,000-piece collection, which includes work by René Magritte, Alexander Calder, Bruce Nauman, Sol LeWitt, Franz Kline, and June Leaf. The museum hosts a party ($14) with live music and hors d'oeuvres from 6 to 10 PM on the first Friday of every month. | 220 E. Chicago Ave. | 312/280–2660 | www.mcachicago.org | $8, free Tues. | Tues. 10–8, Wed.–Sun. 10–5.

★ **Navy Pier.** No matter the season, Navy Pier is a fun place to spend a few hours. Constructed in 1916 as a commercial-shipping pier, it was renamed in honor of the Navy in 1927 (the Army got Soldier Field). The once deserted pier contains shopping promenades; an outdoor landscaped area with pretty gardens, a fountain, a carousel, a 15-story Ferris wheel, and an ice-skating rink; Crystal Gardens, one of the country's largest indoor botanical parks; an IMAX theater; an outdoor beer garden; and myriad shops, restaurants, and bars. Navy Pier is also the home port for a number of tour and dinner cruises. | Grand Ave. at the lakefront | 312/595–7437 | www.navypier.com | Daily 6 AM–11 PM.

At the **Chicago Children's Museum,** "hands-on" is the operative concept. This brightly colored 57,000-square-ft Navy Pier anchor encourages kids to play educational video games, climb through multilevel tunnels, run their own television stations, and, if their parents allow it, get all wet. Some favorites are an early childhood exhibit with a child-size neighborhood complete with a bakery, service station, and construction site; an art studio; science exhibits on such subjects as recycling and inventing; and an activity-filled exhibit that provides children and adults with tools for addressing prejudice and discrimination. | 312/527–1000 | www.chichildrensmuseum.org | $6.50, free Thurs. 5–8 | Tues.–Sun. 10–5.

The **Chicago Shakespeare Theatre** resides in an elegant round building with a bright neon sign. | 312/595–5600.

The lakefront **Skyline Stage** is a 1,500-seat vault-roof theater.

Pumping Station. Water is still pumped to 390,000 city residents at a rate of about 250 million gallons per day from this Gothic-style structure, which, along with the very similar Water Tower across the street, survived the Great Chicago Fire of 1871. The station is also a drop-in tourist information center, which includes a coffee stand, a gift shop, and a Hot Tix booth that sells discounted tickets for many city stage productions. | 811 N. Michigan Ave. | 312/742–8811 | Daily 7:30 AM–7 PM.

Tribune Tower. In 1922 *Chicago Tribune* publisher Colonel Robert McCormick chose a Gothic design for the building that would house his paper, after rejecting a slew of functional modern designs. Embedded in the exterior wall of the tower are chunks of material taken from other famous buildings. Look for labeled blocks from Westminster Abbey, the Alamo, St. Peter's Basilica, the White House, the Berlin Wall, and the moon, among others; some of these bits and pieces were gifts to McCormick, and others were "secured" by the *Trib*'s foreign correspondents. There are also inspirational quotations engraved in the building. On the ground floor, behind plate-glass windows, are the studios of WGN radio, part of the *Chicago Tribune* empire, which also includes WGN-TV, cable-television stations, and the Chicago Cubs. | 435 N. Michigan Ave. | 312/222–3232 | www.chicagotribune.com.

Water Tower. This famous Michigan Avenue structure, completed in 1867, was originally built to house a 137-ft standpipe that equalized the pressure of the water pumped by the similar pumping station across the street. Oscar Wilde uncharitably called it "a castellated monstrosity with salt and pepper boxes stuck all over it." Nonetheless, it remains a Chicago landmark and a symbol of the city's spirit of survival following the fire of 1871, when it was one of the few structures not destroyed. | 806 N. Michigan Ave.

Lincoln Park

The city's oldest and most popular park is one of a number of lakefront greenbelts that were wisely created as a refuge for city dwellers. Within and near Lincoln Park are a number of appealing attractions.

Chicago Historical Society. Chicago's oldest cultural institution (founded in 1856) is housed in a stately brick Georgian building dating to 1932 that was updated in 1971 with a striking addition facing Clark Street. The historical society's permanent exhibits include the much-loved Diorama Room, which portrays scenes from Chicago's history and has been a part of the lives of generations of Chicago children. Other attractions are Chicago's first locomotive (which you may board), collections of costumes, and the popular Illinois Pioneer Life Gallery, where there are daily crafts demonstrations by costumed docents. | 1601 N. Clark St. | 312/642–4600 | www.chicagohistory.org | $5, free Mon. | Mon.–Sat. 9:30–4:30, Sun. noon–5.

Lincoln Park Zoo. Begun in 1868 with a pair of swans donated by New York's Central Park, this very popular 35-acre urban zoo grew through donations of animals from wealthy Chicago residents and the purchase of a collection from the Barnum and Bailey Circus. Lincoln Park Zoo is particularly noted for its Great Ape House; the 24 gorillas are considered the finest collection in the world. The spectacular glass-dome Regenstein Small Mammal and Reptile House has simulated jungle, river, and forest environments for animal residents, including the much-loved koalas. In addition, the zoo has a large-mammal house (elephants, giraffes, black rhinos), a primate house, a bird house complete with a lush free-flight area and a waterfall, a huge polar bear pool with two bears, plus several rare and endangered species, such as the spectacle bear (named for the eyeglasslike markings around its eyes). There's also the children's zoo, the Farm in the Zoo (farm animals and a learning center with films and demonstrations), and the Conservation Station, with hands-on activities. | 2200 N. Cannon Dr. | 312/742–2000 | Free | Daily 9–5.

North Avenue Beach. One of the city's most popular warm-weather destinations, North Avenue Beach is packed with volleyball players and sunbathers on summer weekends. | Lakefront at North Ave.

★ **Peggy Notebaert Nature Museum.** You'll walk among hundreds of Midwest species of butterflies and learn about the impact of rivers and lakes on daily life at this modern, tall-window-filled museum. It's geared toward kids, with educational computer games to play and water tubes to get wet in. But even jaded adults will have trouble restraining their excitement when bright-yellow butterflies land on their shoulders. The Children's Gallery is designed to teach three- to eight-year-olds about the environment. The gift shop is chock-full of interesting hands-on gifts. | 2430 N. Cannon Dr. | 773/755–5100 | www.chias.org | $6, free Tues. | Weekdays 9 AM–4:30 PM, weekends 10–5.

★ **Second City.** Such talents as Joan Rivers, the late John Belushi, Bill Murray and *Saturday Night Live* comedienne Rachel Dratch used this improvisational comedy club as a training ground. Improv sets after the main stage show are free even if you didn't attend the show and generally begin around 10:30 PM. | 1616 N. Wells St. | 312/337–3992 | www.secondcity.com.

Hyde Park

★ **Museum of Science and Industry.** Constantly updating itself with new exhibits—such as Genetics–Decoding Life, which shows how scientists can make frogs' eyes glow and explores the pros and cons of genetic engineering—the museum is a sprawling open space, with 2,000 exhibits on three floors. You can walk through the middle of a 20-ft tall model of the human heart, explore a cantilevered Boeing 727, and make noises in the acoustically perfect Whispering Gallery. The museum also has the world's first permanent exhibit on HIV and AIDS, plus Lego MindStorms and the Idea Factory. Be sure to study the museum map to decide how you want to use your time.

Of special interest for families is the Imagination Station on the lower level, with hands-on activities for children up to age 12. The Omnimax Theater shows science- and space-related films on a giant five-story screen. The museum's classical revival building was designed in 1892 by D. H. Burnham & Company as a temporary structure to house the Palace of Fine Arts of the World's Columbian Exposition. It's the fair's only surviving building. On nice days, the giant lawn out front is almost as entertaining as the museum itself, with hordes of sunbathers and kite flyers; Lake Michigan is across the street. | 5700 S. Lake Shore Dr. | 773/684–1414 | www.msichicago.org | $9 | Late May–early Sept., daily 9–5:30; early Sept.–late May, weekdays 9:30–4, weekends 9:30–5:30.

University of Chicago. The University of Chicago was built through the largesse of John D. Rockefeller. Coeducational from the beginning, it was known for progressive education. The university's stately Gothic-style quadrangles recall the residential colleges in Cambridge and Oxford, England, and the Ivy League schools of the East Coast, but the U of C retains a uniquely midwestern quality.

The university's schools of economics, law, business, and medicine are world famous, and the University of Chicago hospitals are leading teaching institutions. Perhaps the most world-altering event to take place at U of C was the first self-sustaining nuclear chain reaction, created here in 1942 by Enrico Fermi and his team of physicists under an unused football stadium.

The University's visitor center, on the first floor of Ida Noyes Hall, provides maps, publications, and information on university events. Campus tours, which leave from the visitor center, are given to the general public daily at 10:30 AM and again on Friday at 1:30 PM. A self-guided tour of campus architecture, *A Walking Guide to the Campus,* is available for purchase in the University of Chicago bookstore. | Visitor Center: Ida Noyes Hall, 1212 E. 59th St. | 773/702–9739 | www.uchicago.edu | Weekdays 9–5.

Dining

Greater Downtown

The Berghoff. German. This longtime city favorite holds the city's first liquor license. A menu of German classics (Wiener schnitzel, sauerbraten) is augmented by American favorites and, in keeping with the times, lighter dishes and even salads. | 17 W. Adams St. | 312/427–3170 | Closed Sun. | $11–$18 | AE, MC, V.

Lou Mitchell's. American/Casual. This diner, a destination since 1923, specializes in high-fat breakfasts and comfort-food lunches. Though out-the-door waits are common, tables turn rapidly and staffers dole out doughnut holes and Milk Duds to pacify pangs. | 565 W. Jackson Blvd. | 312/939–3111 | No dinner | $8–$14 | AE, V.

The Parthenon. Greek. *Saganaki,* the Greek flaming cheese dish, was invented here in the late 1960s. Known for its festive atmosphere, happy customers, and hearty, inexpensive food. | 314 S. Halsted St. | 312/726–2407 | $10–$15 | AE, D, DC, MC, V.

Near North

Billy Goat Tavern. American/Casual. The late comedian John Belushi immortalized the Goat's short-order cooks on *Saturday Night Live* for barking, "No Coke! Pepsi!" and "No fries! Cheeps!" at customers. Griddle-fried "cheezborgers" are the featured chow. | 430 N. Michigan Ave., lower level | 312/222–1525 | $4–$6 | No credit cards.

Flat Top Grill. Contemporary. This crowded, narrow spot is one of the city's best do-your-own stir-fry places. You can fill your bowl from an assortment of fresh vegetables, meat, and fish; ladle on the sauce of your choice; and watch a chef stir-fry it on a hot griddle. | 319 W. North Ave. | 312/787–7676 | No lunch Mon.–Thurs. | $12 | AE, D, DC, MC, V.

Fox & Obel Food Market Cafe. Café. This riverside gourmet market treats its prepared food with the same reverence for fine and organic foodstuffs as it does its grocery inventory. Service is cafeteria style, but selections are decidedly more sophisticated. Only a block from Navy Pier. | 401 E. Illinois St. | 312/379–0112 | $7–$8 | AE, D, MC, V.

Joe's Be-Bop Cafe and Jazz Emporium. Barbecue. Hear live jazz nightly at this casual barbecue restaurant and outdoor café, whose ribs are proving as popular as some of Chicago's finest. Or is it the delightful Navy Pier lake views? Kids' menu available. | 600 E. Grand Ave. | 312/595–5299 | Reservations not accepted | $7–$19 | AE, D, DC, MC, V.

River North

Ed Debevic's. American/Casual. This tongue-in-cheek re-creation 1950s diner is busy from morning 'til midnight. Gum-snapping waitresses in garish costumes trade quips and snide remarks with customers, but it's all in good humor. | 640 N. Wells St. | 312/664–1707 | Reservations not accepted | $3–$8 | AE, D, DC, MC, V.

★ **Pizzeria Uno/Pizzeria Due.** Italian. Chicago deep-dish pizza got its start at Uno in 1943, with Due following a few years later. Only a block apart, the two sibling restaurants serve the same pizza; check in at both to see which has the shorter wait. Uno: | 29 E. Ohio St. | 312/321–1000 | Due: 619 N. Wabash Ave. | 312/943–2400 | $15–$20 | AE, D, DC, MC, V.

Lincoln Park and North

★ **Ann Sather.** Scandinavian. All four branches of this light, airy Swedish restaurant, mobbed for weekend breakfast, emphasize home-style food and service. Dinner is available only at the Belmont Avenue location. Whichever meal you come for, don't leave without sampling their signature cinnamon rolls. | 5207 N. Clark St. | 773/271–6677 | No dinner | 929 W. Belmont Ave. | 773/348–2378 | 3416 N. Southport Ave. | 773/404–4475 | No dinner | 2665 N. Clark St. | 773/327–9522 | No dinner | $9–$13 | AE, MC, V.

Mama Desta's Red Sea. Ethiopian. The stewlike dishes at this Ethiopian spot intriguingly combine herbs and spices with complex aromas and interesting textures. Food such as spicy chicken, lamb stew, and pureed lentils is flavorful, earthy, and simple. Instead of relying on silverware, diners use spongy, slightly sour flatbread to scoop up the chef's creations. | 3216 N. Clark St. | 773/935–7561 | No lunch Mon.–Thurs. | $6–$10 | AE, DC, MC, V.

Piece. Pizza. The antithesis of Chicago-style deep-dish pizza, Piece's flat pies mimic those made famous in New Haven, Connecticut. Stylish salads make fine starters, and house-brewed beers pair perfectly with the chow. Local families as well as neighborhood hipsters converge at this spot, generally crowded though it occupies a vast former garage. | 1927 W. North Ave. | 773/772–4422 | $9–$15 | AE, D, MC, V.

Thai Classic. Thai. This attractive, spotless restaurant, just a few blocks south of Wrigley Field, stands out with its good service and meticulously prepared dishes. Bargain hunters enjoy the $10.95 buffet, available Saturday afternoon and all day Sunday. It can be very difficult to park here when the Cubs are playing, so plan accordingly. | 3332 N. Clark St. | 773/404–2000 | $6–$13 | AE, D, DC, MC, V.

South

Army and Lou's. Southern. First-rate home-cooked soul food has earned a stellar reputation for this South Side institution. The fried chicken is arguably the city's best; barbecued ribs, roast turkey, turnip and mustard greens, and crunchy fried catfish are other standouts. The setting is surprisingly genteel for such down-home fare: waiters glide about in tuxedo shirts and bow ties, and tables have starched white cloths. | 420 E. 75th St. | 773/483–3100 | Closed Tues. | $7–$20 | AE, D, DC, MC, V.

Hong Min. Chinese. Low prices and well-prepared food are the hallmarks of this no-frills Chinatown mainstay. The menu embraces everything from chop suey to stir-fried lobster; insiders tout the fresh oysters. Bring your own beer and wine. | 221 W. Cermak Rd. | 312/842–5026 | $7–$20 | MC, V.

Manny's Coffee Shop and Deli. American/Casual. Locals and visitors alike may bemoan the dearth of delis in Chicago, but this classic cafeteria on the Near South Side is the real deal. Favorites include thick pastrami sandwiches, soul-nurturing matzo-ball soup, and piping-hot potato pancakes. Search for seating in two teeming rooms and pay as you leave. | 1141 S. Jefferson St. | 312/939–2855 | Reservations not accepted | Closed Sun. No dinner | $6–$10 | No credit cards.

Lodging

Greater Downtown

Hostelling International–Chicago. A historic loft building in the South Loop area houses dormitory-style rooms and two private rooms that go for about $120 per night. Unlike many other hostels, this one has such amenities as 24-hour security and Internet kiosks. Restaurant, dining room, gym, recreation room, laundry facilities, meeting rooms; no room TVs, no smoking | 24 E. Congress Pkwy. | 312/360–0300 | fax 312/360–0313 | www.hichicago.org | 500 dorm beds (summer season), 250 dorm beds (academic year), limited private rooms | $28–$32 | MC, V.

Near North

Cass Hotel. The Cass is a favorite for those looking for cheap sleeps just a short walk from North Michigan Avenue shopping and River North nightlife. Rooms are small and functional, and all bathrooms have modern vanities, fixtures, and tubs. Ask for one of the king or double rooms equipped with a refrigerator. Phones with data ports are available on request. The $1.99 breakfast in the lobby coffee shop is a steal. Restaurant, coffee shop, in-room data ports, some minibars, some refrigerators, cable TV, hair salon, bar, laundry facilities, parking (fee) | 640 N. Wabash Ave. | 312/787–4030 or 800/227–7850 | fax 312/787–8544 | www.casshotel.com | 150 rooms | $74–$104 | AE, D, DC, MC, V.

River North

Best Western River North. The undistinguished exterior and outdated deco-inspired lobby are more than offset by large and reasonably priced guest rooms that include black-and-white tile bathrooms. Parking is free, a cost-saving rarity downtown. The sofa sleepers in the suites and the indoor pool make it a family favorite. Restaurant, pizzeria, room service, in-room data ports, in-room safes, some refrigerators, cable TV, indoor pool, exercise equipment, gym, sauna, bar, dry cleaning, business services, meeting room, free parking, no-smoking floor | 125 W. Ohio St. | 312/467–0800 or 800/727–0800 | fax 312/467–1665 | www.bestwestern.com/rivernorthhotel | 125 rooms, 25 suites | $89–$169 | AE, D, DC, MC, V.

HoJo Inn. On a main thoroughfare in downtown Chicago, this classic L-shape, two-story motor lodge stands as a campy vestige of another era. The rooms are well maintained, the staff is pleasant, parking is free, and the location is just a short walk from a cluster of theme restaurants like Hard Rock Cafe. Coffee shop, some refrigerators, cable TV, free parking, no-smoking rooms | 720 N. LaSalle St. | 312/664–8100 | fax 312/664–2365 | www.hojo.com | 67 rooms, 4 suites | $125–$135 | AE, D, DC, MC, V.

Lincoln Park and North

Best Western Hawthorne Terrace. Tucked into the heart of the Lake View community, this hotel is easy to overlook. The American Colonial lobby and street-level outdoor terrace are the best parts of the property, and the only public areas other than a small exercise room. In-room data ports, some in-room hot tubs, some microwaves, some refrigerators, cable TV, gym, laundry facilities, business services, parking (fee) | 3434 N. Broadway | 773/244–3434 or 888/675–2378 | fax 773/244–3435 | www.hawthorneterrace.com | 46 rooms, 13 suites | $139–$169 | AE, D, DC, MC, V.

City Suites Hotel. Two-thirds of this affordable, art deco hotel consists of suites, each of which has a separate sitting room and a pullout couch. A free Continental breakfast, afternoon cookies, and a newspaper are available daily. The hotel is on a busy street in the Lake View neighborhood, so if noise is a concern, request a room on the east side of the building. Room service, in-room data ports, some microwaves, some refrigerators, cable TV, some in-room VCRs, hair salon, dry cleaning, laundry facilities, concierge, parking (fee) | 933 W. Belmont Ave. | 773/404–3400 or 800/248–9108 | fax 773/404–3405 | www.cityinns.com | 16 rooms, 29 suites | $139–$179 | AE, D, DC, MC, V.

Days Inn Lincoln Park North. This well-kept Days Inn in the lively Lincoln Park neighborhood is a real find. A complimentary Continental breakfast is served in a room off the lobby with a pressed-tin ceiling and brass chandeliers. Cheery floral bedspreads and light furniture brighten up the basic rooms. For about $15 extra a night, you can upgrade to a business room. All guests have free use of a nearby health club. Restaurant, some in-room data ports, in-room safes, microwaves, refrigerators, cable TV, bar, laundry facilities, laundry service, business services, meeting room, parking (fee), no-smoking rooms | 644 W. Diversey Pkwy. | 773/525–7010 or 888/576–3297 | fax 773/525–6998 | www.lpndaysinn.com | 129 rooms, 4 suites | $126–$146 | AE, D, DC, MC, V.

Arts and Entertainment

Dance

Hubbard Street Dance Chicago. Chicago's most notable success story in dance mixes classical ballet techniques, theatrical jazz, and contemporary styles. | 312/850–9744.

Joffrey Ballet of Chicago. Having emerged as Chicago's premier classical dance company, Joffrey Ballet garners acclaim for fine-tuned performances such as its uniquely American production of *The Nutcracker.* | 312/739–0120.

Film

★ **Chicago Outdoor Film Festival.** Every July through August, Grant Park shows movies on Tuesday nights. Bring a picnic dinner and a blanket and watch classic films under the stars. | 500 S. Columbus Dr. | 312/742–7529.

Gene Siskel Film Center. The center specializes in unusual current films, revivals of rare classics, and film festivals. | 164 N. State St. | 312/846–2800.

Music

BLUES

In the years following World War II, Chicago-style blues grew into its own musical form, flourishing during the 1950s. You can still find the South Side clubs where it all began, but since 1970 the blues has migrated to the North Side and attracted new devotees among largely white audiences.

Blue Chicago. Two bars are within two blocks of each other. Both have good sound systems, regularly book female vocalists, and attract a cosmopolitan audience. One cover gets you into both bars. | 536 N. Clark St. | 312/661–0100 | 736 N. Clark St. | 312/642–6261.

In the basement of the **Blue Chicago Store,** Saturday night is family night, with live blues, no alcohol, and no smoking. | 534 N. Clark St. | 312/661–1003.

JAZZ

Jazz Institute Hot Line. Jazz thrives all around town. Call for a recorded listing of upcoming live performances. | 312/427–3300.

★ **Andy's.** A favorite after-work watering hole with a substantial bar menu, Andy's has live, local jazz daily. In addition to the evening performances, there's a jazz program at noon on weekdays—a boon for music lovers who aren't night owls. | 11 E. Hubbard St. | 312/642–6805.

Jazz Showcase. The second-oldest jazz club in the country presents national and international names in jazz, and mostly acoustic groups. This serious no-smoking club, bedecked with photos of all the jazz greats who've played it, is one of the best places to hear jazz in Chicago. Children under 12 are admitted free for the Sunday matinee. | 59 W. Grand Ave. | 312/670–2473.

OPERA

Lyric Opera of Chicago. Top-flight productions star the big voices of the opera world, and it has sold out all of its superb performances for more than a dozen years. Don't worry about understanding German or Italian; English translations are projected above the stage. The season at the Ardis Krainik Theatre in the Civic Opera House runs September–March. | 20 N. Wacker Dr. | 312/332–2244.

ORCHESTRAS

Chicago Symphony Orchestra. Music director Daniel Barenboim conducts September–June at Orchestra Hall. | 220 S. Michigan Ave. | 312/294–3000 or 800/223–7114.

Civic Orchestra of Chicago. The CSO's training orchestra performs a repertoire similar to that of the parent organization and works with the same guest conductors. Performances are free, but advance tickets are required. | 220 S. Michigan Ave. | 312/294–3000 or 800/223–7114.

Theater

Road-show productions of Broadway hits do come to Chicago, but the theater scene's true vigor springs from the multitude of small ensembles that have made a home here. Tickets to shows are best bought at the venue to avoid convenience fees and possibly score a suddenly-available prime seat.

Hot Tix. Several booths throughout the city and suburbs sell discount tickets to shows. Same-day half-price tickets for about 140 city and suburban theaters are available. Note that tickets for weekend and Monday shows go on sale Friday. | 312/554–9800 | www.hottix.org.

Goodman Theatre. One of the oldest and best theaters in Chicago is known for its polished performances of classic and contemporary works starring well-known actors. | 170 N. Dearborn St. | 312/443–3800.

Lookingglass Theatre Company. This ensemble, cofounded by David Schwimmer of *Friends* fame, produces physically—and artistically—daring works. Plans call for the company to move to a new theater in the Chicago Water Works building on Michigan Avenue in mid-2003. | Ruth Page Theater, 1016 N. Dearborn St. | 773/477–9257.

★ **Steppenwolf Theatre Company.** With a commitment to ensemble collaboration and artistic risk, Steppenwolf has won national acclaim for its cutting-edge acting style and its consistently successful productions. Illustrious alumni, who often return to participate in productions, include John Malkovich, Gary Sinise, Joan Allen, and Laurie Metcalf. | 1650 N. Halsted St. | 312/335–1650.

Shopping

The Second City delivers plenty of first-class shopping. Look for discount jewelry and watches in the Loop, designer boutiques on Oak Street, and funky antiques on Lincoln Avenue. Character still counts in Chicago, too, and all around town are specialty shops offering personal service and goods that convey the city's uniqueness—whether you're looking for Frank Lloyd Wright reproductions or blues recordings.

Loop

One of two major downtown shopping areas, the Loop has most shops centered on State Street, which is striving to regain the stature it had when it was immortalized as "State Street, that great street." It's anchored by two of the city's major department stores: **Carson Pirie Scott** (1 S.) and **Marshall Field's** (111 N.). (Pick up a box of Field's signature Frango Mints, one of the city's most popular edible souvenirs, for your favorite chocolate lover.)

The blocks surrounding the intersection of Wabash Avenue and Madison Street are designated as Jewelers Row; five high-rises cater to the wholesale trade, but many showrooms sell to the public at prices 25%–50% below retail.

Illinois Artisans' Shop. Head here for a unique find or two. The store, which is closed weekends, culls the best jewelry, ceramics, glass, and African-American dolls from craftspeople around the state and sells them at reasonable prices. | James R. Thompson Center, 100 W. Randolph St. | 312/814–5321.

★ **Chicago Music Mart.** Nearly a dozen stores are devoted to all things musical—instruments, CDs, sheet music, and music-theme gifts and souvenirs. Stop by at lunchtime to rest your feet and hear a free concert. | 333 State St. | 312/362–6700.

Michigan Avenue

The other downtown shopping district, Michigan Avenue, heralded as the Magnificent Mile, is by contrast the city's most glamorous shopping area. It stretches from the Chicago River (400 N.) to Oak Street (1000 N.). A visit to Chicago wouldn't be complete without a tour of the world-class stores on this strip, which range from big department stores like **Neiman Marcus** (737 N. Michigan Ave.) and **Barneys New York** (25 E. Oak St.) to exclusive designer boutiques like **Jil Sander** (48 E. Oak St.) and **Ultimo** (114 E. Oak St.). A free map of the Mag Mile area is available at hotels and tourist information centers.

American Girl Place. A must-stop for legions of little girls is the phenomenally successful doll company's only retail store (products are sold through catalog and Internet business). There's easily a day's worth of activities for visitors here, who can shop at the boutique, take in a live musical revue, and have lunch or afternoon tea at the café, where dolls can partake in the meal at their own "sassy seats." Be prepared for long lines just to get in during high shopping seasons. | 111 E. Chicago Ave. | 312/255–9876.

Chicago Architecture Foundation. Stylish reminders of the city and its notable architecture take the form of everything from books to neckties and toys. | John Hancock Center, 875 N. Michigan Ave. | 312/751–1380.

★ **City of Chicago Store.** For a souvenir selection that goes beyond T-shirts and snow globes, check out this shop, where the unusual picks range from street signs to bricks from the old Comiskey Park. It's also a good source for guidebooks and posters. | 163 E. Pearson St. | 312/742–8811.

River North and North

Other neighborhoods worth a visit include **River North,** which is contained by the Chicago River on the south and west, Clark Street on the east, and Oak Street on the north. It's home to art galleries, high-end antiques shops, home furnishings stores, and clothing boutiques. All have a distinctive style that fits in with this artsy area. It's also a wildly popular entertainment district where you'll find touristy theme restaurants peddling logo merchandise as aggressively as burgers.

The upscale residential neighborhood of **Lincoln Park** entices with its mix of distinctive boutiques, most notably along Armitage Avenue between Orchard Street (700 W.) and Kenmore Avenue (1050 W.), where stores filled with clothing, tableware, jewelry and gifts beg to be visited. There are some equally enticing shops on Halsted Street and Webster Avenue.

Lake View, a diverse area just north of Lincoln Park, has spawned a number of worthwhile shopping strips. Clark Street between Diversey Avenue (2800 N.) and Addison Street (3600 N.) has myriad clothing boutiques and specialty stores. Farther north on Halsted Street between Belmont Avenue (3200 N.) and Addison Street (3600 N.) are more gift shops and boutiques—several with a gay orientation—as well as a smattering of vintage-clothing and antiques stores. In West Lake View, distinctive boutiques have sprung up on Southport Avenue between Belmont Avenue (3200 N.) and Grace Street (3800 N.). Broadway between Diversey Avenue and Addison Street also claims its share of intriguing shops.

The side-by-side neighborhoods of **Bucktown and Wicker Park,** whose vortex of energy is the intersection of North, Damen, and Milwaukee avenues, is home to trendy coffeehouses, nightclubs, and restaurants catering to resident musicians and artists. Scads of edgy clothing boutiques, art galleries, home design ateliers, alternative music stores, and antiques shops dot the area, too, making it a shopping destination that deserves a solid chunk of time. The neighborhood is very youth-oriented and still a bit gritty, so it's not for everyone. Many stores don't open until at least 11 AM, some shops are closed on Monday and Tuesday, and hours can be erratic.

Sports and Outdoor Activities

Beaches

Chicago has about 20 mi of lakefront, most of it sand or rock beach. Beaches are open to the public daily from 9 AM to 9:30 PM, Memorial Day–Labor Day, and many beaches have changing facilities.

Chicago Park District. The parks provide lifeguard protection during daylight hours throughout the swimming season. The beaches' water is usually too cold for swimming at other times of the year. | 312/747–2200 | www.chicagoparkdistrict.com.

North Avenue Beach. This beach attracts many athletes. There are bathrooms, changing facilities, and showers. The south end of this beach has plenty of lively volleyball action in summer and fall. | 1600–2400 North, Lincoln Park.

Oak Street Beach. You can expect it to be mobbed with trendy singles and people-watchers on any warm summer day at this beach, which probably rates as Chicago's most popular. There are bathrooms, but for official changing facilities you'll have to make the walk to the North Avenue Beach bathhouse. The concrete breakwater that makes up the southern part of Oak Street Beach is a busy promenade on hot summer nights. | 600–1600 North, Near North.

Bicycling

There are many scenic routes along the lake, downtown, and in greater Chicago. Chicago's **lakefront bicycle path** extends about 20 mi, with fabulous views of the lake and the skyline. Keep in mind that the path can get very crowded during typical rush hours and weekends, particularly in the summer, and it's shared by in-line skaters and walkers.

Chicago Park District. Contact the Park District for maps. | 312/747–2200 | www.chicagoparkdistrict.com.

On the Route. You can rent a bike for the day or by the hour from On the Route, which stocks a large inventory of bicycles, including children's bikes. It also supplies helmets and other safety equipment. | 3146 N. Lincoln Ave. | 773/477–5066.

Bike Chicago. They'll deliver a bike to your hotel and pick it up after your ride. Fees start at $7.75 per hour and $30 a day. It also runs a free, two-hour lakefront tour daily, weather permitting. | 600 E. Grand Ave. | 312/755–0488 or 800/915–2453 | www.bikechicago.com/home.asp.

Boating

The lakefront harbors are packed with boats, but if you're not familiar with Great Lakes sailing, it's best to leave the navigating to an experienced skipper.

Chicago Sailing Club. Sailboat lessons and rentals are available. The club focuses on sailing instruction for all levels and includes a program on keeping your boat in tip-top shape. | Belmont Harbor | 773/871–7245 | www.chicagosailingclub.com.

Lincoln Park Lagoon. For a more placid water outing, try the paddleboats, just north of Farm in the Zoo. | 2021 N. Stockton Dr., Lincoln Park | 312/742–2038.

Bowling

What's the Midwest without bowling?

Diversey River Bowl. Rock out to live music while you roll in the 36 lanes at Rock n' Bowl. | 2211 W. Diversey Pkwy. | 773/227–5800 | www.drbowl.com.

Waveland Bowl. Check out the newly remodeled Waveland for 24-hour bowling with 40 lanes. | 3700 N. Western Ave. | 773/472–5902 | www.wavelandbowl.com.

In-line Skating

In-line skating is a popular lakefront pastime. If you're skating the lakefront path, keep to the right and watch your back for bicyclists. Skating is also allowed on Daley Bicentennial Plaza. You can rent blades from **Bike Chicago** (☞ Bicycling).

Running

The 18-mi lakefront path accommodates joggers, bicyclists, and skaters, so you'll need to be attentive while you admire the views. You can pick up the path at Oak Street Beach (across from the Drake Hotel), at Grand Avenue underneath Lake Shore Drive, or by going through Grant Park on Monroe Street or Jackson Boulevard until you reach the lakefront. On the **lakefront path** joggers should stay north of McCormick Place. Muggers sometimes lurk in the comparatively empty stretch between the convention center and Hyde Park.

Chicago-Area Runners Association. Various groups hold organized races. Call for schedules. | 312/666–9836 | www.cararuns.org.

Essential Information

When to Go

If your principal concern is comfortable weather for touring the city, consider a visit in spring or fall, when moderate temperatures make it a pleasure to be out and about. Summertime brings outdoor recreation, although temperatures will climb into the 90°s in hot spells, and the humidity can be high. Winters can see raw weather and the occasional news-making blizzard, and temperatures in the teens are to be expected; come prepared for the cold. Yet mild winters, with temperatures in the 30°s, are common, too, and many indoor venues allow you to look out on the cold in warm comfort.

FESTIVALS AND SEASONAL EVENTS

WINTER

Dec.: **Christmas Around the World.** Trees decorated in the traditional styles of more than 40 countries adorn the Museum of Science and Industry. | 773/684–1414.

SPRING

Mar.: **St. Patrick's Day Parade.** The Chicago River is dyed green, shamrocks decorate the street, and the center stripe of Dearborn Street is painted the color of the Irish from Wacker Drive to Van Buren Street. | 312/942–9188.

SUMMER

June: **Chicago Blues Festival.** Blues greats from Chicago and around the country star in this popular four-day, three-stage event held in Grant Park. | 312/744–3315.

Taste of Chicago. Vendors in Grant Park dish out pizza, cheesecake, and other Chicago specialties to 3½ million people over the course of this 10-day festival, which includes entertainment. | 312/744–3315.

July: **Fireworks along the Lakefront.** Bring a blanket and a portable radio to listen to the 1812 Overture from Grant Park at dusk. | 312/744–3315.

Aug.: **Air and Water Show.** This show along North Avenue Beach thrills viewers with precision-flying teams and antique and high-tech aircraft going through their paces. | 312/744–3315.

AUTUMN

Oct.: **Chicago Marathon.** The race begins in Grant Park at Columbus and Balbo streets and follows a course through the city. | 312/243–3274.

Nov.: **Magnificent Mile Lights Festival.** A block-by-block illumination of hundreds of thousands of tiny white lights along Michigan Avenue and Oak Street kicks off the holiday season. | 312/642–3570.

Bargains

CityPass. To save money on sightseeing, buy a Chicago CityPass, which costs $39. The passes are good for nine days from the day of first use and include admission to the Art Institute of Chicago, the Field Museum, the Museum of Science and Industry, the Adler Planetarium, the Shedd Aquarium, and the Sears Tower Skydeck. You can buy the pass at any one of the participating attractions. | www.citypass.com.

Visitor Pass. For savings on bus fare, purchase a Chicago Transit Authority (CTA) Visitor Pass, good for unlimited city bus rides in one-, two-, three- and five-day increments for $5–$18. (Children under seven ride for free.) Passes can be purchased in advance online or by phone, as well as at airport CTA stations and city visitor centers. | 888/YOUR-CTA | www.transitchicago.com.

Tours

BOAT TOURS

The season usually runs from May through September. Some companies have evening cruises as well as daytime tours.

★ **Chicago Architecture Foundation River Cruise.** The trip highlights more than 50 sights. The cost is $21 from Monday through Friday, $23 on Saturday, Sunday, and holidays; reservations are recommended. | 312/922–3432 for information; 312/902–1500 for tickets | www.architecture.org.

Shoreline Marine. You can also use the Shoreline Water Taxi to see some of Chicago's favorite destinations: Sears Tower, Navy Pier, and Shedd Aquarium. The fleet of taxis makes frequent departures from 10:30 until 6 daily from Memorial Day to Labor Day. The fare is just $6. | 312/222–9328 | www.shorelinesightseeing.com.

Windy of Chicago Ltd. You can get a blast from the past on the *Windy,* a 148-ft ship modeled on old-time commercial vessels. Passengers may help the crew or take a turn at the wheel as you sail Lake Michigan. The cost is $25. | 312/595–5555.

WALKING TOURS

Chicago Architecture Foundation. The foundation has by far the largest selection of guided tours, with more than 50 itineraries covering everything from department stores to Frank Lloyd Wright's Oak Park buildings. | 312/922–3432 | www.architecture.org.

★ **Chicago Office of Tourism.** A new, free service pairs visitors with an official Chicago Greeter, a resident volunteer who will lead you on a two- to four-hour walk of any of Chicago's neighborhoods and favorite attractions. | 312/744–2400; 800/226–6632; 312/744–2947 TTY; 800/406–6418 TTY | www.ci.chi.il.us/CulturalAffairs/Tourism.

Friends of the Chicago River. Saturday-morning tours walk along the river. The organization also has maps of the walking routes, available for a small donation. | 312/939–0490 | www.chicagoriver.org.

Visitor Information

Chicago Office of Tourism | 78 E. Washington St., Chicago 60602 | 312/744–2400; 800/226–6632; 800/406–6418 TTY | www.ci.chi.il.us/culturalaffairs/tourism.

Mayor's Office of Special Events, General Information, and Activities | 121 N. LaSalle St., Room 703, Chicago 60602 | 312/744–3315 | fax 312/744–8523.

Arriving and Departing

BY AIR

Airports

O'Hare International Airport (ORD). The major gateway to Chicago is 20 mi northwest of downtown. | 773/686–2200 | www.ohare.com.

Midway Airport (MDW). Midway is about 7 mi southwest of downtown and primarily serves budget airlines. | 773/838–0600 | www.chicago-mdw.com.

Airport Transportation

Car: Driving to and from O'Hare takes about an hour; the drive to and from Midway takes at least 45 minutes. From O'Hare, follow the signs to I–90 east (Kennedy Expressway), which merges with I–94 (Edens Expressway). From Midway, follow the signs to I–55 east, which leads to I–90.

Public Transit: Chicago Transit Authority (CTA) trains are the cheapest way to and from the airports. In O'Hare Airport the Blue-line station is in the underground concourse between terminals. Travel time to the city is about 45 minutes. At Midway Airport the Orange-line El runs to the Loop. Train fare is $1.50.

Shuttle: Airport Express. Coaches provide service from both airports to major downtown and Near North hotels. The trip downtown from O'Hare takes a half hour or longer, depending on traffic conditions and your destination; the fare is $20, $36 round-trip. The trip downtown from Midway takes about a half hour; the fare is $15, $27 round-trip. | 312/454–7800 or 800/654–7871 | www.airportexpress.com.

Omega Shuttle. Vans travel between O'Hare and Midway, with departures every hour and a fare of $20. Travel time is roughly an hour. | 773/483–6634 | www.omegashuttle.com.

Taxi: Metered taxicab service is available at both O'Hare and Midway. Trips to and from O'Hare incur a $1 surcharge. Expect to pay about $25–$35 plus tip from O'Hare to Near North and downtown locations, about $17–$27 plus tip from Midway.

BY BUS

Greyhound Lines has nationwide service to its main terminal in the Loop at 630 W. Harrison St. and to neighborhood stations.

BY CAR

The Kennedy Expressway, which merges I–90 and I–94, is the main artery into downtown Chicago. Exiting at Monroe or Washington Street will provide easy access to the Loop and most downtown attractions; the Ohio Street exit will point you toward Near North destinations. Lake Shore Drive (U.S. 41), a wonderfully scenic but less accessible option, hugs Lake Michigan and can get you to the same areas from just east of downtown.

BY TRAIN

Union Station. Amtrak offers nationwide service to Chicago's Union Station. | 225 S Canal St., in the Loop.

Getting Around

BY CAR

Chicago traffic is often heavy, on-street parking is nearly impossible to find, parking lots are expensive, congestion creates frustrating delays, and other drivers may be impatient with those who are unfamiliar with the city and its roads. In these circumstances you could find a car to be a liability rather than an asset. Instead, you may want to opt for the city's network of buses and rapid transit rail, or readily available taxis and limousines (the latter often priced competitively with metered cabs).

Parking

Most of Chicago's streets have metered parking, but during peak hours it's hard to find a spot. Most meters take quarters, buying as little as 15 minutes in high-traffic areas, up to an hour in less crowded neighborhoods. Some neighborhoods, such as the area of Lake View known as Wrigleyville, enforce restricted parking and will tow cars without a permit. Many major thoroughfares restrict parking during peak travel hours, generally 9–11 AM heading toward downtown and 4–6 PM heading away. Read street signs carefully to determine whether a parking spot is legal.

BY PUBLIC TRANSIT

Chicago Transit Authority (CTA)

Chicago's extensive public transportation network includes buses and rapid transit trains, both subway and elevated (the latter known as the El).

The CTA fare structure is as follows: The basic fare for rapid transit trains and buses is $1.50, and transfers are 30¢. Transit cards can be purchased in preset denominations of $10 ($11 worth of rides) or $20 ($22 worth of rides) at many local grocery stores, currency exchanges, and stations. You can also purchase a transit card of any denomination over $1.50 at any CTA stop. If you pay cash and do not use a transit card, you must buy a transfer when you first board the bus or train. Transfers can be used twice within a two-hour time period. Transfers between CTA train lines are free—no transfer card is needed. Transit cards may be shared.

Exact fares must be paid in cash (dollar bills or coins; no change given by turnstiles on train platforms or fare boxes on buses) or by transit card. Visitor passes are another option. For $5 a one-day pass offers 24 hours of unlimited CTA riding from the time you first use it. Visitor passes are sold at hotels, museums, and other places tourists frequent, plus all transit card booths. A two-day pass is $9, a three-day pass is $12, and a five-day pass is $18. | 312/836–7000; 888/968–7282 for advance sales of visitor passes | www.transitchicago.com.

Bus: City buses generally stop on every other corner northbound and southbound (on State Street they stop at every corner). Eastbound and westbound buses generally stop on every corner. Buses from the Loop generally run north–south.

Pace runs suburban buses in a six-county region; these connect with the CTA and use CTA transit cards, transfers, and passes.

Subway and the El: Each of the seven CTA train lines has a color name as well as a route name. Most, but not all, rapid transit lines operate 24 hours; some stations are closed at night. In general, late-night CTA travel is not recommended. Pick up the brochure "Downtown Transit Sightseeing Guide" for hours, fares, and other pertinent information.

Metra Commuter Trains

Metra commuter trains serve the city and surrounding suburbs. Metra trains use a fare structure based on the distance you ride. A Metra weekend pass costs $5 and is valid for rides on any of the eight operating lines all day on weekends, except for the South Shore line.

The Metra Electric railroad has a line close to Lake Michigan; its trains stop in Hyde Park. Its commuter rail system has 11 lines to suburbs and surrounding cities including Aurora, Elgin, Joliet, and Waukegan; one line serves the North Shore suburbs, and another has a stop at McCormick Place. Trains leave from a number of downtown terminals. | 312/322–6777 | www.metrarail.com.

BY TAXI

You can hail a cab on just about any busy street in Chicago. Available taxis are sometimes indicated by an illuminated rooftop light. Chicago taxis are metered, with fares beginning at $1.60 upon entering the cab and $1.40 for each additional mile. A charge of 50¢ is made for each additional passenger between the ages of 12 and 65. There is no extra baggage charge. Taxi drivers expect a 15% tip.

Checker Taxi | 312/243–2537. **Flash Cab** | 773/561–1444. **Yellow Cab Co.** | 312/829–4222.

Pennsylvania

Revised and Updated by Laura Knowles Callanan

GETTYSBURG

"The world will little note, nor long remember, what we say here, but it can never forget what they did here." These words from Abraham Lincoln's famous address were delivered in Gettysburg to mark the dedication of its national cemetery in November 1863. Four months earlier, from July 1 to 3, there were some 51,000 American casualties in the bloodiest battle of the Civil War. The resulting Confederate defeat is regarded by many historians as the turning point of the war.

Today, cannons and monuments line the roadsides memorializing the famous battle. Covering over 5,000 acres, the Gettysburg National Military Park contains more than 40 miles of scenic avenues winding around the landmarks of the battle. The National Cemetery in particular is a well-shaded spot for a lovely summer stroll. The tourist district at the southern end of town offers several museums and shops, and the historic downtown area contains more than 100 buildings restored to their original Civil War-era charm. In all, more than 1,000 markers and monuments commemorate the battle. Those who want to skip from the Civil War era to the mid–20th century can visit the home of former president Dwight D. Eisenhower, which is right next to the park. The fruit orchards of Adams County, just north of town, are especially beautiful to drive through in May.

Exploring

Gettysburg National Military Park

There are few landmarks showing the history of the United States as touching as the field where troops from the North and South met and decided the fate of the Civil War. More than 51,000 soldiers were killed, wounded, or captured at the Battle of Gettysburg, making it the bloodiest battle of the Civil War. The self-guided trails make it an excellent opportunity for families with children to learn about American history. In all, the park has more than 6,000 acres and 1,300 monuments to state units. There are markers and memorials scattered throughout the park. Cannons stand along the 35 mi of scenic battlefields and avenues. You can visit 20 museums and attractions dedicated to the battle. In the first week of July, thousands of volunteers dress in period uniforms and reenact the three-day battle, which started July 1, 1863.

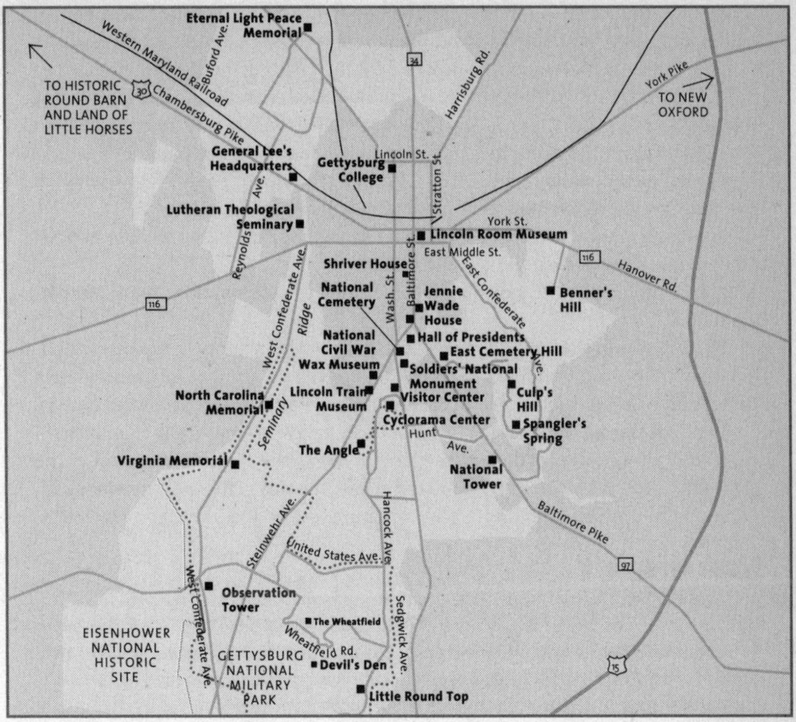

| 97 Taneytown Rd. | 717/334–1124 | fax 717/334–1891 | www.nps.gov/gett | Free | Park grounds and roads daily 6 AM–10 PM.

The ★**visitor center** contains the Gettysburg Museum of the Civil War, with one of the world's largest collections of Civil War items, Gettysburg-related memorabilia, and the Electric-Map battle-orientation program. The audiovisual program, displayed on a giant relief map of the battlefield, gives you an overview of the field, three days of battle, and who the major combatants were. | Museum free, Electric Map $3 | Mid-June–mid-Aug., daily 8–6; mid-Aug.–mid-June, daily 8–5.

It was on **East Cemetery Hill** that General Winfield Scott Hancock rallied beaten Union troops on July 1, 1863. Some Federal troops took up positions behind the stone walls that border the hill while artillery men dug barricades for their guns. By the morning of July 2, Cemetery Hill had become one of the most heavily fortified positions on the field. That night, the "Louisiana Tigers" broke the Union line here and charged up the slope to attack the cannon on top of the hill. Both Union and Confederate armies had severe losses in that fighting.

On the southern end of Cemetery Ridge, **Little Round Top** is another key area of the battlefield. Strewn with loose rocks and large boulders, the hill was a natural position from which to defend this important end of the Union line. Soldiers from both sides died in battle here on July 2, 1863.

Devil's Den marks the Union position on the second day of battle, July 2. The Confederate troops pushed the Union forces from this area.

Charge and countercharge on the afternoon of July 2, left the **wheat field** and nearby woods strewn with more than 4,000 dead and wounded. The thousands of troops who fought in this area compared the fighting to a whirlpool, a stream of eddies and tides that flowed around the 19 acres of George Roses's wheatfield.

Culp's Hill was the important anchor for the right flank of the Union line at Gettysburg. The battle fought here on July 3, 1863, ended with the Confederate Army retreating across Rock Creek, leaving the woods filled with dead and wounded. For the next 50 years, the dying trees on Culp's Hill bore scars of the battle.

The primary Confederate position west of Gettysburg for the final two days of the battle was **Seminary Ridge.** Confederate batteries still stand here.

The **Angle** marks the Union position on July 3 where the Federal soldiers stopped Confederate general George E. Pickett's charge.

President Franklin Delano Roosevelt dedicated the **Eternal Light Peace Memorial** in 1938.

The **Gettysburg National Cemetery** contains more than 7,000 interments, including more than 3,500 from the Civil War. It is also where President Abraham Lincoln delivered the Gettysburg Address in the dedication ceremonies on November 19, 1863.

The **Cyclorama Center** contains the Gettysburg Cyclorama, a 360-ft-long circular oil-on-canvas painting depicting *Pickett's Charge,* the climactic moment of the three-day battle. Completed and exhibited in 1884, it is one of the last surviving cycloramas in the United States. There is a 20-minute film on the battle and exhibits.

Near the Park

★ **A. Lincoln's Place.** *A. Lincoln Speaks,* a one-man performance, shows President Abraham Lincoln's life from birth through the Gettysburg Address. Actor Jim Getty has been depicting Lincoln since 1978, and there are photo and question-and-answer sessions after the performances. | Battle Theater, 571 Steinwehr Ave. | 717/334–6049 or 717/334–8003 | fax 717/334–4932 | www.gettysburg.com/gcvb/lincoln.html | $7 | Mar.–Nov.; call for show times.

★ **Eisenhower National Historic Site.** This is only place President and Mrs. Dwight D. Eisenhower ever owned as a home. In 1951, the Eisenhowers, looking forward to retirement, purchased the Allen Redding farm adjoining Gettysburg National Military Park. During Eisenhower's presidency, the 230-acre country estate was used as a weekend retreat and as a meeting place for world leaders. There is an 11-minute video and exhibits on Eisenhower's life. | 250 Eisenhower Farm La. | 717/338–9114 | fax 717/338–0821 | www.nps.gov/eise | $5.75 | Apr.–Oct., daily 9–4; Jan. and Nov.–Mar., Wed.–Sun. 9–4.

★ **General Lee's Headquarters.** General Robert E. Lee established his personal headquarters in this old stone house, which dates from the 1700s. On July 1, 1863, Lee made plans for the Battle of Gettysburg in this house. The home now holds a collection of Civil War artifacts and has a museum store. | 401 Buford Ave. | 717/334–3141 | fax 717/334–1813 | www.civilwarheadquarters.com | $3 | Mar.–Nov., daily 9–5; extended summer hrs.

Gettysburg College. Founded in 1832, this church-affiliated liberal arts college has a 200-acre campus with an undergraduate enrollment of 2,400. The administration building is listed on the National Register of Historic Places. It served as a hospital for the wounded of both sides during the Battle of Gettysburg. | 300 N. Washington St. | 717/337–6000 or 800/431–0803 | fax 717/337–6145 | www.gettysburg.edu | Free | Daily.

Historic Round Barn and Farm Market. Built in 1914, this Adams County landmark 8 mi west of Gettysburg off Route 30 really is round. Regional arts and crafts are sold, and in summer you can buy locally grown produce and flowers. | 298 Cashtown Rd., 17307 | 717/334–1984 | Free | June–Oct.

Jennie Wade House. Jennie Wade was the only civilian casualty in the Battle of Gettysburg, and her home and its furnishings have been preserved. The museum tells the story of Jennie and shows a snapshot of life in the Civil War era. | 758 Baltimore St., 17325 | 717/334–4100 | $5.95 | Daily 9–6.

Land of Little Horses. One of the world's largest herds of Falabella miniature horses lives at this amusement park. Daily events include pig races, carousel rides, saddle rides, train rides, and an arena show. There's also a museum and nature area with more than 100 animals. | 125 Glenwood Dr., 17325 | 717/334–7259 | $7 | Late May–late Aug., Mon.–Sat. 10–5, Sun. noon–5; Apr.–late May and Sept.–Oct., Sat. 10–5, Sun. noon–5.

★ **Lincoln Room Museum.** The Willis House is where Abraham Lincoln stayed and completed his Gettysburg Address on November 18, 1863. The furnishings in the home are original. | 12 Lincoln Sq. | 717/334–8188 | fax 717/338–9491 | www.gettysburg.com | $3.50 | Late May–early Sept., daily 9–8; early Sept.–late May, Sun.–Thurs. 10–5, Fri.–Sat. 10–8.

Lincoln Train Museum. This ride re-enacts the journey of President Lincoln as he traveled from Washington, D.C. to Gettysburg to give his famed Gettysburg Address, as actors portray reporters and distinguished officials. You can also visit an 1890 caboose, model train display, and military rail collection. | 425 Steinwehr Ave. | 717/334–5678 or 717/334–6296 | fax 717/334–6913 | www.gettysburgaddress.com | $5.95 | Late May–early Sept., daily 9–9; Mar., daily 10–5; Apr. and early Sept.–late Sept., daily 9–7; Oct.–Nov., daily 9–5.

Lutheran Theological Seminary. Founded in 1826, this is the oldest Lutheran seminary on the continent. In 1863, during the Battle of Gettysburg, the buildings on the 52-acre campus played a role first as an observatory for Union soldiers, then as a signal station for the Confederates, and finally as a hospital for the wounded of both armies. | 61 Seminary Ridge | 717/338–3008 or 800/658–8437 | fax 717/334–3469 | www.ltsg.edu/sem/ | Free | Weekdays 8:30–4:30.

National Civil War Wax Museum. The Civil War audiovisual presentation has more than 200 life-size figures in 30 scenes including a battle-room auditorium, a reenactment of the Battle of Gettysburg, and an animated Abraham Lincoln giving the Gettysburg Address. | 297 Steinwehr Ave. | 717/334–6245 | fax 717/334–9686 | www.e-gettysburg.cc | $5.50 | daily Late May–early Sept., daily 9–9; Mar.–Apr. and early Sept.–Dec., daily 9–5; Jan.–Feb., weekends 9–5.

Schriver House. The home of Henrietta and George Washington Schriver has been restored to show what civilian life was like in the Battle of Gettysburg. Schriver was a local hero during the Civil War, and the home tour showcases the attic where Confederate sharpshooters hid (two were killed), as well as Schriver's Saloon, operated out of the basement. | 309 Baltimore St., 17325 | 717/337–2800 | www.schriverhouse.com | $5.75 | Apr.–Nov., Mon.–Sat. 10–5, Sun. noon–5; Dec. and Feb.–Mar., weekends noon–5. Groups of 10 or more with advance reservation Tues.–Sun. 10–5.

Soldiers' National Museum. The headquarters for Union general Oliver O. Howard during the Battle of Gettysburg, this building became the Soldiers National Orphanage after the war and now has 60 displays of more than 5,000 Civil War items. | 777 Baltimore St. | 717/334–4890 or 717/334–6296 | fax 717/334–9100 | www.gettysburgaddress.com | $5.95 | June–early Sept., daily 9–9; Mar.–Apr. and mid-Oct.–late Nov., daily 9–5; May and early Sept.–mid-Oct., daily 9–7.

Dining

The predominant Pennsylvania Dutch ancestry in the area is reflected on dinner menus in such dishes as chicken and dumplings or *Snitz un Knepp* (a pie made with dried apples). Restaurants serve fresh locally grown fruits and vegetables, and menus feature items "cooked from scratch."

★ **Blue Parrot Bistro.** Eclectic. Here's a great place to take a group with dissimilar eating tastes. White linen tablecloths cover each table, but the food ranges from pita pizza and creative homemade soups and salads to eggs benedict, fried rice with vegetables, and porterhouse steaks. As the name suggests, parrot decorations fill a main dining room and a smaller side room. Both rooms have bars and there's also a pool table. | 35 Chambersburg St., 17325 | 717/337–3739 | Closed Sun. and Mon. | $10–$25 | AE, D, DC, MC, V.

Dobbin House. Continental. Listed on the National Register of Historic Places, this tavern and inn occupies the oldest building in Gettysburg. It was a stop on the Underground Railroad and a hospital during the Civil War. You can order a meal like those eaten in the 1700s from servers in period clothing and enjoy it while reclining under a bed canopy, part of the restaurant's seating area. Choose from prime rib, roast duck over apples with a citrus-orange sauce, or a pork tenderloin with raspberry sauce. For dessert there's apple pie and pecan pie. Kids' menu. | 89 Steinwehr Ave. | 717/334–2100 | fax 717/334–6905 | No lunch | $16–$34 | Reservations essential | AE, D, MC, V.

Dunlap's Restaurant and Bakery. American. This casual family restaurant is owned by a couple who fell in love with the town and bought the restaurant after visiting their son at Gettysburg College. You can get burgers, sandwiches, and salads, but save room for a piece of freshly baked cake or pie. | 90 Buford Ave., 17325 | 717/334–4816 | $5–$10 | D, MC, V.

★ **Farnsworth House Inn.** Southern. You can eat like a Civil War soldier on leave: wild game pie, peanut soup, pumpkin fritters, and spoon bread. The historic home has more than 100 bullet holes from the war. You are invited to tour the attic full of Civil War memorabilia and see the sharpshooter's post. Kids' menu. | 401 Baltimore St., 17325 | 717/334–8838 | Reservations essential | $8–$15 | AE, D, MC, V.

Gettysbrew Restaurant and Brewery. Contemporary. Housed in a building that was used as a field hospital by the Confederate Army during the Civil War, Gettysbrew has a patio overlooking the surrounding farmland where many Civil War battles took place. This spot is known for its beer cheese soup, buffets with cold salads and hot entrées, and handcrafted root beer and sodas. Kids' menu. | 248 Hunterstown Rd. | 717/337–1001 | No lunch weekdays | $10–$15 | D, MC, V.

Herr Tavern and Publick House. Continental. Built in 1815, this tavern survived a direct hit on its second floor from artillery during the Battle of Gettysburg, and it served as the first Confederate hospital. The dining room has a view of the Gettysburg battlefield. Choose from cream of crab soup, prime rib, and chicken Chesapeake stuffed with crabmeat and Mornay sauce. End your meal with homemade cheesecake, pecan pie, or apple dumplings. Eat on the porch overlooking nearby farmland. Kids' menu. | 900 Chambersburg Rd. | 717/334–4332 | No lunch Sun. | $14–$26 | D, MC, V.

Historic Cashtown Inn. American. The menu at this historic 1797 inn is reminiscent of home-cooked food from the Civil War era, with choices such as steaks, seafood, pecan-crusted chicken, and crabcakes. The restaurant is in an old building with walk-up porch that was once a stagecoach stop, 8 mi west of downtown Gettysburg. | 1325 Old Rte. 30, 17310 | 717/334–9722 or 800/367–1797 | www.cashtowninn.com | Closed Mon. No lunch Sun. | $8–$15 | AE, D, MC, V.

Lincoln Diner. American. Locals flock to the Lincoln Diner for its cheesecake, as well as cakes, pies, and Greek pastries. Menu choices include the anytime-of-day breakfast and a daily special. | 32 Carlisle St., 17325 | 717/334–3900 | $4–$8 | No credit cards.

Lodging

★ **Best Western Gettysburg Hotel.** This 1797 white-brick building in the center of town served as the summer White House during the Eisenhower administration. Restaurant, room service, in-room data ports, some in-room hot tubs, some refrigerators, cable TV, pool, hot tub, bar, laundry service, business services. | 1 Lincoln Sq. | 717/337–2000 | fax 717/337–2075 | www.webscaper.com/getty | 83 rooms, 23 suites | $105–$165 suites | AE, D, DC, MC, V.

Brickhouse Inn Bed and Breakfast. Guest rooms in this 1898 brick Victorian are furnished with antiques and reproductions, yet the Brickhouse welcomes children of all ages. You can relax in one of two formal parlors. Room TVs are available upon request. Some room TVs; no smoking | 452 Baltimore St., 17325 | 717/338–9337 or 800/864–3464 | fax 717/338–9265 | www.brickhouseinn.com | 7 rooms | $90–$140 | AE, D, MC, V.

★ **Farnsworth House Inn.** This inn is an early 19th-century Federal brick house that Confederate sharpshooters occupied during the Battle of Gettysburg. You can take a tour of the house and cellar, rumored to be haunted. Rooms have Victorian furnishings and some have claw-foot bathtubs. An art gallery and bookstore are on the premises. Restaurant, library, shops, business services; no room phones, no room TVs | 401 Baltimore St. | 717/334–8838 | fax 717/334–5862 | www.farnsworthhousedining.com | 11 rooms | $95–$160 | AE, D, MC, V.

Holiday Inn Express. Next to a family fun center with miniature golf, this hotel is 3 mi from the National Military Park and less than a mile from downtown. Complimentary Continental breakfast. Picnic area, in-room data ports, some microwaves, some refrigerators, cable TV, indoor pool, hot tub. | 869 York Rd. (U.S. 30), 17325 | 717/337–1400 | fax 717/337–1400 ext. 301 | www.hiexpress.com | 51 rooms | $89–$119 | AE, D, DC, MC, V.

Quality Inn. Next door to the Gettysburg National Park Visitor's Center, this hotel is 1 mi south of downtown. In-room data ports, in-room hot tubs (some), kitchenettes (some), cable TV, putting green, pool, indoor pool, exercise equipment, hot tub, sauna, bar, laundry facilities. | 380 Steinwehr Ave., 17325 | 717/334–1103 | fax 717/334–1103 | www.qualityinn.com | 109 rooms | $79–$110 | AE, D, DC, MC, V.

Camping

Artillery Ridge Campground. You can pitch a tent or park an RV a mile south of the Gettysburg National Military Park Visitor Center. Horse owners can even bring their horses on vacation with them. Pool, fishing, bicycles, horseback riding. | 45 tent sites, 105 camper or RV sites | 610 Taneytown Rd., 17325 | 717/334–1288 | $13–$21 | D, MC.

Shopping

Gettysburg has numerous shops that sell handmade crafts and furniture, antiques, gifts, Civil War memorabilia, and books. In the tourist district, many shops along Steinwehr Avenue have bullets and relics excavated from the battlefield. A few shops you might want to visit are Mel's Antiques and Collectibles (33 Foth Alley), Arrow Horse International Market and Antiques (51 Chambersburg St.), Codori's Gift Shop (2 York St.), Irish Brigade Gift Shop (504 Baltimore St.), the Horse Soldier (777 Baltimore St.), and Farnsworth Military Impressions (401 Baltimore St.).

Homemade quilts and furniture, handcrafted by the local Amish community, can be found scattered along Route 30 south of town. Stop at one of the many roadside markets north of Gettysburg for peaches, apples, sweet white corn, tomatoes and other fresh produce at bargain prices.

Sports and Outdoor Activities

Biking

Marked bicycle routes offer a great way to discover the battlefield at your own pace.

Gettysburg Bicycle and Fitness. Rental rates are $7 per hr and $25 per day. Maps are also available. | 307 York St. | 717/334–7791.

Hiking and Walking

A number of trails can be found on the Gettysburg battlefield, including the High Water Mark Trail (1 mi; begins at the Cyclorama Center); the Big Round Top Loop Trail (1 mi); and paths winding through the enormous rocks, caves, and crevices that hid Confederate sharpshooters in Devil's Den. For a longer hike, inquire about the 9-mi Billy Yank Trail or the 3½-mi Johnny Reb Trail. For a more contemplative experience, plan an early morning or evening walk through the National Cemetery, near the spot where Abraham Lincoln delivered the Gettysburg Address. Few others will be present at this time of day, leaving you alone with the ghosts of the past.

Horseback Riding

Trail riding across the battlefield is available.

National Riding Stables. National Riding Stables at Artillery Ridge Campground has trails marked for horseback riding.| 610 Taneytown Rd. | 717/334–1288.

Skiing

Liberty Mountain Resort. Also known as Ski Liberty, the 1,410-ft mountain has a 600-ft vertical drop, 16 trails, and eight lifts. The longest run is 5,200 ft. | 78 Country Club Trail, Carroll Valley 17320 | 717/642–8282 | www.skiliberty.com | $32–$49 | Dec.–Mar., weekdays 9 AM–10 PM, weekends 8 AM–10 PM.

Essential Information

When to Go

Summer months and weekends can be quite crowded at this popular destination. Crowds begin thinning out after Labor Day, but weekends are still busy through November, and the action picks up again beginning on Easter Sunday. The best hotel rates are November through March, but if you visit then, be aware that some museums close during the winter months.

In August, the maximum temperature averages about 90°F, with high humidity. January and February are cold, with an average high of 30°. Spring and fall months bring changeable weather, with many warm days but brisk, cool nights.

FESTIVALS AND SEASONAL EVENTS

SPRING

May: **Apple Blossom Festival.** Take an orchard tour, eat apple foods, buy handmade crafts, and watch various performers entertain during the three days of this festival at South Mountain Fairgrounds in Biglerville. | 717/677–7444.

SUMMER

June–July: **Civil War Heritage Days.** Events commemorating the anniversary of the Battle of Gettysburg include lectures by historians and memorabilia collectors' shows. There's also entertainment, a firefighters' festival, and fireworks. | 717/334–6274.

AUTUMN

Oct.: **Apple Harvest Festival.** The emphasis is on apples and products like apple cider, caramel apples, and apple butter. There are free hayrides, scarecrow making, and crafts all at South Mountain Fairgrounds in Biglerville. | 717/677–9413.

Bargains

The Gettysburg area's chief attraction—the battlefield park itself—charges no admission fee. Also, the park service offers free walks and lectures that are not widely advertised, so be sure to ask at the visitor center for topics and schedules.

Tours

Auto-tour maps can be picked up at the visitor center; auto-tour tapes, which can be bought or rented at the numerous tour centers, re-create the historic three-day battle with sound effects as you drive through the battlefield at your own pace.

Gettysburg Railway. Explore the countryside on this 1-hr and 45-min ride a on a diesel train. The theme rides include the Civil War, a ride with Lincoln, dinner trips, fall foliage, a Santa train, an Easter train, and a Halloween ghost train. | 106 N. Washington St. | 717/334–6932 or 888/948–7246 | fax 717/334–4746 | www.gettysburgrail.com | $20 | Thurs.–Sun. 10–3.

Gettysburg Tour Center. This is the departure point for two-hour narrated tours of the battlefield. Tours on the open-air double-decker buses cost $16.95. | 717/334–6296.

★ **Ghosts of Gettysburg Candlelight Walking Tours.** Guides take you on one of three different evening tours through sections of Gettysburg. The tours were planned by ghost historian Mark Nesbitt and take you outside houses and buildings and to cemeteries where the dead lie, though sometimes not so peacefully. Tours are on foot, but guides can be arranged to accompany private tour-bus groups. | 717/337–0445 | www.ghostsofgettysburg.com | $6.

Visitor Information

Gettysburg–Adams County Chamber of Commerce | 18 Carlisle St., Suite 203, 17325 | 717/334–8151 | www.gettysburg-chamber.org.

Gettysburg Convention and Visitors Bureau | 31 Carlisle St. | 717/334–6274 | www.gettysburg.com.

Arriving and Departing

BY AIR

Airports

Harrisburg International Airport (MDT). | 717/948–3900 | www.flyhia.com.

Airport Transportation

Car rentals are available at the airport, including from Avis, Hertz, National Car Rental and Thrifty Car Rental.

Pick up the Pennsylvania Turnpike (I–76) from the airport and head west to Route 15, which leads about 40 mi south to Gettysburg.

BY CAR

Gettysburg's major east–west corridor is Route 30, and from the north or south, Route 15.

Getting Around

BY CAR

A car is the most practical means of touring the Gettysburg area, since it encompasses a large area. However, the best way to explore downtown is on foot. Parking downtown can sometimes be a problem; the Race Horse Alley Parking Plaza off Stratton Street, behind the Gettysburg Hotel, offers covered, lighted parking at a nominal fee.

BY PUBLIC TRANSIT

Trolley

Gettysburg Battlefield Bus Tours. A trolley serves Gettysburg's downtown area. The fare is $1, paid to the trolley driver. | 717/334-6296 | www.gettysburgbattlefieldtours.com.

Revised and Updated by Carrie Miner

GRAND CANYON NATIONAL PARK

When Theodore Roosevelt first visited the Grand Canyon in 1903, he said: "Leave it as it is. You cannot improve on it. What you can do is keep it for your children, your children's children, and for all who come after you, as the one great sight which every American . . . should see." Five years later President Roosevelt proclaimed the canyon, which resides entirely within Arizona's borders, a national monument—a full four years before Arizona earned statehood.

This geologic wonder stretches 227 mi long, gapes up to 18 mi at its widest point, and plummets a full mile down, revealing the earth's history in layered pages of colored stone. The Grand Canyon is a relatively new geologic feature on the topography of the 9,000-ft Colorado Plateau. Somewhere between 5 and 20 million years ago, after a period of uplift, the Colorado River settled on its present course. When the river broke through the hard Kaibab formation, it quickly chiseled deep into the soft sandstone layers, revealing 2 billion years of volcanic and sedimentary strata, which can be seen today from the North and South rims.

Exploring

Grand Canyon National Park

Grand Canyon National Park encompasses not just the great gorge itself but also vast areas of scenic countryside along the North and South rims. The South Rim, 91 mi from Flagstaff on U.S. 180 at an elevation of 7,000 ft, is the most accessible part of the park; however, it also sees 90% of the 5 million visitors who come to see the Grand Canyon each year. The North Rim, 210 mi from Flagstaff looping around the divide near the Utah border, sits 1,300 ft higher than the South Rim on the forested Kaibab Plateau.

Hours: The South Rim is open year-round. Canyon View Information Plaza is open daily 8 to 6 from late May through early September and daily 8 to 5 from early September through late May. The North Rim is open mid-May through mid-October, and the visitor center is open daily 8 to 6.

Fees: It costs $20 per car to enter the park. Individuals arriving by motorcycle, bicycle, or foot pay $10. Backcountry permits are $10 plus $5 per person per night.

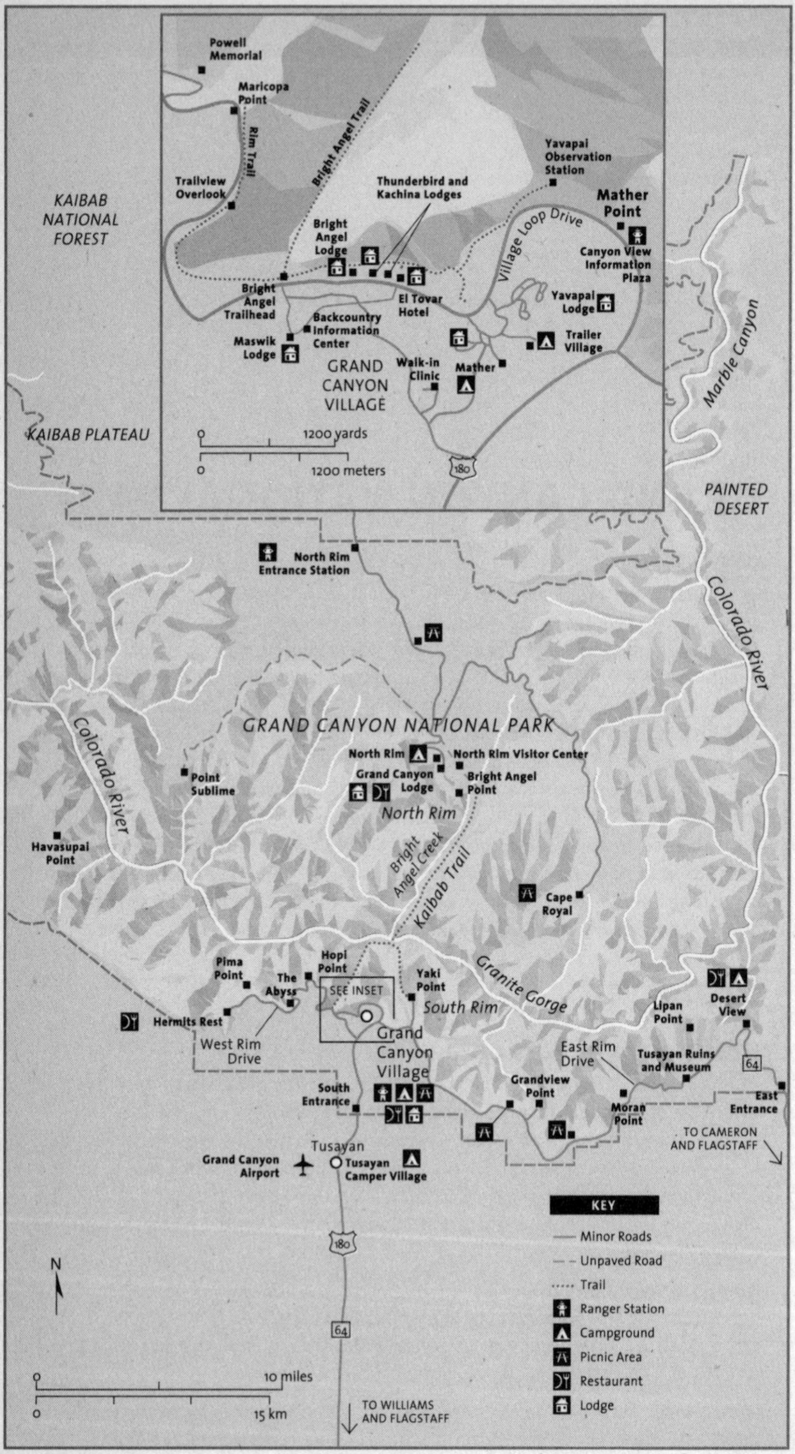
Powell Memorial
Maricopa Point
Rim Trail
Trailview Overlook
Bright Angel Trail
Yavapai Observation Station
Thunderbird and Kachina Lodges
Mather Point
Village Loop Drive
Bright Angel Lodge
Canyon View Information Plaza
Bright Angel Trailhead
El Tovar Hotel
Yavapai Lodge
Backcountry Information Center
Maswik Lodge
Trailer Village
GRAND CANYON VILLAGE
Walk-in Clinic
Mather
1200 yards
1200 meters
180
KAIBAB NATIONAL FOREST
KAIBAB PLATEAU
Marble Canyon
PAINTED DESERT
North Rim Entrance Station
Colorado River
GRAND CANYON NATIONAL PARK
North Rim
North Rim Visitor Center
Grand Canyon Lodge
Bright Angel Point
Point Sublime
North Rim
Havasupai Point
Bright Angel Creek
Kaibab Trail
Cape Royal
Granite Gorge
Pima Point
Hopi Point
The Abyss
SEE INSET
Yaki Point
South Rim
Desert View
Lipan Point
Hermits Rest
West Rim Drive
Grand Canyon Village
East Rim Drive
Tusayan Ruins and Museum
64
South Entrance
Grandview Point
Moran Point
East Entrance
TO CAMERON AND FLAGSTAFF
Tusayan
Grand Canyon Airport
Tusayan Camper Village
KEY
Minor Roads
Unpaved Road
Trail
Ranger Station
Campground
Picnic Area
Restaurant
Lodge
N
10 miles
15 km
TO WILLIAMS AND FLAGSTAFF

SCENIC DRIVES

Cape Royal Road. On the North Rim, a drive to a pair of the area's best-loved canyon vistas awaits you. Starting at Grand Canyon Lodge, drive north on the road for a couple of miles, and bear left at the fork. Continue north 11 mi to Point Imperial—at 8,803 ft, it's the highest vista on either rim, with views of much of the canyon plus thousands of square miles of the surrounding countryside. After stopping here, backtrack the 11 mi to the fork and, instead of going back to the lodge, head southeast on the road to Cape Royal, about a 15-mi drive. The drive back to Grand Canyon Lodge is 23 mi.

★ **Desert View Drive.** This 25-mi road, formerly called East Rim Drive, leads to several of the South Rim's most spectacular turnouts. To get to the drive, turn right about 3 mi north of the South Entrance station. Two miles east is the left turn for the short, well-marked road leading to Yaki Point (except for December–January, when you can drive to Yaki Point, you must take the shuttle). Next, travel about 7 more mi east to Grandview Point, which reveals a group of buttes, including Krishna Shrine and Vishnu Temple, as well as a short stretch of the Colorado River below. Other stops along the route include Moran Point, Tusayan Ruin and Museum, Lipan Point, and Desert View and Watchtower.

SIGHTS TO SEE

Canyon View Information Plaza. The orientation center near Mather Point provides pamphlets and resources to help you plan your sightseeing. Park rangers are on hand to answer questions and aid in planning excursions. A daily schedule for ranger-led hikes and evening lectures is posted on a bulletin board inside. | East side of Grand Canyon Village | 928/638–7888 | Late May–early Sept., daily 8–7; early Sept.–late May, daily 8–5; hrs may vary.

★ **Desert View and Watchtower.** From the top of the 70-ft stone-and-mortar watchtower, which stands at an elevation of 7,430 ft, even the muted hues of the distant Painted Desert to the east and the Vermilion Cliffs rising from a high plateau near the Utah border are visible. | About 23 mi east of Grand Canyon Village on Desert View Dr. | 928/638–2736 | 25¢ to climb the Watchtower | Daily 8–7 or 8–8 in summer, daily 9–5 in winter.

Hermits Rest. This westernmost viewpoint and Hermit Trail, which descends from it, were named for the "hermit" Louis Boucher, a 19th-century French-Canadian prospector who had a number of mining claims and a roughly built cabin down in the canyon. Canyon views from here include Hermit Rapids and the towering cliffs of the Supai and Redwall formations. The stone building at Hermits Rest sells curios and refreshments. | About 8 mi west of Hermit Road Junction on Hermit Rd.

★ **Kolb Studio.** Built in 1904 by the Kolb brothers as a photographic workshop and residence, this building provides a view of Indian Gardens, where, in the days before a pipeline was installed, Emery Kolb descended 3,000 ft each day to get the water he needed to develop his prints. Kolb was doing something right; he operated the studio until he died in 1976 at age 95. The gallery here has changing exhibitions of paintings, photography, and crafts. There's also a bookstore. | About 1/4 mi west of Hermit Road Junction on Hermit Rd. | 928/638–7888.

A few feet away is the **Bright Angel Trailhead,** the starting point for perhaps the best-known trail to the bottom of the canyon.

★ **Lipan Point.** Here at the canyon's widest point, you can get an astonishing visual profile of the gorge's geologic history, with a view of every eroded layer of the canyon. It also marks the spot where you can see more views of the Colorado River than at any other lookout point on the South Rim. | About 25 mi east of Grand Canyon Village on Desert View Dr.

Lookout Studio. Built in 1914 to compete with the Kolbs' photographic studio, the building was designed by architect Mary Jane Colter. The combination lookout point and gift shop has a collection of fossils and geologic samples from around the world. An upstairs loft provides another excellent overlook into the mighty gorge below. | About ¼ mi west of Hermit Road Junction on Hermit Rd.

Mather Point. You'll likely get your first glimpse of the canyon from this viewpoint, one of the most impressive and accessible on the South Rim. Named for the National Park Service's first director, Stephen Mather, this spot yields extraordinary views of the Grand Canyon, including deep into the Inner Gorge and numerous buttes: Wotan's Throne, Brahma Temple, and Zoroaster Temple among others. The Grand Canyon Lodge, on the North Rim, is almost directly north from Mather Point and only 10 mi away—yet you have to drive nearly 210 mi to get from one spot to the other. | Near Canyon View Information Plaza.

Navajo Point. A possible site of the first Spanish view into the canyon in 1540, this peak is also at the highest natural elevation (7,498 ft) on the South Rim (the top of the Desert View Watchtower, at 7,500 ft, beats it by 2 ft as the highest point). | About 21 mi east of Grand Canyon Village on Desert View Dr.

North Rim. The Grand Canyon's more remote rim overlooks vistas as dramatic as those you can see from the South Rim. Higher in elevation and less visited than the southern part of the national park, the North Rim has a distinctly different feel, with taller forests and crisper weather. The North Rim is open mid-May through mid-October.

The walk to **Bright Angel Point** is only 1 mi round-trip, but it's an exciting trek, accented by sheer drops on each side of the trail. In a few spots where the route is extremely narrow, metal railings ensure visitors' safety. | At North Rim visitor center.

GRAND CANYON SCENERY AND WILDLIFE

It's no wonder the Grand Canyon is popular with geologists. Almost 2 billion years' worth of the earth's history is written between the colored layers of sedimentary rock that are stacked from the river bottom to the top of the plateau. The South Rim's Coconino Plateau is fairly flat, at an elevation of about 7,000 ft, and covered with stands of piñon and ponderosa pine, juniper, and Gambel oak. On the Kaibab Plateau on the North Rim, Douglas fir, spruce, quaking aspen, and more ponderosa pine trees prevail. In spring, you're likely to see asters, sunflowers, and lupine in bloom at both rims.

Eighty-eight mammal species inhabit the park, as well as 300 species of birds, 24 kinds of lizards, and 24 kinds of snakes. The rare Kaibab squirrel is found only on the North Rim, and the pink Grand Canyon rattlesnake lives at lower elevations within the canyon. Both are unique to the Grand Canyon. Hawks and ravens are visible year-round, usually coasting on the wind above the canyon. In spring, summer, and fall, mule deer are abundant at the South Rim, even aggressive. Don't be tempted to feed them; it's illegal, and it will disrupt their natural habits and increase your risk of being bitten.

Both sunrise and sunset in the park are spectacular when skies are clear. In any season, some of the best spots to enjoy or photograph them are along Hermit Road west of Grand Canyon Village and Yaki and Lipan points between the Village and Desert View, and Cape Royal on the North Rim.

From **Cape Royal,** the southernmost viewpoint on the North Rim, you'll see a large slice of the Grand Canyon. The 1-mi (round-trip) Cliff Springs trail starts here. Half a mile to the north is Angels Window, a giant erosion-formed natural bridge. | 23 mi southeast of North Rim visitor center.

The highest vista point (elevation 8,803 ft) at either rim, ★**Point Imperial** offers magnificent views of the canyon, the Painted Desert to the east, the Little Colorado River to the southeast, the distant Vermilion Cliffs to the north, and the 10,000-ft Navajo Mountain to the northeast in Utah. | About 11 mi northeast of North Rim visitor center.

North Rim Visitor Center. Situated across from the Grand Canyon Lodge, this center displays a few exhibits on the canyon and provides information of nature walks, children's programs, and ranger-led activities. | Williams | 928/638–7864 | Free | Mid-May–mid-Oct., daily 8–6.

Pima Point. Enjoy a bird's-eye view of Tonto Platform and Tonto Trail, which winds its way through the canyon for more than 70 mi. Also to the west, two dark, cone-shape mountains—Mt. Trumbull and Mt. Logan—are visible on the North Rim on clear days. They rise in stark contrast to the surrounding flat-top mesas and buttes. | About 7 mi west of Hermit Road Junction on Hermit Rd.

Trailview Overlook. Look down on a dramatic view of the Bright Angel and Plateau Point trails as they zigzag down the canyon. In the deep gorge to the north flows Bright Angel Creek, one of the few permanent tributary streams of the Colorado River in the region. Toward the south is an unobstructed view of the distant San Francisco Peaks, as well as of Bill Williams Mountain (on the horizon) and Red Butte (about 15 mi south of the canyon rim). | About 2 mi west of Hermit Road Junction on Hermit Rd.

★ **Tusayan Ruin and Museum.** The museum contains evidence of early human habitation in the Grand Canyon and information about ancestral Puebloan people. *Tusayan* comes from a Hopi phrase meaning "country of isolated buttes," which certainly describes the scenery. The partially intact rock dwellings here were occupied for roughly 20 years around AD 1200 by 30 or so Native American hunters, farmers, and gatherers. They eventually moved on, like so many others, perhaps pressured by drought and depletion of natural resources. A museum and a bookstore display artifacts, models of the dwellings, and exhibits on modern tribes of the region. Free 30-minute guided tours—as many as five a day in summer, fewer in winter—are given daily. | About 20 mi east of Grand Canyon Village on Desert View Dr. | 928/638–2305 | Free | Daily 9–5.

Yaki Point. Stop here for an exceptional view of Wotan's Throne, a majestic flat-top butte named by François Matthes, a U.S. Geological Survey scientist who developed the first topographical map of the Grand Canyon. Due north is Buddha Temple, capped by limestone. Newton Butte, with its flat top of red sandstone, lies to the east. | About 2 mi east of Grand Canyon Village on Desert View Dr.

Attractions Nearby

★ **Glen Canyon National Recreation Area.** This huge preserve covers more than 1,500 square mi in northeastern Arizona and southern Utah, including Lake Powell, which has more than 1,900 mi of shoreline. South of Lake Powell, the landscape gives way to the Echo Cliffs, orange sandstone formations rising up to 1,000 ft above the surrounding desert. At Bitter Springs, Highway 89 ascends the cliffs and provides a spectacular view of the Kaibab Plateau and Vermilion Cliffs. The Carl Hayden Visitor Center at Glen Canyon Dam, 2 mi west of Page, has a three-dimensional map of the area; from May to October you can also take tours of the dam, which creates Lake Powell every hour on the half hour 8–5. | Visitor center: U.S. 89 and Scenic View Dr., Page | 928/608–6404 | www.nps.gov/glca | $5 per vehicle | Visitor center late May–early Sept., daily 8–6; early Sept.–late May, daily 8–5.

★ **Grand Canyon Railway.** First established in 1901, the railway still transports passengers the 65 mi from Williams to the Grand Canyon in railcars that date from the 1920s. There are several classes of service; some tickets include food and beverages. The train depot in the park is conveniently located next to the Bright Angel Lodge, near the attractions and free shuttles of the South Rim. Take time to visit the small railroad museum and vintage railcar at the depot in Williams. Children will also enjoy the free Wild West show held daily at 9 AM at the depot. | Williams Depot, 233 N. Grand Canyon Blvd., Williams | 928/773–1976 or 800/843–8724 | www.thetrain.com | $54.95–$139.95. Depot free | Departs daily at 10 AM, returning to Williams at 3:30.

Lees Ferry. Most Colorado River rafting trips begin at this site, which is at a sharp bend in the river about 5 mi northeast of the town of Marble Canyon. Named for John D. Lee, who constructed the first ferry to cross the Colorado here in 1872, the spot was a ferry crossing until 1928, when Navajo Bridge was built over Marble Canyon. | Off U.S. 89A, Marble Canyon | Free | Daily.

★ **Pipe Spring National Monument.** In 1870, Mormon leader Brigham Young established the church's southern cattle operation in Pipe Springs and built the fortlike structure known as Winsor Castle. This 40-acre monument, 14 mi southwest of Fredonia, is now a memorial to western pioneer life. In summer there are living-history demonstrations of frontier life in the 1870s, including such activities as ranching, weaving, and cheese making. The fort was never used for its original purpose of fending off hostile Indian attacks because a treaty was signed before it was finished. However, in 1871 it did become the first telegraph station in the Arizona territory. | 401 N. Pipe Springs Rd., Fredonia | 928/643–7105 | $3 | Daily 8–5.

Dining

In Grand Canyon

Bright Angel Restaurant. Continental. Casual with rustic charm, this restaurant serves up the best breakfast on the South Rim and is a favorite for its hearty lunch and dinner menus as well. | Bright Angel Lodge, Grand Canyon Village | 928/638–2631 | Reservations not accepted | $4–$12 | AE, D, DC, MC, V.

★ **El Tovar Dining Room.** Continental. El Tovar Hotel has the best restaurant for miles, but don't expect the quality to be commensurate with the prices. Modeled after a 19th-century European hunting lodge, the classic construction of hand-hewn logs and beamed ceilings is worth seeing, but the food is hit or miss. The Continental menu, served southwestern style, changes seasonally. Breakfast also available. | El Tovar Hotel, Grand Canyon Village | 928/638–2631 ext. 6432 | Reservations essential | $17–$25 | AE, D, DC, MC, V.

Grand Canyon Lodge Dining Room. American. The historic lodge houses a huge, high-ceiling dining room with spectacular views and very good food; you might find pork medallions, red snapper, or spinach linguine with red clam sauce on the dinner menu. However, because it is the only fine dining room on the North Rim, dinner reservations should be made one to two months in advance during the busy summer season. Breakfast also available. | Grand Canyon Lodge, Bright Angel Point | 928/638–2611 | Reservations essential | Closed mid-Oct.–mid-May | $12–$28 | AE, D, DC, MC, V.

Grand Canyon Lodge Snack Bar. American/Casual. Dining choices are very limited on the North Rim, so this is your best bet for a meal on a budget. The selections—hot dogs, burgers, sandwiches, yogurt—are standard but sufficient. | Grand Canyon Lodge, Bright Angel Point | 928/638–2611 | Reservations not accepted | Closed mid-Oct.–mid-May | $3–$7 | AE, D, DC, MC, V.

Near the Park

Crazy Jug Restaurant. American/Casual. This homey diner serves standard American dishes, including breakfast. | 467 S. Main St., Fredonia | 928/643–7712 | Closed mid-Nov.–mid-Apr. | $4–$9 | AE, MC, V.

Cruisers Café 66. American/Casual. Route 66 icons fill this renovated gas station, formerly Tiffany's Lube Lounge. The menu and the spirit of the place remain lively—be sure to check out the old gasoline logos and the old gas pumps. | 233 W. Rte. 66, Williams | 928/635–2445 | $7–$10 | AE, DC, MC, V.

Lees Ferry Lodge Restaurant. American. Paintings and photographs of fish and fishermen adorn the walls of this restaurant in rustic Lees Ferry Lodge. The filet mignon and the barbecue pork ribs are winners, as is the house specialty, trout. Breakfast also available. | U.S. 89A, mile marker 54½, Marble Canyon | 928/355–2231 | $8–$20 | MC, V.

Pancho McGillicuddy's. Mexican. Originally the Cabinet Saloon, this restaurant is on the National Register of Historic Places. Gone are the spittoons and pipes—this dining room now serves up food Mexican style. | 141 Railroad Ave., Williams | 928/635–4150 | $8–$17 | MC, V.

Lodging

In Grand Canyon

Bright Angel Lodge. This rustic hostelry built by the Fred Harvey Company in 1935 sits just a few yards back from the canyon rim. It has rooms in the main lodge plus in quaint cabins to the side. Restaurant, hair salon; no TV in some rooms | Grand Canyon Village | 303/297–2757 reservations; 928/638–2631 switchboard | fax 303/297–3175 | 30 rooms, 42 cabins | $56–$109 | AE, D, DC, MC, V.

Phantom Ranch. Mule riders and hikers frequent this no-frills lodging at the bottom of the Grand Canyon. There's a dormitory ($21 per person) accessible only to hikers; cabins are exclusively for mule riders. Restaurant; no room phones, no room TVs | On the canyon floor | 303/297–2757 reservations; 928/638–2631 switchboard | fax 303/297–3175 | 4 dormitories, 9 cabins | $21–$69 | AE, D, MC, V.

Near the Park

Cliff Dwellers Lodge. Built in 1949, this dining and lodging complex sits at the foot of the Vermilion Cliffs. Rooms in the modern motel building are attractive and clean. Restaurant, cable TV; no room phones | U.S. 89A, 9 mi west of Navajo Bridge, Marble Canyon | 928/355–2228 or 800/433–2543 | fax 928/355–2229 | www.cliffdwellerslodge.com | 22 rooms | $64–$74 | D, DC, MC, V.

Fray Marcos Hotel. Western art by a local artist decorates the grand lobby of this hotel, which has a huge flagstone fireplace. Southwestern-style rooms have large bathrooms. Restaurant, cable TV, pool, gym, hot tub, bar, business services | 235 N. Grand Canyon Blvd., Williams | 928/635–4010 or 800/843–8724 | fax 928/635–2180 | 196 rooms | $79–$119 | AE, D, MC, V.

The Grand Hotel. Opened in 1998, this stone and timber structure in the heart of the Tusayan strip has clean, generic motel rooms, each with one king or two twin beds. Restaurant, cable TV, indoor pool, hot tub | Rte. 64, Tusayan 86023 | 928/638–3333 | fax 928/638–3131 | 120 rooms | $99–$159 | AE, MC, V.

Jacob Lake Inn. Basic cabins and standard motel units—without phones or TVs—are available at this 5-acre complex in Kaibab National Forest. The bustling lodge center, complete with grocery store, is a popular stop for those heading to the North Rim.

Restaurant, coffee shop, shop; no room phones, no room TVs. | U.S. 89A, Jacob Lake | 928/643–7232 | www.jacoblake.com | 14 rooms, 22 cabins | $69–$122 | AE, D, DC, MC, V.

Mountainside Inn. This motel on 27 acres is one of the better-maintained in town. Hiking trails crisscross the property. Restaurant, picnic area, room service, some microwaves, some refrigerators, cable TV, pool, hot tub, hiking, bar, some pets allowed (fee) | 642 E. Bill Williams Ave., Williams | 928/635–4431 | fax 928/635–2292 | www.mtnsideinn.com | 96 rooms | $86–$125 | AE, D, DC, MC, V.

Camping

In Grand Canyon

★ **Desert View Campground.** Situated on the East Rim Drive near the Watchtower, this popular campground is known for its spectacular views of the canyon. It fills up fast, though, and there is a seven-day limit. The campground is primitive, but there are nearby facilities. Flush toilets, drinking water, fire grates, ranger station, service station | 50 sites | 26 mi east of visitor center | No phone. | $10 | Reservations not accepted | May–Oct.

Mather Campground. Located 1 mi south of the visitor center, this central campground offers the most modern camping conveniences in the park. It is open year-round with a seven-day limit and is just a short walk to Mather Point on the South Rim. Flush toilets, drinking water, laundry facilities, showers, fire grates, ranger station | 320 sites | Grand Canyon Village 86023 | 800/365–2267 reservations | $10–$15 | Reservations essential.

North Rim Campground. Canyon views and choice rim sites make this one of the most beautiful campgrounds on either rim. Rim sites are $5 more than the standard sites but both have good views. Flush toilets, drinking water, fire grates, showers, ranger station | 83 sites | 3 mi north of North Rim entrance | 800/365–2267 | $15–$20 | Reservations required | May–Oct.

Near the Park

DeMotte Campground. This campground is operated by the U.S. Forest Service. It's relatively primitive, but after a night under the stars at an elevation of 8,760 ft, you will wonder why you don't camp out more often. Nearby hiking trails through Kaibab National Forest add to the outdoor experience. Pit toilets, drinking water, fire grates | 23 sites | Rte. 67, 7 mi north of North Rim entrance, Fredonia | 928/643–7298 | $10 | Reservations not accepted | Mid-May–mid-Oct.

Kaibab Lodge Camper Village. In a wooded area popular with cross-country skiers, this is the closest campground with full hook-ups to the North Rim. Flush toilets, full hook-ups, drinking water, showers, fire grates, picnic tables, public telephone | 80 full hook-ups, 50 tent sites | Rte. 67, ¼ mi south of U.S. 89A | 928/643–7804, 928/526–0924 or 800/525–0924 | $12–$22 | Mid-May–mid-Oct.

Shopping

There are plenty of places within the park to purchase supplies and souvenirs, especially on the South Rim. Just keep in mind that prices increase the closer you are to the park and that you can find Grand Canyon souvenirs as far south as Flagstaff. On the flip side, money spent at park facilities is turned around as capital for continuing improvements within the park proper.

Hopi House. This beautiful shop, housed in an adobe structure, sells high-quality jewelry, pottery, rugs, and kachinas. | Adjacent to El Tovar Hotel in Grand Canyon Village | 928/638–2631.

Verkamp's. This shop, adjacent to El Tovar Hotel, is the best place on the South Rim to buy inexpensive souvenirs like T-shirts, postcard books, and videos of the canyon. The store also has Native American jewelry. | Grand Canyon Village | 928/638–2242.

Sports and Outdoor Activities

Hiking and Backpacking

Bright Angel and South Kaibab are the two most popular trails on the South Rim, but rangers can help you design a trip that best suits your abilities. Under no circumstances attempt a day hike from the rim to the river and back. Remember that when it's 80° on the South Rim, it's 110° on the canyon floor.

Backcountry Office. Overnight hikes in the Grand Canyon require a permit that can be obtained only in person or by written or faxed request to the Backcountry Office. The permit costs $10 plus $5 per person per night, and the office's free *Backcountry Trip Planner* can answer your hiking questions. Find hiking maps and more information at their Web site. | Bright Angel Lodge, Grand Canyon, 86023 | 928/638–7875 | fax 928/638–2125 | www.nps.gov/grca.

★ **Bright Angel Trail.** This well-maintained trail is one of the most popular and scenic hiking paths from the South Rim to the bottom of the canyon (9 mi). Originally a bighorn sheep path and later used by the Havasupai, it was widened late in the 19th century for prospectors and has since become an avenue for mule and foot traffic. Rest houses are equipped with water at the 1½- and 3-mi points from May through September and at Indian Gardens year-round. Plateau Point, about 1½ mi from Indian Gardens, is as far as you should go on a day hike. Bright Angel Trail is the least intimidating footpath into the canyon, but because the climb out from the bottom is an ascent of 5,510 ft, the trip should be attempted only by those in good physical condition and should be avoided in midsummer due to extreme heat. The top of the trail, a tight set of switchbacks, can be icy in winter. Note that you will be sharing the trail with mule trains, which have the right-of-way and sometimes leave unpleasant surprises in your path.

Rim Trail. The most popular walking path at the South Rim is 12-mi (one-way) Rim Trail, which runs along the edge of the canyon from the first overlook on Desert View Drive to Hermits Rest. This walk, which is paved to Maricopa Point, allows visits to several of the South Rim's historic landmarks.

Horseback Riding and Mule Rides

Mule rides provide an intimate glimpse into the canyon for those who have the time, but not the stamina, to see the canyon on foot. Children must be eight years old and able to mount and dismount on their own. All riders must be in good health, weigh less than 200 pounds, and be at least 4′7″ tall. Reservations are essential for all of the rides listed.

Apache Stables. Both horseback riding and mule rides are available here. One-hour and two-hour guided trail rides leave from stables at Moqui Lodge near Tusayan into Kaibab National Forest daily. A four-hour ride travels through the forest and provides great views of the East Rim. The stables open in March, and rides are offered, weather permitting, through the end of November. | U.S. 180 | 928/638–2891 | $30.50–$95.50 | www.apachestables.com.

★ **Grand Canyon National Park Lodges Mule Rides.** Guided mule rides include a day trip to Plateau Point or the overnight trip to Phantom Ranch. | Bright Angel Lodge, Grand Canyon | 928/638–3283 | $128–$345 | May–Sept., daily.

Rafting

White-water trips down the Colorado River and through the Grand Canyon are said by most rafting aficionados to be the adventure of a lifetime. Make reservations well in advance and be aware that white-water excursions aren't accessible to children under eight. Trips range 3–14 days in length. Reservations are essential for all of the trips listed below.

★ **Canyoneers.** With a reputation for high quality and a roster of 4- to 15-day trips, this outfitter is popular with those who want to include some hiking as well. The five-day "Best of the Grand" includes a hike down to Phantom Ranch. | Flagstaff | 928/526–0924 or 800/525–0924 | www.canyoneers.com | $695–$2,895 | Apr.–Sept.

Diamond River Adventures. Owned and operated by a mother-and-daughters team, Diamond River offers both oar-powered and motorized river trips from 4 to 14 days. | Page | 928/645–8866 or 800/343–3121 | www.diamondriver.com | $600–$2,200 | May–Sept.

Essential Information

When to Go

High season is from mid-May to mid-October. If you visit during early spring or late fall the crowds won't be as intense; however, the weather in spring and fall is unpredictable at best. If you decide to visit during the crowded summer months, you might need to make reservations up to six months in advance. Another option is a winter visit to the South Rim (the North Rim is closed in winter). Snow on the ground only enhances the site's sublime beauty, which might make up for the increased chances of encountering snow, icy roads, and a below-zero wind-chill factor. It's always a good idea to call Grand Canyon National Park (928/638–7888) to check on the road conditions.

FESTIVALS AND SEASONAL EVENTS

WINTER

Feb.: **Winterfest.** More than 100 winter events—including sled-dog races, ski competitions, sleigh rides, broom ball, ice skating, and snow sculpture—celebrate the season of snow and ice in Flagstaff. | 928/774–4505.

SPRING

May: **Rendezvous Days.** The Buckskinner Mountain Men, a group of frontier explorer and trapper reenactors, open a trading post, demonstrate frontier activities, and entertain with a black powder shoot during Memorial Day weekend in Williams. | 928/635–4061 or 800/863–0546.

May–Sept.: **Celebration of Native American Art.** Exhibits of work by Zuni, Hopi, and Navajo artists are displayed all summer long at the Museum of Northern Arizona and at the Coconino Center for the Arts, both in Flagstaff. | 928/774–5211 or 928/779–6921.

SUMMER

June: **Flagstaff Heritage Days.** Get your kicks on Route 66 with 12 days of events commemorating "America's Mother Road," which travels through downtown Flagstaff. | 928/779–7611 or 800/217–2367.

Bargains

Purchasing the National Park Pass, which will admit you to any designated National Park Service–administered site for 12 months from the date of purchase, for $50 can be a money saver when you consider that just the standard admission to Grand Canyon National Park is $20 for seven days.

Many of the Grand Canyon National Park Ranger programs and Junior Ranger programs are free of charge (☞ Tours).

Nearby Towns

Tusayan, the gateway to the park's South Entrance, was developed to accommodate Grand Canyon visitors and is ideal if you want to get up and be at the South Rim by early morning. Cheaper, bigger, and with more cultural sights to see, **Flagstaff** and **Williams** are popular second choices, though they're both more than an hour away from the Grand Canyon by car (Williams is closer by 20 mi). Flagstaff, just 15 mi southwest of the beautiful San Francisco Peaks, has two observatories, a good symphony, and Northern Arizona University. Williams, named for Bill Williams, a trapper in the 1820s and '30s, was founded when the railroad passed through it in 1882.

Marble Canyon marks the geographical beginning of the Grand Canyon at its northeastern tip and is a good stopping point if you are driving U.S. 89 to the North Rim. Also nearby is Lees Ferry, where most Colorado River rafting trips through the canyon begin. **Fredonia,** a small community of about 1,200, approximately an hour's drive north of the Grand Canyon, is often referred to as the gateway to the North Rim; it's also relatively close to Zion and Bryce Canyon national parks.

Tours

Junior Ranger Program. Park rangers teach children ages 4–14 how to use field guides, binoculars, magnifying glasses, and other exploration tools on this one-hour ranger-led program. | Canyon View Information Plaza | 928/638–7888 | Free | Tues., Thurs., Sat., and Sun. at 9 AM.

★ **Papillon Helicopters.** The world's largest helicopter sightseeing company, Papillon offers three different tours leaving from the South Rim's Grand Canyon Airport: the 30-minute North Canyon tour, the 50-minute Imperial tour, and the day-long Havasupai excursion. Excursions from the Grand Canyon West Airport combine a helicopter cruise with a pontoon boat ride on the Colorado River. Special charters and flights from Las Vegas are also available. | 928/638–2419 or 800/528–2418 | fax 928/638–3235 | www.papillon.com | $109–$436.

Ranger Programs. The National Park Service sponsors a variety of orientation activities, such as daily guided hikes and talks, at both the North and South rims. The focus may be on any aspect of the canyon—from geology, flora, and fauna to history and early inhabitants. For schedules, go to the South Rim's Canyon View Information Plaza or the Grand Canyon Lodge at the North Rim Visitor Center. | 928/638–7888 or 928/638–7864 | www.nps.gov/grca | Free | Call for hrs.

Visitor Information

Grand Canyon National Park | Box 129, Grand Canyon 86023 | 928/638–7888 | fax 928/638–7797 | www.nps.gov/grca.

Flagstaff Visitor Center | 1 E. Rte. 66, Flagstaff 86001-5588 | 928/774–9541 or 800/842–7293 | www.flagstaff.az.us. **Fredonia Town Office** | 25 N. Main St., Fredonia 86022 | 928/643–7241. **Grand Canyon Chamber of Commerce** | Box 3007, Grand Canyon 86023 | 928/527–0359 | www.grandcanyonchamber.com. **Kaibab National Forest** | 800 S. 6th St., Williams 86046 | 928/635–8200. **Page/Lake Powell Chamber of Commerce (Marble**

Canyon) | 644 N. Navajo, Dam Plaza, Box 727, Page 86040 | 928/645–2741 or 888/261–7243 | www.page-lakepowell.com. **Williams Visitors Center and Chamber of Commerce** | 200 W. Railroad Ave., Williams 86046 | 928/635–4061 or 800/863–0546 | www.williamschamber.com.

Arriving and Departing

BY AIR

Airports

Phoenix Sky Harbor International Airport (PHX). Phoenix is 247 mi south of the Grand Canyon's South Rim. | 602/273–3300 | www.phxskyharbor.com.

McCarran International Airport (LAS). Las Vegas, Nevada, is 276 mi from the popular South Rim. | 702/261–5211 | www.mccarran.com.

Grand Canyon National Park Airport (GCN). This airport is just 6 mi south of the Grand Canyon's South Rim, but no major airlines land here. | 928/638–2446.

Airport Transportation

Phoenix Sky Harbor International Airport is served by Advantage, Alamo, Avis, Budget, Courtesy, Dollar, Enterprise, Hertz, National, and Thrifty. At McCarran International Airport, you can rent a car from Alamo, Avis, Budget, Dollar, Hertz, National, Payless, Sav-mor, and Thrifty.

BY BUS

Greyhound Lines serves both Flagstaff and Williams.

Flagstaff Bus Station. | 399 S. Malpais La. | 928/774–4573.

Williams Bus Station. | 1050 N. Grand Canyon Blvd. | 928/635–0870.

BY CAR

Approaching the South Rim from the south on I–40, take Route 64 north from Williams, which merges with U.S. 180 at Valle. This highway dead-ends at the South Entrance Road at Grand Canyon National Park. To reach the North Rim from I–40, take U.S. 89 out of Flagstaff for 105 mi and then turn left on U.S. 89 ALT, which curves west toward Jacob Lake. Take the juncture of Route 67 south 45 mi where it dead-ends at the North Rim entrance. If you are coming from Nevada on I–15, take Route 9 east to Route 59, which turns into Route 389 at the Utah-Arizona border. At Jacob Lake, take the junction heading north on Route 67, which leads directly to the North Rim at Grand Canyon National Park.

Getting Around

BY CAR

If you decide to use your own vehicle on the South Rim, be aware that, while parking is free once you pay the $20 park entrance fee, it can be difficult to find a spot, especially during peak hours of the busiest summer weeks. Pick up a free copy of *The Guide* at the Canyon View Information Center for a listing of the parking lots on the South Rim. The small lot near the intersection of Center and Village Loop Road often has open spots when the other lots are full. Other good options include the large lot in front of the general store near Yavapai Lodge or the Maswik Transportation Center lot, which is served by the shuttle bus that makes its rounds to all of the parking areas on the South Rim. Parking is not allowed along the roadside, with the exception of marked areas. To download a map of shuttle stops and parking areas, check out the Parking section on the web at www.nps.gov/grca/grandcanyon or call 928/638–7888 or 888/411–7623 for road conditions.

BY PUBLIC TRANSIT

In summer, South Rim roads are congested, and it's often easier, and sometimes required, to park your car and take the free shuttle, which operates year-round (weather permitting) on three routes: Hermit Road (formerly West Rim Drive), the Village Route, and Kaibab Trail Route. From March through November, only the shuttle is allowed on the 8-mi Hermit Road. The ride is free, and bus stops are clearly marked throughout the park. Shuttle service is not available on the North Rim.

Wyoming

Revised and Updated by Candy Moulton

GRAND TETON NATIONAL PARK

Your jaw will probably drop the first time you see the Teton Range jutting up from the Jackson Hole valley floor. With no foothills to get in the way, you will have a close-up view of magnificent, jagged peaks capped with snow—even before you step out of your car. This massif is long on natural beauty. Guarding the Jackson Hole Highway (U.S. 89) like brawny, behemoth sentinels, these mountains have served as a backdrop to mountain men, cattle barons, conservationists, Hollywood cowboys, and political summit meetings. The Indians call them Teewinot—"many pinnacles." Nineteenth-century French trappers called them Les Trois Tetons—"the three breasts." The most prominent Tetons rise north of Moose Junction: 11,901-ft Nez Perce, 12,804-ft Middle Teton, 13,770-ft Grand Teton, 12,928-ft Mt. Owen, and 12,325-ft Teewinot Mountain, south to north. Before your eyes, mountain glaciers creep imperceptibly down 12,605-ft Mt. Moran. Large and small lakes are strung along the range's base, multicolored wildflowers cover the valley floor, and Wyoming's great abundance of wildlife is almost always present.

Exploring

Grand Teton National Park

Lacking the geysers, roadside wildlife, and summer traffic jams of its northern neighbor, Yellowstone National Park, Grand Teton draws a hardier sort of wilderness enthusiast: this is prime hiking, climbing, and rafting country. Jackson Lake is good for water sports like boating and fishing.

Hours: The park is open 24 hours a day, seven days a week, year-round.

Fees: Park entrance fees, payable at the Moose, Granite Canyon, and Moran entrances, are $20 per car, truck, or RV; $15 per motorcycle or snowmobile; and $10 per person entering on foot or bicycle. Your pass is good for seven days in both Grand Teton and Yellowstone parks. Annual park passes are $40.

SCENIC DRIVES

Antelope Flats Road. Off Jackson Hole Highway 1 mi north of Moose Junction, this road wanders eastward over rolling plains and sagebrush flats that are home to pronghorn,

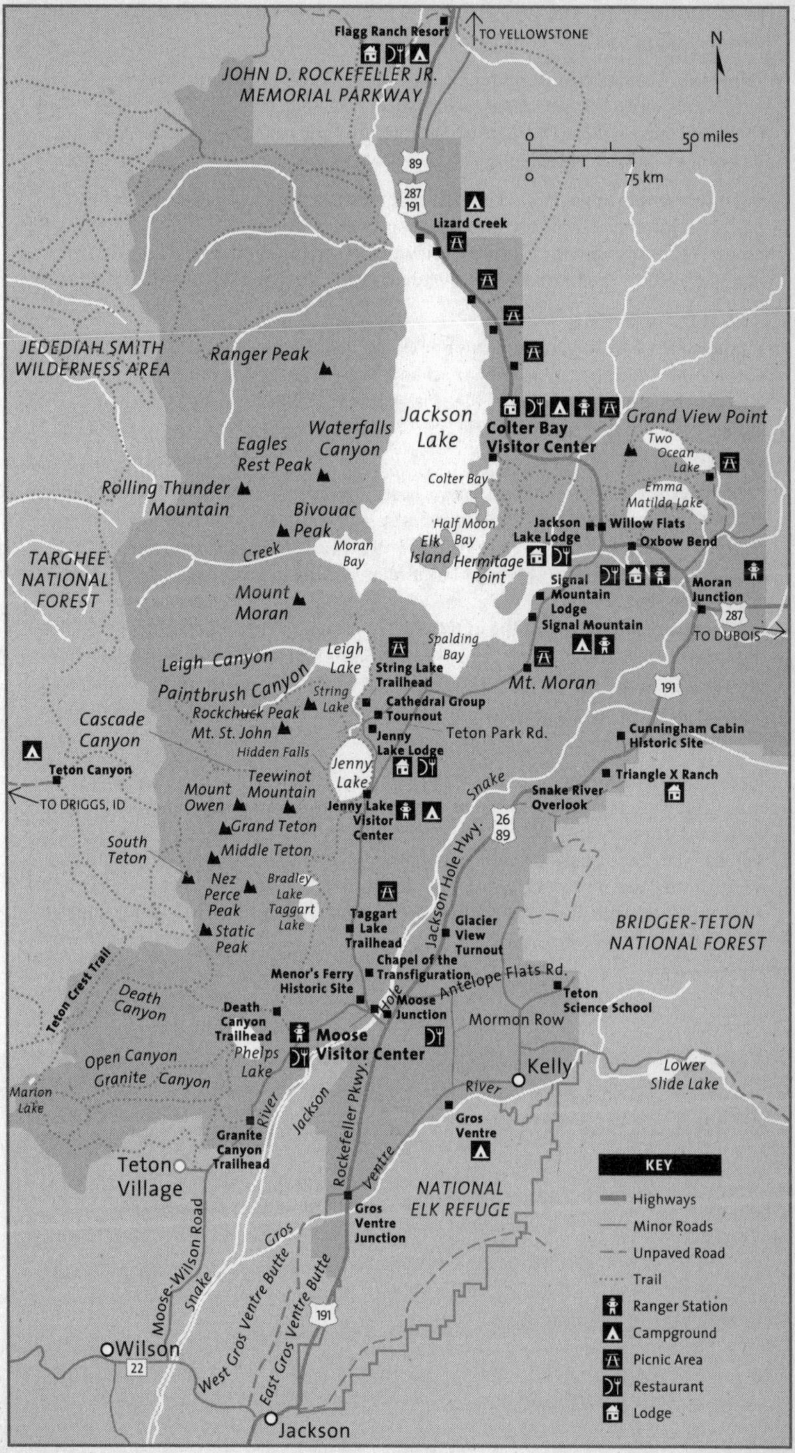

Flagg Ranch Resort
TO YELLOWSTONE
N
JOHN D. ROCKEFELLER JR. MEMORIAL PARKWAY
0 50 miles
0 75 km
89
287 191
Lizard Creek
JEDEDIAH SMITH WILDERNESS AREA
Ranger Peak
Jackson Lake
Waterfalls Canyon
Eagles Rest Peak
Colter Bay Visitor Center
Grand View Point
Two Ocean Lake
Colter Bay
Emma Matilda Lake
Rolling Thunder Mountain
Bivouac Peak
Half Moon Bay
Jackson Lake Lodge
Willow Flats
Oxbow Bend
Creek
Moran Bay
Elk Island
Hermitage Point
TARGHEE NATIONAL FOREST
Signal Mountain Lodge
Moran Junction
Mount Moran
Signal Mountain
287
TO DUBOIS
Spalding Bay
Leigh Lake
Leigh Canyon
String Lake Trailhead
Mt. Moran
Paintbrush Canyon
String Lake
Cathedral Group Tournout
191
Rockchuck Peak
Cascade Canyon
Mt. St. John
Jenny Lake Lodge
Teton Park Rd.
Cunningham Cabin Historic Site
Hidden Falls
Teton Canyon
Jenny Lake
Triangle X Ranch
Teewinot Mountain
Snake
Snake River Overlook
TO DRIGGS, ID
Mount Owen
Jenny Lake Visitor Center
Grand Teton
26 89
South Teton
Middle Teton
Jackson Hole Hwy.
Nez Perce Peak
Bradley Lake
Taggart Lake
Static Peak
Taggart Lake Trailhead
Glacier View Turnout
BRIDGER-TETON NATIONAL FOREST
Teton Crest Trail
Chapel of the Transfiguration
Menor's Ferry Historic Site
Antelope Flats Rd.
Death Canyon
Hole
Moose Junction
Teton Science School
Death Canyon Trailhead
Moose Visitor Center
Mormon Row
Phelps Lake
Open Canyon
Granite Canyon
Kelly
Lower Slide Lake
Marion Lake
River
Jackson
Rockefeller Pkwy.
Gros Ventre
Granite Canyon Trailhead
Teton Village
Ventre
NATIONAL ELK REFUGE
Gros Ventre Junction
KEY
Highways
Minor Roads
Unpaved Road
Trail
Ranger Station
Campground
Picnic Area
Restaurant
Lodge
Gros
Moose-Wilson Road
Snake
West Gros Ventre Butte
East Gros Ventre Butte
191
Wilson
22
Jackson

bison, and moose. The road intersects Mormon Row, where you can see abandoned homesteaders' barns and houses from the turn of the 20th century.

★ **Jenny Lake Scenic Drive.** Providing the park's best roadside close-ups of the Tetons, this road winds south through groves of lodgepole pine and open meadows. Roughly 2 mi down the one-way road, the Cathedral Group Turnout faces the 13,770-ft Grand Teton (the range's highest peak), flanked by 12,928-ft Mt. Owen and 12,325-ft Mt. Teewinot.

Signal Mountain Road. This exciting drive climbs 700 ft along a 5-mi stretch of switchbacks. As you travel through forest you can catch glimpses of Jackson Lake and Mt. Moran. The trip ends with a sweeping view of Jackson Hole and the entire 40-mi Teton Range. Sunset is the most scenic time to make the climb up Signal Mountain.

SIGHTS TO SEE

★ **Chapel of the Transfiguration.** This tiny chapel built in 1925 is still a functioning Episcopal church. Couples come here to exchange vows with the Tetons as a backdrop, and tourists come to take photos of the small church with its awesome view. | ½ mi off Teton Park Rd., 2 mi north of Moose Junction | Late May–late Sept., Sun. services at 8 and 10 AM.

Colter Bay Visitor Center. The auditorium hosts several free daily programs about Indian culture and natural history. Daily at 11 and 3, a 30-minute "Teton Highlights" ranger lecture provides tips on park activities. | 2 mi off U.S. 89/191/287, 5 mi north of Jackson Lake Junction | 307/739–3594 | Mid-May–mid-June and Sept., daily 8–5; mid-June–early Sept., 8–8.

Spend an hour or two at the **Indian Arts Museum,** which has examples of Plains Indian weapons and clothing. June through September, you can see crafts demonstrations by tribal members, take ranger-led tours of the museum, and listen to a daily 45-minute ranger program on Native American culture (early June to early September).

Cunningham Cabin Historic Site. At the end of a gravel spur road, an easy ¾-mi trail runs through sagebrush around Pierce Cunningham's 1890 log cabin homestead. Cunningham, an early Jackson Hole homesteader and civic leader, built his cabin in Appalachian dogtrot style, joining two halves with a roofed veranda. Watch for badgers, coyotes, and Uinta ground squirrels in the area. The site is open year-round, and a pamphlet is available at the trailhead. | ½ mi off Jackson Hole Hwy., 6 mi south of Moran Junction | Year-round.

GRAND TETON WILDLIFE

Your best chance to see wildlife is in the early morning or late evening (think dawn and dusk), along forest edges. Elk are the region's most common large mammals. The best place to view elk in summer is on Teton Park Road; find elk in winter south of the park on the National Elk Refuge, where some 7,500 of the animals spend the colder months. Oxbow Bend and Willow Flats are good places to look for moose, beaver, and otter any time of year. Pronghorn and bison appear in summer along Jackson Hole Highway and Antelope Flats Road, and black bear inhabit the forests along lake shores and the backcountry, although sightings are not common. Birds include bald eagles and ospreys, which can be spotted along the Snake River throughout the year. In addition, there are killdeer in marshy areas and trumpeter swans, mallards, and Canada geese on the river and nearby ponds.

Jackson Lake. The biggest of Grand Teton's glacier-scooped lakes, this body of water in the northern reaches of the park was enlarged by construction of the Jackson Lake Dam in 1906. You can fish, sail, and windsurf on the lake, or hike trails near the shoreline. Three marinas (Colter Bay, Leeks, and Signal Mountain) provide access for boaters, and several picnic areas, campgrounds, and lodges overlook the lake. | U.S. 89/191/287 from Lizard Creek to Jackson Lake Junction, and Teton Park Rd. from Jackson Lake Junction to Signal Mountain Lodge.

Jenny Lake. Named for the Native American wife of mountain man Beaver Dick Leigh, this alpine lake south of Jackson Lake draws boaters to its pristine waters and hikers to its tree-shaded trails. | Jenny Lake Rd., 2 mi off Teton Park Rd. 12 mi north of Moose Junction.

★ **Menor's Ferry Historic Area.** The ferry on display is not the original, but it's an accurate re-creation of the craft built by Bill Menor in the 1890s, and it demonstrates how people crossed the Snake River before bridges were built. The original buildings used by Menor house historical displays, including a photo collection; one building has been turned into a small general store. You can pick up a pamphlet for a self-guided tour. | ½ mi off Teton Park Rd., 2 mi north of Moose Junction | Year-round.

Moose Visitor Center. The center has exhibits of rare and endangered species and the geology and natural history of the Greater Yellowstone area. In the auditorium you can see a video called *The Nature of Grand Teton* and other videos on topics that range from geology to wolves. | Teton Park Rd., ½ mi north of Moose Junction | 307/739–3399 | Sept.–June, daily 8–5; July–Sept., daily 8–7.

★ **Oxbow Bend.** This spot overlooks a quiet backwater left by the Snake River when it cut a new southern channel. White pelicans stop here on their spring migration (many stay on through summer), trumpeter swans visit frequently, and great blue herons nest amid the cottonwoods along the river. Use binoculars to search for bald eagles, ospreys, moose, beaver, and otter. | U.S. 26/89/191/287, 2 mi east of Jackson Lake Junction.

Attractions Nearby

For additional attractions nearby, *see* Yellowstone National Park chapter.

National Bighorn Sheep Interpretive Center. The local variety is known as the Rocky Mountain bighorn, but you can learn about all kinds of bighorn sheep here. Wildlife-viewing tours are conducted in winter. | 907 Ramshorn Ave., Dubois | 307/455–3429 or 888/209–2795 | $2; $5 per family | Late May–early Sept., daily 9–8; early Sept.–late May, daily, call for hrs; wildlife viewing tours mid-Nov.–Mar.

National Elk Refuge. More than 7,000 elk spend winter in the National Elk Refuge, which was established in 1912 to rescue starving herds. The animals migrate to the refuge grounds in late fall and remain until early spring. Trumpeter swans live here, too, as do bald eagles, coyotes, and wolves. In winter you can take a wagon or sleigh ride through the herd. In summer, migration means that there are fewer big-game animals here, but you likely will see waterfowl and you can also fish on the refuge. | 2820 Rungius Rd., Jackson | 307/733–5771 | www.fws.gov | Sleigh rides $8 | Year-round; sleigh rides mid-Dec.–Apr.

Dining

In Grand Teton

Chuckwagon Steak and Pasta House. Steak. Across from Colter Bay Marina in a sprawling, pine-shaded building, the extremely popular restaurant draws families staying at Colter Bay as well as sightseers from Jackson Lake boat tours with its convenient location. | 2 mi off U.S. 89/191/287, 5 mi north of Jackson Lake Junction | 307/543–2811 | Closed late Sept.–late May | $10–$18 | AE, DC, MC, V.

Dornan's. Barbecue. Hearty portions of beef, beans, potatoes, stew, and lemonade or hot coffee are the standbys at Dornan's, which is easily identified by its tepees. Locals know this spot for the barbecue cooked over wood fires. You can eat your chuck-wagon meal inside the tepees if it happens to be raining or windy; otherwise, sit at outdoor picnic tables with views of the Snake River and the Tetons. Lunch is served year-round in the pizza parlor, but the chuck wagon operates September–May only. | 10 Moose Rd., off Teton Park Rd. at Moose Junction | 307/733–2415 | www.dornans.com | $8–$19 | AE, D, DC, MC, V.

Jackson Lake Lodge Pioneer Grill. American/Casual. With an old-fashioned soda fountain, friendly service, and seats along a winding counter, this eatery is favored by families and senior citizens. | U.S. 89/191/287, ½ mi north of Jackson Lake Junction | 307/543–2811 ext. 1911 | Closed early Oct.–late May | $3.25–$11.75 | AE, DC, MC, V.

Picnic Areas. The park has 11 designated picnic areas, each with tables, grills, pit toilets, and water pumps or faucets. In addition to those listed here you can find picnic areas at Colter Bay Village campground, Colter Bay visitor center, Cottonwood Creek, the east shore of Jackson Lake Moose visitor center, and South Jenny Lake trailhead and String Lake trailhead.

North of Colter Bay, four scenic roadside picnic spots dot the **east shore of Jackson Lake.** | U.S. 89/191/287, 6 mi, 8 mi, 9 mi, and 12 mi north of Jackson Lake Junction.

One of the park's most isolated and uncrowded picnic sites is about 6 mi northwest of the Moran entrance station at the east end of **Two Ocean Lake.** A mile north of the entrance station turn east onto Pacific Creek Road, and about 2 mi in from U.S. 26/89/181 take a left (turning north) on the first dirt road. Two Ocean Lake is about 2 mi down the dirt road. | Off Pacific Creek Rd., 2 mi east of U.S. 26/89/191.

Near the Park

Though the park itself has some excellent restaurants, don't miss dining in Jackson, the hub of the Rocky Mountain culinary world. You can find selections such as beef, wild game, fish, or fowl in all price ranges. Steaks are usually cut from grass-fed Wyoming beef.

★ **Bar J Chuckwagon.** American/Casual. This may be the best value in Jackson Hole. You get a full ranch-style meal served outdoors, plus a complete western show featuring song, stories, and even cowboy poetry. The dinner and show take place under cover, so don't let the weather keep you away. Reservations recommended. | 4200 Bar J Chuckwagon Rd., off Teton Village Rd., 3 mi west of Teton Village | 307/733–3370 | www.barjchuckwagon.com | Closed Oct.–late May. No lunch | $16–$24 | D, MC, V.

Billy's Giant Hamburgers. American/Casual. Sharing an entrance with Cadillac Grille, Billy's is 1950s-style, with a few booths and a bunch of tall tables with high stools. Though you can choose from a variety of sandwiches, Billy's specialty is big—really big—burgers, which are really, really good. | 55 N. Cache Dr., Jackson | 307/733–3279 | $6–$15 | AE, MC, V.

Cowboy Cafe. American. This small downtown restaurant serves homemade food, including sandwiches and steaks, buffalo burgers, chicken, pork, and fish. | 115 Ramshorn Ave., Dubois | 307/455–2595 | $7–$13 | MC, V.

Jedediah's House of Sourdough. American/Casual. Friendly, noisy, and elbow-knocking, this restaurant a block east of the town square in a historic home caters to the big appetite. Try the sourdough pancakes, called sourjacks, or Teton taters and eggs. There's a kids' menu and outdoor deck dining. Breakfast also served. | 135 E. Broadway Ave., Jackson | 307/733–5671 | $10–$18 | AE, D, MC, V.

Lodging

Grand Teton National Park doesn't have Yellowstone Park's variety of inexpensive lodgings. A larger choice of lower-priced properties can be found in nearby Jackson and Teton Village ski resort (open in summer), 12 mi north of Jackson on the Moose-Wilson road. Rates at Teton Village—but not in Jackson—are often $10–$40 higher during the winter ski season.

In Grand Teton

Colter Bay Village. Near Jackson Lake, this complex of western-style cabins—some with one room, others with two or more—is within walking distance of the lake. The property has splendid views and an excellent marina and beach for the windsurfing crowd (you'll need a wet suit). The tent cabins aren't fancy and they share communal baths, but they do keep the wind and rain off. There's also a 113-space RV park. 2 restaurants, lake, boating, fishing, hiking, bar, shops, laundry facilities, some pets allowed; no room TVs | 2 mi off U.S. 89/191/287, 5 mi north of Jackson Lake Junction | 307/733–3100 or 800/628–9988 | fax 307/543–3143 | 166 cabins, 66 tent cabins, | $69–$129 1- to 3-bedroom cabins, $34 tent cabins | Closed late Sept.–late May | AE, DC, MC, V.

Dornan's Spur Ranch Cabins. Near Moose visitor center in Dornan's all-in-one shopping-dining-recreation development, these one- and two-bedroom cabins have great views of the Tetons and the Snake River. Each of the log cabins has a full kitchen as well as a generously sized living-dining room and a furnished porch with a Weber grill in summer. Restaurant, boating, hiking, bar, shops; no room TVs | 10 Moose Rd., off Teton Park Rd. at Moose Junction | 307/733–2522 | fax 307/739–9098 | www.dornans.com | 12 cabins | $140–$210 | AE, D, DC, MC, V.

★ **Moulton Ranch Cabins.** Along Mormon Row, these cabins—one used to be a granary—stand a few dozen yards south of the famous Moulton Barn, which you see on brochures, jigsaw puzzles, and photographs of the park. The land was once part of the T. A. Moulton homestead, and the cabins are still owned by the Moulton family. The quiet property has views of both the Teton Range and the Gros Ventre Range, and the owners can regale you with stories about the early homesteaders. Picnic area, hiking; no room TVs, no smoking | Off Antelope Flats Rd., U.S. 26/89/191, 2 mi north of Moose Junction | 307/733–3749 or 208/529–2354 | fax 307/733–1664 or 208/523–3161 | www.srv.net/~iblake/moulton | 5 cabins | $75–$135 | Closed Sept.–May | MC, V.

Near the Park

Reservation Services. You can reserve rooms near the park through two agencies.

Jackson Hole Central Reservations handles hotels as well as B&Bs. | Box 510, Teton Village 83025 | 307/733–4005 or 800/443–6931 | www.jacksonholeresort.com.

You can make reservations for most motels in Jackson through **Resort Reservations.** | 110 Buffalo Way, Suite B (Box 12739), Jackson 83002 | 307/733–6331 or 800/329–9205 | www.jacksonhole.net.

Antler Inn. Like real estate agents say, location, location, location are the three things that matter, and few motels in Jackson are as convenient to the town square as this one, just a block south. The motel rooms are standard, but some have fireplaces. In-room data ports, cable TV, hot tub, sauna, laundry, some pets allowed, no-smoking rooms | 43 W. Pearl St., Jackson | 307/733–2535 or 800/483–8667 | fax 307/733–2002 | www.antlerinn.com | 110 rooms | $98–$130 | AE, D, MC, V.

Intermountain Lodge. Modern, small log cabins nestled among cottonwood trees have basic, comfortable furnishings. Each cabin houses two units; the rooms have showers but no bathtubs. Picnic area, kitchenettes, cable TV, hot tub, volleyball, laundry facilities; no smoking | 34 Ski Hill Rd., Dubois | 208/354–8153 | fax 208/354–2998 | www.tetonvalleychamber.com | 14 rooms | $49–$69 | AE, D, MC, V.

Stagecoach Motor Inn. This downtown motel has a large backyard and play area, including a replica stagecoach for kids to climb on, but the play area is bordered by Pretty Horse Creek, so young children require some supervision. Some rooms have full kitchens and many have refrigerators. Picnic area, refrigerators, cable TV, pool, hot tub, playground, laundry facilities, airport shuttle, some pets allowed (fee) | 103 E. Ramshorn Ave., Dubois | 307/455–2303 or 800/455–5090 | fax 307/455–3903 | 47 rooms, 9 suites | $60–$78 rooms, $70–$100 suites | AE, D, MC, V.

Camping

In Grand Teton

Check in at National Park Service campsites as early as possible—sites are assigned on a first-come, first-served basis. You can camp in the park's backcountry year-round, provided you have the requisite permit and are able to gain access to your site. Between June 1 and September 15, backcountry campers in the park are limited to one stay of up to 10 days. You can reserve a backcountry site for a $15 nonrefundable fee by faxing a request to the backcountry permit office at 307/739–3438 or by writing to the office at Box 170, Moose 83012. You can also take a chance that the site you want will be open when you show up, in which case you pay no fee. Campfires are prohibited in the backcountry except at designated lakeshore campsites.

Colter Bay Campground. Busy, noisy, and filled by noon, this campground has both tent and trailer or RV sites—and one great advantage: it's centrally located. Try to get a site as far from the nearby cabin road as possible. This is the only National Parks–operated campground in the park that has hot showers. The maximum stay is 14 days. Flush toilets, dump station, drinking water, laundry facilities, showers, bear boxes, fire grates, picnic tables | 238 sites | 2 mi off U.S. 89/191/287, 5 mi north of Jackson Lake Junction | 307/543–3100 | $12 | Reservations not accepted | AE, D, MC, V | Mid-May–late Sept.

★ **Jenny Lake.** Wooded sites and Teton views make this the most desirable campground in the park, and it fills early. The small, quiet facility allows tents only and limits stays to a maximum of seven days. Flush toilets, drinking water, bear boxes, fire grates, picnic tables | 49 tent sites | Jenny Lake Rd., ½ mi off Teton Park Rd., 8 mi north of Moose Junction | no phone | $12 | Reservations not accepted | No credit cards | Late May–late Sept.

Near the Park

When the campgrounds in the park are full you can usually find a campsite in one of several commercial Jackson Hole campgrounds or in nearby Bridger-Teton and Targhee national forests. Outside the park there are RV-and-tent campgrounds as well as roadside campgrounds and backcountry sites.

Bridger-Teton National Forest. There are 45 developed campgrounds in the forest, though none have hook-ups or showers. A few campgrounds have corrals, and most have drinking water. You can reserve in advance for some of the campsites. Pit toilets, fire pits, picnic tables | Rte. 26/287 east of Moran Junction; Rtes. 89 and 189 south of Jackson; U.S. Forest Service Reservations, 340 N. Cache St. (Box 1888), Jackson 83001 | 307/739–5500 or 800/280–2267 | fax 307/739–5010 | www.fs.fex.us/btnf | Free–$15 | No credit cards | June–Nov., depending on area.

Shopping

Inside the park you can buy basic items, from food to souvenirs. Outside the park, particularly in Jackson, shopping opportunities abound. Bustling Town Square is surrounded by storefronts that house a mixture of galleries, specialty shops, and outlets (most of them small-scale) with moderate to expensive prices.

Sports and Outdoor Activities

Bicycling

Jackson Hole's long, flat profile and mountain scenery attract 10-speed and mountain bikers of all skill levels. Teton Park Road and Jackson Hole Highway are generally flat with long, gradual inclines and have well-marked shoulders. Grand Teton has few designated bike paths, so cyclists should be very careful when sharing the road with vehicles, especially RVs and trailers. A bike lane allows for northbound bike traffic along the one-way Jenny Lake Loop Road, a one-hour ride. The River Road, 4 mi north of Moose, is an easy four-hour mountain-bike ride along a ridge above the Snake River. Bicycles are not allowed on trails or in the backcountry.

Hoback Sports. There are bike rentals and tours including family-style outings to the National Elk Refuge, or intermediate or advanced tours from the top of Snow King Mountain. | 40 S. Millward St. | 307/733–5335.

Bird-Watching

Teton-country birds include bald eagles and osprey, which nest near Oxbow Bend throughout summer. White pelicans also stop at the Oxbow on their northerly migration in spring. Nearby Willow Flats is host to similar bird life plus sandhill cranes. You can see trumpeter swans at Oxbow Bend and Two Ocean Lake. Look for songbirds, such as pine and evening grosbeaks and Cassin's finches, in surrounding open pine and aspen forests. Similar songbirds inhabit Grandview Point, as do blue and ruffed grouse. Keep binoculars handy while traveling along Antelope Flats Road: you may spot red-tailed hawks and prairie falcons. At Taggart Lake you'll see woodpeckers, bluebirds, and hummingbirds. In all more than 300 species of birds inhabit the park.

Boating

Motorboats are allowed on Jenny, Jackson, and Phelps lakes. On Jenny Lake, there's an engine limit of 7horsepower. You can launch your boat at Colter Bay, Leek's Marina, Signal Mountain, and Spalding Bay.

Colter Bay Marina. All types of services are available to boaters, including free parking for boat trailers and vehicles, free mooring, boat rentals, guided fishing trips, and fuel. The marina, on Jackson Lake, is operated by the Grand Teton Lodge Company. | 2 mi off U.S. 89/191/287, 5 mi north of Jackson Lake Junction | 307/543–2811 | Mid-May–mid-Oct.

Signal Mountain Lodge Marina. The marina rents pontoon boats, deck cruisers, motorboats, and canoes by the hour or for full- or half-day cruising. You can also obtain fuel, oil, and overnight mooring. | Teton Park Rd., 3 mi south of Jackson Lake Junction | 307/543–2831 | Canoes $9 per hr, motorboats $20 per hr, runabouts $36 per hr, pontoon boats $54 per hr. Mooring $20 per night | Mid-May–mid-Oct.

Fishing

Rainbow, brook, lake, and native cutthroat trout inhabit the park's waters. The Snake's 75 mi of river and tributary are world-renowned for their fishing.

Wyoming Fishing License. To fish in Grand Teton National Park you need a license. A day permit for nonresidents is $10 and an annual permit is $65 plus a $10 conservation stamp; for state residents a license costs $15 per season plus $10 for a conservation stamp. You can buy a fishing license at Colter Bay Marina, Moose Village Store, Signal Mountain Lodge, and at area sporting-goods stores.

You can also get a license direct from the **Wyoming Game and Fish Department.** | 360 N. Cache St. (Box 67), Jackson, 83001 | 307/733–2321.

Grand Teton Lodge Company. The park's major concessionaire operates guided Jackson Lake fishing trips that include boat, guide, and tackle. The company also offers guided fly-fishing trips on the Snake River. Make reservations at the activities desks at Colter Bay Village or Jackson Lake Lodge, where trips originate. | Colter Bay Marina or Jackson Lake Lodge | 307/543–2811, 307/543–3100, or 800/628–9988 | fax 307/543–3143 | www.gtlc.com | $104–$350 | June–Sept.

Hiking

Much of the spectacular mountain scenery of Grand Teton is best seen by hiking. You can get trail maps and information about hiking conditions from rangers at the park visitor centers at Moose, Jenny Lake, or Colter Bay. Popular trails are those around Jenny Lake, the Leigh and String lakes area, and Taggart Lake Trail, with views of Avalanche Canyon. Other trails let you experience the Grand Teton backcountry on longer hikes lasting from a few hours to several days. You can also do some off-trail hiking in the park. Pick up backcountry trail information from any ranger station or visitor center. Frontcountry or backcountry, you may see moose and bears, but keep your distance. Pets are not permitted on trails or in the backcountry, but you can take them on paved frontcountry trails so long as they are on a leash no more than 6 ft long.

Colter Bay Nature Trail Loop. This very easy 1¾-mi round-trip excursion treats you to views of Jackson Lake and the Tetons. As you follow the level trail from Colter Bay visitor center and along the forest's edge, you may see moose and bald eagles. Allow yourself two hours to complete the walk. | 2 mi off U.S. 89/191/287, 5 mi north of Jackson Lake Junction.

★ **Jenny Lake Trail.** You can walk to Hidden Falls from Jenny Lake ranger station by following the mostly level trail around the south shore of the lake to Cascade Canyon Trail. Jenny Lake Trail continues around the lake for 6½ mi. It's an easy trail that will take you two to three hours depending on how fast you walk. | South Jenny Lake Junction, ½ mi off Teton Park Rd., 8 mi north of Moose Junction.

Horseback Riding

Colter Bay Village Corral. Grand Teton Lodge Company offers one-, two-, and three-hour rides from Colter Bay Village Corral and from Jackson Lake Corral to a variety of destinations. Some rides include breakfast or dinner eaten along the trail. | Colter Bay Corral is 2 mi off U.S. 89/191/287, 5 mi north of Jackson Lake Junction; Jackson Lake Corral is ½ mi north of Jackson Lake Junction | 307/543–2811, 307/543–3100, or 800/628–9988 | fax 307/543–3143 | www.gtlc.com | Short rides $25–$38, breakfast rides $40, dinner rides $45 | June–Aug.

River Expeditions

If you're floating the Snake River on your own, you are required to purchase a permit that costs $10 per raft and is valid for the entire season. Permits are available year-round at Moose visitor center and at Colter Bay, Signal Mountain, and Buffalo (near Moran entrance) ranger stations in summer. Before you set out, check with park rangers for current conditions.

You may prefer to take one of the many guided float trips through calm-water sections of the Snake; outfitters pick you up at the float trip parking area near Moose visitor center for a 10- to 20-minute drive to upriver launch sites. All concessionaires provide ponchos and life preservers. Early morning and evening floats are your best bets for wildlife viewing, but be sure to carry a jacket or sweater. Float season runs mid-May to mid-September.

Grand Teton Lodge Company Snake River Float Trips. This company operates exclusively within Grand Teton National Park. Choose from a scenic float trip, one that also includes lunch, or an evening trip that includes a steak-fry dinner. Make reservations at the activities desk at Colter Bay Village or Jackson Lake Lodge. | 307/543–2811, 307/543–3100, or 800/628–9988 | fax 307/543–3143 | www.gtlc.com | Scenic float $39.50, lunch float $46, steak-fry float $52 | June–Aug.

Skiing

Grand Teton National Park has some of North America's finest and most varied cross-country skiing. Ski the gentle 3-mi Swan Lake–Heron Pond Loop near Colter Bay visitor center, the mostly level 9-mi Jenny Lake Trail, or the moderate 4-mi Taggart Lake–Beaver Creek Loop and 5-mi Phelps Lake Overlook trail, which have some steep descents. Advanced skiers should head for the Teton Crest Trail. In winter all overnight backcountry travelers must register at park headquarters in Moose to obtain a free permit.

Jackson Hole Mountain Resort. When the snow is right, this is truly one of the great downhill skiing experiences in America. Jackson is a place to appreciate both as a skier and as someone who likes to watch extreme skiing. World-class racers like Olympic champion skier Tommy Moe and snowboarder Rob King will regularly train here. The resort claims 2,500 skiable acres. And although Jackson is best known for its advanced to extreme skiing, it is also a place where imaginative intermediates can go exploring and have the time of their lives. The tram to the summit of Rendezvous Peak provides access to 4,139 vertical ft of skiing, resulting in arguably the longest continuous runs in the United States. The runs for beginners and intermediate skiers are somewhat limited, but there are good snowboard runs and a half pipe. Box 290, Teton Village 83025 | 307/733–2292 or 800/333–7766 | www.jacksonhole.com | $40 | Early Dec.–mid-Apr., daily 9–4. Tram tours May–late Sept., daily 9–5.

Snowmobiling

Designated unplowed sections of Teton Park Road are open to snowmobiles, but you must first purchase an annual $15 permit at a park entrance station. The speed limit within the park is 45 mph.

Flagg Ranch Resort. The resort north of Grand Teton rents snowmobiles that you can ride directly into Grand Teton and Yellowstone national parks. It will also provide transportation to the Jackson-area snowmobile trails and offers snowcoachtours into Yellowstone National Park. | John D. Rockefeller Jr. Memorial Pkwy., 4 mi north of Grand Teton National Park boundary | www.flaggranch.com | 307/543–2861 or 800/443–2311 | Snowmobile rentals $140–$195 per day, snowcoach tours $109 | Nov.–Mar.

Essential Information

When to Go

The park is open year-round, though many services are curtailed in winter. All interior park roads are generally open from early May through late October. Before Memorial Day and after late September services in the park are limited, but Moose visitor center stays open all winter, except on Christmas Day.

Summer is definitely high season in Grand Teton National Park. Around 4 million visitors travel through the region; July and August are the park's most crowded months. In Jackson dining and lodging rates are generally highest in summer. The lowest rates and smallest crowds can be found in spring and fall, both in the park and throughout the surrounding area, but note that some services won't be available. In

April most of Teton Park Road is open to bicyclists, in-line skaters, and hikers only, an off-season treat for observers of wildlife. When park lodgings and visitor services are closed for winter the crowds in the park are genuinely sparse. Most of Teton Park Road is closed late October through early May, but Jackson Hole Highway remains open, providing access to cross-country ski trails and frozen Jackson Lake. However, because of the popularity of the excellent downhill skiing in the area, winter is a very busy time around Teton Village and in Jackson. Winter dining and lodging rates at Teton Village are often higher than in summer.

FESTIVALS AND SEASONAL EVENTS

WINTER

Dec.: **Torchlight Parades.** Skiers celebrate Christmas and New Year's Eve with torchlight parades at Snow King Mountain in Jackson and at Jackson Hole Mountain Resort. | 307/739–2770 or 307/733–5200.

SPRING

May: **Old West Days** in Jackson include a rodeo, Native American dancers, a western swing dance contest, and cowboy poetry readings. | 307/733–3316 or 800/782–0011.

SUMMER

May–Aug.: **Teton County Historical Society** sponsors monthly field trips each spring and summer to regional sites such as pioneer ranches. | 307/733–9605.

July–Aug.: **Grand Teton Music Festival.** A schedule of symphony orchestra performances is presented at Walk Festival Hall in Teton Village and outdoors near Jackson Hole Resort. There's also a winter concert schedule. | 307/733–1128 or 800/959–4863.

Aug.: **Wind River Rendezvous.** Near Dubois, modern-day mountain men known as buckskinners gather to re-create a camp like those of the fur-trapping era. | 307/455–2556.

AUTUMN

Sept.–Oct.: **Jackson Hole Fall Arts Festival.** Special events include poetry readings and dance performances. Jackson's many art galleries have special exhibits and programs. | 307/733–3316.

Bargains

Free ranger-led activities usually originate at Moose and Colter Bay visitor centers. They include guided walks, naturalist tours, photography workshops, and campfire programs. Some otherwise expensive lodgings offer shoulder-season (Apr.–May and mid-Oct.–late Nov.) specials. Lodging is generally less expensive in Teton Village during the summer because high season there is during winter, when the ski resort is in full swing.

Nearby Towns

The major gateway to Grand Teton National Park is **Jackson,** often mistakenly referred to as Jackson Hole. Actually, Jackson Hole is the mountain-ringed valley that houses Jackson and much of Grand Teton National Park. The community of roughly 7,000 permanent residents hosts around 4 million visitors annually. Expensive homes and fashionable shops have sprung up all over, but Jackson manages to maintain at least part of its true western character. There's a lot to do here, both downtown (museums, art galleries, fine dining, western dancing) and in the surrounding countryside (hiking, climbing, floating down the Snake River). If it's skiing you're after, **Teton Village** is the place for you. It's not an incorporated city or town; rather, Teton Village is a cluster of businesses and lodging properties that centers on the facilities of the Jackson Hole Ski Resort—a tramway, gondola, and various other lifts. The community resounds with the clomp of ski boots in winter and to the strains of the Grand Teton Music Festival in summer.

On the "backside of the Tetons," as eastern Idaho is known, **Driggs** is a western gateway to Yellowstone Country and Grand Teton National Park. Easygoing and rural, Driggs resembles the Jackson of a few decades ago. From here you have to cross a major mountain pass to reach the park; note that the pass is sometimes closed in winter by avalanches.

If you prefer an easier drive into the park but want to avoid the hubbub of Jackson and Teton Village, you can stay in **Dubois,** about 55 mi east of Jackson. The least known of the gateway communities to Grand Teton and Yellowstone, this town of 1,000 has all the services of the bigger towns. In Dubois you can still get a room for the night during the peak summer travel period without making a reservation weeks or months in advance (though it's a good idea to call a week or so before you intend to arrive).

Tours

Jackson Lake Cruises. Grand Teton Lodge Company runs 1½-hour Jackson Lake scenic cruises from Colter Bay Marina throughout the day as well as breakfast cruises, and sunset steak-fry cruises. One cruise, known as Fire and Ice, shows how forest fires and glaciers have shaped the Grand Teton landscape. | 2 mi off U.S. 89/191/287, 5 mi north of Jackson Lake Junction | 307/543–3100, 307/543–2811, or 800/628–9988 | www.gtlc.com | Scenic cruise $15, breakfast cruise $28, steak-fry cruise $46 | Mid-May–mid-Sept.

Ranger Walks. Rangers lead free walks throughout the park in summer, from a one-hour lakeside stroll at Colter Bay to a three-hour hike from Jenny Lake. Call for itineraries, times, and reservations or get details at visitor centers. | 307/739–3300 or 307/739–3400 TDD | Free | Early June–early Sept.

Young Naturalist Program. Children ages 8–12 learn about the natural world of the park as they take an easy 2-mi hike with a ranger. Kids should wear old clothes and bring water, rain gear, and insect repellent. The hike, which takes place at Jenny Lake or Colter Bay, is 1½ hours long and is limited to 12 children. Parents must pick up children promptly at 3 PM. | Jenny Lake: meet at flag pole at visitor center; Colter Bay: meet at visitor center | 307/739–3300 | Free | Mid-June–mid-Aug., daily 1:30.

Visitor Information

For general information about the park, contact **Grand Teton National Park** | Box 170, Moose, 83012 | 307/739–3300; 307/739–3400 TDD | www.nps.gov/grte. For information on activities at Jackson Lake, contact **Colter Bay Visitor Center** | 2 mi off U.S. 89/191/287, 5 mi north of Jackson Lake Junction | 307/739–3594. For information on lodging, dining, and tours in the park contact the park's largest concessionaire, contact **Grand Teton Lodge Company** | Box 240, Moran, 83013 | 307/543–2811, 307/543–3100, or 800/628–9988 | fax 307/543–3143 | www.gtlc.com.

Dubois Chamber of Commerce | Box 632, Dubois, WY 82513 | 307/455–2556 | fax 307/455–3168 | www.duboiswyoming.org. **Eastern Idaho Yellowstone/Teton Territory Visitor Information Center** | 505 Lindsay Blvd. (Box 50498), Idaho Falls, ID 83402 | 208/523–1010 or 800/634–3246 | fax 208/523–2255 | www.idahofallschamber.com. **Jackson Chamber of Commerce** | Box E, Jackson 83001 | 307/733–3316 | fax 307/733–5585 | www.jacksonholechamber.com. **Jackson Hole and Greater Yellowstone Visitor**

Center | 532 N. Cache St., Jackson | 307/733–3316 | www.fs.fed.us/jhgyvc. **Teton Valley Chamber of Commerce** | 75 North Main St. (Box 250), Driggs, ID 83422 | 208/354–2500 | fax 208/354–2500 | www.tetonvalleychamber.com. **Wyoming Division of Tourism** | I-25 at College Dr., Cheyenne, 82002 | 307/777–7777 or 800/225–5996 | fax 307/777–2877 | www.wyomingtourism.org.

Arriving and Departing

BY AIR

Airports

Jackson Hole Airport (JAC). This airport, within the park and 8 mi north of Jackson off U.S. 89, receives daily flights connecting through Denver and Salt Lake City. | 307/733–7682.

Airport Transportation

Some lodgings provide free airport shuttle service.

Car: Rental cars are available at the airport from Alamo, Avis, Budget, Dollar, Hertz, Thrifty, and Leisure Rentals.

Taxi: Buckboard Transportation. One-way taxi fare from the airport to Jackson is $12, and one-way taxi fare from the airport to Teton Village is $22. | 307/733–1112 or 800/791–0211.

BY CAR

The Jackson Hole Highway (U.S. 26–89–191) is open all year from Jackson to Moran Junction, east over Togwotee Pass (U.S. 26–287) and north to Flagg Ranch, 2 mi south of Yellowstone Park's south entrance (closed in winter).

Getting Around

BY CAR

The best way to see Grand Teton National Park is by car. Unlike Yellowstone's Grand Loop, Grand Teton's road system doesn't allow for easy tour-bus access to all the major sights. Only a car will get you close to Jenny Lake, into the remote east Jackson Hole hills, and to the top of Signal Mountain. You can stop at many points along the roads within the park for a hike or a view. Jackson Hole Highway (U.S. 89–191) runs the entire length of the park, from Jackson to Yellowstone National Park's south entrance (it's also U.S. 26 south of Moran Junction and Route 287 north of Moran Junction). This road is open all year from Jackson to Moran Junction and north to Flagg Ranch, 2 mi south of Yellowstone. Also open year-round, U.S. 26–287 runs east from Dubois over Togwotee Pass to the Moran entrance station, a drive of about one hour.

North Carolina, Tennessee

Revised and Updated by Susan Reigler

GREAT SMOKY MOUNTAINS NATIONAL PARK

The landscape is mysterious and majestic. But it's accessible rather than remote. Natural assets and proximity to several metro areas help make the Great Smoky Mountains National Park the most-visited national park, welcoming more than 9 million people a year. The park is certainly big enough to handle this influx. Established in 1934, the National Park is composed of 520,000 acres (60 mi long and 20 mi wide) equally distributed over eastern Tennessee and western North Carolina.

Found here are the largest tracts of old-growth forest in the eastern United States (some 200,000 acres), as well as the tallest mountains. It's not just one forest either. Five different woodland systems compose the Smoky Mountain landscape. The mountains were called Shaconage ("place of blue smoke") by the region's first inhabitants, the Cherokee, for the blue-gray haze, a result of plant respiration, that clings to the wooded slopes much of the time. For its extraordinary biodiversity and stunning landscape, Great Smoky Mountains National Park has been designated a United Nations International Biosphere Reserve and a World Heritage Site.

Exploring

Great Smoky Mountains National Park

In the 200 years before it was declared a national park, the Smoky Mountains region was settled by 18th- and 19th-century pioneers and partially deforested by timber companies in the early 20th century. Today the interior is managed as a wilderness preserve. There are many camping facilities and interpretive programs but few other services. Two roads traverse the park: a portion of U.S. 441 called the Newfound Gap Road, and Little River Road, which leads to a pioneer historic area called Cades Cove. At the park's edges are the gateway resort towns of Gatlinburg, Tennessee, and Cherokee, North Carolina, which have extensive visitor facilities.

Hours: The park is open year-round.

Fees: There are no entrance fees.

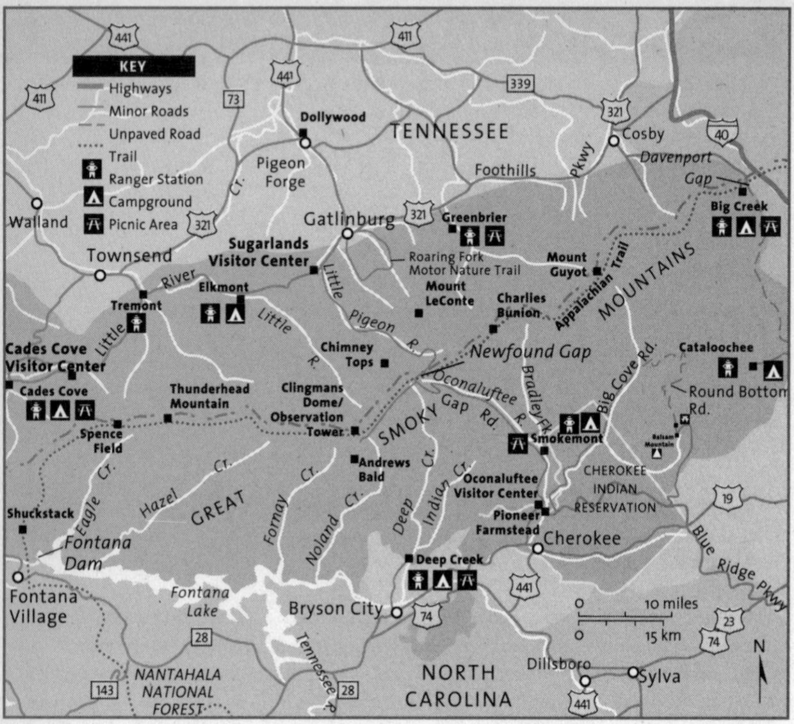

SCENIC DRIVES

Cades Cove Loop Road. Skirting the edge of a broad valley containing open pastures and a preserved pioneer settlement, this 11-mi road is the park's most popular auto tour. This can be a crowded trip in peak season, but you can take a break from the traffic jam by pulling off at the mid-point of the loop and walking the 5-mi round-trip Abrams Fall trail.

★ **Clingmans Dome Road.** The views of wave after wave of mountain ridges receding into the distance characterize this 7-mi road, which will take you to a paved trail leading to the park's highest peak. The Spruce-Fir Self-Guiding Nature Trail through the cool, damp forest is ½ mi long.

Newfound Gap Road. This 33-mi route snakes along the spine of the Great Smoky Mountains connecting the towns of Cherokee, North Carolina, and Gatlinburg, Tennessee. You'll ascend about 3,000 ft through all the forest types of the park, from the hardwoods found in the valleys to the spruce and fir forests of the highest elevations. There are several roadside pullouts offering the chance to look out over the terrain. At Newfound Gap itself, there's a parking area for access to the Appalachian Trail, exhibits about the park, and rest rooms.

Roaring Fork Motor Nature Trail. This 5-mi drive starts in Cherokee Orchard and winds along a fast-flowing stream through a new-growth forest. One of the highlights is the Place of a Thousand Drips, where hundreds of tiny underground springs create a very unusual mountainside waterfall.

SIGHTS TO SEE

Appalachian Trail. The trail crosses the highway at Newfound Gap, and even if you're not a serious hiker, you'll enjoy a short walk along this famous pathway. Unfortunately, heavy usage and soil erosion have worn down the trail to solid rock in places (☞ Hiking and Backpacking).

★ **Cades Cove.** West of the Sugarlands Visitor Center along Little River Road, this carefully preserved historic area reflects the heritage of pioneer settlers. For many years, families who lived here were virtually isolated from the rest of the world. You can follow an 11-mi loop road through the area, stopping at the visitor center, where displays depict life here as it once was. Also along the way are hewn-log houses, small churches with their historic burial grounds, and a working gristmill. The loop road is open daily, weather permitting. | 12 mi south of Townsend on Laurel Creek Rd. | 865/448–2472 | Visitor center and gristmill mid-Apr.–Oct., daily | Free.

Clingmans Dome. At 6,643 feet, this is the highest peak in Tennessee. A seven-mi spur road extends to Clingmans Dome from Newfound Gap, but keep in mind that this road is generally closed in winter. A rather steep pathway that is not too arduous leads to a mountaintop observation tower from which, weather permitting, you'll see the mountains sweeping in every direction. | About 25 mi south of Gatlinburg off Newfound Gap Rd. Follow spur road sign.

Newfound Gap. About midway along the Newfound Gap Road at a 5,048-ft elevation, the Gap marks the boundary dividing North Carolina and Tennessee. On a clear day, views from this majestic site on the crest of the Great Smokies are extraordinary. | About 15 mi southeast of Gatlinburg on Newfound Gap Rd.

POCKET FIELD GUIDE: THE SMOKIES

Ecological Communities: The greatest diversity of plant and animal life, not just in the United States but anywhere in the world outside of tropical rain forests, is found here. More than 5,000 species of fungi, plants, and animals (including more than 300 new to science) have been identified since 1997 by a continuing research project designed to inventory the flora and fauna of the park. The reason for the extraordinary biodiversity lies in the five types of forest that occur in the park. Lining the valleys are hardwoods dominated by tulip poplar (beloved of log cabin builders because it's termite-proof), sweet gum, red maple, and dogwood. Along the stream banks you'll find hemlocks casting their protective branches over the water. The dry ridges along the middle altitudes of the park are covered in oak, hickory, and pine. As you climb from 3,500 to 5,500 ft, the northern hardwood mix of sugar maple, American beech, and yellow birch takes over. And above 4,500 ft, the park's highest elevations, you can't be blamed for thinking you may have driven north to Maine instead of south to Tennessee. Red spruce and Fraser fir are the dominant trees.

Flora: There are more than 130 species of trees. In the forest understory, you'll see flowering scrubs such as azalea and rhododendron. Blooming at different times from late March to mid-October are some 1,500 species of wildflowers, including jack-in-the-pulpit, spring beauty, lady slipper, Indian paintbrush and blue gentian.

Fauna: Bird-watchers will be delighted by being able to spot more than 230 species of birds (more than 110 of these breed within park boundaries). Reptiles and amphibians abound. There are even 30 species of salamanders, making the Smokies the unofficial Salamander Capital of the World. A total of 65 species of mammals live in the park, including the black bear. Please do not feed the bears. Park officials are very serious about this. Fines range up to $5,000 and six months in prison for feeding a bear.

Oconaluftee Visitor Center. The visitor center is just inside the park's southern entrance. The adjacent Mountain Farm Museum consists of a collection of vintage structures—main house, barn, storage bins, smokehouse—suggesting the rugged, self-sufficient lifestyle of mountain people during the late 19th century. During the peak season, craftsfolk demonstrate pioneer skills. | About 2 mi north of Cherokee on U.S. 441 | 828/497–9146 | Free | Mid-Mar.–mid-Nov., daily.

Half a mile north off Newfound Gap Road, cornmeal is produced the old-fashioned way by water-powered wheels and may be purchased at **Mingus Mill.** | No phone.

Sugarlands Visitor Center and **The Great Smoky Mountains National Park Headquarters.** At the park entrance, 2 mi south of Gatlinburg, Tennessee, on U.S. 441, you can get an introduction to the park through an audiovisual presentation and displays highlighting the wildlife, plants, and geological formations of the Smokies. From mid-April to October, rangers give campfire programs and other illustrated talks. | 107 Park Headquarters Rd. | 865/436–1200 | Free | Daily.

Near the Park

CHEROKEE

★ **Museum of the Cherokee Indian.** One of the best Native American museums in the United States has displays and artifacts that cover 12,000 years. Computer-generated images, lasers, specialty lighting, and sound effects help re-create events in the history of the Cherokee: for example, at one exhibit you'll see children stop to play a butter-bean game while adults shiver along the snowy Trail of Tears. The museum has an art gallery, a gift shop, and an outdoor living exhibit of Cherokee life in the 15th century. | U.S. 441 at Drama Rd. | 828/497–3481 | www.cherokeemuseum.org | $8 | June–Aug., Mon.–Sat. 9–8, Sun. 9–5; Sept.–May, daily 9–5.

Oconaluftee Indian Village. Guides in native costumes will lead you through a re-created village of 225 years ago while other reenactors demonstrate traditional skills such as weaving, pottery, canoe construction, and hunting techniques. | U.S. 441 at Drama Rd. | 828/497–2315 | www.dnet.net/~cheratt | $12 | Mid-May–late Oct., daily 9:30–5.

Smoky Mountain Gold and Ruby Mine. Every mountain county has significant deposits of gems and minerals, and at this mine on the Qualla Boundary, you can search for gems such as aquamarines. Children love panning, precisely because it can be wet and messy. Here they're guaranteed a find. Gem ore can be purchased, too: gold ore costs $5 per bag. | U.S. 441 N | 828/497–6574 | $4–$10, depending on gems | Mar.–Nov., daily 10–6.

GATLINBURG

Dollywood. Singer Dolly Parton's popular amusement park in nearby Pigeon Forge embodies the country superstar's own flamboyance—plenty of Hollywood flash mixed with simple country charm that you either love or hate. There are 118 acres of rides (including car chases and water slides) plus live musical entertainment. As you might expect of Dolly's park, there's country music, but there's also gospel and '50s rock-and-roll shows. | 1020 Dollywood La., Pigeon Forge | 865/428–9488 or 800/365–5996 | www.dollywood.com | $34.25; free next day on tickets purchased after 3 | Mid-Apr.–Oct., daily 9–6; extended hrs mid-June–mid-Aug. Closed Tues. and Thurs. May and Sept., Thurs. in Oct.; call for varying hrs Nov.–Dec.

★ **Gatlinburg Sky Lift.** Open ski-lift benches take you more than 500 feet up the side of Crockett Mountain for panoramic views across the mountains. Gatlinburg and the Little Pigeon River shrink into toy-landscape dimensions below. | 865/436–9100 | www.gatlinburgskylift.com | $9 | Apr.–Oct., 9 AM–10 PM; Nov.–Mar., 9–5.

Ober Gatlinburg Tramway. One of America's largest aerial tramways departs every 20 minutes from downtown Gatlinburg and takes 120 riders directly to the Ober

Gatlinburg Ski Resort and Amusement Park atop Mt. Harrison. The 15-minute trip offers an impressive panorama of Gatlinburg and the Smokies. | 1001 Parkway | 865/436–5423 | www.obergatlinburg.com | $9.

Dining

In the Smokies

There are no restaurants in the park, so plan either to eat in one of the nearby towns or to bring your own picnic.

Picnic Areas. Picnicking is permitted throughout the park, and there are several areas set aside with tables and fire rings. Most picnic areas have pavilions, which may be reserved for $20. Always keep food locked in your car if you are not actually preparing or eating a meal. Wildlife, including bears, can be attracted by food. All food and trash must be completely removed from a site after picnicking. Feeding the wild animals is strictly prohibited, for your safety and theirs. Call for a complete list of sites as well as reservations. | 800/365–2267.

There are 81 sites in the meadow-side **Cades Cove,** all of which have tables and fire rings. Many are wheelchair accessible. Rest rooms and drinking water are available. Closing time is 8 PM May through August and sunset the rest of the year. | Just before the beginning of the Cades Cove loop road.

This wooded spot next to scenic **Deep Creek** is popular with rafters. The facility has 15 tables, four elevated grills, rest rooms, changing rooms, and drinking water. A pavilion can be reserved for up to 70 people. | North of Bryson City, North Carolina.

Near the Park

CHEROKEE

Hemlock Inn. Contemporary. Even if you're not a guest at the inn, which is built on a small mountain that overlooks three valleys, you can make a reservation for dinner Monday through Saturday and for lunch on Sunday. The fixed-price all-you-can-eat meals are prepared with regional foods, including locally grown fruits and vegetables and mountain honey. | Galbraith Creek Rd., 1 mi north of U.S. 19, Bryson City 28713 | 828/488–2885 | fax 828/488–8985 | Closed Nov.–mid-Apr. | $15 | D, MC, V.

★ **Nantahala Village Restaurant.** American. This roomy rock-and-cedar restaurant with front-porch rocking chairs is about 10 mi southwest of Cherokee and is a local favorite. The food isn't fancy, but the choices—trout, chicken, country ham, and even some vegetarian options—are good and filling. Sunday brunch has some surprises, including *huevos rancheros* (tortilla with fried eggs and salsa) and eggs benedict. | 9400 U.S. 19 W, Bryson City | 828/488–9616 or 800/438–1507 | Closed late Nov.–early Mar. | $10–$20 | MC, V.

GATLINBURG

Pancake Pantry. American. This restaurant, with its century-old brick, polished-oak paneling, rustic copper accessories, and spacious windows, is a family favorite. Austrian apple-walnut pancakes covered with apple cider compote, black walnuts, apple slices, sweet spices, powdered sugar, and whipped cream are a house specialty. Other selections include omelets, sandwiches, and fresh salads. Box lunches are available for mountain picnics. | 628 Parkway | 865/436–4724 | Reservations not accepted | No dinner | $7–$10 | No credit cards.

Smoky Mountain Trout House. Seafood. Of the 15 distinctive trout preparations to choose from at this cozy restaurant, an old favorite is trout Eisenhower: panfried, with cornmeal breading and served with bacon-and-butter sauce. Prime rib, country ham, and grilled chicken are also on the menu. | 410 Parkway. | 865/436–5416 | Reservations not accepted | No lunch | $12–$22 | AE, DC, MC, V.

Lodging

In the Smokies

★ **LeConte Lodge.** This rustic retreat near the top of 6,593-ft Mt. LeConte is the only overnight facility in the park. And the only way to get to it is to hike or ride horseback up a 5½-mi-long trail. Nonetheless, it's booked up to a year in advance. There's no electricity, so lighting is provided by kerosene lamps. The only sounds are of wind stirring the branches of the fir trees and birds singing. A small library, a selection of games, and comfortable chairs for reading provide recreation. Family-style meals are served in the lodge dining hall. Flush toilets; no showers, no room phones, no room TVs. | 1 3-bedroom lodge sleeps 6, 1 2-bedroom lodge sleeps 10, 6 cabins sleep 4 each | 250 Apple Valley Rd. | 865/429–5704 | fax 865/774–0045 | $111 | Reservations essential | Closed Dec.–Mar. | No credit cards.

Near the Park

CHEROKEE

Holiday Inn Cherokee. Guest rooms are standard chain fare, but the staff at this well-equipped, full-service facility is very friendly. The Chestnut Tree restaurant has dinner buffets that are veritable groaning boards, and the native crafts shop, the Hunting Ground, with works by local artists, is a nice touch. Restaurant, cable TV, indoor pool, wading pool, sauna, recreation room, shop, playground, business services, meeting room | U.S. 19, 28719 | 828/497–9181 or 800/465–4329 | fax 828/497–5973 | www.hicherokee.com | 150 rooms, 4 suites | $76–$96 | AE, D, DC, MC, V.

GATLINBURG

Holiday Inn Sunspree Resort. This complex offers kids and adults plenty to do and also has family programs. All rooms have a coffeemaker, and there is a general store. The hotel is two blocks from the convention center. 2 restaurants, refrigerators, cable TV, 2 pools (1 indoor), hot tub, gym, sauna, bar, video game room, laundry facilities, meeting rooms. | 520 Historic Nature Trail, 37738 | 865/436–9201 or 800/465–4329 | fax 865/436–7974 | www.sixcontinentshotels.com | 400 rooms | $69–$119 | AE, D, DC, MC, V.

Park Vista Resort Hotel. Set on a mountain ledge, this large hotel has modern, lavishly decorated public areas and spacious, elegant guest rooms, each with a balcony overlooking colorful gardens, the town of Gatlinburg, the Little Pigeon River, and the mountains beyond. Nonetheless, this white, semicircular contemporary tower is a jarring sight in the Great Smoky Mountains. Restaurant, 2 indoor pools, wading pool, hot tub, sauna, lounge, sports bar, meeting rooms. | 705 Cherokee Orchard Rd., 37738 | 865/436–9211 or 800/421–7275 | fax 865/436–5141 | www.parkvista.com | 306 rooms, 6 suites | $70–$130 | AE, DC, MC, V.

Rainbow Motel. This small, neat, well-maintained lodging is within walking distance of downtown Gatlinburg. Cabins have hot tubs, fireplaces, full kitchens, decks, and swings. Family-owned and -operated, Rainbow Motel is a pleasant choice for budget-minded vacationers. Microwaves, cable TV with VCRs, pool. | 390 E. Parkway (3 blocks east of U.S. 441), Box 1397, 37738 | 865/436–5887 or 800/422–8922 | www.rainbowmotelandrentals.com | 40 rooms, 10 cabins | $35–$65; $75–$125 cabins | D, MC, V.

Camping

In the Smokies

For further information, or to make reservations in advance, contact the park service. | 800/365–2267 | www.nps.gov.

★ **Abrams Creek.** This small campground ringed by hemlock forest is near the banks of Abrams Creek. Flush toilets, fire grates, picnic tables | 16 sites | Off Hwy. 129 and the foothills Pkwy. | $12 | Mid-Mar.–Oct.

★ **Balsam Mountain.** At an elevation of more than 5,330 ft, this is the highest campground in the park. Flush toilets, fire grates, picnic tables | 46 sites | Off Heintooga Rd. and the Blue Ridge Pkwy. | $14 | Mid-May–mid-Oct.

Cades Cove. If your don't want to go too high in the park, stay at this valley-view campground. Historic buildings and rolling pastures are nearby. Flush toilets, fire grates, picnic tables, general store | 161 sites | Off Laurel Creek Rd. | $14–$17 | Reservations essential in summer | Year-round.

Near the Park

Little River Village Campground. Private and heavily wooded campsites are in Townsend, Tennessee. Configured for tents or RVs, the 67 RV sites have complete hook-ups. Flush toilets, full hook-ups, laundry facilities, deli, playground, pool | 67 full hook-ups | 8533 Rte. 73 | 865/448–2241 | $13–$26 | Year-round.

Yogi-in-the-Smokies. This large campground in Cherokee, North Carolina, caters to RVs. Sites are heavily wooded, and many are along the Raven Folk River. Some sites have full hook-ups; most have water and electricity; 10 are primitive. Recreation room. Flush toilets, full hook-ups, partial hook-ups (water and electricity), laundry facilities, general store, playground | 250 sites | 317 Galamore Bridge Rd. | 828/497–9151 | $21–$32 | Apr.–Oct.

Shopping

Cherokee

On the Cherokee Reservation, in the shadow of the Smoky Mountains, elders pass on to children the secrets of finger weaving, wood carving, and mask and beaded-jewelry making. Their work, intricate and colorful, is ageless, a connective thread to a time that predates the United States by thousands of years.

Medicine Man Crafts. This downtown Cherokee shop is one of several selling authentic Cherokee crafts items. | U.S. 441 | 828/497–2202.

Gatlinburg

With more than 400 specialty shops, Gatlinburg is a browsing heaven. You can also visit the local trout farms around the town.

The mountain towns of East Tennessee are known for Appalachian folk crafts, especially wood carvings, cornhusk dolls, pottery, dulcimers, and beautiful handmade quilts.

Great Smoky Arts and Crafts Community. A collection of 80 shops and craftspeople's studios is strung along 8 mi of rambling country road. Begun in 1937, the community includes workers in leather, pottery, weaving, hand-wrought pewter, stained glass, quilt making, hand carving, marquetry, and more. Everything sold here is made on the premises by the community members. Also here are two restaurants and the popular Wild Plum Tearoom. | Off U.S. 321, 3 mi east of Gatlinburg | 865/671–3600 | www.smokymtnarts-crafts.com. For more information: Box 807, Gatlinburg 37738.

Sports and Outdoor Activities

Hiking and Backpacking

To get the deepest appreciation of the beauty of the Smokies, lace up your hiking boots. Trails vary in difficulty from short, paved walks of ½ mi or less to the rugged terrain of the 68 mi of the Appalachian Trail that snakes diagonally across the park from the northeast to the southwest corner.

Backcountry Reservation Office. You must have a backcountry permit (no fee) if you plan to stay on the trails overnight. The bear-proof shelters along the Appalachian Trail are in great demand and are rationed, so you must register for them by telephone at least one month in advance. Call for both permits and for trail shelter reservations. | 865/436–1231.

Appalachian Trail. An unusually elevated and scenic portion of the famous trail runs along high ridges in the Great Smoky Mountains National Park. Serious hikers wishing to walk its entire stretch in the park can enter at Davenport Gap at the eastern end of the park or Fontana Dam at the southwestern end. It will take six to eight days to complete the trail, and there are shelters along the trail about a day's walk apart.

Deep Creek–Indian Creek Loop. At 4 mi, this is a relatively short trail, but it is rich with rushing streams that spill over rock ledges. Gravity and geology conspire to create veils of shimmering mist that hang over the lush greenery of the mountainsides.

★ **Ramsey Cascade Trail.** The 8-mi round-trip trail offers an intimate introduction to the old-growth forest of massive tulip poplars and hemlocks. Deeper into the forest you'll find the park's highest waterfall, the 100-ft Ramsey Cascade. The trail climbs 2,375 ft in 4 mi, but the effort in the calves and knees is rewarded with magical scenery.

Horseback Riding

Smoky Mountain Stables. Guided horseback rides head into the Great Smoky Mountains National Park from March through November. | U.S. 321 N | 865/436–5634.

Rafting

There are water tours for visitors of all ages and abilities. You can choose to shoot the rapids of white-water rivers or float along still water in inflatable kayaks.

Rafting in the Smokies. This outfitter offers guided white-water raft trips from March through October. | 865/436–5008 or 800/776–7238.

Skiing and Snowboarding

Ober Gatlinburg Ski Resort. Skiers and snowboarders have their choice of eight trails on 32 acres on Mt. Harrison. There are three chairlifts, two quad, and one double, and when temperatures drop, snow-making equipment blankets all of the trails. A ski school offers instruction on all levels. | 1001 Parkway | 865–436–5423 or 800/251–9202 | www.obergatlinburg.com/ski.htm | Daily.

Essential Information

When to Go

Dogwoods and hosts of wildflowers bloom from late April to mid-May. June and July bring mountain laurel, flame azalea, and rose, purple, and white rhododendrons. The primrose, sweet shrub, Indian paintbrush, Queen Anne's lace, Turk's Cap lilies, and minuscule bluets last all summer and into September. Toward late September at higher elevations, the sumac turns deep scarlet, heralding the approach of autumn. Foliage generally peaks about mid-October in the higher altitudes and lasts into early November along the intermediate and lower slopes. Numerous varieties of hardwood trees produce brilliant colors—gold, red, russet, deep scarlet, and dazzling yellow.
There is no bad or wrong time of year to visit the park. However, during July, August, and October, you may want to avoid driving the Newfound Gap Road on weekends; traffic during these peak seasons can slow to a snail's pace. Even during the summer,

the weather can be crisp and cool at higher elevations. Winter temperatures can vary from moderate to bitterly cold, but the Newfound Gap Road remains open unless there's ice and snow, and the park has a certain solitary beauty—and it's uncrowded.

FESTIVALS AND SEASONAL EVENTS

SPRING

Apr.: **Spring Wildflower Pilgrimage.** A three-day program consists of conducted nature walks, motorcades, and photographic tours that traverse both the North Carolina and Tennessee sides of the park and a designated wildlife sanctuary. In addition to field trips for those with a botanical bent, there are also bird, insect, spider, amphibian, and geological jaunts offered. | 865/436–1200.

May: **Gatlinburg Scottish Festival.** Pipe and drum bands, professional athletes, Highland dancing, and sheepdog demonstrations are featured, along with games and contests. | 865/457–2986.

SUMMER

June: **Dulcimer and Harp Festival.** This celebration of old-fashioned music and dancing takes place in nearby Crosby 15 mi from Gatlinburg. | 865/487–5543.

July: **Fourth of July Pow-Wow.** Native American dance and crafts demonstrations as well as athletic competitions take place on the tribal ceremonial grounds behind the Museum of the Cherokee Indian. | 828/497–3481 or 800/438–1601.

AUTUMN

Sept.: **Mountain Lights Festival.** Held on the third Saturday of September at the Oconaluftee Visitor Center, this festival centers on rural arts such as making apple butter, apple cider, sorghum molasses, and soap. | 865/436–1200.

Bargains

The best bargain is the park itself; admission to the Great Smoky Mountains National Park is free. Seasonal nature programs are also free and are conducted by park rangers at visitor centers and campgrounds. These programs sometimes involve short walks (including sunset and twilight treks), while others are illustrated talks.

Nearby Towns

The 50,000-acre Cherokee reservation in North Carolina is known as the Qualla Boundary, and the town of **Cherokee,** one of the gateways to the Smokies, is its capital. Truth be told, there are two Cherokees. There's the Cherokee with the sometimes tacky pop culture, designed to appeal to the masses of tourists, many of whom are visiting the nearby National Park. But there's another Cherokee that explores the rich heritage of the tribe's Eastern Band. Although now relatively small in number—tribal enrollment is 12,500—these Cherokee and their ancestors have been responsible for keeping alive the Cherokee culture. They are the descendants of those who hid in the Great Smoky Mountains to avoid becoming part of the Trail of Tears, the forced removal of the Cherokee Nation to Oklahoma in the 19th century.

Gateway city to Great Smoky Mountains National Park, **Gatlinburg,** popular with honeymooners and families, has steadily expanded from a remote little Tennessee town with a sprinkling of hotels, chalets, and mountain crafts shops to the sprawling network of mini-golf courses and homemade-candy "shoppes" it is today. During the summer, the town is clogged with visitors, complete with the annoyances of traffic jams and packed restaurants. Nevertheless, Gatlinburg is Tennessee's premier mountain resort town and is set in the narrow valley of the Little Pigeon River—actually a turbulent mountain stream.

Tours

Great Smoky Mountains Railroad. The historic rail line that snakes through the woodlands of North Carolina dates from the 1840s. Passengers ride in restored vintage coaches, club cars, dining cars, and (for the truly adventurous) open cars ideal for photographing the dramatic scenery. Gourmet, Santa, and Mystery rides are offered with the seasons. Fees are $28–$65 and up, and trips last from 2 to 6½ hours. | 800/882–1061 or 865/453–0734 | www.gsmr.com.

Smoky Mountain Tour Connection. In Pigeon Forge, Smoky Mountain Tour offers guided treks through East Tennessee back roads, the Smoky Mountains, and to major East Tennessee sites. | 800/882–1061.

Visitor Information

Great Smoky Mountains National Park Headquarters | 107 Park Headquarters Rd., Gatlinburg, TN 37738 | 865/436–1230 | www.nps.gov/grsm.

Cherokee Visitors Center | U.S. 441 Business | 828/497–9195 or 800/438–1601 | www.cherokee-nc.com.

Gatlinburg Chamber of Commerce | Box 527, Gatlinburg 37738 | 800/822–1998 | www.gatlinburg-tennessee.com.

Smoky Mountain Host of NC | 4437 Georgia Rd., Franklin 28734 | 828/369–9606 or 800/432–4678 | www.visitsmokies.org.

Arriving and Departing

BY AIR

Airports

Asheville Regional Airport (AVL). Approximately an hour's drive from Cherokee, AVL is served by Midway Connections, Atlantic Southeast Airlines, ComAir, and US Airways. | 828/684–2226 | www.ashevilleregionalairport.com.

McGhee Tyson Airport (TYS). TYS is in Tennessee, about an hour away from Gatlinburg. | 865/970–2773 | www.tys.org.

Airport Transportation

All major rental car companies operate at both airports.

BY BUS

Greyhound/Carolina Trailways serves Asheville and Knoxville.

BY CAR

In Tennessee, if you are coming from the east (I–81), take I–40 to Exit 407 (Sevierville) to TN Route 66 south and continue to U.S. 441 south. Follow U.S. 441 to the park. From I–40 in Knoxville, take Exit 386B onto Highway 129 south (Alcoa/Maryville). At Maryville, travel on U.S. 321 north through Townsend and continue on TN Highway 73 to the park.

In North Carolina, from I–40, take Route 19 west through the Maggie Valley, where you'll pick up U.S. 441 north at Cherokee. Follow U.S. 441 north into the park.

Getting Around

BY CAR

There are more than 270 mi of paved and gravel roads winding throughout the ½ million acres of the national park. Do remember that you are not going to go fast. Most roads, though well maintained, are narrow and steep. The top speed limit is 30 mph. When you are going downhill, you'll want to shift to a lower gear in order to save wear and tear your brakes. If you have an automatic transmission, use L or 2. Also allow plenty of distance between you and the car in front of you. And be aware that wildlife can and will wander onto the roadways. Be especially watchful for deer and elk during the fall mating season. Roads are open year-round, but some sections may be closed in the winter if ice and/or snow make them unsafe.

Arkansas

Revised and Updated by Ruth Mitchell

HOT SPRINGS AND THE OZARKS

Midway between the Appalachians and the Great Plains lie the velvety hills of Arkansas, a land of simple pleasures where crooked highways wind their way through peaceful mountain towns. One such settlement is Hot Springs, which grew up almost a century ago around a series of legendary geothermal springs revered by Native Americans and later by European settlers for the water's medicinal powers. Congress established Hot Springs Reservation in 1832, which makes it the oldest park currently in the National Park system—40 years older than Yellowstone National Park. Casino gambling flourished during the town's heyday in the 1910s and '20s, drawing the likes of Al Capone, Andrew Carnegie, Jack Dempsey, and Babe Ruth. Today, the gambling is limited to horse racing at Oaklawn Park, but bathers still come by the thousands to enjoy the park and its history. A multitude of attractions, the Ouachita National Forest, and five area lakes make this a popular tourist destination.

No matter what road you take north to get to Eureka Springs in the Ozarks, you'll find the vistas and scenery stunning. Folded inside of wooded ridges, this charming Victorian town seems to have been overlooked by time. You'll find scores of gingerbread houses tucked away on shady back streets, but there's more than an authentic historic experience here. The shopping is rich and varied, with lots of local artists whose galleries and shops line serpentine Spring Street.

Exploring

Hot Springs National Park

The ancient forests and rivers of the quartz-rich Ouachita (pronounced *wash*-i-taw) Mountains cradle Hot Springs, where 47 thermal springs were encountered by Spanish explorer Hernando de Soto in 1541. It was known as "the Valley of the Vapors" by Native Americans and later nicknamed "the Spa City."

The national park covers about 5,500 acres in and near the town of Hot Springs. Its heart is Bathhouse Row on Central Avenue, composed of eight turn-of-the-20th-century spa buildings with two open thermal springs behind Maurice Bathhouse. The visitor center in the Fordyce Bathhouse contains exhibits showing the spa town's

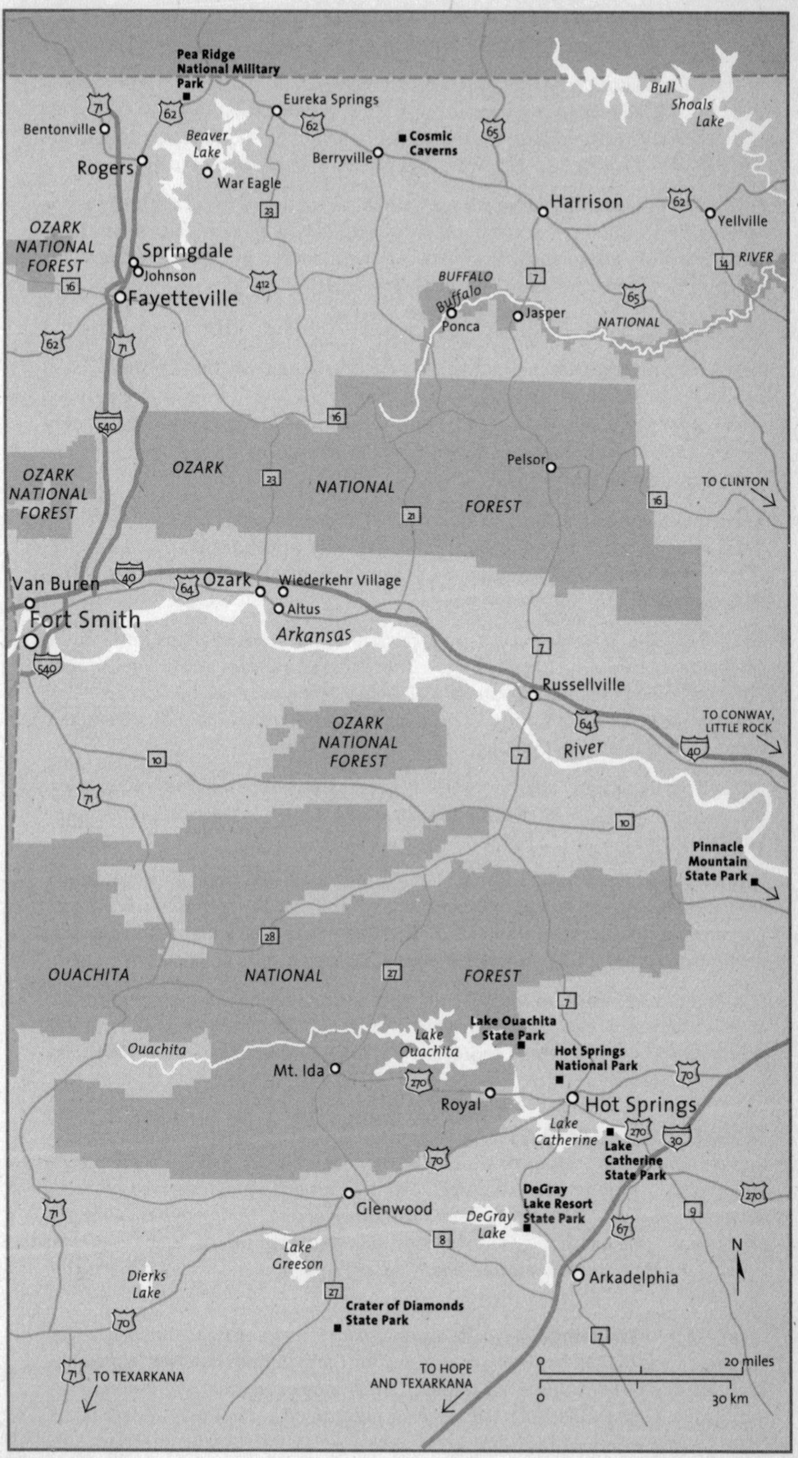
Pea Ridge National Military Park
Eureka Springs
Bull Shoals Lake
Bentonville
Beaver Lake
Cosmic Caverns
Berryville
Rogers
War Eagle
Harrison
Yellville
OZARK NATIONAL FOREST
Springdale
Johnson
Fayetteville
BUFFALO
Buffalo
RIVER
Ponca
Jasper
NATIONAL
OZARK
NATIONAL
FOREST
Pelsor
TO CLINTON
Van Buren
Ozark
Wiederkehr Village
Altus
Fort Smith
Arkansas
Russellville
TO CONWAY, LITTLE ROCK
River
Pinnacle Mountain State Park
OUACHITA
NATIONAL
FOREST
Lake Ouachita State Park
Ouachita
Lake Ouachita
Mt. Ida
Hot Springs National Park
Royal
Hot Springs
Lake Catherine
Lake Catherine State Park
Glenwood
DeGray Lake Resort State Park
DeGray Lake
Lake Greeson
Dierks Lake
Arkadelphia
Crater of Diamonds State Park
TO TEXARKANA
TO HOPE AND TEXARKANA
N
0
20 miles
0
30 km

history. The park also has a campground, scenic drives, 30 mi of hiking trails, a hot-water cascade, and picnic areas in mountains and gorges surrounding the town.

★ **Buckstaff Bathhouse.** A 1912 National Historic Landmark, Buckstaff is one of only six hotels and spas still providing old-fashioned mineral baths. | 509 Central Ave. | 501/623–2308 | www.buckstaffbaths.com | Thermal mineral baths $16.50, massage $18 | Mar.–Nov., Mon.–Sat. 7–11:45 and 1:30–3; Dec.–Feb., weekdays 7–11:45 and 1:30–3, Sat. 7–11:45.

★ **Fordyce Bathhouse.** The fully restored bathhouse continues its legacy today as the national park's visitor center and museum; stained-glass windows and an ornate fountain grace the interior along with original facilities. There's also a bookstore and an orientation film. | 369 Central Ave. | 501/624–3383 | Free | Daily 9–5.

Hot Springs

Within the historic district, which you can easily walk, you will find a host of tourist activities, art galleries, crafts shops, and antique stores. Hot Springs is the boyhood home of former U.S. President Bill Clinton. If you love water and beautiful scenery, there are five crystal-clear lakes nearby. Enjoy a white-water trip, or go canoeing and fishing on area rivers.

Arkansas Alligator Farm and Petting Zoo. See hundreds of alligators, some 10 ft long, plus deer, pygmy goats, llamas, lambs, and ostriches, at this popular (and the city's oldest) museum. | 847 Whittington Ave. | 501/623–6172 or 800/750–7891 | hotspringsusa.com/gatorfarm | $4 | Daily 9:30–5.

★ **Garvan Woodland Gardens.** On a 210-acre peninsula on Lake Hamilton, this impressive botanical garden has architecturally distinguished pavilions and bridges, in addition to cascading streams and waterfalls. The whole family will enjoy the ADA-accessible sights. Follow the signs from the 270 Bypass. | 550 Arkridge Rd. | 800/366–4664 | www.garvangardens.org | $7 | Daily.

Hot Springs Mountain Tower. Enjoy the breeze and the sights from the famous tower that overlooks 140 mi of parkland and mountains. | Fountain St. and Hot Springs Mountain Dr. | 501/623–6035 | $4 | Daily.

★ **Magic Springs and Crystal Falls.** A combination theme and water park, this venue, with attractions ranging from Dr. Dean's Rocket Machine to the Crystal Cove Wave pool, will provide family entertainment all day long. | 1701 Hwy. 70 E | 501/624–0100 | www.magicsprings.com | $28.96 | Summer, daily; spring and fall, weekends.

★ **Mid-America Science Museum.** Explore science and nature through interactive exhibits at the Mid-America Science Museum, which is affiliated with the Smithsonian. | 500 Mid-America Blvd. | 501/767–3461 or 800/632–0583 | www.direclynx.net/~masm | $6 | Tues.–Sun. 10–5.

Nearby Attractions

★ **Crater of Diamonds State Park.** The only diamond mine in North America offers a rare opportunity to hunt for diamonds and other precious and semiprecious stones. Keep what you find; digging tools are for rent. There's a visitor center with exhibits, campsites, picnic areas, a café, gift shop, 2½ mi of hiking trails, interpretive programs, and even trout fishing. | 209 State Park Rd., Murfreesboro | 870/285–3113 | www.arkansasstateparks.com | $5 | Daily.

Lake Catherine State Park. Stay in the historic, modernized, and fully equipped housekeeping cabins built by the Civilian Conservation Corps during the Great Depression. There are also RV hook-ups, tent camping, rental camp equipment, swimming, boating, fishing, a store and seasonal restaurant, playground, picnic areas, and pavilions. | 1200 Catherine Park Rd. | 501/844–4176 | www.arkansasstateparks.com | Free | Daily.

Lake Ouachita State Park. This is the largest man-made lake in the state and one of the prettiest. You can swim, ski, scuba dive, rent a boat, fish, hike trails, and take part in interpretive programs. Fully equipped housekeeping cabins, RV and tent campsites, picnic areas, a marina with boat rentals and supplies, a store, and a snack bar are also available. | 5451 Mountain Pine Rd., Mountain Pine | 501/767–9366 | www.arkansasstateparks.com | Free | Daily.

Ouachita National Forest. With 1.6 million acres, this national forest has many hiking trails, including the 223-mi-long Ouachita National Recreation Trail, which runs from Talimina, Oklahoma, to Pinnacle Mountain State Park near Little Rock. You can canoe, fish, and go white-water rafting on the rivers. There are picnic sites; mountain-bike, ATV, and horseback-riding trails; as well as scenic drives. Call for directions from Hot Springs. | 501/321–5202 | www.fs.fed.us | Free | Daily.

Scenic Highway 7. Widely known as one of the 10 most beautiful drives in the U.S., Highway 7 leads north from Hot Springs toward Eureka Springs, through the beautiful Ouachita and Ozark mountains to Harrison, joining Highway 62 to Eureka Springs and Highway 65 to Branson, Missouri.

Eureka Springs

Eureka Springs has been a tourist town since its earliest days as a Victorian-era spa. Shady streets zigzag up the sides of Ozark hollows, revealing old-fashioned small-town homes, fences of limestone walls, lush gardens, and fern-lined springs.

Enjoy the scenic mountain drives, visit colorful caverns, or take part in outdoor activities. The town's schedule is packed with music, crafts and other shows, festivals, and events, while shoppers enjoy the many arts, crafts, antiques, galleries, boutiques, and gift shops available.

★ **Eureka Springs Gardens.** The magnificent Blue Spring is the focal point upon which a beautiful 33-acre botanical garden has been built. The Gardens are on Scenic Highway, 5½ mi from Highway 62 west. | 479/253–9256 | $6.75 | Apr.–Oct., 9–6; Nov.–Mar., 9–5.

Eureka Springs Historical Museum. Learn about the colorful past and people of this Victorian village through artifacts, photos, and furnishings. From Highway 62, turn onto Highway 23 north. The museum is the first three-story stone building on the left. | 95 S. Main St. | 479/253–9417 | $2.50 | Mon.–Sat. 9:30–4, Sun. 11–4.

Eureka Springs Model Railroad Co. Delight in the miniature world of toy trains and other nostalgic toys. On display is one of the world's largest exhibits of Marklin model trains. | 127 Spring St. | 479/253–2525 or 866/507–6665 | www.railroadtrain.com | Deli and store 8:30–5:30; tours at 10 AM.

Quigley's Castle. One of the curiosities of the Ozarks, this unusual home was begun in 1943 and took two decades to complete. The owner's extensive rock collection was used as a construction material. Bare earth borders on the first floor are planted with tropical plants that grow up into the second story. Fossil, butterfly, crystal, arrowhead, and glassware collections have to be seen to be believed. | 4 mi south of town on Hwy. 23 | No phone | www.quigleyscastle.com | $5.50 | Apr.–Oct., Mon.–Wed. and Fri.–Sat. 8:30–5.

★ **Thorncrown Chapel.** The stunning architecture of this 48-ft-tall glass chapel is synergistic with its woodland setting. The American Institute of Architects voted the chapel one of the top 10 buildings of the 20th century. The chapel is about 3 mi west of downtown. | 12968 Hwy. 62 W | 479/253–7401 | www.thorncrown.com | Donations only | Apr.–Nov., 9–5; Mar.–Dec., 11–4. Call for a schedule of services.

★ **Turpentine Creek Wildlife Refuge.** Lions and tigers and bears, oh my! This exceptional shelter and rescue for lions, tigers, and other large cats in distress from across the United

States is located on 450 acres. It's 7 mi outside of town on Highway 23. | 239 Turpentine Creek La. | 479/253–5841 | www.turpentinecreek.org | $10 | Daily 9–dusk.

Nearby Attractions

Cosmic Cavern. No one has ever discovered the bottom of the Ozarks' largest underground lake system. This privately owned cavern is 6 mi northeast of Berryville on Highway 21, halfway between Branson, Missouri, and Eureka Springs. | 6386 Hwy. 21 N, Berryville | 870/749–2298 | $10 | Daily 8–5.

Pea Ridge National Military Park. This is the sight of the largest Civil War battle west of the Mississippi River. A 7-mi self-guided tour leads visitors around its 4,300 acres. The visitor center includes a museum, an informational film, and a bookstore. Pea Ridge Military Park is 8 mi east of Rogers. | 15930 Hwy. 62 W, Garfield | 479/451–8122 | www.nps.gov/peri | $2 per person or $4 per vehicle | Daily.

Dining

Although traditional pork barbecue is widespread, Cajun and Creole foods are prevalent as well as country cooking—chicken or beef served with vegetables, gravy, and corn bread, often with fruit cobbler for dessert.

Hot Springs

The Brick House. American. Tucked inside a historic structure at the end of Bathhouse Row, this cozy place serves up hearty steaks, burgers, sandwiches, and salads. The prime-rib sandwich is delectable. | 80 Central Ave. | 501/321–2926 | Closed Sun. | $6–$20 | AE, MC, V.

Cajun Boilers. Cajun. At this casual place on the shore of busy Lake Hamilton, dock space is provided along with the food. Eat like a real Cajun with such options as crawfish pie, étouffée, and other seafood favorites. | 2806 Albert Pike Hwy. | 501/767–5695 | Closed Sun.–Mon. No lunch | $6–$27 | AE, D, DC, MC, V.

Grannie's Kitchen. American. Everyone enjoys Grannie's home-cookin' specials like fried chicken, chicken fried steak, and white beans and ham. All dinners come with three vegetables, hot rolls, or corn bread. | 362 Central Ave. | 501/624–6183 | $5–$10 | D, MC, V.

La Hacienda. Mexican. This festive restaurant with its fabrics hung from the ceiling and brightly painted chairs has a full menu of Mexican favorites. Try the *carne asada a la diabla con queso*—beef sirloin or chicken grilled with salsa, chorizo, and cheese. The white cheese dip is outstanding. | 4723 Central Ave. | 501/525–8203 | $8–$16 | AE, D, MC, V.

★ **McClard's Bar-B-Q.** Barbecue. Nothing's changed since the 1940s at this sparkling-clean stucco building, where you nearly always have to wait for a seat. But the waits are short, as veteran servers speed orders of smoked meat, hot tamales, shakes, fries, and more to happy diners. Everything from beans to slaw to fries is homemade, and the place is known for barbecue ribs. | 505 Albert Pike | 501/624–9586 | Closed Sun.–Mon. | $10–$15 | No credit cards.

Eureka Springs

C C Cinnamon. American. This is a great place to people-watch. Sit on the outdoor deck overlooking downtown Eureka and munch on cinnamon rolls or cool off with a cream cone. At lunch there are a variety of sandwiches on homemade bread. | 12½ S. Main St. | 479/253–8004 | Closed Jan.–Feb. and Sun. No dinner | $3–$6 | No credit cards.

★ **Ermilio's Italian Home Cooking.** Italian. One of the best Italian restaurants in the area, Ermilio's is warm and cozy, and the staff is friendly. Sink your chops into the amazing shrimp Provençal or choose from 10 sauces and eight different pastas. Chicken marsala and filet mignon are favorites as well. | 26 White St., 72632 | 479/253–8806 | No lunch | $8–$22 | MC, V.

Grandma's Beans & Cornbread. Southern. This country-style home-cooking restaurant sits next to the Pine Mountain Jamboree. As the name suggests, the highlight of the menu is beans and corn bread, also served with cobblers and soups. | 200 Village Cir. | 479/253–6561 | Closed Sun. | $3–$4 | No credit cards.

Mud Street Café. American. In the heart of town, down just one flight of stairs, this dining room has a turn-of-the-20th-century oak bar with beveled mirrors as its centerpiece. There's local art on the walls, oak tables, and colorful hand-painted chairs. The excellent food—wraps, quiche, and burgers—is served in copious portions. Be sure to order a coffee or dessert, too. | 22 S. Main St. | 479/253–6732 | www.mudstreetcafe.com | Closed Wed. No dinner. | $5–$8 | AE, D, MC, V.

Myrtie Mae's. American. This place has been around since the 1920s, and it is still serving up Myrtie's recipes. Enjoy the favorites, such as strip steak, rainbow trout, red snapper, barbecue breast of chicken, and veal cutlet. You can take in a view of the Ozark valley while you eat. | 207 W. Van Buren St. | 479/253–9768 | $7–$15 | AE, D, MC, V.

Pancake's Family Restaurant. Southern. Breakfast is served anytime, and aren't you glad. Try the breakfast bar for $4.99. You won't get bored looking around, either. The restaurant resembles an old Studebaker dealership and is filled with antique toys, airplanes hanging from the ceiling, and pictures of the famous car. | Hwy. 62 E, 72632 | 479/253–6015 | Closed Jan.–Feb. No dinner Mar.–Apr. or Nov.–Dec.; closed Wed. and Sun. night. | $7–$9 | D, MC, V.

Sparky's Roadhouse Café. American. Enjoy the funky knickknacks while you feast on specialty sandwiches, like spicy sausage grilled with sautéed bell peppers and onions, or enjoy hefty burgers, like the guacamole burger. An abundance of creative sides and starters includes Cuban black beans or French goat cheese. The chicken and goat cheese quesadillas melt in your mouth. | 41 Van Buren St. | 479/253–6001 | Closed Sun. | $4–$15 | D, MC, V.

Lodging

Hot Springs

Arlington Resort Hotel and Spa. If you wish to "take the cure," you can do it in the mineral baths at this landmark with views of Hot Springs National Park. 3 restaurants, cable TV, driving range, putting green, tennis courts, 2 pools, exercise equipment, hair salon, hot tub, massage, spa, bar, laundry facilities, business services. | 239 Central Ave., 71901 | 501/623–7771; 800/643–1502 reservations (outside Arkansas) | fax 501/623–2243 | www.arlingtonhotel.com | 484 rooms | $88–$118 | AE, DC, MC, V.

The Austin Hotel and Convention Center. You'll have a hard time missing this hotel, which towers over downtown Hot Springs. The Maxwell Blade Magic Show, music at the Bathhouse Show, and the town's famous mineral water baths are each about two blocks away. Restaurant, cable TV, indoor-outdoor pool, hot tub, spa, bar, business services. | 305 Malvern Ave., 71901 | 501/623–6600 | fax 501/624–7160 | www.theaustinhotel.com | 200 rooms | $79–$89 | AE, D, DC, MC, V.

Clarion Resort on the Lake. Enjoy water sports, scenic views, and accessibility to area attractions. Restaurant, some refrigerators, cable TV, tennis courts, pool, boating, bar, playground, laundry facilities, business services, some pets allowed. | 4813 Central Ave., 71913 | 501/525–1391 or 800/432–5145 | fax 501/525–0813 | www.clariononthelake.com | 151 rooms | $79.95–$99.95 | AE, D, MC, V.

Eureka Springs

Country Mountain Inn. On the edge of town, this comfortable inn provides a Continental breakfast in an antiques-filled, lodge-style great room. Kids will enjoy the playground while mom and dad kick back in comfortable rooms. Picnic area, cable TV, pool, playground | 4112 E. Van Buren St. (Hwy. 62 E) | 800/626–7120 or 479253–7120 | www.countrymountaininn.com | 33 rooms | $99 | D, MC, V.

Dinner Bell Ranch and Resort. Horseback riding, hayrides, and chuck-wagon dinners are some of the activities you can enjoy while staying in modern, themed cabins. Pets are welcome to stay, too, and can even participate on the trail rides if well behaved. Rates quoted are for two; extra guests are $10 each. In-room hot tubs, kitchens, cable TV, some pets allowed; no smoking | Rockhouse Road, Rte. 1 (Box 543, 72632) | 800/684–3324 | www.eureka-net.com/dinnerbell | 4 cabins | $139–$149 | D, MC, V.

Domestic Tranquility. Just outside of town, you'll find attractively decorated Ozark cabins set on several wooded acres where the kids can stretch their legs. Pet the ponies and feed the chickens and rabbits. Rates quoted for two; extra guests are $10 each. In-room hot tubs, kitchens, cable TV, some pets allowed | 21031 Hwy. 62 W, 72632 | 479/253–8223 | www.domestictranquility.com | 4 cabins (multiple occupancy) | $100 D, MC, V.

5 OJO Inn. In a town filled with ornate Victorian B&Bs, this lovely inn does not shy away from guests with older children, despite the presence of lots of beautiful antiques. Common areas include books and games for kids as well. An extraordinary gourmet breakfast is served every day at 9 AM. Some in-room hot tubs, refrigerators, cable TV; no smoking | 10 rooms | 5 Ojo St. | 800/656–6734 | www.5ojo.com | $85–$139 | MC, V.

Camping

Hot Springs

DeGray Resort State Park. Just 20 mi south of Hot Springs on Route 7 is a 14,000-acre lake. There is a 96-room lodge, a marina with boat rentals, waterskiing, a public golf course, and hiking. Bathrooms, partial hook-ups (electric and water), dump station, showers, picnic tables, barbecue areas, swimming (lake) | 113 sites | Rte. 3 (Box 490, Bismarck 71929) | 501/865–2851 | www.degray.com | $16.

Hot Springs National Park. The only campground in the national park is in scenic Gulpha Gorge, 2 mi from downtown. Flush toilets, dump station, drinking water, grills, picnic tables, public telephone | 43 sites | Off Rte. 70B | 501/624–3383 | $10 | Reservations not accepted | No credit cards.

Eureka Springs

Hidden Cove RV & Cabins. On the shores of beautiful Beaver Lake, this shady campground has a boat-launch ramp as well as a fully air-conditioned and heated shower house. There's country music around the campfire. Full hook-ups, showers, fire pits, picnic tables, camping rooms, tent camping, cabins. | 15 full hook-ups | 709 C.R. 1089 | 479/253–2939 | $19.95 tent sites, $21.95 RV sites.

Lake Leatherwood Park. With 1,600 acres, this municipal park is the second largest of its kind in the United States. A 100-acre, spring-fed lake provides the perfect setting for lots of recreational activities. The park offers boat rental, hiking trails, fishing, and cabins. The historic rest rooms, built by the WPA, are only open in season. Flush toilets, full hook-ups, partial hook-ups (electric and water), dump station, drinking water, showers, fire pits, picnic tables, electricity, general store, playground, swimming (lake)

| 4 hook-ups, 23 tent sites; 4 cabins | 2 mi west of Eureka Springs on Hwy. 62 | 479/253-8624 | $12–$20 hook-ups, $10–$12 tent sites; $70–$80 cabins | MC, V | Mar.–Nov.

Shopping

Both Hot Springs and Eureka Springs offer diverse and quality shopping in the Historic Districts. Art galleries, fine clothing, antiques, as well as crafts and foods of the region await. In Hot Springs you will also find a mall and even some outlet stores along Route 7. In Hot Springs rock shops have items unique to the region, while in Eureka there are crafts indigenous to the Ozarks, and good values on handmade pottery, quilts, and locally created art can be found in both towns.

Sports and Outdoor Activities

Canoeing

Arkansas is well known for its scenic rivers, which provide canoeing enthusiasts with a wide range of experience-level streams. Most rivers are at their prime for canoeing in spring and early summer. The state tourism department (www.arkansas.com) distributes a comprehensive floater's guide to Arkansas with all the information you will need.

★ **Buffalo National River.** Imposing limestone bluffs and pristine, free-flowing water make this river—which in 1972 became the first federally-protected waterway—a popular float trip. Along the way lie historic sites—hollows, caves, and trails used by Native Americans, pioneers, Civil War soldiers, and outlaws. Elk herds have also been successfully reintroduced to the area. There are outfitters near almost every access point as well as campsites, rental cabins, motels, guest ranches, and commercial stables. | 870/741-5443 | www.nps.gov/buff.

Kings River. This scenic, gentle canoe trip generally takes four to eight hours. Springtime is considered best for a float. This scenic river winds through overhanging hardwood forests and not only provides a good ride, but outdoor enthusiasts will enjoy spotting some of the local flora and fauna. Deer, beaver, and raccoon are plentiful, and ferns, wild azaleas, and umbrella magnolias abound.

Buffalo Camping and Canoeing. This full-service canoe and shuttle service is in Gilbert. | 479/439-2888 | www.gilbertstore.com.

Eureka Springs Outfitters. Canoes, kayaks, bikes, snorkels, and fins are available for rent. | 8190 Hwy. 221 S | 479/253-2346 or 888/811-3591 | www.eureka-net.com/adventure/outfitters.

Fishing

Area lakes harbor largemouth and smallmouth bass, bream, and catfish. There are trout streams in the Ozark National Forest not far from Eureka Springs.

Arkansas Game and Fish Commission. Contact the Game and Fish Commission for fishing guides. | 2 Natural Resources Dr., Little Rock 72205 | 501/223-6300 | www.agfc.state.ar.us.

Hiking

Arkansas has well-marked trails galore, a good many of them concentrated around the Buffalo National River and in the Ouachita and Ozark national forests.

Ozark National Forest. More than 1 million acres of national forest cover northwestern Arkansas. The forest offers three spectacular multiple-use trails for horseback riding, mountain biking, hiking, and all-terrain vehicles. | 479/968-2354 | www.fs.fed.us/oonf/ozark.

Horseback Riding

There are a number of riding stables in both Hot Springs and Eureka Springs. Both areas offer interesting trail rides along streams and wooded acreage.

Dinner Bell Ranch. Although a number of different trail rides are available at this resort in Eureka Springs, you might find that one of the most fun is the "Saddle and Paddle." You ride one hour on horseback to the King's River, where you will trade your horse for a canoe and float for 7 mi to Trigger Gap. Your car awaits you at the end of the trip. Bring your swim suit, fishing gear, and camera. | Rockhouse Rd. (Rte. 1, Box 543) | 479/253–2900 or 800/684–3324 | www.eureka-net.com/dinnerbell.

Rock Hounding

The Hot Springs area was well known to Native American tribes, who would trade for the coveted "honing" stones. There are also large crystal deposits, and of course nearby is the only diamond mine in North America. There are a number of crystal mines where families can dig for crystals and other semiprecious stones.

Coleman Mines. This family-owned operation, just 14 mi north of Hot Springs in Jessieville, is one of the oldest in the area. | 501/984–5453 | www.colemanquartz.com.

Water Sports

Swimming is good at Buffalo Point on the Buffalo River, south of Yellville on Route 14. Boats can be rented for waterskiing on Lake Hamilton, Lake Ouachita, and DeGray Lake.

Kahuna Bay. Rent party barges, ski boats, or Jet-Skis,or go parasailing. | 4904 Central Hot Springs | 501/520–5700.

Essential Information

When to Go

Temperatures average in the 40s in winter, and summer days can be rather warm, averaging in the 90s at the height of the season. The fall foliage attracts droves of visitors, which drives up rates, especially in Eureka Springs. The busiest time in Hot Springs is racing season (late January–April), when hotel rates jump noticeably.

FESTIVALS AND SEASONAL EVENTS

WINTER

Year-Round: **Hot Springs Gallery Walk.** On the first Friday of every month, enjoy strolling along the beautiful historic district of Hot Springs while viewing the works of resident artists. Music and complimentary refreshments are often provided. | 501/321–2277.

Jan.: **Eagle Watch Weekend on Beaver Lake.** On the last full weekend of the month, the *Belle of the Ozarks* runs eagle-watch cruises that include guides, lectures, and plenty of bald eagles. There are three two-hour cruises a day (11 AM, 1 PM, 3 PM) on this 50-passenger boat, and they sell out quickly. The trips leave from Rockybranch Marina on Beaver Lake near Eureka Springs. | 501/253–6200 or 800/552–3803.

Jan.–Apr.: **Oaklawn Jockey Club Thoroughbred Horse Racing.** Horse racing in Hot Springs is an integral part of the cultural scene in the winter and early spring, with live and simulcast Thoroughbred racing since 1904. Children under 16 are not allowed, however. | 501/623–4411.

SPRING

May: **Eureka Springs May Festival of the Arts.** The month kicks off with the "Art-Rageous" parade and later includes a gallery tour called "White Street Walk," in which local artists open their homes and studios to show their work. You'll find plenty of exhibitions, workshops, special arts events, contests, and other activities along the main drag of this suddenly big small town. You can walk or grab the open-air trolley. | 888/855–7823.

SUMMER

Apr.–Oct.: **The Great Passion Play.** More than 6 million people over the past 34 years have attended this elaborate outdoor drama in Eureka Springs depicting Christ's final week. | 479/253–8559 | www.greatpassionplay.com.

June–July: **Opera in the Ozarks.** Since 1950, an international cast has presented three major productions "in rep" with orchestra at Inspiration Point just outside of Eureka Springs. A new multi-million-dollar facility is planned for the future. Seating is reserved. | 479/253–8595 or 479/253–8737 | www.opera.org.

AUTUMN

Sept.: **Eureka Springs Jazz Festival.** Top-name musicians present world-class music in venues all over town. Some acts are free. | 479/253–6258.

Hot Springs Film Festival. If you're a culture maven, you can feast on American and international films, humanities forums, lectures and question-and-answer periods following the films, visiting Academy Award–winning filmmakers, scholars, and celebrities. | 501/321–4747.

Bargains

Everyone likes a bargain. In Hot Springs one of the best values around is the bath and massage package because the rates are regulated by the National Park Service (☞ Hot Springs National Park). Arkansas also provides regional brochures through the State Park system. Available at any tourist information center, these brochures contain discounts on area attractions.

Tours

Belle of the Ozarks. Take an excursion along 12 mi of Beaver Lake shoreline, and you'll get some sense of the history of the lake, the Ozarks, and local Native American heritage. Plus there's a loop around a pristine 200-acre wildlife game-preserve island. The trip takes 75 minutes, and admission is $14. Open May–October, Thursday–Sunday. Take Highway 62 west to Highway 187; then Highway 187 to Mundell Road, which ends at Starkey Park. | Starkey Marina off U.S. 62 W | 800/552–3803 or 479/253–6200 | www.estc.net/belle.

★ **Eureka Springs and North Arkansas Railway.** All aboard for a scenic train ride along a stream and through the woods. Enjoy a delicious lunch or dinner with fresh-cut flowers and linen tablecloths. Reservations for meals are suggested. The ride is $9; it's $17.95 for lunch and $26.95 for dinner. Trains run April–October, Monday–Saturday 9–5. The historic depot is on Highway 23 N. | 299 N. Main St. | 479/253–9623 | www.esnarailway.com.

National Park Duck Tours. Take a 90-minute ride on WWII amphibious duck vehicles through downtown Hot Springs and onto Lake Hamilton. The $12 rides are available daily March–November and on winter weekends. | 418 Central Ave. | 501/321–2911 or 800/682–7044 | www.angelfire.com/ar2/nationalparkducks.

Olden Days Carriage Services. What could be better than getting acquainted with Eureka Springs by listening to tidbits of history while riding through town aboard an old-fashioned horse-pulled carriage? Just look for the carriages between Café Santa Fe and Sonny's Pizzeria on North Main Street. The tour is a mere $25 per couple and $40 for two couples. Available daily 'til 10 PM year-round. | N. Main St. | 800/296–2157 or 479/253–1737 | www.oldendayscarriageservices.com.

Visitor Information

Eureka Springs Visitors Bureau | Box 522, 72632 | 479/253–7333 | www.eurekasprings.org. **Hot Springs Convention and Visitors Bureau** | 134 Convention Blvd., 71902 | 800/922–6478 | www.hotsprings.org. **Hot Springs National Park** | 369 Central Ave., 71902 | 501/624–2701 | www.nps.gov/hosp.

Arriving and Departing

BY AIR

Airports

Little Rock National Airport–Adams Field (LIT). Most air traffic into and out of Arkansas goes through this airport. | 501/372–3439 | lrn-airport.com.

Northwest Arkansas Regional Airport (XNA). This regional airport is closer to Eureka Springs. | 472/205–1000 | xna.com.

Airport Transportation

Bus: Airport Shuttle. Daily shuttle service between the Little Rock National Airport–Adams Field and Hot Springs is around $28 per person one-way. | 800/643–1505.

Car: Rental cars are available from Avis, Budget, Hertz, National, and Thrifty at the Northwest Arkansas Regional Airport.

BY BUS

Greyhound Lines runs two buses daily between Little Rock and Hot Springs.

BY CAR

Two major interstate highways cross Arkansas. I–40 runs east and west; I–30 runs diagonally northeast to southwest. I–71 connects to I–40 serving as a link in northwest Arkansas. U.S. 65 is a scenic drive; it also goes through the north section of the state. U.S. 79 and U.S. 65 lead in from Louisiana.

Getting Around

BY CAR

A car is essential for visiting Hot Springs and the Ozarks, although Bathhouse Row in Hot Springs and Eureka Springs' central district are best explored on foot. Find a place in one of the lots in the heart of town to park and walk the historic district. The parking surrounding the Tourist Information Center is free. From the Tourist Information Center on Central Avenue, turn left on Highway 7 for 7 mi out to Lake Hamilton and a plethora of water activities.

In Eureka Springs, traffic can get very congested. Walking or trolley riding is recommended for in-town activities, but you'll need a car for enjoying outlying activities or visiting Beaver Lake.

BY PUBLIC TRANSIT

Trolley

The motorized trolleys that travel the streets of both Hot Springs and Eureka Springs are a great way to see everything, especially on crowded weekends.

Eureka Springs Trolley. Ride up and down the steep hills to shopping, galleries, and other attractions on five different routes. Tickets are available at the downtown depot, lodgings, and many shops for $3.50. Trolleys run from March through December from 9 to 6. | 137A W. Van Buren St., 72632 | 479/253–9572 | www.cityofeurekasprings.org.

Hot Springs Trolley. These free public trolleys run every 20 minutes during the summer season. Park for free at the new Transportation Plaza on Broadway two blocks south of Bathhouse Row and ride the trolley to virtually any destination in the Historic Downtown district. There are easily spotted regular trolley stops throughout the downtown area for your convenience. | 501/321–2006.

Nevada

Revised and Updated by Mike Weatherford

LAS VEGAS

For 50 years, up until the early 1990s, the name Las Vegas was synonymous with adult entertainment, and even that revolving mostly around gambling. But then came a sudden, drastic period of reinvention. As modest '50s-era casinos were demolished to make way for towering "mega-resorts," the city attempted to remake itself as a family destination, adding roller coasters, animal attractions, and arcades. The makeover didn't really take, as evidenced by a recent explosion in topless shows and after-hours nightclubs. But in the big picture, Las Vegas seems to have arrived at a happy medium. In the new century it's neither theme park nor Sin City but rather a resort destination. It appeals to both the gambler and the non-gambling spouse, the conventioneer as well as the weekend warrior, the family seeking a cheap hub for access to the region's national parks and the family that wouldn't mind spending a full week on the Strip.

Exploring

The Strip, the 3½-mi stretch of Las Vegas Boulevard South between Russell Road and Sahara Avenue, is the heart of Las Vegas. Its soul is the downtown area north of the Strip, whose core is Fremont Street. By exploring these two areas, you'll experience both the commercial lifeblood and pioneer spirit of this most flamboyant of American cities.

South Strip

Excalibur Hotel and Casino. This 1990 creation of the Mandalay Resort Group might be described as "King Arthur does Las Vegas." The over-the-top medieval theme is continued inside, with staff members in costume and such place-names as the Court Jester's Stage and Sir Galahad's Prime Rib House. | 3850 Las Vegas Blvd. S | 702/597–7777 or 800/937–7777 | www.excaliburlasvegas.com.

Fantasy Faire, a midway of carnival games, has six different movie and motion simulators, including a virtual roller coaster. | Film Rides $4 each | Daily 10–10.

Upstairs from the casino is the **Renaissance Village,** which has shops, theme restaurants, a huge buffet, and an open stage where jugglers, puppeteers, and magicians perform.

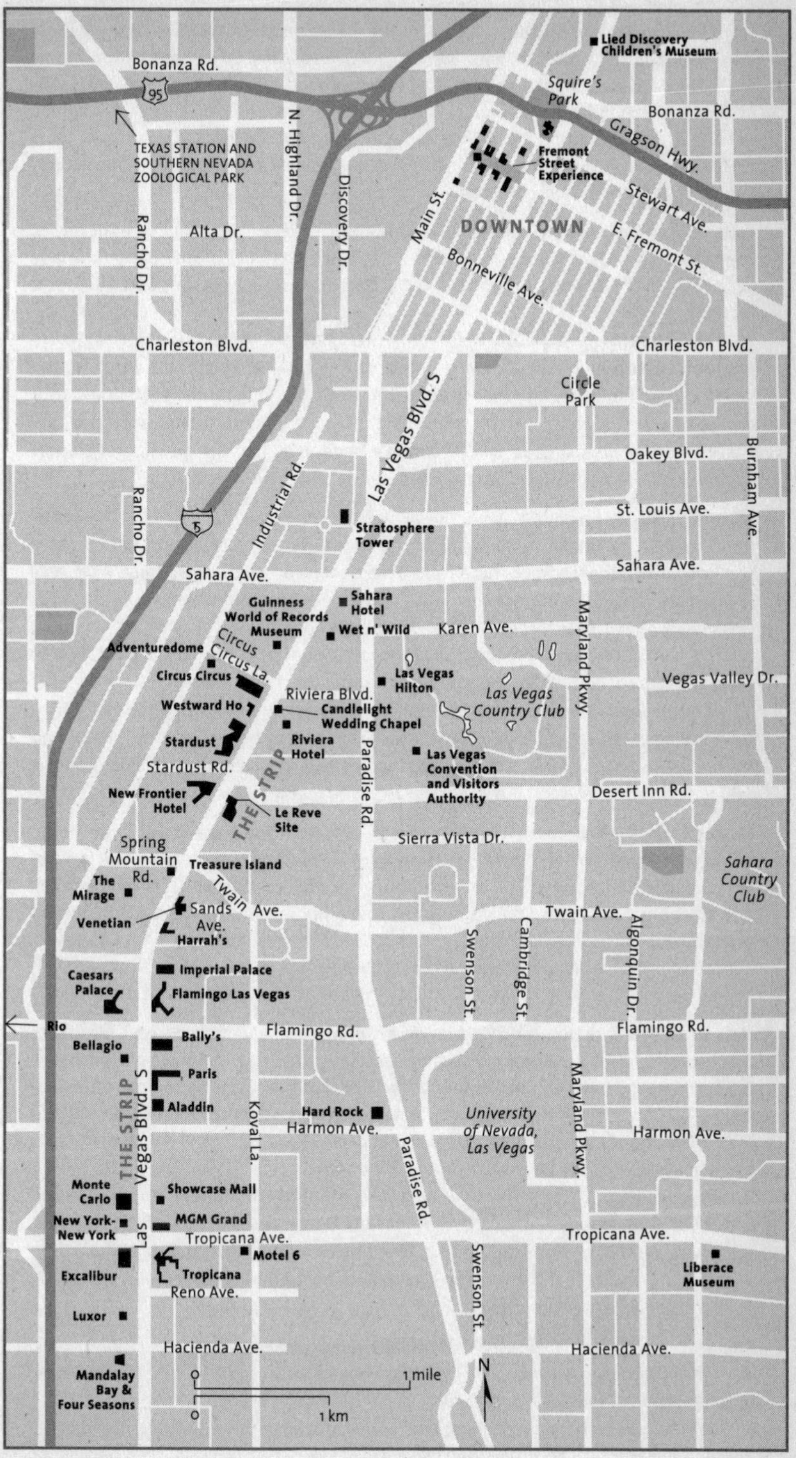

Bonanza Rd.
95
TEXAS STATION AND SOUTHERN NEVADA ZOOLOGICAL PARK
N. Highland Dr.
Discovery Dr.
Lied Discovery Children's Museum
Squire's Park
Bonanza Rd.
Gragson Hwy.
Fremont Street Experience
Stewart Ave.
Main St.
DOWNTOWN
E. Fremont St.
Bonneville Ave.
Alta Dr.
Rancho Dr.
Charleston Blvd.
Charleston Blvd.
Las Vegas Blvd. S
Circle Park
Oakey Blvd.
Burnham Ave.
Industrial Rd.
St. Louis Ave.
15
Rancho Dr.
Stratosphere Tower
Sahara Ave.
Sahara Ave.
Guinness World of Records Museum
Sahara Hotel
Wet n' Wild
Karen Ave.
Maryland Pkwy.
Adventuredome
Circus Circus La.
Circus Circus
Las Vegas Hilton
Vegas Valley Dr.
Riviera Blvd.
Las Vegas Country Club
Westward Ho
Candlelight Wedding Chapel
Stardust
Riviera Hotel
Paradise Rd.
Las Vegas Convention and Visitors Authority
Stardust Rd.
New Frontier Hotel
THE STRIP
Le Reve Site
Desert Inn Rd.
Sierra Vista Dr.
Spring Mountain Rd.
Treasure Island
Sahara Country Club
The Mirage
Twain Ave.
Sands Ave.
Twain Ave.
Venetian
Harrah's
Swenson St.
Cambridge St.
Algonquin Dr.
Imperial Palace
Caesars Palace
Flamingo Las Vegas
Rio
Flamingo Rd.
Flamingo Rd.
Bellagio
Bally's
Paris
Aladdin
Hard Rock
University of Nevada, Las Vegas
Harmon Ave.
Harmon Ave.
Maryland Pkwy.
Koval La.
THE STRIP
Las Vegas Blvd. S
Paradise Rd.
Monte Carlo
Showcase Mall
New York-New York
MGM Grand
Tropicana Ave.
Tropicana Ave.
Excalibur
Motel 6
Tropicana
Liberace Museum
Reno Ave.
Swenson St.
Luxor
Hacienda Ave.
Hacienda Ave.
Mandalay Bay & Four Seasons
0
1 mile
0
1 km
N

★ **Hard Rock Hotel and Casino.** A haven for the young and hip, the Hard Rock is a high-class rock-and-roll museum, with memorabilia from every rock decade adorning its walls. The Hard Rock is cozy by megaresort standards and a favorite hiding spot for many of the music and film stars of today. The hotel's pool area is a tropical beach–inspired oasis featuring a floating bar, private cabanas, and poolside blackjack. In recent years it's become a favorite filming location for MTV. | 4455 Paradise Rd. | 702/693–5000 or 800/693–7625 | www.hardrockhotel.com.

Luxor Hotel-Casino. In Luxor, the folks at Mandalay Resort Group have built one of the modern wonders of the world—a 36-story black glass and bronze pyramid, made with 13 acres of black glass. | 3900 Las Vegas Blvd. S | 702/262–4000 or 800/288–1000 | www.luxor.com.

The "Passport to Adventure" for the entertainment attractions in the Luxor's **Pharaoh's Pavilion** is all-inclusive—it gets you an IMAX movie; the "Search for the Obelisk" ride film; entry into the reproduction of King Tutankhamen's tomb; and your choice of a virtual roller-coaster ride or the movie *The Great Pharaohs.* Stop by the vast two-story video arcade, too. | Pharaoh's Pavilion attractions $4–$8.95; Passport to Adventure $23.95 | Sun.–Thurs. 9 AM–11 PM, Fri.–Sat. 9 AM–midnight.

★ **Mandalay Bay Resort and Casino.** The 43-story, $950 million Mandalay Bay Resort has 3,700 rooms. The hotel falls on the high side for a typical family budget, but bargains can be found in the summer. There's a 10-acre lagoon complete with a huge wave pool (8-ft waves, roughest waters on the Strip) and a stage for summer concerts. | 3950 Las Vegas Blvd. S | 702/632–7777 or 877/632–7400 | www.mandalaybay.com.

The **House of Blues,** an 1,800-seat theater and a 600-seat restaurant, is also here; the restaurant walls are covered with Louisiana Delta folk art.

At **Shark Reef,** a 105,000-square-ft facility holds some 2 million gallons of seawater housing exotic creatures large and small. The journey begins in temple ruins and makes its way to the bowels of a sunken galleon, where sharks swim below, above, and around the skeleton ship. | Shark Reef $13.95 | Daily 10 AM–11 PM.

MGM Grand. With more than 5,000 rooms, the MGM Grand is the largest hotel in the world, a self-proclaimed "City of Entertainment" sprawling over 112 acres. The front of the property is adorned with a 100,000-pound bronze lion statue that stands 45 ft tall and sits atop a 25-ft pedestal. Inside you'll find a habitat for live lions, a full ½ mi of restaurants, ball rooms, nightclubs, and shops—even a research center for CBS Television, where you can screen potential new shows. | 3799 Las Vegas Blvd. S | 702/891–1111 or 800/929–1111 | www.mgmgrand.com | Lion Habitat free | Lion Habitat daily 11–10.

★ **New York–New York Hotel and Casino.** The exterior of the $460 million, 2,000-plus-room megaresort is a mini-Manhattan skyline, complete with a 150-ft Statue of Liberty. The Big Apple theme continues inside, with an art deco lobby, a casino pit themed after Central Park, a Coney Island–theme arcade, and a food court patterned after Greenwich Village. ESPN Zone is the champion of all sports cafés. | 3790 Las Vegas Blvd. S | 702/740–6969 or 800/693–6763 | www.nynyhotelcasino.com.

Roller-coaster aficionados, take note: the **Manhattan Express** is a real rocker. While being whisked past great views of the faux New York skyline, you climb 15 stories, dive 75 ft, climb then dive 144 ft, do a 360-degree somersault, and do a "heartline twist" that simulates the sensation one gets in a jet doing a barrel roll. | $10 | Daily 10 AM–11 PM (weather permitting).

Showcase Mall. This mall has several specialty shops, a movie theater, and Gameworks, a multi-level young-adult arcade. | 3785 Las Vegas Blvd. S | 702/736–7611 | Sun.–Thurs. 10 AM–midnight, Fri.–Sat. 10 AM–1 AM.

Gameworks is the biggest, most boisterous arcade in town, with more than 300 arcade-style games. | 702/432–4263 | Free entry, $25 per 2 hrs of play.

M&M's World is four stories of fun that will melt in your mouth, not in your hand. The store offers plenty of candy-coated treats (including an Ethel M. Chocolates outlet for more upscale sweet tooths) plus everything from T-shirts to limited-edition lithographs. There's also the M&M Academy, featuring interactive exhibits and a free 3-D movie. | 702/736–7611 | M&M Academy Sun.–Mon. and Thurs. 11–6, Fri.–Sat. 10:40–8.

Center Strip

Aladdin Hotel and Casino. It took Queen Scheherazade 1,001 nights to woo her husband—nearly five months longer than it took to build the $1.4 billion, 2,567-room Aladdin. A 50-ft waterfall cascades down a sandstone cliff fronting the property. Doors off the elevated sidewalk offer a choice of walking into the casino or a shopping mall. | 3667 Las Vegas Blvd. S | 702/736–0111 or 877/333–9474 | www.aladdincasino.com.

The **Desert Passage** is a $300 million complex of 135 shops ensconced in minarets, onion domes, and other Moorish architecture. | 702/866–0703 or 888/800–9474 | www.desertpassage.com.

★ **Bellagio Las Vegas.** The $1.8 billion, 3,000-room Bellagio is one of the most opulent and expensive hotel-casinos ever built. Walking into the lobby, you're confronted with a fantastic and colorful 2,000-square-ft glass sculpture called *Fiori di Como,* by famed artist Dale Chiluly. It's composed of more than 2,000 individually blown glass pieces and cost upward of $10 million. Bellagio has some of the most exclusive and beautiful stores in the world, including Giorgio Armani, Chanel, Gucci, Prada, and Tiffany & Co. Note: no one under 18 is allowed in Bellagio unless staying at the hotel. | 3600 Las Vegas Blvd. S | 702/693–7111 or 888/744–7687 | www.bellagio.com.

A 12,500-square-ft conservatory, the **Bellagio Botanical Gardens** is full of living flowers, shrubs, trees, and other plants.

Stretching 900 ft across Bellagio's lake is a signature outdoor spectacle: the $30 million **Fountains of Bellagio** water ballet, made famous by an appearance in the 2001 remake of *Ocean's Eleven.* More than 1,000 fountain nozzles, 4,500 lights, and 27 million gallons of water combine to dazzle audiences with dancing waters choreographed to popular music. There's a show every 30 minutes from 2 PM to midnight.

The **Gallery of Fine Art** displays rotating exhibits arranged with museums, other galleries, and private collectors. | $15 | Sun.–Thurs. 10–6, Fri.–Sat. 10–9.

Caesars Palace. A 20-ft statue of Caesar greets visitors to this iconic hotel-casino. Two people-movers transport you from the Strip into the hotel-casino complex. Having undergone major expansions in its 35-year history, the complex covers a vast area, including two casinos and numerous restaurants and entertainment venues. | 3570 Las Vegas Blvd. S | 702/733–7900 or 800/223–7277 | www.caesarspalace.com.

The ★**Forum Shops at Caesars** is a shopping mall–entertainment complex designed to resemble an ancient Roman streetscape. It houses roughly 100 retailers and eateries, including Abercrombie & Fitch, Emporio Armani, Gucci, Hugo Boss, Louis Vuitton, Virgin Megastore, FAO Schwartz, Spago, and the Cheesecake Factory. Overhead is a painted sky that changes throughout the day from airy clouds to stunning sunsets to star-studded nights. The mall also has a number of entertainment options, including two pretty astounding animatronic statue shows. There's also the Race for Atlantis, the most sophisticated digital thrill ride in town. | Race for Atlantis $10 | Forum Shops and Race for Atlantis Sun.–Thurs. 10 AM–11 PM, Fri.–Sat. 10 AM–midnight.

Imperial Palace Hotel and Casino. Festooned with carved dragons and wind-chime chandeliers, this casino has a distinctly Asian feel. | 3535 Las Vegas Blvd. S | 702/731–3311 or 800/634–6441 | www.imperialpalace.com.

On the fifth level of the hotel's parking garage (catch the elevator at the back of the casino) is the **Imperial Palace Automobile Museum,** a collection of more than

200 antique, classic, and special-interest vehicles. | $6.95; coupons for free admission usually handed out in front of hotel-casino | Daily 9:30 AM–11:30 PM.

Mirage Hotel and Casino. The signature volcano erupts very 15 minutes from dusk to midnight. Just inside the resort's front entrance is a lush rain forest. Palm trees, cascading waterfalls, meandering lagoons, and exotic tropical flora are housed under a 100-ft-high dome, and a 20,000-gallon aquarium provides a stunning backdrop to the front desk. | 3400 Las Vegas Blvd. S | 702/791–7111 or 800/627–6667 | www.mirage.com.

Behind the Mirage, seven Atlantic bottlenose dolphins live in a 2½-million-gallon saltwater **Dolphin Habitat,** the largest in the world. | Secret Garden and Dolphin Habitat $10; Dolphin Habitat alone $5 on Wed. and daily after 3:30 | Weekdays 11–7, weekends 10–7.

Next to the habitat is the **Secret Garden of Siegfried and Roy,** a palm-shaded sanctuary for the veteran magicians' exotic creatures, including snow-white tigers, white lions, and an Asian elephant. Many of the animals are used in the duo's evening stage spectacular. | Secret Garden and Dolphin Habitat $10 | Mon.–Tues. and Thurs.–Fri. 11–5, weekends 10–5 | Closed Wed.

Paris Las Vegas. This $785 million homage to the City of Lights tries to reproduce all the charm of the French capital. | 3655 Las Vegas Blvd. S | 702/739–4111 or 888/226–5687 | www.parislasvegas.com.

The 50-story **Eiffel Tower,** built almost exactly to a half-size scale, rises above it all; the Eiffel Restaurant is on the 11th floor, and three legs of the tower come right through the casino roof, resting heavily on its floor. A glass elevator ascends to the tower's small observation deck (a small caged catwalk) at the 460-ft level. | $9 | Daily 10 AM–1 AM.

Cobblestone "streets" meander through **Le Boulevard** shopping district, where you can purchase everything from fine jewelry to freshly baked breads and pastries; bread delivery men ride through on bicycles, singing "Alouette" in operatic voices.

Treasure Island Las Vegas. Treasure Island appeals to a younger and more family-oriented clientele than its sister hotel the Mirage. | 3300 Las Vegas Blvd. S | 702/894–7111 or 800/944–7444 | www.treasureisland.com.

The free ★**Treasure Island Pirate Show,** performed six times a night (weather cooperating), is a must-see, one of the top attractions in Las Vegas. The show rages with spectacular pyrotechnics, an impressive sound system, and major stunts. Don't bet on the British; the pirates always score the knockout blow. | Free | Performances begin at 5:30 and run every 90 minutes until 10 (11:30 Fri.–Sat.).

Venetian Resort-Hotel-Casino. This meticulously themed hotel re-creates Italy's most romantic city with reproductions of various Venetian landmarks. | 3355 Las Vegas Blvd. S | 702/733–5000; 702/642–6440 wax museum; 800/494–3556 | www.venetian.com.

The **Grand Canal Shops** is a 90-store mall. Gondolas (ride for $10 per person, same-day reservations usually required) ply the waterway, steered by serenading gondoliers. The canal ends at a colossal reproduction of St. Mark's Square. The complex also includes Warner Bros. Stage 16, a dining, retail, and entertainment complex.

The intimate **Guggenheim-Hermitage Museum** displays masterworks from the Guggenheim and Hermitage collections. | $15 | Daily 9:30–8:30.

Madame Tussaud's Wax Museum features more than 100 wax figures, many celebrating Sin City's past—classic Vegas crooners such as Tom Jones, Frank Sinatra, and Tony Bennett are among those replicated here. | $12.50 | Daily 11–7, 10–10.

North Strip

Circus Circus. Circus Circus opened in 1968, with the then unique idea of appealing to the families. Under the pink-and-white big top, the clowns, trapeze stars, high-wire artists, unicyclists, and aerial dancers perform daily every 30 minutes from 11 AM to midnight. | 2880 Las Vegas Blvd. S | 702/734–0410 or 800/634–3450 | www.circuscircus-lasvegas.com.

Behind the hotel-casino is the **Adventuredome,** a 5-acre indoor amusement park covered by a pink dome. Inside are the world's largest indoor roller coaster (the double-loop, double-corkscrew Canyon Blaster), a flume ride, a laser-tag room, and other rides and games. | Free entry, individual rides $2–$5 or all-day wristbands $16.95 | Mon.–Thurs. 10–6, Fri.–Sat. 10 AM–midnight, Sun. 10–8.

A **carnival midway** has old-time fair games (dime toss, milk can, bushel basket) along with clown-face painting, a video arcade with more than 200 games, fun-house mirrors, corn dogs, and pizza. | Daily 10 AM–midnight.

Las Vegas Hilton. The Hilton is just off the Strip and is adjacent to the Las Vegas Convention Center. | 3000 W. Paradise Rd. | 702/732–5111 or 800/774–1500 | www.lv-hilton.com.

The biggest attraction at the Hilton is **Star Trek: The Experience,** a $70 million museum and interactive theater–motion-simulator ride. During the ride, the audi-

EXCURSIONS WITH THE KIDS

Of the roughly 35 million visitors to Las Vegas each year, 12% are under 21. If you're the parent of one of these too-young-to-gamble tourists, you know that the hotel pool will only occupy them for so long. Fortunately, there's lots for kids to do in Vegas, and any of the following destinations is sure to be a hit.

Las Vegas Natural History Museum. The museum has displays of mammals from Alaska to Africa and has rooms full of sharks (including live ones), birds, dinosaur fossils, and hands-on exhibits. The Young Scientists area has child-oriented interactive displays such as the Dig-A-Fossil area, Rub-A-Dino, a Paleontologist Lab, and a robotic baby dinosaur youngsters can control. | 900 Las Vegas Blvd. N | 702/384–3466 | $5.50 adults, $3 children 4–12 | Daily 9–4.

Lied Discovery Children's Museum. One of the largest children's museums in the nation, at roughly 25,000 square ft, the Lied (pronounced *leed*) contains more than 100 hands-on exhibits covering the sciences, arts, and humanities. In the Desert Discovery area for children age five and under, youngsters are entertained and educated with a number of hands-on interactive displays, including Boulder Mountain, where children don hard hats and mine soft-sculpture boulders in geometric shapes. | 833 Las Vegas Blvd. N | 702/382–3445 | www.ldcm.org | $6 adults, $5 children 1–17 | Tues.–Sun. 10–5.

Mountasia Family Fun Center. This amusement park in Green Valley, a fast-growing suburb in southeastern Las Vegas, has two 18-hole miniature-golf courses, a roller-skating rink, go-carts, bumper boats, and an arcade with 75 video games. | 2050 Olympic Ave., Henderson | 702/454–4386 | $4.50 per ride, fun package $15 (only available on Fri.) | Mon.–Thurs. 3 PM–9 PM, Fri. 3 PM–11, Sat. 11–11, Sun. noon–9.

Zoological-Botanical Park. Five minutes from downtown, you'll find the last family of Barbary apes in the United States, along with chimpanzees, eagles, ostriches, emus, parrots, wallabies, flamingos, endangered cats (including tigers), and every species of venomous reptile native to southern Nevada. One exhibit features species native to Nevada such as coyotes, golden eagles, and deer; an underwater exhibit stars a 7-ft-long alligator named Elvis. | 1775 N. Rancho Dr. | 702/648–5955 | $5.95 | Daily 9–5.

ence is kidnaped by the Klingons and beamed into the 24th century and onto the bridge of the Starship *Enterprise.* | www.startrekexp.com | $24.99 | Daily 11–11.

Sahara Hotel and Casino. The line between old Las Vegas and new is clear at the Sahara. The former Rat Pack haunt—and current host of "The Rat Pack Is Back," a fun impersonator's showcase—manages to encompass both old-school swank and the popular NASCAR Café. | 2535 Las Vegas Blvd. S | 702/737–2111 or 800/634–6666; NASCAR Café 702/737–2750 | www.saharahotelandcasino.com.

Near the NASCAR Café is **Cyber Speedway,** a $15 million virtual-reality race car-driving experience, where 3-D motion-simulator rides make audience members feel as though they're driving on the Las Vegas Motor Speedway or the Las Vegas Strip. | Rides $8 | Weekdays 10–10, weekends 10 AM–11 PM.

Speed–The Ride uses magnetic technology to propel riders through a tunnel, around a loop, and into and out of the casino at speeds of more than 70 mph. Then you do the entire thing again—backward. | Rides $8 | Weekdays 10–10, weekends 10 AM–midnight.

Stratosphere Hotel Tower and Casino. The view from the tower and the thrill rides at the top make it worth the extra effort to get to this hotel-casino, which occupies a sort of no-man's land a few blocks north of the northern end of the Strip. | 2000 Las Vegas Blvd. S | 702/380–7777 or 800/380–7732 | www.stratlv.com.

The tower view has no peer—you'll be looking down at Las Vegas from the top of the tallest ★**observation tower** in the United States, dominating the Las Vegas skyline at 1,149 ft.

High above the Las Vegas Strip are the Stratosphere's two **thrill rides:** Big Shot and the High Roller roller coaster. | Big Shot $11, High Roller $9 (includes tower elevator); both rides and tower $15. | Sun.–Thurs. 10 AM–1 AM, Fri.–Sat. 10 AM–2 AM.

Downtown

If you've never traveled north of the Stratosphere Tower, you're missing a vital piece of Las Vegas. Downtown Las Vegas is where Sin City was born. The street's patron saints, the 50-ft-tall neon cowboy Vegas Vic and his gal Vegas Vickie, still welcome visitors with a sincere "howdy."

At the east end of Fremont Street, Neonopolis opened in summer 2002 as a retail complex aimed at revitalizing downtown. It boasts a collection of unusual neon signs rescued and restored from various parts of the country.

★ **Fremont Street Experience.** Fremont Street has one of Vegas's most spectacular sights—this four-block-long light canopy. In essence the largest electronic sign in the world, the Experience employs 2.1 million lights and a 540,000-watt sound system. Free outdoor concerts on select weekends and street venders now complement the light show. | Fremont St. from Main to 4th St. | 702/678–5600 | www.vegasexperience.com.

Hoover Dam

★ Congress authorized the funding of the $175 million dam in 1928 for two purposes: flood control and the generation of electricity. Named the Civil Engineering Monument of the Millennium by the American Society of Civil Engineers, the dam is 727 ft high (the equivalent of a 70-story building) and 660 ft thick at the base (about the length of two football fields). Construction required 4.4 million cubic yards of concrete—enough to build a two-lane highway from San Francisco to New York. | U.S. 93 east of Boulder City | Bureau of Reclamation 702/293–8000 | www.lc.usbr.gov | Daily 9–5.

Guided tours have been replaced by the **Discovery Tour,** which allows you to see the power-plant generators, the Nevada Intake Tower, the visitor center, the old Exhibit Building, and other vantage points at your own pace. | Discovery Tour $10.

Dining

The Strip

Grand Lux Cafe. American/Casual. The Venetian's 24-hour operation is a member of the same family as the Cheesecake Factory. Grand Lux offers such items as Asian nachos, oven-roasted mussels, and Mongolian steak. | The Venetian Resort-Hotel-Casino, 3355 Las Vegas Blvd. S | 702/414–3888 | $8–$26 | AE, D, DC, MC, V.

Il Fornaio. Italian. Cross the Central Park footbridge, and you'll come to this cheery and bright Italian café. You can dine "outdoors" on the patio by the pond. An exhibition kitchen prepares fresh fish, wood-oven pizzas, and pasta. | New York–New York Hotel and Casino, 3790 Las Vegas Blvd. S | 702/650–6500 | Green Valley Ranch Station Casino, 2197 Paseo Verde Pkwy., Henderson | 702/614–5283 | $10–$25 | AE, MC, V.

Rock Lobster. Contemporary. There's everything from lobster club sandwiches and lobster tacos to $65 lobster dinners, but this restaurant, owned by the China Grill group, also serves such favorites as steak, shrimp-and-scallop sauté, and even hamburgers. Huge video walls show music clips, and a conveyor belt runs plates of sushi along the central bar. | Mandalay Bay Resort and Casino, 3950 Las Vegas Blvd. S | 702/632–7405 | $7–$65 | AE, D, DC, MC, V | No lunch.

Downtown

Carson Street Cafe. American/Casual. The Golden Nugget is widely considered one of the gems of Downtown, and the Carson Street Cafe does it proud. Standbys on the lunch and dinner menus include rainbow trout, southern fried chicken, and slabs of baby-back ribs. | Golden Nugget Hotel and Casino, 129 E. Fremont St. | 702/385–7111 | $8–$20 | AE, D, DC, MC, V.

Paradise Road

Gordon Biersch Brewing Co. American/Casual. This Palo Alto import is popular with both singles and the power-lunch crowd, thanks to its trendy warehouse look and location in the Hughes Center office park. Entrées range from pasta and wood-oven pizza to pan-seared ahi tuna and old-fashioned meat loaf with beer-mustard gravy. | 3987 Paradise Rd. | 702/312–5247 | $10–$20 | AE, D, DC, MC, V.

Mr. Lucky's 24/7. American/Casual. The hippest casino coffee shop in Las Vegas has banks of slot machines bearing the likenesses of Jimi Hendrix and Sid Vicious. Menu items in this bubbly, circular café range from vegetable omelets to baby-back ribs. The garlic mashed potatoes are superb. It's open 24 hours, seven days a week. | Hard Rock Hotel and Casino, 4455 Paradise Rd. | 702/693–5000 | $8–$14 | AE, D, DC, MC, V.

Boulder Strip

The Broiler. American. Station Casinos has emerged as one of the front-running off-Strip casino organizations. Branches of the Broiler, its good, inexpensive steak and seafood house, are found at both the Palace and Boulder stations. Both locations have excellent soups, breads, and a salad bar, which set the stage for medium-price mesquite-grilled steaks, veal, and chicken. | Boulder Station Hotel and Casino, 4111 Boulder Hwy. | 702/432–7777 | Palace Station Hotel and Casino, 2411 W. Sahara Ave. | 702/367–2411. | $15–$39 | AE, D, MC, V.

West Side

Carnival World Buffet. Eclectic. This was one of the first Las Vegas buffets with separate theme areas; the buffets-within-a-buffet here serve up fresh Mexican, Italian, Chinese, Japanese, American, and other ethnic specialties under one large and colorful roof. | Rio All-Suite Hotel and Casino, 3700 W. Flamingo Rd. | 702/252–7777 | $16 | AE, D, DC, MC, V.

Little Buddha. Pan-Asian. France's Buddha Bar, world famous for its food and music, now has a branch, Little Buddha, in Las Vegas. The kitchen produces such Pacific Rim wonders as Hawaiian smoked potstickers, wok-fried salt and pepper calamari and frog's legs, and curry shrimp in banana leaf. | The Palms, 4321 W. Flamingo Rd. | 702/942–7777 | $10–$24 | AE, D, DC,MC, V.

Henderson

Feast Around the World. Eclectic. This buffet has a similar name as those at some of Station Casinos' other properties, but there's no mistaking that the company has improved its offerings with each new casino. A huge display of fresh produce and the use of natural stone and careful lighting lend a decidedly upscale touch. Specialty stations include a Mongolian grill, Italian, Mexican, and American. | Green Valley Ranch, 2300 Paseo Verde Pkwy. | 702/614–5283 | $12 | AE, D, DC, MC, V.

Lodging

The Strip

Flamingo Las Vegas. This 3,466-room behemoth has a central location that makes it a perfect "dormitory" for its more heavily themed neighbors. But it has one stellar calling card of its own; a lovely 15-acre pool park, with pools connected by water slides. The spacious rooms offer expansive views of the Strip. 8 restaurants, in-room safes, cable TV, 4 tennis courts, 3 pools, health club, spa, lounge, casino, showroom, shops, business services, meeting room | 3555 Las Vegas Blvd. S | 702/733–3111 or 800/732–2111 | www.flamingolv.com.

Harrah's Las Vegas Casino & Hotel. In 1997 Harrah's added a 35-story, 1,000-room tower and retail and restaurant space, expanded the casino, and replaced the facade, all to the tune of $250 million. The rooms are modest and have lavender doors, gray walls, blue bedspreads and matching curtains, and dark-wood furniture. 7 restaurants, in-room data ports, cable TV, pool, health club, hair salon, spa, lounge, casino, showroom, business services, meeting rooms. | 3475 Las Vegas Blvd. S 89109 | 702/369–5000 or 800/427–7247 | fax 702/369–5008 | www.harrahs.com | 2,651 rooms, 49 suites | $59–$149 | AE, D, DC, MC, V.

Stardust Hotel and Casino. Emblazoned with an amazing amount of neon, the 2,500-room Stardust is owned by the Boyd Corporation, the operators of middle-market hotels that emphasize slots, low table minimums, and good deals on food. The tower rooms offer a great view of the Strip or the hotel garden and pool area and are among the largest in town. 6 restaurants, in-room data ports, in-room safes, cable TV, 2 tennis courts, 2 pools, health club, lounge, casino, showroom, meeting room, car rental, laundry service, no-smoking rooms | 3000 Las Vegas Blvd. S 89109 | 702/732–6111 or 800/634–6757 | fax 702/732–6257 | www.stardustlv.com | 2,500 rooms | $39–$119 | AE, DC, MC, V.

Tropicana Resort and Casino. The Trop is a beautifully landscaped hotel-casino, with an especially lush 5-acre pool area, including a meandering swimming pool, swim-up bars, and a child-pleasing 110-ft-long water slide. Rooms vary in size, but all have rattan furnishings and some even have a terrace (a plus for families). 5 restaurants, in-room safes, cable TV, 4 tennis courts, 3 pools, health club, massage, spa, racquetball, lounge, casino, showroom, business services, meeting room | 3801 Las Vegas Blvd. S 89109 | 702/739–2222 or 888/826–8767 | fax 702/739–2448 | www.tropicanalv.com | 1,708 rooms, 200 suites | $49–$129 | AE, D, DC, MC, V.

Beyond the Strip

Alexis Park Resort Hotel. Halfway between the convention center and the airport, this is a favorite spot for conventioneers who want as "normal" a living experience as possible during their business trip. There are no slots and no gaming tables; rooms are clean and adequate and all come with wet bars. Restaurant, in-room data ports, cable TV, 9-hole putting green, 2 tennis courts, 3 pools, spa, lounge | 375 E. Harmon Ave. 89109 | 702/796–3300 or 800/582–2228 | fax 702/796–0766 | www.alexispark.com | 500 suites | $79–$109 | AE, D, DC, MC, V.

Sam's Town Hotel and Gambling Hall. This simple yet busy hotel is close to the desert—it's on the Boulder Strip, 6 mi from downtown. The food is good, plentiful, and inexpensive. The newer rooms are built around a nine-story glass-roof atrium filled with live trees, a rock waterfall, and babbling brooks. Inside they are fairly standard, with queen-size beds and soothing colors. 8 restaurants, cable TV, pool, bowling, lounge, casino, meeting rooms | 5111 Boulder Hwy., 89122 | 702/456–7777 or 800/634–6371 | fax 702/454–8014 | www.samstownlv.com | 650 rooms | $44–$99 | AE, D, DC, MC, V.

Downtown

Golden Nugget Hotel and Casino. At the best hotel downtown, red rugs flow over white marble; the lobby and large public area have columns, etched-glass windows, and fresh flowers in gold-plated vases. The well-kept rooms are modern and comfortable. The pool is the biggest and best downtown. 7 restaurants, in-room safes, cable TV, pool, health club, spa, lounge, casino, showroom, meeting room | 129 E. Fremont St., 89101 | 702/385–7111 or 800/634–3454 | fax 702/386–8362 | www.goldennugget.com | 1,805 rooms, 106 suites | $59–$179 | AE, D, DC, MC, V.

Main Street Station Casino, Brewery & Hotel. Gobs of antiques, collectibles, and memorabilia, including Theodore Roosevelt's Pullman railroad car, adorn this hotel. Guest rooms, accented in dark wood, antiques, and gold-framed mirrors, continue the theme. Make sure to get one on the south side of the building, facing Main Street—it's hard to get away from the noise of I–15 on the north side. There's a free shuttle service to the Strip. 4 restaurants, in-room data ports, in-room safes, cable TV, lounge, casino, meeting rooms | 200 N. Main St., 89101 | 702/387–1896 or 800/713–8933 | fax 702/386–4421 | www.mainstreetcasino.com | 406 rooms | $40–$170 | AE, DC, MC, V.

Camping

Circusland RV Park. The only RV park right on the Strip, Circusland makes for easy access to Las Vegas's main drag. Pets are allowed. Flush toilets, full hook-ups, dump station, drinking water, laundry facilities, showers, public telephone, general store, pool | 399 full hook-ups | 500 Circus Circus Dr. | 702/794–3757 or 800/444–2472 | fax 702/792–2280 | $19–$35 | AE, D, DC, MC, V.

Silverton RV Park. Like the casino it's named for, the Silverton RV Park is all about down-home charm. Just to the southwest of the Strip, the park has telephone and cable hook-ups for every stall. There's also a recreation room and a shuttle to the Strip. Pets are allowed. Flush toilets, full hook-ups, dump station, drinking water, laundry facilities, showers, general store, pool | 460 sites | 3333 Blue Diamond Rd. | 702/263–7777 or 800/588–7711 | fax 702/897–4208 | www.silvertoncasino.com | $20 | AE, D, DC, MC, V.

Arts and Entertainment

Afternoon Shows

Mac King. King stands apart from the other magic shows on the Strip by offering a one-man hour of low-key, self-deprecating humor and the kind of "close-up" magic that often requires more skill than the "cabinet tricks" of the larger shows. | Harrah's Las Vegas Casino & Hotel, 3475 Las Vegas Blvd. S | 702/369–5111 | $14.95 | Tues.–Sat. 1 PM and 3 PM.

The Illusionary Magic of Rick Thomas. If you want your children to see a Las Vegas–style magic show without paying Siegfried & Roy–level prices, Rick Thomas's well-paced revue offers an overview of the basic stage illusions and even throws in a white tiger. | Tropicana Resort and Casino, 3801 Las Vegas Blvd. S | 702/739–2222 | $16.95–$21.95 | Sat.–Thurs. 2 PM and 4 PM.

Evening Revues

★ ***Blue Man Group: Live at Luxor.*** Three men in utilitarian uniforms, their heads bald and gleaming from cobalt blue greasepaint, commit twisted "science projects." Angular spaghetti western music complements the Blue Men's signature percussion instruments made from PVC pipe. | Luxor Hotel-Casino, 3900 Las Vegas Blvd. S | 702/262–4400 | www.blueman.com | $65–$100 | Nightly 7 and 10.

Mystère. This new-age circus performed by Cirque du Soleil is the premier family show in town. The music is rousing and haunting, the acrobatics chilling, and the dance numbers inspiring. Treasure Island Hotel and Casino, | 3300 Las Vegas Blvd. S | 702/894–7722 | $88 | Wed.–Sun. 7:30 PM and 10:30 PM.

★ ***O.*** *O* is the pronunciation of *eau,* French for "water," and water is everywhere—1.5 million gallons of it, 12 million pounds of it. The intense and nonstop action of Cirque du Soleil takes place above, within, and even on the surface of the water. | Bellagio, 3600 Las Vegas Blvd. S | 702/693–7111 | $93–$121 | Fri.–Tues. 7:30 PM and 10:30 PM.

The Second City. On a Strip filled with stand-up comedy clubs, Chicago's ensemble comedy institution is a breath of fresh air. Five performers present favorite sketches from Second City's 40-year archives and pull audience members into improvisational games. | Flamingo Las Vegas, 3555 Las Vegas Blvd. S | 702/733–3333 | $27.95 | Tues. and Thurs.–Sun. 8 PM and 10:30 PM, Wed. and Fri. 8 PM.

Siegfried and Roy at the Mirage. The magic duo, synonymous with Las Vegas, have performed on the Strip since the 1960s. They have made elephants and motorcycles disappear and have levitated each other as well as the lions and signature white tigers. | Mirage Hotel and Casino, 3400 Las Vegas Blvd. S | 702/792–7777 | $100.50 | Sun.–Tues. 7:30 PM, Fri.–Sat. 7:30 PMand 11 PM.

Tournament of Kings. In an unusual show, the audience eats a basic dinner (no utensils) while cheering for fast horses, jousting, and swordplay. It's a wonderful family show—especially for families with pre-adolescents, who get to make a lot of noise. | Excalibur Hotel and Casino, 3850 Las Vegas Blvd. S | 702/597–7600 | $39.95 | Nightly 6 and 8:30.

Shopping

The Strip

Caesars Palace rules the retail market with the **Forum Shops at Caesars** and the **Appian Way,** which includes everything from lingerie to linguine. The **Desert Passage at the Aladdin** tried to give the Forum Shops a run for its heavily themed money, but traffic has suffered with the Aladdin's financial woes.

For one-stop souvenir shopping, go to **Bonanza,** the "World's Largest Gift Shop," at the corner of Sahara Avenue.

Malls and Department Stores

Belz Factory Outlet World. Just a few miles away from the Strip's most exclusive and expensive shopping areas is one of the country's largest discount malls. This 580,000-square-ft world of shopping choices includes two food courts and a full-size carousel. | 7400 Las Vegas Blvd. S | 702/896–5599 | www.belz.com.

Fashion Show Mall. On Las Vegas Boulevard south next to the New Frontier, the mall was getting a monstrous makeover in 2002, including the arrival of Las Vegas's first Nordstrom's. | 3200 Las Vegas Blvd. S | 702/369–8382 | www.thefashionshow.com.

Sports and Outdoor Activities

Bicycling

Las Vegas Valley has a handful of good, long rides. One popular trip is the jaunt out to Red Rock Canyon on West Charleston Boulevard; it's 11 mi from the Rainbow Boulevard intersection to the Red Rock Visitors Center.

Mountain biking is limited primarily to Mt. Charleston and the Bristlecone Trail, accessible at the top of the Lee Canyon ski area parking lot. It's a 6-mi loop and climbs 1,400 ft (☞ Hiking).

Bowling

The Castaways Hotel & Bowling Center. With 106 lanes, this is the world's largest bowling alley. It hosts the oldest stop on the PBA professional tour, held every January. | 2800 E. Fremont St. | 702/385–9153.

Fishing

Lake Mead is the place to fish for largemouth and striped bass, channel catfish, crappie, bluegill, and various types of trout. The lake is stocked with a half-million rainbow trout regularly, and at least a million fish are harvested every year. You can fish here 24 hours a day, year-round (except for posted closings). Limits are 5 trout, 6 largemouth bass, 15 crappie, 20 striped bass, and 25 catfish. Nonresident licenses are $12 a day or $51 for the year.

Golf

The Bali Hai Golf Club carries the bragging rights as the only golf course right on the Strip. Otherwise, there are many courses on the outskirts of the city, and a few scattered around Summerlin, Henderson, Primm Valley, and Lake Las Vegas. Most hotel concierges will help you reserve tee times.

Angel Park. This intensely popular course has a 36-hole Arnold Palmer–designed layout. Call two months prior to set up your tee times at this municipal course; fees range from $135 to $160. | 100 S. Rampart Blvd. | 702/254–4653.

Craig Ranch. The 50-year-old public course is short (6,000 yards, par 70) and narrow, with 11,000 trees. It's also the most inexpensive course in Las Vegas, a mere $18 to walk 18 holes ($26 to ride). | 628 W. Craig Rd. | 702/642–9700.

Hiking and Walking

Mt. Charleston. In summer, hikers escape the heat by traveling 45 minutes into the mountains, where the U.S. Forest Service maintains more than 50 mi of marked hiking trails for all abilities. Trails range from ¼-mi long (the Robber's Roost and Bristlecone Loop trails) to the extremely strenuous 10-mi North Loop Trail, which reaches the Mt. Charleston summit at 11,918 ft; the elevation gain is 3,500 ft.

The Mt. Charleston Wilderness Area is part of the Toiyabe National Forest; for information, contact the **U.S. Forest Service.** | 2881 S. Valley View Blvd., Suite 16, Las Vegas 89103 | 702/873–8800 | www.fs.fed.us.

★ **Red Rock Canyon Recreation Area.** In winter, when skiing is the outdoor activity of choice on Mt. Charleston, hikers head to Red Rock, which encompasses 83,100 acres of Bureau of Land Management recreation lands. Hiking runs the gamut from short discovery trails for children to all-day routes up the sandstone to various mountain peaks. | W. Charleston Blvd. | 702/363–1922 | www.redrockcanyon.blm.gov.

For guided group hikes in Red Rock Canyon, contact the local chapter of the **Sierra Club.** | 702/363–3267.

Horseback Riding

Sagebrush Ranch. Sagebrush offers one- and two-hour guided rides as well as breakfast and dinner trail rides. The one-hour ride is $25, the two-hour ride is $50. The ranch caters to families, and riding helmets are provided. | 12000 West Ann Rd. | 702/645–9422.

Rafting

Black Canyon, just below Hoover Dam, is the place for river running near Las Vegas. You can launch a raft here on the Colorado River year-round. The 11-mi run to Willow Beach on the Arizona side is reminiscent of rafting the Grand Canyon, with its vertical canyon walls, bighorn sheep on the slopes, and feeder streams and waterfalls coming off the bluffs. The water flows at roughly 5 mph, but some rapids, eddies, and whirlpools can cause difficulties, as can head winds, especially for inexperienced rafters.

U.S. Bureau of Reclamation. If you want to go rafting in Black Canyon on your own, you must apply for a $5 permit. Permits are issued immediately. The bureau will also send a list of guides and outfitters. | Box 60400, Boulder City 89006 | 702/293–8204.

Skiing and Snowboarding

Las Vegas Ski and Snowboard Resort. Southern Nevada's skiing headquarters is a mere 47 mi northwest of downtown Las Vegas; depending on traffic it can take as little as an hour to get from the Strip to an elevation of 9,500 ft. "Ski Lee," as it's affectionately known, is equipped with three double chairlifts, a ski school, a ski shop, rental equipment, and a day lodge with a coffee shop and lounge. There are 40 acres of groomed slopes. The longest run is 3,000 ft, with a vertical drop of more than 1,000 ft. Ski-lift rates are $28. | Mt. Charleston, Hwy. 156 | 702/646–0008.

Water Sports

All water sports in the Las Vegas area are centered on Lake Mead.

Lake Mead Resort and Marina. You can choose from a variety of motorboats (and water-ski equipment) for rent by the hour or day. | 322 Lakeshore Rd., Boulder City | 702/293–3484.

Essential Information

When to Go

Las Vegas is a year-round destination. Except for the first three weeks in December and some of the hottest summer weekdays, you can assume that Las Vegas will be running at full speed. The Strip is especially jam-packed for three-day weekends, the Super Bowl, the NCAA Final Four, and Cinco de Mayo. The week between Christmas and New Year's is the most crowded of the year. In addition, certain conventions and sporting events such as NASCAR have a citywide impact, causing room prices to soar.

In April and May, daytime temperatures are delightful, in the 70s and 80s. In September and October, the summer heat has abated, and the pools remain open. Winter brings windy and chilly days and surprisingly cold nights. Summer is a time of dry, uncomfortably hot weather (sometimes literally 110°F in the shade).

FESTIVALS AND SEASONAL EVENTS

WINTER

Dec.: **National Finals Rodeo.** The Super Bowl of rodeos runs for nine days at the Thomas and Mack Center. | 702/731–2115.

New Year's Eve. In the new century, New Year's has been celebrated by a synchronized fireworks display from one end of the Strip to the other. The tradition is so young that it's not set in stone; there is annual debate over whether the street party's benefits justify its massive expense. | 702/382–6397.

SPRING

Mar.: **NASCAR Winston Cup Race.** The race is the largest sporting event of the year in Nevada. Some 135,000 racing fans converge on Las Vegas to watch the grueling 400-mi race on the 1½-mi track, with top national drivers competing for $3 million in prize money. | 702/644–4443.

AUTUMN

Oct.: **Pro Bull Riders Finals.** The top 50 bull riders compete for a $1 million purse. | 702/891–7272 or 800/929–1111.

Las Vegas Invitational Golf Tournament. This five-day event is played on three courses, with television coverage. | 702/382–6616.

Bargains

Hotel rooms, food, drink, and entertainment often cost less than what they would in other cities, simply because the highly profitable casinos bankroll all the other vacation necessities. Las Vegas is renowned for its cheap and ample buffets; you can find breakfast for as little as 99¢ or a steak dinner for $5; you can drink alcoholic beverages for free in all the casinos as long as you're playing the tables. "Archi-tainment" is a word that's been coined to describe heavily themed environments and free attractions that make the casinos stand out from one another; circus acts, exploding volcanoes, and pirate shows are among the free come-ons. To tour the Strip inexpensively, take the local bus or trolley, both of which creep through the brightly lit district for a small fare.

Tours

Gray Line Tours. City tours trips to Red Rock Canyon, Lake Mead, and Valley of Fire and longer trips to the Grand Canyon and Death Valley are available. | 702/384–1234 or 800/634–6579.

Sundance Helicopters. Helicopters do two basic tours in and around Las Vegas: a 20-minute flyover of the Strip and a several-hour trip out to the Grand Canyon and back. | 702/736–0606 | www.helicoptour.com.

Visitor Information

Las Vegas Convention and Visitors Authority | 3150 Paradise Rd. 89109 | 702/892–0711 | fax 702/892–2824. **Las Vegas Chamber of Commerce** | 3720 Howard Hughes Pkwy. 89109 | 702/735–1616 | fax 702/735–2011.

Arriving and Departing

BY AIR

Airports

McCarran International Airport (LAS). The gateway to Las Vegas is immediately east of the southern end of the Strip. | 702/261–5733 | www.mccarran.com.

Airport Transportation

Shuttle: This is the cheapest way from McCarran to your hotel. The service is shared with other riders and costs $5–$7 per person to the Strip, $6–$8 to downtown, and $8–$12 to outlying "locals" casinos.

Taxi: The trip to most hotels on the Strip should cost less than $11–$18.

BY BUS

Greyhound serves Las Vegas at the bus terminal downtown, on 200 S. Main St.

BY CAR

More than a third of Las Vegas visitors on any given weekend are coming from California on the crowded Interstate 15. Northern California visitors may choose to come down from Reno on state Highway 95. Arizona visitors will come through Kingman on Interstate 40 and state Highway 93 or Laughlin, Nevada, on state Highway 95.

Getting Around

BY CAR

Las Vegas is an easy city to navigate. The principal north–south artery is Las Vegas Boulevard (I–15 runs roughly parallel to it, less than a mile to the west). A 5-mi stretch of Las Vegas Boulevard South is known as the Strip, where a majority of the city's hotels and casinos are clustered. Many of the major streets running east–west (Tropicana Avenue, Flamingo Road, Desert Inn Road, Sahara Avenue) are named for the casinos built at their intersections with the Strip.

Because the capacity of the streets of Las Vegas has not kept pace with the city's incredible growth, traffic can be slow. To avoid it, try the streets that parallel Las Vegas Boulevard: Paradise Road to the east and Industrial Road to the west.

Parking

Free self-parking garages as well as valet parking for the price of a tip are available at virtually every hotel.

BY PUBLIC TRANSIT

Bus

Citizens Area Transit (CAT). CAT runs local buses throughout the city, but most visitors only ride CAT buses up and down the Strip or to the Downtown Transportation Center. The Strip buses stop on the street in front of all the major hotels every 15 minutes (in a perfect world) 24 hours a day. The fare is $2 (exact change required, but $1 bills are accepted). The schedule for all buses other than those along the Strip is 5:30 AM–1:30 AM daily; the fare is $1.25. Since traffic is quite haphazard along the Strip, buses supposedly running every 15 minutes can take 25 to 30 minutes to show up. | 702/228–7433.

BY TAXI

The fare is $2.30 on the meter when you get in, plus $1.80 for every mile. No fees are assessed for luggage, but taxis leaving the airport are allowed to add an airport surcharge of $1.30.

Desert Cab | 702/376–2687. **Whittlesea Blue Cab** | 702/384–6111. **Yellow** and **Checker Cab** | 702/873–2000.

Kentucky, Indiana, Illinois

Revised and Updated by Joanne Cleaver

THE LINCOLN TRAIL

Stretching from the green hills of northern Kentucky to Indiana's Ohio River valley and to the wide-open prairies of southern and central Illinois, the Lincoln Trail conjures up images of log cabins, tiny farms surrounded by split-rail fences, and prairie air scented with wood smoke. Exaggerations? Not really, for you don't have to walk too far from your car to find all of these on the historic Lincoln Trail.

Abraham Lincoln's presence is still felt along the strip of middle America now known as the Lincoln Trail; dozens of spots along the trail, countless historical markers, and three national historic sites pay homage to the slain president's memory. The Abraham Lincoln Birthplace National Historic Site, near Hodgenville, Kentucky, enshrines in a large granite memorial the tiny log cabin where Lincoln was born. Remote southern Indiana's Lincoln Boyhood National Memorial marks the farm where Lincoln and his family labored for 14 difficult years. And in Springfield, Illinois, where he practiced law for 24 years, the Lincoln Home National Historic Site preserves the only home he ever owned; the place where he received word of his election to the presidency in 1860; and his grave.

Much of the region cut by the Lincoln Trail is rural, dotted with small towns and neat, orderly farms. Even Springfield, the Illinois prairie capital known as Mr. Lincoln's Hometown, is surrounded by seemingly endless cornfields. You won't find much glitter along the Lincoln Trail: except for Springfield, which bustles when the legislature is in session, the pace is slow and life is fairly sedate.

Exploring

Abraham Lincoln was born in Hodgenville in 1809 and spent his early childhood in the then-frontier of Kentucky. Despairing of the never-ending land-title disputes, Lincoln's father, Thomas, moved his small family to southern Indiana in 1816. In Indiana, Thomas's wife and Abraham's mother, Nancy Hanks Lincoln, died and Thomas returned to Kentucky to marry Sarah Bush Johnston. She and her three children returned with him to the farm that is now the Lincoln Boyhood site. Though the family flourished in Indiana, Thomas Lincoln moved them again, in 1830, to Illinois. Shortly thereafter, Abraham Lincoln struck out on his own, trying his hand at a variety of occupations—among them, postmaster and store clerk—in newly settled New Salem, Illinois. When he was elected to the Illinois legislature, he sat in session in

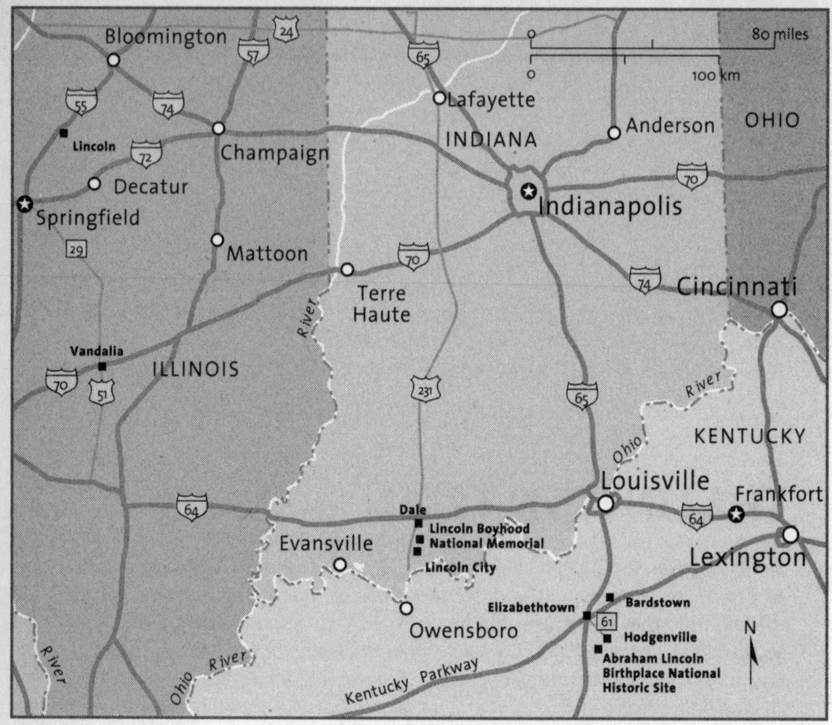

the old state capital in Vandalia. Springfield was rapidly emerging as the seat of politics and commerce for central Illinois, however, and it was there that Lincoln finally settled down, establishing a thriving law practice, marrying, buying a house, and campaigning for president. After his assassination, his body was laid to rest in Oak Ridge Cemetery in Springfield.

Historic sites along the trail capture Lincoln's social and economic rise from a child in a rough-hewn cabin to a lawyer and family man in a tidy, two-story clapboard house in a frontier town that was fast growing into a regional and political center. That's why it is most meaningful to organize the trip to parallel the chronology of Lincoln's life. If time is short, concentrate on the Springfield area, as the contrast between frontier New Salem and up-and-coming Springfield crystallizes the pre-presidential accomplishments of this unique American icon.

Kentucky

★ **Abraham Lincoln Birthplace National Historic Site.** Fifty-six steps, one for each year of the president's life, lead up to the granite memorial, which houses a one-room log cabin—a replica of Lincoln's birthplace. Above the portals is carved "With malice toward none, with charity for all," quoted from Lincoln's address to an Indiana Regiment in March 1865. The memorial, which opened in 1911, is on the grounds of a 110-acre park that was part of the original Thomas Lincoln farm. There are also hiking trails and picnic areas. The visitor center houses exhibitions about, and artifacts of, the Lincoln family, including the family Bible, and has a short film about Lincoln's boyhood. | 2995 Lincoln Farm Rd., Hodgenville 42748 | 270/358–3137 | www.nps.gov/abli | Free | Late May–early Sept., daily 8–6:45; early Sept.–late May, daily 8–4:45.

Kentucky Railway Museum. The KRM, about 6 mi north of Hodgenville on U.S. 31E, owns 17 mi of the old Louisville and Nashville Lebanon branch of the now-defunct regional L&M railroad. The collection of railroad artifacts and memorabilia includes model trains and layouts, steam and first-generation diesel locomotives, and more than 80 pieces of rolling stock. The KRM also operates a 22-mi train ride through the scenic and historic Rolling Fork River valley—May through December (except Mon.) and only weekends after September. Reenactments of Civil War skirmishes and train robberies are conducted on selected weekends. For $25 you can ride in the locomotive's cab; coach fares range from $12.50 to $15. | New Haven Depot U.S. 31E, New Haven 40051 | 502/549–5470 or 800/272–0152 | fax 502/549–5472 | www.kyrail.org | $3 | May–Dec.

★ **Lincoln's Boyhood Home.** This reconstructed cabin rests on the site where Lincoln lived from age 2 to 8 and is furnished with antiques from the period. In 2002, the home was purchased by the National Park Service and may be undergoing renovations—and thus be closed—periodically. | 7120 Bardstown Rd., Hodgenville 42748 | 270/358–3137 | $1 | Apr.–Oct. 9–5.

Lincoln Jamboree. It's billed as Kentucky's number one country music showplace—bluegrass music lovers have been flocking to this foot-stomping hoedown since 1954. Traditional and contemporary country music is the entertainment at this family-oriented center where a regular band is featured plus guest performers. The Lincoln Jamboree restaurant is also on the premises. Saturday evening performances begin at 8 PM; reservations are recommended. | 2579 Lincoln Farm Rd., Hodgenville 42748 | 270/358–3545 | $8 | Tues.–Sun.

Lincoln Museum. Twelve dioramas with 21 life-size wax figures portray phases of Abraham Lincoln's life from cabin living to Ford's Theatre. The 94-year-old preserved building with original floors and fittings is part of the Civil War Preservation Trust, which maintains a number of historic sites and trails related to the war. It is filled with memorabilia including Civil War artifacts, artwork, and documents. | 66 Lincoln Sq., Hodgenville 42748 | 270/358–3163 | www.lincolnmuseumky.org | $3 | Mon.–Sat. 8:30–4:30, Sun. 12:30–4:30.

Indiana

Lincoln Boyhood National Memorial. Abraham Lincoln spent 14 years of his youth in the hinterlands of southern Indiana near the Ohio River, a few miles from his birthplace in Hodgenville, Kentucky. Lincoln's mother, Nancy Hanks Lincoln, is buried here. A cabin has been reconstructed on the southwest corner of the original Thomas Lincoln property; split rail fences surround the garden, and there are farm animals such as the family would have had. Frontier family life is re-created from May through October, offering children a chance to peek into the cabin's sleeping loft, taste corn pone baked in the fireplace, and pet the animals. A high-spirited musical drama, *Young Abe Lincoln,* brings Lincoln's boyhood years to life. | Lincoln City 47552 | 812/937–4541 | www.nps.gov/libo | $2 per vehicle residents, $5 nonresidents.

Lincoln State Park. This 1,700-acre state park includes housekeeping cabins, campground, 10 mi of hiking trails, a nature center, and a small lake. It's less than 1 mi from Lincoln Boyhood National Memorial and 13 mi east of Santa Claus town center. | Rte. 162, Lincoln City 47552 | 812/937–4710 | www.state.in.us/dnr/statepar | $2 per vehicle residents, $5 nonresidents | Daily.

Illinois

Lincoln Depot. Lincoln bid farewell to Springfield at this depot as he left for Washington, D.C., in 1861. You can look at two restored waiting rooms (one for women and one for the luggage and tobacco-spitting men), displays of people and places close to Lincoln, and an audiovisual show that re-creates the 12-day trip to his inauguration. | Monroe St., Springfield 62701 | 217/544–8695 or 217/788–1356 | Free | Apr.–Aug., daily 10–4.

★ **Lincoln–Herndon Law Office Building.** Lincoln practiced law at this office downtown from 1843 to 1852. Visits to the building are by guided tours only and include a video and a stop at a re-created 1846 post office. | 1 Old State Capitol Plaza, 6th and Adams Sts., Springfield 62701 | 217/785–7289 | $2 suggested donation | Mar.–Oct., daily 9–5; Nov.–Feb., daily 9–4.

★ **Lincoln Home National Historic Site.** Just three blocks from the town square is the only home Lincoln ever owned. The house is furnished to closely replicate the furnishings and decor at the time when Lincoln was elected president, based on painstaking and ongoing research. This is the most popular site in Springfield, so arrive early at the excellent visitor center, a block west of the actual house, to pick up a free ticket that will admit you into the house at a certain time. As you wait, stroll the three-by-two-block neighborhood, which is gradually being restored to replicate the neighborhood as it was when Lincoln and Mary Todd lived there. Exhibits on the restoration process and about the people who spent nearly two decades as the Lincolns' neighbors are being installed in the houses as the restorations are completed. | Visitor center: 426 S. 7th St., Springfield 62701 | 217/492–4241 ext. 221 | fax 217/492–4648 | www.nps.gov/liho | Free | Mar.–Sept., daily 8–6; Oct.–Feb., daily 8–5.

Lincoln Memorial Garden and Nature Center. Wooded trails (five for hiking) and a nature center are 10 mi south of Springfield, on the south bank of Lake Springfield. | 2301 E. Lake Dr., 62707 | 217/529–1111 | fax 217/529–0134 | www.lmgnc.com | Free | Garden daily dawn–dusk; nature center Tues.–Sat. 10–4, Sun. 1–4.

★ **Lincoln Tomb State Historic Site.** This tomb in the Oak Ridge Cemetery is the final resting place of the Lincoln family. It's 16 blocks north of the Old State Capitol. | 1500 Monument Ave., Springfield 62702 | 217/782–2717 | fax 217/524–3738 | Free | Mar.–Oct., daily 9–5; Nov.–Feb., daily 9–4.

★ **Lincoln's New Salem State Historic Site.** About 20 mi northwest of Springfield is the reconstructed village where Lincoln spent his early adulthood. In summer volunteers in period dress re-create village life and host many special events that capture the activities and spirit of frontier life. Summer is also the season for a corny but touching musical of Lincoln's young adulthood in the outdoor amphitheater. | Rte. 97 near Petersburg | 217/632–4000 | www.lincolnsnewsalem.com | Free | Nov.–Feb., Wed.–Sun. 8–4; Mar.–Oct., Wed.–Sun. 9–5.

★ **Old State Capitol State Historic Site.** Lincoln worked in this building for 23 years, trying cases and using its law library. He made his famous "House Divided" speech in its Hall of Representatives. | 1 Old State Capitol Plaza, Springfield 62701 | 217/785–7960 | fax 217/557–0282 | $2 suggested donation | Mar.–Oct., daily 9–5; Nov.–Feb., daily 9–4.

Springfield Children's Museum. Kids and adults alike can enjoy the exhibits on art, architecture, health, and nature at this museum a block east of the Old State Capitol. | 619 E. Washington St., Springfield 62701 | 217/789–0679 | fax 217/789–0682 | $3 | Mon., Wed., and Fri. 10–4; Thurs. 10–7; weekends 11–4.

★ **Under the Prairie.** Just 20 mi north of Springfield on I–55, in the hamlet of Elkhart, an outstanding museum of frontier archaeology opened in summer 2002. Professionally produced by accomplished archaeologists, the museum showcases artifacts from the earliest days of European discovery of Illinois, discovered in the last 10 to 15 years on private land. These items are the precise type that Lincoln would have used daily in his childhood and in New Salem. An adjoining coffeehouse serves up homemade cinnamon rolls and coffee. | 109 Governor Oglesby St., 62634 | 217/947–2522 | fax 217/529–0134 | Donation requested. | Wed.–Sun. 10–4.

Dining

Kentucky

Joel Ray Sprowls' Restaurant. Southern. Joel Ray's is in the same building as the popular Saturday-night Lincoln Jamboree Country Music Show (2½ mi south of downtown Hodgenville). It's definitely "country," with a mix of Lincoln memorabilia, country artifacts, and country music items. Lunch- and dinner-menu choices at this cafeteria always include fried chicken and could include salmon cakes, meat loaf, pork chops, or chicken and dumplings. Breakfast is also available. | 2579 Lincoln Farm Rd. (U.S. 31E), Hodgenville 42748 | 270/358–3545 | Closed Mon. | $5 | No credit cards.

Illinois

Augie's Front Burner. Contemporary. Chef-owner Augie describes his cooking as "American with an attitude," offering such innovations as macadamia nut–encrusted salmon and pan-roasted ostrich fillet. This airy artsy place is on the west side of Old State Capitol Plaza. | 2 W. Old State Capitol Plaza, Springfield | 217/544–6979 | Closed Sun. No lunch Sat. | $12–$21 | AE, D, DC, MC, V.

Café Brio. Eclectic. Recipes from Mexico, the Caribbean, and the Mediterranean make up the menu at this colorful restaurant, where the margaritas are made with fresh lime juice. Try the rotolo, a puff pastry filled with mushrooms, three cheeses, and basil pesto, served atop a roasted tomato and kalamata olive sauce. Weekend brunch. | 524 E. Monroe St., Springfield 65801 | 217/544–0574 | No dinner Sun. | $10–$18 | AE, MC, V.

★ **Maldaner's.** Contemporary. Established in 1883, this is the oldest restaurant in Springfield (it's been at this location in the center of town for more than a century). Legislators, lobbyists, businesspeople, and tourists come here for the beef Wellington and pistachio-roasted salmon. Other menu items include grilled rib eye, filet of beef, Portobello mushrooms, roasted chicken, and rack of lamb. You can dine on the sidewalk in summer. | 222 S. 6th St., Springfield 62701 | 217/522–4313 | www.maldaners.com | Closed Sun. No lunch Sat., no dinner Mon. | $13–$20 | AE, MC, V.

Sebastian's. Eclectic. This late 1800s painted-brick establishment is sandwiched between the old and new capital buildings. You can eat in the candlelit dining room, with its brass fixtures and a terrazzo fountain, or take the marble staircase down into the bar and sit at the marble-top tables. Try the shrimp stuffed with jack cheese and chipotle dipping sauce, a signature dish that lures diners from miles away. | 221 S. 5th St., Springfield 62701 | 217/789–8988 | Closed Sun. No lunch | $12–$18 | AE, D, DC, MC, V.

Lodging

The state park systems of Kentucky and Indiana run state park resorts that are friendly and reasonably priced. In addition, they offer a wide and varied menu of activities ranging from kids' nature talks to ranger-led hikes. These resorts are extremely popular with in-the-know Midwest travelers and book up quickly. Reservation policies vary by resort, so it's best to check with the respective state park departments in advance. For Indiana, go to www.state.in.us/dnr/parklake/ and for Kentucky check out www.state.ky.us/agencies/parks. Even if you don't stay at one of the parks, try to stop in for a down-home dinner at one of the lodges, which typically feature country-style food served in dining rooms that often enjoy spectacular scenic views.

Kentucky

Cruise Inn Motel. This small motel is close to the Lincoln attractions in Hodgenville. Cable TV. | 2768 Lincoln Farm Rd., Hodgenville 42748 | 270/358–9998 | 10 rooms | $38–$43 | MC, V.

Olde Gait Farm Bed & Breakfast. From this 1917 Victorian farm house walk across the road and hike the pastures and woods at Abraham Lincoln's Boyhood Home. The commons area has a TV, phone, and fireplace; there's also a separate reading parlor. Explore the barn, help groom the horses, bird-watch, or do nothing but swing on the veranda. Also available are horseback-riding lessons. Stalls are available if you bring your own horse ($15 per night). Kids sharing your room are $15 extra. Hiking, horseback riding; no room phones, no room TVs. | 7281 Bardstown Rd., Hodgenville, 42748 | 502/549–7348 or 877/548–7348 | 3 rooms | $90 | No credit cards.

Indiana

Santa's Lodge Resort. Though you won't find Dancer or Prancer or Rudolph tramping around this rustic, two-story cedar resort built in 1995, you will find a Christmas theme, a pond for fishing and paddleboat rides, and a free shuttle to local attractions. Rooms are mistletoe-free, although a candy cane is left on your pillow at bedtime. Complimentary Continental breakfast. In-room data ports, some in-room hot tubs, cable TV, pond, exercise equipment, boating, fishing, laundry facilities, business services. | 91 W. Christmas Blvd., 47579 | 812/640–7895 or 800/640–7895 | www.santaslodge.com | 87 rooms | $90–$150 | AE, D, MC, V.

Illinois

Days Inn. Just two blocks west of Lake Springfield is this modern motel in the southeast section of town. It has free shuttle service to Capital Airport and the train station, as well as complimentary Continental breakfast. Picnic area, some in-room data ports, some microwaves, some refrigerators, cable TV, pool, laundry service, business services, airport shuttle, some pets allowed (fee). | 3000 Stevenson Dr., 62703 | 217/529–0171 or 800/329–7466 | fax 217/529–9431 | www.daysinn.com | 153 rooms | $68 | AE, D, DC, MC, V.

Henry Mischler House Bed & Breakfast. Across from the Lincoln Home National Historic Site, this inn has hand-carved oak banisters, Victorian wallpaper, and lace curtains. The rooms are all furnished with antiques; all have private baths, though some require a short walk down the hall. Cable TV | 802 E. Edwards St., 62703 | 217/525–2660 | www.mischlerhouse.com | 4 rooms, 1 suite | $75–$95 | AE, D, MC, V.

Inn at 835 Bed & Breakfast. In the heart of Springfield's historic district, but a bit of a hike on foot from the Lincoln sites, this inn's rooms are furnished with antiques, such as brass and four-poster beds and claw-foot tubs, and have verandas and ceiling fans. Select wines are served in the sitting room evenings. Some in-room hot tubs, cable TV with video games, laundry facilities. | 835 S. 2nd St., 62704 | 888/217–4835 | www.innat835.com | 8 rooms, 2 suites | $109–$149 rooms, $169–$189 suites | AE, D, MC, V.

Camping

Kentucky

Rough River Dam State Resort Park. About a 45-minute drive due west from the Lincoln Birthplace National Historic site in Hodgenville, this campground has it all, including an airstrip. It is open year-round and offers a marina with boat slips, mini-golf and a 9-hole course, as well as some facilities for the disabled. The park also has a lodge and cottages. Flush toilets, partial hook-ups (electric and water), dump station, drinking water, showers, fire pits, picnic tables, public telephone, playground, pool. | 66 partial hook-ups, 20 tent sites | KY 79 | 800/325–1713 | $16 partial hook-ups, $10 tent sites | Apr.–Oct.

Indiana

Lincoln State Park. Adjacent to the Lincoln Boyhood Memorial, this state park is set in the same rolling woods that Lincoln traversed as a boy. The memorial, with its working pioneer farm, is not even five minutes away by car, and there is boating on the lake. The state park offers housekeeping cabins, and bathhouses are available for those using camper sites. Pit toilets, partial hook-ups (electric), dump station, drinking water, grills, picnic tables, general store, swimming (lake). | 150 partial hook-ups, 120 tent sites | Hwy. 162 | 866/622–6746 | www.camp.in.gov | $22 partial hook-ups, $10 tent sites | MC, V | Apr.–Oct.

Illinois

Lincoln's New Salem State Historic Site Campground. Settle in at the campsite adjacent to New Salem and enjoy a leisurely exploration of the piney woods surrounding the re-created frontier village. It's also convenient for taking in the evening outdoor drama about Lincoln's years in New Salem, because campers can just walk back to their sites rather than drive half an hour to a Springfield hotel. Flush toilets, partial hook-ups (electric), dump station, showers, drinking water, fire pits, picnic tables, public telephone, playground. | 100 partial hook-ups, 100 tent sites | Rte. 97 near Petersburg | 217/632–4003 | www.lincolnsnewsalem.com | $11 partial hook-ups, $8 tent sites | No credit cards | Apr.–Oct.

Shopping

Gift shops at the various Lincoln historic sites are a treasure trove of books about the Civil War, Lincoln, Mary Todd Lincoln, and pioneer life. Those operated by the National Park Service also offer pioneer children's toys, crafts kits, activity kits, and other items that let kids ages 3 to 12 get in the spirit of frontier life.

Sports and Outdoor Activities

Boating

Kentucky and southern Indiana are dotted with lakes. Fishing and boating are very popular here, so there are plenty of rentals available, particularly around state and county parks.

Lincoln State Park, Indiana. A network of small lakes offers plenty of shoreline for boating and fishing. Canoes, paddleboats, and rowboats can be rented at the park. | Rte. 162 Lincoln City, IN 47552 | 812/937–4710.

Caving

Southern Indiana is honeycombed with caves that are just the right size for a short family excursion.

Harrison-Crawford Wyandotte Complex, Indiana. The surface terrain here isn't spectacular, because the good stuff is underground. Several caves are rigged for public access. With the requisite array of stalactites and other formations, they offer an excellent opportunity for a introduction to cave tours. | 7240 Old Forest Rd., Corydon, IN 47118 | 812/738–2782.

Hiking

Rolling hills and scenic small rivers—and one big one, the Ohio—crisscross western Kentucky and southern Indiana.

Adams Wildlife Sanctuary, Illinois. This small nature preserve in Springfield offers easy-to-navigate trails through prairie and woods—ideal for kids, who also like the wildlife exhibits. | 2315 E. Clear Lake, Springfield 62703 | 217/544–5781 | www.springfield.k12.il.us/adamswildlife.

Lincoln Park, Illinois. Perfect for sedate strolls, the garden's botanical exhibits explain native Illinois flora. | 1601 N. 5th St. | 217/522–5431.

Riverside Park, Illinois. This spacious park on the edge of Springfield offers golf and seasonal family activities. | 4105 Sand Hill Rd. | 217/789–2353.

Essential Information

When to Go

July and August are the trail's hottest months, when maximum temperatures often reach the upper 80s or higher, with high humidity. Winters see modest snowfall and average temperatures in the upper 20s, although freezing rain often falls. Although the summer (June–August) is peak season, the region is perhaps loveliest in autumn, when the crowds thin out, the heat and humidity are lower, and the land is ablaze with color.

FESTIVALS AND SEASONAL EVENTS

WINTER

Feb.: **Lincoln's Birthday Commemoration.** Speeches, concerts, programs, and a luncheon In Hodgenville, Kentucky, mark February 12, the birthday of the 16th president. | 270/358–3411.

Feb.–Mar.: **Maple Syrup Time.** Demonstrations of maple-syrup making from sap gathering to sugaring down take place weekends from the middle of February to the middle of March at the Lincoln Memorial Garden and Nature Center. The center is 10 mi south of Springfield on the south bank of Lake Springfield. | 217/529–1111.

SUMMER

June: **International Carillon Festival.** Carillon artists from all over the world perform at evening concerts at the Thomas Rees Memorial Carillon in Springfield. There's a $2 admission charge; special rates for students. | 217/753–6219.

Aug.: **Illinois State Fair.** This annual fair showcases livestock and produce from all over the state, as well as nationally known performers, and plenty of food, rides, and exhibits. It all happens at the State Fairgrounds (I–55, Exit 100) the first two weeks of the month from 7 AM–midnight. There's a $3 entrance fee; kids 12 and under are free. | 217/782–6661.

AUTUMN

Oct.: **Lincoln Days Celebration.** This festival of family activities in Hodgenville occurs on the second weekend of the month and includes games, crafts, food, and music. | 502/358–3411.

Bargains

Rural Kentucky, Indiana, and Illinois are lightly populated and are off the beaten path for tour groups, so there are few opportunities for organized events. However, though you must have your own car to trace the Lincoln Trail, you'll find that small-town prices make this a trip that's easy on your pocketbook. Keep an eye out for farm stands, Boy Scout pancake breakfasts, and other slices of American life that can add charm to your day while preserving your checkbook. Check with the Springfield

Convention and Visitors Bureau (☞ Visitor Information) for a schedule of festivals and events that include packages at local hotels.

Visitor Information

Kentucky Department of Travel Development | Capital Plaza Tower, 500 Mero St., Suite 2200, Frankfort, KY 40601 | 502/564–4930 or 800/225–8747 | www.kentuckytourism.com. **Indiana Tourism Development Division** | 1 N. Capitol, Suite 700, Indianapolis, IN 46204-2288 | 888/365–6946 | www.enjoyindiana.com. **Springfield Convention and Visitors Bureau** | 109 N. 7th St., Springfield, IL 62701 | 217/789–2360 or 800/545–7300 | www.visit-springfieldillinois.com.

Arriving and Departing

BY AIR

Airports

Louisville International Airport–Standiford Field (SDF). Five miles south of downtown Louisville, Kentucky, this airport has scheduled daily flights by major U.S. carriers. | 502/368–1515 | www.louintlairport.com.

Springfield Capital Airport (SPI). This airport 5 mi north of downtown Springfield, Illinois, is served by regional carriers. | 217/788–1060 | www.flyspi.com.

Airport Transportation

The only practical way to traverse Lincoln's life through these rural regions is by car. To follow in his footsteps in chronological order, start in Hodgenville, an hour's drive south of Louisville, and follow the interstate highways west, making frequent diversions to specific historic sites via local routes. One logical option is to fly into Louisville and rent a car, returning it at the Springfield, Illinois, airport. The following car rental companies are located at Louisville's Standiford Field: Avis, Budget, Dollar, Enterprise, Hertz, National, and Thrifty. Three of these—Avis, Budget, and Hertz—are also located at Capital Airport in Springfield.

BY CAR

A car is the most practical means of touring the Lincoln Trail. I–65 intersects Kentucky from north to south and passes near Hodgenville's Lincoln attractions. For travelers heading to Indiana's Lincoln Boyhood National Memorial, I–64 crosses southern Indiana from east to west. In Illinois, I–55 passes through Springfield, and I–74 and I–70 lead to other Lincoln sites.

Getting Around

BY CAR

The Lincoln Trail is a drive through small towns and rolling hills in Kentucky and Indiana and small towns and flat farmland in Illinois. Rest stops occur about every 50 mi on the interstate highways. Traffic is relatively light. Restaurants and hotels are largely fast food, family dining, and moderately priced, as they also cater to the local populations. Parking at each of the major Lincoln historic sites is ample, though there are sometimes clogs of chartered tour buses and flocks of school children on field trips. The major sites and museums are largely handicapped accessible, though it can be tough navigating a wheelchair or stroller over the wide, unpaved paths of the Lincoln Boyhood Home in Indiana and New Salem in Illinois.

California

Revised and Updated by Kristina Brooks

LOS ANGELES

Don't believe everything you've heard about Los Angeles. Sure, there are earthquakes, riots, endless freeways, and, of course, the smog. But the City of Angels is still a place where dreams are easy to conjure, between the pounding surf of the Pacific Ocean to the west and the majestic mountain ranges to the east. Artists talk about the special quality of light here; tourists revel in the palm tree–fringed boulevards and glorious weather.

The city offers a kaleidoscope of wonders, from vibrant ethnic enclaves to playgrounds of the very rich and famous to surfing and blading opportunities galore. It's a city where Disneyland, Universal Studios, the La Brea Tar Pits, Hollywood, and countless other attractions beckon visitors year-round. While Angelenos may pride themselves on setting national trends (think health food, yoga, and exercise clothing as fashion statement), they also tend to live up to the laid-back stereotype and are usually more than willing to give directions, advice, or beach reports. In short, Los Angeles is an easy city in which to be a tourist, and with nearly 25 million visitors annually, you will not stand out—even with a camera around your neck.

With nearly 3.7 million residents and 467 square mi of desert, mountains, and beaches, L.A. is many things to many people. Although you won't be able to see or do it all here, you'll doubtless have fun trying.

Exploring

In a city whose residents think nothing of a 50-mi commute to work, visitors have their work cut out for them. Be prepared to put miles on your rental car and become very familiar with your L.A. map. Choose adjacent neighborhoods when planning the day's adventures. Neighborhoods, below, are given in roughly west to east order, with areas farther outside of L.A. (the Valley, Pasadena, Long Beach, and Anaheim) listed separately.

Santa Monica, Venice, and Malibu

The coastal communities of Santa Monica, Venice, and Malibu have their differences, from wealthy Malibu to liberal Santa Monica to the bohemian-seedy mix of Venice. What they share, however, is cleaner and cooler coastal air and plenty of opportunities to get out and enjoy life.

Marina del Ray. Just south of Venice, this enormous man-made marina with moorings for 10,000 boats is a brilliant sight on a sunny day. Small "Mother's Beach" (Marina Beach) has calm, protected waters ideal for young children.

To arrange marina and dining cruises, call **Hornblower Dining Yachts** in Fisherman's Village. | 13755 Fiji Way, Marina del Rey | 310/301–6000 or 310/301–9900 | www.hornblower.com.

Santa Monica Pier. Eateries, souvenir shops, a psychic adviser, arcades, and rides dot this pier below Palisades Park, where free concerts are held in summer. The pier's trademark is a 1922 Looff carousel. | Colorado Ave. and the ocean, Santa Monica | 310/458–8900 | www.santamonicapier.org.

Third Street Promenade. Just a whiff away from the Pacific Ocean, this pedestrian-only street is lined with boutiques and chain stores, movie theaters, clubs, pubs, and restaurants. Day or night, wacky street performers, missionaries, and protesters work the crowds, while vendor cart operators cast a tolerant eye. | 3rd St. between Wilshire Blvd. and Broadway, Santa Monica.

★ **Venice Boardwalk.** This is a slice of L.A. that shouldn't be missed. Year-round action includes bikini-clad skaters who put on impromptu demonstrations, vying for attention with magicians, fortune tellers, a chain-saw juggler, and street artists. A local bodybuilding club works out on the adjacent "Muscle Beach," or you can get your own workout by renting skates or bicycles at the south end of the boardwalk.

The Westside

Westside districts like West Los Angeles, Westwood, Bel-Air, Brentwood, and Pacific Palisades share high concentrations of plastic surgeons and BMWs. The Westside, however, is also rich cultural territory. UCLA's Westwood campus and the Getty Center in Brentwood are just 3 mi apart.

★ **The Getty Center.** High atop a hill, the Getty affords fabulous views of the city, the ocean and Catalina Island beyond. A tram ferries you up from the parking level to the Getty itself. While spectacular architecture and imaginative gardens preoccupy most visitors, some actually go for the art. The permanent collections include European paintings, drawings, sculpture, illuminated manuscripts, and photographs. Parking reservations ($5) are required weekdays before 4 PM, for large groups, and for events. If possible, reserve a few weeks ahead, but same-day reservations are sometimes possible. Alternately, take public transportation (MTA No. 561 or Santa Monica Big Blue Bus No. 14). | 1200 Getty Center Dr. | 310/440–7300 | www.getty.edu | Free, parking $5 | Tues.–Sun. 10–6.

University of California, Los Angeles (UCLA). The parklike UCLA campus makes for a fine stroll. Of special interest are the Franklin Murphy Sculpture Garden and the Mildred Mathias Botanic Garden. Campus maps and information are available at drive-by kiosks at major entrances (the main entrance is on Westwood Boulevard). Advance reservations for free walking tours (Monday–Saturday) are required (310/825–8764). Campus parking is $6. | Le Conte, Hilgard, and Gayley Aves. and Sunset Blvd. border the campus | www.ucla.edu.

The changing exhibits at the **UCLA Fowler Museum of Cultural History** showcase world cultures and arts, especially those of Africa, Asia, Oceania, and Native and Latin America. | 310/825–4361 | $5, free Thurs. | Wed. and Fri.–Sun. noon–5, Thurs. noon–8.

Although small, the **UCLA Hammer Museum** has a rich permanent collection of old masters and French Impressionists and Postimpressionists. It also houses 35,000 graphic arts pieces, including drawings by Michelangelo and Rembrandt. | 310/443–7000 | $4.50, free Thurs. 3-hr parking $2.75 with validation.

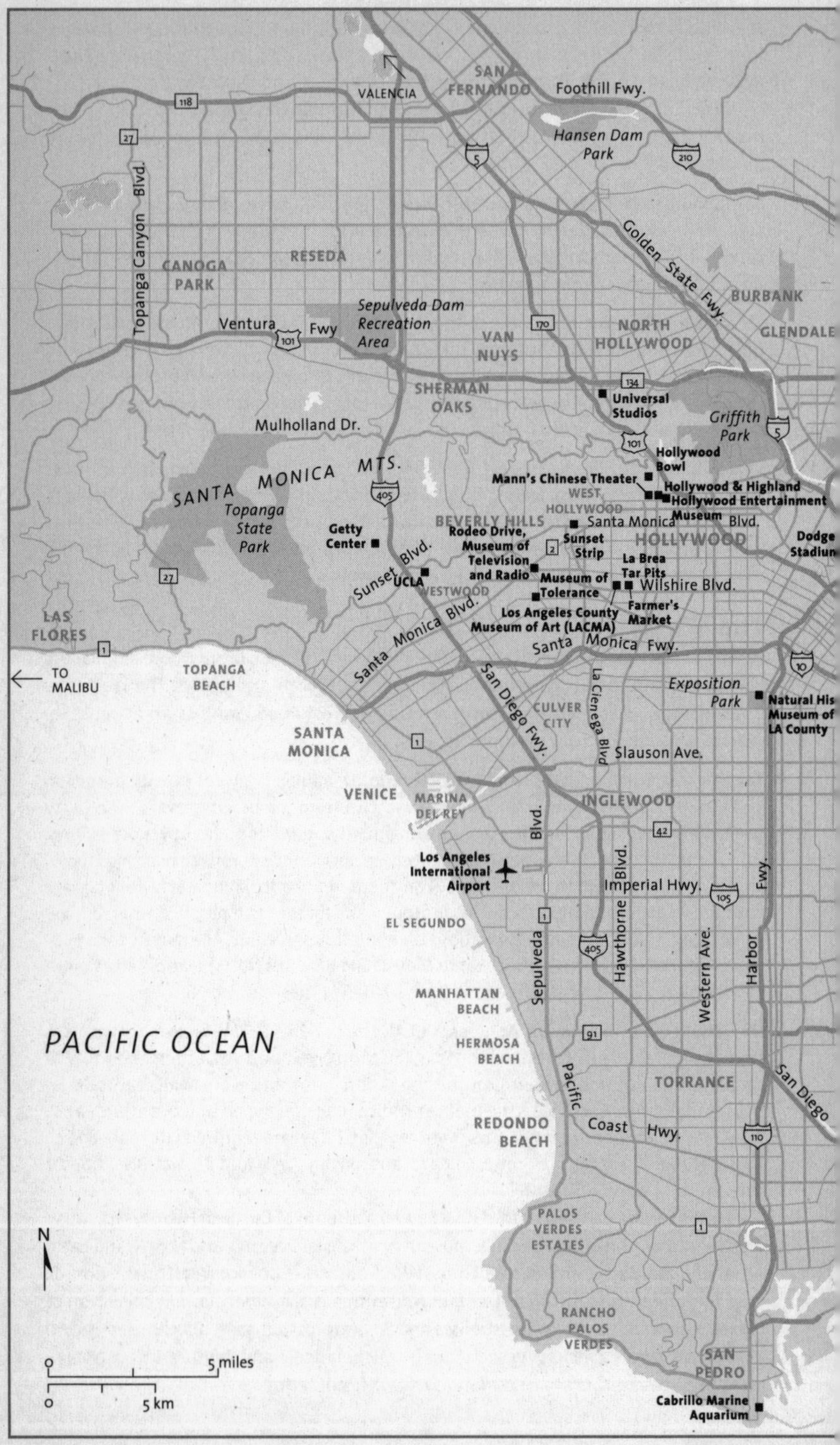

VALENCIA
SAN FERNANDO
Foothill Fwy.
118
27
Hansen Dam Park
5
210
Topanga Canyon Blvd.
Golden State Fwy.
RESEDA
CANOGA PARK
BURBANK
Sepulveda Dam Recreation Area
Ventura
101
Fwy
VAN NUYS
170
NORTH HOLLYWOOD
GLENDALE
SHERMAN OAKS
134
Universal Studios
Griffith Park
Mulholland Dr.
Hollywood Bowl
SANTA MONICA MTS.
Mann's Chinese Theater
405
WEST HOLLYWOOD
Hollywood & Highland
Hollywood Entertainment Museum
Topanga State Park
Getty Center
BEVERLY HILLS
Santa Monica Blvd.
Rodeo Drive, Museum of Television and Radio
HOLLYWOOD
Dodge Stadium
Sunset Strip
2
La Brea Tar Pits
Sunset Blvd.
UCLA
Museum of Tolerance
Wilshire Blvd.
WESTWOOD
Farmer's Market
Los Angeles County Museum of Art (LACMA)
LAS FLORES
Santa Monica Blvd.
Santa Monica Fwy.
1
TOPANGA BEACH
TO MALIBU
10
San Diego Fwy.
La Cienega Blvd
Exposition Park
Natural His Museum of LA County
CULVER CITY
SANTA MONICA
Slauson Ave.
VENICE
MARINA DEL REY
INGLEWOOD
42
Los Angeles International Airport
Imperial Hwy.
105
EL SEGUNDO
Sepulveda Blvd.
Hawthorne Blvd.
Western Ave.
Harbor Fwy.
MANHATTAN BEACH
PACIFIC OCEAN
91
HERMOSA BEACH
Pacific Coast Hwy.
TORRANCE
San Diego
REDONDO BEACH
110
PALOS VERDES ESTATES
N
RANCHO PALOS VERDES
SAN PEDRO
0
5 miles
0
5 km
Cabrillo Marine Aquarium

SAN GABRIEL MOUNTAINS
Angeles Crest Hwy.
2
Mt. Wilson
San Gabriel Reservoir
LA CAÑADA FLINTRIDGE
Glendale Fwy.
Rose Bowl
PASADENA
Norton Simon Museum
OLD TOWN PASADENA
Huntington Library
Forest Lawn Memorial Park
Pasadena Fwy.
110
SAN MARINO
ALHAMBRA
SAN GABRIEL
San Gabriel R.
Foothill Fwy.
210
39
5
EL MONTE
San Bernardino Fwy.
10
Union Station, Olvera Street
MONTEREY PARK
60
LA PUENTE
Pomona Fwy.
Valley Blvd.
Santa Ana Fwy.
Rosemead Blvd.
San Gabriel River Fwy.
WHITTIER
ROWLAND HEIGHTS
HUNTINGTON PARK
710
72
19
DOWNEY
42
105
LA HABRA
90
Orange Fwy.
Long Beach Fwy.
COMPTON
Los Angeles R.
57
Riverside Fwy.
91
Knott's Berry Farm
605
Lincon Ave.
LAKEWOOD
ANAHEIM
Disneyland
Santa Ana R.
El Dorado Park
55
Pacific Coast Hwy.
Queen Mary
Long Beach Aquarium of the Pacific
LONG BEACH
San Diego Fwy.
Harbor Blvd.
SANTA ANA
Costa Mesa Fwy.
1

Beverly Hills and Century City

Beverly Hills means expensive boutiques on Rodeo Drive; sky-high real estate prices; legendary hotels; high-powered restaurants; and—most of all—movie stars. Star-gazing visitors thus flock to the neighborhood, hoping for a close encounter with glamour.

Bordering Beverly Hills to the southwest is Century City, home to the Century City Shopping Center, the Shubert Theater, and 20th Century Fox Studios, while to the northeast is West Hollywood, home to Sunset Strip (still going strong) and a melange of nightclubs, gay discos, restaurants, art galleries, and interior design stores.

Museum of Television & Radio. This sleek museum houses 100,000 programs spanning eight decades. Search for your favorite commercials and television and radio shows on computers; then watch or listen to them in an adjacent room. Look for special exhibits of television- and radio-related art and costumes, as well as frequent seminars with television and radio cast members. | 465 N. Beverly Dr. | 310/786–1000 | www.mtr.org | $6 | Wed. and Fri.–Sun. noon–5, Thurs. noon–9.

Museum of Tolerance. Using interactive technology, this museum challenges visitors to confront bigotry and racism. One affecting section covers the Holocaust, and Anne Frank artifacts are part of the permanent collection. Advance reservations are advised (especially for Fridays, Sundays, and holidays). | 9786 W. Pico Blvd. | 310/553–8403 | www.wiesenthal.com/mot | $9 | Sun. 11–5, Mon.–Thurs. 11:30–4, Fri. 11:30–1 (Fri. 11:30–3 Apr.–Oct.).

★ **Rodeo Drive.** The section of Rodeo between Santa Monica and Wilshire boulevards offers free gawking and window-shopping at Tiffany & Co., Cartier, Gucci, Armani, Prada, and the like. | www.rodeodrive.com.

Museum Row and the Farmers Market

Just east of Fairfax Avenue in the Miracle Mile district is Museum Row, a three-block stretch of Wilshire Boulevard with five disparate museums and a prehistoric tar pit to boot. A few blocks away, the historic and newly revamped Farmers Market is a great place to start the day with coffee, pastries and people-watching. Finding parking along Wilshire Boulevard can present a challenge any time of day, so get advice from the information phone lines of most attractions.

★ **Farmers Market.** Since 1934, the Farmers Market has been an L.A. institution. With more than 110 stalls and 20 restaurants, and close to CBS Television Studios, the market is a major hub for stars and stargazers, tourists and locals. An electric trolley shuttles between Farmers Market and the Grove, an adjacent open-air shopping-and-entertainment center that opened in 2002. Parking is free. | 6333 W. 3rd St. | 323/933–9211 | www.farmersmarketla.com | May–Oct., Mon.–Sat. 9–7, Sun. 10–6; Nov–Apr., Mon.–Sat. 9–6:30, Sun. 10–5.

★ **La Brea Tar Pits.** Unexpectedly, the world's richest Ice Age fossil sites are smack dab in the middle of L.A. About 40,000 years ago, more than 600 species (like American mastodons and California saber-tooths) became trapped in sticky asphalt and eventually entombed. Dinosaur fans, be warned: these fossils date from millions of years *after* the dinosaur era. View the outdoor pits for free. | Hancock Park | www.tarpits.org.

The **Page Museum at the La Brea Tar Pits** displays fossils from the tar pits. | 5801 Wilshire Blvd. | 323/934–7243 | www.pagemuseum.org | $6 | Weekdays 9:30–5, weekends 10–5.

Los Angeles County Museum of Art (LACMA). LACMA's collection of more than 150,000 works from around the world is considered the most comprehensive in the western United States. Five buildings with mainly non-European art surround a central courtyard. LACMA West, a historic 1939 Streamline Moderne Building, houses a Latin American gallery (especially deep in modern Mexican masters like Diego Rivera) and the Experimental Gallery, geared toward children and families, who may enjoy interactive technologies more than paintings on a wall. | 5905 Wilshire Blvd. | 323/857–6000; 323/857–0098 TDD | www.lacma.org | $7, free 2nd Tues. of month | Mon.–Tues. and Thurs. noon–8, Fri. noon–9, weekends 11–8.

Petersen Automotive Museum. The world's largest automotive museum is, quite naturally, in L.A. Rare and classic cars, trucks, and motorcycles are all here. Rotating exhibits include Hollywood-celebrity and movie cars (for example, Fred's rockmobile from *The Flintstones* movie). A children's interactive Discovery Center illustrates the mechanics of the automobile. | 6060 Wilshire Blvd. | 323/930–2277 | www.petersen.org | $7 | Tues.–Sun. 10–6.

Hollywood

For many years, the famed HOLLYWOOD sign loomed above a neighborhood more seedy than glamorous. But since 2000, Hollywood has undergone some serious revitalization, bringing back the glamour of its heyday. If you have any star-struck family members, allot at least a half day to "do" Hollywood, including the new Hollywood & Highland complex, the Hollywood Entertainment Museum, the Hollywood Walk of Fame, and Mann's Chinese Theatre. It's a crowded area, so spring for the $10 parking lot off Highland Avenue, under Hollywood & Highland. And don't forget a camera!

Griffith Park. At 4,100 acres, Griffith Park is the largest municipal park in the nation and contains some major L.A. highlights. | Daily 6 AM–10 PM.

Most famously, the **Griffith Observatory and Planetarium** offers terrific views of the city (and the skies), but its $52 million renovation won't be complete until 2005. Call or check the Web site for more information. | 323/664–1191 | www.griffithobs.org.

The 80-acre **Los Angeles Zoo,** known for its breeding of endangered species like the California condor, is in the northeast corner of the park. | 323/664–6400 | www.lazoo.org | $8.25 | Daily 10–5.

Adjacent to the zoo is the **Autry Museum of Western Heritage,** at the junction of the Ventura Freeway (Highway 134) and the I–5. | 323/667–0988.

Kids may be most enamored of **Travel Town,** a collection of vintage locomotives and railroad cars with a ride-on choo-choo train. | 323/662–5874.

Hollywood & Highland. This megamillion-dollar hotel-retail-entertainment complex embodies the glamour and fantasy of the movies. Sweeping "Miss America" steps lead between floors of the open-air mall with branches of designer shops and chain stores. On the upper level, Babylon Court is presided over by a pair of 33-ft-high elephants. For a perfect photo opportunity on clear days, an arch frames the HOLLYWOOD sign. Next door, the Academy Awards are finally doled out in Hollywood, in the gorgeous Kodak Theatre. Abundant underground parking is accessible from Highland Avenue. There's also a Metro Red Line stop. | Hollywood Blvd. and Highland Ave. | 323/960–2331 | www.hollywoodandhighland.com | Parking $10.

Hollywood Entertainment Museum. A multimedia presentation and interactive exhibits along the one-hour guided tour trace the evolution of Hollywood, from the low-tech silent era to today's hyper-tech world of special effects. Highlights include sets from television shows such as the original *Star Trek* and the bar from *Cheers,* into which the series' stars carved their names. | 7021 Hollywood Blvd. | 323/465–7900 | www.hollywoodmuseum.com | $8.75 | Mon.–Tues. and Thurs.–Sun. 11–6.

★ **Hollywood Walk of Fame.** Along this mile-long stretch of Hollywood Boulevard's sidewalk, entertainment legends' names are embossed in brass at the center of pink stars.

Look for Charlie Chaplin at 6751 Hollywood, Marilyn Monroe at 6774 Hollywood (in front of McDonald's), Michael Jackson at 6927 Hollywood, and John Wayne at 1541 Vine.

Contact the **Hollywood Chamber of Commerce** for celebrity-star locations and information on future star installations (for real, live celebrity sightings). | 7018 Hollywood Blvd. | 323/469–8311 | www.hollywoodcoc.org.

Mann's Chinese Theatre. The former "Grauman's Chinese," a fantasy of Chinese pagodas and temples, is a Hollywood institution. Although you have to buy a movie ticket to appreciate the interior trappings, the courtyard is open to the public. Here you'll see cement hand- and footprints from more than 160 celebrities, along with some oddball imprints, like the one of Jimmy Durante's nose. | 6925 Hollywood Blvd. | 323/461–3331.

Downtown

Downtown L.A. may be an afterthought for most visitors, yet this area is not only the financial core of the city but its cultural and historical soul as well. Several under-utilized museums as well as dynamic ethnic enclaves coexist in the downtown L.A. area. If you tire of educational enrichment, relax and watch the wedding photography in Exposition Park's beautiful rose gardens (closed January–mid-March) after grabbing lunch at one of the museum's eateries.

★ **Cathedral of Our Lady of the Angels.** Opened in 2002, this $200 million, 12-story cathedral overlooking the Hollywood Freeway (I–101) is the new mother church of the country's largest Roman Catholic archdiocese. Its architecture and interior are awe-inspiring. | 555 W. Temple St. | 213/680–5200 | www.olacathedral.org | Weekdays 6:30 AM–7 PM, Sat. 9–5, Sun. 7–5.

California African-American Museum. The museum's collection documents the African-American experience from Emancipation and Reconstruction through the 20th century, with an emphasis on history in the West and California. | 600 State Dr. | 213/744–7432 | www.caam.ca.gov | Free, parking $6 | Tues.–Sun. 10–5.

California Science Center. Ogle Tess, the 50-ft animatronic star of the exhibit Body Works; build a structure to see how it stands up to an earthquake; or ride a high-wire bicycle to learn about gravity. An IMAX theater shows science-related films. | 700 State Dr. | 323/724–3623; 213/744–2019 IMAX | www.casciencectr.org | Free, except for IMAX (prices vary); parking $6 | Daily 10–5.

ESSENTIALS FOR YOUR CAR

Cell phone numbers of other family members.

Phone number at your next destination.

Driving directions for your family's route.

Music tapes or CDs; books on tape.

Tool kit.

Extra water; windshield-wiper fluid.

Motor oil; coolant or anti-freeze.

Spare tire.

Cooler with drinks and snacks.

Maps.

Your auto-club membership card.

Natural History Museum of Los Angeles County. The third-largest natural history museum in the United States has a rich collection of prehistoric fossils and extensive bird, insect, and marine-life exhibits. The terrific Ralph M. Parsons Discovery Center for children has hands-on exhibits and a (live) insect zoo. | 900 Exposition Blvd. | 213/763–3466 | www.nhm.org | $8, free 1st Tues. of month; parking $6 | Weekdays 9–5, weekends 10–5.

★ **Olvera Street.** A one-block tiled walkway, overhung with grapes and bounded by shops and restaurants, lively Olvera Street offers vendor carts with Mexican wares, strolling mariachis, and a melting pot of visitors. At the Plaza between Main and Los Angeles streets, folk dancers often perform on weekends.

The **Olvera Street Visitors Center** is open Monday–Saturday 10–3. | 622 N. Main St. | 213/628–1274 | www.olvera-street.com.

Chinatown is just north of Olvera Street, bounded by Yale, Bernard, Ord, and Alameda streets.

San Fernando Valley

There are other valleys in the Los Angeles area, but this is *the* Valley of Valley Girl fame. Large portions of the Valley are bedroom communities of suburban tract homes and shopping centers, but most of the major film and television studios are also located here.

Six Flags Magic Mountain. If you're a true thrill seeker looking for "monster" rides, this is the place for you. In fact, Six Flags set a Guiness Book world record for most roller coasters (15) when it opened **X** in 2002. Shows and parades, along with rides for younger kids, fill out a long day at this park, less than an hour north of L.A. | Magic Mountain Parkway, off I–5, 25 mi northwest of Universal Studios | 661/255–4100 | www.sixflags.com | $43 | Daily, except some winter weekdays; call for hrs.

Universal Studios Hollywood. This theme park provides a sensational introduction to the principles of special effects. Seated aboard a comfortable tram, with state-of-the-art sound and LCD monitors, you can experience the parting of the Red Sea; meet a 30-ft-tall version of King Kong; be attacked by the ravenous killer shark of *Jaws* fame; and come face-to-face with an evil mummy. Narrated, hour-long tours traverse the 420-acre complex all day long. There are also several entertainment attractions based on Universal films and television shows. The 20-minute *Spider-Man Rocks!* show is one of the best. | 100 Universal City Plaza | 818/622–3801 | www.universalstudios.com | $45, parking $7 | Mid-June–early Sept., daily 8–10; early Sept.–mid June, daily 9–7.

CityWalk is a separate venue open to the non-park-going public. There's a slew of shops, restaurants, nightclubs, and movie theaters, including IMAX–3-D.

Warner Bros. Studios. Two-hour tours at this major studio center in Burbank involve a lot of walking, so dress comfortably. Tours are more technically oriented than the ones at Universal and take in the back-lot sets, prop construction department, and sound complex. Daily fare varies based on TV and movie production schedules. Reservations are required; children under eight are not admitted. | 4000 Warner Blvd., Burbank | 818/846–1403 or 818/954–1744 | www.wbsf.com | $32 | Tours weekdays 9–3 on the half hr.

Pasadena Area

Although part of the general Los Angeles sprawl, Pasadena is a historically distinct city with several gemlike museums and some world-class shopping. To reach Pasadena from downtown Los Angeles, drive north on the Pasadena Freeway (I–110). From Hollywood and the San Fernando Valley use the Ventura Freeway (Highway 134, east).

★ **Huntington Library, Art Collections, and Botanical Gardens.** Railroad tycoon Henry E. Huntington's home, dating from the early 1900s, is near the California Institute of Technology (Cal Tech) campus. The library contains more than 600,000 books and some 300 manuscripts, including such treasures as a Gutenberg Bible, George Washington's genealogy in his own handwriting, and first editions by Ben Franklin and Shakespeare. Two galleries hold collections of British paintings and American paintings and decorative arts. The 150-acre grounds are fabulous for strolling and include gardens with desert, Japanese, rose, and Shakespeare themes. | 1151 Oxford Rd., San Marino | 626/405–2100; 626/405–2141 recorded information | www.huntington.org | $10, free 1st Thurs. of month | Tues.–Fri. noon–4:30, weekends 10:30–4:30.

Norton Simon Museum. In the 1950s, Norton Simon started collecting the works of Degas, Renoir, Gauguin, and Cézanne. Today the Norton Simon Museum is one of the finest small museums anywhere, with a collection that spans more than 2,000 years of Western and Asian art. The outdoor sculpture garden with a natural pond was inspired by Claude Monet's Giverny. | 411 W. Colorado Blvd., Pasadena | 626/449–6840 | www.nortonsimon.org | $6 | Wed.–Thurs. and Sat.–Mon. noon–6, Fri. noon–9.

Old Town Pasadena. Revitalized in the 1990s, this area has restored 19th-century brick buildings with a contemporary overlay. Plentiful cafés and restaurants share space with chain stores, boutiques, and specialty bookstores. In the evenings and on weekends, streets are packed with people and Old Town crackles with energy. The 12-block historic district is anchored along Colorado Boulevard, between Pasadena Avenue and Arroyo Parkway.

Long Beach

Long Beach began as a seaside resort in the 19th century. During the early part of the 20th century, an oil boom brought midwesterners and Dust Bowlers in search of a better life. Bust followed boom, but a long-term redevelopment program has led to a revitalized community with several worthy attractions.

Long Beach Aquarium of the Pacific. Nestled along Long Beach's harbor, this aquarium has 17 major exhibit tanks and 30 smaller focus tanks of Pacific Ocean marine animals (some 10,000 creatures). Discovery Labs allow you to touch sea creatures, and an outdoor play area helps work off kids' excess energy. | 100 Aquarium Way | 562/590–3100 | www.aquariumofpacific.org | $16.95 | Daily 9–6.

Queen Mary. The largest passenger ship ever built, the 85,000-ton *Queen Mary* was launched in 1934 as a floating treasure of art deco splendor. The former first-class passenger quarters are now a hotel. Both guided and self-guided tours of the ship are available. On board are several restaurants and shops, an art gallery, and even a wedding chapel. You can ride the Metro Blue Line to Long Beach from downtown L.A., then catch a shuttle to the ship. | Pier J | 562/435–3511 | www.queenmary.com | $10 adults; guided tours additional; parking $5 | Daily 10–6, Sat. until 9 in summer.

Anaheim Vicinity

Since Walt Disney chose this once quiet farming community in Orange County for the site of his first amusement park in 1955, Disneyland has attracted more than 450 million visitors. Today, Anaheim's tourist center includes Edison International Field, home of the Anaheim Angels baseball team; Arrowhead Pond, where the Mighty Ducks hockey team plays and major rock concerts are held; and Knott's Berry Farm. Off the I–5, Anaheim is 26 mi southeast of Los Angeles.

★ **Disneyland.** If a trip to the "Happiest Place on Earth" is on your itinerary, rest assured you will not be bored: on 85 acres, there are eight theme lands with more than 60 major rides, 50 shops, and 30 restaurants. If you want a park overview, board the Disneyland

Railroad at the park entrance for a tour of all the lands. Highlights include Mickey and Minnie photo-ops in **Mickey's Toontown**; Sleeping Beauty's Castle and It's a Small World in **Fantasyland**; the popular Jungle Cruise and the Indiana Jones Adventure in **Adventureland**; Splash Mountain, Disney's steepest, wettest adventure, in **Critter Country**; Space Mountain and Toy Story's new Buzz Lightyear stage show in **Tomorrowland.** Besides the eight lands, daily live-action shows and parades are indelible crowd-pleasers. Arrive early to secure a good view; if there are two shows scheduled for the day, the second one tends to be less crowded. At the entrance, brochures with maps list show and parade times.

During the summer, Disneyland is mobbed with visitors, and popular rides may require up to a two-hour wait. Off-season (September–May) and mid-week visits are recommended. Otherwise, try to arrive early (the box office opens a half hour before the park), and head for popular rides first. The Fastpass allows you to reserve a place in line at the park's more popular attractions. If you plan to visit for more than a day, three- and four-day Park Hopper tickets that grant same-day "hopping" privileges between Disneyland and Disney's California Adventure are economical. | 1313 Harbor Blvd., Anaheim | 714/781–4565 | www.disneyland.com | $43, parking $7 | Daily. Hrs vary seasonally; call for schedule.

Disney's California Adventure. This 55-acre theme park next to Disneyland opened in 2001 and celebrates the Golden State with three theme areas: **Paradise Pier, Hollywood Pictures Backlot,** and **Golden State.** If you're looking for thrills, the California Screamin' roller coaster takes its riders from 0 to 55 mph in about four seconds and proceeds through scream tunnels, steeply angled drops, and a 360-degree loop. You can play for prizes at Who Wants to Be a Millionaire—Play It!, a replica of the game show's set. There's also a working 1-acre farm and winery, a 40,000-square-ft animation exhibit, Broadway-style theater, nature trail, and tortilla factory. Like its sister park, California Adventure has a daily parade. Retail shops and restaurants are plentiful. | 1313 Harbor Blvd., Anaheim | 714/781–4565 | www.disneyland.com | $43 | Daily; hrs vary seasonally (call for schedule).

Downtown Disney. Open to the non-park-going public, this 20-acre promenade of dining, shopping, restaurants, and nightclubs connects the Disneyland Resort hotels and theme parks. Sports fans gravitate to ESPN Zone, with American grill food, interactive video games, and 175 screens telecasting worldwide sports events. There is also a 12-screen AMC multiplex theater and promenade shops selling everything from Disney goods to fine art. | Disneyland Dr. between Ball Rd. and Katella Ave., Anaheim | 714/300–7800 | www.disneyland.com | Free | Daily 7 AM–2 AM; hrs at shops and restaurants vary.

Knott's Berry Farm. Down the road from the mouse empire in Anaheim, Knott's Berry Farm is California's second-largest amusement park, with 150 acres and more that 165 rides, shows, shops, restaurants, and other diversions in six theme areas. Built on the site where the boysenberry was invented, this attraction is 25 mi south of Los Angeles along the I–5. Although intended as an excursion into Old West history, Knott's Berry Farm is increasingly going the high-tech route with entertainments like Supreme Scream, the tallest descending thrill ride in the world. If you stay late, watch for the new laser and pyrotechnic show over Reflection Lake. | 8039 Beach Blvd., between La Palma Ave. and Crescent St., 2 blocks south of Hwy. 91, Buena Park, | 714/220–5200 | www.knotts.com | $40 | June–mid-Sept., daily 9 AM–midnight; mid-Sept.–May, weekdays 10–6, Sat. 10–10, Sun. 10–7; closed during inclement weather.

Dining

L.A.'s restaurants reflect both the city's well-deserved reputation for culinary innovation and its rich ethnic cornucopia. Not only are many of the country's superstar chefs in residence, but there are also many unheralded chefs who delight Angelenos with the cuisines of their native Shanghai, Oaxaca, Tuscany, and beyond. So whether you are looking for a culinary adventure or just a really good burger, expect to be satisfied here.

Santa Monica, Venice, and Malibu

Gladstone's 4 Fish. Seafood. Proclaiming itself the most popular restaurant along the Pacific coast, Gladstone's has a sprawling indoor dining area and spacious outdoor deck. You'll still probably have a wait if you arrive at high mealtime. Much of the seafood is mesquite-grilled, but you can also get fish chowder, seafood salads, or enormous burgers for lunch. Portions are huge (split them for kids). | 17300 Pacific Coast Hwy. (at Sunset Blvd.), Malibu/Pacific Palisades | 310/573–0212 | $15–$45 | AE, DC, MC, V.

Gaucho Grill. Argentine. On the 3rd Street Promenade, this busy, noisy restaurant specializes in Argentinian grilled chicken and steak. Curlicue fries, salads, and sandwiches round out the menu. Gaucho Grill also has branches in Hollywood, Studio City, Brentwood, and Glendale (call for locations). Reservations for 5 or more essential. | 1251 3rd St. Promenade | 310/394–4966 | $8–$16 | AE, DC, MC, V.

Sidewalk Café. Eclectic. It's worth waiting in line for a table at Venice Beach's Sidewalk Café. The food is fine (burgers, pizza, sandwiches, salads, burritos), but what's better is the prime location for watching Venice's free spirits parade past your patio table. | 1401 Ocean Front Walk | 310/399–5547 | Reservations not accepted | $6–$12 | AE, MC, V.

The Westside

The Apple Pan. American/Casual. When only a burger and fries will do, head for the Apple Pan. It's a small diner where everyone sits around a U-shape counter that surrounds an open kitchen. You may have to wait, but service is fast and the cooks put on a good show. Save room for a big slice of apple pie with or without ice cream. | 10801 W. Pico Blvd., West L.A. | 310/475–3585 | Reservations not accepted | Closed Mon. | $5–$10 | No credit cards.

Beverly Hills and Century City

★ **Ed Debevic's.** American/Casual. A '50s-style diner with *attitude*, this is the kind of place where the waitress sits at your table while you order. The decor is chrome and Formica, while the menu offers tasty burgers, onion rings, chili fries, and fountain drinks. | 134 N. La Cienega Blvd. | 310/659–1952 | $5–$15 | MC, V.

Nate 'n' Al's. Delicatessens. A famous gathering place for Hollywood comedians and Beverly Hills shoppers, Nate 'n' Al's has regulars bantering with waitresses who serve first-rate matzo-ball soup, lox and scrambled eggs, and deli sandwiches. The room is large and the tables roomy, but expect a wait at peak hours. Free parking. | 414 N. Beverly Dr. | 310/274–0101 | Reservations not accepted | $8–$12 | AE, MC, V.

Museum Row and the Farmers Market

★ **Canter's.** Delicatessens. This granddaddy of L.A. delicatessens (open since 1928) pickles its own corned-beef pastrami and has an in-house bakery. Next door is the Kibitz Room, where there's live music every night. | 419 N. Fairfax Ave. | 323/651–2030 | Reservations not accepted | $11–$17 | MC, V.

Gumbo Pot. Cajun/Creole. This outdoor Cajun-Creole café in the Farmers Market serves a mean, spicy gumbo rich in shrimp and chicken. Come, too, for corn-battered shrimp, jambalaya, and *beignets*. | 6333 W. 3rd St. | 323/933–0358 | Reservations not accepted | $5–$10 | MC, V.

Hollywood Vicinity

East India Grill. Indian. This popular café serves traditional, zesty Indian food with a California edge. Traditional dishes such as green-coconut and tomato-based curries are served, along with imaginative alternatives like tandoori chicken salad and mango ribs. There's free garage parking. | 345 N. La Brea Ave. | 323/936–8844 | $7–$13 | AE, MC, V.

El Cholo. Mexican. Packing them in since the '20s, El Cholo serves large portions of L.A.-Mex standards, like chicken enchiladas and *carnitas* (shredded fried pork). A hand-painted adobe ceiling and outdoor patio with a fountain provide atmosphere for enjoying margaritas and all kinds of tacos, some of which you make yourself. There's valet and meter parking. | 1121 S. Western Ave. | 323/734–2773 | $12–$15 | AE, DC, MC, V.

Hard Rock Cafe. American/Casual. You'll spy the 1959 green Caddy plunging through the roof outside and, most likely, the line out the door. This branch of the international chain, outfitted in rock memorabilia, is ripe for star-gazing. If you don't mind the noise and crowds, the food is consistently good (burgers, salads, barbecue chicken and ribs). | 8600 Beverly Blvd., in the Beverly Center | 310/276–7605 | Reservations not accepted | $9–$22 | AE, DC, MC, V.

Hollywood Hills Coffee Shop. American/Casual. Surprisingly good food and sometimes-famous diners make this little café a find. Breakfast choices include huevos rancheros and cheese blintzes, while dinner selections include vegetarian, meat, or fish options. | 6145 Franklin Ave. | 323/467–7678 | Reservations not accepted | $7–$18 | MC, V.

Roscoe's House of Chicken 'n' Waffles. Southern. This is *the* place for real down-home southern cooking. Just ask the patrons, who drive from all over the L.A. basin for Roscoe's bargain-price fried chicken, waffles, and grits. | 1514 N. Gower St. | 323/466–9329 | Reservations not accepted | $5–$9 | AE, D, DC, MC, V.

Downtown

Mon Kee Seafood Restaurant. Chinese. In Chinatown, this bustling, plain two-room restaurant's specialty is Hong Kong–style fresh seafood like garlic crab, steamed catfish, or shrimp in spicy salt. Large tables are available, but be prepared for a wait. | 679 N. Spring St. | 213/628–6717 | $9–$17 | AE, DC, MC, V.

La Golondrina. Mexican. Housed in the city's historic first brick building, La Golondrina has indoor and outdoor seating that enables diners to choose between privacy or access to Olvera Street performers and people-watching. House specialties include fajitas, chiles relleno, and charbroiled fresh fish. An all-you-can-eat buffet is served weekdays at lunch. | W–17 Olvera St. | 213/628–4349 | $8–$15 | AE, D, DC, MC, V.

Philippe the Original. American/Casual. This downtown landmark near Union Station and Chinatown has been serving its famous French dip sandwich (made with beef, pork, ham, lamb, or turkey on a freshly baked roll) since 1908. Sawdust on the floor and long, wooden tables encourage diners to behave like one big, noisy family. The home cooking includes hearty breakfasts, an enormous pie selection, and one of America's last dime cups of coffee. | 1001 N. Alameda St. | 213/628–3781 | Reservations not accepted | $7–$12 | No credit cards.

San Fernando Valley

Paty's. American. Near NBC, Warner Bros., and the Disney Studio, this homey coffee shop is reliable, affordable, and ideally located if you're hungry after a studio tour. Breakfasts include plump omelets and homemade biscuits. For lunch or dinner there are hearty, comforting dishes such as Swiss steak, roast turkey, and beef stew. | 10001 Riverside Dr. | 818/761–0041 | Reservations not accepted | $6–$13 | AE, DC, MC, V.

Wolfgang Puck Cafe. Contemporary. Sample the creations of L.A.'s most famous chef, Wolfgang Puck, at this attractive café along Universal's CityWalk. Reasonably priced specialties like pizzas, pastas, and rotisserie chicken will allay any fears about weird gourmet foods. | 1000 Universal Center Dr. | 818/985–9653 | Reservations not accepted | $10–$23 | MC, V.

Long Beach

Johnny Rockets. Contemporary. If you're touring the *Queen Mary* or the Aquarium of the Pacific, grab a free shuttle to downtown Long Beach and hop off at this '50s-retro burger joint. Indulge in burgers, hot dogs, chili fries, and fountain drinks in a family atmosphere. | 245 Pine Ave. | 562/983–1332 | Reservations not accepted | $4–$8 | AE, D, MC, V.

Lodging

Like real estate, hotel selection in L.A. can be summed up in three words: location, location, location. Hotels near LAX, Long Beach, Santa Monica, Marina del Rey, Venice, and Beverly Hills are along or near the beaches; Westside hotels are near Beverly Hills and Hollywood; San Fernando Valley hotels are convenient for Universal Studios or Hollywood; downtown L.A. is still frequented mostly by conventioneers and business travelers; and Anaheim is the place to be for Disneyland and other Orange County attractions. If you have a car, parking is an expense to consider, as most hotels charge for the privilege and some resorts have valet parking only.

Los Angeles International Airport

Furama Hotel Los Angeles. In a quiet residential area, the Furama is convenient to jogging paths, tennis, and golf. Most rooms have views of the pool, the airport, or the city. A shuttle service goes to LAX (about 1 mi), Marina del Rey, Venice Beach, and the Santa Monica Mall. Happy-hour snacks are served weeknights in the lounge. Restaurant, room service, cable TV with movies, 2 gyms, hot tub, bar, baby-sitting, laundry service, concierge, concierge floor, Internet, business services, meeting room, parking (fee), no-smoking floor | 8601 Lincoln Blvd. | 310/670–8111 or 800/225–8126 | fax 310/337–1883 | www.furama-hotels.com | 760 rooms, 6 suites | $120 | AE, D, DC, MC, V.

Summerfield Suites by Wyndham. There's room to spread out in these one- and two-bedroom extralarge suites with living-room sleeper sofas. Cook in the fully outfitted kitchens or on the gas grills outside. The staff will stock your refrigerator with groceries (you'll only pay for the groceries). There are also plenty of restaurants within walking distance. Weeknights the hotel hosts a happy hour with complimentary drinks and snacks. Room service, in-room data ports, cable TV, in-room VCRs, pool, gym, hot tub, basketball, laundry facilities, laundry service, Internet, business services, meeting rooms, free parking, no-smoking rooms | 810 S. Douglas Ave. | 310/725–0100 or 800/996–3426 | fax 310/725–0900 | www.wyndham.com | 122 suites | $179 | AE, D, DC, MC, V.

Santa Monica and Venice

Best Western Marina Pacific Hotel & Suites. This hotel faces the Pacific and one of the world's most vibrant boardwalks: the Strand. Nestled among Venice's art galleries, shops, and offbeat restaurants, there's always something to do. The marina is a stroll away, and racquetball and tennis courts are nearby. Some rooms have balconies and views of the beach. Continental breakfast is complimentary. Dining room, in-room data ports, refrigerators, cable TV, laundry service, meeting room, parking (fee), no-smoking rooms | 1697 Pacific Ave. | 310/452–1111 or 800/421–8151 | fax 310/452–5479 | www.mphotel.com | 57 rooms, 35 suites | $99–$159 | AE, D, DC, MC, V.

Hotel California. Welcome to the Hotel California, where you can enjoy the warmth of a private guest house with a prime location on Ocean Avenue. Private gated beach access leads you to the biggest swimming hole in the West. Reasonable rates make it a very popular choice, especially summer weekends. Some kitchens, refrigerators, cable TV, some in-room VCRs, parking (fee), no-smoking room | 1670 Ocean Ave. | 310/393–2363 or 866/571–0000 | fax 310/393–1063 | www.hotelca.com | 18 rooms, 8 suites | $99–$169 | AE, DC, MC, V.

★ **Loews Santa Monica Beach Hotel.** It's a splurge, but this family-oriented hotel may be worth it. Right on the beach, two blocks from the Santa Monica Pier and three blocks from the Promenade, the location couldn't be better. Dramatic design elements include a five-story glass atrium and a glass-domed pool ranging both indoors and outdoors. Kids ages 5 to 12 can join the "Splash Club" for supervised morning and evening activities ($5 per hour) or choose to check out books, video games, or board games on their own time. Kids under 18 stay free in their parents' room, or, in summer, in a connecting room for half price. 2 restaurants, café, room service, in-room data ports, minibars, cable TV, health club, hair salon, hot tub, massage, sauna, spa, steam room, beach, windsurfing, bicycles, bar, baby-sitting, laundry service, concierge, business services, meeting room, travel services, car rental, parking (fee), no-smoking floor | 1700 Ocean Ave. | 310/458–6700 or 800/235–6397 | fax 310/458–6761 | www.loewshotels.com | 321 rooms, 19 suites | $210–$460 | AE, D, DC, MC, V.

The Westside

Best Western Royal Palace. This smallish hotel is right off I–405, making it convenient to ocean beaches, LAX, and Beverly Hills (all within 6–10 mi). Suites have microwaves and refrigerators; Continental breakfasts are complimentary; and kids under 12 stay free with parents. Room service, refrigerators, cable TV, pool, gym, hot tub, sauna, billiards, laundry facilities, meeting room, free parking, no-smoking rooms | 2528 S. Sepulveda Blvd. | 310/477–9066 or 800/251–3888 | fax 310/478–4133 | www.bestwesternroyalpalace.com | 23 rooms, 32 suites | $84–$159 | AE, D, DC, MC, V.

Doubletree Hotel. Amid the high-rise condos of Wilshire Corridor, this tastefully appointed 19-story hotel blends in well. Midway between Westwood Village and Beverly Hills, the Doubletree is an ideal choice for visitors to the UCLA campus (there's a free shuttle). Fresh chocolate-chip cookies await you upon check-in. Restaurant, room service, in-room data ports, cable TV with video games, pool, gym, bar, dry cleaning, laundry service, concierge, Internet, meeting room, parking (fee), no-smoking rooms | 10740 Wilshire Blvd. | 310/475–8711 | fax 310/475–5220 | www.doubletreelawestwood.com | 294 rooms, 8 suites | $129–$159 | AE, D, DC, MC, V.

Beverly Hills

Beverly Hills Plaza Hotel. Space is not a problem at this all-suite hotel. Outdoor gardens with a waterfall and koi pond are lovely. You'll find kitchens, movies, and Nintendo in the suites; VCRs can be rented at the front desk. Restaurant, in-room safes, minibars, cable TV, pool, gym, hot tub, bar, laundry service, concierge, business services, parking (fee) | 10300 Wilshire Blvd. | 310/275–5575 or 800/800–1234 | fax 310/278–3325 | www.placestostay.com | 116 suites | $185 | AE, D, DC, MC, V.

Beverly Terrace Hotel. Rooms are basic (except for the leopard-print bedspreads), and bathrooms have shower stalls instead of tubs, but the price is right. The hotel borders Beverly Hills and West Hollywood, close to the Sunset Strip. Complimentary Continental breakfast is served outside by the pool. Trattoria Amici, the on-site Italian restaurant, is known to attract some of the neighborhood's high-profile clientele. Some refrigerators, cable TV, pool, free parking, some pets allowed (fee); no smoking | 469 N. Doheny Dr. | 310/274–8141 or 800/842–6401 | fax 310/385–1998 | www.beverlyterracehotel.com | 39 rooms | $95–$165 | AE, D, DC, MC, V.

Hollywood Vicinity

Highland Gardens Hotel. Just blocks from the Walk of Fame and a few minutes' drive from the Sunset Strip, this three-story, '60s-style hotel has basic but spacious sleeping areas. For charm, it has a large, sparkling pool and lush, if somewhat overgrown, tropical gardens. Some kitchenettes, refrigerators, room TVs, pool, laundry facilities, free parking, no-smoking rooms | 7047 Franklin Ave. | 323/850–0536 or 800/404–5472 | fax 323/850–1712 | www.highlandgardenshotel.com | 70 rooms, 48 suites | $75–$95 | AE, MC, V.

Magic Castle Hotel. In a 1908 Victorian mansion that is also the clubhouse of the Academy of Magical Arts, this hotel enables you to secure reservations to the exclusive Magic Castle restaurant and magic shows (jacket and tie are required for both). Although close to the action of Hollywood, the Magic Castle's relaxing pool and pagoda seem far from the city. For quick trips downtown or to Universal Studios, there's a Red Line stop a few blocks away. In-room safes, some kitchenettes, refrigerators, cable TV, pool, laundry facilities, free parking | 7025 Franklin Ave. | 323/851–0800 or 800/741–4915 | fax 323/851–4926 | www.magiccastlehotel.com | 10 rooms, 30 suites | $79 | AE, D, DC, MC, V.

Downtown

Inntowne Hotel. This modern, three-story hotel is on 2 acres dotted with palm trees. The convention center and Staples Center are 1½ blocks away; downtown restaurants and nightlife are within walking distance. Cable TV, pool, laundry facilities, car rental, parking (fee), no-smoking rooms | 913 S. Figueroa St. | 213/628–2222 or 866/629–3388 | fax 213/623–1350 | www.inntownela.net | 170 rooms | $85 | AE, D, DC, MC, V.

★ **Westin Bonaventure Hotel & Suites.** This 35-story futuristic complex has five circular glass towers, each with its own outside glass elevator (seen in several movies). Tourists come to gawk even if they're *not* staying here. Some 40 shops and restaurants encircle the lower floors. Swimming in the outdoor pool on the fourth floor, surrounded by skyscrapers, is one of those uniquely L.A. experiences. 17 restaurants, room service, in-room data ports, minibars, cable TV, pool, health club, hair salon, spa, indoor track, 5 bars, laundry service, concierge, business services, meeting room, car rental, travel services, parking (fee), no-smoking floor | 404 S. Figueroa Ave. | 213/624–1000 or 800/228–3000 | fax 213/612–4800 | www.westin.com | 1,354 rooms, 135 suites | $159–$319 | AE, D, DC, MC, V.

San Fernando Valley and Vicinity

Sheraton Universal. If you want to be first in line at Universal Studios (and maybe spot some stars in your hotel lobby), head for this 21-story Sheraton. Walk or take the free tram to Universal Studios, and ask about special package deals that include passes for the studio tour. Kids under 16 stay free with their parents. Restaurant, room service, in-room data ports, in-room safes, minibars, cable TV, pool, gym, hot tub, bar, laundry service, concierge, business services, meeting room, car rental, parking (fee), no-smoking floor | 333 Universal Terrace Pkwy. | 818/980–1212 or 800/325–3535 | fax 818/985–4980 | www.starwood.com | 436 rooms and suites | $149–$219 suites | AE, D, DC, MC, V.

Sportsmen's Lodge. This five-story, English country–style inn has grounds with waterfalls, a swan-filled lagoon, and a gazebo. Overlooking the gardens, the Lodge restaurant is a Valley favorite for brunch; live entertainment and happy hour bring in the crowds from nearby TV studios on weekends. Golf, tennis, and Universal City are nearby. Discount tickets and a complimentary shuttle to Universal Studios are available. 3 restaurants, room service, in-room data ports, cable TV, pool, gym, hair salon, outdoor hot tub, bar, dry cleaning, laundry facilities, laundry service, airport shuttle, car rental, travel services, free parking, no-smoking floors | 12825 Ventura Blvd. | 818/769–4700 or 800/821–8511 | fax 818/769–4798 | www.slhotel.com | 177 rooms, 13 suites | $118–$154 | AE, D, DC, MC, V.

Long Beach

Hotel *Queen Mary.* The legendary *Queen Mary* passenger ship transports you to a bygone era. First-class staterooms and suites are decorated in art deco style. Children, especially, are enthralled by the experience of shipboard lodging and exploring. Take a self-guided tour of the venerable vessel during the day, or for an extra fee, tour the Scorpion submarine docked next to the ship. 3 restaurants, room service, cable TV, gym, massage, spa, bar, shops, laundry service, business services, meeting rooms, car rental, free parking, parking (fee), no-smoking floor | 1150 Queens Hwy., Pier H | 562/435–3511 or 800/437–2934 | fax 562/432–7674 | www.queenmary.com | 300 staterooms, 8 suites | $109–$129 | AE, DC, MC, V.

Anaheim

Disneyland Hotel. One of three Disney hotels, this family favorite may have kids thinking this *is* the Magic Kingdom. Disney characters stroll through the dining rooms, there's a 5,000-square-ft swimming hole (Never Land Pool), a waterfall, ponds, and caves, plus a game arcade to keep them busy for hours. Other area hotels are cheaper, but, if your vacation centers on Disneyland, this is awfully convenient. Early admission vouchers for Disneyland (1½ hours before general admission) are available for most days. Children 17 and under stay free with parents. 5 restaurants, room service, in-room data ports, in-room safes, minibars, refrigerator, 10 tennis courts, 5 pools, 2 hot tubs, exercise room, beach, 2 bars, laundry service, concierge, business services, car rental, travel services, airport shuttle, parking (fee), no-smoking rooms | 1150 Magic Way, Anaheim | 714/778–6600 | fax 714/956–6582 | www.disneyland.com | 990 rooms, 62 suites | $170–$255 | AE, D, DC, MC, V.

Arts and Entertainment

Film

Some of the country's most historic and beautiful theaters are found in L.A., hosting both first-run and revival films. Admission to first-run movies is about $9, but it can be lower for discount matinees and theaters or higher for specialty venues like IMAX theaters.

ART AND REVIVAL HOUSES

★ **American Cinematèque Lloyd E. Rigler Theatre at the Egyptian.** The 1922 Egyptian Theater screens classics and new indies. | 6712 Hollywood Blvd., Hollywood | 323/466–3456 | www.egyptiantheatre.com.

Silent Movie Theater. Pre-talkies return to the big screen with live musical accompaniment. | 611 N. Fairfax Ave., Fairfax District | 323/655–2520 | www.silentmovietheater.com.

MOVIE PALACES

Mann's Chinese Theatre. Open since 1929, this is perhaps the world's best-known theater, with its cement walkway marked with movie stars' foot- and handprints and its gala premieres. | 6925 Hollywood Blvd., Hollywood | 323/464–8111.

Pacific Cinerama Dome. The futuristic, geodesic theater was the first U.S. theater designed specifically for the enormous screen and magnificent sound system of Cinerama. | 6360 Hollywood Blvd., Hollywood | 323/466–3401.

Pacific's El Capitan. Across the street from Mann's Chinese Theatre, this classic art deco masterpiece has been meticulously renovated by Disney. | 6838 Hollywood Blvd., Hollywood | 323/467–7674.

Music

Los Angeles Philharmonic. The orchestra offers both adult fare and a kids' concert series at the new Walt Disney Concert Hall. | 323/850–2000 | www.laphil.org.

The new (in 2003) **Walt Disney Concert Hall,** designed by Frank Gehry, is a $274 million facility with state-of-the-art acoustics. | Grand Ave. and 1st St., Downtown.

In the summer, the Philharmonic plays at the **Hollywood Bowl,** an outdoor amphitheater in Griffith Park that also hosts jazz, pop, and world music acts. Park-and-Ride buses to the Bowl leave from various locations around town. | 2301 Highland Ave., Hollywood | 323/850–2000 | www.hollywoodbowl.com.

Television

For **free tickets** to tapings, call one of the television networks or the offices of Paramount Pictures. Free tickets are also available outside Mann's Chinese Theatre in Hollywood, at Universal Studios Hollywood, and along Ocean Front Walk on Venice Beach. Many shows do not admit children or have minimum age requirements.

ABC–TV | 818/506–0067.

CBS–TV | 213/852–2458.

NBC–TV | 818/840–3537.

Paramount Pictures | 213/956–5577.

Audiences Unlimited also distributes free tickets by mail or by reservation over the Internet only. | 100 Universal City Plaza, Bldg. 153, Universal City 91608 | 818/506–0043 | www.tvtickets.com.

NBC Television Studios. NBC, in "lovely downtown Burbank," also offers behind-the-scenes tours of TV-show sets as well as wardrobe and makeup departments, with perhaps a star or two at work. All ages are welcome, but toddlers won't last through an hour of walking and listening. Tours are given weekdays 9–4. | 3000 W. Alameda Ave., Burbank | 818/840–3537 | www.ohwy.com/ca/n/nbcstudi.html | $6.

Theater

As you'd imagine, L.A. has a vibrant theater scene. Check listings at **Now Playing** (www.reviewplays.com) and **Theatre League Alliance** (www.theatrela.org), which also offers WebTIX, where you can buy tickets on-line the day of the performance at half-price or less.

Geffen Playhouse. New plays, many of them on their way to or from Broadway, are showcased in the summer. | 10886 Le Conte Ave., Westwood | 310/208–5454.

Los Angeles Music Center. Four major venues share space here. The LA Opera, housed in the Dorothy Chandler Pavilion, will have a new neighbor when the LA Philharmonic moves into the new Walt Disney Concert Hall. | 135 N. Grand Ave., Downtown | 213/972–7211 | www.musiccenter.org.

Pantages Theatre. A former home of the Academy Awards telecast, the art deco theater presents large-scale Broadway musicals such as *The Lion King*. | 6233 Hollywood Blvd., Hollywood | 323/468–1770 | www.nederlander.com.

Santa Monica Playhouse. The playhouse puts on children's favorites like *Beauty and the Beast*. | 1211 4th St., Santa Monica | 310/394–9779.

Shopping

Shopping in L.A. is more than a pastime, as residents strive to find the best deal, the latest trend, or the most exclusive boutique. Visitors will have no trouble finding shops in which to lighten their wallets. One of the most fun areas for picking up trinkets is **Olvera Street,** where vendor carts with Mexican goods tempt adults and kids alike.

Santa Monica and Venice

Less frenetic and status-conscious than Beverly Hills, Santa Monica is ideal for leisurely shopping. Most shopping activity takes place at the **3rd Street Promenade,** between Broadway and Wilshire Boulevard; **Main Street** between Pico Boulevard and Rose Avenue; and along the boutiques-lined **Montana Avenue,** from 9th to 17th Street. Parking is next to impossible in Santa Monica on Wednesday, when some streets are blocked off for the Farmers Market.

Now that Julia Roberts has bought a house in artsy Venice, it's destined to become ever more popular. Try window-shopping along **Abbot Kinney Boulevard.**

Beverly Hills and Century City

Shopping in Beverly Hills centers on the three-block stretch of **Rodeo Drive** between Santa Monica and Wilshire boulevards and the streets surrounding it. Places you've always heard about—Tiffany, Cartier, Versace, Gucci, and many more—are all (expensively) here. There's no charge for looking, but some exclusive boutiques require an appointment. Department stores like Barneys, Neiman Marcus, and Saks are along **Wilshire Boulevard.**

To the west, Century City is where entertainment executives and industry types do their serious shopping. In general, it's more affordable than Beverly Hills. There are also plenty of restaurants and live theaters, as well as a 14-screen AMC movie complex.

Hollywood Vicinity

In Hollywood, the shopping focus is on **Hollywood & Highland.** Outside this retail megaplex, on La Brea Avenue especially, you'll find plenty of trendy, quirky, and hip merchandise, from records to furniture and clothing. To the west, the very popular shopping area of **West Hollywood** offers record stores along Sunset Boulevard, pricey antiques stores and galleries on Melrose Place, and upscale boutiques on Robertson Boulevard and upper Melrose Avenue. South of Hollywood the funky **★Melrose Avenue** is a bohemian shopping district and great people-watching venue. Teens in gothic black, multipierced slackers, and aspiring actors and musicians scour the vintage-clothing shops. The L.A. section, from North Highland to Sweetzer, has anything from used clothing to fetish wear and vintage shoes.

Fred Segal. A longtime L.A. fashion landmark (a second branch opened in Santa Monica), Fred Segal is a collection of eclectic mini-boutiques, specializing in items unavailable elsewhere—European Levi lines, up-and-coming L.A. designers, and the like. All that is hot and hip in clothing, jewelry, shoes, and accessories is here, with the requisite star sighting or two as a bonus. | 8101 Melrose Ave. | 323/651–4129.

Hollywood Magic Shop. This Tinseltown institution sells costumes year-round and has a wide selection of tricks, jokes, and novelties. | 6614 Hollywood Blvd. | 323/464–5610.

Downtown

Several huge shopping venues are downtown: the **Flower Mart** (742 Maple Avenue), the **Jewelry District** (between Hill Street and Broadway, from 5th to 8th Street), and the **Fashion District** (roughly between I–10 and 7th Street and San Pedro and Main streets). **Santee Alley,** in the Fashion District, is an open-air market with everything from knockoff designer wear to sunglasses. Ethnic shopping areas also abound, from colorful **Olvera Street** to the nearby neighborhoods of **Chinatown, Koreatown,** and, a little farther south and west, **Leimert Park** (between Crenshaw and Leimert boulevards and 43rd Street and Vernon Avenue), an African-theme shopping area.

Pasadena

In Pasadena, the stretch of Colorado Boulevard between Pasadena Avenue and Arroyo Parkway, known as **Old Town,** is a popular pedestrian shopping mecca where fashionable chain stores such as Crate & Barrel and J. Crew share the street with trendy boutiques. A few blocks west on Colorado between Los Robles and Marengo avenues, the new open-air "urban village," **Paseo Colorado,** mixes residential, retail, dining, and entertainment spaces.

Malls and Markets

Beverly Center. The sophisticated neon-touched mall, anchored by Macy's and Bloomingdale's, has chain and upscale stores on three levels. Check out the terrific view of the city from the eighth-floor terrace. | 8500 Beverly Blvd., at Beverly, La Cienega, and San Vicente Blvds. and 3rd St., West Hollywood | 310/854–0070.

Century City Shopping Center & Marketplace. Set among office buildings on what used to be Twentieth Century Fox film studios' back lot, this open-air mall has an excellent roster of upscale shops, moored by Macy's and Bloomingdale's. Across from Bloomie's is the Marketplace of eateries and vendor carts. | 10250 Santa Monica Blvd. | 310/277–3898.

★ **Santa Monica Farmers Market.** The biggest farmers' market in L.A. fills four large blocks every Wednesday from 9 to 2. A smaller market Saturday 8:30–1 is geared toward organic produce. | Arizona and 3rd Sts., Santa Monica | 310/458–8712.

Sports and Outdoor Activities

Beaches

From Malibu to Orange County, the Los Angeles area has miles of beaches along the Pacific Coast Highway—PCH for short—suited for swimming, surfing, or strolling. Los Angeles County beaches (or state beaches operated by the county) all have year-round lifeguards, and many have showers, rest rooms, and public parking (for a fee).

From downtown, reach the coast by taking the Santa Monica Freeway (I–10) due west. Once you reach the end of the freeway, I–10 runs into the PCH, where you can head north or south. MTA buses run from downtown to the coast along Pico, Olympic, Santa Monica, Sunset, and Wilshire boulevards.

While most beaches are great for swimming, be aware that pollution, particularly after storms, can make some areas unhealthful. Call ahead for **beach conditions** (310/457–9701 Malibu; 310/578–0478 Santa Monica; 310/379–8471 South Bay area), or check beach ratings at www.healthebay.org. The following beaches are listed in north–south order:

Topanga Canyon State Beach. Topanga has good surfing at the western end (at the mouth of the canyon). Close to a busy section of the PCH and rather narrow, Topanga is teeming with teenagers. Fishing and children's swings are available. | 18700 block of PCH, Malibu | 310/577–5700 | Parking, lifeguard (year-round, except only as needed in winter), rest rooms, food concessions.

★ **Santa Monica State Beach.** One of L.A.'s most popular beaches, this wide and sandy beach is adjacent to the Santa Monica Pier. Be prepared for crowds at the pier and on the beach on summer weekends, when parking becomes an expensive ordeal. The beach has a playground, volleyball courts, and lots of bikers and rollerbladers zipping along the path at the beach's northern boundary. | 1642 Promenade (PCH at California Incline), Santa Monica | 310/577–5700 | Parking, lifeguard (year-round), rest rooms, showers.

Venice City Beach. Swimming is an afterthought at Venice Beach, where the boardwalk features acrobatic rollerbladers, magicians, muscle builders, street artists, and some of L.A.'s most hotly contested pickup games on the nearby basketball courts. You can rent a bike or some in-line skates and hit the Strand. | West of Pacific Ave., Venice | 310/577–5700 | Parking, rest rooms, showers, food concessions.

Redondo County Beach. The Redondo Beach Pier marks the starting point of this wide, sandy, family-packed beach, which continues south for about 2 mi. Restaurants, shops, excursion boats, and pier fishing are regular features, while rock and jazz concerts take place at the pier every summer. | Torrance Blvd. at Catalina Ave., Redondo Beach | 310/372–2166 | Parking, lifeguard, rest rooms, showers, food concessions, volleyball.

Mother's Beach. On Alamitos Bay in Long Beach, this calm beach in a protected marina is ideal for children. Nearby kayak rentals allow the adventurous to explore the canals of Naples (California, not Italy). An adjacent park has playground equipment for kids too young to kayak. | Appian Way at 2nd St., Long Beach | Parking, lifeguard, rest rooms, showers, food concessions.

Bicycling and In-line Skating

Los Angeles is a prime location for biking and blading year-round. The **South Bay Bike Path** runs 22 mi along the Pacific Ocean from Pacific Palisades (north of Santa Monica) south to Redondo Beach. The most crowded biking areas are along the Santa Monica and Venice beaches, while the latter is also the unofficial in-line skating capital of L.A.—and possibly the world.

Los Angeles County Parks and Recreation Department. Check here for bike trail maps. | 433 S. Vermont Ave., 4th floor, Los Angeles 90020 | 213/738–2961.

Perry's. For bike rentals, Perry's has three locations along the Strand; try Perry's Cafe & Sports Rentals. | 1200 The Promenade, Santa Monica | 310/485–3975.

Boardwalk Skates. For in-line skates, try Boardwalk. | 201½ Ocean Front Walk, Venice | 310/450–6634.

Boating and Kayaking

Balboa Boat Rentals. The biggest boating town is Newport Beach, and you can rent kayaks, sailboats, and small motorboats in the harbor at Balboa. Rented boats are not allowed out of the bay. | 949/673–7200.

Malibu Ocean Sports. Across from the pier at Malibu Point, Malibu Ocean Sports has kayak rentals, lessons, and organized cruises. | 22935 PCH, Malibu | 310/456–6302.

Marina Boat Rentals. In Marina del Rey's Fisherman's Village, try here for single and double kayaks as well as speed boats, cruisers, and sailboats, by the hour or half-day. | 13719 Fiji Way | 310/574–2822.

Fishing

Shore fishing and surfcasting are excellent on many area beaches, and pier fishing is popular because no license is necessary to fish off public piers. Local charter companies offer boat excursions (and, often, whale-watching excursions as well), and most will sell you a fishing license ($7 per day) and rent tackle. The **Santa Monica** and **Redondo Beach piers** have bait-and-tackle shops with everything you'll need.

Del Rey Sport Fishing runs excursions for $25 per half day. | 13759 Fiji Way, Marina del Rey | 310/822–3625.

Golf

There are seven public 18-hole courses in Los Angeles, and the county runs some good ones, too.

Los Verdes Golf Course. If you want a course with a cliff-top view of the ocean—time it right and you can watch the sun set behind Catalina Island—visit this county-run, par-71 course. | 7000 W. Los Verdes Dr., Rancho Palos Verdes | 310/377–7370.

Hiking

Nursery Nature Walks. Walks are geared to families with children under age eight; $5 requested donation per family. | 1440 Harvard St., Santa Monica | 310/998–1151.

Santa Monica Mountains National Recreation Area. National Park Service rangers and docents lead free guided hikes daily. | 818/597–9192.

Surfing

Surfing is the quintessential southern California sport, but, if you're not a strong swimmer, you should start with a lesson. Surf shops with rentals are plentiful at surfing beaches like Zuma (north of Malibu), Topanga Canyon, or Surfrider, just north of the Malibu pier. Most rent long, short, and miniboards from $18 per day and wet suits from $8 per day.

L.A. County Lifeguards. For the best waves, call the pre-recorded surf-conditions hot lines. | 310/457–9701 Malibu; 310/578–0478 Santa Monica; 310/379–8471 Manhattan, Redondo, and Hermosa beaches.

Malibu Ocean Sports. Across from the pier at Malibu Point, Ocean Sports offers surfing lessons. | 22935 PCH | 310/456–6302.

Essential Information

When to Go

Almost any time of year is the right time to visit Los Angeles; the climate is generally warm year-round and the sun shines 329 days a year. While November–March is the rainy season, showers are usually brief. July through September are the hottest, smoggiest months, but temperatures vary by as much as 25° from the cooler coastal areas to the broiling interior valleys. Prices skyrocket and reservations are a must when tourism peaks during summer months or for the Rose Bowl game and the Academy Awards.

FESTIVALS AND SEASONAL EVENTS

WINTER

Jan.: **Tournament of Roses Parade and Football Game.** This world-famous parade is an extravaganza of floats (adorned with 6 million flowers), marching bands, and 300 equestrians. You can view the floats up-close after the parade at a site adjacent to Pasadena High School at Sierra Madre and Washington boulevards; admission is $2. The Rose Bowl game, of course, follows the parade. | 626/449–7673.

Feb.: **Chinese New Year.** Los Angeles's large Chinese-American community heralds the new year with a parade, beauty pageant, street fair, and fun run. | 213/617–0396.

SPRING

Apr.: **Fiesta Broadway.** Held the week before Cinco de Mayo, this fiesta stretches along 36 blocks. Find food, mariachi music, folkloric dancing, and kids' games along Broadway between 1st Street and Olympic Boulevard. | 310/914–0015.

SUMMER

July–Aug.: **Festival of the Arts and Pageant of the Masters.** The works of 160 artists are exhibited in a juried show in Laguna; the unique accompanying pageant brings masterpieces of art and sculpture to life with real people posing in costume. | 949/494–1145.

AUTUMN

Nov.: **Doo Dah Parade.** Pasadena's riotous spoof of the annual Rose parade features the Lounge Lizards, dressed as reptiles and lip-syncing Frank Sinatra favorites, and West Hollywood cheerleaders in drag. | 626/440–7379.

Bargains

CityPass. This $59 pass covers the two-hour Starline Hollywood Tour, Universal Studios (by itself a $43 ticket), American Cinematèque at the Egyptian Theatre, the Hollywood Entertainment Museum, the Petersen Automotive Museum, the Museum of Television and Radio, and the Gene Autry Museum of Western Heritage. Buy CityPass at the aforementioned venues. An added bonus: your CityPass booklet contains actual tickets, so you can avoid long lines. | www.citypass.net/hollywood.

Tours

★ **Los Angeles Sightseeing Cruises' Whale Watching Cruises.** Sign on to follow the annual migration of the Pacific gray whale along California's coastline. From late December through mid-April, whale-watching boats leave San Pedro harbor for 2½-hour tours twice daily on weekdays and four times daily on weekends and holidays. $15 for adults. | 800/900–8188 | www.2seewhales.com.

Starline Tours of Hollywood. Starline Tours picks up passengers from area hotels and from Mann's Chinese Theater for half- to full-day tours ($29–$87). Destinations include Universal Studios, Sea World, Knott's Berry Farm, stars' homes, Disneyland, Tijuana, and other attractions. | 323/463–3333 or 800/959–3131 | www.starlinetours.com.

Visitor Information

Los Angeles Visitors Information Center | 685 S. Figueroa St. | 213/689–8822 | www.visitlanow.com. **Anaheim/Orange County Visitor and Convention Bureau** | 800 W. Katella Ave., Box 4270, Anaheim | 714/765–8888.

Arriving and Departing

BY AIR

Airports

Los Angeles International Airport (LAX). The third-busiest airport in the world, the major gateway to L.A., is serviced by more than 85 major airlines. | 310/646–5252 | www.lawa.org/lax/laxframe.html.

Burbank/Glendale/Pasadena Airport (BUR). This is the next most convenient airport to points in L.A. | 2627 N. Hollywood Way, Burbank | 818/840–8830 or 818/840–8847.

Ontario International Airport (ONT). ONT is about 35 mi east of Los Angeles. | Airport Dr. and Vineyard Ave. | 909/937–2700.

John Wayne/Orange County Airport (SNA) | 18601 Airport Way, Santa Ana | 949/252–5006 and **Long Beach Airport (LGB)** | 4100 Donald Douglas Dr. | 562/570–2600 are other options.

Airport Transportation

LAX provides free bus service between terminals, and most car rental companies offer gratis shuttles to their nearby parking lots. Some hotels, especially those near the airport, provide free airport shuttles for their guests.

Bus: It will take roughly an hour to ride a MTA bus from LAX to downtown, and the fare is $1.35. Consult the MetroTrip Planner on the MTA's Web site before leaving home.

Car: About 40 rental car companies operate out of LAX. Most provide phone links near the baggage claim area to request free shuttle service to off-airport locations. Catch shuttles at the lower/arrival level, and get detailed driving directions at the rental agency office. Driving times from LAX to different parts of the city vary: about 25 minutes to downtown, 20 minutes to Santa Monica, 30 minutes to Beverly Hills, and 35–40 minutes to Van Nuys or Sherman Oaks (the central San Fernando Valley). From the Burbank Airport, it's 20 minutes to downtown, 40 minutes to Santa Monica, 35–40 minutes to Beverly Hills, and 15 minutes to the central San Fernando Valley.

Shuttle: Shared-ride vans offer door-to-door service; check with the company for rates.

Prime Time Shuttle | 800/733–8267. **SuperShuttle** | 323/775–6600, 310/782–6600, or 800/258–3826 | www.supershuttle.com.

Taxi: Taxis are the most convenient but most expensive way to get to the city from the airport. At taxi stands outside terminals on the lower/arrival level, you'll be given a ticket with typical fares to major destinations.

Independent Cab Co. offers a $25 flat rate from LAX to West Hollywood. | 213/385–8294 or 800/521–8294 | www.taxi4u.com.

BY BUS

Greyhound stops in downtown Los Angeles at its main terminal, 1716 E. 7th St.

BY CAR

Los Angeles is at the western terminus of I–10, a major east–west highway that runs all the way to Florida. Interstate 5 runs north–south through California, up to San Francisco (about 400 mi away) and down to San Diego (about 100 mi away). More scenic but slower routes from San Francisco include Highway 101 and Pacific Coast Highway 1. Interstate 15, which angles southwest from Las Vegas, also runs down to San Diego.

BY TRAIN

Union Station. Built in 1939, Union Station in downtown Los Angeles is a gorgeous facility that blends Spanish colonial revival and art deco design. Here you'll find both Amtrak and regional Metrolink trains. | 800 N. Alameda St. | 213/683–6979.

Getting Around

BY CAR

Although sprawling and traffic-clogged, L.A. at least has wide streets and abundant parking garages. Get a good map, and be aware that a number of major streets have similar-sounding names (like Beverly Drive and Beverly Boulevard) or exactly the same name (San Vicente Boulevard in West L.A., Brentwood, Santa Monica, and West Hollywood). Take major streets to avoid dead ends and detours, and get clear directions and stick to them.

California Highway Patrol | 323/906–3434; 800/427–7623 for road conditions.

Parking

Illegally parked cars are ticketed and/or towed very quickly in Los Angeles (the minimum ticket is $35). Some public lots are free; otherwise prices vary from 25¢ per half hour (in public lots) to $2–$25 per day. Downtown and Century City garage rates may reach $25 an hour, although prices drop on weekends. Many restaurants offer valet parking for $3–$5 or an optional tip. Metered parking is also widely available for 25¢ for 15 minutes to one hour.

BY PUBLIC TRANSIT

Bus

Let's face it: in L.A., the car is king. Sometimes, though, a bus may be your best option: for example, visiting the Getty Center with no prior parking reservation, going to Universal Studios, or venturing into downtown.

Metropolitan Transit Authority (MTA). MTA service is available at all hours, but keep in mind that heavy traffic might throw off scheduled times. An MTA bus ride costs $1.35, plus 25¢ for each transfer (exact change required). | 213/626–4455 or 800/266–6883 | www.mta.net.

The **Metropolitan Transit Authority DASH (Downtown Area Short Hop)** minibuses have six circular routes in Hollywood, Mid-Wilshire, and the downtown area. Buses stop every two blocks or so and make pickups at five-minute intervals. You pay 25¢ every time you get on. Buses generally run weekdays 6 AM–7 PM and Saturday 10 AM–5 PM. The Downtown Discovery Route (DD) makes a continuous loop among downtown sites; Route E is a shopper's tour with stops in the Broadway, Jewelry, and Fashion districts, as well as at two downtown malls. | 213/626–4455 or 310/808–2273.

Big Blue Bus. The Santa Monica Municipal Bus Line, aka the Big Blue Bus, is a pleasant and inexpensive (50¢) way to navigate the Westside, where the MTA lines leave off. Transfers are free from one Big Blue Bus to another; to MTA or Culver CityBus it's 25¢. There's also an express bus to and from downtown L.A. and the Tide Shuttle bus (25¢) that runs between Main Street and the 3rd Street Promenade, stopping at hotels along the way. | 310/451–5444.

Train

Metrolink. Surface light rail lines, Metro Rail Blue and Red Lines, operate from 5 AM–11 PM. The Red Line has two segments: one running west from downtown to Wilshire and Western, one running northwest from downtown through Hollywood to Universal City and North Hollywood. The Blue Line runs from downtown south to Long Beach. The fare is $1.35 one-way. | 800/371–5465 or 213/347–2800 | www.metrolinktrains.com.

BY TAXI

Don't even try to hail a cab on the street in Los Angeles. Instead, phone one of the many taxi companies. The metered rate is $1.60 per mile, with a starting rate from $1.90 to $2.50 per fare. Beware that distances between sights in L.A. can be vast, so cab fares add up quickly. One relative bargain, though: for a $4 flat fare, up to four passengers may use a taxi to visit downtown attractions within the "One Fare Zone," bounded by the Harbor Freeway (I–110) to the west, Main Street to the east, Pico Boulevard to the south, and the Hollywood Freeway (U.S. 101) to the north.

Bell Cab | 888/235–5222 | www.bellcab.com. **Independent Cab Co.** | 800/521–8294 | www.taxi4u.com. **Yellow Cab/LA Taxi Co-Op** | 800/200–1085 or 800/200–0011.

Kentucky

Revised and Updated by Susan Reigler

MAMMOTH CAVE NATIONAL PARK

Mammoth Cave National Park, in south-central Kentucky, has something you can't lay eyes on anywhere else on the planet: a hole in the ground with hundreds of miles of winding subterranean passages. (The second-longest cave on earth, Optimisticeskaya, in Ukraine, is barely a *quarter* as long as Mammoth.) It's a first-class natural wonder, as reliably awe-inspiring as that other famous hole in the ground, the Grand Canyon.

The cave's marvels range from 192-ft-high Mammoth Dome to 105-ft-deep Bottomless Pit; from a rugged climb called Mt. McKinley to a drifting voyage on the River Styx, 360 ft down, where eyeless fish swim; from a saltpeter mine abandoned after the War of 1812 to a tuberculosis hospital abandoned after an ill-advised experiment in 1843; from an unforgiving passage called Fat Man's Misery to a vaulting chamber known as—what else?—the Grand Canyon.

More than 350 mi of caverns have been found under the 80-square-mi park, and you can take ranger-led tours underground. Above ground, rangers sponsor other activities and cultural events, and you can hike, canoe, picnic, camp, or bird-watch. Mammoth Cave is also an International Biosphere Reserve and a World Heritage Site.

Exploring

Mammoth Cave National Park

The longest natural underground system in the world was hollowed out through the limestone over 350 million years. Humans are newcomers by comparison. Spearheads recovered from the cave have been dated to a mere 12,000 years old.

The cave was an important source for saltpeter, a major ingredient in gunpowder, during the War of 1812. It supplied three quarters of the powder used by U.S. troops against the British. Mining stopped after the war, and the tourists began to arrive. Stagecoaches and a railway brought the first visitors.

In 1839, Dr. John Croghan of Louisville bought Mammoth Cave; terms of the deed also gave Croghan ownership of Stephen Bishop, a black slave who remains the most famous guide in the cave's history. An enthusiastic explorer, Bishop was the

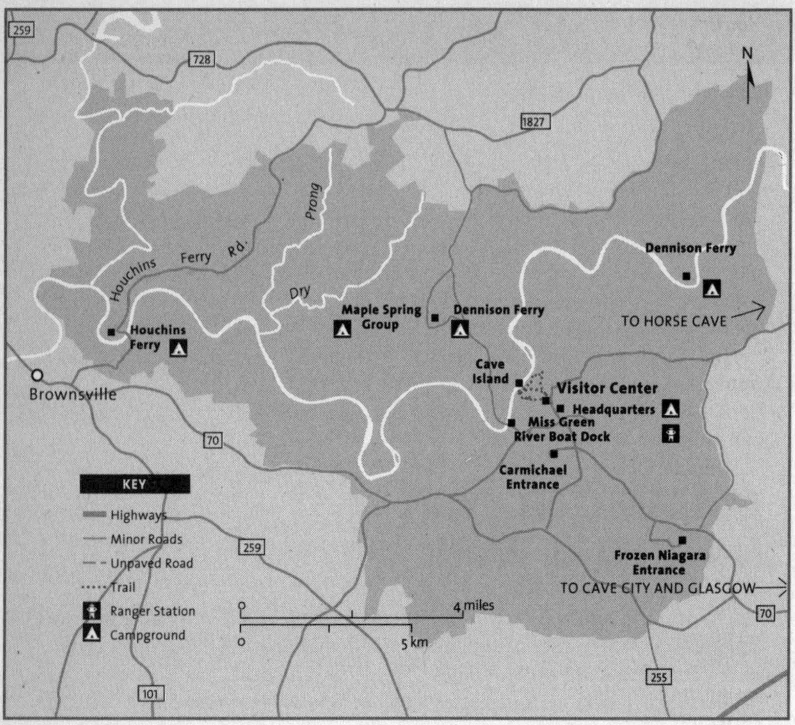

first person to discover the unique eyeless fish and crayfish living in the deep, underground waters. He was a popular and knowledgeable guide until his death in 1857.

Tuberculosis was a major health concern in the mid-1800s, and in 1842, Dr. Croghan began housing patients in custom-built huts inside the cave, under the premise that the cave air, with a year-round temperature of 54°F, might be beneficial to consumptives. Unfortunately, all the patients eventually died of the disease, either while still in residence or soon after leaving Mammoth Cave. The program was abandoned in 1843. The tourism business continued to thrive, however. In the 1850s, Edmund Booth, a well-known actor, gave readings in the cave, and Jenny Lind, the so-called Swedish Nightingale, sang in one of its chambers.

The property was handed down through the Croghan family until 1926, when the last descendant, Serena Croghan Rogers, died. Several area businessmen then lobbied Congress to have the area designated as a national park. Mammoth Cave became the nation's 26th national park in 1941. It's still the only one in Kentucky.

It is possible to see the cave in half a day and be on your way. It is preferable, however, to linger in the park and explore the riches of "the surface world." As this cluttered planet goes, Mammoth Park is still a fairly pristine place. If you get off the beaten path, it's possible to recapture a bit of the Kentucky that the 19th-century visitors knew.

Visitor Center. At the center of the park, the Mammoth Cave Visitor Center has maps and descriptions of tours and hikes. The cave tours depart from here. This is also where you can pick up your permit for backcountry hiking. Schedules of walks led by the park rangers, evening programs, and show times for films and slide shows in the center auditorium are available here, too. | 270/758–2328 | Daily 8–5.

Hours: The park is open 24 hours a day, every day, year-round.

Fees: There is no entrance fee to the park grounds. The prices for cave tours are detailed below (☞ Cave Tours).

CAVE TOURS

There are tours designed for all ages and physical abilities. They can last from a little over an hour to 6½ hours. Admission prices vary, and not all tours are offered every day. Call ahead for reservations. | 270/758–2328 or 800/967–2283.

★**Frozen Niagara** is one of the more spectacular tours, winding among enormous pits and domes and the great dripstone formation that resembles a rock-hewn waterfall. The two-hour tour is described as strenuous, so don't take it unless you are prepared to descend about 300 steps and climb through steep terrain. | $8.

The **Historic** tour focuses on the cave's human history. Inside, you'll see artifacts from Native Americans and European cave explorers, ruins of early mining operations, and other evidence of human presence. You must be able to climb rock stairs and a 130-step steel tower. The tour is about two hours long. | $8.

The **Mobility Impaired** tour accommodates those who might not be able to negotiate the steps and inclines on other tours. An elevator descends to passageways accessible to wheelchairs. The tour is 1¼ hours long. | $7.

Even though there are some steps on the **Travertine** tour, it is one of the least physically demanding, and adults with small children are usually able to take it. Sights include the Frozen Niagara, Crystal Lake, and the Drapery Room. Tour time is about 1¼ hours. | $7.

The educational ★**Trog** tour, focusing on the cave's ecology and geology, is designed for children 8 to 12 (proof of age required). Long pants and hiking shoes are required; knee pads are recommended. Helmets and lights are provided. The tour lasts 2½ hours. Parents must accompany their children for the first 15 minutes and pick them up punctually at tour's end. | $10.

★**Violet City Lantern Tour** is a lantern tour along the early explorers' route and includes the remains of saltpeter mining, traces of prehistoric activity, huts that were used for tuberculosis patients in the 1800s, and some of the largest rooms in the park. The tour takes about three hours and is physically demanding. | $9.

MAMMOTH CAVE SCENERY AND WILDLIFE

The cave is home to more than 40 species of animals that have evolved to live underground. These troglobites, as they are called, include pale, and often blind, crayfish, beetles, other assorted invertebrates, and the blind fish Amblyopsis spelaea. Dozens of species of bats use the cave for shelter, including the endangered gray and Indiana bats.

Along the backcountry trails, you can spot red foxes, opossums, raccoon, and rabbits. A variety of birds will trill in startled protest when strangers invade their territory.

Wildflowers bloom throughout the park from April through September, 200 species in all. Spring brings trillium and the humble daisy; midsummer, the rarer orchid. In August, honeysuckle fills the air with its extravagant sweetness. And in September, the primrose dots the woods with color.

The 7 mi of forest trails, leading from the visitor center, contain some very old, unusually large sycamores, beeches, and tulip poplars. Along the far ridge, stands of oaks and hickories abound. The Big Woods, off Little Jordan Road, is considered virgin forest. Its trees loom up, darkly austere, impenetrable.

Ganter Cave. Within park boundaries, this less-traveled cave is open to qualified cavers, only. Requirements are stiff for safety reasons. Groups are limited to four to nine adults, with one experienced caver for every two novices. Approval is needed from the Chief Ranger's Office. | 270/758–2251.

SCENIC DRIVES

Green River Ferry Road. Most of the aboveground landscape at Mammoth Cave is heavily wooded. So spring, when the dogwoods and redbuds are blooming, and fall, when the leaves are awash in red and gold, are best for a driving tour. If you drive from the South Entrance along the Green River Ferry Road, you can take in the forest and then enjoy a view up and down the tranquil Green River during a ferry ride across the water.

Joppa Motor Trail. Southwest of the visitor center, this drive is an excellent place to catch a glimpse of wild turkeys and the region's white-tailed deer. The winding route offers views down deep ravines. It's open seasonally, so ask at the visitor center about access.

Attractions Nearby

CAVE CITY

Crystal Onyx Cave and Campgrounds. Beautiful formations such as delicate crystalline draperies and rimstone pools adorn Crystal Onyx Cave. Stalactites, stalagmites, and onyx formations, including columns, are other highlights. There's also a Native American burial ground with remains dating from 680 BC. | 8709 Happy Valley Rd., Cave City 42127 (Exit 53 off I–65 to Hwy. 90) | 270/773–2359 | www.mammothcave.com | $4.50–$6.50, cave tours | Feb.–Dec., daily.

Diamond Caverns. You'll experience enormous stalactites and stalagmites, projecting onyx peaks, and rock palaces, up close and personal. Guided tours are given every 1½ hours. | Box 250, Park City 42160, 1 mi from Park City on Mammoth Cave Pkwy. | 270/749–2233 | fax 270/749–3423 | www.diamondcaverns.com | $10 | Daily.

Mammoth Cave Chair Lift and Guntown Mountain. A re-created 1880s frontier boomtown comes to life with mock gunfights, a saloon, music, and magic shows. There's also a chairlift up the mountain. Drive to Exit 53 off I–65 and follow the signs to the fun. | Box 236, Cave City 42127 | 270/773–3530 | fax 270/773–5176 | www.guntownmountain.com | $13.95 | May and mid-Aug.–early Oct., weekends; June–mid-Aug. and early Oct.–mid-Oct., daily.

GLASGOW

Barren River Dam and Lake. Maintained by the Army Corps of Engineers, this dam rises 146 ft and is 3,970 ft long. The dam has created a 10,000-acre lake (noted for its bass fishing) across Barren and Allen counties. Facilities include boat ramps, as well as picnicking, swimming, and camping areas. | 11088 Finney Rd., Glasgow 42141 | 270/646–2055 | Daily 6:30–4.

Barren River Lake State Resort Park. This park, covering more than 2,000 acres, features a lodge, a swimming pool, riding stables, nature trails, and a marina serving the lake. There are also 22 two-bedroom cottages to rent, and tent and trailer sites. Other recreational facilities include tennis courts, bicycle trails, and an 18-hole golf course. | 1149 State Park Rd., Lucas 42156 | 270/646–2151 or 800/325–0057 | www.kystateparks.com/agencies/parks/barren.htm | Fees for camping and golf | Daily.

HORSE CAVE

American Cave Museum/Hidden River Cave. Hidden River Cave's entrance can be viewed from a free Main Street overlook in downtown Horse Cave. Closed as a tourist attraction in 1943 because of pollution, it is now reopened after a long conservation effort, which has even lured back rare blind cave fish. The cave has a subterranean river flowing 100 ft below the city and a turn-of-the-20th-century waterworks. The museum's science and history displays include exhibits about Mammoth Cave, Horse Cave, cave exploring, groundwater, Floyd Collins, and saltpeter mining. A guided cave tour leaves the museum every hour. Nearby is the American Cave Museum's two-story environmental education center. The "cave" exhibit, complete with stalactites and stalagmites, has displays on the cultural and natural resources associated with caves. | E. Main St., Horse Cave 42749 | 270/786–1466 | www.kdu.com/acm.html | $8 | Early Sept.–late May, 9–5; late May–early Sept., 9–7.

Horse Cave Theatre. A regional theater company presents up to six new and established plays per season by Kentuckian and nationally known playwrights in the renovated Thomas Opera House, a 343-seat facility built in 1911. Call ahead to arrange a tour of backstage. | 101 E. Main St., Horse Cave 42749 | 270/786–1200 or 800/342–2177 | fax 270/786–5298 | June–Nov.

★ **Kentucky Down Under/Mammoth Onyx Cave.** The outback of Australia is re-created here in Kentucky Cave country. Visitors can roam through a field of kangaroos or learn an ancient aboriginal dance. Other wildlife includes brightly colored tropical birds, wallabies, wombats, and emus. The guided cave tour features unusual onyx formations. | 3700 L&N Turnpike Rd., Horse Cave 42749 | 270/786–2634 or 800/762–2869 | www.kdu.com | $16 | Daily.

Dining

In Mammoth Cave National Park

Mammoth Cave Hotel Restaurant. Southern. This pleasant, busy restaurant at the inn features southern fare, such as country ham, and generous, country-style breakfasts. | Mammoth Cave | 270/758–2225 | AE, DC, MC, V.

Picnic Areas. The four campgrounds at the park (Dennison Ferry, Headquarters Campground, Houchins Ferry, and Maple Springs Campground) all have picnic tables, each with its own fire grate, at each of their campsites.

Headquarters Campground is near the visitor center and is open spring through fall. It includes an open picnic shelter that seats 80 and that can be rented for $50 per day. There's also an enclosed shelter accommodating 50 that can be rented for $75 per day. Running water and flush toilets are features of the campground and its picnic areas.

Near the Park

CAVE CITY

Joe's Diner. American. This diner-grill caters to tourists visiting nearby Mammoth Cave. There's grilled chicken and sandwiches and a variety of burgers. Food is served with a smile and in a hurry so as to hasten your journey to the cave. | 1004 Mammoth Cave Dr., Cave City 42127 | 270/773–3186 | Closed Mid-Sept.–mid-May.

GLASGOW

Bolton's Landing. American. This gray-and-blue-frame family restaurant boasts a completely made-from-scratch menu, which includes angel biscuits and country ham Alfredo. A kids' menu is also available. | 2433 Scottsville Rd. (U.S. 31 E), Glasgow 42141 | 270/651–8008 | Closed Sun. No lunch Sat. | $7–$17 | AE, D, DC, MC, V.

HORSE CAVE

The Bookstore. Southern. Fifteen tables share one large room with a used-book store. One wall is decorated with old Horse Cave photographs, and of course there is plenty of interesting reading material. This locals' favorite has breakfast with biscuits and gravy and a lunch standard of meat and two veggies. Specialties are fried chicken, catfish, and country ham. | 111 Water St., Horse Cave 42749 | 270/786–3084 | No dinner Sun. | $6–$14 | D, MC, V.

Lodging

In Mammoth Cave National Park

★ **Mammoth Cave Hotel.** The wood-trimmed, two-story hotel inside the park is designed to blend in with the surrounding landscape. Most rooms have balconies or patios, and there are several two-bedroom suites, just right for families. An arched bridge leads from the main building to the Mammoth Cave Park Visitor Center. 2 restaurants, cable TV, tennis courts, laundry facilities, business services, some pets allowed. | Hwy. 70, Mammoth Cave 42259 | 270/758–2225 | fax 270/758–2301 | www.mammothcavehotel.com | 110 rooms | $68 | AE, DC, MC, V.

Mammoth Cave Hotel Cottages. These one-room cottages furnished in the Early American style are 1/4 mi from the main hotel. They have air-conditioning and electric heat. Room TVs; no room phones | Hwy. 70, Mammoth Cave 42259 | 270/758–2225 | fax 270/758–2301 | www.mammothcavehotel.com | 10 cottages | $64 | Mar.–Nov. | AE, DC, MC, V.

Near the Park

CAVE CITY

Best Western Kentucky Inn. After a day at Mammoth Cave, drive 10 mi east to Exit 53 off I–65 and you'll enjoy a bright, cheerful room with bordered wallpaper at this one-story modern motel. The lobby is formal with a Victorian-style burgundy and green theme. Cable TV, pool, wading pool, laundry facilities. | 1009 Doyle Ave., Cave City 42717 | 270/773–3161 | fax 270/773–5494 | www.bestwestern.com | 50 rooms | $30–$40 | AE, D, DC, MC, V.

Park Mammoth Resort. This 2,000-acre resort is 20 minutes from Mammoth Cave National Park and other cave-country attractions. The lobby is rustic and has an old-fashioned organ and fireplace. The lodge is at the intersection of I–65 and U.S. 31 west. Dining room, in-room data ports, cable TV, 2 18-hole golf courses, miniature golf, 2 tennis courts, indoor pool, wading pool, sauna, playground, business services. | U.S. 31 W, Park City 42160 | 270/749–4101 | fax 270/749–2524 | 92 rooms | $60 | AE, D, DC, MC, V.

Parkview Motel. Rock your troubles away on the front porch at Cave City's oldest motel. All rooms have been decorated in a comfortable country style, including one "dollhouse" efficiency completely outfitted with kitchen appliances and utensils. The motel sits on 5 acres of well-manicured lawn and provides a complimentary Continental breakfast. Mammoth Cave Park is only 2 1/2 mi away. Restaurant, grill, picnic area, room TVs, pool. | 3906 Mammoth Cave Rd., Cave City 42127 | 270/773–3463 or 877/482–2262 | www.parkviewmotel.com | 10 rooms, 6 cabins, 1 efficiency cabin | $28–$44 | D, MC, V.

Rose Manor Bed & Breakfast. This two-story brick Victorian offers spacious rooms with private baths, aromatherapy, a non-alcoholic beverage bar, late-night snack, traditional country breakfast, a commons area with video and CD library. Out front there is usually a horse carriage for hire. You can also arrange for a therapeutic massage. Some in-room hot tubs; no room TVs | 204 Duke St., Cave City 42127 | 270/773–4402 or 888/621–5900 | mammothcave.com/rose.htm | 5 rooms | $90–$110 | No credit cards.

Camping

In Mammoth Cave National Park

Four campgrounds within the park allow you to camp near your car. Twelve more backcountry sites are available to hikers on foot (☞ Hiking and Backpacking). All are in beautiful, natural settings. Like the park itself, the campgrounds are less crowded before Memorial Day and after Labor Day. Even in summer, however, they are run on a first-come, first-served basis. The exception, Maple Springs Campgrounds, which accommodates horses, requires reservations.

★ **Houchins Ferry Campground.** Your car is the only reminder of civilization at this small campsite, 14 mi from headquarters, on the west side of the park. Portable toilets, fire grates, picnic tables | 12 sites | Mammoth Cave National Park, Mammoth Cave 42259 | 270/758–2212 | www.nps.gov/maca | $15 | No reservations | AE, D, MC, V.

Maple Springs Campground. Because of the hitching posts, which lend an Old West flavor, these campgrounds, north of Green River, are the park's most popular. Three of the sites are designated for groups with horses, and there's parking for horse trailers. Portable toilets, fire grates, picnic tables. | 7 sites | Mammoth Cave National Park, Mammoth Cave 42259 | 270/758–2212 | www.nps.gov/maca | $25 | Reservations essential | AE, D, MC, V.

Sports and Outdoor Activities

Bicycling

A gentle-grade, mile-long bike trail runs from Headquarters Campground to Carmichael Entrance Road, skirting the edge of a bluff and passing through shaded woodlands. No bicycles are for rent in the park, however, so visitors must bring their own.

Boating and Canoeing

Almost 30 mi of the Green and Nolin rivers are open to boaters and canoeists in the park. Unfortunately, there are no boats for rent, so visitors must provide their own crafts. The most popular boat trip launches at Dennison Ferry Campground and floats down the Green River to Houchins Ferry. The trip, which takes about six hours, passes scenic woodlands and dramatic bluffs. No launch fees or permits are required for boating. However, you do need a Coast Guard–approved life preserver for each person on board.

Fishing

Fishing is available year-round on both the Green and Nolin rivers. Within the park, you don't need a fishing license, but all other Kentucky state regulations apply. Check at the visitor center for specifics. If you drop a line in the water, you are likely to catch musky, bass, white perch, or catfish.

Hiking and Backpacking

Nearly 100 mi of hiking trails are found in the North and South sides of the park, as well as those originating near the visitor center. There are 30 trails in all, ranging in length from under 1 to about 10 mi and are graded easy to strenuous, according to hills and inclines. Ask for trail maps at the visitor center.

Backcountry Use Permit. Camping at backcountry sites requires a permit, obtainable for free at the visitor center. | 270/758–2212.

Cave Island Nature Trail. This mile-long path begins at the cave mouth and winds through the woods past the River Styx Springs, named for its black-colored waters. En route, see limestone deposits shaped like jagged ice crystals.

Heritage Trail. This ¾-mi path, not far from the visitor center, makes for a pleasant afternoon stroll. Along the way, see wildflowers, trees, and the Old Guides Cemetery, where the first cave explorers are buried. Stop at Sunset Point, a spectacular lookout, in time to watch the sun go down.

Horseback Riding

Horseback riding is allowed on all trails north of the Green River (except Ganter Cave Trail) in Mammoth Cave National Park. Trailer parking is available at Lincoln trailhead and across the road from Maple Springs Campground.

Jesse James Riding Stables. Horses are available for rent by the half hour for trail rides on the 300 acres of property adjoining the stables. | Rte. 70 W, Cave City 42127 | 270/773–2560.

Essential Information

When to Go

Mid-March to mid-April is the best time to visit the park. Redbud and dogwood trees are in bloom, and springtime temperatures average 65°. Be aware, though, that temperatures can climb well into the 80s and dip down into the 30s. Five inches of rainfall are normal for this time of year, with occasional severe thunderstorms. Because the park is only moderately crowded in early spring, cave tours are not fully booked—though reservations are always advisable—and the hotels offer their off-season rates, at least until April 15.

Fall is also a glorious time in the park. The weather cools, the crowds thin out, and the trees are ablaze with color. If you're just interested in viewing the caves, winter is the time to do so (the tours are underbooked, and you have the guides to yourself), but organized park activities are sharply curtailed, and the area seems to sink into hibernation.

FESTIVALS AND SEASONAL EVENTS

WINTER

Dec.: **Christmas Sing in the Cave.** Subterranean holiday music is performed by a local choir. | 270/758–2328 or 800/967–2283.

SPRING

Apr.: **Springfest.** Wildflower walks and other nature activities punctuate a weekend of folk and bluegrass concerts and arts-and-crafts exhibitions in the national park. | 270/758–2328 or 800/967–2283.

SUMMER

Apr.–Oct.: **Kentucky Down Under/Kentucky Taverns.** Exhibits of Australian animals such as wallabies and wombats are the focus of this festival. There's a 45-minute guided tour of the cave. | 800/762–2869.

June: **Walking Horse Show.** It's a horse of a different kind—not the state's Thoroughbred, but spectacular nonetheless. Held annually one weekend of the month in Cave City. | 270/773–3131, 270/773–2188, or 800/346–8908.

AUTUMN

Oct.: **Colorfall.** The park's cultural heritage is the focus for this weekend of crafts demonstrations, archaeological talks and tours, and oral history and genealogy seminars. | 270/758–2328 or 800/967–2283.

Bargains

At Campfire Circles held most evenings from spring through fall, the rangers speak gratis about the region's plants and animals and the cave's distinctive history. For a leisurely stroll of an hour and a half, join the Wildflower Walks, offered free to acquaint visitors with the park's seasonal blossoms. For more details about Campfire Circles and Wildflower Walks, stop by the visitor center (☞ Exploring). The park's extensive nature trails, of course, are there for the asking.

Another option is to take a ferry ride across Green River at the Green River or Houchins dock. Ferries operate daily, except under high-water conditions, at no charge.

Nearby Towns

Cave City is the center of the state's famous limestone cave region. It also has the highest concentration of commercial attractions in the area. **Glasgow,** founded by Scottish settlers in 1799 near a large spring, is the county seat and commercial center of Barren County. It's also the town nearest Barren River State Resort Park and Barren Lake, both recreational destinations in this part of the state, and it is just 1½ mi from Mammoth Cave National Park. **Horse Cave,** the largest town in Hart County, was named for the large cave around which it grew. An underground river provided energy for an electricity generator as early as the late 1800s.

Tours

★ ***Miss Green River* Boat Trip.** This is an hour-long river tour on a twin-diesel-powered boat. Departing from inside the park and following the Green River, the route passes through valleys rich in wildlife, including white-tailed deer, beavers, and wild turkeys. The $4 trips are available April–October. | 270/758–2328 or 800/967–2283 | fax 270/758–2349 | www.mammoth.cave.national-park.com/tours.htm.

Visitor Information

Mammoth Cave National Park | Box 7, Mammoth Cave 42259 | 270/758–2328 or 800/967–2283 | www.nps.gov/maca.

Cave City Tourist and Convention Commission | Box 518, Cave City 42127 | 270/773–3131 or 800/346–8908. **Glasgow/Barren County Chamber of Commerce** | 118 E. Public Square, Glasgow, 42141 | 270/651–3161 or 800/264–3161. **Hart County Chamber of Commerce** | Box 688, Munfordville 42765 | 270/524–2892.

Arriving and Departing

BY AIR

Airports

Nashville International Airport (BNA). Nashville is about 90 mi from the park. | 615/275–1675 | www.nashintl.com.

Louisville International Airport (SDF). Louisville, another option with many scheduled flights, is also about 90 mi away from Mammoth Cave. | 502/367–4636 | www.louintlairport.com.

Airport Transportation

You'll need to rent a car; both airports have Alamo, Avis, Budget, Dollar, Hertz, National, and Thrifty branches.

BY BUS

Greyhound Lines offers bus service to Cave City, 10 mi from Mammoth Cave National Park.

BY CAR

Coming from either north or south, I-65 provides the best access. From the north, take Exit 53 at Cave City to Route 70 west and drive 9 mi to the park's visitor center. From the south, take Exit 48 at Park City to Route 255 west and drive 8 mi to the visitor center. Cumberland Parkway runs through hardwood ridge country, a more scenic, less direct route.

Getting Around

BY CAR

You will need a car to explore Kentucky cave country and Mammoth Cave National Park. The speed limit within the park is 15 mph. Mammoth Cave is popular with bicyclists, so do watch for them. Beware of deer and other animals on the roads, too. Free parking is provided in many areas of the park, including near cave entrances, campgrounds, and at the park lodge and cottages. Parking lots are available at trailheads, as well.

Louisiana

Revised and Updated by Paul Greenberg

NEW ORLEANS

For most visitors, New Orleans means Mardi Gras, the French Quarter, electrifying jazz, and great food. New Orleans is both an old-fashioned town with 10 historic districts and a major international destination with a thriving port and an insouciant, fun-loving soul. Its party-town reputation is well founded—local folks eagerly celebrate anything at the drop of a hat. New Orleanians love their city. They treasure tradition, bask in the sultry semitropical climate, and look at life with a laid-back attitude that makes New Orleans seem a close cousin to her Caribbean neighbors.

Sometime during your visit to New Orleans, find a wrought-iron balcony or an oak-shaded courtyard or a columned front porch and sit quietly, favorite beverage in hand, at 6 AM. At this hour, when the moist air sits most heavily upon the streets, New Orleans is a city of mesmerizing tranquillity. By noon, early morning calm confronts big-city chaos: with all there is to see and hear and eat and drink and do, the old, mystical, weighty spirit in the city's air can at times be frustrating, seeming to hold you and everyone around you from accomplishing anything too quickly or efficiently. But when it also keeps you from really caring, then you have found the true secret of New Orleans, the reason why most locals can't imagine living anywhere else.

To experience this fun-filled city, you can begin with the usual tourist attractions, but you must go beyond them to linger in a corner grocery store, sip a cold drink in a local joint, or chat with a stoop-sitter. New Orleanians, for all their gripes and grumbling, love their city. They treasure custom and tradition, take in stride the heat and humidity of a semitropical climate, and look at life with a laid-back attitude.

Exploring

French Quarter

The French Quarter is alive with the sights, sounds, and everything else one might expect to find in a major entertainment hub. However, it's also a residential neighborhood. It consists of historic blocks lush with wrought iron and greenery that seems to sprout from every crevice.

★ **Aquarium of the Americas.** More than 7,000 aquatic creatures swim in 60 displays ranging from 500 to 500,000 gallons of water. Woldenberg Riverfront Park, which surrounds the aquarium, is a tranquil spot with a view of the Mississippi. Package tickets for the

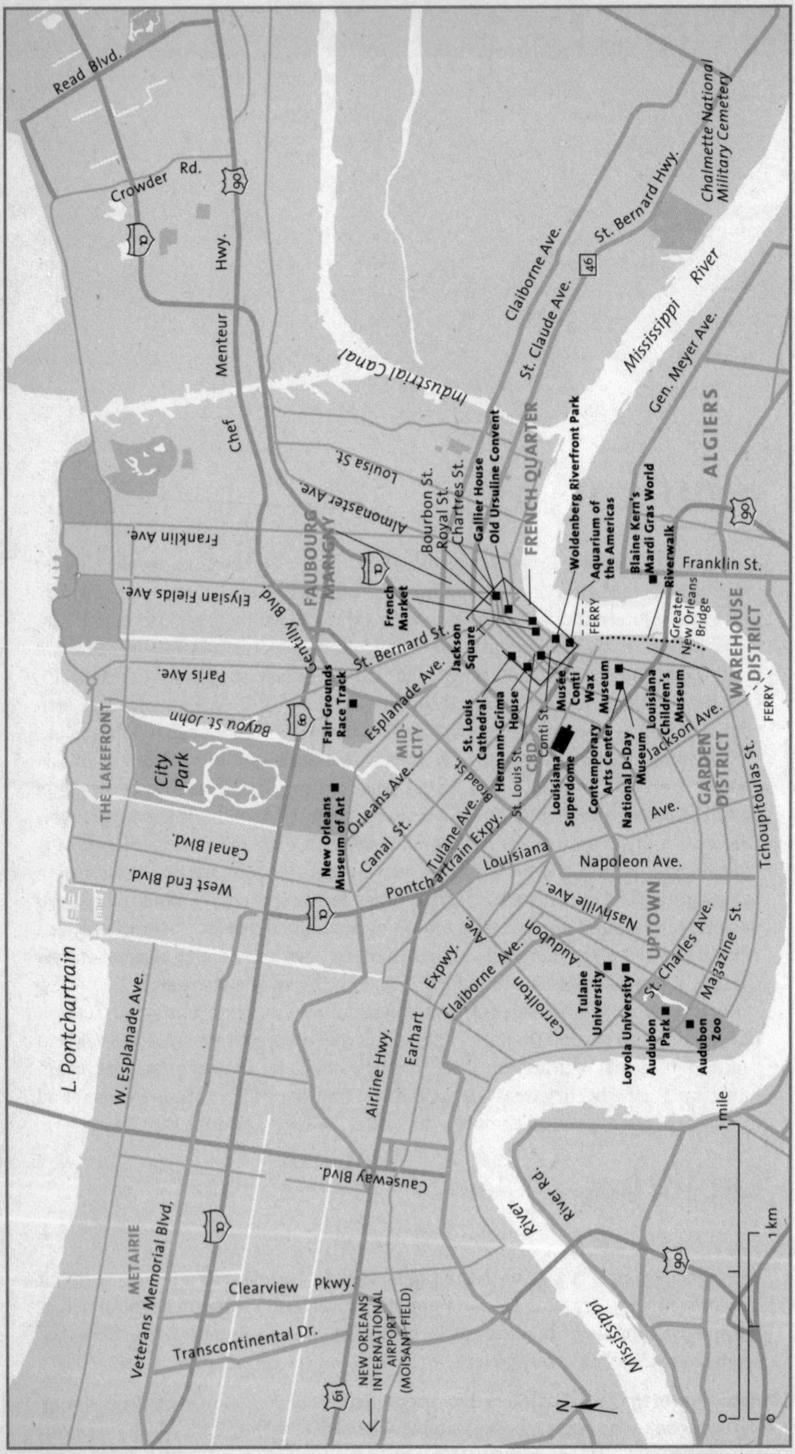
L. Pontchartrain
THE LAKEFRONT
METAIRIE
Read Blvd.
Crowder Rd.
Chef Menteur Hwy.
Industrial Canal
Franklin Ave.
Elysian Fields Ave.
Paris Ave.
Bayou St. John
City Park
Canal Blvd.
West End Blvd.
W. Esplanade Ave.
Veterans Memorial Blvd.
Causeway Blvd.
Clearview Pkwy.
Transcontinental Dr.
NEW ORLEANS INTERNATIONAL AIRPORT (MOISANT FIELD)
Airline Hwy.
Earhart Expwy.
Pontchartrain Expy.
Gentilly Blvd.
FAUBOURG MARIGNY
Louisa St.
Almonaster Ave.
Claiborne Ave.
St. Claude Ave.
St. Bernard Hwy.
Chalmette National Military Cemetery
Mississippi River
Gen. Meyer Ave.
ALGIERS
Franklin St.
FRENCH QUARTER
Bourbon St.
Royal St.
Chartres St.
Gallier House
Old Ursuline Convent
Woldenberg Riverfront Park
Aquarium of the Americas
Blaine Kern's Mardi Gras World
Riverwalk
FERRY
Greater New Orleans Bridge
WAREHOUSE DISTRICT
French Market
Jackson Square
St. Bernard St.
Esplanade Ave.
Fair Grounds Race Track
MID-CITY
New Orleans Museum of Art
Orleans Ave.
Canal St.
Tulane Ave.
Broad St.
St. Louis Cathedral
Hermann-Grima House
St. Louis St.
Conti St.
CBD
Musée Conti Wax Museum
Louisiana Superdome
Contemporary Arts Center
National D-Day Museum
Louisiana Children's Museum
Jackson Ave.
GARDEN DISTRICT
Tchoupitoulas St.
Louisiana Ave.
Napoleon Ave.
Nashville Ave.
UPTOWN
Claiborne Ave.
Audubon
Carrollton
Tulane University
Loyola University
St. Charles Ave.
Magazine St.
Audubon Park
Audubon Zoo
River Rd.
Mississippi River
1 mile
1 km
0
N
90
10
61
46

aquarium and a river cruise are available outside the aquarium. You can also combine tickets for the aquarium and the Entergy IMAX Theater or for the aquarium, a river cruise, and the Audubon Zoo (found uptown in Audubon Park) in a package; or you can take the river cruise by itself. | 1 Canal St. | 504/581–4629 | www.auduboninstitute.org | Aquarium $13.50; combination ticket with IMAX $17.25; combination ticket for aquarium, zoo, and round-trip cruise $30 | Aquarium Sun.–Thurs. 9:30–6 (last entry at 5), Fri.–Sat. 9:30–7 (last entry at 6).

Beauregard-Keyes House. This stately 19th-century mansion with period furnishings was the temporary home of Confederate general P. G. T. Beauregard. The house and grounds had severely deteriorated in the 1940s when novelist Frances Parkinson Keyes moved in and helped restore it. | 1113 Chartres St. | 504/523–7257 | $5 | Mon.–Sat. 10–3, tours on the hr.

Canal Street. At 170 ft, this is the widest main street in the United States and one of the liveliest. In the early 1800s, after the Louisiana Purchase, the French Creoles residing in the French Quarter were segregated from the Americans who settled upriver from Canal Street. The communities had separate governments and police systems, and what is now Canal Street—and, most specifically, the central median running down Canal Street—was neutral ground between them. Today, animosities between these two groups are history, but the term "neutral ground" has survived as the name for all medians throughout the city.

★ **French Market.** The sounds, colors, and smells here are alluring: street performers, ships' horns on the river, pralines, muffulettas, sugarcane, and Creole tomatoes. Originally a Native American trading post, later a bustling open-air market under the French and Spanish, the market begins at Ursulines Street; after a block or so, the fresh produce sold by New Orleans–area farmers and local goods gives way to a flea market. | Daily 7–7, depending on weather.

Gallier House. Famous New Orleans architect James Gallier designed this as his family home in 1857. Take a moment to look through the carriageway; it may be the only one in the city with a carriage parked in it. Call for daily tour schedule. | 1132 Royal St. | 504/525–5661 | www.gnofn.org~hggh | $6, combination ticket with Hermann-Grima House $10 | Tours weekdays 10–3:30.

Hermann-Grima House. This Georgian-style house is one of the largest and best-preserved examples of American architecture in the Quarter. Cooking demonstrations on the open hearth are held here all day Thursday from October through May. | 820 St. Louis St. | 504/525–5661 | www.gnofn.org~hggh | $6, combination ticket with Gallier House $10 | Tours weekdays 10–3:30.

★ **Jackson Square.** Surrounded by historic buildings and filled with plenty of the city's atmospheric street life, the heart of the French Quarter is today a beautifully landscaped park.

Among the notable buildings around the square is St. Louis Cathedral. Two Spanish colonial–style buildings, the Cabildo and the Presbytère, flank the cathedral. The handsome rows of brick apartments on either side of the square are the Pontalba Buildings. Dozens of artists hang their paintings on the park fence and set up outdoor studios where they work on canvases. Musicians, mimes, tarot-card readers, and magicians surround the square. | Park daily 8–at least 6 PM.

Jean Lafitte National Park Visitor Center. This center has free visual and sound exhibits on the customs of various ethnic groups in the state, as well as information-rich daily history tours of the French Quarter. The tours leave at 9:30 AM and are free. | 419 Decatur St. | 504/589–2636 | Daily 9–5.

Le Petit Théâtre. Since 1916 this building has housed a community-based theater group that produces numerous plays each season. It also hosts the Tennessee Williams Festival each spring. | 616 St. Peter St. | 504/522–9958.

Louisiana Office of Tourism. In addition to maps and hundreds of brochures about sights in the city and its environs, this information center has guides who can answer questions. | 529 St. Ann St. | 504/568–5661 | Daily 9–5.

Musée Conti Wax Museum. The history of New Orleans and Louisiana unfolds in colorful vignettes in this fun museum. Local legends are captured in life size at seminal moments. Written and audio explanations supplement the visual scenes. | 917 Conti St. | 504/525–2605 | www.get-waxed.com | $6.75 | Mon.–Sat. 10–5:30, Sun. noon–5:30.

New Orleans Historic Voodoo Museum. A large collection of artifacts and information on voodoo as it was—and still is—practiced in New Orleans is here in a two-room, rather home-grown museum. | 724 Dumaine St. | 504/523–7685 | www.voodoomuseum.com | Museum $7, tours $22 | Daily 10–8.

Old Ursuline Convent. The Ursulines were the first of many orders of religious women who came to New Orleans and founded schools, orphanages, and asylums. Their original convent was built in 1734 and is now the oldest French colonial building in the Mississippi valley. The formal gardens, church, and first floor of the old convent are open for guided tours. | 1100 Chartres St. | 504/529–2651 | $5 | Tours Tues.–Fri. at 10, 11, 1, 2, and 3; weekends at 11:15, 1, and 2.

★ **St. Louis Cathedral.** The oldest active cathedral in the United States, this church at the heart of the old city is named for the 13th-century French king who led two crusades. The current building, which replaced two former structures destroyed by fire, dates from 1794, although it was remodeled and enlarged in 1851. | 615 Père Antoine Alley | 504/525–9585 | www.saintlouiscathedral.org | Free | Tours Mon.–Sat. 9–4:30, Sun. 1–4:30.

Faubourg Marigny and Bywater

The Faubourg Marigny, across Esplanade Avenue from the French Quarter, was developed in the early 1800s by wealthy planter Bernard de Marigny. With architectural styles ranging from classic Creole cottage to Victorian mansion, the Marigny is in effect a residential extension of the Quarter. The streets are more peaceful and the rents a bit cheaper, attracting musicians, artists, and other downtown types. Frenchmen Street is the main street here, lined with music clubs, shops, coffeehouses, and restaurants. The Bywater, a crumbling yet beautiful old neighborhood across Elysian Fields, is a haven to those musicians and artists who find even the Marigny too expensive and overrun.

New Orleans Center for Creative Arts (NOCCA). Many of New Orleans's most talented young musicians, artists, and writers pass through this high school arts program, nurtured by jazz dignitary Ellis Marsalis and now taught by other professional artists from around the country. | 2800 Chartres St. | 504/940–2800.

Studio Inferno Glassworks. This working studio gives demonstrations of glassblowing and casting and sells the results in its gallery. | 3000 Royal St. | 504/945–1878 | Free | Mon.–Sat. 10–5.

Washington Square Park. This park provides a large green space in which to play Frisbee or catch some sun.

Treme

Across Rampart Street from the French Quarter, the neighborhood of Treme (truh-*may*) claims the distinction of being the oldest African-American neighborhood in the country. Once the site of the Claude Treme plantation, it became home to many free people of color during the late 18th and early 19th centuries. Today, Treme is a vibrant and developing area. It can still, however, be unsafe. Unless you are familiar with the area, visit only during the day and stay alert, as this is still a low-income and somewhat risky neighborhood.

Louis Armstrong Park. This large park with its grassy knolls and lagoons is named for native son and world-famous musician Louis Armstrong (1900–71). Congo Square is an inlaid-stone space, where African slaves and free persons of color gathered on Sundays in the 18th and early 19th centuries, which was the only time they were permitted to play their music openly. Neighborhood musicians still congregate here at times for percussion jams. Marie Laveau, the greatly feared and respected voodoo queen of antebellum New Orleans, had her home a block away on St. Ann Street and is reported to have held voodoo rituals here regularly. Adjacent to the park are the Morris F. X. Jeff Municipal Auditorium and Mahalia Jackson Center for the Performing Arts. The park is patrolled by a security detail, but be very careful when wandering, and do not visit after dark. | N. Rampart St. between St. Philip and St. Peter Sts. | Auditorium and performing arts center by event.

St. Louis Cemeteries. New Orleans's "cities of the dead," with rows of crypts like little houses, are one of the city's most enduring images. St. Louis Cemetery #1, the oldest in the city, is an example of the aboveground burial practices of the French and Spanish. Because of the high water level, it was difficult to bury bodies underground without having the coffin float to the surface after the first hard rain. Modern-day burial methods permit underground interment, but many people prefer these ornate family tombs and vaults.

St. Louis Cemetery #2 is four blocks beyond this cemetery, on Claiborne Avenue. St. Louis Cemetery #3 is at the end of Esplanade Avenue, a good drive from here. Although these cemeteries are open to the public, it is dangerous to enter them alone because of frequent muggings inside; group tours are a rational option. | #1: Basin and Conti Sts. | Daily 9–3.

Save Our Cemeteries leads tours every Sunday at 10 AM, or by group appointment, departing from Royal Blend Coffee House at 621 Royal Street. Tickets are $12; reserve by Friday afternoon to be sure of a spot on the tour. | 504/525–3377.

Central Business District (CBD) and the Warehouse District

Bordered by the river, St. Charles Avenue, Poydras Street, and Andrew Higgins Drive and filled with former factories and warehouse buildings, the Warehouse District has exploded over the past decade. Old, abandoned warehouse buildings were renovated to accommodate the 1984 World's Fair, and the stage was set for future development. Today, the neighborhood is dotted with modern renovations of historic buildings, excellent eateries, a growing number of bars and music clubs, and a host of contemporary art galleries as well as the National D-Day Museum, the Ogden Museum of Southern Art, and the Contemporary Arts Center.

The Central Business District (CBD) covers the ground between Canal Street and Poydras Avenue, with some spillover into the Warehouse District's official territory.

★ **Contemporary Arts Center.** Founded in 1976, the center showcases temporary exhibits, often featuring local or regional artists but also welcoming the work of national and international talent. The CAC theater hosts concerts, films, dance, plays, and lectures. | 900 Camp St. | 504/528–3805; 504/528–3800 theater box office | www.cacno.org | $5; free Thurs. | Tues.–Sun. 11–5.

Julia Street. Contemporary art dealers have adopted this strip in the Warehouse District as their own. The street is lined with galleries, flower shops, and modern apartment buildings. The first Saturday evening of each month gallery owners throw open their doors to show off new exhibits, to the accompaniment of wine, music, and general merriment.

★ **Louisiana Children's Museum.** This top-notch Children's Museum is fun and educational. Favorite activities include a mini–grocery store and a giant bubble station. Children with disabilities will find an especially welcoming environment; some exhibits are aimed at increasing awareness of other children's disadvantages. Art teachers lead classes daily; a theater hosts morning programs; and special activities such as jewelry making and storytelling are held each week. A special indoor playground is reserved for toddlers age three and under. | 420 Julia St. | 504/523–1357 | www.lcm.org | $6 | Late Aug.–early June, Tues.–Sat. 9:30–4:30, Sun. noon–4:30; early June–late Aug., Mon.–Sat. 9:30–4:30, Sun. noon–4:30 (last entry at 4).

★ **National D-Day Museum.** The brainchild of historian and writer Dr. Stephen Ambrose, this moving, well-executed examination of World War II covers far more ground than simply the 1944 D-Day invasion of Normandy. The exhibits are spread through a series of small galleries that fill one half of the museum's large, industrial warehouse space; the other half of the warehouse is open, showcasing fighter planes and a replica of the Higgins boat troop-landing craft. | 925 Magazine St. (main entrance on Andrew Higgins Dr.) | 504/527–6012 | www.ddaymuseum.org | $10 | Daily 9–5.

New Orleans School of Glassworks and Printmaking Studio. The School of Glassworks gives demonstrations of all stages of glassmaking and design, printmaking, and silver alchemy in a large warehouse space. | 727 Magazine St. | 504/529–7277 | June–Aug., weekdays 10:30–5; Sept.–May, Mon.–Sat. 10:30–5.

Ogden Museum of Southern Art. This imaginative new museum, scheduled to open spring 2003, has a rooftop garden and centers on a stair hall, which filters natural light through the L-shape series of galleries. More than 1,200 works collected since the 1960s by local developer Roger Ogden will be displayed here. | Entrances at both 615 Andrew Higgins Dr. and 925 Camp St. | 504/539–9600 | www.ogdenmuseum.org | Weekdays 10–5.

Riverwalk Marketplace. This three-block-long shopping-and-entertainment center includes 140 shops and eateries. | 1 Poydras St. | 504/522–1555 | www.riverwalkmarketplace.com | Mon.–Sat. 10–9, Sun. 11–7.

St. Patrick's Church. A stark exterior gives way to a more ornate interior in this first church built in the American sector of New Orleans. | 724 Camp St. | 504/525–4413.

Spanish Plaza. For a terrific view of the river and a place to relax, go behind the World Trade Center at 2 Canal Street to Spanish Plaza. You can hear occasional live music played here, and you can purchase tickets for riverboat cruises.

Garden District

With its beautifully landscaped gardens surrounding elegant antebellum homes, the Garden District lives up to its name. None of the private homes are open to the public on a regular basis, but the occupants do not mind your enjoying the sights from outside the cast-iron fences surrounding their magnificent estates.

Anne Rice's House. The famous novelist's elegant Garden District home is a three-bay Greek Revival, extended over a luxurious side yard. | 1239 1st St.

Christ Church Cathedral. This beautiful Gothic Revival Episcopal church completed in 1887 has windows and steeply pitched gables, architectural details that were precursors to the New Orleans Victorian style. | 2919 St. Charles Ave.

The Rink. This small collection of specialty shops was once the South's first roller-skating rink, built in the 1880s. The Garden District Book Shop stocks regional, rare, and old books. Sometimes the novelist Anne Rice autographs her books here. | Washington Ave. and Prytania St.

Uptown

Lying west of the Garden District, Uptown is the area on both sides of St. Charles Avenue along the streetcar route, upriver from Louisiana Avenue. It includes many mansions similar to those in the Garden District, as well as Loyola and Tulane universities and a large urban park. The St. Charles Avenue streetcar provides a wonderful way to take in this neighborhood.

★ **Audubon Park.** This large, lush stretch of green extends between St. Charles Avenue and Magazine Street, continuing across Magazine Street to the river. It contains the world-class Audubon Zoo, a 1.7-mi track for running, walking, or biking; picnic and play areas; and a golf course, riding stables, a tennis court, and a river view. | 6500 Magazine St. | 504/586–8777 | www.auduboninstitute.org | Park free; combination admission to Aquarium of the Americas downriver and cruise available; round-trip cruise only, $17.50; cruise, zoo, and aquarium $30 | 7-mi river ride to French Quarter and Canal St. daily at 11, 1, 3, and 5.

The ★**Audubon Zoo** uses natural-habitat settings to display and breed animals. It harbors lions, tigers, bears, sea lions, and a family of extremely rare white (albino) alligators. The Louisiana Swamp exhibit re-creates the natural habitat of alligators, nutria (large swamp rodents), and catfish; alligator-feeding time is always well attended, and Sunday afternoons bring live performances by Cajun musicians. | 6500 Magazine St. | 504/581–4629 | $9, combination ticket for zoo and Aquarium of the Americas $17.50 | Daily 9:30–5 (last entry at 4).

Bayou St. John and Mid-City

Above the French Quarter, below the Lakefront, Mid-City is a neighborhood of tremendous ethnic and economic diversity. Here are great restaurants, restored former plantation homes, and crumbling inner-city neighborhoods.

★ **City Park.** One of the largest urban recreation areas in the country is a great place to picnic, walk, or jog. Also included within City Park's boundaries are the Timken Center, New Orleans Botanical Garden, Storyland, Carousel Gardens, New Orleans Museum of Art, tennis courts, and a golf course. | Bordered by City Park Ave., Robert E. Lee Blvd., Marconi Dr., and Bayou St. John | 504/483–4888; 504/483–9422 boat rentals; 504/483–9397 golf facilities | www.neworleanscitypark.com.

Carousel Gardens has a carousel from 1906 that is on the National Register of Historic Places. Surrounding it are a roller coaster, tilt-a-whirl, Ferris wheel, bumper cars, and other rides. A miniature train takes adults and children throughout the area on its own track, and there is a wading pool with bronze statuary. | 504/483–9356 | www.neworleanscitypark.com | General admission $2; unlimited-ride ticket $10 | During Celebration in the Oaks, evenings 5:30–10:30 PM Mar.–May and Sept.–Nov., weekends 10–4; June–Aug., daily 10–4.

The peaceful 10 acres of the **New Orleans Botanical Garden** encompass a tropical conservatory, a water-lily pond, a formal rose garden, azalea and camellia gardens, and horticultural gardens, all decorated with fountains and sculptures by world-renowned local artist Enrique Alferez. Groups can take a guided tour (call ahead for times); otherwise, browse on your own. | 504/483–9386 | $5 | Tues.–Sun. 10–4:30; hrs may vary by season.

At the **New Orleans Museum of Art (NOMA),** the jeweled treasures, particularly some of the famous eggs by Peter Carl Fabergé, are a favorite exhibit, along with European and American paintings, sculpture, drawings, prints, and photography. The museum holds one of the largest glass collections in the country as well as a large collection of Latin American colonial art and a good selection of Japanese painting of the Edo period. | 504/488–2631 | www.noma.org | $6; free Thurs. 10–noon for Louisiana residents | Tues.–Sun. 10–5.

Storyland is a whimsical theme park for children, with 26 storybook exhibits built around fairy-tale characters. | 504/483–9381 | $2 | Weekends only; hrs vary by season (call ahead).

Fair Grounds Race Course. The third-oldest race track in the country, and one of the few remaining independent tracks, sits just off Esplanade Avenue, among the houses of Mid-City. | 1751 Gentilly Blvd. | 504/943–2200 | www.fgno.com | Grandstand $1, Clubhouse $4 | Thurs.–Mon. first post 12:30 PM.

Metairie and the Lakefront

The neighborhood of Old Metairie is part of Orleans Parish and feels like much of Uptown. Most of Metairie, however, has a modern, suburban feel, with mostly lavish homes. Metairie extends to the Lakefront, an area buzzing with bikers, joggers, and especially boaters. On a pretty day, a picnic along the shore includes the spectacle of sailing extravaganzas.

Lake Pontchartrain. This is a popular spot for fishing and boating: in good weather you can see lots of sailboats and Windsurfers. Lakeshore Drive, a road along Lake Pontchartrain, has many park and picnic areas that are generally filled on warm weekends and holidays.

Linear Parkway. Along the south shore of Lake Pontchartrain is the Linear Parkway, a 7½-mi path for biking and hiking.

Longue Vue House and Gardens. Eight acres of beautiful gardens embellished with fountains surround this city estate fashioned after the great country houses of England. | 7 Bamboo Rd. | 504/488–5488 | $10 | Mon.–Sat. 10–4:30, Sun. 1–5.

Algiers Point

Directly across the Mississippi River from the French Quarter and Canal Street, extending out into the river's curve, is the sleepy, historic neighborhood of Algiers Point. Algiers Point is best experienced by walking along its quiet streets, admiring the architecture, and savoring its small-town feel. However, because it is primarily residential and is separated from the main part of the city by the river, it is isolated; you should take the usual precautions for personal safety.

★ **Blaine Kern's Mardi Gras World.** Blaine Kern has for many years been the best-known artist and creator of Mardi Gras floats; he often personally conducts tours through this one-of-a-kind facility. You can watch the artists and builders at work, view a film about Mardi Gras, and buy Carnival memorabilia in the gift shop. A photo of yourself with one of the giant figures used on the floats makes a terrific souvenir, and there's a chest full of costumes for children to try on. | 233 Newton St. | 504/362–8211 | www.mardigrasworld.com | $13.50 (includes cake and coffee) | Daily 9:30–4:30 (hrs vary around Mardi Gras).

Dining

French Quarter

Acme Oyster and Seafood Restaurant. Seafood. This no-nonsense eatery at the entrance to the French Quarter is a prime source for raw oysters on the half shell; great shrimp, oyster, and roast-beef po'boys; and state-of-the-art red beans and rice. | 724 Iberville St. | 504/522–5973 | Reservations not accepted | $5–$12 | AE, DC, MC, V.

Café du Monde. Café. No trip to New Orleans would be complete without a cup of chicory-laced café au lait and a few sugar-dusted beignets in this venerable Creole institution. | French Market, Decatur and St. Ann Sts. | 504/525–4544 | $10 or less | No credit cards.

Central Grocery. Café. This old-fashioned Italian grocery store in the French Quarter produces authentic muffulettas (round loaves of seeded bread with ham, salami, mozzarella) and a salad of marinated green olives. | 923 Decatur St. | 504/523–1620 | $15 or less | No credit cards.

Croissant d'Or. Café. Locals compete with visitors for a table in this colorful, pristine pastry shop, which serves excellent and authentic French croissants, pies, tarts, and custards, as well as an imaginative selection of soups, salads, and sandwiches. Wash them down with real French breakfast coffee, cappuccino, or espresso. Hours are 7 AM to 5 PM daily. | 617 Ursulines St. | 504/524–4663 | $10 or less | MC, V.

Gumbo Shop. Creole. Evocative of old New Orleans, the menu—jambalaya, shrimp Creole and rémoulade, red beans, bread pudding, and seafood and chicken-and-sausage gumbos—is heavily flavored with tradition. | 630 St. Peter St. | 504/525–2486 | $7–$16 | AE, D, DC, MC, V.

Irene's Cuisine. Italian. From Irene DiPietro's kitchen come succulent roasted chicken brushed with olive oil, rosemary, and garlic; tubes of manicotti bulging with ground veal and mozzarella; and big, fresh shrimp, aggressively seasoned and grilled before joining linguine glistening with herbed olive oil. End with an Italian-style baked Alaska, covered with a blue flame of ignited grappa liqueur. | 539 St. Philip St. | 504/529–8811 | Reservations not accepted | Closed Sun. No lunch | $15–$19 | AE, MC, V.

★ **Johnny's Po'boys.** Café. Inside the soft-crust French bread come the classic fillings, including lean boiled ham, well-done roast beef in a garlicky gravy, and crisply fried oysters or shrimp. | 511 St. Louis St. | 504/523–9071 | No dinner Sun. | $15 | No credit cards.

Faubourg Marigny

Mona's Café & Deli. Café. This rather bare and simple spot sells some of the best, basic eastern Mediterranean cooking. Cut open a ball of crunchy fried kibbee and the reward is superbly seasoned beef and lamb. Tabouleh, with lots of parsley and mint flecks, is more than just seasoned bulgur wheat. The gyro sandwiches are meaty and flavorful, too. | 504 Frenchmen St. | 504/949–4115 | $3–$13 | AE, D, MC, V.

★ **Praline Connection.** Creole. Down-home cooking in the southern-Creole style includes fried or stewed chicken, smothered pork chops, barbecue ribs, and collard greens. And the soulful filé gumbo, bread pudding, and sweet-potato pie are among the best in town. To all this add moderate prices, a congenial staff, and a neat-as-a-pin dining room. | 542 Frenchmen St. | 504/943–3934 | 901 S. Peters St., Warehouse District | 504/523–3973. | Reservations not accepted | $7–$14 | AE, D, DC, MC, V.

Central Business District (CBD)

Mother's. Café. Mother's dispenses delicious baked ham and roast-beef po'boys (ask for "debris" on the beef sandwich and the bread will be slathered with meat juices and shreds of meat), home-style biscuits and jambalaya, and a very good chicken gumbo in a couple of dining rooms. | 401 Poydras St. | 504/523–9656 | $7–$11 | No credit cards.

Uptown

★ **Camellia Grill.** American. Locals vie until the early morning hours for one of the 29 stools at the gleaming counter, each place supplied with a large, fresh linen napkin. The hamburger—four ounces of excellent beef on a fresh bun with any number of embellishments—is one of the best in town. Other blue-ribbon dishes are the chili, the fruit and meringue pies, and the garnished omelets. | 626 S. Carrollton Ave. | 504/866–9573 | $15 | No credit cards.

Franky & Johnny's. Seafood. From the kitchen's steaming cauldrons come freshly boiled shrimp, crab, and crawfish, piled high and ready to be washed down with ice-cold beer.

On the day's po'boy roster might be fried crawfish tails or oysters, meatballs in tomato sauce, or roast beef with gravy. | 321 Arabella St. | 504/899–9146 | Reservations not accepted | $15 | D, MC, V.

La Crêpe Nanou. French. French chic for the budget-minded is the style in this welcoming little bistro. The menu is loaded with earthy dishes, led by the filet mignon with one of several classic French sauces and french fries that are really French. Other reliable standbys are the pâté maison, hearty lentil soup, and lavish dessert crepes. | 1410 Robert St. | 504/899–2670 | Reservations not accepted | No lunch | $11–$17 | MC, V.

Martinique. Caribbean. The French Caribbean meets New Orleans in dishes suffused with delicate herbal and spicy flavors, ranging from bracing poached oysters with lime and cayenne to lamb sausage with minted beans. Good, too, are the cod fritters, carrot and leek soup, salmon in pineapple-sesame sauce, and *blaff,* a Martiniquaise bouillabaisse that's perfect for a cool evening. | 5908 Magazine St. | 504/891–8495 | Closed Mon. No lunch | $13–$17 | MC, V.

Mid-City

Angelo Brocato's. Café. Traditional Sicilian fruit sherbets, ice creams, pastries, and candies are the attractions of this quaint little sweetshop that harks back to the time when the French Quarter was peopled mostly by Italian immigrants. | 214 N. Carrollton Ave. | 504/488–1465 | $15 | No credit cards.

Mandina's. Seafood. Butter, hearty seasonings, and tomato sauce are the staples at this neighborhood treasure. The shrimp rémoulade and old-fashioned gumbo are the logical appetizers. Broiled trout and shrimp, wading in seasoned butter, are tasty, as are the fried oysters and shrimp, the seafood or Italian sausage po'boys, and the sweetbread pudding. | 3800 Canal St. | 504/482–9179 | Reservations not accepted | $15 | No credit cards.

Lodging

French Quarter

Hotel Royal. Many rooms in this circa-1830 home are pleasantly oversize; four have balconies overlooking Royal Street and a school playground, two have hot tubs, and each has a coffeemaker and a small refrigerator. Distinctly modern amenities complement high ceilings and antebellum furnishings. The complimentary Continental breakfast comes from the nearby Croissant d'Or. Cable TV, parking (fee) | 1006 Royal St., 70116 | 504/524–3900 or 800/776–3901 | fax 504/558–0566 | www.melrosegroup.com | 30 rooms | $95–$180 | AE, D, DC, MC, V | CP.

Hotel Villa Convento. Although it's just blocks from the Quarter's tourist attractions, shopping, and great restaurants, this guest house is on a surprisingly quaint, quiet street, close to the Old Ursuline Convent. Each morning you can have croissants and fresh-brewed coffee on the lush patio. Furnished with reproductions of antiques, rooms vary in price; some have balconies, chandeliers, or ceiling fans. Cable TV | 616 Ursulines St., 70116 | 504/522–1793 | fax 504/524–1902 | www.villaconvento.com | 25 rooms | $105–$175 | AE, D, DC, MC, V | CP.

Central Business District (CBD)

Comfort Suites Downtown. A boon for budget travelers, this former office building is four blocks from the French Quarter. It has large, well-equipped one-room suites; luxury suites have whirlpool baths. The sauna, hot tub, and free morning paper are pleasant surprises, and the first five local calls are free. In-room safes, microwaves, refrigerators, cable TV, gym, hot tub, sauna, bar, laundry facilities, business services, parking (fee), no-smoking rooms | 346 Baronne St., 70112 | 504/524–1140 or 800/524–1140 | fax 504/523–4444 | www3.choicehotels.com/ires/en-US/hotel/LA071 | 102 suites | $129–$399 | AE, D, DC, MC, V | CP.

Quality Inn—Midtown. A location just west of downtown makes this a popular place to stay during Jazz Fest and City Park golf tournaments. Restaurant, cable TV, pool, hot tub, bar, free parking, no-smoking rooms | 3900 Tulane Ave., 70119 | 504/486–5541 or 800/228–5151 | fax 504/488–7440 | www.qualityinn.com | 96 rooms, 8 suites | $89–$159 | AE, D, DC, MC, V.

Garden District/Uptown

★ **The Chimes Bed and Breakfast.** The Abbyad family maintain a homey environment with all the conveniences found in large hotels: hair dryers, irons, stereos, coffeemakers, and private entrances. Continental breakfast is served in the airy dining room. Cable TV, some pets allowed; no smoking | 1146 Constantinople St., 70115 | 504/488–4640 or 800/729–4640 | fax 504/488–4639 | 5 rooms | $115–$160 | No credit cards | CP.

Quality Inn Maison St. Charles. This is a lovely property in six historic buildings that cluster around intimate courtyards. A complimentary shuttle to the convention center and 24-hour security are among the amenities. Cable TV, pool, hot tub, bar, parking (fee), no-smoking rooms | 1319 St. Charles Ave., 70130 | 504/522–0187 or 800/831–1783 | fax 504/528–9993 | www.qualityinn.com | 129 rooms, 16 suites | $115–$150 | AE, D, DC, MC, V.

St. Charles Guest House. Simple and affordable, this European-style pension is in four buildings one block from St. Charles Avenue. Rooms in the A and B buildings are larger. The small "backpacker" rooms share a bath and do not have air-conditioning. A pleasant surprise is the large swimming pool and deck. Pool; no room phones, no room TVs | 1748 Prytania St., 70130 | 504/523–6556 | fax 504/522–6340 | www.stcharlesguesthouse.com | 36 rooms, 28 with bath | $75–$105 | AE, MC, V | CP.

Metairie

Best Western Landmark Hotel. This 17-story, centrally located hotel has oversize rooms, a top-floor restaurant with a view of the city, and two corporate-level executive floors with special amenities. Pool, cable TV, lounge, free parking | 2601 Severn Ave., 70002 | 504/888–9500 | fax 504/889–5792 | www.nolahotels.com/landmarkbw/index.html | 342 rooms | $90–$119 | D, DC, MC, V.

Westbank

Holiday Inn—Westbank. Don't get confused—the address here is exactly the same as at the Quality Inn Gretna, but this hotel is a few blocks farther along the expressway, on the opposite side of the expressway when coming off the Crescent City Connection Bridge. Golfers stay here during tournaments at the nearby English Turn Golf and Country Club. Restaurant, cable TV, pool, bar, free parking | 100 Westbank Expressway, Gretna 70053 | 504/366–2361 or 800/465–4329 | fax 504/362–5814 | www.holiday-inn.com | 311 rooms, 6 suites | $77–$150 | AE, D, DC, MC, V.

Kenner/Airport

Holiday Inn Select–Airport Holidome. Many of the rooms here face the dome-covered pool area, which is popular with children. It's convenient to I–10 and close to Rivertown, U.S.A., and the *Treasure Chest* riverboat casino. All rooms have hair dryers, irons, and ironing boards. Restaurant, cable TV, pool, gym, hot tub, sauna, bar, meeting room, airport shuttle, free parking | 2929 Williams Blvd., Kenner 70062 | 504/467–5611 or 800/887–7371 | fax 504/469–4915 | www.holiday-inn.com | 303 rooms, 1 suite | $119–$139 | AE, D, DC, MC, V.

Camping

Bayou Segnette State Park. The campsites are in a wooded area of the park; reservations are not accepted for holiday weekends. Furnished loft cabins that sleep from six to eight have screened porches overlooking the bayou; reservations are required for these. The park, which has the state's largest wave pool, is off the Westbank Expressway near the Huey P. Long Bridge. There's also a boat launch. Flush toilets, partial hook-ups (electric and water), dump station, laundry facilities, showers, grills, picnic tables, public telephone. | 98 sites, 20 cabins | 7777 Westbank Expressway, Westwego 70094 | 504/736–7140 or 877/226–7652 | $12–$65 | MC, V.

KOA West. There are a few tent sites as well as large back-in sites for RVs with well-kept grass areas around tree-shaded concrete pads; reservations are recommended. The campground is close to Rivertown, U.S.A., in Kenner (take the Williams Blvd. exit off I–10). Both Grayline and New Orleans tours pick up here for sightseeing, and the campground operates a shuttle bus to the French Quarter. Flush toilets, full hook-ups, dump station, laundry facilities, showers, picnic tables, playground, pool | 6 tent sites, 96 RV sites | 11129 Jefferson Hwy., River Ridge 70123 | 504/467–1792 or 800/562–5110 | fax 504/464–7204 | $30 | AE, D, MC, V.

Arts and Entertainment

Dance

★ **Mid-City Bowling Lanes Rock 'n' Bowl.** The saying "Only in New Orleans . . ." applies to this combination bowling alley–music club near Uptown, in Mid-City. Dancers may spill over into the lanes when a favorite band such as zydeco legend Boozoo Chavis takes the stage. Blues, R&B, rock, swing, and Cajun music are all presented. Thursday is zydeco night, bringing the best musicians in from rural Louisiana. | 4133 S. Carrollton Ave. | 504/482–3133.

★ **Mulate's.** Across the street from the convention center, this large restaurant seats 400, and the dance floor quickly fills with couples twirling and two-stepping to authentic Cajun bands from the countryside. Regulars love to drag first-timers to the floor for impromptu lessons. The home-style Cajun cuisine is quite good, and the bands play until 10:30 or 11 PM. | 201 Julia St. | 504/522–1492.

Music

House of Blues. Despite its name, blues is a relatively small component in the booking policy, which also embraces rock, jazz, country, soul, funk, world music, and more, performed by everyone from local artists to international touring acts. A gospel brunch is a rousing Sunday staple. | 225 Decatur St. | 504/529–2583 concert line.

Louisiana Philharmonic Orchestra. Always good and sometimes excellent, the orchestra performs a wide range of classical works in the Orpheum Theater (129 University Pl.) | 504/523–6530.

Preservation Hall. The jazz tradition that flowered in the 1920s is enshrined in this cultural landmark by a cadre of distinguished New Orleans musicians, most of whom were schooled by an ever-dwindling group of elder statesmen who actually played with Louis Armstrong et al. There is limited seating—many patrons end up squatting on the floor or standing in back—and no beverages are served or allowed. Nonetheless, the legions of satisfied customers regard an evening here as a transcendent New Orleans experience. | 726 St. Peter St. | 504/522–2841 or 504/523–8939.

Theater

Le Chat Noir. Come to the cabaret for a scintillating mix of revues, chanteuses, theater, tango, piano trills, and pop standards. In the heart of the arts district, this cat is sleek, elegant, and eclectic, with plenty of warm wood and cool tile, all polished to the highest gloss. The patrons, whether in their twenties or fifties, are appropriately urbane. | 715 St. Charles Ave. | 504/581–6333.

True Brew Café/True Brew Theater. This airy spot serves coffee, pastries, salads, sandwiches, and cocktails from 6:30 AM on weekdays, 7:30 AM on weekends. Weekends often bring local slapstick theater and cabaret. | 200 Julia St. | 504/524–8441.

Shopping

The fun of shopping in New Orleans is in the many regional items available throughout the city. You can take home some of the flavor of the city: its pralines (pecan candies), seafood (packaged to go), Louisiana red beans and rice, coffee (pure or with chicory), and Creole and Cajun spices (cayenne pepper, chili, and garlic). There are even packaged mixes of such local favorites as jambalaya, gumbo, beignets, and the sweet red local cocktail called the Hurricane. Cookbooks also share the secrets of preparing distinctive New Orleans dishes.

The masks worn at Mardi Gras are popular as gifts, souvenirs, and decorative pieces. Mardi Gras costumes, beads, and doubloons make wonderful gifts, too. Posters, photographs, and paintings on canvas and slate capture scenes in New Orleans. Jewelry, antiques, ceramics, carved wooden toys, kites, jazz umbrellas, and wreaths of dried flowers are often handmade and make lovely gifts and souvenirs.

Many clothing shops sell items popular in the semitropical heat: Panama hats, lacy lingerie, and the ubiquitous T-shirt and sports clothes. The Welcome Center of the New Orleans Metropolitan Convention and Visitors Bureau on the St. Ann Street side of Jackson Square also has pamphlets on shopping.

Shopping Areas

The main shopping areas in the city are the **French Quarter,** with its narrow streets lined with specialty, gift, and antiques shops and art galleries. The charm of this area and its fascinating merchandise should be enjoyed at a leisurely pace.

The **Central Business District (CBD)** has department stores and clothing, specialty, and jewelry shops. Nearby, in the heart of the **Warehouse District,** art and crafts galleries line Julia Street, the premier avenue of the arts for New Orleans.

Along **Magazine Street**'s 5 mi, you can find dozens of intriguing antiques shops, bric-a-brac vendors, used-clothing and -furniture stores, art galleries, and specialists in furniture restoration, interior decorating, and pottery.

Uptown sprinkles neighborhood and specialty shops across several fashionable shopping areas. This area exudes an old-fashioned small-town feeling, where most of the shops are housed in turn-of-the-20th-century cottages.

Sports and Outdoor Activities

Bicycling

Instead of riding the streetcar, you can bike at your own pace past the mansions of St. Charles Avenue to lush Audubon Park. A paved path along the crest of the Mississippi River levee runs from Audubon Park to Jefferson Parish and beyond, affording views of romantically decaying fishing camps, industrial rigs, and the river itself. City Park and the lakefront are other good alternatives.

Bicycle Michael's. Rentals (a major credit card is required for deposit) are available for $5 per hour, or $16 per day. | 622 Frenchmen St. | 504/945–9505 | www.bicyclemichaels.com | $5 per hr, $16 per day.

Boating

City Park. Four-seat paddleboats provide an intimate view of the swampy lagoons. Rental costs $20 per hour, and the dock is to the right behind the New Orleans Museum of Art. | 504/482–4888 or 504/483–9422.

Canoeing

Bayou Sauvage National Wildlife Refuge. Within the eastern limits of New Orleans, the U.S. Fish and Wildlife Service administers a 22,000-acre marshland preserve. Free guided canoe trips are available at the refuge on weekends; these include canoes and gear. Reservations are required. | Off I–10 | 985/646–7555 for information; 985/882–3881 for reservations | Free.

Fishing

Louisiana Department of Wildlife and Fisheries. Residents and nonresidents intending to fish around New Orleans must purchase a license. For licenses or information about fishing regulations, contact the Louisiana Department of Wildlife and Fisheries in advance. Box 98000, Baton Rouge 70898 | 225/765–2800 or 225/765–2887).

City Park. One-day permits (sunup to sundown; $2) allow fishing for perch, catfish, and bass from the shore of the stocked streams in the park. | 504/482–4888.

Essential Information

FESTIVALS AND SEASONAL EVENTS

WINTER

Dec.: **Christmas Eve Bonfires.** The bonfires, legend says, originally were lit by the early settlers to help Papa Noël (the Cajun Santa Claus) find his way to their new homes along the Mississippi levees in St. James Parish. New Orleans Paddle Wheels (504/529–4567) and New Orleans Steamboat (504/586–8777) run boats up the muddy Mississippi for this blazing festival.

Countdown. A huge, televised New Year's Eve celebration in Jackson Square is *the place* to be to ring in the year.

Jan.: **Sugar Bowl Classic.** The city's oldest annual sporting event includes not only one of the biggest college football games of the year but also tennis, basketball, sailing, running, and flag football championship events. | 504/525–8573.

Feb.: **Mardi Gras.** Rollicking, raucous, and ritualistic. Dozens of parades are scheduled nearly every weekend during the Carnival season (January 6–Ash Wednesday) and nightly during the final two weeks. Lundi Gras (Monday) is a full day of free concerts on the downtown riverfront, and Mardi Gras (always the Tuesday before Ash Wednesday) is a full day of street parties, masquerades, and parades throughout the city and suburbs.

SPRING

Tennessee Williams–New Orleans Literary Festival and Writer's Conference. Begun as a forum about the work of Tennessee Williams, this festival has expanded to include a broad range of New Orleans–based authors and writings. Everyone's favorite event? The Stanley and Stella screaming match, which takes place in Jackson Square. | 504/581–1144.

Crescent City Classic. The very popular 10K footrace culminates in a huge party in Audubon Park. | 504/861–8686.

Apr.: **French Quarter Festival.** This is a weekend of free music and entertainment for all ages throughout the Quarter. | 504/522–5730.

New Orleans Jazz and Heritage Festival. Two long weekends of performances by more than 4,000 musicians, authentic Louisiana foods, plus quality arts and crafts attract an international crowd to the Fair Grounds. Sounds of gospel, R&B, jazz, Cajun, zydeco, folk, rock, Latin, African, Caribbean, swing, rap, reggae, and more fill 12 different music venues. | 504/522–4786.

SUMMER

June: **New Orleans Wine and Food Experience.** This is a weekend of tasting, with more than 350 wines and food from 80 restaurants on offer. | 504/529–9463.

July: **Essence Music Festival.** For the past several years, the festival has been held over the Fourth of July weekend in the Louisiana Superdome. This predominately African-American music festival plans to keep coming back indefinitely. | 504/522–4786.

AUTUMN

Nov.: **Celebration in the Oaks.** For many New Orleanians, Christmas just isn't Christmas without the mandatory drive through City Park, with its dazzling and dramatic assortment of lights. | 504/483–9415.

Bargains

Stroll the streets of the French Quarter and watch local artists create their work, especially in and around Jackson Square. Seasonal festivals on the Riverfront often showcase local jazz and Cajun or zydeco musicians and moderately priced foods from local restaurants that set up booths.

Tours

BUS TOURS

New Orleans Tours. City, swamp, and plantation tours and combination city–paddle wheeler outings are available. Full-day plantation tours include guided tours through two antebellum plantation homes along the Mississippi River and a stop for lunch in a Cajun-Creole restaurant outside the city. | 504/592–0560 or 800/543–6332.

Tours by Isabelle. City, swamp, plantation, and combination swamp-and-plantation tours are available. Exploring an exotic Louisiana swamp and traveling into Cajun country is an experience not to be missed. | 504/391–3544 or 888/223–2093.

RIVERBOAT CRUISES

New Orleans Paddle Wheel. Riverwalk is the point of embarkation for a river plantation and battlefield cruise, a river plantation harbor cruise, and a Crown Point swamp tour. There is also an evening jazz dinner cruise from 8 to 10 (boarding at 7 PM). | 504/524–0814.

WALKING TOURS

Friends of the Cabildo. Three-hour general history tours are given daily at 10 and 1:30 by Friends of the Cabildo. The tour price includes admission to two state museums of your choice. | 504/523–3939.

Jean Lafitte National Park. Park rangers give free 1½-hour general history tours of the French Quarter daily at 10:30 AM. | 504/589–2636.

Visitor Information

Greater New Orleans Black Tourism Network | 1520 Sugar Bowl Dr., 70112 | 504/523–5652 or 800/725–5652 | fax 504/522–0785 | www.soulofneworleans.com. **Louisiana Office of Tourism** Box 94291, Baton Rouge 70804-9291 | 800/633–6970 | fax 504/342–8390 | www.louisianatravel.com. **New Orleans and River Region Chamber of Commerce** | 601 Poydras St., 70190 | 504/527–6900 | fax 504/527–6970. **New Orleans Metropolitan Convention & Visitors Bureau** | 1520 Sugar Bowl Dr., 70112 | 504/566–5011 or 800/672–6124 | fax 504/566–5021 | www.neworleanscvb.com; in the U.K., | 20 Barclay Rd., Croydon, Surrey CRO 1JN | 020/8760–0377 | fax 020/8666–0365.

Arriving and Departing

BY AIR

Airports

New Orleans International Airport (MSY). The airport is in suburban Kenner, about 11 mi west of downtown New Orleans. | 504/464–0831 | www.flymsy.com.

Airport Transportation

Car: Take the I–10 expressway (from the CBD, go west to the Airport exit). Allow 90 minutes for the drive during afternoon rush hour.

Public Transit: Louisiana Transit Buses. The trip on a bus from the airport to the Central Business District (CBD) costs $1.50 in exact change. From the CBD, departures for the airport are every 10 to 20 minutes from Elks Place and Tulane Avenue across from the city library. The last bus leaves at 6:30 PM. | 504/818–1077.

Shuttle: New Orleans Tours Airport Shuttle. A one-way ticket from the airport to downtown hotels is $10 per person, and the trip takes about 40 minutes. | 504/522–3500.

Taxi: A cab ride costs $24 from the airport to the CBD for one person and $10 (per passenger) for three or more passengers. Pick-up is on the lower level, outside the baggage claim area.

BY BUS

Union Passenger Terminal. Greyhound serves New Orleans from the terminal in the CBD. | 1001 Loyola Ave. | 504/525–6075 or 800/231–2222.

BY CAR

I–10 runs from Florida to California and passes directly through the city. To get to the CBD, exit at Poydras Street near the Louisiana Superdome. For the French Quarter, look for the Vieux Carré exit.

BY TRAIN

Union Passenger Terminal. Three Amtrak lines arrive at and depart from New Orleans's Union Passenger Terminal. | 1001 Loyola Ave. | 504/528–1610 or 800/872–7245.

Getting Around

BY BOAT AND FERRY

Canal Street Ferry. The ferries, which depart from the foot of Canal Street, cross the river to a part of New Orleans called Algiers. The trip takes about 10 minutes; ferries leave on the hour and half hour and run from 6:30 AM to midnight. | 504/376–8100.

BY CAR

Having a car in New Orleans is no problem—except at Mardi Gras. A car is not needed for sightseeing around the most-visited areas of the city, however.

Parking

Finding a parking space is fairly easy in most of the city, except for the French Quarter. Parking laws throughout the city are dubious, however. If in doubt about a space, pass it up and pay to use a parking lot.

BY PUBLIC TRANSIT

Bus and Streetcar

Regional Transit Authority (RTA). RTA operates public buses with interconnecting lines throughout the city.

The Riverfront streetcar covers a 2-mi route along the Mississippi River, connecting major sights from the end of the French Quarter to the New Orleans Convention Center. This streetcar operates weekdays 6 AM until midnight and weekends 8 AM until midnight, passing each stop every 15 minutes. The St. Charles Avenue streetcar runs the 5 mi from the CBD to Carrollton Avenue 24 hours a day, about every 10 minutes 7 AM–8 PM, every half hour 8 PM–midnight, and every hour midnight–7 AM.

Bus and streetcar fare is $1.25 exact change, plus 25¢ for transfers. Visitor passes, available at hotels, cost $5 for one day, $12 for three days of unlimited rides. | 504/248–3900; 504/242–2600 automated information.

BY TAXI

Cabs are metered at $2.50 minimum plus $1 for each additional passenger and $1.10 per mile.

Checker Yellow Cabs| 504/943–2411. **Liberty Bell Cabs** | 504/822–5974. **United Cabs** | 504/522–9771.

New York

Revised and Updated by Christina Knight

NEW YORK CITY

Attractions crowd close together on the narrow island of Manhattan, and between the world-famous sights you plan to see, you're bound to be pleasantly sidetracked by break-dancing street performers and seductive window displays. Neighborhoods themselves are spectacles with no admission costs. A carnival-like atmosphere reigns in Chinatown, where the sidewalks are jammed with sightseers and locals ogling the unusual vegetables, pungent varieties of fish, and discount wares found in the area's countless shops. In the crazy-quilt pattern of tree-lined Greenwich Village, small restaurants and coffee shops serve as directional markers. Even locals can get lost here when trying to find a piano bar or meet friends for a brunch date. Manhattan's character changes every few blocks, so quaint town houses stand shoulder to shoulder with sleek glass towers, artisan galleries sit around the corner from dusty thrift shops, and chic bistros enliven the storefronts of soot-smudged warehouses. For most kids, the city streets are one big curiosity store en route to must-sees such as the American Museum of Natural History, the Statue of Liberty, or the panorama from either the Empire State Building or the Brooklyn Bridge. When the weather is fine, do like New Yorkers do and dally an hour or two in Central Park, whether to watch the disco-dancing rollerbladers near Sheep's Meadow or the model boats on the Conservatory Water.

Exploring

New Yorkers may seem hurried and brusque, but they will often gladly come to your aid if you need directions. Fifth Avenue is the east–west dividing line for numbered streets: on either side, addresses begin at 1 where a street intersects 5th Avenue. The area below 14th Street was settled before the 1811 grid was decreed—here you'll find West 4th Street intersecting West 11th Street, and Leroy Street turning into St. Luke's Place for one block and then becoming Leroy again. Logic won't help you below 14th Street; only a good street map and good directions will.

Lower Manhattan

Battery Park. Ferries leave from the park's Castle Clinton National Monument to the Statue of Liberty and Ellis Island. The ferry ride is one loop; you can get off at Liberty Island, visit the statue, then reboard any ferry and continue on to Ellis Island. Inside

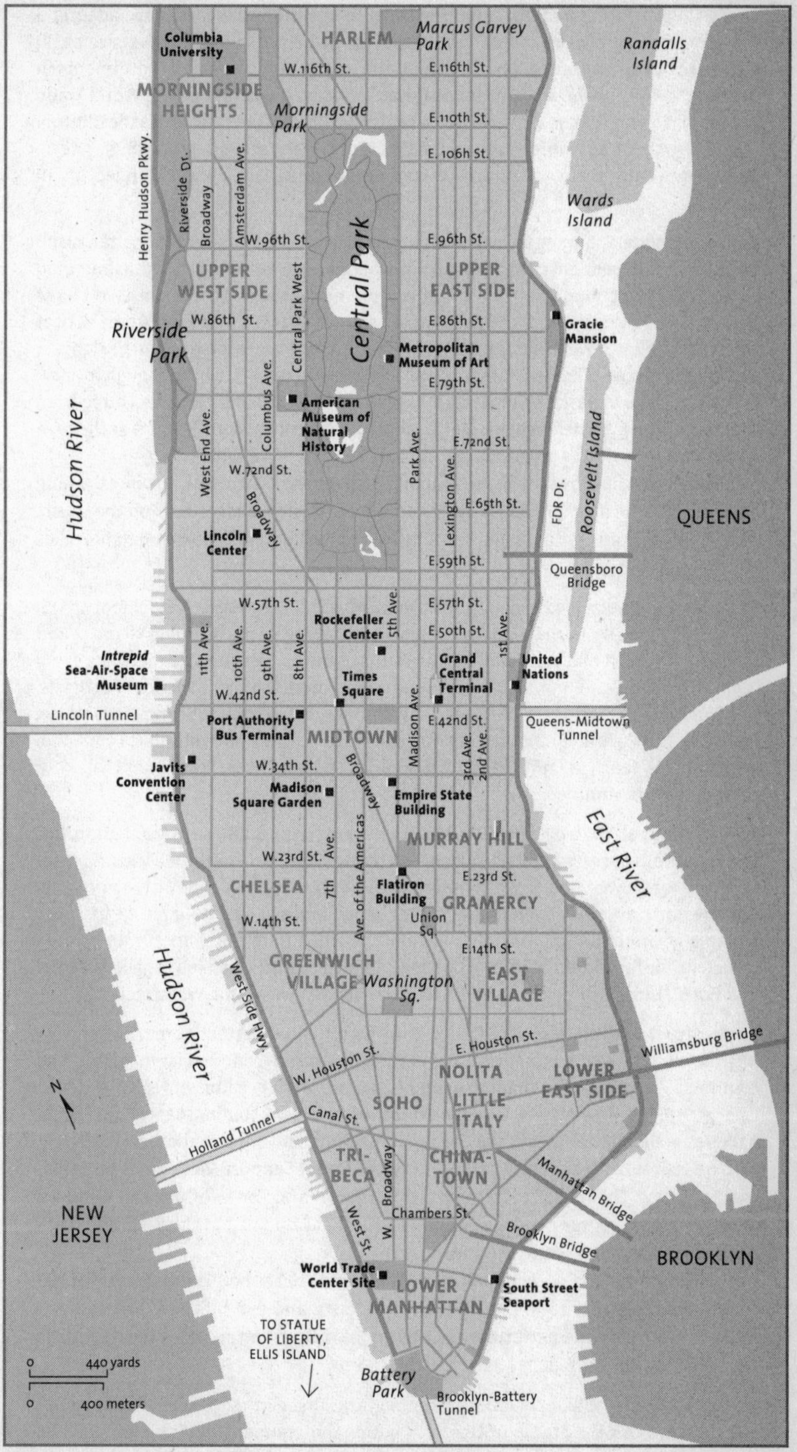
Columbia University
HARLEM
Marcus Garvey Park
Randalls Island
W.116th St.
E.116th St.
MORNINGSIDE HEIGHTS
Morningside Park
E.110th St.
E.106h St.
Henry Hudson Pkwy.
Riverside Dr.
Broadway
Amsterdam Ave.
Wards Island
W.96th St.
E.96th St.
Central Park
UPPER WEST SIDE
UPPER EAST SIDE
Central Park West
W.86th St.
E.86th St.
Gracie Mansion
Riverside Park
Metropolitan Museum of Art
Columbus Ave.
E.79th St.
American Museum of Natural History
Hudson River
West End Ave.
E.72nd St.
Park Ave.
Lexington Ave.
Roosevelt Island
W.72nd St.
Broadway
E.65th St.
FDR Dr.
QUEENS
Lincoln Center
E.59th St.
Queensboro Bridge
W.57th St.
E.57th St.
Rockefeller Center
5th Ave.
E.50th St.
1st Ave.
11th Ave.
10th Ave.
9th Ave.
8th Ave.
Grand Central Terminal
United Nations
Intrepid Sea-Air-Space Museum
Times Square
W.42nd St.
Lincoln Tunnel
Port Authority Bus Terminal
E.42nd St.
Queens-Midtown Tunnel
MIDTOWN
Madison Ave.
3rd Ave.
2nd Ave.
Javits Convention Center
W.34th St.
Broadway
Madison Square Garden
Empire State Building
East River
MURRAY HILL
W.23rd St.
7th Ave.
Flatiron Building
E.23rd St.
CHELSEA
GRAMERCY
Ave. of the Americas
W.14th St.
Union Sq.
E.14th St.
Hudson River
GREENWICH VILLAGE
Washington Sq.
EAST VILLAGE
West Side Hwy.
E. Houston St.
Williamsburg Bridge
W. Houston St.
NOLITA
LOWER EAST SIDE
N
SOHO
LITTLE ITALY
Canal St.
Holland Tunnel
TRI-BECA
Broadway
CHINA-TOWN
Manhattan Bridge
NEW JERSEY
West St.
W. Broadway
Chambers St.
Brooklyn Bridge
BROOKLYN
World Trade Center Site
LOWER MANHATTAN
South Street Seaport
TO STATUE OF LIBERTY, ELLIS ISLAND
0
440 yards
0
400 meters
Battery Park
Brooklyn-Battery Tunnel

Castle Clinton, a Colonial fort, are dioramas of lower Manhattan. Leave adequate time for security checks at the ferry boarding. Large packages and oversize backpacks are not permitted on board. Joining the many memorials and monuments in the park is *The Sphere,* a sculpture that had stood at the center of the World Trade Center plaza for 30 years. | Broadway and Battery Pl. | 212/344–7220 for Castle Clinton; 212/269–5755 for ferry information | Castle Clinton free, ferry $10 | Daily 8:15–5, ferry departures daily every 30 mins 8:30–4:30; more departures and extended hrs in summer.

★ **Brooklyn Bridge.** Spanning the East River, the Brooklyn Bridge connects Manhattan island to the once independent city of Brooklyn. A walk across it is a must for the astounding views. When the bridge opened in 1883 it was promptly crowned the "Eighth Wonder of the World." Its twin Gothic-arch towers, with a span of 1,595½ ft, rise 272 ft from the river below; the bridge's overall length of 6,016 ft made it four times longer than the longest suspension bridge of its day. From roadway to water is about 133 ft, high enough to allow the tallest ships to pass. The roadway is supported by a web of steel cables, hung from the towers and attached to block-long anchorages on either shore. Plaques at the towers explain the bridge's construction.

Pedestrians, in-line skaters, and bicyclists share the boardwalk, so obey the lane markings on the promenade: bicyclists on the north side, pedestrians on the south. A walk across from Centre Street near City Hall to the heart of Brooklyn Heights takes about 40 minutes.

★ **Ellis Island.** Between 1892 and 1924, approximately 12 million people first set foot on U.S. soil at this 27½-acre island's federal immigration facility. By the time Ellis Island closed for good in 1954, it had processed the ancestors of more than 40% of Americans living today. The Ellis Island Immigration Museum holds more than 30 galleries of artifacts, photographs, and taped oral histories that chronicle the immigrant experience. At the American Family Immigration Center, you can search Ellis Island's records for your own ancestors ($5 fee). | 212/363–3200 | www.ellisisland.org | Free. Ferry $10 | Daily 9–5; extended hrs in summer.

St. Paul's Chapel. The oldest (1766) public building in continuous use in Manhattan, this Episcopal house of worship was modeled on London's St. Martin-in-the-Fields. A prayer service here followed George Washington's inauguration as president; Washington's pew is in the north aisle. After September 11, the chapel served as a 24-hour refuge for those working at Ground Zero, which is just across the street from the chapel's 18th-century cemetery. The fence around St. Paul's Chapel has been transformed into a gallery of grief and hope. | Broadway and Fulton St. | 212/602–0800 | www.trinitywallstreet.org.

★ **South Street Seaport Historic District.** This charming cobblestone corner of New York has the city's largest concentration of early 19th-century commercial buildings, and commercial it still is, with chain stores filling a pier's mall. | Visitor center: 211 Water St. | 212/732–7678 for events and shopping information | www.southstseaport.org | Ships, galleries, walking tours, Maritime Crafts Center, films, and other seaport events $5.

The visitor center of the scatter-site **South Street Seaport Museum** is on Schermerhorn Row. The museum offers walking tours, hands-on exhibits, and fantastic creative programs for children, all with a nautical theme. | 212/748–8600 | Apr.–Sept., daily 10–6; Oct.–Mar., Wed.–Mon. 10–5.

Historic ships are docked at **Pier 16.** The Pier 16 ticket booth provides information and sells tickets to the museum, ships, tours, and exhibits. Pier 16 also hosts frequent concerts and performances, has an ice rink in winter, and is the departure point for various cruises.

★ **Statue of Liberty.** Millions of American immigrants first glimpsed their new land when they laid eyes on the Statue of Liberty, a national monument that still ennobles all those who encounter it. *Liberty Enlightening the World,* as the statue is officially named, was sculpted by Frederic-Auguste Bartholdi and presented in 1886 to the United States as a gift from France. Since then she has become a near-universal symbol of freedom and democracy, standing a proud 152 ft high on top of an 89-ft pedestal (executed by Richard Morris Hunt), on Liberty Island in New York Harbor. Emma Lazarus's sonnet *The New Colossus* ("Give me your tired, your poor, your huddled masses . . .") is inscribed on a bronze plaque at the statue's base.

At press time, the museum, pedestal, and stairwell to the crown were closed, but do visit for an inspiring ranger-led tour around the statue. Heightened security measures at the ferry departure point (Castle Clinton at Battery Park) will add time to your trip. | Liberty Island | 212/363–3200; 212/269–5755 for ferry information | www.nps.gov/stli | Free Ferry $10 | Daily 9–5; extended hrs in summer.

World Trade Center site. On September 11, 2001, terrorist hijackers steered two commercial jets into the World Trade Center's 110-story towers, demolishing them and five outlying buildings and killing nearly 3,000 people. Dubbed Ground Zero, the fenced-in 16-acre work site has become a pilgrimage site of sorts for visitors, who cluster at every viewpoint along the secured area's perimeter, though the main viewing area is Liberty Street. People from around the world leave notes, candles, photographs, baseball caps, and other mementos at impromptu memorials.

The World Trade Center (WTC) was a seven-building, 12-million-square-ft complex resembling a miniature city, with more than 430 companies from 28 countries engaged in a wide variety of commercial activities, including banking and finance, insurance, transportation, import and export, customs brokerage, trade associations, and representation of foreign governments. The daytime population of the WTC included 50,000 employees and 100,000 business and leisure visitors. The twin towers were New York's two tallest buildings, the fourth tallest in the world. The two 1,350-ft towers, designed by Minoru Yamasaki and built in 1972–73, were more engineering marvel than architectural masterpiece, but at night they were indeed beautiful strokes on the Manhattan skyline. The best place to observe the work site is Liberty Street (8 AM–9 PM). | Liberty St., between Church and Greenwich Sts.

Chinatown, Little Italy, and the Lower East Side

Visually exotic and full of inexpensive wares and gadgets, Chinatown is a vital community where roughly a quarter of the city's 400,000 Chinese lives. Mott Street below Canal Street is a main drag. Since the late 20th century, Chinatown has spilled into Little Italy to the north and the formerly Jewish Lower East Side to the east. Orchard Street on the Lower East Side has both discount clothing stores and young designers' boutiques.

Lower East Side Tenement Museum. Step back in time and into the 1863 tenement building at 97 Orchard Street, where you can view the apartments of immigrant families who arrived between 1878 and 1935. The tour through the Confino family apartment is designed for children. Reservations are suggested for the guided tour. The museum also leads a walking tour around the Lower East Side. If you wish to forego the tours, you can watch a free historical slide show as well as a video with interviews of Lower East Side residents past and present. The gallery (free) has changing exhibits. Tours are limited to 15 people. | 90 Orchard St., at Broome St. | 212/431–0233 | Tenement and walking tours, each $9; Confino apartment tour $8 | Museum Mon.–Sun. 11–5:30; tenement tour Tues.–Fri. every 30 mins 1–4, weekends every 30 mins 11–4:30; Confino apartment tour weekends hourly noon–3; walking tour Apr.–Dec., weekends 1 and 2:30.

Greenwich Village

"The Village" is one of the most vibrant parts of the city. Except for a few pockets of adult-entertainment shops on Christopher Street, the Village is as scrubbed as posher neighborhoods.

Washington Square Park. NYU students, street musicians, skateboarders, jugglers, chess players, and bench warmers generate a maelstrom of playful activity in this $9^1/_2$-acre park. Two shady playgrounds attract gaggles of youngsters, dog owners congregate at the popular dog run, and tourists and locals alike are drawn toward the large central fountain.

The triumphal Washington Memorial Arch stands at the foot of 5th Avenue. *Washington at War* on the left and *Washington at Peace* on the right were added in 1916 and 1918, respectively. | 5th Ave. between Waverly Pl. and 4th St.

Midtown

Few streets in America claim as many landmarks as midtown Manhattan's central axis, 42nd Street, from Times Square, Bryant Park, and the main branch of the New York Public Library on its western half to Grand Central Terminal and the United Nations on its eastern flank. After years of seediness, the street has made a dazzling comeback with reopened theaters, new museums, chain restaurants, and arcades.

★ **Empire State Building.** This pencil-slim silhouette is a symbol for New York City and, perhaps, the 20th century. The art deco behemoth opened in April 1931 after a mere 13 months of construction. In 1951 a TV transmittal tower was added to the top, raising the total height to 1,472 ft. Ever since the 1976 American bicentennial celebration, the top 30 stories have been spotlighted at night with seasonal colors. The 86th-floor observatory (1,050 ft high) is open to the air (expect heavy winds) and spans the building's circumference; on clear days you can see up to 80 mi. | 350 5th Ave., at E. 34th St. | 212/736–3100 | www.esbnyc.com | $9 | Weekdays 10 AM–midnight, weekends 9:30 AM–midnight; last elevator up leaves at 11:15 PM.

★ **GE Building.** The tallest tower in Rockefeller Center is more than just the backdrop to the Channel Gardens, Prometheus, and the ice-skating rink—it's also the backdrop to the Rockefeller Center Christmas tree. The 70-story (850-ft-tall) building is the headquarters of the NBC television network. Inside the lobby is a monumental mural by José María Sert, *American Progress.* The *Today* show is broadcast from ground-floor studios at the southwest corner of 49th Street and Rockefeller Plaza. Crowds gather each morning outside its windows between 7 and 9, hoping for a moment of national air time with the weatherperson. To tour the area on your own, grab a free "Walking Tour of Rockefeller Center" pamphlet at the GE Building's lobby information desk. | 30 Rockefeller Plaza, between W. 49th and W. 50th Sts. | 212/332–6868 | www.rockefellercenter.com.

The two-level, monitor-spiked NBC Experience Store, directly across West 49th Street from the *Today* studio, is the departure point for 70-minute tours of the **NBC Studios** and of Rockefeller Center itself. Ticket information for other NBC shows is available here as well. | Tour $17.50 | Children under 6 not permitted | Tours depart from NBC store at street level of GE Bldg. every 15 mins Jan.–late Nov., Mon.–Sat. 8–7, Sun. 9–4:30; late Nov.–Dec., Mon.–Sat. 7–10, Sun. 7–9.

Grand Central Terminal. Grand Central is not only the world's largest railway station (76 acres) and the nation's busiest (500,000 commuters and subway riders use it daily), it's also one of the world's greatest public spaces. The south side of East 42nd Street is the best vantage point from which to admire Grand Central's dramatic beaux arts facade. At the top are a graceful clock and a crowning sculpture, *Transportation,* which depicts Mercury flanked by Hercules and Minerva. Doors on Vanderbilt Avenue and on East 42nd Street lead to the cavernous main concourse. Overhead, a celestial map of the zodiac constellations covers the robin's egg–blue ceiling (the major stars actually glow with fiber-optic lights).

The Municipal Arts Society leads architectural tours of the terminal from the central information kiosk, which is topped by a four-faced clock. | Main entrance: E. 42nd St.

at Park Ave. | 212/935–3960 | www.grandcentralterminal.com | Tour free (donations accepted) | Tours Wed. at 12:30; meet in front of information kiosk on main concourse.

***Intrepid* Sea-Air-Space Museum.** Formerly the USS *Intrepid*, this 900-ft aircraft carrier is serving out its retirement as the centerpiece of Manhattan's only floating museum. An A-12 Blackbird spy plane, lunar landing modules, helicopters, seaplanes, and other aircraft are on deck. Docked alongside, and also part of the museum, are a strategic-missile submarine; a Vietnam-era destroyer; and several other naval veterans. For an extra thrill (and an extra $5), kids can try the Navy Flight Simulator and "land" an aircraft onboard. | Hudson River, Pier 86, 12th Ave. and W. 46th St. | 212/245–0072 | www.intrepidmuseum.org | $12; free to active U.S. military personnel | May–Sept., weekdays 10–5, weekends 10–6; Oct.–Apr., Tues.–Sun. 10–5; last admission 1 hr before closing.

★ **Times Square.** Whirling in a chaos of competing lights and advertisements, Times Square is New York's white-hot energy center. Hordes of people jostle for space on the sidewalks to walk and gawk at the two-story-high cups of coffee that actually steam; a 42-ft-tall bottle of Coca-Cola; huge billboards of underwear models; superfast digital displays of world news and stock quotes; on-location network studios; and countless other technologically sophisticated allurements. Zoning actually *requires* that buildings be decked out with ads, as they have been for nearly a century. The "square" is two triangles formed by the angle of Broadway slashing across 7th Avenue between West 42nd and 47th streets. Times Square (the name also applies to the general area, beyond the intersection of these streets) has been the city's main theater district since the turn of the 20th century: from West 44th to 51st Street, the cross streets west of Broadway are lined with some 30 major theaters.

Throngs of teens gather each afternoon in front of MTV's studios in the heart of the square, hoping to be chosen to be part of the show *Total Request Live*. *TRL* is broadcast live from the second-floor glass windows at West 44th Street and Broadway. | W. 42nd to W. 47th St. at Broadway and 7th Ave.

United Nations Headquarters. Officially an "international zone," not part of the United States, the U.N. Headquarters is a working symbol of global cooperation. An hour-long guided tour (given in 20 languages) is the main attraction; it includes the General Assembly, the Security Council Chamber, the Trustee Council Chamber, and the Economic and Social Council Chamber, though some rooms may be closed on any given day. Displays on war, nuclear energy, and refugees are also part of the tour. Free tickets to assemblies are sometimes available on a first-come, first-served basis before sessions begin; pick them up in the General Assembly lobby. The public concourse has a post office where you can mail letters with U.N. stamps. | Visitor entrance: 1st Ave. and E. 46th St. | 212/963–7713 | www.un.org | Tour $8.50 | Tours daily 9:30–4:45; hr-long tours in English leave General Assembly lobby every 30 mins | Children under 5 not admitted.

Upper East Side

Once known as Millionaires' Row, the stretch of 5th Avenue between East 79th and 104th streets has been fittingly renamed Museum Mile, for it now contains New York's most distinguished cluster of cultural institutions.

★ **Metropolitan Museum of Art.** The largest art museum in the western hemisphere (spanning four blocks, it encompasses 2 million square ft), the Met is one of the city's supreme cultural institutions. Its permanent collection of nearly 3 million works of art from all over the world includes objects from the Paleolithic era to modern times. The Met's awesome Egyptian collection includes papyrus pages from the Egyptian Book of the Dead, stone coffins engraved in hieroglyphics, and mummies. The collection's centerpiece is the Temple of Dendur, an entire Roman-period temple (circa 15 BC). The Costume Institute has changing and increasingly popular exhibits of clothing and fashion that focus on subjects ranging from undergarments to Gianni Versace.

The Met offers more than you can reasonably see in one visit. Focus on two to four sections and know that, somewhere, there's an empty exhibit that just might be more rewarding than the one you can't see due to the crowds. Walking tours and lectures are free with your admission contribution. Tours covering various sections of the museum begin about every 15 minutes on weekdays, less frequently on weekends; they depart from the tour board in the Great Hall. | 5th Ave. at 82nd St. | 212/535–7710 | www.metmuseum.org | $10 suggested donation | Tues.–Thurs. and Sun. 9:30–5:30, Fri.–Sat. 9:30–9.

Central Park

Without this beloved park's 843 acres of meandering paths, tranquil lakes, ponds, and open meadows, New Yorkers might be a lot less sane. The park, which opened in 1859, was designed by Frederick Law Olmsted and Calvert Vaux, the founders of the landscape architecture profession in the United States. Horse-drawn carriages are for hire at Grand Army Plaza or any other major intersection of Central Park South at 59th Street between 5th Avenue and Columbus Circle. Rates are $34 for the first half hour and $10 for each additional quarter hour for up to four people.

Belvedere Castle. Standing regally atop Vista Rock, Belvedere Castle was built in 1872. Since 1919 it has been a U.S. Weather Bureau station. Inside the tower, the Henry Luce Nature Observatory has nature exhibits, children's workshops, and educational programs. Free discovery kits containing binoculars, maps, and sketching materials are available. | Mid-park at 79th St. Tranverse | 212/772–0210 | Free | Apr.–Oct., Tues.–Sun. 9–5; Nov.–Mar., Tues.–Sun. 10–4.

Central Park Wildlife Center. A leisurely visit to this small menagerie, home to about a hundred species, will take only about an hour. The biggest specimens here are the polar bears. The Tisch Children's Zoo has interactive, hands-on exhibits where you can pet domesticated animals. There's also an enchanted forest area, designed to thrill the six-and-under set. Above a redbrick arcade outside the zoo is the Delacorte Clock, decorated with mechanical animals that rotate and hammer their bells when the clock chimes its tune every half hour. | Entrance at 5th Ave. and E. 64th St. | 212/439–6500 | www.wcs.org/zoos | $3.50 | Apr.–Oct., weekdays 10–5, weekends 10:30–5:30; Nov.–Mar., daily 10–4:30 | No children under 16 admitted without adult.

★ **Conservatory Water.** The sophisticated model boats that sail this Renaissance revival–style stone basin are raced each Saturday morning at 10, spring through fall. At the north end is one of the park's most beloved statues, José de Creeft's 1960 bronze sculpture of Alice in Wonderland, sitting on a giant mushroom with the Mad Hatter, March Hare, and leering Cheshire Cat in attendance; children clamber all over it. On the west side of the pond, a bronze statue of Hans Christian Andersen, the Ugly Duckling at his feet, is the site of storytelling hours on summer weekends. A concession in the brick pavilion here rents model boats. | East side of park, from E. 73rd to E. 75th St.

Friedsam Memorial Carousel. Remarkable for the size of its hand-carved steeds—all 57 are three-quarters the size of real horses—this carousel was built in 1908 and moved here from Coney Island in 1951. Today it's considered one of the finest examples of turn-of-the-20th-century folk art. | Mid-park, south of 65th St. Transverse | 212/879–0244 | $1 | Apr.–Oct., daily 10–6; Nov.—Mar., daily 10–4:30, weather permitting.

Upper West Side

★ **American Museum of Natural History.** With 42 exhibition halls and more than 32 million artifacts and specimens, this is the world's largest and most important museum of natural history. Three spectacular dinosaur halls on the fourth floor use real fossils and interactive computer stations to present interpretations of how dinosaurs and pterodactyls might have behaved. The Hall of Human Biology and Evolution's wondrously detailed dioramas trace human origins back to the 4-million-year-old "Lucy" skeleton. For a taste of what the museum was like before computers and other high-tech wizardry were introduced, visit the softly lighted Carl Akeley Hall of African Mammals, where a small herd of elephants is frozen in time and surrounded by early 20th-century dioramas.

The Hayden Planetarium is home to the Rose Center for Earth and Space, which has two major exhibits. In addition, its Sky Theater—using "all-dome video"—transports you from galaxy to galaxy. After the show, you descend a spiral walkway that tracks 13 billion years of the universe's evolution. | Central Park W at W. 79th St. | 212/769–5200 for museum tickets and programs; 212/769–5100 for museum general information | www.amnh.org | Museum $10 suggested donation; museum and planetarium show combination tickets $19. Prices may vary for special exhibitions | Sun.–Thurs. 10–5:45, Fri.–Sat. 10–8:45.

Films at the **IMAX Theater** cost $15 and include museum admission. | 212/769–5034 for show times.

Dining

Chinatown and Little Italy

Sweet 'n' Tart Cafe & Restaurant. Chinese. You'll be handed four different menus at this multilevel restaurant. One lists an extensive selection of dim sum prepared to order; another offers special dishes organized according to principles of Chinese

TREATS FOR THE KIDS

If you want to leave the chain-eatery experience back home, be aware that New York restaurants can be ill-equipped to handle families with young children. Waiters aren't used to braking for wayward tots, and little room between tables makes staying seated and low-volume conversation a courtesy to other diners. However, there are family-friendly options and plenty of fun snack stops to keep the younger set happily full.

Chinatown:

Chinatown Ice Cream Factory flavors include lychee and ginger, as well as the familiar chocolate and vanilla. | 65 Bayard St., between Mott and Elizabeth Sts. | 212/608–4170.

Greenwich Village:

Cones scoops European-style gelato. | 272 Bleecker St., between 6th and 7th Aves. | 212/414–1795.

Cowgirl Hall of Fame serves corn dogs and Frito pie (a slit-open bag of corn chips drowned with spicy chili) in a kitschy dining room. | 519 Hudson St., at W. 10th St. | 212/633–1133.

Peanut Butter & Co. has more than 10 varieties of peanut butter sandwiches, all served with carrot sticks and potato chips. | 240 Sullivan St., between Bleecker and W. 3rd Sts. | 212/677–3995.

Midtown West:

Jekyll & Hyde, a macabre multilevel fantasy world of trick doors, animated skeletons, and so-so food, will appeal to the budding Stephen Kings in your brood. | 1409 6th Ave., between W. 57th and W. 58th Sts. | 212/541–9505.

Mars 2112 takes you on a five-minute bumpy spaceship ride to Mars prior to the arrival of decent food served up by Trekkie waitstaff. | 1633 Broadway, at W. 51st St. | 212/582–2112.

medicine; a third lists standards, such as hot-and-sour soup; and the final one lists curative "teas" (more like soups or fruit shakes, really). | 20 Mott St., between Chatham Sq. and Pell St. | 212/964–0380 | $4–$16 | AE accepted at 20 Mott St. location; no credit cards at other locations.

The **original café,** with a more limited menu, is up the street, and some think it has better food. | 76 Mott St., at Canal St. | 212/334–8088.

SoHo and NoLita (North of Little Italy)

Lombardi's. Italian. Brick walls, red-and-white check tablecloths, and the aroma of thin-crust pies emerging from the coal oven set the mood for some of the best pizza in Manhattan. The mozzarella is always fresh, resulting in an almost greaseless slice, and the toppings, such as homemade meatballs, pancetta, or imported anchovies, are also top quality. | 32 Spring St., between Mott and Mulberry Sts., SoHo | 212/941–7994 | $12–$25 | No credit cards.

Rialto. American. If your family is large enough, you might just score a half-circle burgundy banquette (especially if you arrive before 7 PM). It's a good vantage point from which to watch the attractive crowd filling the shabby-chic room with pressed-tin walls. Dishes such as wild mushroom sausage or rosemary roasted chicken are interesting without being fussy. The lovely back garden is a great spot for summer dining. | 26 Elizabeth St., between E. Houston and Prince Sts. | 212/334–7900 | $9–$21 | AE, MC, V.

Soho Steak. French. This French bistro offers a creative, mostly meat menu at reasonable prices. The tables in the small dining room are so close together they might as well be communal. Before ordering, eye your neighbor's braised oxtail raviolo (a single ravioli) or filet mignon with potato Roquefort *galette,* spinach, and foie gras mousse. There are a couple of selections from the sea, as well as a quiet weekend brunch. | 90 Thompson St., between Prince and Spring Sts. | 212/226–0602 | $15–$18 | No credit cards.

Greenwich Village

Caffe Rafaella. Café. Parchment-paper lamp shades adorned with fluttering red fringe, variously hued marble-top tables, and an antiques-store assortment of chairs make this one of the homiest cafés in the city. The menu is fairly diverse. | 134 7th Ave. S, between 10th and Charles Sts. | 212/929–7247 | $7–$12 | No credit cards.

★ **Grange Hall.** American. Updated all-American cuisine, affordable prices, a friendly bar, and a WPA-style mural attract a lively crowd to this former speakeasy on one of Greenwich Village's most charming, tucked-away streets. Order one of the small plates, such as potato pancakes with chive-spiked sour cream, for starters before moving on to an entrée such as the center-cut pork chops or maple-glazed salmon. | 50 Commerce St., at Barrow St. | 212/924–5246 | Reservations essential | $12–$20 | AE, MC, V.

Le Figaro Cafe. Café. A major Beat hangout long ago, Le Figaro attracts herds of tourists and students now. On the weekend there's live jazz, but during the week (Wednesday and Thursday) you have to suffer karaoke. Middle Eastern music and belly dancers entertain in the back room on Sunday night. | 184 Bleecker St., at MacDougal St. | 212/677–1100 | $6–$17 | MC, V.

Moustache. Middle Eastern. There's always a crowd waiting outside for one of the copper-top tables here. The pitas—steam-filled pillows of dough rolled before your eyes and baked in a searingly hot oven—are the perfect vehicle for tasty salads like a lemony chick-pea and spinach. Although the service can be slow, it's always friendly. | 90 Bedford St., between Barrow and Grove Sts. | 212/229–2220 | 265 E. 10th St., between Ave. A and 1st Ave., East Village | 212/228–2022 | $8–$12 | No credit cards.

East Village and Lower East Side

Katz's Delicatessen. Delicatessens. Everything and nothing has changed at Katz's since it first opened in 1888, when the neighborhood was dominated by Jewish immigrants. The rows of Formica tables, the long self-service counter, and such signs as SEND A SALAMI TO YOUR BOY IN THE ARMY are all completely authentic. What's different are the area's demographics, but the locals still endure the fluorescent lighting and a little old-school attitude for succulent hand-carved corned beef and pastrami sandwiches, soul-warming soups, juicy hot dogs, crisp half-sour pickles. You may recognize the place from *When Harry Met Sally.* | 205 E. Houston St., at Ludlow St. | 212/254–2246 | $6–$12 | AE, MC, V.

★ **Mogador Cafe.** Moroccan. Whether it's for the Middle Eastern breakfast or belly dancing on Wednesday night, East Villagers don't mind a wait in this cozy café. The menu occasionally strays beyond its staples of couscous and hummus with dishes such as butternut squash ravioli. | 101 St. Marks Pl., between 1st Ave. and Ave. A | 212/677–2226 | $7–$15 | AE, MC, V.

Second Avenue Deli. Delicatessens. Memorabilia inside and Hollywood-style stars embedded in the sidewalk outside commemorate the luminaries of the Yiddish theaters that once reigned along this stretch of 2nd Avenue. The kosher deli's bevy of Jewish classics includes chicken in the pot, matzo-ball soup, and chopped liver. A better pastrami sandwich you can't find (don't ask for it lean). | 156 2nd Ave., at E. 10th St. | 212/677–0606 | $15–$25 | AE, DC, MC, V.

Murray Hill and the Flatiron District

City Bakery. Café. One of the major draws of this self-service bakery–restaurant is the kids' corner and the pricey salad bar—a large selection of impeccably fresh food including whole sides of baked salmon, roasted vegetables, and pasta salads. Much of the produce comes from the nearby farmers' market. | 3 W. 18th St., between 5th and 6th Aves. | 212/366–1414 | Closed Sun. No dinner | $3–$10 | AE, MC, V.

Eisenberg's Sandwich Shop. American/Casual. Since the 1930s this narrow coffee shop with its time-worn counter and cramped tables has been providing the city with some of the best tuna, chicken, and egg salad sandwiches. During the lunch rush counter workers shout orders at one another down the line. They still use the cryptic language of soda jerks and diner cooks, in which "whisky down" means rye toast and "Adam and Eve on a raft" means two eggs on toast. Stick to sandwiches; the soups come from a can. Be sure to walk up to 23rd Street for the picture-perfect view of the Flatiron Building. | 174 5th Ave., between E. 22nd and E. 23rd Sts. | 212/675–5096 | Closed Sun. | $4–$8 | AE.

Mandoo Bar. Korean. This appealing little dumpling shop is a welcome addition to Little Korea's main drag, which is filled mostly with huge eateries lit up with neon and fluorescent lighting. You can watch the ladies making dumplings in the window on your way to one of the blond-wood cafeterialike tables in the back. There are plenty of dumplings, or *mandoo,* to choose from, such as broiled shrimp and sea cucumber, Korean kimchee, beef, pork, or leek. There are also traditional noodle and rice dishes and a couple of specialties like *tangsuyook*—fried pork with sweet-and-sour sauce. | 2 W. 32nd St. | 212/279–3075 | $6–$11 | AE, MC, V.

Pongal. Indian. Vegetarian. One of the city's most authentic Indian restaurants is also vegetarian-only and kosher. Try the spicy, potato-filled samosas or chickpea-battered vegetable pakoras. One of the restaurant's specialties is *dosas*—giant, wafer-thin, crisp crepes made from fermented grains such as lentil and rice and filled with spiced potatoes. | 110 Lexington Ave., between E. 27th and E. 28th Sts. | 212/696–9458 | 81 Lexington Ave., at E. 26th St. | 212/696–5130 | $9–$11 | No credit cards.

Republic. Pan-Asian. Diners share picnic-style tables at this innovative Asian noodle emporium, which looks like a cross between a downtown art gallery and a Japanese school cafeteria. The young waitstaff dressed in black T-shirts and jeans hold remote-control ordering devices to speed the already speedy service. The spicy coconut chicken soup and the Vietnamese-style barbecued pork are particularly delicious. | 37A Union Sq. W, between E. 16th and E. 17th Sts. | 212/627–7172 | $6–$9 | AE, DC, MC, V.

Midtown West

Carnegie Deli. Delicatessens. Although not what it once was, this no-nonsense deli is still a favorite of out-of-towners. The portions are so huge you feel like a child in a surreal culinary fairy tale. Two giant matzoh balls come in a bowl of soup, the knishes hang off the edge of the plates, and some combination sandwiches are so tall they are held together with bamboo skewers, not toothpicks. Don't miss the cheesecake, to our palates the best (and, of course, biggest) in the city. You pay for that excessive amount of food, but you can take home what you don't eat. | 854 7th Ave., between 54th and 55th Sts. | 212/757–2245 | $15–$20 | No credit cards.

★ **Grand Sichuan.** Chinese. This regional Chinese restaurant serves a vast menu of specialties you won't find anywhere else. The emphasis is on fiery Sichuan (Szechwan) cooking, but Cantonese, Hunan, Shanghai, and even American Chinese food are represented (a handy treatise on Chinese food and guide comes with the menu). Spicy dan dan noodles, shredded potatoes in vinegar sauce, crab soup dumplings, and minced pork with cellophane noodles or fermented green beans are among the hauntingly delicious dishes. | 745 9th Ave., between W. 50th and W. 51st Sts. | 212/582–2288 | $7–$15 | AE, MC, V.

Island Burgers and Shakes. American/Casual. Belly-busting burgers rule at this bright and cheery café with multicolored round tables and funky chairs. If you're in the mood for even more calories, the tempting selection of milk shakes is extremely hard to pass up. The only drawback is that there are no french fries—you'll have to settle for potato chips. | 766 9th Ave., between W. 51st and W. 52nd Sts. | 212/307–7934 | $7–$10 | No credit cards.

Mangia–57th Street. Mediterranean. Office workers looking for out-of-the-ordinary take-out come here for sandwiches and salads that include fresh mozzarella, prosciutto, foccacia, grilled eggplant, and sun-dried tomatoes. In the sit-down restaurant upstairs, small pizzas and pastas are a regular feature, and special dishes might include grilled swordfish with puttanesca sauce or rib-eye steak with porcini mushrooms. It's one of the most reasonably priced lunches in midtown. | 50 W. 57th St., between 5th and 6th Aves. | 212/582–5882 | Closed weekends. No dinner | $6–$12 | AE, D, DC, MC, V.

★ **Virgil's Real BBQ.** Barbecue. Neon, wood, and Formica set the scene at this massive roadhouse in the theater district. Start with stuffed jalapeños or buttermilk onion rings with blue-cheese dip. Then go for the "pig out"—a rack of pork ribs, Texas hot links, pulled pork, rack of lamb, chicken, and more. If you prefer seafood, the New Orleans–style barbecued shrimp are giant and tasty. | 152 W. 44th St., between 6th Ave. and Broadway | 212/921–9494 | Reservations essential | $13–$22 | AE, MC, V.

Upper East Side

Comfort Diner. American/Casual. Looking for a quick, casual, and satisfying meal? Comfort Diner is glad to oblige, with a menu of typical American fare like buffalo wings, Caesar salad, grilled chicken club sandwich, macaroni and cheese, meat loaf, and burgers. The pies and cakes are baked fresh daily. | 142 E. 86th St., at Lexington Ave. | 212/426–8600 | 214 E. 45th St., between 2nd and 3rd Aves., Midtown East | 212/867–4555 | $6–$12 | D, DC, MC, V.

Le Pain Quotidien. Café. This international Belgian chain brings its homeland ingredients with it, treating New Yorkers to crusty breads and delicious jams. Best of all is the Belgian chocolate sweetening the café mochas and hot chocolate. For a more substantial meal, take a seat at the long wooden communal table and sample hearty sandwiches. | 1131 Madison Ave., between E. 84th and E. 85th Sts. | 212/327–4900 | 833 Lexington Ave., between E. 63rd and E. 64th Sts. | 212/755–5810 | 100 Grand Street, at Mercer St., SoHo | 212/625–9009 | $6–$13 | No credit cards.

Serendipity 3. American/Casual. A neighborhood favorite since 1954, this fun ice cream parlor bedecked with stained-glass lamps also dishes out excellent burgers, foot-long hot dogs, French toast, omelets, salads, and special sandwiches. However, most people come for the huge, naughty, and decadent sundaes, as well as Serendipity's most famous dessert—frozen hot chocolate (now available in a mix you can prepare at home). It's a good break after a sweep through nearby Bloomingdale's. | 225 E. 60th St., between 2nd and 3rd Aves. | 212/838–3531 | $7–$19 | AE, DC, MC, V.

Upper West Side

★ **Cafe Mozart.** Café. Images of Mozart cover the walls at this festive spot near Lincoln Center. Patrons stop in before or after a night at the opera or ballet to sample the specialties—luscious desserts including linzer torte and banana mousse cake. Cappuccino, espresso, and hot chocolate are also available, as well as a variety of soups, salads, and sandwiches. Playing up the café's musical theme, classical and jazz pianists perform regularly. | 154 W. 70th St., between Broadway and Columbus Ave. | 212/595–9797 | $9–$19 | AE, DC, MC, V.

Gabriela's. Mexican. For authentic Mexican cuisine at rock-bottom prices, these modest cantinas are the way to go. The menu is filled with such interesting choices as tacos with marinated roast pork, and tamales stuffed with mushrooms and other vegetables. Ceramic parrots hang from the ceiling in the noisy and festive dining room. Parents with small children particularly appreciate Gabriela's for its welcoming attitude. | 311 Amsterdam Ave., at W. 75th St. | 212/875–8532 | $7–$18 | AE, DC, MC, V.

Ollie's. Chinese. This no-frills Chinese chain is a blessing for locals and Lincoln Center patrons in search of a quick budget meal. The best dishes are the noodle soups and the dim sum prepared by speedy chefs whose nimble maneuverings you can watch while you wait for a table. The portions are generous. | 1991 Broadway, at W. 67th St. | 212/595–8181 | 2315 Broadway, at W. 84th St. | 212/362–3111 | 200 W. 44th St., at Broadway, Midtown West | 212/921–5988 | $5–$15 | AE, MC, V.

Lodging

Chinatown

Holiday Inn Downtown. Oversize arched windows, high ceilings, and a classic exterior remain in this former factory building, but the lobby mixes marble and Asian accents. Europeans and young budget travelers are drawn by the reasonable rates and proximity to Little Italy, TriBeCa, and SoHo. Asian business travelers come for the dim sum at Pacifica Restaurant. The rooms are clean and well maintained and the staff works hard to please. Restaurant, room service, in-room data ports, cable TV, room TVs with movies, bar, dry cleaning, laundry service, concierge, parking (fee); no-smoking floors | 138 Lafayette St., at Howard St. | 212/966–8898 or 800/465–4329 | fax 212/966–3933 | www.holidayinn-nyc.com | 215 rooms, 12 suites | $139–$219 | AE, D, DC, MC, V.

Murray Hill

Herald Square Hotel. Sculpted cherubs on the facade and vintage magazine covers adorning the common areas hint at this building's previous incarnation as *Life* magazine's 1886 headquarters. Rooms are basic and clean; all have TVs and phones with voice mail. There's no concierge and no room service, but nearby restaurants will deliver. In-room safes, cable TV, Internet, some pets allowed; no-smoking rooms | 19 W. 31st

St., between 5th Ave. and Broadway | 212/279–4017 or 800/727–1888 | fax 212/643–9208 | www.heraldsquarehotel.com | 120 rooms | $99–$120 | AE, D, MC, V.

Pickwick Arms Hotel. This no-frills but convenient East Side establishment is regularly booked solid by bargain hunters. Privations you endure to save a buck start and end with the Lilliputian size of some rooms, all of which have cheap-looking furnishings. However, some rooms look over the Manhattan skyline, and all are renovated on a regular basis. There's also a rooftop garden. Café, in-room data ports, some refrigerators, bar, parking (fee) | 230 E. 51st St., between 2nd and 3rd Aves. | 212/355–0300 or 800/742–5945 | fax 212/755–5029 | www.pickwickarms.com | 360 rooms, 175 with bath | $125–$145 | AE, DC, MC, V.

Quality Hotel East Side. The least antiseptic of Manhattan's three Apple Core hotels is on a pleasant residential block and has sunny rooms done in primary colors. A small gym and a tiny business center with a credit card–operated fax, photocopier, and computer are in the basement. Café, in-room data ports, in-room safes, cable TV with movies and video games, exercise equipment, gym, business services, parking (fee); no-smoking floors | 161 Lexington Ave., at E. 30th St. | 212/545–1800 or 800/567–7720 | fax 212/481–7270 | www.applecorehotels.com | 79 rooms | $89–$209 | AE, D, DC, MC, V.

Red Roof Inn. Two blocks from the Empire State Building, Penn Station, Madison Square Garden, and Macy's, this new edition to the Korean Restaurant Row has pleasant rooms and a mezzanine bar overlooking the smart lobby. Weekday newspapers are free, as is the Continental breakfast. In-room data ports, microwaves, refrigerators, cable TV with movies and video games, health club, bar, dry cleaning, laundry service, concierge, Internet, business services, meeting rooms, parking (fee); no-smoking rooms | 6 W. 32nd St., between 5th Ave. and Broadway | 212/643–7100 or 800/567–7720 | fax 212/643–7101 | www.applecorehotels.com | 171 rooms | $89–$209 | AE, D, DC, MC, V.

Midtown West

★ **Belvedere Hotel.** This hotel off the theater district has some fun with its art deco café and playful floor patterning, but more important are the rooms large enough for kitchenettes and two full beds. Most windows have views of the street and some skyline, rather than of an inner courtyard. Café, room service, in-room data ports, in-room safes, kitchenettes, microwaves, refrigerators, cable TV with movies and video games, in-room VCRs, shop, dry cleaning, laundry facilities, concierge, Internet, business services, parking (fee) | 319 W. 48th St., between 8th and 9th Aves. | 212/245–7000 or 888/468–3558 | fax 212/245–4455 | www.newyorkhotel.com | 398 rooms, 2 suites | $135–$250 | AE, D, MC, V.

Hotel Edison. This offbeat old hotel is a popular stop for tour groups from the United States and abroad. The simple guest rooms are clean and fresh, but the bathrooms show their age. The loan-shark murder scene in *The Godfather* was shot in what is now Sophia's restaurant, and the pink-and-blue plaster Edison Café is a theater-crowd landmark. Restaurant, coffee shop, cable TV, gym, 2 bars, dry cleaning, Internet, meeting rooms, airport shuttle, parking (fee); no-smoking floors | 228 W. 47th St., between Broadway and 8th Ave. | 212/840–5000 or 800/637–7070 | fax 212/596–6850 | 770 rooms, 30 suites | $145 | AE, D, DC, MC, V.

Portland Square Hotel. You can't beat this theater district old-timer for value, given its clean, simple rooms, which invite with flower-print bedspreads and curtains. James Cagney once lived in the building, and—as the story goes—a few of his Radio City Rockette acquaintances lived upstairs. Everything from the gilt-edged entryway to the original detailing evokes old New York. Rooms on the east wing have oversize bathrooms. In-room safes, cable TV, gym, Internet, laundry facilities | 132 W. 47th St., between 6th and 7th Aves. | 212/382–0600 or 800/388–8988 | fax 212/382–0684 | www.portlandsquarehotel.com | 142 rooms, 112 with bath | $125 | AE, MC, V.

Quality Hotel and Suites. This small pre-war hotel shares its block with a plethora of Brazilian restaurants and is near many theaters and Rockefeller Center. The rooms are very plain, but most are well maintained and clean. This block is one of midtown's most deserted at night, so be alert. Cafeteria, in-room data ports, in-room safes, cable TV with movies and video games, hair salon, bar, business services, meeting rooms, parking (fee); no-smoking rooms | 59 W. 46th St., between 5th and 6th Aves. | 212/790–2710 or 800/567–7720 | fax 212/290–2760 | www.applecorehotels.com | 193 rooms, 20 suites | $89–$229 | AE, D, DC, MC, V.

Arts and Entertainment

Time Out New York offers a comprehensive weekly listing of amusements by category. The Friday *New York Times* "Weekend/Movies and Performing Arts" section runs columns that can clue you in to what's in the air. The "Goings On About Town" section of *New Yorker* contains ruthlessly succinct reviews of theater, dance, art, music, film, and nightlife. You may also get good tips from a suitably au courant hotel concierge.

Broadway

Broadway—not the Statue of Liberty or even the Empire State Building—is the city's number one tourist attraction. This theater district is roughly bounded by West 41st and West 52nd streets, between 7th and 9th avenues, where bright lights shine on newly restored theaters, gleaming entertainment complexes, theme stores, and restaurants. *Playbill*'s Web site, www.playbill.com, is a good resource for both daily news and feature articles on Broadway and off-Broadway theater. It also links to the other theater-oriented sites, seating charts for all Broadway theaters, and access to Tele-Charge services.

TICKETS

It's always a good idea to purchase tickets in advance. Tickets for weekend Broadway-show matinees are tougher to secure than for those on Wednesday. Web sites usually have links to individual theater seating charts so you can see where your seats are before you buy a ticket. Generally, the box office is the best place to buy tickets, since in-house ticket sellers make it their business to know about their theaters and can point out (on a chart) where you'll be seated.

The Broadway Line. This service gives information about show times, theater addresses, and ticket prices. Once you've heard the information you seek, the line can connect you directly to Tele-Charge or Ticketmaster to buy tickets. | 888/276–2392 toll-free; 212/302–4111 in the tristate area.

Broadway Ticket Center. Open daily 8–8 at the Times Square Visitors Center, the Broadway Ticket Center has descriptions and videotaped excerpts from shows, theater location maps, and a box office that handles tickets for all Broadway shows (except *The Lion King*) and several off-Broadway shows. Tickets are usually full-price, with a $4.50 handling charge per ticket. | 1560 Broadway, between W. 46th and W. 47th Sts. | no phone.

TKTS. The two locations of New York's best-known discount-ticket source sell day-of-performance tickets for Broadway and off-Broadway plays at 25%–50% off the usual price (plus a $2.50 service fee). You can pay with cash or traveler's checks only. For evening performances Monday–Saturday, the Times Square booth is open from 3 to 8; for Wednesday and Saturday matinee performances, from 10 to 2; for Sunday matinee and evening performances, from 11 to 7:30. Lines here can be long.

The South Street Seaport TKTS office in lower Manhattan is open Monday through Saturday from 11 to 6 and Sunday from 11 to 3:30. For matinees (on Wednesday,

Saturday, and Sunday), you have to purchase tickets the day before the performance (which means matinee tickets are available to downtown customers before customers in midtown). | W. 47th St. and Broadway, Midtown West | 186 Front St., Lower Manhattan | 212/221–0013, | tdf.org.

Performing Arts Centers

City Center. This theater has a neo-Moorish look (it was built in 1923 by the Ancient and Accepted Order of the Mystic Shrine) and presents major dance troupes such as Alvin Ailey and Paul Taylor, as well as concert versions of classic American musicals. | 131 W. 55th St., between 6th and 7th Aves., Midtown West | 212/581–1212 | www.citycenter.org.

Lincoln Center. This unified complex of pale travertine is the largest performing arts center in the world—so large it can seat nearly 18,000 spectators at one time in its various halls. The complex's three principal venues are grouped around the central Fountain Plaza. | W. 62nd to W. 66th St., Broadway to Amsterdam Ave., Upper West Side | 212/546–2656 | www.lincolncenter.org.

The **New York State Theater** is home to the New York City Ballet and the New York City Opera. | 212/870–5570.

Metropolitan Opera, the titan of American opera companies, commands a massive stage at the **Metropolitan Opera House** | 212/362–6000.

Avery Fisher Hall is host to the New York Philharmonic Orchestra. | 212/875–5030.

Intimate **Alice Tully Hall** is home of the Chamber Music Society of Lincoln Center. Jazz at Lincoln Center, directed by Wynton Marsalis, also has a wide range of programming and special events here. | 212/875–5050.

★ **Radio City Music Hall.** One of the jewels in the crown of Rockefeller Center is also America's largest indoor theater. Opened in 1932, it astonished the hall's Depression-era patrons with its 60-ft-high foyer, ceiling representing a sunset, and 2-ton chandeliers. Its year-round schedule now includes major performers, awards presentations, and special events, along with its own Christmas and Easter extravaganzas featuring the fabled Rockettes. Very popular one-hour tours of the theater are offered daily. | 1260 6th Ave., at W. 50th St., Midtown West | 212/247–4777 | www.radiocity.com.

Shopping

T-shirts are probably the least expensive souvenir, as street vendors around the theater district often hawk three for $10. Knickknack stores in the theater district offer the same sort of items you'll find at the airport, only cheaper.

SoHo

Once an abandoned warehouse district, then lined with artists' studios and galleries, the streets of SoHo are now packed with high-rent boutiques and national chains. Big fashion guns such as Louis Vuitton, Chanel, and Prada have established themselves; a flock of makeup stores also swept in. Much to the distress of longtime residents, the mall element (Victoria's Secret, Old Navy, J. Crew, French Connection, and many more) has a firm foothold; however, there are still many unique shops, especially for housewares and clothing. The streets east of Lafayette make up NoLita, where pricey one-of-a-kind stores and inexpensive small eateries remain the rule.

5th Avenue

Fifth Avenue from Rockefeller Center to Central Park South still wavers between the money-is-no-object crowd and an influx of more accessible stores. The flag-bedecked

Saks Fifth Avenue faces Rockefeller Center, which harbors branches of Banana Republic and J. Crew as well as smaller specialty shops. The perennial favorites will eat up a lot of shoe leather: Cartier jewelers and Salvatore Ferragamo, at 52nd Street; Takashimaya (a pristine branch of Japan's largest department store), at 54th Street; Tiffany and Bulgari jewelers, at 57th Street; and Bergdorf Goodman, at 58th Street. Allow plenty of time for the funhouse of toys, F.A.O. Schwarz, also at 58th Street. Exclusive design houses such as Prada and Gucci are a stone's throw from the über-chain Gap and a souped-up branch of good old Brooks Brothers. Swedish retailer H&M adds affordable designer knockoffs to the mix.

57th Street

The angular, white-glass Louis Vuitton Moët Hennesy headquarters sits on the north side of East 57th Street between 5th and Madison avenues; it houses branches of Louis Vuitton, Christian Dior, and Bliss, the SoHo-born superspa. These glamazons are surrounded by big-name art galleries and other swank flagships such as Burberry and Chanel, but the block is no longer limited to top-echelon shopping. More affordable stores, including Levi's and NikeTown, sit cheek by jowl with the couture houses.

Department Stores

Bloomingdale's. The main floor is a stupefying maze of cosmetic counters, mirrors, and black walls. Get past this, and you'll find some good buys on dependable designers, bedding, and housewares. | 1000 3rd Ave., main entrance at E. 59th St. and Lexington Ave., Midtown East | 212/355–5900.

Macy's. Macy's headquarters store claims to be the largest retail store in America; expect to lose your bearings at least once. Fashion-wise, there's a concentration on the mainstream rather than the luxe. | Herald Sq., Broadway at W. 34th St., Midtown West | 212/695–4400.

Pearl River Mart. The three floors of this Asian department store are packed with everything from tatami slippers and karate pants to bamboo steamers, parasols, and porcelain tea sets—and it's all pretty cheap. In spring 2003 another store will open on Broadway between Broome and Grand streets. | 277 Canal St., at Broadway, Chinatown | 212/431–4770 | 200 Grand St., between Mott and Mulberry Sts., Chinatown | 212/966–1010.

Saks Fifth Avenue. The choice of American and European designers at this apparel-only department store is impressive. Nearly every New Yorker visits at least once a year—to line up to see the windows' mechanical Christmas displays. | 611 5th Ave., between E. 49th and 50th Sts., Midtown East | 212/753–4000.

Essential Information

When to Go

New York is a city to experience on foot, and though a year-round destination, it's probably most difficult to fully appreciate in the coldest months of January and February. The summer calendar is jammed with free open-air performances. The hot, humid days of August (when the temperature can reach 100°F) are particularly unpleasant; even so, you may need a second layer for the ubiquitous air-conditioning. September heralds the arrival of dry "champagnelike" weather, and autumn is mild and comfortable.

FESTIVALS AND SEASONAL EVENTS

WINTER

Dec.: **First Night.** You don't have to spend hours outdoors with the masses in Times Square waiting for the ball to drop. On New Year's Eve the city also sponsors free events in alcohol-free venues throughout the boroughs. | 212/788–2000.

SPRING

Mar./Apr.: **Ringling Bros. and Barnum & Bailey Circus.** The Greatest Show on Earth sets down in Madison Square Garden every year. | 212/465–6741.

Apr.: **The Cherry Blossom Festival.** Fluffy clouds of pink at Brooklyn Botanic Garden are the backdrop to Taiko drumming concerts, traditional Japanese dance, lessons in calligraphy, and bento box lunches. | 718/623–7200.

SUMMER

June–Aug.: **Summer Stage.** Free weekday evening and weekend afternoon performances and readings take place near the East 72nd entrance to Central Park. Arrive early for a seat or spot on the ground. | 212/360–2777.

AUTUMN

Nov.: **Macy's Thanksgiving Day Parade.** Huge balloons float down Central Park West from West 77th Street to Broadway and Herald Square. The day-before viewing of the balloons' inflation has become an event in its own right. | 212/494–4495.

Bargains

CityPass. This packet of tickets to the Empire State Building, Guggenheim Museum, the American Museum of Natural History, the Museum of Modern Art, the Whitney Museum of American Art, Circle Line Cruises, and the Intrepid Sea-Air-Space Museum will save you half the cost of each individual ticket. The packet is good for nine days from first use. You can buy a CityPass at any of the participants' ticket offices. | 888/330–5008 | www.citypass.com.

High 5 for the Arts. Teens can buy $5 tickets to all sorts of performances, which are sold on-line, and also at Ticketmaster outlets in the city, including at music stores such as HMV and Tower Records. Tickets are either for a single teen (Fridays and weekends) or for a teen and his or her guest of any age (Monday–Thursday). These $5 tickets cannot be bought over the phone or at the venue box offices. With the $5 museum pass, a teen can bring a guest of any age to participating museums any day of the week; these tickets are available only at the Ticketmaster outlets. | 212/750–0555 ext. 200; 212/445–8587 for hot line and mailing list | www.high5tix.org.

Tours

BOAT TOURS

Circle Line Cruise. Narrated daily tours show off the city's skyline and harbor. A 35-mi circumnavigation of the island takes three hours and costs $24; Semi-Circle cruises, limited tours, cost $20. | 212/563–3200 | www.circleline.com.

NY Waterway. Harbor cruises run year-round and cost $19; the Twilight Cruise operates from May through late December. | 800/533–3779 | www.nywaterway.com.

Seaport Liberty Cruises. Several cruises leave from South Street Seaport's Pier 16. Daily, hour-long sightseeing tours of New York Harbor and lower Manhattan cost $13. | 212/630–8888 or 212/563–3200 | www.circleline.com.

BUS TOURS

Gray Line New York. You can "hop-on, hop-off" these double-decker bus tours, which include a Harlem gospel tour and evening drives through the city. Packages include entrance fees to attractions and one-day MetroCards. | 800/669–0051 | www.graylinenewyork.com.

New York Double-Decker Bus Tours. Board an authentic London double-deck bus year-round, 9 AM–6 PM in summer, 9 AM–3 PM in winter. Tickets, which are valid for boarding and reboarding all day for five days, cost $26 for a downtown loop, $26 for an uptown loop, and $40 for a combination ticket. | 718/361–5788 | www.nydecker.com.

WALKING TOURS

Big Onion Walking Tours. The wise-cracking Ph.D. candidates of Big Onion Walking Tours lead themed tours in addition to neighborhood walks. | 212/439–1090 | www.bigonion.com.

Downtown Alliance. The Downtown Alliance offers free, history-rich tours of the Wall Street area on Thursday and Saturday at noon. | 212/606–4064 | www.downtownny.com.

Visitor Information

Big Apple Greeters | 1 Center St., Suite 2035, New York 10007 | 212/380–8159 | www.bigapplegreeter.org. **Downtown Alliance** | 120 Broadway, Suite 3340, 10271 | 212/566–6700 | www.downtownny.com. **NYC & Company–Convention & Visitors Bureau** | 810 7th Ave., 3rd floor, between W. 52nd and W. 53rd Sts., 10019 | 212/484–1200 | www.nycvisit.com. **Times Square Visitors Center** | 1560 Broadway, between 46th and 47th Sts., | 212/768–1560 | www.timessquarebid.org.

Arriving and Departing

BY AIR

Airports

LaGuardia Airport (LGA). LaGuardia, in the borough of Queens, is the closest airport to Manhattan. | 718/533–3400 | www.laguardiaairport.com.

JFK International Airport (JFK). JFK is also in Queens. | 718/244–4444 | www.jfkairport.com.

Newark International Airport (EWR). Newark is in nearby Newark, New Jersey. | 973/961–6000 or 888/397–4636 | www.newarkairport.com.

Airport Transportation

Note that if you arrive after midnight at any airport, you will likely wait a very long time for a taxi. Call a car service, as there is no bus or van shuttle service at that time.

Car Service: The driver will often meet you on the concourse or in the baggage-claim area and help you with your luggage. Rates are often comparable to taxi fares, but some car services will charge for waiting time at the airport. To eliminate these expenses, other car services require that you telephone their dispatcher again when you land. New York City Taxi and Limousine Commission rules require that all car services be licensed and pick up riders only by prior arrangement, if possible *at least* a half day before your flight's departure.

Carmel Car Service | 212/666–6666 or 800/922–7635. **Manhattan International Limo** | 718/729–4200 or 800/221–7500. **Skyline** | 212/741–3711 or 800/567–5957. **Tel Aviv Car and Limousine Service** | 212/777–7777 or 800/222–9888.

Public Transit from LaGuardia: Triboro Coach Corp. The Q-33 line travels from LaGuardia to the Jackson Heights subway stop in Queens, where you can transfer to the E or F train; it also stops at the Roosevelt Avenue–Jackson Heights station, where you can pick up the 7 subway line to midtown. The cost is $1.50. | 718/335–1000 | www.triborocoach.com.

Public Transit from JFK: AirTrain JFK. The Port Authority's AirTrain links JFK to the Howard Beach subway station (the A line). In 2003, AirTrain JFK will also serve Jamaica Station (where the Long Island Railroad station connects to Manhattan's Penn Station). AirTrain JFK will run 24 hours. From mid-town Manhattan, the longest trip to JFK will be via the A train (roughly under an hour); the quickest trip will be with the Long Island Railroad (under 45 minutes). | 718/244–4444 | www.jfkairtrain.com.

Public Transit from Newark: AirTrain Newark. From the airport terminals, AirTrain Newark connects to New Jersey Transit at the Newark International Airport Station. Travel time to Penn Station in Manhattan is approximately 20 minutes and the fare is $11.55. AirTrain runs from 5 AM to 2 AM daily. | 888/397–4636 or 800/626–7433 | www.airtrainnewark.com.

New Jersey Transit Airlink. Buses leave Newark Airport every 20 to 30 minutes from 6:15 AM to 1:45 AM, for Penn Station in Newark, New Jersey. The ride takes about 20 minutes, and the fare is $4 (be sure to have exact change). From there, you can catch PATH trains, which run to Manhattan 24 hours a day. The fare for PATH trains is $1.50. | 973/762–5100 | www.njtransit.state.nj.us.

Shuttle: Shuttle services generally pick up passengers from a designated spot along the curb at the airport.

Gray Line Air Shuttle. Bus service travels to major Manhattan hotels from each of the three airports. | 212/315–3006 or 800/451–0455 | www.graylinenewyork.com.

New York Airport Service. Buses shuttle between JFK and LaGuardia airports and Grand Central Terminal, Port Authority Bus Terminal, Penn Station, and hotels between 33rd and 57th streets in Manhattan. Costs for bus shuttles range between $10 and $15. | 718/875–8200 | www.nyairportservice.com.

Olympia Trails. Buses leave Newark for Grand Central Terminal and Penn Station in Manhattan about every 20 minutes until midnight. The trip takes roughly 45 minutes, and the fare is $11. | 212/964–6233 or 718/622–7700 | www.olympiabus.com.

SuperShuttle. Vans travel to and from all airports. These blue vans will stop at any private residence or hotel. For travel to the airport, SuperShuttle requests 24-hour advance notice. Fares range from $13 to $22. Make arrangements for any company at the airport's ground transportation counter or via a courtesy phone. | 212/258–3826 | www.supershuttle.com.

Taxi: From JFK to destinations in Manhattan, taxis charge a flat fee of $35 plus tolls (which may be as much as $4), plus tip. Trips to other locations in New York City run on the meter. Taxis to Manhattan from LaGuardia cost $15–$30 plus tip and tolls and take 30–40 minutes.

Taxis to Manhattan from Newark cost $35–$55 plus tolls ($8) and take 20 to 45 minutes. From Manhattan, there's an extra $10 surcharge.

BY BUS

Port Authority Terminal. Most long-haul and commuter bus lines feed into the Port Authority. | 625 8th Ave., between W. 40th and W. 42nd Sts. | 212/564–8484 | www.panynj.gov.

BY TRAIN

Grand Central Terminal. Commuters from New York State and Connecticut take Metro-North Commuter Railroad to Grand Central. | E. 42nd St. between Vanderbilt and Lexington Aves. | 212/340–2210 | www.grandcentralterminal.com.

Metro-North Commuter Railroad | 212/532–4900 | www.mta.nyc.ny.us/mnr.

Penn Station. Amtrak trains arrive at Penn Station. The Long Island Railroad and New Jersey Transit commuter trains also terminate here. | from W. 31st to W. 33rd St., between 7th and 8th Aves. | no phone.

Amtrak | 800/872–7245 | www.amtrak.com.

Long Island Railroad | 718/217–5477 | www.mta.nyc.ny.us/lirr.

New Jersey Transit | 973/762–5100 | www.njtransit.com.

Getting Around

BY BOAT

New York Water Taxi. In addition to serving commuters, the Water Taxi shuttles tourists to the city's many waterfront attractions. The hop-on, hop-off ticket (good for 24 hours) for adults is $15. | 212/742–1969 | www.newyorkwatertaxi.com.

NY Waterway. Service between the World Financial Center on the Hudson River to Pier 11 on Wall Street is free. | 201/902–8700 or 800/533–3779 | www.nywaterway.com.

BY PUBLIC TRANSIT

Metropolitan Transit Authority (MTA)

The subway and bus networks are thorough and a single fare is only $1.50, but be prepared to carry strollers up and down steps. For frequent bus and subway travel, buy a MetroCard, which provides free transfers between bus and underground travel and with each swipe allows you two hours to complete your trip. MetroCards are sold at all subway stations and at some stores. Buy a seven-day unlimited-ride MetroCard ($17) if you will make more than 12 trips. The one-day unlimited-ride Fun Pass ($4) is good from the day of purchase through 3 AM the following day and is only sold by neighborhood MetroCard merchants and MetroCard vending machines at stations (not through the station booth attendant). The pay-per-ride MetroCard is available in any denomination between $3 and $80. Pay-per-ride cards worth $15 or more receive a 10% free-ride credit (for example, you get 11 rides for the price of 10). The advantage of pay-per-ride over unlimited ride is that the card can be shared between riders; unlimited-ride MetroCards can only be used once at the same station or bus route in an 18-minute period.

Most subway station entrances have MetroCard vending machines (usually near the token booth) that accept credit cards, ATM/debit cards, and cash. Coin-size tokens are used for transport fare as well and are sold at subway booths. MTA Travel Information Center: | 718/330–1234 | www.mta.nyc.ny.us; MTA Status information hot line | 718/243–7777, updated hourly.

Bus: Most city buses go up or down the north–south avenues, or east and west on the major two-way crosstown streets. Service is infrequent late at night, and traffic jams can make rides maddeningly slow. Certain bus routes offer "Limited-Stop Service" during weekday rush hours, which saves travel time by stopping only at major cross streets and transfer points. A sign posted at the front of the bus indicates it has limited service.

To find a bus stop, look for a light-blue sign (green for a limited bus) on a green pole; bus numbers and routes are listed, with the stop's name underneath. Pay your fare when you board, with exact change in coins (no pennies, and no change is given), with a token, or with a MetroCard. When paying by token or cash, you can ask the driver for a free transfer coupon, good for one change to an intersecting route. Legal transfer points are listed on the back of the slip. Transfers have time limits of at least two hours. You cannot use the transfer to enter the subway system. Route maps and schedules are posted at many bus stops.

Subway: The 714-mi subway system operates 24 hours a day. It's cheaper than a cab, and during the workweek it is often faster than either taxis or buses. The trains are clean and well lighted. Most entrances are at street corners and are marked by lampposts. Subway lines are designated by numbers and letters. Some lines run "express" and skip stops, and others are "locals" and make all stops. Each station entrance has a sign indicating the lines that run through the station. Some entrances are also marked "Uptown Only" or "Downtown Only." One of the most frequent mistakes visitors make is taking the train in the wrong direction. Maps of the full subway system are posted in every train car and usually on the subway platform. You can pick up free maps at token booths. Pay your subway fare at the turnstile, using a subway token or a MetroCard.

You can transfer between subway lines an unlimited number of times where lines intersect. If you use a MetroCard to pay your fare, you can also transfer to intersecting MTA bus routes for free. Transfers generally have time limits of two hours.

BY TAXI AND CAR SERVICE

Yellow taxis run on a meter, while car services charge a flat fee. By law, car services are not allowed to pick up passengers unless you call for one first. Always determine the fee beforehand when using a car-service sedan.

Taxis are usually easy to hail on the street or from a taxi rank in front of major hotels. You can see if a taxi is available by checking its rooftop light; if the center panel is lit and the side panels are dark, the driver is ready to take passengers. Taxi fares cost $2 for the first 1/5 mi, 30¢ for each 1/5 mi thereafter, and 20¢ for each minute not in motion. A 50¢ surcharge is added to rides begun between 8 PM and 6 AM.

Direct your cab driver by the cross streets of your destination (for instance, "5th Avenue and 42nd Street"), rather than the numerical address, which means little to many drivers. Save your taxi receipt should you later realize you forgot something in the cab. The receipt may make tracking down your belonging through the Taxi and Limousine Commission easier.

Carmel | 212/666–6666. **Highbridge Car Service** | 212/927–4600. **New York City Taxi and Limousine Commission** | 212/NYC–TAXI. **Tel-Aviv** | 212/777–7777.

New York and Ontario, Canada

Revised and Updated by Jack Kohane

NIAGARA FALLS

Nearly everyone who sees Niagara Falls is struck by the wonder of it. Though not among the world's highest waterfalls, Niagara Falls is, for sheer volume of water, unsurpassed at more than 750,000 gallons per second in the summer. The falls are responsible for the invention of alternating electric current, and they run one of the globe's largest hydroelectric developments. And it really is all that water, fuelled by four of the Great Lakes—Superior, Michigan, Huron, and Erie—flowing into the fifth, Ontario, that ranks Niagara as one of the planet's natural wonders.

Niagara Falls has inspired artists for centuries. The English painter William H. Bartlett, who visited here in the mid-1830s, noted that "you may dream of Niagara, but words will never describe it to you." And cynics have taken their own stab at Niagara Falls, calling it everything from "water on the rocks" to "the second major disappointment of American married life" (Oscar Wilde). The thundering cascades were dramatically immortalized by Hollywood in 1953, when Marilyn Monroe starred as a steamy siren, luring her jealous husband down to the crashing cascades in the film *Niagara*.

The malls, amusement parks, hotels, tacky souvenir shops, and flashy wax museums that surround the falls today attest to the region's maturation into a world-class tourist attraction. But despite the hoards of visitors jostling unceremoniously for the best photographic vantage point, the astounding beauty of the falls remains undiminished, and unending.

Exploring

On the boundary between the United States and Canada, part of the world's longest unfortified borders, Niagara Falls is the geological handiwork of three major cataracts: the American and Bridal Veil Falls in New York State, and the Horseshoe Falls in Ontario, Canada.

You'll probably want to see the U.S. side first. Park in the lot on Goat Island near the American Falls, and walk along the path beside the Niagara River. This is the point where the flow becomes increasingly turbulent as it approaches the big drop-off of nearly 200 ft. Be sure to go down to the lower level of Goat Island so you can nudge up beside Bridal Veil Falls.

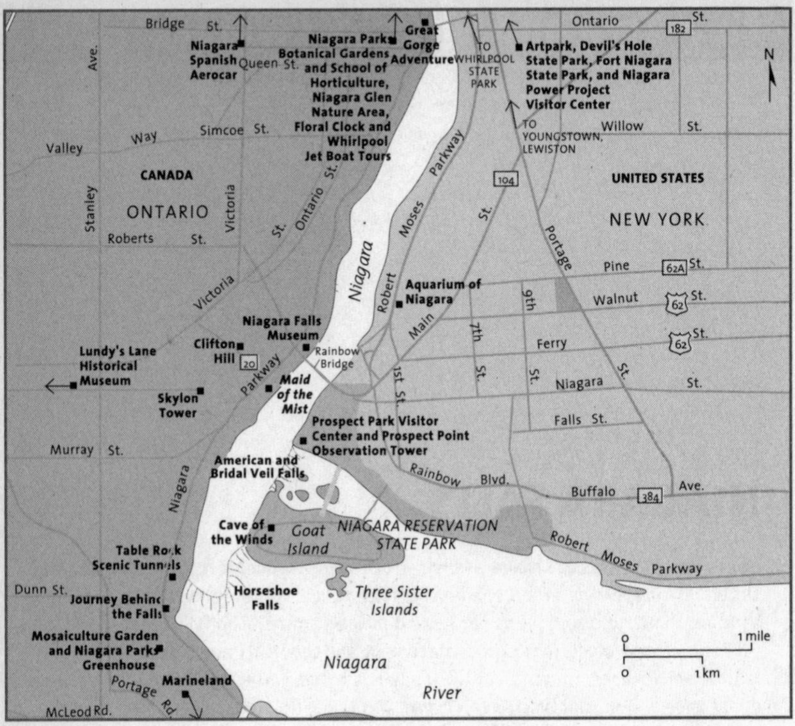

After experiencing the falls from the U.S. cliffside, walk or drive across Rainbow Bridge to the Canadian side, where you can get a panoramic view of the American Falls and a close-up of the Horseshoe Falls. Park your car in any of several lots on the Canadian side, and hop onto one of the People Mover buses, which run continuously to all the sights along the river. If you're in a daring mood, the *Maid of the Mist* boat takes you to the foot of the falls, close enough to get soaked in the spray.

Although the grandeur of the falls will likely be the focus of your trip, the surrounding area is well worth seeing. Stateside is the historic community of Lewiston. Farther north, where the river opens into Lake Ontario, are the scenic villages of Youngstown, one of the first communities to be settled after Niagara Falls.

The land north of the falls in Canada is composed primarily of orchards and vineyards, and fertile sod to some of the country's top wines. Be sure to check out the **wine tours** to sample the local libations.

Château des Charmes | 905/262–4219 | www.chateaudescharmes.com.

Hillebrand Estate Winery | 905/468–4929 or 888/609–4442 | www.hillebrand.com.

Inniskillin Wines | 905/468–3554 or 888/466–4754 | www.inniskillin.com.

Niagara Falls

Native North Americans called it "Onguiaahram," or "Thundering Waters." For hundreds of years, visitors to Niagara Falls have marveled at the sheer immensity of this surging wall of water. Its awe-inspiring views today are enhanced by early misty mornings, sun-streaked rainbows that arch over the Niagara Gorge during the daytime, and its grand after-dark illumination by spotlights that penetrate the night sky.

From the early 18th century, dozens of challengers have plummeted over the falls in boats and barrels. Nobody survived until 1901, when schoolteacher Annie Taylor emerged from her barrel and asked, "Did I go over the falls yet?" The stunts were finally outlawed in 1912, although every year another brave (or foolhardy) soul attempts the plunge and hopes to live to tell the tale.

★ ***Maid of the Mist* Boat Tour.** View the three falls from up close and personal during a spectacular 1½-hour ride on this world-famous boat tour. Waterproof clothing is provided. To reach the boat launch in New York, take the elevator in the Prospect Point Observation Tower, which descends to the base of the falls. On the Ontario side, board at the foot of Clifton Hill. | 151 Buffalo Ave., Prospect Park | 716/284–8897 or 905/358–5781 | www.maidofthemist.com | $9.50 or C$12.25 | Apr.–late May, daily 9:45–5:45; late May–Aug., daily 9–7; Sept.–late Oct., weekdays 9:45–4:45.

New York

Aquarium of Niagara. Dive into Niagara's other water wonder. This is a close encounter with more than 1,500 aquatic animals, including sharks, piranha, sea lions, and moray eels. The aquarium has sea-lion demonstrations daily and an outdoor harbor–seal exhibit. | 701 Whirlpool St. | 716/285–3575 or 800/500–4609 | fax 716/285–8513 | www.aquariumofniagara.org | $6.75 | Late May–early Sept., daily 9–7; early Sept.–late May, daily 9–5.

★ **Artpark.** Niagara Falls' premier performing arts center offers reasonably priced world-class musical theater, dance, classical, pop, and jazz concerts. The center is in a 202-acre state park in Lewiston, 7 mi north of the falls. | 450 S. 4th St., Lewiston | 716/754–4375 or 800/659–7275 | www.artpark.net | Call for schedule.

Devil's Hole State Park. You can hike to the Niagara Gorge in this park overlooking the whirlpool and the New York State Power Plant 4 mi north of the falls. You can also fish. Rest rooms are closed in winter. Follow signs from Robert Moses Parkway. | Devil's Hole State Park | 716/284–5778 | Free | Daily dawn–dusk.

Fort Niagara State Park. You'll find picnic tables, shelters, swimming, nature programs, hiking, fishing, tennis, a boat-launch site, and a playground in this park, which surrounds Fort Niagara. In winter there is cross-country skiing, snowmobiling, and sledding slopes. In Youngstown, 10 mi north of Niagara Falls. | Rte. 18F, Youngstown | 716/745–7273 | $5 per vehicle June–early Sept. free rest of yr | Daily.

Just minutes from the falls, **Old Fort Niagara,** a stone fort dating from 1726, hosts colorful displays of cannon and musket firings, historical reenactments, 18th-century military demonstrations, and archaeological programs. There's a museum shop and snack bar. Follow signs from Robert Moses Parkway. | Fort Niagara State Park, Youngstown | 716/745–7611 | www.oldfortniagara.org | $7 | Nov.–Mar., daily 9–4:30; Apr. and Oct., daily 9–5:30; June, weekdays 9–6:30, weekends 9–7:30; July–Aug., daily 9–7:30; May and Sept., weekdays 9–5:30, weekends 9–6:30.

Niagara Power Project Visitor Center. Niagara Falls generates power at one of the largest hydroelectric plants in the world. The self-touring and newly renovated visitor center has hands-on exhibits, including a working model of a hydropower turbine, computer games, and an explanation of how hydroelectric power is generated. Free parking. | 5777 Lewiston Rd. (Rte. 104) | 716/286–6661 or 866–697–2386 | www.nypa.gov | Free | Daily 9–5.

Niagara Reservation State Park. This state park around Niagara Falls includes Prospect Point, Goat Island, Luna Island at Bridal Veil Falls, and Three Sisters Island. Witness the nightly illumination of the falls from here, and check out the visitor center and the observation tower and elevator, which takes you to the base of the falls. Follow signs from Robert Moses Parkway. | Niagara Reservation State Park | 716/278–1770 | $5 per vehicle | Daily.

The **Cave of the Winds Trip** is a guided excursion along special walkways at the base of Bridal Veil Falls. Waterproof clothing is provided. | Cave of the Winds Facility Building, Goat Island | 716/278–1730 | $6 | May–Oct., daily 8–8.

Goat Island provides access to Bridal Veil Falls, Three Sisters Islands, and Top of the Falls restaurant. It's a wonderful spot for a quiet walk and a close-up view of the rapids. | 716/278–1762 | Daily.

The **Prospect Park Visitor Center** provides tourist information, exhibits, a garden, and a snack bar. The giant-screen "thrill film" *History of Niagara* gets your attention with a virtual-reality helicopter simulator ride. | Prospect Park, | 716/278–1762 | Free | Sun.–Thurs. 8 AM–8:15 PM, Fri.–Sat. 8 AM–10:15 PM.

The 282-ft-high ★**Prospect Point Observation Tower** offers dramatic views of all three falls. A glass-walled elevator takes you above the falls and descends to the base for a boat tour. At the Niagara Reservation on the U.S. side of the falls; follow signs from Robert Moses Parkway. | Prospect Park | 716/278–1762 or 716/278–1750 | 50¢ | Daily.

Whirlpool State Park. Set 2 mi north of the falls, this park has nature trails, fishing, a stairway down to the gorge, and hiking. There are great views of the giant whirlpool and lower rapids. Follow signs from Robert Moses Parkway. | Whirlpool State Park | 716/278–1762 | Free | Daily dawn–dusk.

Ontario

★ **Casino Niagara.** Set in an architectural design reminiscent of the 1920s, this casino includes 2,700 slot machines, video poker machines, and 135 gambling tables. Within the casino are several restaurants, an all-you-can-eat buffet, and lounges. Valet parking or Park N' Ride shuttle service is available. | 5705 Falls Ave. | 888/946–3255 or 905/374–3598 | www.discoverniagara.com | Daily.

Clifton Hill. The most glitzy commercial district of Niagara Falls is opposite the American Falls. Referred to as the "Street of Fun," there's plenty of family entertainment on this two-block section.

At the **Great Canadian Midway,** more than 250 interactive games jam the 70,000-square-ft entertainment facility for adults and kids. There are 30 televisions, bowling, billiards, and a simulated roller-coaster ride. Try the tram ride through a haunted house called Ghost Blasters, where scary spirits will try to dodge your laser-guided pistols. | 905/358–3676 | www.cliftonhill.com.

Guinness Museum of World Records | 905/356–2299, 905/356–2238, 905/374–6601, or 905/358–3061 | www.guinnessniagarafalls.com.

Movieland Wax Museum | 905/358–3061.

Ripley's Believe It or Not Museum and the new Ripley's Moving Theatre | 905/356–2238, | www.ripleysniagara.com.

Floral Clock. The 40-ft-diameter "living" face is planted in a different design twice every season. One of the world's largest floral clocks, it is a short distance (downriver) from the Botanical Gardens and School of Horticulture on the Niagara Parkway.

Great Gorge Adventure. Take an elevator to the bottom of the Niagara Gorge, where you can walk on a boardwalk beside the torrent of the Niagara River. The gorge is rimmed by sheer cliffs as it enters the giant whirlpool. Nature interpreters explain the geology and the formation of the raging rapids. | Niagara Pkwy., 3 km (2 mi) north of falls | 905/371–0254 or 877/642–7275 | www.niagaraparks.com | C$5.75 | Jan.–May, 9–5; June–Sept., 9–9; Oct.–Dec., 9–5.

★ **Journey Behind the Falls.** Your admission ticket includes use of rubber boots and a hooded rain slicker. An elevator takes you to an observation deck that provides a fish's-eye view of the Canadian Horseshoe Falls and the Niagara River. From there a walk through three tunnels cut into the rock takes you behind the wall of crashing water. | Tours begin at

Table Rock House, Queen Victoria Park | 905/371–0254 or 877/642–7275 | C$7 | Mid-June–early Sept., daily 9 AM–11 PM; early Sept.–mid-June, daily 9–5.

Lundy's Lane Historical Museum. This two-story limestone building dating from 1874 is on the site of one of the fiercest battles in the War of 1812. There are displays of the lives of settlers of that era and native artifacts as well as military attire, including tunics and cross-belt plates. | 5810 Ferry St. | 905/358–5082 | www.lundyslanemuseum.com | C$1.60 | May–Nov., daily 9–4; Dec.–Apr., weekdays noon–4.

★ **Marineland.** This theme park with a marine show, wildlife displays, and rides is 1½ km (1 mi) south of the falls. The daily marine show includes performing killer whales, dolphins, harbor seals, and sea lions. A new 20-acre aquarium complex features three separate aquariums housing sharks, an ocean reef, and freshwater fish from around the world. Children can pet and feed members of a herd of 500 deer. Marineland is signposted from Niagara Parkway or reached from the Queen Elizabeth Way by exiting at McLeod Road (Exit 27). | 8375 Stanley Ave. | 905/356–9565 | www.marinelandcanada.com | Admission varies with season. | May–June and Sept., daily 10–5; Oct., daily 10–4:30; July–Aug., daily 9–6.

Mosaiculture Garden and Niagara Parks Greenhouse. Thousands of living plants are sculpted into life-size creatures, including moose, bears, and geese in flight. | Niagara Pkwy. south of Horseshoe Falls | 905/371–0254 or 800/642–7275 | www.niagaraparks.com | C$4.50 | Seasonally.

Niagara Falls IMAX Theatre/The Daredevil Adventure Gallery. You can see the wonder of the falls up close and travel back in time for a glimpse of its 12,000-year-old history with *Niagara: Miracles, Myths and Magic*. The movie screen, Canada's largest, is more than six stories high. The Daredevil Adventure Gallery chronicles the expeditions of those who have tackled the falls. | 6170 Fallsview Blvd. | 905/374–4629 | www.imaxniagara.com | C$12 | Daily 11–8; movies every hr on the hr.

Niagara Parks Botanical Gardens and School of Horticulture. The school has been graduating professional gardeners since 1936. The art of horticulture is celebrated by its students with 100 acres of immaculately maintained gardens. | 2565 Niagara Pkwy. | 905/371–0254 or 877/642–7275 | www.niagaraparks.com | Botanical Gardens free | Daily dawn–dusk.

Within the Botanical Gardens is the **Niagara Parks Butterfly Conservatory,** one of North America's largest collections of free-flying butterflies—at least 2,000 are protected in a lush rain-forest setting by a glass-enclosed conservatory. The climate-controlled conservatory operates year-round and contains 50 species from around the world. | 905/371–0254 | $8.50.

Niagara Spanish Aero Car. In operation since 1916, the cable car crosses the whirlpool basin in the Niagara Gorge. This trip is not for the fainthearted, but there's no better way to get an aerial view of the gorge, whirlpool, the rapids, and the hydroelectric plants. | Niagara Pkwy., 4½ km (3 mi) north of the falls | 905/371–0254 or 877/642–7275 | www.niagaraparks.com | C$6 | Mid-June–early Sept., daily 9–9; early Sept.–Nov., shorter hrs, weather permitting.

★ **Skylon Tower.** Rising 775 ft above the falls, it's the best view of both the great Niagara Gorge and the entire city. An indoor-outdoor observation deck (visibility to 80 mi) facilitates the view. Amusements for children plus a revolving dining room are other reasons to visit. | 5200 Robinson St. | 905/356–2651 or 800/814–9577 | www.skylon.com | C$8.50 | Mid-June–early Sept., daily 8 AM–midnight; early Sept.–early June, daily 10–10.

★ **Whirlpool Jet Boat Tours.** A wet and wild thrill ride veers around and hurdles white-water rapids that follow Niagara canyons up to the great wall of roiling waters just below the falls. Full-length splash suit and boots provided. Not for children under four. Departures from Niagara-on-the-Lake and Queenston, Canada, and Lewiston, New York. | 61 Melville

St., Niagara-on-the-Lake, Ontario | 905/468–4800 or 888/438–4444 | www.whirlpooljet.com | C$52 | May–Oct. 8–5.

Dining

Scattered among the well-represented fast-food chains in Niagara are numerous respectable restaurants. The ethnic restaurants, particularly Italian, are very good. You can also find excellent Continental cuisine. Casual dress is acceptable in the establishments listed, and reservations are not necessary.

While the American dollar's current exchange is much more than the Canadian dollar, keep in mind that Canadian restaurants do tend to be a little more expensive than their American counterparts.

New York

★ **Buzzy's New York Style Pizza & Restaurant.** Pizza. Buzzy's, an institution since 1953, serves up 30 different pies, calzones, subs, and hoagies. For the adventurous eater, the chicken wings and chicken fingers—fresh, not frozen—come with blue cheese dip and a choice of 10 sauces, including one called Suicide. | 7617 Niagara Falls Blvd. | 716/283–533 | www.pizzapass.com/buzzys | $6–$15 | AE, MC, V.

Clarkson House. American. Along with delicious steaks and lobsters, there's a lot of history in this restaurant, which is housed in an antiques-filled 19th-century building. Reservations are essential on weekends. Kids' menu. | 810 Center St., Lewiston | 716/754–4544 | $11–$38 | AE, D, MC, V.

Como Restaurant. Italian. Since 1927, the Antonacci family has been serving traditional dishes from the south of Italy like veal à la Francesca, chicken cacciatore, and veal parmigiana. The interior evokes Italy with a stone fireplace and grapes hanging from the ceiling. Sunday brunch. Kids' menu. | 2220 Pine Ave. (U.S. 62A) | 716/285–9341 | www.fallscasino.com/como | $8–$18 | AE, D, MC, V.

Fyfe and Drum American. Historic Youngstown, the first settlement to grow outside of Fort Niagara in the 1700s, is the picturesque colonial village setting for this circa 1840 inn and restaurant. This local favorite for steaks, shepherd's pie, pastas and vegetarian entrées is 15 mi south of Niagara Falls. Lunch specials start at $5.50. | 440 Main St., Youngstown | 716/745–3907 | www.fyfe-and-drum.com | $11–$14 | D, MC, V.

Goose's Roost American. Casual homey describes this roost, where the seafood platters are oceanic and the prime beef on Weck (actually a salted caraway-seed roll—and a western New York bakery tradition) is a specialty. Open for breakfast, lunch, dinner. Kids' menu. | 343 4th St. | 716/282–6255 | $9–$13 | AE, MC, V.

Olde Fort Inn. Continental. This colonial inn in Youngstown is known for barbecued ribs, Angus beef, and Maryland crab cakes. Bread and desserts are homemade. Near Artpark in Youngstown, 15 mi south of Niagara Falls. Early-bird dinners served 4–6 PM. Friday fish fry. Kids' menu. | 110 Main St., Youngstown | 716/745–7141 | www.oldefortinn.com | Closed Mon. No lunch | $10–$25 | AE, MC, V.

★ **Top of the Falls.** American. A panoramic way to dine, this spot, situated just feet away from the brink of the falls, lives up to its name. The view is awesome, as is the thick New York strip steak and signature Buffalo Wrap (crispy chicken fingers, hot sauce, lettuce, and blue cheese in a flour tortilla). Kids' menu. | Niagara Reservation State Park, Goat Island | 716/278–0340 | $13–$20 | AE, D, MC, V.

Ontario

Beef Baron. American. As the name implies, this is the place for prime rib. Set amid dark wood paneling and lush red carpets, its signature steaks (26–30 ounces) are thick and priced to weight. Pastas are sumptuous, as is the rack of lamb. A kids' menu and lunchtime specials make this a tranquil and tasty stopover in a hectic day of touring. | 5019 Centre St. | 905/356–6110 | www.beefbaronrestaurant.com | C$10–C$30 | AE, D, DC, MC, V.

Casa d'Oro. Italian. It looks a little like a Disney version of a Venetian castle, but ornate wall sconces, fireplaces, wine casks, and huge faux-marble and bronze sculptures are somehow not out of place in Niagara Falls. The Roberto family has been serving steak, seafood, and traditional Italian specialties here for 30 years. Folks come here for the gigantic portions of prime rib, T-bones, fillets, and the hefty Lasagna Roberto. After dinner, you can cross a painted bridge that spans a water-filled moat to the Rialto nightclub's raised dance floor. | 5875 Victoria Ave. | 905/356–5646 | www.thecasadoro.com | C$17–C$36 | AE, D, DC, MC, V.

Casa Mia. Italian. Casa Mia is a lovely off-the-tourist-track Italian villa 10 minutes from the center of town. All the pasta is kitchen-made. If you've ever wondered what real cannelloni is like, try these light pasta pancakes, filled with coarse-ground veal and spinach. The veal chop is pan-seared with sage and truffle oil. | 3518 Portage Rd. | 905/356–5410 | www.casamiaristorante.com | C$20–C$36. | AE, MC, V.

Skylon Tower. American. The view from the Revolving Dining Room, perched 775 ft overlooking the Horseshoe Falls, is breathtaking, and the food is good, too. Traditionally prepared rack of lamb, baked salmon, steak, and chicken make up the list of entrées. It's an eclectic crowd, with people in cocktail wear and casual clothes seated side-by-side. Even with a reservation, there may be a short wait. | 5200 Robinson St. | 905/356–2651 or 800/558–2041 | www.skylon.com | C$23–C$40 | AE, DC, MC, V.

Table Rock. Canadian. Run by Niagara Parks, Table Rock serves inoffensive, standard U.S.–Canadian fare in an amazing setting. The dining room, in the rear of a two-story souvenir shop, offers tourist comfort food such as Caesar salads, baked salmon, pasta primavera, and beef and chicken burritos. | Just above Scenic Tunnels | 905/354–3631 | C$21–C$31 | AE, DC, MC, V.

21 Club. Steak. Whether you come to the casino for baccarat or the slots, dining at this elegant restaurant is no gamble. The menu has solid, high-end American steak-house fare and some Italian specialties. You'd have to search far to find a more delectably grilled 24-ounce Canadian porterhouse steak. | Casino Niagara, 5705 Falls Ave. | 905/374–3598 | C$22–C$38 | AE, DC, MC, V.

Yukiguni. Japanese. This spot is popular with locals and Japanese tourists because of its reasonable lunch specials, which include miso soup, fresh salad, and such entrées as juicy pepper-flavored chicken skewers. Other menu options include tempura soba, thin buckwheat noodles that come with shrimp and vegetable tempura; and steamed smoked eel, served on rice in a round stacked lacquer box. | 5980 Fallsview Blvd. | 905/354–4440 | C$10–C$17 | AE, DC, MC, V.

Lodging

For a complete listing of bed-and-breakfasts, check with the convention and visitor's bureaus in both New York and Ontario.

The **Western New York Bed & Breakfast Association** represents member B&Bs in Buffalo and Niagara Falls, New York. | www.bbwny.com.

Niagara Region Bed-and-Breakfasts represents more than 30 member B&Bs in Niagara Falls, Canada. | 905/358–8988.

New York

Elizabeth House. This three-story, Georgian-style home built in 1922 has a backyard, deck, patio, and pool. On chilly days, you can curl up with a book in the library or listen to music in the sunroom. Rooms have floral-pattern fabrics, lace insets in the windows, and antique furnishings. Breakfast is complimentary. Pool, library; no room TVs. | 327 Buffalo Ave., 14303 | 716/285–1109 | www.elizabethhousebandb.com | info@elizabethhousebandb.com | 4 rooms (2 with shared bath) | $60–$100 | AE, MC, V.

Fallsview Travelodge Hotel. True to Niagara Falls' honeymoon tradition, some rooms have king-size beds and red, heart-shaped hot tubs. Just one block east of the falls, this property in an 11-story brown-brick historic building has some rooms with views of the upper Niagara River. Restaurant, some refrigerators, cable TV, bar, business services, some pets allowed. | 201 Rainbow Blvd., 14303 | 716/285–9321 or 800/876–3297 | fax 716/285–2539 | www.niagarafallstravelodge.com | 200 rooms | $69–$199 | AE, D, DC, MC, V.

Holiday Inn–Grand Island. This resort-type hotel with an adjacent golf course and marina is on Grand Island, about 12 mi south of Niagara Falls. Some rooms have views of the Niagara River. Restaurant, cable TV, 2 pools, wading pool, gym, hot tub, massage, bar, playground, business services. | 100 White Haven Rd., Grand Island 14072 | 716/773–1111 or 800/465–4329 | fax 716/773–1229 | www.sixcontinentshotels.com | 262 rooms | $129–$159 | AE, D, DC, MC, V.

Howard Johnson Inn at the Falls. A block from the falls, you can walk to Cave of the Winds, the Casino Niagara, the Niagara Aquarium, and many other attractions from this chain motel, which offers amenities from children's themed rooms to business services. Restaurant, some in-room hot tubs, cable TV, pool, sauna, laundry facilities. | 454 Main St., 14301 | 716/285–5261 or 800/282–5261 | fax 716/285–8536 | www.hojo.com | 80 rooms | $95–$159 | AE, D, DC, MC, V.

Portage House. This no-frills motel is a good budget choice just a 10-minute drive to the falls, near Artpark and other Lewiston attractions. Cable TV; no room phones. | 280 Portage Rd., Lewiston 14092 | 716/754–8295 | fax 716/754–1613 | 21 rooms | $50–$60 | AE, D, MC, V.

★ **Red Coach Inn.** Established in 1923 and modeled after the Old Bell Inn in Finedon, England, this inn has wood-burning fireplaces and a spectacular view of Niagara Falls' upper rapids. Unique guest rooms—with names like the London Room, Bristol Suite, and Windmere Suite—are furnished with antiques, and there are 12 large, luxurious suites. Continental breakfast is complimentary. Restaurant, room service, some kitchenettes, cable TV, bar, business services. | 2 Buffalo Ave., 14303 | 716/282–1459 | fax 716/282–2650 | www.redcoach.com | 2 rooms, 12 suites | $79–$159 rooms, $119–$219 suites | AE, D, DC, MC, V.

Sands Hotel. This motel is a budget-price alternative for travelers who want a comfortable room and a convenient location for sightseeing. Not just a cookie-cutter roadside motel, this place has retro charm with low-key, friendly service. Picnic area, refrigerators, cable TV, pool. | 9393 Niagara Falls Blvd., 14304 | 716/297–3797 | www.travelbase.com/destinations/niagara-falls/sands-motel/ | sands-motel@travelbase.com | 17 rooms | $28–$75 | AE, D, DC, MC, V.

Ontario

Prices listed exclude 7% GST and 5% room tax.

★ **Brock Plaza Hotel.** Since its opening in the 1920s, this grande dame of Niagara hotels has hosted royalty, prime ministers, and Hollywood stars. Now completely renovated but with glamorous details intact, the imposing, stone-walled Brock is part of the Casino Niagara complex, with indoor access to gaming facilities, the Hard Rock Cafe, and the Rainbow Room restaurant overlooking the falls. It's a handsome landmark affording front-row suites overlooking the falls and is worth the splurge for those with a penchant for the tasteful and the time-honored. 2 restaurants, coffee shop, dining room, room TVs with video games, indoor pool, wading pool, hot tub, sauna, spa, lounge. | 5685 Falls Ave., L2E 6W7 | 905/374–4444 or 800/263–7135 | fax 905–374–9601 | www.niagarafallshotels.com | 233 rooms | C$349 | AE, D, DC, MC, V.

Candlelight Motor Inn. This two-story motel offers good, basic accommodations. Some rooms have whirlpool tubs, others offer heart-shape tubs and slightly fancier decor; the two efficiency suites have small kitchens. Restaurant, room TVs, pool. | 7600 Lundy's La., L2H 1H1 | 905/354–2211 reservations; 905/374–7010; 800/572–0308 | fax 905/358–0696 | www.candlelightniagara.com | 50 rooms | C$79–C$129 | AE, DC, MC, V.

Courtyard by Marriott Niagara Falls. A terrific location—only a block away from the falls and casino—makes this 10-story hotel a traveling family's lodging favorite. There are two-room family suites, and for pure romanticism it's hard to beat the hot tub and fireplace rooms. Restaurant, room TVs with video games, 2 pools (indoor and outdoor), hot tub, health club, spa, meeting rooms. | 5950 Victoria Ave., L2G 3L7 | 905/358–3083 or 800/771–1123 | fax 905/358–8720 | www.nfcourtyard.com | 258 rooms | C$189–C$500 | AE, D, DC, MC, V.

Lincoln Motor Inn. A pleasant landscaped courtyard gives this motor inn, within walking distance of the falls, an intimate feeling. Connecting family suites sleep up to a dozen. Facilities include an extra-large heated pool and an outdoor heated whirlpool. A golf course is nearby. Restaurant, room TVs, pool, hot tub | 6417 Main St., L2G 5Y3 | 905/356–1748 or 800/263–2575 | fax 905/356–7531 | 57 rooms | C$129–C$230 | AE, MC, V.

★ **Sheraton on the Falls.** This is the only hotel located directly across from the falls. The falls views are spectacular, as is the view. There's direct access to Casino Niagara, part of the 20-acre Falls Avenue complex linking most major downtown attractions. 2 restaurants, room TVs with movies and video games, pool, spa, health club, meeting rooms | 5875 Falls Ave., L2E 6W7 | 905/374–4444 or 800/263–7135 | fax 905/374–9606 | www.niagarafallshotels.com | 670 rooms | C$99–C$349 | AE, D, DC, MC, V.

Stoneleigh Bed & Breakfast. A B&B of rustic stone and stucco, that's less than a mile from the falls, is convenient to downtown and attractions, without the noise. The Gorge View and River View rooms offer the best vistas beyond the falls. Some room TVs, some pets allowed; no smoking. | 5127 River St., L2E 3G8 | 905/357–5116 | www.stoneleigh.ca | 3 rooms | C$75–C$140 | AE, MC, V.

Shopping

Arts and Crafts

If you're in the market for nontraditional keepsakes, the **Niagara, NY Arts and Cultural Center (NACC)** houses the studios of more than 50 local artists. Paul Hanover, a noted NACC painter, has his oils and acrylic originals of historic Niagara hanging in the offices of both President George W. Bush and Canada's Prime Minister Jean Chrétien. Local Tuscaroran First Nations artist Rosemary Hill produces old-fashioned raised glass beadwork sewn onto purses, pin cushions, and picture frames, and inspired by native traditions. NACC runs the on-site gallery and a gift shop where these and other creations are displayed and available for purchase. | 1201 Pine Ave., at Portage Rd. | 716/282–7530 | www.naccarts.net.

In and around Niagara Falls, Ontario, several major **arts-and-crafts fairs** showcase Canadian artists and artisans. | www.tourismniagara.com.

Outlets and Souvenirs

Between 15 million and 18 million visitors—many of them avid shoppers—come to Niagara Falls annually. Niagara factory outlets offer up to 70% off retail prices on top-quality manufacturers' goods and are easy to reach by foot or car, and group tours are available.

Canada One Factory Outlets, on the Canadian side about 1 mi north of the falls, lets the American buck go further with 40 specialty brand-name retail stores. | 7500 Lundy's La. | 905/356–8989 or 866/284–5781 | fax 905/356–1767 | www.canadaoneoutlets.com.

Factory Outlet Mall has more than 150 brand-name stores and is just 7 mi from the falls. | 1900 Military Rd., Niagara Falls, NY | 716/297–0933 | fax 716/297–6460 | www.primeoutlets.com.

Rainbow Center Factory Outlet is a one-block walk from the falls. | 302 Rainbow Blvd., Niagara Falls, NY | 716/285–9758 or 716/285–5525.

★ **Souvenir City.** Not your average souvenir shop, this memento mecca is actually four stores, including the regular T-shirt and postcard variety, and also a First Nations crafts store, a chocolate factory, and a marketplace selling everything from Cuban cigars to good old-fashioned Canadian maple syrup. | 4199 River Rd. | 905/357–1133.

Sports and Outdoor Activities

Bicycling

Biking through the Niagara region in any direction leads to adventure. On the American side, most bike tours wheel down to Whirlpool Park and Devil's Hole Park and then on to the Niagara Reservation State Park. In Canada, the approximately 30-mi Niagara River Recreation Trail follows the Niagara River from Fort Erie to Niagara-on-the-Lake, stretching across beautiful parkland, over small bridges, and to strategic lookouts. Bring along sunscreen and sunglasses, and always dress for the season. Stiff-soled running shoes for hard pedaling and the occasional hiking over rough terrain are recommended.

Bikes and Hikes of Niagara. This New York outfitter offers guided and self-guided tours of 3 to 12 mi that pedal to most of the main local sights. Rental rates: with guided 1-hour tour $25, 2-hour tour $35; self-guided 2-hour tour $12. | 526 Niagara St. | 716/278–0047 or 716/471–9422 | www.bikesandhikes.com.

Cupolo's Sports Bicycle Rental. In Ontario, Cupolo's provides mountain-bike rentals and directions to all city and environs bike trails. Rates: C$3 per hour; C$15 per day; helmets C$3 per hour or C$5 per day. Rental of children's strollers and tandem bikes also available. | Ferry St., near corner of Stanley Ave. | 905/356–4850 | www.cupolosports.com.

★ **Steve Bauer Bike Tours.** Indulge in a guided bike tour of the wineries of Niagara. The all-inclusive two-night package covers accommodations, all meals, wine-tasting stops, and spa treatments at a local resort, along with fruits and snacks en route. A great country-side outing. | 77 Queenston St., Queenston, Ontario | 905/562–0788 | www.stevenbauer.com.

Essential Information

When to Go

High season runs from Memorial Day through Labor Day, when most cultural activities take place and the falls' boat rides are operating. Consequently, tourists abound and hotel prices are highest. Summer temperatures range from 75°F to 85°F, with occasional light rainfall. The area near the falls is always misty, a natural refresher in the summertime. Very hot, humid days are infrequent. Winter temperatures create ice-covered tree branches and rocks that sparkle, and the railings and bridges turn almost crystalline.

FESTIVALS AND SEASONAL EVENTS

WINTER

Nov.–Jan.: **Festival of Lights.** Seventy trees are illuminated with 34,000 lights in the Ontario parklands near the Rainbow Bridge; there's also "The Enchantment of Disney," lighted displays based on Disney characters. The falls are illuminated nightly from 5 to 10 PM.

SPRING

Apr.–Nov.: **Shaw Festival.** Held just 12 mi north of Niagara Falls, Ontario, this world-renowned theater festival features the works of George Bernard Shaw and his contemporaries in three theaters. | 905/468–2172 or 800/511–7429.

SUMMER

Aug.: **Hands-on History.** The entire family can experience living history at Old Fort Niagara by participating in 18th-century games and activities. | 716/745–7611.

AUTUMN

Oct.: **Niagara's Apple Country Festival.** Here's a chance to sample fresh farm produce, see historical agricultural displays, join in children's activities—all apple-themed. Takes place in nearby Lockport, New York. | 716/433–3828.

Bargains

Masterpass coupon book. If you plan to visit the majority of the Niagara Reservation State Park attractions, Masterpass grants admission to the six major New York State park attractions. Sold mid-May–October, the pass can be purchased at Niagara Reservation parking booths and visitor center, Grand Island Official Information Center, and designated locations in the Niagara Frontier state parks. | $23.

Money Matters

CURRENCY

Throughout this chapter, prices are given in American dollars ($) for all goods and services available in New York, and prices are given in Canadian dollars (C$) for all goods and services available in Ontario.

U.S. dollars are accepted in much of Canada (especially in communities like Niagara Falls that are near the border). However, to get the most favorable exchange rate, exchange at least some of your money into Canadian funds at a bank or other financial institution. The units of currency in Canada are the Canadian dollar (C$) and the cent, in almost the same denominations as U.S. currency (C$5, C$10, C$20, C1¢, C5¢, C10¢, C25¢, etc.). The C$1 and C$2 are no longer used; they have been replaced by C$1 and C$2 coins.

TAXES

A goods and services tax (GST) of 7% applies on virtually every transaction in Canada except for the purchase of basic groceries. In addition to the GST, Ontario levies a provincial sales tax of 8%.

You can get a GST refund on purchases taken out of Canada and on short-term accommodations of less than one month, but not on food, drink, tobacco, car or motorhome rentals, or transportation; rebate forms, which must be submitted within 60 days of leaving Canada, may be obtained from certain retailers, duty-free shops, customs officials, or from the Canada Customs and Revenue Agency. Always save your original receipts from stores and hotels (not just credit card receipts), and be sure the name and address of the establishment shows on the receipt. In order for you to be eligible for a refund, receipts must total at least $200, and each individual receipt must show a minimum purchase of $50. The process of getting reimbursed is rather long and complicated, but for those spending lots of Canadian dollars, it may be worth the trouble.

Canada Customs and Revenue Agency | Visitor Rebate Program, Summerside Tax Center, 275 Pope Rd., Suite 104, Summerside, PE C1N 6C6 | 902/432–5608; 800/668–4748 in Canada | www.ccra-adrc.gc.ca.

Tours

Bedore Tours. Of the various tours offered from April to late October, the four-hour US/Canada Boat and Van tour is the most popular family outing. It views or visits the *Maid of the Mist* boat, the American and Canadian falls, the lower rapids, giant whirlpool, Table Rock, and numerous observation spots. | 716/285–7550 or 800/538–8433 | www.niagarafallslive.com/bedore_tours_inc.htm.

Niagara Glen Horticultural Department. Located 4 mi due north of the falls, the Horticultural Department runs free guided geological hikes from late April to November down all the paths of the Niagara River to the bottom. Proper footwear, suitable for steep and rugged terrain, is recommended. | 905/356–2241 or 877/642–7275.

Niagara Helicopters Ltd. A 12-minute flight takes you over the giant whirlpool, up the Niagara Gorge, and past the American Falls, then banks around the curve of the Horseshoe Falls. The fare is C$95 for adults; family rates are available. No reservations accepted. Open daily year-round (weather permitting). | 905/357–5672 or 800/281–8034 | www.niagarahelicopters.com.

Visitor Information

New York

Niagara Falls USA Chamber of Commerce | 345 3rd St., 14303 | 716/285–9141 | fax 716/285–00941. **Niagara Falls Convention & Visitors Bureau** | 310 4th St., 14303 | 716/285–2400 or 800/421–5223 | fax 716/285–0809 | www.nfcvb.com.

Ontario

Ontario Tourism | 905/282–1721 or 800/668–2746 | www.ontariotravel.net. **Niagara Falls Tourism** | 5515 Stanley Ave., at Hwy. 420, Niagara Falls, Ontario L2G 3X4 | 905/356–6061 or 800/563–2557 | fax 905/356–5567 | www.niagarafallstourism.com.

Arriving and Departing

BY AIR

Airports

Buffalo Niagara International Airport (BUF). This is the primary point of entry by air for Niagara Falls. | 716/630–6000 | www.nfta.com.

Niagara Falls International Airport (IAG). Many charter tours use this airport as their hub. | 716/297–4494 | www.nfta.com.

Airport Transportation

Bus: Niagara Falls Metro Buses run between the Buffalo and Niagara airports and downtown Niagara Falls. The bus ride to Niagara Falls from Buffalo International Airport requires a brief stopover in downtown Buffalo and costs about $2. Bus fare from Niagara International Airport costs $1.25.

Taxi: Taxi service from Buffalo Niagara International Airport to Niagara Falls, New York, costs approximately $46.

BY BUS

Visitor Information Center. The center, next to the convention center at 4th and Niagara streets, houses the Greyhound Lines bus station in New York. The station will be relocating, but at press time future location information was not available. | 343 4th St. | 716/282–1331.

Bus Station. In Ontario, this is a hub for the Canada Coach, Empire Trailway, Gray Coach, Greyhound, and Peter Pan lines. | 4555 Erie Ave. | 905/356–1179.

BY CAR

Access from the east and south is primarily via I–90, the New York State Thruway. The expressway spur, I–190, leads from 1–90 at Buffalo, across Grand Island to the Robert Moses Parkway into Niagara Falls. Approaches from the west are via a number of highways in Canada, including the Queen Elizabeth Way (QEW), with three bridges funneling traffic stateside.

BY TRAIN

The Amtrak station in New York is just beyond downtown Niagara Falls, at the intersection of Lockport Road and Hyde Park Boulevard. The Amtrak station will be relocating, but at press time the location of the new station was unavailable. Check Amtrak's Web site for schedules and stations.

VIA Rail. The station in Canada, at 4267 Bridge Street, is within walking distance of the falls. | 800/561–3949 to contact VIA Rail from the U.S.; 888/842–7245 reservations from Canada | www.viarail.com.

Getting Around

BY BICYCLE

Bicycles (☞ Sports and Outdoor Activities) are often a practical way to get around the traffic congestion in the downtown core.

BY CAR

To avoid bridge traffic caused by Canadian shoppers invading the malls on weekends, travel to Canada in the morning and return home in the late afternoon or evening. But once you've arrived in Niagara Falls, on either side of the border, there really isn't much need for a car. Public transit systems and tour vehicles, which pass the major sites, take away the worry of getting directions and finding a parking space. If you opt for a self-guided scenic drive, the most pleasing route along the American rim of the falls is the Robert Moses Parkway. It's a toll-free road that skirts the edge of the gorge with signs indicating key observation points where you can park (free of charge) and take in the different vistas. That's much the same when driving along Ontario's picturesque Niagara Parkway, the main arterial roadway into and out of the city of Niagara Falls (which eventually links up with the major east–west highways). Remember the speed limits in Canada are posted in kilometers per hour as opposed to miles per hour. The speed limit on most city streets is 50 kph (30 mph); on most highways, the speed limit is posted as 100 kph (60 mph). A rule of thumb is to multiply the posted speed limit by six and then divide by 10 to convert the posted kph to mph.

Parking

There's plenty of free parking for most attractions in Niagara Falls, New York, including the aquarium, the Niagara Power Project Visitor Center and Old Fort Niagara. But many of the larger parks, such as Artpark, Prospect Point, and Niagara Falls State Park, do charge $5 for all-day parking. Depending on the time of day and the season, parking on the Ontario side can be at a premium. Weekends during warm-weather months are always busiest, and it's wise to plan ahead and arrive early in the morning to snag the prime locations. Some attractions offer convenient free parking, such as beside the Floral Clock, Butterfly Conservatory, and the Niagara Spanish Aero Car. The falls parking lot is located opposite the Canadian falls and fills up the quickly. Rates are C$10 for cars, C$11 for RVs for the entire day (9 AM–midnight), but with no in-out privileges. The Rapids View parking area is farther away, about a 30-minute walk to the falls, and charges C$9 for both cars and RVs. If you are parking here, the price includes a free shuttle bus to the falls.

BY PUBLIC TRANSIT

New York

Viewmobile. A 40-minute guided trolley (train on wheels) ride circles Goat Island, making five stops. The Niagara Reservation State Park operates this service, and the cost is $5. | 716/278–1770.

Metro Bus. This system serves the Greater Niagara Falls area. | 716/285–9319 | www.nfta.com.

Ontario

People Mover. The Niagara Parks Commission operates these buses in Niagara Falls, Ontario. The People Mover is a "loop" transportation system that allows tourists to get on and off all day at any of 12 stops along the Niagara River. The cost is $3 for adults and $1.50 for children ages 6–12. Children under six ride free. Sightseers traveling to Ontario by auto pay $8, which includes parking and a People Mover ticket for everyone in the car. People Mover buses operate mid-May–mid-October from 9 AM until 11 PM. | 905/356–2241.

Niagara Transit. This bus system operates the Niagara Falls Shuttles. A shuttle ticket allows all-day transfers to and from various sites around downtown Niagara Falls, Ontario.| 905/356–1179.

BY TAXI

New York

Blue United Taxi. In downtown Niagara Falls, New York, fares are metered within the city, while the flat fare to ride to Canada is $17.50. | 716/285–3333.

Ontario

Niagara Taxi. In Niagara Falls, Ontario, a taxi ride within the city is metered pricing; from the Rainbow Bridge to the Floral Clock, 6 mi north, costs C$16; to Niagara Falls, New York, is C$18; and to Buffalo Niagara International Airport is C$60. | 905/357–4000 or 800/363–4900.

5-0 Taxi Service. This service has a specially equipped van for tourists traveling with wheelchairs. | 905/358–3232.

ON FOOT

All downtown Niagara Falls, New York, attractions are within a 10- to 15-minute walk. After exploring the American side you can even walk across the Rainbow Bridge into Canada. Most of the Canadian attractions, however, are a 20- to 30-minute walk; so for most visitors, riding the People Mover is preferable, after you've finished exploring Queen Victoria Park.

Revised and Updated by Anne Dubuisson Anderson

PHILADELPHIA AND THE PENNSYLVANIA DUTCH COUNTRY

Almost a century after English Quaker William Penn founded Philadelphia in 1682, the city became the birthplace of the nation and the home of its first government. Today, Philadelphia is synonymous with Independence Hall, the Liberty Bell, cheese steaks, friendly neighborhoods, and world-class museums.

Although Philadelphia is the fifth-largest city in the nation (1.6 million people live in the city, 5.8 million in the metropolitan area), it maintains a small-town feeling. It's a cosmopolitan, exciting, but not overwhelming city, a town that's easy to explore on foot yet big enough to keep surprising even those most familiar with it.

The plain and fancy live side by side in Lancaster County, some 65 miles west of Philadelphia—an area more popularly known as Pennsylvania Dutch Country. The county is home to the nation's largest population of Plain people (Amish, Mennonite, and Brethren), descendants of German and Swiss immigrants who came to the area to escape persecution; they have thrived over the years while maintaining their own cuisine, language, and traditions. They shun the amenities of modern civilization, such as electricity and cars, preferring to use kerosene or gas lamps, and to drive horse-drawn carriages.

In addition to exploring the Amish way of life along the county's tranquil country lanes, you can also tour a pretzel factory in historic Lititz and visit the many railroad-theme attractions in Strasburg.

Exploring

Philadelphia

Any visit to Philadelphia, whether you have one day or several, should begin in the Historic District, which comprises the attractions of Independence National Historical Park. From this neighborhood, you can walk to the riverfront development, Penn's Landing, where you can explore the city's shipbuilding and navigation history at the Independence Seaport Museum and on two historic battleships. You can spend a whole day in each of the museums that line Philadelphia's grand boulevard, the Benjamin Franklin Parkway. If your time is limited, choose according to

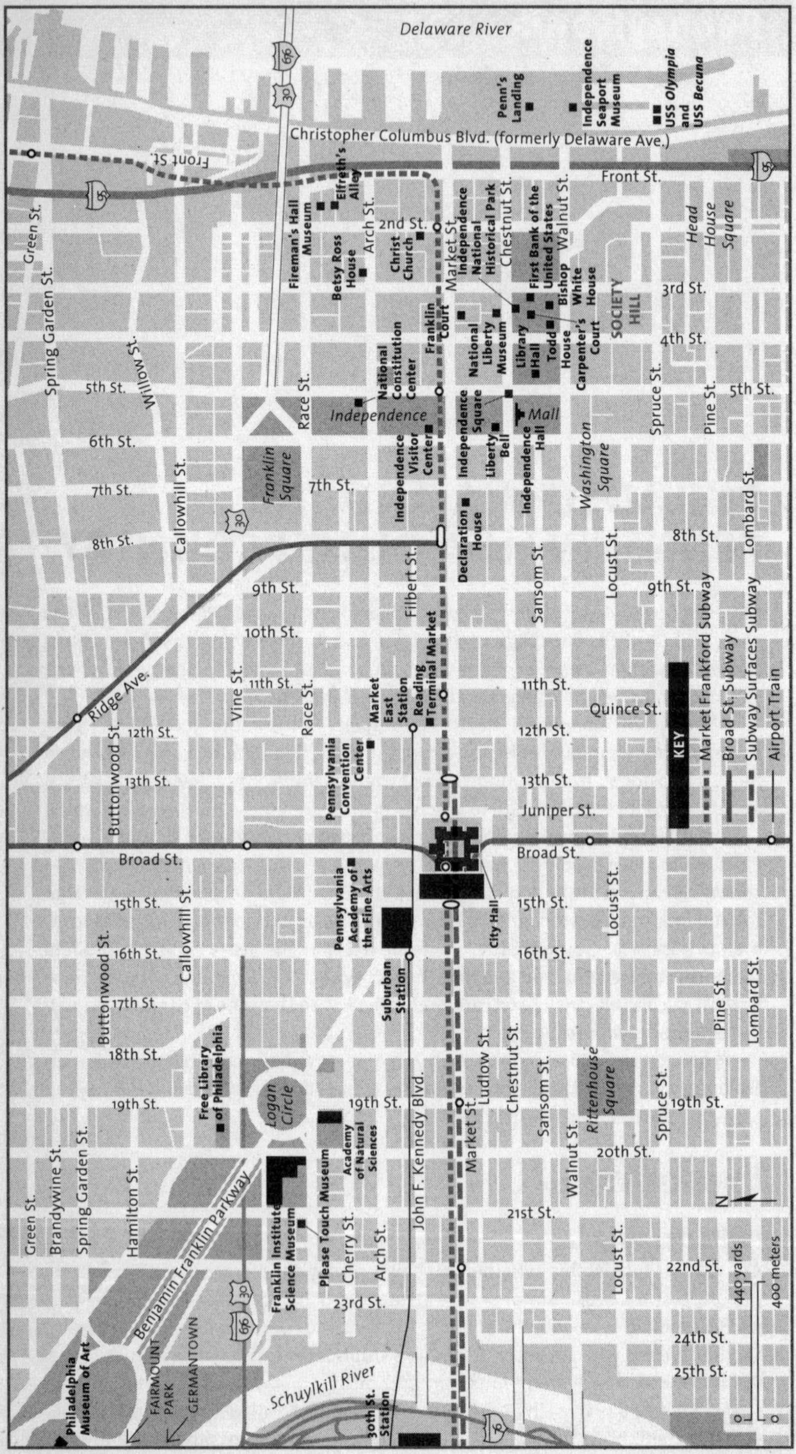
Delaware River
Penn's Landing
Independence Seaport Museum
USS Olympia and USS Becuna
Christopher Columbus Blvd. (formerly Delaware Ave.)
Front St.
Elfreth's Alley
Fireman's Hall Museum
Betsy Ross House
Arch St.
2nd St.
Christ Church
Market St.
Independence National Historical Park
Chestnut St.
First Bank of the United States
Walnut St.
Bishop White House
Head House Square
3rd St.
Society Hill
Franklin Court
National Liberty Museum
Library Hall
Todd House
Carpenter's Court
4th St.
Green St.
Spring Garden St.
Willow St.
5th St.
Race St.
National Constitution Center
Independence Mall
Independence Square
Liberty Bell
Independence Hall
Spruce St.
Pine St.
6th St.
Franklin Square
Independence Visitor Center
Washington Square
Callowhill St.
7th St.
Declaration House
Lombard St.
8th St.
Locust St.
Filbert St.
Sansom St.
9th St.
10th St.
Reading Terminal Market
Market East Station
Ridge Ave.
11th St.
Vine St.
Quince St.
Pennsylvania Convention Center
12th St.
Buttonwood St.
13th St.
Juniper St.
KEY
Market Frankford Subway
Broad St. Subway
Subway Surfaces Subway
Airport Train
Broad St.
Pennsylvania Academy of the Fine Arts
City Hall
15th St.
16th St.
Suburban Station
17th St.
18th St.
Free Library of Philadelphia
Logan Circle
19th St.
Academy of Natural Sciences
John F. Kennedy Blvd.
Ludlow St.
Rittenhouse Square
20th St.
Brandywine St.
Hamilton St.
Benjamin Franklin Parkway
Franklin Institute Science Museum
Please Touch Museum
Cherry St.
21st St.
22nd St.
23rd St.
24th St.
25th St.
440 yards
400 meters
N
Philadelphia Museum of Art
Fairmount Park
Germantown
Schuylkill River
30th St. Station

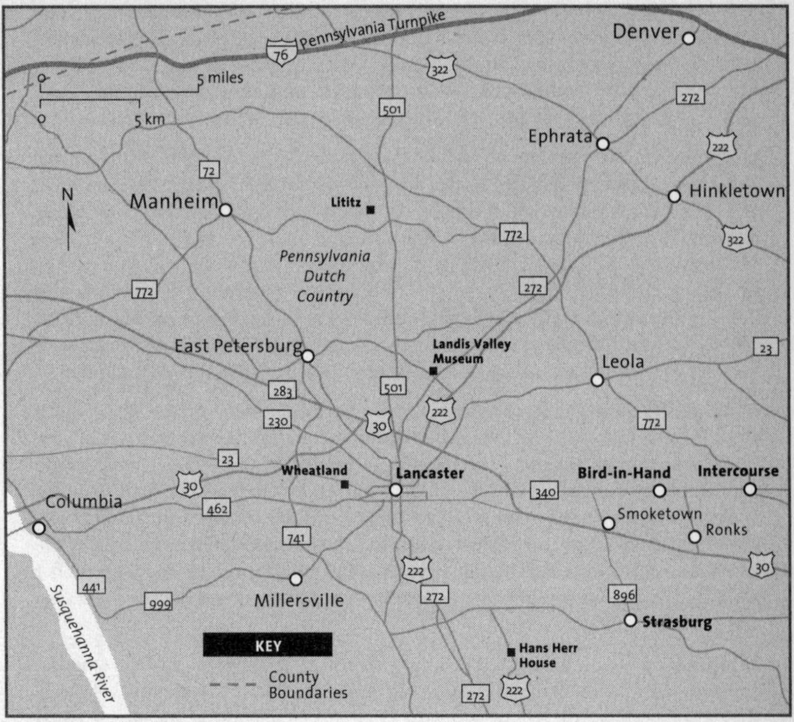

your interests: art, science, or natural history. If you are looking for a respite from the city, head to tranquil, historic Fairmount Park.

HISTORIC DISTRICT

Philadelphia is the birthplace of the United States, the home of the country's first government, and nowhere is the spirit of those miraculous early days—the boldness of conceiving a brand-new nation—more palpable than along the cobbled streets of the city's most historic district.

Most of the buildings that feature prominently in the nation's founding have been restored, and others have been reconstructed on their original sites. Today the park covers 42 acres and holds close to 40 buildings. The city's most historic area is now also one of its loveliest.

★ **Betsy Ross House.** Every American school child learns of Betsy Ross's contribution to the nation's founding. It's easy to find this little brick house with the gabled roof: just look for the 13-star flag displayed from its second-floor window. Whether Betsy Ross—who worked in her family's flag making and upholstery business—actually lived here and whether she really made the first Stars and Stripes is debatable. Nonetheless, the house, built about 1760, is a good example of a Colonial Philadelphia home and is fun to visit. The eight-room house overflows with artifacts such as a family Bible and Betsy Ross's chest of drawers and reading glasses. | 239 Arch St. | 215/686–1252 | www.ushistory.org/betsy/flaghome.html | $2 donation requested | Tues.–Sun. 10–5.

Carpenters' Hall. This handsome, patterned red-and-black brick building dating from 1770 was the headquarters of the Carpenters' Company, a guild founded to support carpenters, who were both builders and architects in this era, and to aid their families. In September 1774 the First Continental Congress convened here and addressed a declaration of rights and grievances to King George III. Today re-creations of Colonial settings include original Windsor chairs and candle sconces and displays of 18th-century carpentry tools. The Carpenters' Company still owns and operates the building. | 320 Chestnut St. | 215/925–0167 | www.nps.gov/inde/carpenters-hall.html | Free | Jan.–Feb., Wed.–Sun. 10–4; Mar.–Dec., Tues.–Sun. 10–4.

Christ Church. The Anglicans of the Church of England built a wooden church on this site in 1697. The congregation included 15 signers of the Declaration of Independence. The bells and the soaring 196-ft steeple, the tallest in the Colonies, were financed by lotteries run by Benjamin Franklin. Brass plaques mark the pews of George and Martha Washington, John and Abigail Adams, Betsy Ross, and others. As you pass by Christ Church Burial Ground located two blocks west of the church, toss a penny onto Ben Franklin's grave. Local legend says this will bring you good luck. | 2nd St. north of Market St. | 215/922–1695 | www.christchurchphila.org | Mar.–Dec., Mon.–Sat. 9–5, Sun. 1–5; Jan.–Feb., Wed.–Sat. 9–5, Sun. 1–5; services Sun. at 9 and 11, Wed. at noon.

Declaration House. In a second-floor room that he had rented from bricklayer Jacob Graff, Thomas Jefferson (1743–1826) drafted the Declaration of Independence in June 1776. The bedroom and parlor in which Jefferson lived that summer are re-created here with period furnishings. The display on the Declaration of Independence shows some of the changes Jefferson made while writing it. You can see Jefferson's original version—which would have abolished slavery had the passage not been stricken by the committee that included Benjamin Franklin and John Adams. | 7th and Market Sts. | 215/925–7877 | www.nps.gov/inde/declaration-house.html | Free | Hrs vary; check Web site or inquire at visitor center.

★ **Elfreth's Alley.** The alley, the oldest continuously occupied residential street in America, dates to 1702. Much of Colonial Philadelphia resembled this area, with its cobblestone streets and narrow two- or three-story brick houses. | Front and 2nd Sts. between Arch and Race Sts. | 215/574–0560 | www.elfrethsalley.org | Alley free, museum $2 | Jan., Sat. 10–4, Sun. noon–4; Feb.–Dec., Tues.–Sat. 10–4, Sun. noon–4.

Fireman's Hall Museum. Housed in an authentic 1876 firehouse, this museum traces the history of fire fighting, from the volunteer company founded in Philadelphia by Benjamin Franklin in 1736 to the professional departments of the 20th century. The collection includes early hand- and horse-drawn fire engines, such as an 1815 hand pumper and a 1907 three-horse Metropolitan steamer; fire marks (18th-century building signs marking them as insured for fire); uniforms; and other memorabilia. | 147 N. 2nd St. | 215/923–1438 | www.angelfire.com/pa4/firemanshall | Free; donations welcome | Tues.–Sat. 9–4:30.

Franklin Court. In 1763, at the age of 57, Benjamin Franklin (1706–1790) built his first permanent home in Philadelphia, in a courtyard off Market Street. This underground museum on the site of the house is an imaginative tribute to a Renaissance man: scientist and inventor (of bifocals and the lightning rod), philosopher and writer, savvy politician and successful businessman. Pick up a telephone to hear his thoughts or to listen to what his contemporaries really thought of him. Don't forget to get a letter hand-stamped with a "B. FREE FRANKLIN" cancellation. | 314–322 Market St., or enter from Chestnut St. walkway | 215/597–8974 | www.nps.gov/inde/Franklin_Court | Free | Mar.–Nov., daily 9–5; Dec.–Feb., 10–4.

★ **Independence Hall.** The birthplace of the United States, this redbrick building with its clock tower and steeple is one of our nation's greatest icons. The delegates to the Second Continental Congress met in the hall's Assembly Room in May 1776, united in anger over the blood that had been shed when British troops fired on citizens in Concord, Massachusetts. In this same room George Washington was appointed commander in chief of the Continental Army, Thomas Jefferson's eloquent Declaration of Independence was signed, and later the Constitution of the United States was adopted.

Here the first foreign minister to visit the United States was welcomed; the news of Cornwallis's defeat was announced, signaling the end of the Revolutionary War; and, later, John Adams and Abraham Lincoln lay in state. The memories this building holds linger in the collection of polished muskets, the silver inkstand used by delegates to sign the Declaration of Independence, and the "Rising Sun" chair in which George Washington sat. | Chestnut St. between 5th and 6th Sts. | 215/597–8974 | www.nps.gov/inde/indep-hall.html | Free | Sept.–June, daily 9–5; July–Aug., daily 9–8.

Independence Visitor Center. A visit to the area should begin here at the city's official visitor center. On hand are park rangers to answer questions and distribute maps and brochures on park sites and other historic locations. There's also a fully staffed concierge and trip-planning desk, which will provide information on other attractions, from the Philadelphia Museum of Art to the Philadelphia Zoo, as well as a reservation and ticketing service. Pick up a tiny Liberty Bell reproduction at the well-stocked souvenir shop. | 6th St., between Market and Arch Sts. | 215/965–7676 or 800/537–7676 | www.independencevisitorcenter.com | Sept.–June, daily 9–5; July–Aug., daily 9–6.

★ **Liberty Bell.** The bell fulfilled the biblical words of its inscription when it rang to "proclaim liberty throughout all the land unto all the inhabitants thereof," beckoning Philadelphians to the State House yard to hear the first reading of the Declaration of Independence. Ordered in 1751 and originally cast in England, the bell cracked during testing and was recast in Philadelphia by Pass and Stow two years later. To keep it from falling into British hands during the Revolution—they would have melted it down for ammunition—the bell was spirited away by horse and wagon to Allentown, 60 mi to the north. The bell is the subject of much legend; one story says it cracked when tolled at the funeral of Chief Justice John Marshall in 1835. Actually, the bell cracked slowly over a period of years. It was repaired but cracked again in 1846 and was then forever silenced. It was called the State House Bell until the 1830s, when a group of abolitionists adopted it as a symbol of freedom and renamed it the Liberty Bell. The Liberty Bell complex houses a bell chamber, an interpretive exhibit area with historic displays and memorabilia, and a covered area for waiting in line. | 6th and Chestnut Sts. | 215/597–8974 | www.nps.gov/inde/liberty-bell.html | Free | Sept.–June, daily 9–5; July–Aug., daily 9–8.

★ **Lights of Liberty.** Put on a pair of 3-D sound wireless headsets and view high-definition five-story projections on the area's historic buildings. This one-hour multimedia show, which dramatizes the events that led up to the American Revolution, takes you back to British Philadelphia in 1763 at Franklin Court, the site of Ben Franklin's home, and culminates in the grand finale at Independence Hall on July 8, 1776, with the first public reading of the Declaration of Independence. The show features special effects and a stirring musical score recorded by the Philadelphia Orchestra. There are six shows per hour; call for reservations and schedule. | PECO Energy Liberty Center, 6th and Chestnut Sts. | 215/542–3789 or 877/462–1776 | www.lightsofliberty.org | $17.76 | Apr.–Oct., daily, from just after dark, weather permitting.

National Constitution Center. Scheduled to open on July 4, 2003, this 132,000-square-ft museum will bring the U.S. Constitution alive through a series of highly interactive exhibits tracing the development and adoption of the nation's landmark guiding document. The heart of the sprawling museum, "The Story of We the People," takes you from the American Revolution through the Constitution's ratification to major events in the nation's constitutional history. Later, you can play the role of a Supreme Court justice deciding an important case, and walk among the framers in Signers Hall, where you can decide whether to add your signature to the list of founding fathers. | 525 Arch St. | 215/923–0004 | www.constitutioncenter.org | $5 | Daily 9–5.

National Liberty Museum. Using interactive exhibits, video, and works of art, the museum aims to combat bigotry in the United States by putting a spotlight on the nation's rich traditions of freedom and diversity. Galleries celebrate outstanding

Americans, including 19 Nobel Peace Prize winners, as well as heroes from around the world. A 6-ft pyramid, in the exhibit From Conflict Resolution to Harmony, shows us that there are three sides to every conflict, while Sandy Skoglund's colorful Jelly Bean People is a reminder that we're all the same inside regardless of the color of our skin. | 321 Chestnut St. | 215/925–2800 | www.libertymuseum.org | $5 | Tues.–Sun. 10–5.

PENN'S LANDING

The spot where William Penn stepped ashore in 1682 is the hub of a 37-acre riverfront park. Walk along the waterfront and you'll see scores of pleasure boats moored at the marina and cargo ships chugging up and down the Delaware. You can visit a maritime museum and historic marine vessels. A short ferry ride across the river will take you to the attractions of Camden, New Jersey, which include an aquarium, a children's garden, and the USS *New Jersey.*

Battleship New Jersey. The World War II–era USS *New Jersey,* one of the most decorated battleships in the history of the U.S. Navy, is now a floating museum Docked in Camden, New Jersey, it is across from the Philadelphia Naval Shipyard, which built and launched it in 1942. A two-hour guided tour takes you around the upper and lower decks of the ship, which was involved in a long list of Pacific operations, including the Marshalls, Iwo Jima, and Okinawa. | Beckett St. at the Delaware River, Camden, NJ | 856/966–1652 | www.battleshipnewjersey.org | $20 | Oct.–Mar., 9–3, Apr.–Sept., 9–5.

★ **Independence Seaport Museum.** At Philadelphia's maritime museum, you can climb in the gray, cold wooden bunks used in steerage; unload cargo from giant container ships with a miniature crane; weld and rivet a ship's hull; or even hop in a scull and row along the Schuylkill. The "What Floats Your Boat" exhibit is a fun introduction to the art and craft of boatbuilding. You can test boat models in the water and build your own boat frame. | 211 S. Columbus Blvd., at Walnut St. | 215/925–5439 | seaport.philly.com | $8 includes museum and USS Becuna and USS Olympia; $21.50 includes museum, USS Becuna, USS Olympia, fare on RiverLink Ferry and New Jersey State Aquarium. Free Sun. 10 AM–noon | Daily 10–5.

RiverLink Ferry. This passenger ferry makes a 12-minute trip across the Delaware River; it travels back and forth between the Independence Seaport Museum at Penn's Landing and Camden's waterfront attractions, including the New Jersey State Aquarium, the Camden Children's Museum, and the battleship *New Jersey.* You'll get a picturesque view of Philadelphia's skyline and the Ben Franklin Bridge. | Penn's Landing near Walnut St. | 215/925–5465 | www.riverlinkferry.org | $5 round-trip; $21.50 includes RiverLink fare, Independence Seaport Museum, USS Becuna, USS Olympia, and New Jersey State Aquarium | Apr.–mid-Nov., daily. Departs from Camden every 40 mins 9:40–5:40, from Philadelphia every 40 mins 10–5:20.

USS *Becuna.* You can tour this 318-ft-long "guppy class" submarine, which was commissioned in 1944 and conducted search-and-destroy missions in the South Pacific. The guides—all World War II submarine vets—tell amazing stories of what life was like for a crew of 88 men, at sea for months at a time, in these claustrophobic quarters. Then you can step through the narrow walkways, climb the ladders, and glimpse the torpedoes in their firing chambers. | Penn's Landing at Spruce St. | 215/922–1898 | www.phillyseaport.org | $21.50 includes admission to USS Becuna, USS Olympia, the Independence Seaport Museum, fare on RiverLink Ferry and New Jersey State Aquarium | Daily 10–5.

USS *Olympia.* Commodore George Dewey's flagship at the Battle of Manila in the Spanish-American War is the only remaining ship from that war. Dewey entered Manila Harbor after midnight on May 1, 1898. At 5:40 AM, he told his captain, "You may fire when ready, Gridley," and the battle began. By 12:30 the Americans had destroyed the entire Spanish fleet. The *Olympia* was the last ship of the "New Navy" of the 1880s and 1890s, the beginning of the era of steel ships. You can tour the entire restored ship, including the officers' staterooms, engine room, galley, gun batteries, pilothouse, and conning tower. | Penn's Landing at Spruce St. | 215/922–1898 | www.phillyseaport.org | $21.50 includes admission to USS Olympia, USS Becuna, the Independence Seaport Museum, fare on RiverLink Ferry and New Jersey State Aquarium | Daily 10–5.

CENTER CITY AND BENJAMIN FRANKLIN PARKWAY

Philadelphia's downtown area, known as Center City, is a bustling mixture of historic architecture, old-fashioned town squares, and dramatic new high-rises. Here, too, are indoor and outdoor shopping plazas and the legendary Reading Terminal Market.

The Benjamin Franklin Parkway is the city's Champs-Elysées. Alive with colorful flowers, flags, and fountains, this 250-ft-wide boulevard is crowned by a Greco-Roman temple on a hilltop—the Philadelphia Museum of Art. Other museums, institutions, hotels, and apartment buildings line the road, competing with each other in grandeur. Here you'll also find the Free Library of Philadelphia, housed in a building whose design was copied from the palaces on Paris's Place de la Concorde.

Academy of Natural Sciences. The world-famous dioramas of animals from around the world displayed in their natural habitats give this natural history museum an old-fashioned charm; the latest discoveries give it drawing power. The most popular attraction is the state-of-the-art Dinosaur Hall, with reconstructed skeletons of a Tyrannosaurus rex and the latest paleontological find—the giganotosaurus, the biggest meat-eating dinosaur ever discovered. The fossils here date as far back as 160 million years ago. Other drawing cards are Living Downstream, an interactive watershed model with multimedia kiosks featuring a role-playing game called Tough Choices; the Big Dig, where you can dig for real fossils; and the live butterflies that flutter all around you in a tropical rain-forest setting. Outside-In is an interactive children's nature museum where kids can crawl through a log, investigate a real bee hive, and touch a tarantula. Short presentations for children with live animal demonstrations take place several times a day. If you're keeping track of Philadelphia firsts, note that the academy, the oldest science research institution in the Western Hemisphere and a world leader in the fields of natural science research, education, and exhibition, was founded in 1812; the present building dates from 1868. | 19th St. and Benjamin Franklin Pkwy. | 215/299–1000 | www.acnatsci.org | $9 | Weekdays 10–4:30, weekends 10–5.

Clothespin. Claes Oldenburg's 45-ft-high, 10-ton steel sculpture stands in front of the Center Square Building. Lauded by some and scorned by others, this pop-art piece contrasts with the traditional statuary so common in Philadelphia. | 15th and Market Sts.

Eastern State Penitentiary Historic Site. Designed by John Haviland and built in 1829, Eastern State was at the time the most expensive building in America; it influenced penal design around the world and was the model for some 300 prisons from China to South America. The massive hulk, with 30-ft-high, 12-ft-wide walls and a hub-and-spoke floor plan, was created to promote a revolutionary and controversial concept: the reform of prisoners through solitary confinement, in accordance with the Quaker belief that if prisoners had light from heaven (in their private exercise yard), the word of God (the Bible), and honest work, they would reflect and repent. Charles Dickens came to America in 1842 to see Niagara Falls and Eastern State; he became its most famous detractor, insisting that solitary confinement was cruel. Before it closed in 1971, the prison was home to Al Capone, Willie Sutton, and Pep the Dog, who killed the cat that belonged to a governor's wife. The guides on the hourly tours of the unrestored structure (you must wear hard hats) tell terrific anecdotes and take you on a visit to Death Row. | 22nd St. and Fairmount Ave. | 215/236–3300 | www.easternstate.org | $7; children under 7 not allowed | Early May–late May and early Sept.–Oct., weekends 10–5; late May–early Sept., Wed.–Sun. 10–5; guided tours on the hr.

First Union Science Park. Discover the principles of gravity, energy, and physics while playing with the colorful interactive displays in this outdoor playground behind the Franklin Institute. | 21st St. between Winter and Race Sts. | Free with admission to Franklin Institute or Please Touch Museum | Early May–late Oct., daily 9–4:30.

★ **Franklin Institute Science Museum.** Founded more than 175 years ago to honor Benjamin Franklin, the institute is a science museum that is as clever as its namesake, thanks to an abundance of dazzling hands-on exhibits. To make the best use of your time, study the floor plan before you begin exploring. You can sit in the cockpit of a T-33 jet trainer, trace the route of a corpuscle through the world's largest artificial heart (15,000 times life size), and ride to nowhere on a 350-ton Baldwin steam locomotive. The many exhibits cover energy, motion, sound, physics, astronomy, aviation, ships, mechanics, electricity, time, and other scientific subjects. You'll also find a working weather station and the world's largest pinball machine. The Fels Planetarium has shows about the stars, space exploration, comets, and other phenomena, plus laser light shows choreographed to rock-and-roll favorites on Friday and Saturday nights (the last show's at midnight). The Mandell Center includes the Cyberzone computer lab, with 20 computers linked to the Web; Material Matters, a chemistry lesson; and the Tuttleman IMAX Theater, with a 79-ft domed screen and a 56-speaker high-tech sound system. One don't-miss: the 30-ft statue of Benjamin Franklin. | 20th St. and Benjamin Franklin Pkwy. | 215/448–1200; 215/448–1388 for laser-show hot line | www.fi.edu | Ticket packages $9.75–$14.75 | Daily 9:30–5, Mandell Center and Omniverse Theater open until 9 Fri.–Sat.

Free Library of Philadelphia. With its grand entrance hall, sweeping marble staircase, 30-ft ceilings, enormous reading rooms with long tables, and spiral staircases leading to balconies, this Greek Revival building looks the way libraries should. The Rare Book Room is a beautiful suite housing first editions of Dickens, ancient Sumerian clay tablets, illuminated medieval manuscripts, and more modern manuscripts, including Poe's *Murders in the Rue Morgue* and "The Raven." With 100,000 books for children from preschool to eighth grade, the Children's Department houses the city's largest collection of children's books in a made-for-kids setting. Historical collections include copies of the Hardy Boys and Nancy Drew series, over which adults wax nostalgic. The department also sponsors story hours and film festivals. | 19th St. and Benjamin Franklin Pkwy. | 215/686–5322 | www.library.phila.gov | Call for hrs.

Logan Circle. One of William Penn's five squares, Logan Circle was originally a burying ground and the site of a public execution by hanging in 1823. It found a fate better than death, though. The water-spouting frogs will now greet you at the square's majestic centerpiece, the Swann Fountain.

★ **Pennsylvania Academy of the Fine Arts.** This High Victorian Gothic structure is a work of art in itself. Designed in 1876 by the noted and sometimes eccentric Philadelphia architects Frank Furness and George Hewitt, the multicolor stone-and-brick exterior is an extravagant blend of columns, friezes, and Richardsonian Romanesque and Moorish flourishes. The interior is just as lush, with rich hues of red, yellow, and blue and an impressive staircase. The nation's oldest art school and museum (founded in 1805) displays a fine collection that ranges from the Peale family, Gilbert Stuart, Benjamin West, and Winslow Homer to Andrew Wyeth and Red Grooms. The permanent collection is supplemented by constantly changing exhibitions of sculpture, paintings, and mixed-media artwork. | 118 N. Broad St., at Cherry St. | 215/972–7600 | www.pafa.org | $5; free Sun. 3–5 | Tues.–Sat. 10–5, Sun. 11–5.

★ **Philadelphia Museum of Art.** The city's premier cultural attraction is one of the country's leading museums. Actually, one of the greatest treasures of the museum is the building itself. Constructed in 1928 of Minnesota dolomite, it's modeled after ancient Greek temples but on a grander scale. You can enter the museum from the front or the rear;

choose the front, and you can run up the 99 steps made famous in the movie *Rocky* (Rocky ran up only 72).

The museum has several outstanding permanent collections: the John G. Johnson Collection covers Western art from the Renaissance to the 19th century; the Arensberg and A. E. Gallatin collections contain modern and contemporary works by artists such as Brancusi, Braque, Matisse, and Picasso. The most spectacular "objects" in the museum are entire structures and great rooms moved lock, stock, and barrel from around the world: a 12th-century French cloister, a 16th-century Indian temple hall, a 16th-century Japanese Buddhist temple, a 17th-century Chinese palace hall, and a Japanese ceremonial teahouse. Among the other collections are costumes, Early American furniture, and Amish and Shaker crafts. An unusual touch—and one that children especially like—is the Kienbusch Collection of Arms and Armor.

Every Sunday the museum hosts a children's event, which may include live musical performances, make-and-take art projects, and special tours for young visitors. | 26th St. and Benjamin Franklin Pkwy. | 215/763–8100; 215/684–7500 for 24-hr taped message | www.philamuseum.org | $8; free Sun. 10–1 | Tues. and Thurs.–Sun. 10–5, Wed. and Fri. 10–8:45.

Please Touch Museum. Philadelphia's children's museum, one of the country's best, is designed for youngsters ages one to seven. Highlights include Alice's Adventures in Wonderland, a 2,300-square-ft re-creation of Wonderland that encourages children to develop problem-solving and literacy skills; Sendak, an interactive exhibit of oversize settings and creatures from books by celebrated author-illustrator Maurice Sendak; and SuperMarket Science, with large shopping and kitchen play settings and a lab where science and math-related demonstrations are held. The museum also has a child-size television studio, an exhibit on transportation, a farm-theme area for toddlers, and interactive theater shows. | 210 N. 21st St. | 215/963–0667 | www.pleasetouchmuseum.org | $8.95 | Sept.–June, daily 9–4:30; July–Aug., daily 9–6.

★ **Reading Terminal Market.** The market is nothing short of a historical treasure and a food heaven to Philadelphians and visitors alike. One floor beneath the former Reading Railroad's 1891 train shed, the sprawling market has more than 80 food stalls and other shops, selling items from hooked rugs and handmade jewelry to South American and African crafts. Here, amid the local color, you can sample Bassett's ice cream, Philadelphia's best; down a cheese steak, a bowl of snapper soup, or a soft pretzel; or nibble Greek, Mexican, and Indian specialties. From Wednesday through Saturday the Amish from Lancaster County cart in their goodies, including Lebanon bologna, shoofly pie, and scrapple. Many stalls have their own counters with seating; there's also a central eating area. If you want to cook, you can buy a large variety of fresh food from fruit and vegetable stands, butchers, fish stores, and Pennsylvania Dutch markets. | 12th and Arch Sts. | 215/922–2317 | www.readingterminalmarket.org | Mon.–Sat. 8–6.

Rittenhouse Square. Once grazing ground for cows and sheep, Philadelphia's most elegant square is the perfect place to relax, play, stroll, and people-watch in between visits to the parkway museums. If you want to join the office workers who have lunch-hour picnics in the park, you'll find scores of restaurants and sandwich shops along Walnut, Sansom, and Chestnut streets east of the square. | Walnut St. between 18th and 19th Sts.

FAIRMOUNT PARK

Stretching from the edge of downtown to the city's northwest corner, Fairmount Park is the largest landscaped city park in the world. With more than 8,500 acres and 2 million trees (someone claims to have counted), the park winds along the banks of the Schuylkill River—which divides it into west and east sections—and through parts of the city. Quite a few city dwellers consider the park their backyard. On weekends the 4-mi stretch along Kelly Drive is crowded with joggers, bicycling moms and dads with children strapped into kiddie seats atop the back wheel, hand-holding senior citizens out for some fresh air, collegiate crew teams sculling along the river, and budding artists trying to capture the sylvan magic just as Thomas Eakins once did.

Fairmount Park encompasses natural areas—woodlands, meadows, hills, two scenic waterways, and a forested 5½-mi gorge. It also contains tennis courts, ball fields, playgrounds, trails, exercise courses, the Philadelphia Zoo, and some historic Early American country houses that are operated by the Philadelphia Museum of Art and open to visitors.

You can tour by car (get a good city map), starting near the Philadelphia Museum of Art. Signs help point the way, and the historic houses have free parking. Before you set out, call **Park House Information** (215/684–7926) to find out which historic houses are open that day and what special events are planned. Another option is to take the narrated tour given by Philadelphia Trolley Works (board it at the Philadelphia Museum of Art or at John F. Kennedy Plaza, at 16th Street and John F. Kennedy Boulevard). The trolley bus visits many of these sites, and you can get on and off all day for $10. Also, the Philadelphia Museum of Art has a **two-hour guided tour** of three park houses. For tickets, call 215/235–7469.

Boathouse Row. These architecturally varied 19th-century buildings—in Victorian Gothic, Gothic Revival, and Italianate styles—house the rowing clubs that make up the "Schuylkill Navy," an association of boating clubs organized in 1858. The view of the boathouses from the west side of the river is splendid—especially at night, when they're outlined with hundreds of small lights. The row's newest addition, Lloyd Hall, has a gymnasium, bicycle and skate rentals in season, and a two-story café overlooking the river. | Kelly Dr., East Fairmount Park.

Japanese House. This reconstructed 16th-century samurai's dwelling, built in Japan, was exhibited temporarily at the Museum of Modern Art in New York, then reassembled here in 1958. The house itself and the waterfall, gardens, Japanese trees, and pond make a serene contrast to the busy city. The house is called Shofu-So, which means "pine breeze villa." It has a roof made of the bark of hinoki, a cypress that grows only in the mountains of Japan. Call ahead to see if a traditional tea ceremony is scheduled. | Lansdowne Dr. east of Belmont Ave., West Fairmount Park | 215/878–5097 | www.shofuso.org | $2.50 | May–Oct., Tues.–Sun. 10–4.

★ **Philadelphia Zoo.** Chartered in 1859 and opened in 1874, America's first zoo is home to more than 2,000 animals representing six continents. At each exhibit an old-fashioned Talking Storybook provides narration when activated by an elephant-shape key. The Amphibian and Reptile House houses 87 species, from 15-ft-long snakes to frogs the size of a dime. You'll want to save a lot of time for the state-of-the-art 2½-acre Primate Reserve, an enchanting playhouse for langurs, gorillas, and nine other primate species from around the world. The zoo is also home to rare white lions; Carnivore Kingdom, where meat eaters prowl just inches away; a terrific Bird House; and the African Plains, stomping ground of giraffes and zebras. The Rare Animal Conservation Center houses a collection of rare and endangered species, including Matschie's tree kangaroos and blue-eyed lemurs, along with seriously ugly naked mole rats. Children can climb inside a four-story tree, hatch from an egg, and ride a dinosaur in the Treehouse. The Children's Zoo has pony rides and a barnyard animal petting and feeding area. Take a ride in the Zooballoon—a 124-ft tall grounded helium balloon that soars 400 ft. On a clear day, from its gondola, you can see as far as the Atlantic Ocean. | 34th St. and Girard Ave., West Fairmount Park | 215/243–1100 | www.phillyzoo.org | Ticket packages $12.95–$27.90 | Feb.–Nov., weekdays 9:30–5, weekends 9:30–6; Dec.–Feb., daily 10–4.

The Wissahickon. Of the Philadelphia areas that William Penn encountered, the Wissahickon has changed the least. In the northwestern section of Fairmount Park, the

Wissahickon Creek carved out this gorge—5½ mi of towering trees, cliffs, trails, and animals. You can easily visualize the Leni-Lenape who lived here and gave the creek its name.

You will feel far away from the city as you walk or bike along **Forbidden Drive,** a dirt-and-gravel pathway along the west side of the creek. Mountain bikers will exalt at the rugged trails along both sides of the creek, and strollers can enjoy the many statues and the covered bridge—the last still standing within the borders of a major American city—along the route.

You'll need a car to get here: from downtown, take the Schuylkill Expressway west to the Lincoln Drive–Wissahickon Park exit (Exit 32). Follow Lincoln Drive to Allen's Lane, and then turn right. At Germantown Avenue turn left, go about a mile, turn left at Springfield Avenue, and follow it to the end.

NEARBY ATTRACTIONS

★ **University Museum of Archaeology and Anthropology.** Indiana Jones, look out! Rare treasures from the deepest jungles and ancient tombs make this one of the finest archaeological-anthropological museums in the world. On the University of Pennsylvania campus in West Philadelphia, the collection of more than a million objects, gathered largely during worldwide expeditions by University of Pennsylvania scholars, includes a 12-ton sphinx from Egypt, a crystal ball once owned by China's Dowager Empress, the world's oldest writing (Sumerian cuneiform clay tablets), and the 4,500-year-old golden jewels from the royal tombs of the kingdom of Ur. The museum has a superb collection of Chinese monumental (large-scale) art and more than 400 artifacts in its Ancient Greek World section. *Canaan and Ancient Israel* showcases ancient pottery, statuary, jewelry, weapons and more, with some artifacts dating from as early as 3000 BC, and includes a full-scale reconstruction of a house of the biblical period. Children run to *The Egyptian Mummy: Secrets and Science* and to *Living in Balance: The Universe of the Hopi, Zuni, Navajo, and Apache.* The museum has two gift shops and a café. | 33rd and Spruce Sts. | 215/898–4001 | www.upenn.edu/museum | $5, free Sun. | Early Sept.–late May, Tues.–Sat. 10–4:30, Sun. 1–5; late May–early Sept., Tues.–Sat. 10–4:30.

★ **Valley Forge National Historical Park.** Twenty miles northeast of downtown Philadelphia is the location of the 1777–78 winter encampment of General George Washington and the Continental Army. Stop first at the visitor center to see the 18-minute orientation film (shown every 30 minutes), view exhibits, and pick up a map for a 10-mi self-guided auto tour of the attractions in the 3,600-acre park. Stops include reconstructed huts of the Muhlenberg Brigade and the National Memorial Arch, which pays tribute to the soldiers who suffered through the brutal winter.

While the British occupied Philadelphia, Washington's soldiers were forced to endure horrid conditions here—blizzards, inadequate food and clothing, damp quarters, and disease. Many men deserted, and although no battle was fought at Valley Forge, 2,000 American soldiers died. The troops did win one victory that winter—a war of will. The forces slowly regained strength and confidence under the leadership of Prussian drillmaster Friedrich von Steuben. In June 1778 Washington led his troops away from Valley Forge in search of the British. Fortified, the Continental Army was able to carry on the fight for five years more.

The park contains 6 mi of jogging and bicycling paths and hiking trails, and you can picnic at any of three designated areas. A leisurely visit to the park takes no more than half a day. | Rtes. 23 and 363 | 610/783–1077 | www.nps.gov/vafo | Washington's headquarters $2, park free | Visitor center and Washington's headquarters, daily 9–5; park grounds daily dawn–dusk.

Pennsylvania Dutch Country

Lancaster, in roughly the center of Lancaster county, has plenty to see and also makes a good base for exploring the surrounding countryside. East of the city, between Routes 340 and 23 in towns with names such as Intercourse, Blue Ball, Paradise, and Bird-in-Hand, lives most of Lancaster County's Amish community. Strasburg, to the southeast, has sights for train buffs. About 12 mi north of Lancaster, is the lovely historic town of Lititz.

When you are visiting among the Amish, remember to respect their values. They believe that photographs and videos with recognizable reproductions of them violate the biblical commandment against making graven images. You will likely be asked to refrain from photographing or making videos of the Amish, and you should comply.

LANCASTER

Near the heart of Pennsylvania Dutch Country, Lancaster is a colorful small city that combines the Colonial past with the Pennsylvania Dutch present. During the French and Indian War and the American Revolution, its craftsmen turned out fine guns, building the city's reputation as the arsenal of the Colonies. On September 27, 1777, Lancaster became the national capital for a day, as Congress fled the British in Philadelphia. Today markets and museums preserve the area's history. East of town on U.S. 30 are some of the area's more commercial attractions, such as miniature golf and fast-food eateries.

Dutch Wonderland. The 44 acres of games, water slides, and rides at this amusement park are suited for families with younger children. Most rides are tame. Diving shows, an animated bear show, and concerts supplement the rides. | 2249 U.S. 30, east of Lancaster | 717/291–1888 | www.dutchwonderland.com | Unlimited rides $46.95 | Late May–early Sept., daily 10–6 or later; early Sept.–Oct. and Easter–late May, weekends 10–6.

Heritage Center Museum. The Old City Hall has been reborn as the Heritage Center. Discover the culture and history of the region through such artifacts as dolls, quilts, paintings, and Pennsylvania long rifles of the Pennsylvania German settlers. | King and Queen Sts. on Penn Sq. | 717/299–6440 | www.lancasterheritage.com | Donation requested | May–Dec., Tues.–Sat. 10–5.

★ **Landis Valley Museum.** This is an outdoor museum of Pennsylvania German rural life and folk culture before 1900. You can visit more than 15 historical buildings, from a farmstead to a country store. There are demonstrations of skills such as spinning and weaving, pottery making, and tinsmithing, the products of which are for sale in the Weathervane Shop. | 2451 Kissel Hill Rd. | 717/569–0401 | www.landisvalleymuseum.org | $7, family $19 | Mar.–Dec., Mon.–Sat. 9–5, Sun. noon–5.

INTERCOURSE

Intercourse is a center of Amish life. Many places that help you better understand this community can be found between here and Bird-in-Hand. The town is at the intersection, or intercourse, of two roads (today's Routes 340 and 772), which is how it got its name in Colonial times.

★ **People's Place.** A "people-to-people interpretation center" provides an excellent introduction to the Amish, Mennonite, and Hutterite communities. A 30-minute multiscreen slide show titled *Who Are the Amish?* has close-ups of Amish life and perceptive narration. There's a bookstore, too. | 3513 Old Philadelphia Pike/Rte. 340 | 717/768–7171 or 800/390–8436 | www.thepeoplesplace.com | $8 | Late May–early Sept., Mon.–Sat. 9:30–8; early Sept.–late May, Mon.–Sat. 9:30–5.

20Q (short for 20 Questions), an interactive family museum, highlights the differences between Amish and Mennonite societies. Children can try on bonnets and play in the "feeling box." Don't miss the collection of wood carvings by Aaron Zook.

BIRD-IN-HAND

This village, like many others, took its name from the sign on an early inn and tavern. Today it is a center for the Pennsylvania Dutch farming community.

Abe's Buggy Rides. Abe chats about the customs of the Pennsylvania Dutch during the course of a 2-mi spin down country roads in an Amish carriage. | 2596 Old Philadelphia Pike | 717/392–1794 | $10 | Mon.–Sat. 9 AM–dusk.

Amish Experience. A multimedia theatrical presentation tells the history of the Amish, using 3-D sets, multiple screens, and special effects. In *Jacob's Choice,* the teenage main character struggles between traditional ways and the temptations of the present. A $25.95 package includes the show "The Amish Country Homestead" and Amish Country Tours, a bus tour of the farmlands. | Rte. 340 between Bird-in-Hand and Intercourse at Plain & Fancy Farm | 717/768–8400 | www.amishexperience.com | $6.95, combination ticket with Amish Country Homestead $10.50 | Apr.–June, Mon.–Sat. 8:30–5, Sun. 10–5; July–Oct., Mon.–Sat. 8:30–8, Sun. 10:30–5; Nov.–Mar., daily 10–5; shows on the hr.

STRASBURG

Although settled by French Huguenots, the village of Strasburg is today a community of Pennsylvania Dutch. It's best known as the railroad center of eastern Pennsylvania; railroad buffs can easily spend a day here.

Choo-Choo Barn, Traintown, USA. It all began as a family hobby in 1945 with a single train chugging around the Groff family Christmas tree. This 1,700-square-ft display of Lancaster County in miniature has 18 trains in O-gauge and 130 animated scenes, including an authentic Amish barn raising, a huge three-ring circus with animals and acrobats, and a blazing house fire with fire engines rushing to the disaster. Periodically, the overhead lights dim, and it becomes night, when streetlights and locomotive headlights glow in the darkness. | Rte. 741 | 717/687–7911 | www.choochoobarn.com | $5 | Apr.–Dec., daily 10–5.

★ **National Toy Train Museum.** The showplace of the Train Collectors Association displays antique and 20th-century model trains. The museum has five huge operating layouts, with toy trains from the 1800s to the present, plus nostalgia films and hundreds of locomotives and cars in display cases. Take the children to see the special hands-on layouts every Friday from June through August. | Paradise La. just north of Rte. 741 | 717/687–8976 | www.traincollectors.org | $3 | May–Oct. and Christmas wk, daily 10–5; Apr. and Nov.–mid-Dec., weekends 10–5.

★ **Railroad Museum of Pennsylvania.** Seventy-five pieces of train history on display here include 13 colossal engines built between 1888 and 1930; 12 railroad cars, among them a Pullman sleeper; sleighs; and railroad memorabilia documenting the history of Pennsylvania railroading. More than 50 of the pieces of equipment are kept indoors in the Rolling Stock Hall. | Rte. 741 | 717/687–8628 | www.rrmuseumpa.org | $7 | May–Oct., Mon.–Sat. 9–5, Sun. noon–5; Nov.–Apr., Tues.–Sat. 9–5, Sun. noon–5.

Strasburg Rail Road. Take a scenic 45-minute round-trip excursion through Amish farm country from Strasburg to Paradise on a rolling antique chartered in 1832 to carry milk, mail, and coal. Called America's oldest short line, the Strasburg run has wooden coaches pulled by an iron steam locomotive. You can lunch in the dining car or buy a box lunch in the restaurant at the station and have a picnic at Groff's Grove along the line. There are seasonal Santa, Pumpkin, and Easter Bunny train rides. | Rte. 741 | 717/687–7522 | www.strasburgrailroad.com | $11 | Mid-Feb.–mid-Apr. and Nov.–mid-Dec., weekends noon–2; mid-Apr.–Oct., weekdays 11–4, weekends 11–5 or later; dinner train boards at 6:30. Trains depart every hr, depending on season; call for schedule.

LITITZ

Lititz was founded in 1756 by Moravians who settled in Pennsylvania to do missionary work among the Native Americans. Its tree-shaded main street, lined with 18th-century cottages and shops selling antiques, crafts, clothing, and gifts, is a fine place for a walk. Around the main square are the Moravian communal residences, a church dating from 1787, and a hospital that treated the wounded during the Revolutionary War.

Julius Sturgis Pretzel House. At the oldest pretzel bakery in the United States, pretzels are twisted by hand and baked in brick ovens the same way Julius Sturgis did it in 1861. At the end of the 20-minute guided tour, you can try your hand at the almost extinct art of pretzel twisting. | 219 E. Main St. | 717/626–4354 | www.sturgispretzel.com | $2 | Mon.–Sat. 9–5.

Wilbur Chocolate Company's Candy Americana Museum and Factory Candy Outlet. The first thing you notice in Lititz is the smell of chocolate emanating from the Wilbur Chocolate Company, which has a small museum of candy-related memorabilia and a large retail store. | 48 N. Broad St. | 717/626–3249 | www.wilburbuds.com | Free | Mon.–Sat. 10–5.

Dining

Philadelphia

HISTORIC AREA

The Continental Restaurant and Martini Bar. American/Casual. Don't be discouraged by the name—this sunny, casual spot with a varied menu is a good choice for families before the late-night bar crowd takes over. Simple food from fish-and-chips to filet mignon is fancifully prepared. A number of vegetarian entrées are also available. | 134 Market St. | 215/923–6069 | $6–$17 | AE, MC, V.

Pizzicato. American/Casual. As the name implies, you can find wonderful brick-oven pizza here, but you can also find a full range of contemporary takes on traditional dishes from mushroom tagliatelle to veal chops stuffed with Portobello and red pepper. There's outdoor seating in season and chairs upstairs. | 248 Market St. | 215/629–5527 | $7–$20 | AE, D, MC, V.

CENTER CITY

Marathon Grill. American. At this upscale diner, you can choose anything from grilled brie to jalapeño peppers to top your cheeseburger and design your own drink at the smoothie and espresso bar. The menu also includes classic entrées such as filet mignon and tuna steak. | 16th and Sansom St. | 215/569–3278 | Closed Mon. | $6–$10 | AE, MC, V.

Ocean City. Chinese. Lacquered ducks and roast pork cuts hang in the window of this restaurant on the eastern periphery of Chinatown, a large, bright place that covers all bases on its huge menu, although it leans heavily toward Cantonese. Fish tanks of creatures, including eels, meant for cooking line the entryway. Banquets for 10 or more people (reserve ahead) are an outstanding specialty. Order one of these, and course after course of well-known—and several lesser-known but well-prepared—dishes comes flying to the table. | 234 N. 9th St. | 215/829–0688 | $6–$16 | AE, MC, V.

Rachael's Nosheri. Delicatessens. All the standard Jewish deli fare appears here, both on the menu and as decoration, such as jars of cucumbers in various stages of pickling. The menu, in typical deli style, is comprehensive with lists of smoked fish and smoked meats, too, for stuffed sandwiches and platters. The take-out business caters to apartments and businesses in the area, but a neat cluster of tables anticipates those people who prefer to polish off their food on the premises. Only breakfast and lunch are served. | 120 S. 19th St. | 215/568–9565 | Closed Sun. No dinner | $5–$8 | AE, D, DC, MC, V.

★ **Reading Terminal Market.** Eclectic. A Philadelphia treasure, the Reading Terminal Market contains a profusion of more than 80 stalls, shops, lunch counters, and food emporiums in a huge, exciting indoor market. You can choose from numerous raw ingredients and prepared foods—Chinese, Greek, Mexican, Japanese, Thai, Middle Eastern, Italian, soul food, vegetarian, and Pennsylvania Dutch. Food options also include an extensive salad bar, seafood spots, a deli, baked goods, specialty hoagie and cheese-steak shops, a sushi bar, and the outstanding Bassetts ice cream counter. Get here early to beat the daily lunch rush. | 12th and Arch Sts. | 215/922–2317 | Closed Sun. | $2–$8.

The **Down Home Diner** inside the market has farm-style breakfasts and lunches (and dinner until 8, except Sunday). The market is open Monday to Saturday 8 to 6.

Sang Kee Peking Duck House. Chinese. Sang Kee dishes up the most delicious noodle soups in town. Egg or rice noodles come in different widths with duck, pork, or beef brisket. If you wish, you can have your soup with both noodles *and* overstuffed, tender wontons. Other traditional foods, besides the house specialty duck, are carried from the kitchen with more speed than style. Beer is available. | 238 N. 9th St. | 215/925–7532 | Reservations not accepted | $6–$14 | No credit cards.

Morning Glory Diner. American. Although the Morning Glory bills itself as a diner and offers many diner touches such as big mugs of steaming coffee (although the mugs are pewter), the place was transformed from a couple of storefronts and departs from tradition in other ways as well: big breakfasts come with mammoth homemade biscuits, but if you want toast, you pay extra. Tasty turkey meat loaf is a specialty—frequently topped off with nippy, homemade catsup—that reflects the sparky contemporary style of the owners. | 735 S. 10th St. | 215/413–3999 | Closed Mon. | $7–$15 | No credit cards.

Pennsylvania Dutch Country

LANCASTER

J'M's Bistro. American/Casual. The local favorite is known for being relaxed and friendly. You can choose from a wide variety of well-prepared foods, including crab cakes, salads, gourmet pizzas, mussels, and rack of lamb. | 377 N. Queen St. | 717/392–5656 | No lunch weekends. | $6–$18 | AE, MC, V.

INTERCOURSE

Kling House. American. The Kling family home has been converted into a pleasant, casual restaurant that serves innovative breakfast and lunch selections. The turkey Reuben and sausage platter are favorites, as are the *knepp* (ham) entrées, which come with a complimentary appetizer of red-pepper jam and cream cheese with crackers. The soups are homemade, and desserts are luscious. A children's menu is available. Dinner is served seasonally. Call first. | Kitchen Kettle Village, Rtes. 340 and 772 | 717/768–8261 | Closed Sun. | $5–$12 | D, MC, V.

BIRD-IN-HAND

Amish Barn Restaurant. American. Pennsylvania Dutch cuisine is served family style, which means generous helpings of meat and produce, breads, and pies are brought to your table in big bowls or platters. You can also choose from an à la carte menu. Apple dumplings and shoofly pie are specialties. Breakfast is available, too. No liquor is served. | 3029 Old Philadelphia Pike/Rte. 340, between Bird-in-Hand and Intercourse | 717/768–8886 | $6–$15 | AE, D, MC, V.

★ **Bird-in-Hand Family Restaurant.** American. This family-owned diner-style restaurant has a good reputation for hearty Pennsylvania Dutch home cooking. The menu is à la carte, but there's a lunch buffet weekdays. It's an excellent place to sample local specialties such as apple dumplings and chicken potpie. No liquor is served. | 2760 Old Philadelphia Pike/Rte. 340 | 717/768–8266 | Closed Sun. | $6–$10 | MC, V.

★ **Miller's Smorgasbord.** American. The spread here is lavish, with a good selection of Pennsylvania Dutch foods. The breakfast buffet (served daily June through October and on weekends November through May) is sensational, with omelets, pancakes, and eggs cooked to order, fresh fruits, pastries, bacon, sausage, potatoes, and much more. | 2811 Lincoln Hwy. E/U.S. 30, Ronks | 717/687–6621 | $7–$11 | AE, D, MC, V.

Lodging

Philadelphia

HISTORIC AREA

Comfort Inn Downtown. The reasonable price is the most noteworthy draw here, with complimentary Continental breakfast as an additional lure at this 10-story hotel. Decor is contemporary, with oak furniture and a mauve color scheme. Tucked between the Benjamin Franklin Bridge, Columbus Boulevard, and I–95, the inn has more noise than charm—but if you have a room on an upper floor facing the river, you'll enjoy a good view of the Benjamin Franklin Bridge lighted up at night. A nice plus is the courtesy van service to Center City; foot power brings you to the nearby Betsy Ross House, historic Elfreth's Alley, or to the RiverLink Ferry. Room TVs, lobby lounge, laundry service, meeting rooms, parking (fee), no-smoking rooms | 100 N. Columbus Blvd., 19106 | 215/627–7900 or 800/228–5150 | fax 215/238–0809 | www.comfortinn.com | 185 rooms | $89–$149 | AE, D, DC, MC, V | CP.

CENTER CITY

Best Western Center City. A bit far from the heart of Center City, but within an easy walk of the Philadelphia Museum of Art, this old-timer (in relative terms) of a motel was renovated a few years ago but is still a bit tired, with rooms done in navy blue. The best views from the guest rooms face south toward the flag-draped Benjamin Franklin Parkway and the downtown skyline. This is still a relative bargain in a city where prices have been rising quickly. Restaurant, in-room data ports, room TVs, pool, gym, sports bar, laundry service, meeting rooms, free parking, no-smoking rooms | 501 N. 22nd St., 19130 | 215/568–8300 or 800/528–1234 | fax 215/557–0259 | www.bestwestern.com | 179 rooms, 4 suites | $109 | AE, D, DC, MC, V.

Crowne Plaza Philadelphia City Center. This is a good choice for those who want to be in the center of the action. It is a close walk to both the parkway museums and the benches of Rittenhouse Square. The good-size guest rooms in the 25-floor hotel have a contemporary decor. Restaurant, snack bar, in-room data ports, room TVs, pool, gym, laundry service, meeting rooms, free parking, no-smoking rooms | 1800 Market St., 19103 | 215/561–7500 or 800/227–6963 | fax 215/561–4484 | www.philadelphia.crowneplaza.com | 445 rooms, 2 suites | $80–$229 | AE, D, DC, MC, V.

Pennsylvania Dutch Country

BIRD-IN-HAND

Bird-in-Hand Family Inn. The rooms are simple, clean, and comfortable, and the staff is friendly at this family-run motel. The property offers a host of recreational opportunities. Restaurant, room TVs, refrigerators, miniature golf, tennis court, outdoor pool, indoor pools, lake, gym, hot tub, bicycles, basketball, playground | 2740 Old Philadelphia Pike/Rte. 340, 17505 | 717/768–8271 or 800/537–2535 | fax 717/768–1768 | www.bird-in-hand.com/familyinn | 125 rooms, 4 suites | $72–$105 | AE, D, DC, MC, V.

STRASBURG

Fulton Steamboat Inn. Named after Lancaster native Robert Fulton, who built the first passenger steamer, in 1807, this inn is at one of Lancaster County's busiest intersections, across from Rockvale Square Outlets. It's designed to look just like a steamboat: the upper deck has whirlpool baths and private outdoor decks; the no-smoking middle deck has staterooms with two queen-size beds; and the lower deck has nautical-theme cabins with bunk beds. Restaurant, refrigerators, indoor pool, gym, hot tub | 96 rooms, 5 suites | Rtes. 30 and 896 (Box 333), 17579 | 717/299–9999; 800/922–2229 outside Pennsylvania | fax 717/299–9992 | www.fultonsteamboatinn.com | $75–$125 | AE, MC, V.

Mill Stream Country Inn and Restaurant. Long a popular choice, this freshly renovated motel overlooks a picturesque stream. Breakfast is available in the restaurant, but alcohol is not served. Guests have exercise privileges at the Willow Valley Family Resort in Lancaster. Pool | Rte. 896, 17576 | 717/299–0931 | fax 717/295–9326 | www.millstreamcountryinn.com | 49 rooms, 3 suites | $59–$139 | AE, D, MC, V | BP.

Strasburg Village Inn. This circa-1788 house in the heart of town has rooms elegantly appointed in the Williamsburg style. Most have a canopy or four-poster bed; three have a whirlpool bath. A sitting/reading room is on the second floor; an old-fashioned porch overlooks Main Street. Room TVs | 1 W. Main St., 17579 | 717/687–0900 or 800/541–1055 | www.strasburg.com | 5 rooms, 5 suites | $79–$99 | AE, D, MC, V | BP.

Camping

Pennsylvania Dutch Country

Historic Mill Bridge Village and Campresort. This campground is attached to a restored 18th-century village that was home to Herr's Grist Mill. Campers are given free admission to the village, with its ice cream parlor, craftsman and Amish schoolhouse, and a complimentary buggy ride. There's fishing nearby. Flush toilets, full hook-ups, dump station, showers, fire pits, picnic tables, snack bar, public telephone, general store | 100 hook-ups | S. Ronks Rd., ½ mi south of U.S. 30, Ronks 17579 | 717/687–8181 or 800/645–2744 | www.millbridge.com | $26–$39 | MC, V | Apr.–Oct.

Spring Gulch Resort Campground. Glorious farmland and forest are the setting for the pleasantly shaded campsites and a limited number of rental cottages at $84 to $127. A full schedule of weekend activities includes country dances and chicken barbecues. There's also plenty to do on your own—facilities include miniature golf, tennis, spa, fishing, volleyball, and a recreation room. Flush toilets, full hook-ups, dump station, showers, fire pits, picnic tables, 2 pools, swimming (lake) | 400 hook-ups, 4 cottages | 475 Lynch Rd., New Holland 17557 | 717/354–3100 or 800/255–5744 | www.springgulch.com | $25–$39 | MC, V.

Shopping

Philadelphia

From antiques to fine cheese to funky clothes, you can find what you are looking for by strolling through Philadelphia's diverse downtown neighborhoods. There are also two indoor Center City malls.

Antiques Row. These three blocks of Pine Street have dozens of antiques stores and curio shops, many specializing in expensive period furniture and Colonial heirlooms. | Pine St. between 9th and 12th Sts.

Gallery at Market East. A block north of Chestnut Street is Philadelphia's landmark effort at urban renewal–cum–shopping and America's first enclosed downtown shopping mall. The four-level glass-roof structure near the Pennsylvania Convention Center contains 150 mid-price retailers. It includes 40 food outlets and two department stores—JCPenney and Strawbridge's, which has somewhat higher-quality merchandise. Strawbridge's, now part of the May Company chain, is home-grown; it was founded by prominent local businessmen Justus C. Strawbridge and Isaac Clothier. | Market St. between 8th and 11th Sts. | 215/925–7162.

Italian Market. It's more Naples than Philadelphia: vendors crowd the sidewalks and spill out onto the streets; live crabs and caged chickens wait for the kill; picture-perfect produce is piled high. The market dates back to the turn of the 20th century, when it was founded by Italian immigrants. You'll find imported and domestic products, kitchenware, fresh pastas, cheeses, spices, meats, fruits and vegetables, and dry goods. These days the market has lost some of its charm; food stalls share the already crowded street with vendors selling bootleg CDs, logo T-shirts, and dollar-store bargains, but it's still enjoyable to stroll and to duck into a cheese or spice shop. | 9th St. between Washington Ave. and Christian St. | www.phillyitalianmarket.com | Tues.–Sat. 9–late afternoon, Sun. 9–12:30.

Shops at Liberty Place. This upscale complex at 16th and Chestnut streets features a food court and popular stores including Benetton, Barami, the Coach Store, J. Crew, Speedo Authentic Fitness, the Body Shop, and Country Road Australia. More than 60 stores and restaurants are arranged in two circular levels within a strikingly handsome 90-ft glass-roof atrium. | 1625 Chestnut St. | 215/851–9055.

South Street. For some of the most entertaining people-watching in the city, head to South Street, just south of Society Hill. Hot-pink-haired teens vie for space with moms wheeling strollers on this bustling strip. More than 300 unusual stores—high-fashion clothing, New Age books, music and health food, avant-garde art galleries, and 100 restaurants line the area. Most shops are open in the evening. You'll find a few of the national chains, but 95% of the stores are individually owned, selling things you won't find in the mall back home. | South Street between Front and 9th Streets.

Pennsylvania Dutch Country

Shoppers in Lancaster County can find everything from farmers' markets to several hundred outlet stores. The county's main arteries, U.S. 30 and Route 340, are lined with gift shops and outlets. Some outlets are factory stores, with top-quality goods at good discounts.

On Sunday antiques hunters frequent the huge antiques malls along Route 272 between Adamstown and Denver. As many as 5,000 dealers may turn up on Extravaganza Days, held in late spring, summer, and early fall. You can spend hours browsing among old books and prints and looking at Victorian clothing, pewter, silver, pottery, and lots of furniture. Or you can stop in a store along a country road to shop for the crafts and handmade quilts for which the area is famous. Galleries, boutiques, roadside stands, and farmers' markets abound, with a temptingly wide variety of merchandise.

★ **Central Market.** Beginning with open-air stalls in 1742, Central Market is where locals shop for fresh fruit and vegetables, meats (try the Lebanon bologna), flowers, and baked goods such as sticky buns and shoofly pie. The current Romanesque building, in the heart of town, was constructed in 1889 and is one of the oldest covered markets in the country. It's a good place to pick up food for a picnic. | Penn Sq. | 717/291–4723 | Tues. and Fri. 6–4:30, Sat. 6–2.

Essential Information

When to Go

Late spring and early fall are the best times to visit. The area can be uncomfortably hot and humid in the summer, with temperatures ranging from 75° to 95°, and freezing cold in winter, when snowfalls average 21 inches and the temperature ranges from 26° to 49°. On summer weekends, you'll find the main tourist attractions crowded with busloads of visitors. In October, visitors flock to Pennsylvania Dutch Country to see the fall foliage. In September and in spring, the atmosphere as well as the climate are comfortable and welcoming, with temperatures ranging from 50° to 76°.

FESTIVALS AND SEASONAL EVENTS

WINTER

Jan.: **Mummers Parade.** This day-long event kicks off the New Year as some 30,000 sequined and feathered paraders—members of string bands, "fancies," comics and fancy brigades—march west on Market Street to City Hall in downtown Philadelphia. | 215/965–7676 or 800/537–7676.

SPRING

Mar.: **Philadelphia Flower Show.** The nation's largest and most prestigious indoor flower show transforms the Philadelphia Convention Center with lush acres of whimsical garden displays. | 215/988–8800.

SUMMER

June: **Elfreth's Alley Fete Days.** This is the time for open houses on America's oldest continuously occupied street, along with food and fife-and-drum music. | 215/574–0560.

July: **Sunoco Welcome America Festival.** Philadelphia's premier event celebrates America's birthday in America's birthplace. Highlights of the more than 80 free happenings are big-name outdoor concerts, fireworks and music in front of the Philadelphia Museum of Art, a patriotic parade on the Parkway, the awarding of the Philadelphia Liberty Medal, a Family Festival, a Summer Mummers Parade, and a costumed reenactment at Ft. Mifflin. | 215/683–2201.

Bastille Day Celebration. The storming of the Bastille is reenacted at the Eastern State Penitentiary, highlighted by an appearance by Marie-Antoinette. | 215/236–3300.

Bargains

CityPass. If you're planning to visit some of Philadelphia's top museums, look into CityPass, which offers 50% savings on admission to five attractions and is valid for nine days. The pass costs $30 and covers the Academy of Natural Sciences, the Franklin Institute Science Museum, the Independence Seaport Museum, the Philadelphia Zoo, and the Philadelphia Trolley Tour. You can buy the pass at any of the attractions; because the passes are tickets, you also avoid any ticket lines. | www.citypass.com.

In Lancaster County, festivals, quilt and farm-equipment auctions, flea markets, and chicken-corn soup or ox-roast suppers are frequently staged to raise money for the volunteer fire company crews and attract large numbers of Amish people. The events offer good, cheap, home-cooked foods and inexpensive entertainment. The Pennsylvania Dutch Convention & Visitors Bureau (☞ Visitor Information) publishes a calendar of these almost weekly events.

Tours

PHILADELPHIA

American Trolley Tours. Tours run every 45 minutes between 9 and 3:45 and take approximately two hours; the cost is $14. American Trolley offers free pickup at major hotels as well as historic sites and the Pennsylvania Convention Center. | 215/333–2119 | www.americantrolleytours.com.

Centipede Tours. Walking tours of Independence Park are led by guides in Colonial dress. Tours of the city's ethnic heritage and of its circles and squares are also available. | 215/735–3123 | www.centipedeinc.com.

LANCASTER COUNTY

Amish Country Tours. The most popular tour is the two-hour Amish farmlands trip, with stops at a farmhouse, a wine tasting, and shopping for crafts; tours to Hershey are available on Tuesday. | Rte. 340 at Plain & Fancy Farm, between Bird-in-Hand and Intercourse | 717/768–3600 or 800/441–3505.

Mennonite Information Center. Local Mennonite guides join you in your car to teach you about their religion and customs as they guide you down country roads. | 2209 Millstream Rd., Lancaster | 717/299–0954 | www.mennoniteinfoctr.com.

Visitor Information

Greater Philadelphia Tourism Marketing Corporation | 215/599–0776 or 888/467–4452 | www.gophila.com. **Independence Visitor Center** | 6th St. between Market and Arch Sts. | 215/925–6101 | www.independencevisitorcenter.com. **Pennsylvania Office of Travel and Tourism** | 717/787–5453; 800/847–4872 for brochures | www.experiencepa.com.

Pennsylvania Dutch Convention & Visitors Bureau | 501 Greenfield Rd., Lancaster 17601 | 717/299–8901 or 800/735–2629 | www.padutchcountry.com.

Arriving and Departing

BY AIR

Airports

Philadelphia International Airport (PHL). The airport is 8 mi from downtown, in the southwestern part of the city. | 215/937–6800 for operator and lost and found; 800/745–4283 for arrival and departure times and gate assignments | www.phl.org.

Airport Transportation to Philadelphia

Bus: Shuttle buses cost $10 and up per person and will make most requested stops downtown as well as to the suburbs. You can make shuttle arrangements at the centralized ground transportation counter in the baggage claim areas.

Car: Allow at least a half hour, more during rush hour, for the 8-mi trip between the airport and Center City. By car the airport is accessible via I–95 south or I–76 east.

Public Transit: SEPTA (Southeastern Pennsylvania Transportation Authority). The Airport Rail Line R1 leaves the airport every 30 minutes from 6:10 AM to 12:10 AM. The trip to Center City takes about 20 minutes and costs $5. Trains serve the 30th Street, Suburban (Center City), and Market East stations. | www.septa.com.

Taxi: Taxis at the airport are plentiful but expensive—a flat fee of $20 plus tip. Follow the signs in the airport and wait in line for a taxi.

Getting Around Philadelphia

BY CAR

With the exception of a few wide streets (notably the Benjamin Franklin Parkway, Broad Street, Vine Street, and part of Market Street), streets in Center City are narrow and one-way. Philadelphia's compact 2-square-mi downtown is laid out in a grid. The traditional heart of the city is Broad and Market streets, where City Hall stands. Market Street divides the city north and south; 130 South 15th Street, for example, is in the second block south of Market Street. North–south streets are numbered, starting with Front (1st) Street, at the Delaware River, and increasing to the west. Broad Street, renamed the Avenue of the Arts, is the equivalent of 14th Street. The diagonal Benjamin Franklin Parkway breaks the grid pattern by leading from City Hall out of Center City into Fairmount Park.

Parking

Parking in Center City can be tough. A spot at a parking meter, if you're lucky enough to find one, costs 25¢ per 15 minutes. Parking garages are plentiful, especially around Independence Hall, City Hall, and the Pennsylvania Convention Center, but can charge up to $1.50 per 15 minutes and up to $20 or so for the day. Police officers are vigilant about ticketing illegally parked cars, and fines begin at $25. Fortunately the city is compact, and you can easily get around downtown on foot or by bus after you park your car.

BY PUBLIC TRANSIT

Bus

PHLASH. The distinctive purple minibuses you'll see around Center City are SEPTA's convenience line for visitors, the PHLASH. The 33 stops in the loop run from the Philadelphia Museum of Art on the Benjamin Franklin Parkway through Center City to Penn's Landing. Since a ride on the PHLASH costs $2 for a one-way ticket, consider the handy all-day, unlimited-ride pass available for $4. These buses run daily from 10 AM to midnight in summer, 10 to 6 mid-September to mid-may. There's service every 10 minutes. | 215/474–5274 | www.septa.com.

BY TAXI

Cabs cost $1.80 at the flag throw and then $1.80–$2.30 per mile. They are plentiful during the day downtown—especially along Broad Street and near hotels and train stations. At night and outside Center City, taxis are scarce. Your best bet is to go to a hotel and have the doorman hail a taxi for you. Or, you can call for a cab, but they frequently show up late and occasionally never arrive. Be persistent: calling back if the cab is late will often yield results. The standard tip for cabdrivers is 15% of the total fare.

Olde City Taxi | 215/338–0838. **Quaker City Cab** | 215/728–8000. **Yellow Cab** | 215/922–8400.

Getting Around Lancaster County

A car is the easiest way to explore the many sights in the area; it also lets you get off the main roads and into the countryside. Lancaster County's main arteries are U.S. 30 (also known as the Lincoln Highway) and Route 340 (sometimes called the Old Philadelphia Pike). Some pleasant back roads can be found between Routes 23 and 340. Remember that you must slow down for horse-drawn buggies when you're driving on country roads.

California

Revised and Updated by Rob Aikins

SAN DIEGO

San Diego is a big city with a small-town feel. With more than 1 million people, San Diego is second in population among California cities and encompasses roughly 400 square mi of land and sea. Its most popular attribute may be its 70 mi of beaches, but the inland mountains and deserts offer much to the outdoor enthusiast, including near perfect weather year-round.

The San Diego area, the birthplace of California, was claimed for Spain by explorer Juan Rodríguez Cabrillo in 1542 and eventually came under Mexican rule. You'll find reminders of San Diego's Spanish and Mexican heritage throughout the region—in architecture and place-names, in distinctive Mexican cuisine, and in the historic buildings of Old Town.

The city experienced a major growth boom when the U.S. Navy built a destroyer base in the 1920s. While not as evident as when sailors bar-hopped at waterfront dives, the military's presence can still be felt. Today, the tourist industry has become a major force behind the economy as visitors come to enjoy the natural beauty, the sunny weather and friendly atmosphere.

Although the city has numerous world-class museums and attractions, it is quite possible that you could come and never set foot inside any of them. Instead, many opt to take advantage of nearly every type of outdoor activity available, from surfing to sailing, golf to kayaking or just plain soaking in the sun.

Without question, San Diego is one of the most appealing destinations in the United States and, whether your vacation takes you across the county or no further than the nearest beach towel, you're sure to understand why the locals say they'd never live anywhere else.

Exploring

Balboa Park

Overlooking downtown and the Pacific Ocean, 1,200-acre Balboa Park is the cultural heart of San Diego, where you'll find more than 25 museums and attractions, including the Natural History Museum, Museum of Art, Aerospace Museum, a Miniature Railroad and the San Diego Zoo. Cultivated and wild gardens are an integral part of Balboa Park, thanks to the "Mother of Balboa Park," Kate Sessions, who made sure

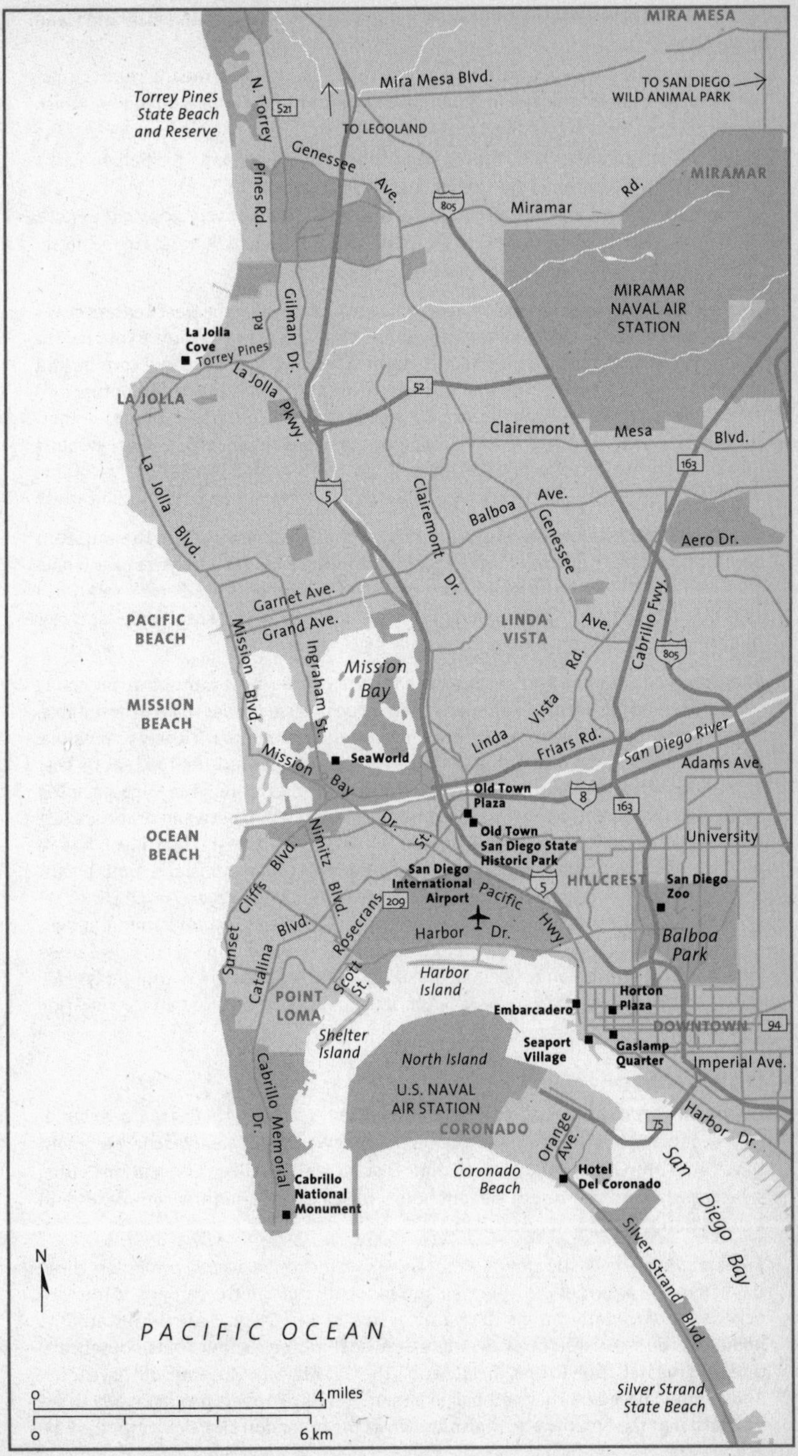

MIRA MESA
Mira Mesa Blvd.
TO SAN DIEGO WILD ANIMAL PARK
Torrey Pines State Beach and Reserve
N. Torrey Pines Rd.
521
TO LEGOLAND
Genessee Ave.
805
Miramar Rd.
MIRAMAR
MIRAMAR NAVAL AIR STATION
Gilman Dr.
La Jolla Cove
Torrey Pines Rd.
La Jolla Pkwy.
52
LA JOLLA
Clairemont Mesa Blvd.
163
La Jolla Blvd.
5
Clairemont Dr.
Balboa Ave.
Genessee Ave.
Aero Dr.
Garnet Ave.
Grand Ave.
PACIFIC BEACH
LINDA VISTA
Cabrillo Fwy.
Mission Blvd.
Ingraham St.
Mission Bay
MISSION BEACH
Linda Vista Rd.
Friars Rd.
San Diego River
Adams Ave.
SeaWorld
Mission Bay Dr.
Old Town Plaza
8
163
OCEAN BEACH
Nimitz Blvd.
Old Town San Diego State Historic Park
University
Sunset Cliffs Blvd.
San Diego International Airport
HILLCREST
San Diego Zoo
209
Pacific Hwy.
Rosecrans St.
Catalina Blvd.
Harbor Dr.
Balboa Park
Harbor Island
Scott St.
POINT LOMA
Embarcadero
Horton Plaza
DOWNTOWN
94
Shelter Island
Seaport Village
Gaslamp Quarter
Imperial Ave.
North Island
U.S. NAVAL AIR STATION
CORONADO
Cabrillo Memorial Dr.
Orange Ave.
75
Harbor Dr.
Hotel Del Coronado
Coronado Beach
San Diego Bay
Cabrillo National Monument
Silver Strand Blvd.
N
PACIFIC OCEAN
0
4 miles
0
6 km
Silver Strand State Beach

the park was planted with thousands of palms, purple-blossoming jacaranda, and other trees.

Many of the park's Spanish colonial revival buildings were meant to be temporary exhibit halls for the Panama-California International Exposition of 1915, which celebrated the opening of the Panama Canal. Fortunately, city leaders realized the value of the buildings and incorporated them into their plans for Balboa Park's acreage, which had been set aside by the city founders in 1868.

Parking is abundant and free, although you may not find a spot very close to the Prado, where the majority of the museums are. Free trams run from parking lots to the museums approximately every 10 minutes, 9:30–5:30 daily.

Reuben H. Fleet Science Center. Children and adults alike enjoy the Fleet Center's clever interactive exhibits, which are sneakily educational. You can reconfigure your face to have two left sides, or, by replaying an instant video clip, watch yourself coming and going at different speeds. The IMAX Dome Theater screens exhilarating nature and science films. The SciTours simulator is designed to take you on virtual voyages—stomach lurches and all. | 1875 El Prado | 619/238–1233 | www.rhfleet.org | Gallery exhibits $6.75; Gallery exhibits and one IMAX film $11.50; Gallery exhibits and two IMAX films $15 | Mon.–Thurs. 9:30–5, Fri.–Sat. 9:30–8, Sun. 9:30–6 (hrs vary seasonally; call ahead).

San Diego Natural History Museum. After a multiyear renovation, the museum includes numerous interactive displays for all ages, including a full-size gray whale skeleton and the Foucault pendulum, designed to demonstrate Earth's rotation. | 1788 El Prado | 619/232–3821 | www.sdnhm.org | Exhibits $5–$7 | Early Sept.–late May, daily 9:30–4:30; late May–early Sept., daily 9:30–5:30.

San Diego Zoo. Balboa Park's—and perhaps the city's—most famous attraction is its 100-acre zoo. Nearly 4,000 animals of some 800 diverse species roam in hospitable, expertly crafted habitats that replicate natural environments as closely as possible. Open-air trams can whisk you around 85% of the exhibits, but the zoo is at its best when you wander the paths, such as the one that climbs through the huge, enclosed Scripps Aviary, where brightly colored tropical birds swoop between branches just inches from your face. The zoo's simulated Asian rain forest, Tiger River, has 10 exhibits with more than 35 species of animals; tigers, Malayan tapirs, and Argus pheasants wander among the collection of exotic trees and plants. | 2920 Zoo Dr. | 619/231–1515 | www.sandiegozoo.org | $19.50 includes zoo, Children's Zoo, and animal shows; $32 includes above, plus 40-min guided bus tour and round-trip Skyfari ride; $46.80 pass good for admission to zoo and San Diego Wild Animal Park within 5 days | AE, D, MC, V | May–Sept., daily 9–9; Oct.–Apr., daily 9–4; Children's Zoo and Skyfari ride close earlier.

Downtown

Downtown's revival started in the late 1970s when restoration of its rundown buildings began and the Horton Plaza shopping center was built. Massive redevelopment gave rise to the Gaslamp Quarter Historic District and San Diego Convention Center, which spurred an upsurge of elegant hotels, upscale condominium complexes, and swank, trendy cafés and restaurants.

Embarcadero. The bustle along Harbor Drive's waterfront walkway comes less these days from the activities of fishermen and sailors than from the throngs of tourists, yet the Embarcadero retains the nautical soul of San Diego. Seafood restaurants abound, as do sea vessels of every variety—cruise ships, ferries, tour boats, houseboats, and naval vessels. Due to open in late 2003, the USS *Midway* Museum will have tours and exhibits based on the mothballed behemoth. Day-trippers getting ready to set sail gather at the Broadway Pier, also known as the excursion pier. Tickets for the harbor tours and whale-watching trips are sold here. The terminal for the Coronado Ferry lies just beyond the Broadway pier.

Gaslamp Quarter. The 16-block national historic district between 4th and 6th avenues from Broadway to K Street contains most of San Diego's Victorian-style commercial buildings from the late 1800s, when Market Street was the center of early downtown. The commercial district moved west toward Broadway at the turn of the 20th century, however, and the neighborhood went into decline. Known as the Stingaree district, it was infamous as a seedy port of call for bar-hopping sailors.

History buffs, developers, architects, and artists formed the Gaslamp Quarter Council in 1974. Bent on preserving the district, they gathered funds from various sources and began cleaning up the quarter, restoring significant buildings, and attracting businesses and the public back to the heart of New Town. Their efforts paid off, as the area is now a major destination for tourism.

For additional information about the historic area, call the **Gaslamp Quarter Association** | 619/233–5227 | www.gaslamp.org.

Seaport Village. On a prime stretch of waterfront, the village's three bustling shopping plazas are designed to reflect the architectural styles of early California, especially New England clapboard and Spanish mission. A 1/4-mi wooden boardwalk that runs along the bay and 4 mi of paths lead to specialty shops, snack bars, and restaurants. Seaport Village's shops are open daily 10–9 (10–10 in summer). I. D. Looff crafted the hand-carved, hand-painted steeds on the Broadway Flying Horses Carousel. Strolling clowns, balloon sculptors, mimes, musicians, and magicians are also on hand throughout the village to entertain visitors. | 619/235–4014; 619/235–4013 for events hot line | www.spvillage.com.

Coronado

Although it's actually an isthmus, reached from the mainland via Imperial Beach, Coronado has always seemed like an island—and is often referred to as such. The streets are wide, quiet, and friendly, with lots of neighborhood parks and grand Victorian homes.

Coronado is visible from downtown and Point Loma and accessible via the San Diego–Coronado Bridge. San Diego's Metropolitan Transit System runs a shuttle bus, No. 904, around the island; you can pick it up where you disembark the ferry and ride it out as far as the Silver Strand State Beach. Buses start leaving from the ferry landing at 10:30 AM and run once an hour on the half hour until 6:30 PM.

San Diego Harbor Excursion. You can board the ferry at downtown San Diego's Embarcadero near the Broadway pier. You'll arrive at the Ferry Landing Marketplace. Boats depart every hour on the hour from the Embarcadero and every hour on the half hour from Coronado, Sunday through Thursday 9–9, Friday and Saturday until 10; the fare is $2 each way, 50¢ extra for bicycles. | 619/234–4111.

Hotel Del Coronado. Since its opening in 1888, the "Del" has had a colorful history, integrally connected with that of Coronado itself. The Del's distinctive red-tile peaks and Victorian gingerbread architecture have served as a set for many movies, political meetings, and extravagant social happenings. Fourteen presidents have been guests of the Del, and it is one of San Diego's most prominent landmarks. | 1500 Orange Ave., Coronado | 619/435–6611 | www.hoteldel.com.

Orange Avenue. It's easy to imagine you're on a street in Cape Cod when you stroll along this thoroughfare, Coronado's version of a downtown: the clapboard houses, small restaurants, and boutiques are in some ways more characteristic of New England than of California.

Harbor Island, Point Loma, and Shelter Island

Point Loma protects the center city from the Pacific's tides and waves. It's shared by military installations, funky motels and fast-food shacks, stately family homes, and private marinas packed with sailboats and yachts. Newer to the scene, Harbor and Shelter islands were created out of sand dredged from San Diego Bay in the 1960s. They've become tourist hubs, their high-rise hotels, seafood restaurants, and boat-rental centers looking as solid as those anywhere else in the city.

Cabrillo National Monument. This 144-acre preserve marks the site of the first European visit to San Diego, made by 16th-century explorer Juan Rodríguez Cabrillo (circa 1498–1543). Cabrillo came to this spot in 1542. Government grounds were set aside to commemorate his discovery in 1913, and today the site is one of the most frequently visited of all the national monuments. The entrance pass allows unlimited admissions for one week from date of purchase. | 1800 Cabrillo Memorial Dr. | 619/557–5450 | www.nps.gov/cabr | $5 per car, $3 per person entering on foot or by bicycle | Daily 9–5:15 (call for later summer hrs, which vary).

The **visitor center** presents films and lectures about Cabrillo's voyage, the sea-level tide pools, and migrating gray whales.

The moderately steep 2-mi **Bayside Trail** winds through coastal sage scrub, curving under the cliff-top lookouts and bringing you ever closer to the bay-front scenery, but there is no beach access. The climb back is long but gradual, leading up to the **Old Point Loma Lighthouse.**

Sea creatures abound in the **tide pools** at the foot of the monument's western cliffs. Drive north from the visitor center to the first road on the left, which winds down to the coast guard station and the shore.

Scott Street. Running along Point Loma's waterfront from Shelter Island to the old Naval Training Center on Harbor Drive, this thoroughfare is lined with deep-sea fishing charters and whale-watching boats. It's a good spot from which to watch fisherfolk haul marlin, tuna, and mackerel off their boats or to enjoy fresh seafood in a café.

Mission Bay and the Beaches

The 4,600-acre Mission Bay aquatic park is San Diego's monument to sports and fitness. Admission to its 27 mi of bay-shore beaches and 17 mi of ocean frontage is free.

★ **SeaWorld of California.** One of the world's largest marine-life amusement parks, SeaWorld is spread over 100 bay-front acres. The majority of the exhibits are walk-through marine environments. Various freshwater and saltwater aquariums hold underwater creatures from around the world. Shipwreck Rapids, the park's first adventure ride, offers plenty of excitement—but you may end up getting soaked.

SeaWorld's highlights are its large-arena entertainments. You can arrive 10 or 15 minutes in advance to get front-row seats, and the stadiums are large enough for everyone to get a seat even at the busiest times. The traditional favorite is the Shamu show, with synchronized killer whales bringing down the house; the new Pets Rule! stars household pets, many of which were rescued from shelters, performing all sorts of amazing feats and hijinks.

Since it's hard to come away from here without spending a lot of money on top of the hefty entrance fee and parking tab, consider the two-day entry option, only $4 more than a single-day admission. | 1720 South Shores Rd., near west end of I–8 | 619/226–3815; 619/226–3901 for recorded information | www.seaworld.com | $42.95, 2-day package $46.95; parking $7 | AE, D, MC, V | Daily 10–dusk; extended hrs in summer.

Old Town

San Diego's Spanish and Mexican history and heritage are most evident in Old Town, north of downtown at Juan Street, near the intersection of Interstates 5 and 8. Old Town is the first European settlement in southern California, but the pueblo's true beginnings took place overlooking Old Town from atop Presidio Park, where Father Junípero Serra established the first of California's missions, San Diego de Alcalá, in 1769. On San Diego Avenue, the district's main drag, art galleries and expensive gift shops are interspersed with tacky curio shops, restaurants, and open-air stands selling inexpensive Mexican pottery, jewelry, and blankets.

★ **Old Town San Diego State Historic Park.** The six square blocks on the site of San Diego's original pueblo are the heart of Old Town. Most of the 20 historic buildings preserved or re-created by the park cluster around Old Town Plaza. San Diego Avenue is closed to vehicle traffic here. Worth exploring in the plaza area are the Casa de Bandini, Seeley Stable, Casa de Estudillo, Wells Fargo Museum, and the San Diego Courthouse. | www.parks.ca.gov.

The **Robinson-Rose House** was the original commercial center of old San Diego, housing railroad offices, law offices, and the first newspaper press. In addition to serving as the park's visitor center and administrative center, it now hosts a model of Old Town as it looked in 1872, as well as various historic exhibits. | 619/220–5422.

La Jolla

La Jolla means "The Jewel" in Spanish, and for good reason. The most scenic miles of San Diego's coastline curve into natural coves backed by verdant hillsides covered with homes worth millions.

To reach La Jolla from I–5, if you're traveling north, take the La Jolla Parkway exit, which veers into Torrey Pines Road, and turn right onto Prospect Street. If you're heading south, get off at the La Jolla Village Drive exit, which will also leads into Torrey Pines Road. Traffic is virtually always congested in this popular area.Prospect Street and Girard Avenue, the village's main drags, are lined with expensive shops and cafés.

La Jolla Caves. It's a walk down 145 sometimes slippery steps to Sunny Jim Cave, the largest of the grottoes in La Jolla Cove. The cave entrance is through the Cave Store, a throwback to the 1902 shop that served as the underground portal. | 1325 Cave St. | 858/459–0746 | $2 | Daily 9–dark.

La Jolla Cove. The wooded spread that looks out over a shimmering blue inlet is what first attracted everyone to La Jolla, from Native Americans to the glitterati; it is the village's enduring cachet. You'll find the cove beyond where Girard Avenue dead-ends into Coast Boulevard, marked by towering palms that line a promenade. An underwater preserve at the north end of La Jolla Cove makes the adjoining beach the most popular one in the area.

The **Children's Pool,** at the south end of the park, has a curving beach protected by a seawall from strong currents and waves. Due to a large population of seals, it's not open to swimmers, but it's the best place on the coast to view these engaging creatures.

Walk through **Ellen Browning Scripps Park,** past the groves of twisted junipers to the cliff's edge. You can spread your picnic out on a table at one of the open-air shelters and enjoy the scenery.

North County

A visit to Legoland will take you to Carlsbad, a laid-back beach town with great views, beaches, and shopping. Trek inland through the backcountry to reach the San Diego Wild Animal Park, where you can ride a safari tram through wide-open environments where animals roam free.

★ **Legoland California.** This is a full day of entertainment for pint-size fun-seekers and their parents. The experience is best appreciated by kids ages 2 to 10, who often beg to ride the mechanical horses around the Royal Joust again and again, or take just one more turn through the popular Driving School. Miniland, an animated collection of cities constructed entirely of Lego blocks, captures the imaginations of kids and adults. Other attractions include a castle and pint-size Dragon and Spellbound roller coasters. Kids can climb on and over, operate, manipulate, and explore displays and attractions constructed out of plastic blocks. Stage shows and restaurants with kid-friendly buffets are also part of the mix. | 1 Lego Dr. (exit I–5 at Cannon Rd. and follow signs east 1/4 mi), Carlsbad | 760/918–5346 | www.legolandca.com | $39 | Early Sept.–mid-June, daily 10–5; mid-June–early Sept., daily 9–9.

★ **San Diego Wild Animal Park.** An extension of the San Diego Zoo, this 1,800-acre preserve is designed to protect endangered species of animals from around the world. Exhibits have been carved out of the landscape to represent the animal's natural habitats, including African plains, Australian rain forest, and Asian swamps. The 50-minute Wgasa Bushline Railway is included in the price of admission and will take you on a narrated tour of all the environments. The park also has a number of trails to walk and several entertainingly educational shows. | 15550 San Pasqual Valley Rd., Escondido | 760/747–8702 | www.sandiegozoo.org/wap | $25.95 | Mid-June–early Sept., daily 9–8; early Sept.–mid-June, daily 9–4.

Dining

Downtown

★ **Fish Market.** Seafood. Fresh mesquite-grilled fish is the specialty at this informal restaurant. There's also an excellent little sushi bar and good steamed clams and mussels. The view is stunning: enormous plate-glass windows look directly out onto the harbor. | 750 N. Harbor Dr. | 619/232–3474 | Reservations not accepted | $13–$30 | AE, D, DC, MC, V.

Sammy's Woodfired Pizza. Pizza. Pies may be topped with spicy, Jamaican-style shrimp; lamb sausage with wild mushrooms; and a surprisingly savory team of grilled zucchini and eggplant. The menu offers pastas, meats, and fish as well. | 770 4th Ave. | 619/230–8888 | $9–$18 | AE, MC, V.

The Tin Fish. Seafood. Since all the seating is outdoors, on rare rainy days the staff takes it easy at this eatery across the trolley tracks from the San Diego Convention Center. This is a good spot for grilled and fried fish and shellfish, as well as Mexican-style seafood burritos and tacos. The quality here routinely surpasses that at grander establishments. | 170 6th Ave. | 619/238–8100 | $3–$14 | Reservations not accepted | MC, V.

Uptown

★ **Corvette Diner Bar & Grill.** American/Casual. The absolute San Diego County favorite for children's parties and other family occasions, Corvette Diner features a real Corvette in a kitschy, 1950s-style dining room dominated by vintage movie posters and singing servers. The menu has what you'd expect—macaroni and cheddar, plump burgers, piled-high deli sandwiches, greasy chili-cheese fries, and thick milk shakes. | 3946 5th Ave. | 619/542–1001 | $4–$10 | AE, D, MC, V.

Coronado

Bistro d'Asia. Contemporary. As at a French bistro, the mood is relaxed and the portions generous. The menu overall takes a Chinese point of view but spans the cuisines of East Asia, so that traditional Chinese offerings like the "Buddha's Delight" vegetables and crispy Cantonese panfried noodles are supplemented by spicy, Bangkok-style beef, and a Vietnamese-influenced version of kung pao chicken. | 1301 Orange Ave. | 619/437–6677 | $8–$27 | MC, V.

Harbor Island, Point Loma, and Shelter Island

Hudson Bay Seafood. Seafood. Part of the pleasure in this small, friendly, waterside fish house is watching the day-charter boats arrive at the adjacent dock. The greater pleasure is the food. The restaurant bakes the sourdough rolls in which it sandwiches delicately fried fish fillets or shellfish. The french fries are freshly cut, the fish tacos taste of Mexico, and even the tartar sauce is homemade. | 1403 Scott St. | 619/222–8787 | $6–$11 | MC, V.

Mission Bay and the Beaches

★ **Caffe Bella Italia.** Italian. Contemporary Italian cooking as prepared in Italy is the rule at this simple restaurant. The menu presents Neapolitan-style macaroni with sausage and artichoke hearts in spicy tomato sauce and formal entrées like slices of rare filet mignon tossed with herbs, then topped with arugula and shavings of Parmesan cheese. | 1525 Garnet Ave. | 858/273–1224 | Closed Mon. | $9–$19 | MC, V.

Mission Valley

Ricky's Family Restaurant. American/Casual. Chain feederies haven't driven out San Diego's old-line family restaurants, and this unpretentious place remains dear to the city's heart. This three-meals-daily restaurant serves big portions of unassuming, well-prepared, all-American cooking but is famed for its breakfasts, when savory corned-beef hash and fluffy, strawberry-crowned Belgian waffles are the rule. | 2181 Hotel Circle S | 619/291–4498 | $7–$13 | MC, V.

Old Town

Berta's Latin American Restaurant. Latin. A San Diego rarity—and a surprise in a section of town where the food leans toward the safe and touristy—Berta's serves wonderful Latin American dishes. The wine list showcases good Chilean wines, and the food manages to be tasty and health-conscious at the same time. | 3928 Twiggs St. | 619/295–2343 | $10–$16 | AE, MC, V.

★ **Saffron Noodles and Sate.** Thai. Despite the minimal decor, the comfortable outdoor tables and friendly prices make an attractive package. The simple menu suggests spicy or mild noodle soups; stir-fried noodles with chicken, beef, pork, or turkey; a couple of uncommon Vietnamese and Thai-Indian noodle dishes bathed with aromatic sauces; and grilled sate skewers of chicken, beef, and pork. | 3737 India St. | 619/574–7737 | $6–$9 | MC, V.

La Jolla

Alfonso's of La Jolla. Mexican. Grab a seat on the sidewalk terrace, where you can review the passing parade while munching sizable plates laden with *carne asada*. This marinated, grilled steak is a house specialty and arrives both garnished *tampiqueña*-style with a cheese enchilada, rice, and beans; or chopped as a filling for tacos and quesadillas. The menu extends to typical enchiladas and burritos. | 1251 Prospect St. | 858/454–2232 | $9–$19 | AE, MC, V.

Lodging

San Diego is spread out, so the first thing to consider when selecting lodging is location. Rooms close to the ocean tend to be more expensive. If you plan to sightsee, take into account a hotel's proximity to attractions. High season is summer, and rates are lowest in the fall.

Downtown

Comfort Inn. This three-story stucco property surrounds a parking lot and courtyard. There's nothing fancy about the accommodations, but some rooms on the south side of the hotel have good views of the city skyline. It's close to downtown hot spots and Balboa Park. In-room data ports, microwave, cable TV with movies, hot tub, car rental, business services, airport shuttle, free parking; no smoking. | 719 Ash St., 92101 | 619/232–2525 or 800/404–6835 | fax 619/687–3024 | 45 rooms | $79–$95 | AE, D, DC, MC, V.

★ **Gaslamp Plaza Suites.** On the National Registry of Historic Places, this 11-story structure a block from Horton Plaza was built in 1913 as one of San Diego's first "skyscrapers." Appealing public areas have old marble, brass, and mosaics. Although most rooms are rather small, they are well decorated with dark-wood furnishings that give the hotel an elegant flair. Restaurant, microwaves, refrigerators, cable TV, hot tub, bar, nightclub, parking (fee); no a/c | 520 E St., 92101 | 619/232–9500 or 800/874–8770 | fax 619/238–9945 | 52 suites | $89–$199 | AE, D, DC, MC, V.

Coronado

★ **Crown City Inn & Bistro.** On Coronado's main drag, the Crown City Inn is close to shops, restaurants, and the beach. For the price, it's easily one of the best deals on the island. A public park is across the street. Restaurant, room service, in-room data ports, minibars, microwaves, refrigerators, cable TV with movies, pool, bicycles, laundry facilities, parking (fee); no smoking | 520 Orange Ave., 92118 | 619/435–3116 or 800/422–1173 | fax 619/435–6750 | 33 rooms | $119–$200 | AE, D, DC, MC, V.

Harbor Island, Point Loma, and Shelter Island

Point Loma Travelodge. You'll get the same view here as at the higher-price hotels—for far less money. Of course, there are fewer amenities and the neighborhood isn't as serene, but the rooms—all with coffeemakers—are adequate and clean. In-room data ports, cable TV, pool, free parking; no smoking. | 5102 N. Harbor Dr., 92106 | 619/223–8171 or 800/578–7878 | fax 619/222–7330 | 45 rooms | $72–$95 | AE, D, DC, MC, V.

Ramada Limited San Diego Airport. The location is convenient, although on a busy street, and the rooms with bay views are quite a deal. Continental breakfast, daily newspaper, and local calls are complimentary. There is a heated pool and a bay-view bar with billiards, and there's a free shuttle to area attractions. Restaurant, dining room, cable TV, pool, bar, meeting rooms, airport shuttle, free parking, some pets allowed (fee); no smoking | 1403 Rosecrans St., 92106 | 619/225–9461 or 888/298–2054 | fax 619/225–1163 | 83 rooms | $96–$107 | AE, D, DC, MC, V.

Vagabond Inn–Point Loma. This two-story budget motel is safe, clean, and comfortable, close to the airport, yacht clubs, and Cabrillo National Monument. A daily newspaper and Continental breakfast are included. Restaurant, in-room safes, some kitchens, some refrigerators, cable TV with movies, pool, bar, airport shuttle, free parking; no smoking | 1325 Scott St., 92106 | 619/224–3371 | fax 619/223–0646 | 40 rooms | $78–$95 | AE, D, DC, MC, V.

Mission Bay and the Beaches

Pacific Shores Inn. One of the better motels in the Mission Bay area, this property is less than a half block from the beach. Rooms, some of them spacious, are decorated in a simple contemporary style. Kitchen units with multiple beds are available at reasonable rates. Continental breakfast is included. Kitchenettes, refrigerators, cable TV with movies, pool, laundry service, free parking, some pets allowed (fee); no smoking. | 4802 Mission Blvd., 92109 | 858/483–6300 or 800/826–0715 | fax 858/483–9276 | 55 rooms | $83–$139 | AE, D, DC, MC, V.

Surfer Motor Lodge. This four-story building is right on the beach and directly behind a shopping center with restaurants and boutiques. Rooms are plain, but those on the upper floors have good views. Restaurant, kitchenettes, cable TV, pool, beach, bicycles, laundry service, free parking; no smoking | 711 Pacific Beach Dr., 92109 | 858/483–7070 or 800/787–3373 | fax 858/274–1670 | 52 rooms | $87–$122 | AE, DC, MC, V.

Mission Valley

Days Inn–Hotel Circle. Rooms in this large complex are par for a chain motel but some extras like irons and ironing boards; some units have kitchenettes. Airport, Amtrak, zoo, and SeaWorld shuttles are provided. Restaurant, minibars, refrigerators, cable TV with movies and video games, pool, hair salon, outdoor hot tub, shops, laundry service, meeting rooms, airport shuttle, free parking; no smoking | 543 Hotel Circle S, 92108 | 619/297–8800 or 800/329–7466 | fax 619/298–6029 | 280 rooms | $109–$149 | AE, D, DC, MC, V.

Old Town

Western Inn–Old Town. The three-story Western Inn is decorated in a Spanish motif and is close to shops and restaurants but far enough away from the main tourist drag that you don't have to worry about noise and congestion. There is free Continental breakfast and a barbecue area where you can cook for yourself. A bus, trolley, and Coaster station is a few blocks away. In-room data ports, cable TV, refrigerators, airport shuttle, free parking; no smoking | 3889 Arista St., 92110 | 619/298–6888 or 888/475–2353 | fax 619/692–4497 | 29 rooms, 6 suites | $79–$109 | AE, D, DC, MC, V.

La Jolla

★ **La Jolla Inn.** One block from the beach and near some of the best shops and restaurants, this European-style inn with a delightful staff sits in a prime spot in La Jolla Village. Many rooms (some with kitchenettes) have sweeping ocean views from their balconies; one spectacular penthouse suite faces the ocean, another the village. An upstairs sundeck is a great spot to enjoy the delicious complimentary Continental breakfast. Room service, in-room data ports, kitchenettes, some refrigerators, cable TV with movies, library, shop, dry cleaning, laundry facilities, concierge, business services, free parking; no smoking | 1110 Prospect St., 92037 | 858/454–0133 or 800/433–1609 | fax 858/454–2056 | 21 rooms, 2 suites | $149–$199 | AE, D, DC, MC, V.

Arts and Entertainment

California Ballet Company. High-quality contemporary and traditional works—from story ballets to Balanchine—are performed September–May. | 858/560–6741.

★ **The Globe Theatres.** The oldest professional theater in California performs classics, contemporary dramas, and experimental works. It produces the famous summer Shakespeare Festival at the Old Globe and its sister theaters, the Cassius Carter Centre Stage and the Lowell Davies Festival Theatre. | Simon Edison Centre for the Performing Arts, 1363 Old Globe Way | 619/239–2255.

San Diego Symphony Orchestra. Year-round special events include classics, and summer and winter pops. Concerts are held at Copley Symphony Hall, except the Summer Pops series at the Navy Pier, on North Harbor Drive downtown. | 750 B St. | 619/235–0804.

Shopping

Downtown

Shoppers can enjoy the quaint Seaport Village, with its unique shops, or head to the art galleries and boutiques of the Gaslamp Quarter along 4th and 5th avenues. For a more traditional shopping center, there is always Horton Plaza, the centerpiece of the refurbished downtown and a destination in its own right.

Seaport Village. The waterfront complex includes 75 unique shops and restaurants. Aside from the shops, there are horse and carriage rides, an 1890 Looff carousel, and usually some form of public entertainment. | W. Harbor Dr. at Kettner Blvd. | 619/235–4014.

Westfield Shoppingtown Horton Plaza. This multilevel, open-air shopping, dining, and entertainment complex has department stores, fast-food counters, upscale restaurants, the Lyceum Theater, cinemas, and 140 other stores. Stop by the San Diego City Store to buy a real street sign or other one-of-a-kind souvenir. | 619/238–1596.

Coronado

Unique shops line Orange Avenue, and there's also the Ferry Landing.

Ferry Landing Marketplace. There are 30 shops, plus a Tuesday-afternoon farmers' market. | 1201 1st St., at B Ave.

Old Town

The colorful Old Town historic district recalls a Mexican marketplace. Adobe architecture, flower-filled plazas, fountains, and courtyards decorate the Bazaar del Mundo and Old Town Esplanade, where you'll find international goods, toys, souvenirs, and arts and crafts.

Bazaar del Mundo. Boutiques sell designer items, crafts, fine arts, and fashions from around the world. The best time to visit is during the annual Santa Fe Market in March, when you can browse through collections of jewelry, replica artifacts, wearable-art clothing, pottery, and blankets—all crafted by southwestern artists. | 2754 Calhoun St. | 619/296–3161.

Mission Valley

The Mission Valley–Hotel Circle area, northeast of downtown near I–8 and Route 163, has a few major shopping centers.

Fashion Valley Center. San Diego's upscale shopping mall has lush landscaping, a contemporary Mission theme, and more than 200 shops and restaurants. There's a San Diego Trolley station in the parking lot. The major department stores are Macy's, Nordstrom, Saks Fifth Avenue, Neiman Marcus, and Robinsons-May. | 7007 Friars Rd.

Mission Bay and Beaches

Pacific Beach along Garnet Street offers trendy shops catering to a college age and younger crowd. Mission Beach along Mission Avenue near the roller coaster caters to the beach-going set. For a unique souvenir stop by one of dozens of small, local surf shops. Every beach community in San Diego has a few that sell equipment, apparel and the like, reflecting San Diego's role as a surf capitol. A good example is South Coast Surf Shop on Newport Ave. in Ocean Beach.

Ocean Beach Farmer's Market. Every Wednesday from 4–7 PM, Ocean Beach closes off a long block of its main drag, Newport Ave., so that local farmers, ranchers and flower growers can hawk their products. Walk around and try samples of produce that was picked fresh that same morning. | 4900 block of Newport Ave.

La Jolla

This seaside village has chic boutiques, art galleries, and gift shops lining narrow, twisty streets. One could spend the day shopping without leaving the village.

Westfield Shoppingtown UTC. There are 155 shops, several department stores, a cinema, 25 eateries, and an ice-skating rink. | La Jolla Village Dr., between I–5 and I–805 | 858/546–8858.

Sports and Outdoor Activities

Beaches

The beaches below are listed from south to north.

★ **Coronado Beach.** With the famous Hotel Del Coronado as a backdrop, this stretch of sandy beach is one of San Diego County's largest and most picturesque. It's perfect for sunbathing, people-watching, or playing Frisbee. | From the bridge, turn left on Orange Ave. and follow signs.

Mission Beach. San Diego's most popular beach draws huge crowds on hot summer days. The 2-mi-long stretch extends from the north entrance of Mission Bay to Pacific Beach. The boardwalk is popular with walkers, runners, skaters, and bicyclists. Surfers, swimmers, and volleyball players congregate at the south end. Toward the north end, the beach narrows and the water becomes rougher. The crowds grow thicker and somewhat rougher as well. | Exit I–5 at Garnet Ave. and head west to Mission Blvd. Turn south and look for parking.

★ **La Jolla Cove.** This is one of the prettiest spots in the world. A palm-lined park sits on top of cliffs formed by the incessant pounding of the waves. At low tide the tide pools and cliff caves provide a destination for explorers. Divers and snorkelers can explore the underwater delights of the San Diego–La Jolla Underwater Ecological Reserve. | Follow Coast Blvd. north to signs, or take the La Jolla Village Dr. exit from I–5, head west to Torrey Pines Rd., turn left, and drive downhill to Girard Ave. Turn right and follow signs.

La Jolla Shores. On summer holidays all access routes are usually closed to this popular beach. The lures here are a wide, sandy beach and the most gentle waves in San Diego. A concrete boardwalk parallels the beach. Arrive early to get a parking spot in the lot at the foot of Calle Frescota. | From I–5 take La Jolla Village Dr. west and turn left onto La Jolla Shores Dr. Head west to Camino del Oro or Vallecitos St. Turn right.

Bicycling

On any given summer day Route S21 from La Jolla to Oceanside looks like a freeway for cyclists. Never straying more than a quarter-mile from the beach, it is easily the most popular and scenic bike route around. Those seeking a more leisurely bike adventure should head to the bike paths of Mission Beach or Mission Bay, which are made for cruising.

Mission Beach Club. This shop is right on the boardwalk and rents bikes, skates, and boards of all types. | 704 Ventura Pl. | 858/488–5050.

Boating, Jet-skiing, and Waterskiing

Most bay-side resorts rent equipment for on-the-water adventures.

Bahia Resort Hotel. Boats, kayaks, and equipment are available for rent. | 998 W. Mission Bay Dr. | 858/539–7696.

Coronado Boat Rentals. Coronado has kayaks, Jet Skis, fishing skiffs, and power boats from 15 ft to 19 ft in length as well as sailboats from 18 ft to 36 ft. | 1715 Strand Way | 619/437–1514.

Diving

Enthusiasts the world over come to San Diego to snorkel and scuba-dive off La Jolla and Point Loma. The San Diego–La Jolla Underwater Ecological Park is found at La Jolla Cove. The HMCS *Yukon,* a decommissioned Canadian warship, was intentionally sunk off of Mission Beach. Beware and exercise caution: even experienced divers have become disoriented inside the wreck, which landed upside down.

Diving Locker. San Diego's longest-running dive shop has been a fixture since 1959. | 1020 Grand Ave. | 858/272–1120.

Fishing

The Pacific Ocean is full of corbina, croaker, and halibut. No license is required to fish from a public pier, such as the Ocean Beach and Oceanside piers.

Department of Fish and Game. A fishing license, available at most bait-and-tackle and sporting-goods stores, is required for fishing from the shoreline. | 4949 Viewridge Ave., San Diego 92123 | 858/467–4201.

Fisherman's Landing. A fleet of luxury vessels from 57 ft to 124 ft long offers long-range multiday trips in search of yellowfin tuna, yellowtail, and other deep-water fish. | 2838 Garrison St. | 619/221–8500.

H&M Landing. Fishing trips are scheduled December through March. | 2803 Emerson St. | 619/222–1144.

Golf

Balboa Park Municipal Golf Course. The Balboa Park location makes it convenient for downtown visitors. Greens fees are $33–$38. | 2600 Golf Course Dr. | 858/570–1234.

Coronado Municipal Golf Course. There are 18 holes and views of San Diego Bay and the Coronado Bridge from the back 9 holes. Greens fees are $20–$34. | 2000 Visalia Row, Coronado | 619/435–3121.

Torrey Pines Municipal Golf Course With 36 holes, this is one of the best public golf courses in the United States. There are views of the Pacific from every hole, and it's sufficiently challenging to host the Buick Invitational in February. Greens fees are $65–$105. | 11480 N. Torrey Pines Rd. | 800/985–4653.

Hiking

Guided hikes are conducted regularly through Los Peñasquitos Canyon Preserve and the Torrey Pines State Beach and Reserve.

Mission Trails Regional Parks. Nearly 6,000 acres of mountains, wooded hillsides, lakes, and riparian streams are only 8 mi northeast of downtown. Trails range from easy to difficult. | 1 Father Junípero Serra Tr. | 619/668–3275 | www.mtrp.org.

In-line Skating

The sidewalks at Mission Bay are perfect for roller-blading and skating.

Mission Beach Club. Skates and everything else a beachgoer could need are available for rent here. | 704 Ventura Pl. | 858/488–5050.

Surfing

If you're a beginner, consider paddling in the waves off Mission Beach, Pacific Beach, or La Jolla Shores. More experienced surfers usually head for Sunset Cliffs, the La Jolla reef breaks, or Black's Beach. Many local surf shops rent both surf- and bodyboards and will provide information on qualified surf instruction.

La Jolla Surf Systems. This is your first stop if you want to surf the reefs or beachbreaks of La Jolla. | 2132 Avenida de la Playa | 858/456–2777.

Mission Beach Club. Just steps from the waves, Mission Beach Club rents boards. | 704 Ventura Pl. | 858/488–5050.

Windsurfing

Also called sailboarding, windsurfing is best practiced on smooth waters, like Mission Bay. More experienced windsurfers will enjoy wave-jumping out on the ocean.

Bahia Resort Hotel. Sailboarding rentals and instruction are available. | 998 W. Mission Bay Dr. | 858/488–0551.

Essential Information

When to Go

For the most part, any time of the year is the right time for a trip to San Diego. The climate is generally close to perfect. Typical days are sunny and mild, with low humidity—ideal for sightseeing and for almost any sport that does not require snow and ice. The annual high temperature averages 70°F with a low of 55°F, and the annual rainfall is usually less than 10 inches. Most of the rain occurs in January and February, but precipitation usually lasts for only part of the day or for a day or two at most.

FESTIVALS AND SEASONAL EVENTS

WINTER

Dec.: **December Nights.** More than 125,000 people congregate in Balboa Park on the first Friday and Saturday of December. Attractions include carolers, holiday food, music, dance, handmade crafts for sale, a candlelight procession, and free admission to all the museums. | 619/239–0512.

Wild Animal Park Festival of Lights. Free kid-oriented activities, Christmas caroling, live-animal presentations, and real snow celebrate the season. | 760/796–5615.

SPRING

May: **Fiesta Cinco de Mayo.** Entertainment and booths enliven Old Town San Diego State Historic Park and the Bazaar del Mundo. | 619/220–5427.

SUMMER

June–July: **San Diego County Fair.** This classic county fair in Del Mar has live entertainment, flower and garden shows, a carnival, livestock shows, and Fourth of July fireworks. | 858/793–5555.

July: **U.S. Open Sandcastle Competition.** Sand sculptors of all ages compete at Imperial Beach Pier in one of the largest castle-building events in the United States. | 619/424–6663.

AUTUMN

Oct.: **Founders Day.** Take advantage of free admission to the San Diego Zoo on the first Monday in October. Children get in free the entire month. | 619/234–3153.

Bargains

The International Visitor Information Center (☞ Visitor Information) has a free book, *Rediscover San Diego,* that contains discount coupons to attractions, hotels, and restaurants. SeaWorld, the zoo, and the Wild Animal Park all offer multi-day discounts.

Passport to Balboa Park. The passport provides unlimited admission to 13 park attractions for one week for $30. | 619/232–2054.

San Diego Art + Sol. Packages combine lodging, dining, theater tickets, and museum admission within San Diego County. Deals vary and change frequently; you can order a brochure, but allow four to six weeks for delivery. | 800/270–9283 | www.sandiegoartandsol.com.

Times Arts Tix. Half-price tickets for music, theater, and dance are available here for cash only on the day of the performance. | Horton Plaza | 619/497–5000.

Tours

BOAT TOURS

Hornblower Invader Cruises. One- and two-hour harbor cruises cost $15 and $20 dollars, respectively. Hornblower also offers dinner cruises, price depending on the occasion. | 619/234–8687 | www.hornblower.com.

BUS AND TROLLEY TOURS

Centre City Development Corporation's Downtown Information Center. Free two-hour bus tours explore the downtown redevelopment area, including the Gaslamp Quarter. Groups leave on the first and third Saturday of the month at 10 AM and noon. Advance reservations are necessary. | 619/235–2222 | www.ccdc.com.

Old Town Trolley Historic Tours. The trolley, which leaves every 30 minutes, operates daily 9–4 in winter. It takes the trolley two hours to make a full loop to eight sites, including Old Town, Seaport Village, Marriott Hotel near the Convention Center, Horton Plaza in the Gaslamp Quarter, Coronado, the San Diego Zoo, and El Prado in Balboa Park. The tour is narrated, and you can get on and off as you please at any stop. An all-day pass costs $24 for adults. The company also offers several special-interest tours, like Ghosts & Gravestones and the Seal Tour, aboard an amphibious vehicle that cruises Mission and San Diego bays. The San Diego Passport is good for the regular trolley tour plus admission to the zoo, San Diego Museum of Art, one Hornblower cruise, and other goodies. The cost is $69.95 per person, and the passport is available at visitor centers and is good for one year. | 619/298–8687 | www.trolleytours.com.

WALKING TOURS

The Gaslamp Quarter Historical Foundation. Two-hour historical walking tours of the downtown historic district depart on Saturday at 11 AM ($8). Several fine walking tours are available on weekdays or weekends; upcoming walks are usually listed in the Thursday "Night and Day" section of the *San Diego Union-Tribune.* | 619/233–4692 | www.gaslampquarter.org.

Visitor Information

Balboa Park Visitors Center. | 1549 El Prado | 619/239–0512 | www.balboapark.org | Daily 9–4. **International Visitor Information Center.** | 11 Horton Plaza, at 1st Ave. and F St. | 619/236–1212 | www.sandiego.org | Sept.–May, Mon.–Sat. 8:30–5; June–Aug., Mon.–Sat.

8:30–5, Sun. 11–5. **San Diego Convention & Visitors Bureau** | 401 B St., Suite 1400, 92101 | 619/236–1212 | www.sandiego.org. **San Diego Visitor Information Center** | 2688 E. Mission Bay Dr., off I–5 at the Clairemont Dr. exit | 619/275–8259 | www.infosandiego.com/visitor | Daily 9–dusk.

Arriving and Departing

BY AIR

Airports

San Diego International Airport (SAN). Called Lindbergh Field by locals, this is the major airport in town. It is close to downtown, Shelter Island, and Point Loma. | 619/231–2100 | www.portofsandiego.org.

Airport Transportation

Car: Take Harbor Drive, at the perimeter of the airport, to downtown, which is 3 mi southeast. Take Harbor Drive west to reach Shelter Island and Point Loma. To reach I–5 and I–8, take Harbor Drive west to Nimitz Boulevard, then right on Rosecrans Street. You can reach Mission Bay, La Jolla, and North County via I–5 north. I–8 east leads to Hotel Circle and Mission Valley. To reach Coronado take Harbor Drive east and turn left on Grape Street to reach I–5 south. Take the Highway 75 exit to cross the San Diego–Coronado Bay Bridge.

Public Transit: San Diego Transit Flyer. The cheapest and often most convenient shuttle is the Flyer. These buses will drop you at most downtown businesses and hotels. The fare is $2.25, including transfer to local transit buses and the San Diego Trolley. Have exact fare handy. | 619/233–3004 | www.sdcommute.com.

Shuttle: Cloud 9 Shuttle. The vans will take you wherever you desire. The prices are reasonable and are arranged before leaving. | 800/974–8885 | www.cloud9shuttle.com.

Taxi: Taxi fare is $7–$9 plus tip to most downtown hotels. Fare to Coronado runs about $15 plus tip.

BY BUS

Greyhound Station | 120 W. Broadway | 619/239–8082.

BY CAR

Interstate 5 stretches from Canada to the Mexican border and bisects San Diego. Interstate 8 provides access from Yuma, Arizona, and points east. Drivers coming from Nevada and the mountain regions beyond can reach San Diego on I–15. To avoid traffic on I–5 and on I–15 between I–805 and Escondido steer clear of rush-hour periods.

BY TRAIN

Santa Fe Depot. Amtrak serves downtown San Diego's Santa Fe Depot with daily trains to and from Los Angeles, Santa Barbara, and San Luis Obispo. Connecting service is available in Los Angeles. Amtrak trains stop in San Diego North County at Solana Beach and Oceanside. | 1050 Kettner Blvd. | 619/239–9021.

Getting Around

BY CAR

A car is essential for San Diego's sprawling freeway system. Traffic is particularly heavy during morning and afternoon rush hours, which are generally 6–8:30 AM and 3:30–6 PM. Listen to radio traffic reports for information on the lines waiting to cross the border to Mexico.

Parking

Balboa Park, Cabrillo National Monument, and Mission Bay all have huge free parking lots, and it's rare not to find a space. Lots downtown are plentiful and cost $6–$35 per day. Old Town has large free lots by the Transit Center. Parking is more of a problem in La Jolla and Coronado, where you generally need to rely on hard-to-find street spots or expensive by-the-hour parking lots.

Parking at meters costs $1 an hour; enforcement is 8 AM–6 PM except Sunday. In the evenings and during events it can be difficult to locate parking spaces downtown. Horton Plaza offers two free hours with validation. If you're not going to stay in an area for more than two hours, parking meters generally are the best budget options.

BY PUBLIC TRANSIT

Buses

San Diego County is served by a coordinated, efficient network of bus and rail routes that includes service to Oceanside in the north, the Mexican border at San Ysidro, and points east to the Anza-Borrego Desert. There are two major transit agencies, San Diego Transit and North County Transit District (NCTD).

San Diego Transit. Buses connect with the San Diego Trolley light rail system at the San Diego Zoo, Balboa Park, Lindbergh Field, Mission Beach, Pacific Beach, La Jolla, and regional shopping centers.

San Diego Transit fares range from $1.75 to $2. Discounted fares of 75¢ are available for senior citizens and for people with disabilities. Most transfers are free; request one when boarding. Schedules are posted at each stop, and the buses usually are on time. | 619/233–3004; 619/234–5005 TTY/TDD | www.sdcommute.com for info about all public transit.

North County Transit District (NCTD). NCTD routes serve from La Jolla north to San Clemente, inland to Fallbrook, Pauma Valley, Valley Center, Ramona, and Escondido, with transfer to San Diego Transit buses.

NCTD fares are $1.50. Discounted fares of 75¢ are available for senior citizens and for people with disabilities. Transfers are free; request one when boarding. Schedules are posted at each stop, and the buses usually are on time. | 800/266–6883 for bus and Coaster.

Trolleys

San Diego Transit. The San Diego Trolley light rail system connects with San Diego Transit buses. The trolleys service downtown San Diego, Mission Valley, Old Town, South Bay, the U.S. border, and East County. The trolleys operate seven days a week from about 5 AM to midnight, depending on the station, at intervals of about 15 minutes. Bus connections are posted at each station, and bicycle lockers are available at most. Trolleys can get crowded during morning and evening rush hours. On-time performance is excellent.

San Diego Trolley tickets are priced according to the number of stations traveled. Quick Tripper tickets good for two hours are $1.25 to $2.50; Round Tripper tickets good for a return trip on the date purchased are $2 to $5. Tickets are dispensed from self-service ticket machines at each stop; exact fare in coins is recommended, although some machines accept bills in $1, $5, $10, and $20 denominations. Transfers between buses and/or the trolley are free or require an upgrade if the second fare is higher.

Day Tripper Passes are available for one, two, three, or four days ($5, $8, $10, and $12, respectively), which give unlimited rides on regional buses and the San Diego Trolley. They may be purchased from most trolley vending machines, at the Transit Store, and some hotels. | 619/233–3004; 619/234–5005 TTY/TDD | www.sdcommute.com.

Commuter Rail

Coaster. Coaster commuter trains, which run between Oceanside and San Diego Monday–Saturday, stop at the same stations as Amtrak plus others. One-way fares are $3.50 to $4.75, depending on the distance traveled. The Oceanside, Carlsbad, and Solana Beach stations have beach access. You can pick up Coaster flyers or brochures with detailed itineraries for each stop, including walking directions and connections to local bus service. Trains are typically on time. | 800/262–6883 | www.sdcommute.com.

BY TAXI

Transportation Network. Taxis departing from the airport are subject to regulated fares—all companies charge the same rate (generally $1.80 for the first mile, $1.20 for each additional mile). Fares vary among companies on other routes, however, including the ride back to the airport. If you call ahead and ask for the flat rate you'll get it; otherwise you'll be charged by the mile. The Transportation Network is composed of companies that serve the greater San Diego area, including the airport. Most companies do not serve all areas of San Diego County, so be sure to ask about service to your destination. | 619/239–8061 | www.driveu.com.

California

Revised and Updated by Sharron Wood

SAN FRANCISCO

Bordered by the Pacific Ocean, the Golden Gate Strait, and San Francisco Bay, San Francisco encompasses only about 46 square mi. But it is packed with sights: the majestic Golden Gate and San Francisco–Oakland bridges; the hills and steep streets with cable cars rattling up and down; and exuberant architecture, including pastel-colored Victorian houses, stately mansions, and modern downtown high-rises. Its temperate climate nurtures lush vegetation, and its restaurants are some of the best in the country.

Never a small town, San Francisco went from a settlement of cabins and tents to an instant metropolis during the 1840s gold rush. Since then, this port city has attracted generations of immigrants from around the world, including European, Asian, and Latin American countries. This unusually large number of residents with ties to other cultures flavors the cuisine, commerce, and tenor of the place; it also encourages a tolerance for diversity in customs, beliefs, and lifestyles. As a result, the city's neighborhoods are self-aware and retain strong cultural, political, and ethnic identities. Russian bakeries can still be found in the Richmond District, African-American–owned businesses line Fillmore Street in the Western Addition, and taquerías send their enticing smells through the Mission District.

San Francisco's steep hills are notorious, but they do provide spectacular vistas all over town—the crests of the city's seven main hills offer variations on a theme of astounding beauty. From the top of Telegraph Hill you might see jewel-like Angel Island glittering in the sun or the clouds rolling in to cover the bay in a blanket of fog.

Exploring

"You could live in San Francisco a month and ask no greater entertainment than walking through it," wrote Inez Hayes Irwin, author of *The Californiacs,* an effusive 1921 homage to the state of California and the City by the Bay. Her claim remains true today: as in the 1920s, touring on foot is the best way to experience this diverse metropolis.

San Francisco is a relatively small city. About 800,000 residents live on a 46½-square-mi tip of land between San Francisco Bay and the Pacific Ocean. Yet this compact space is packed with sites of historical and architectural interest. In addition, the neighborhoods

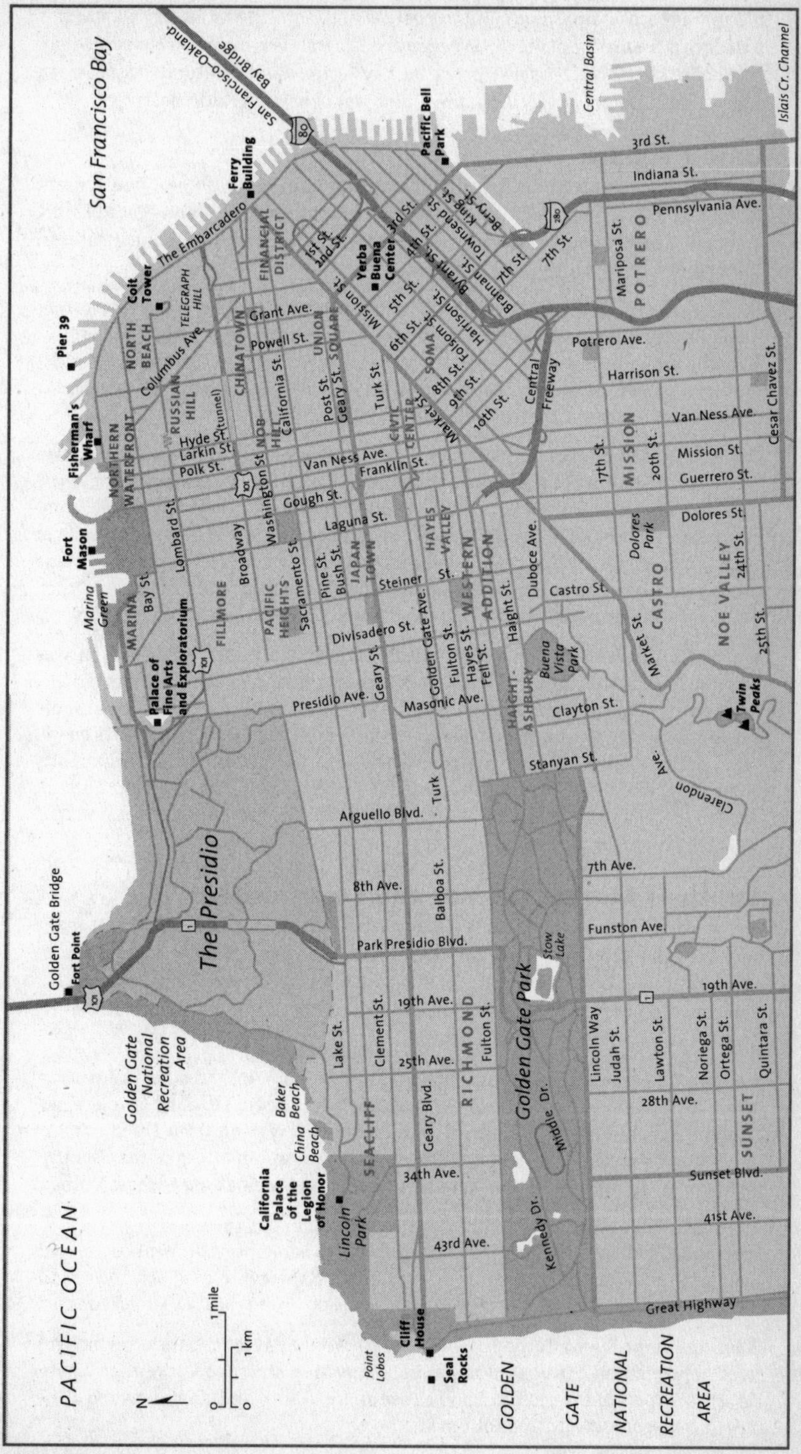

San Francisco Bay
PACIFIC OCEAN
San Francisco–Oakland Bay Bridge
Ferry Building
The Embarcadero
Coit Tower
Pier 39
Fisherman's Wharf
Fort Mason
Marina Green
Palace of Fine Arts and Exploratorium
Golden Gate Bridge
Fort Point
The Presidio
Golden Gate National Recreation Area
Baker Beach
China Beach
California Palace of the Legion of Honor
Lincoln Park
Cliff House
Seal Rocks
Point Lobos
Pacific Bell Park
Yerba Buena Center
Central Basin
Islais Cr. Channel
NORTH BEACH
TELEGRAPH HILL
RUSSIAN HILL
CHINATOWN
FINANCIAL DISTRICT
NOB HILL
UNION SQUARE
CIVIC CENTER
SOMA
NORTHERN WATERFRONT
MARINA
FILLMORE
PACIFIC HEIGHTS
JAPAN TOWN
HAYES VALLEY
WESTERN ADDITION
HAIGHT-ASHBURY
POTRERO
MISSION
CASTRO
NOE VALLEY
RICHMOND
SEACLIFF
SUNSET
Golden Gate Park
Stow Lake
Buena Vista Park
Dolores Park
Twin Peaks
Central Freeway
GOLDEN GATE NATIONAL RECREATION AREA
1 mile
1 km
N

of San Francisco retain strong cultural, political, and ethnic identities. Locals know this pluralism is the real life of the city. Experiencing San Francisco means visiting the neighborhoods: the colorful Mission District, the gay Castro, countercultural Haight Street, swank Pacific Heights, lively Chinatown, and ever bohemian North Beach.

Union Square

The Union Square area bristles with big-city bravado. The city's finest department stores do business here, along with exclusive emporiums like Tiffany & Co., Prada, and Coach. Several dozen hotels within a three-block walk of the square cater to visitors.

Maiden Lane. Known as Morton Street in the raffish Barbary Coast era, this former red-light district reported at least one murder a week during the late 19th century. After the 1906 fire destroyed the brothels, the street emerged as Maiden Lane, and it has since become a semi-chic pedestrian mall stretching two blocks, between Stockton and Kearny streets. | Between Stockton and Kearny Sts.

Union Square. The heart of San Francisco's downtown since 1850, the 2½-acre square takes its name from the violent pro-union demonstrations staged here prior to the Civil War. At center stage, the *Victory Monument,* by Robert Ingersoll Aitken, commemorates Commodore George Dewey's victory over the Spanish fleet at Manila in 1898. Completely renovated in 2002, the once dowdy square now has an open-air stage and central plaza, an outdoor café, gardens, four sculptures by the artist R. M. Fischer, and a visitor information booth. | Between Powell, Stockton, Post, and Geary Sts.

Westin St. Francis Hotel. The second-oldest hotel in the city, established in 1904, was conceived by railroad baron and financier Charles Crocker and his associates as a hostelry for their millionaire friends. After the hotel was ravaged by the 1906 fire, a larger, more luxurious Italian Renaissance–style residence was opened in 1907. The hotel's checkered past includes the ill-fated 1921 bash in the suite of the silent-film comedian Fatty Arbuckle, at which a woman became ill and later died. In 1975 Sara Jane Moore, standing among a crowd outside the hotel, attempted to shoot then-president Gerald R. Ford. | 335 Powell St., at Geary St. | 415/397–7000 | www.westin.com.

South of Market (SoMa) and Embarcadero

Key players in San Francisco's arts scene migrated to this once industrial area in the 1990s. At the heart of the action are the San Francisco Museum of Modern Art (SFMOMA) and the Center for the Arts at Yerba Buena Gardens. Glitzy projects like the Four Seasons Hotel and residential complex coexist uneasily with still-gritty stretches of Mission and Market streets.

Cartoon Art Museum. Krazy Kat, Zippy the Pinhead, Batman, and other colorful cartoon icons greet you at the Cartoon Art Museum. In addition to a 12,000-piece permanent collection, changing exhibits examine everything from the impact of underground comics to the output of women and African-American cartoonists. | 655 Mission St. | 415/227–8666 | www.cartoonart.org | $5 (pay what you wish 1st Thurs. of month) | Tues.–Fri. 11–5, Sat. 10–5, Sun. 1–5.

Metreon. Child's play meets the 21st century at this Sony entertainment center with interactive play areas, a 15-screen multiplex, an IMAX theater, retail shops, and restaurants. | 4th St. between Mission and Howard Sts. | 800/638–7366 | www.metreon.com.

Rooftop@Yerba Buena Gardens. Fun is the order of the day among these brightly colored concrete and corrugated-metal buildings atop Moscone Convention Center South. Also part of the rooftop complex are an ice-skating rink and a bowling alley. | 4th St. between Howard and Folsom Sts.

The historic **Looff carousel** ($2 for two rides) twirls from Sunday through Friday between 10 and 6, Saturday between 10 and 8.

South of the carousel is **Zeum,** a high-tech interactive arts and technology center ($7) geared to children ages eight and over. Zeum is open in summer from Wednesday through Sunday between 11 and 5, in winter on weekends and school holidays from 11 to 5. | 415/777–2800 | www.zeum.org.

★ **San Francisco Museum of Modern Art (SFMOMA).** Mario Botta designed the striking SFMOMA facility, completed in early 1995, which consists of a sienna-brick facade and a central tower of alternating bands of black and white stone. Inside, natural light from the tower floods the central atrium and some of the museum's galleries. Works by Matisse, Picasso, O'Keeffe, Kahlo, Pollock, and Warhol form the heart of the diverse permanent collection. | 151 3rd St. | 415/357–4000 | www.sfmoma.org | $10, free 1st Tues. of each month, ½-price Thurs. 6–9 | Late May–early Sept., Fri.–Tues. 10–6, Thurs. 10–9; early Sept.–late may, Fri.–Tues. 11–6, Thurs. 11–9.

Yerba Buena Gardens. The centerpiece of the SoMa redevelopment area, these two blocks encompass the Center for the Arts, Metreon, Moscone Center, and the Rooftop@Yerba Buena Gardens. A circular walkway lined with benches and sculptures surrounds the East Garden, a large patch of green amid this visually stunning complex. The waterfall memorial to Martin Luther King Jr. is the focal point of the East Garden. | Between 3rd, 4th, Mission, and Folsom Sts. | www.yerbabuena.org | Daily sunrise–10 PM.

Financial District ("The Heart of the Barbary Coast")

It was on Montgomery Street, in the Financial District, that Sam Brannan proclaimed the historic gold discovery that took place at Sutter's Mill on January 24, 1848. The gold rush brought streams of people from across America and Europe, transforming the onetime frontier town into a cosmopolitan city almost overnight. Along with the prospectors came many other fortune seekers. Saloon keepers, gamblers, and prostitutes all flocked to the so-called Barbary Coast (now Jackson Square and the Financial District). By 1917 the excesses of the Barbary Coast had fallen victim to the Red-Light Abatement Act and the ire of church leaders. Since then the red-light establishments have edged upward to the Broadway strip of North Beach, and Jackson Square evolved into a sedate district of refurbished brick buildings decades ago.

Jackson Square. Here was the heart of the Barbary Coast of the Gay '90s. Though most of the red-light district was destroyed in the 1906 fire, old redbrick buildings and narrow alleys recall the romance and rowdiness of the early days. Some of the city's earliest business buildings, survivors of the 1906 quake, still stand in Jackson Square, between Montgomery and Sansome streets. | Between Broadway and Washington and Montgomery and Sansome Sts.

Transamerica Pyramid. The city's most-photographed high-rise is the 853-ft Transamerica Pyramid. Designed by William Pereira and Associates in 1972, the initially controversial icon has become more acceptable to most locals over time. A fragrant redwood grove along the east side of the building, replete with benches and a cheerful fountain, is a placid patch in which to unwind. | 600 Montgomery St. | www.tapyramid.com.

Wells Fargo Bank History Museum. In 1852, during the gold rush, Wells Fargo opened its first bank in the city, and the company established banking offices in the mother-lode camps. The museum displays samples of nuggets and gold dust from mines, a mural-size map of the Mother Lode, original art by western artists Charles M. Russell and Maynard Dixon, mementos of the poet bandit Black Bart, and an old telegraph machine on which you can practice sending codes. The showpiece is the red Concord stagecoach, the likes of which carried passengers from St. Joseph, Missouri, to San Francisco in three weeks during the 1850s. | 420 Montgomery St. | 415/396–2619 | Free | Weekdays 9–5.

Chinatown

Bordered roughly by Bush, Kearny, and Powell streets and Broadway, Chinatown has one of the largest Chinese communities outside Asia. Prepare to have your senses assaulted here. Pungent smells waft out of restaurants, fish markets, and produce stands. Good-luck banners of crimson and gold hang beside dragon-entwined lampposts, pagoda roofs, and street signs with Chinese calligraphy. Honking cars chime in with shoppers bargaining loudly in Cantonese or Mandarin. Add to this the sight of millions of Chinese-theme goods spilling out of the shops along Grant Avenue, and you get an idea of what Chinatown is all about.

Chinatown Gate. Stone lions flank the base of the pagoda-topped gate, the official entrance to Chinatown. The lions and the glazed clay dragons atop the largest of the gate's three pagodas symbolize, among other things, wealth and prosperity. The four Chinese characters immediately beneath the pagoda represent the philosophy of Sun Yat-sen (1866–1925), the leader who unified China in the early 20th century. Sun Yat-sen, who lived in exile in San Francisco for a few years, promoted the notion of friendship and peace among all nations based on equality, justice, and goodwill. | Grant Ave. at Bush St.

Chinese-American National Museum and Learning Center. This airy, light-filled gallery has displays about the Chinese-American experience from 19th-century agriculture to 21st-century food and fashion trends. A separate room hosts rotating exhibits by contemporary Chinese-American artists. Julia Morgan, the architect known for the famous Hearst Castle, designed this handsome redbrick building. | 965 Clay St. | 415/391–1188 | www.chsa.org | $3 | Tues.–Fri. 11–4, weekends noon–4.

Chinese Six Companies. Several fine examples of Chinese architecture can be spotted along Stockton Street, but this is the most noteworthy. With its curved roof tiles and elaborate cornices, the imposing structure's oversize pagoda cheerfully calls attention to itself. The business leaders who ran the six companies, which still exist today, dominated Chinatown's political and economic life for decades. | 843 Stockton St.

Golden Gate Fortune Cookies Co. The workers sit at circular motorized griddles and wait for dollops of batter to drop onto a tiny metal plate, which rotates into an oven. A few moments later out comes a cookie that's pliable and ready for folding. A bagful of cookies—with mildly racy "adult" fortunes or more benign ones—costs $2 or $3. | 56 Ross Alley (west of and parallel to Grant Ave. between Washington and Jackson Sts.) | 415/781–3956 | Daily 10–7.

Tin How Temple. Day Ju, one of the first three Chinese to arrive in San Francisco, dedicated this temple to the Queen of the Heavens and the Goddess of the Seven Seas in 1852. The gold-leaf wood carving suspended from the ceiling depicts the north and east sides of the sea, which Tin How and other gods protect. A statue of Tin How sits in the middle of the back of the temple, flanked by a red lesser god and by a green one. Photography is not permitted, and visitors are asked not to step onto the balcony. | 125 Waverly Pl. | no phone | Free (donations accepted) | Daily 9–4.

North Beach

Novelist and resident Herbert Gold calls North Beach "the longest-running, most glorious American bohemian operetta outside Greenwich Village." Indeed, to anyone who's spent some time in its eccentric old bars and cafés or wandered the neighborhood, North Beach evokes everything from the Barbary Coast days to the no-less-rowdy beatnik era. Italian bakeries appear frozen in time, homages to Jack Kerouac and Allen Ginsberg pop up everywhere, and the modern equivalent of the Barbary Coast's "houses of ill repute," strip joints, do business on Broadway.

★ **City Lights Bookstore.** Finally designated a city landmark in 2001, the hangout of Beat-era writers—Allen Ginsberg and Lawrence Ferlinghetti among them—remains a vital part of San Francisco's literary scene. In 1999 the store, still leftist at heart, unveiled a replica of a revolutionary mural destroyed in Chiapas, Mexico, by military forces. | 261 Columbus Ave. | 415/362–8193 | www.citylights.com.

Coit Tower. Among San Francisco's most distinctive skyline sights, the 210-ft-tall Coit Tower stands as a monument to the city's volunteer firefighters. During the early days of the gold rush, Lillie Hitchcock Coit was said to have deserted a wedding party and chased down the street after her favorite engine, Knickerbocker No. 5, while clad in her bridesmaid finery. She was soon made an honorary member of the Knickerbocker Company. Lillie died in 1929, leaving the city $125,000 to "expend in an appropriate manner . . . to the beauty of San Francisco." Inside the tower, 19 depression-era murals depict economic and political life in California. | Telegraph Hill Blvd., at Greenwich St. or Lombard St. | 415/362–0808 | $3.75 | Daily 10–6.

Telegraph Hill. Telegraph Hill, now capped by Coit Tower, got its name from one of its earliest functions—in 1853 it became the location of the first Morse Code Signal Station. Hill residents have some of the best views in the city, as well as the most difficult ascents to their aeries (the flower-lined steps flanking the hill make the climb more than tolerable for visitors, though). | Between Lombard, Filbert, Kearny, and Sansome Sts.

Nob Hill and Russian Hill

Once called the Hill of Golden Promise, this area was officially dubbed Nob Hill during the 1870s when "the Big Four"—Charles Crocker, Leland Stanford, Mark Hopkins, and Collis Huntington, who were involved in the construction of the transcontinental railroad—built their hilltop estates. But the 1906 earthquake and fire destroyed all the palatial mansions, except for portions of the Flood brownstone. Just a few blocks north of Nob Hill, the old San Francisco families of Russian Hill were joined during the 1890s by bohemian artists and writers. Today, simple studios, spiffy pieds-à-terre, Victorian flats, Edwardian cottages, and boxlike condos rub elbows on the hill. The bay views here are some of the city's best.

★ **Cable Car Museum.** Photographs, old cable cars, signposts, ticketing machines, and other memorabilia dating from 1873 document the history of these moving landmarks. The massive powerhouse wheels that move the entire cable car system steal the show; the design is so simple it seems almost unreal. The gift shop sells cable car paraphernalia. | 1201 Mason St., at Washington St. | 415/474–1887 | www.cablecarmuseum.com | Free | Oct.–Mar., daily 10–5; Apr.–Sept., daily 10–6.

★ **Grace Cathedral.** The seat of the Episcopal Church in San Francisco, this soaring Gothic structure, erected on the site of Charles Crocker's mansion, took 53 years to build. The gilded bronze doors at the east entrance were taken from casts of Ghiberti's Gates of Paradise, which are on the baptistery in Florence, Italy. A black-and-bronze stone sculpture of St. Francis by Beniamino Bufano greets you as you enter. | 1100 California St., at Taylor St. | 415/749–6300 | www.gracecathedral.org | Weekdays 7–5:45, weekends 7–5.

Ina Coolbrith Park. This attractive park is unusual because it's vertical—that is, rather than being one open space, it's composed of a series of terraces up a very steep hill. A poet, Oakland librarian, and niece of Mormon prophet Joseph Smith, Ina Coolbrith (1842–1928) introduced Jack London and Isadora Duncan to the world of books. | Vallejo St. between Mason and Taylor Sts.

Lombard Street. The block-long "Crookedest Street in the World" makes eight switchbacks down the east face of Russian Hill between Hyde and Leavenworth streets. Join the line of cars waiting to drive down the steep hill, or avoid the whole morass and walk down the steps on either side of Lombard. You'll take in super views of North Beach and Coit Tower whether you walk or drive. | Lombard St. between Hyde and Leavenworth Sts.

Pacific Heights and Japantown

Some of the city's most expensive and dramatic real estate—including mansions priced in the millions—is in Pacific Heights. Grand Victorians line the streets, and from almost any point in this neighborhood you get a magnificent view.
Japantown, or "Nihonmachi," is centered on the southern slope of Pacific Heights north of Geary Boulevard between Fillmore and Laguna streets. This area was virtually deserted during World War II, when many of its residents were forced into so-called relocation camps. Though Japantown is a relatively safe area, the Western Addition, which lies to the south of Geary Boulevard, can be dangerous; after dark also avoid straying too far west of Fillmore Street just north of Geary.

Haas-Lilienthal House. A small display of photographs in this elaborate 1886 Queen Anne house, which cost a mere $18,500 to build, makes clear that it was modest compared with some of the giants that fell victim to the 1906 earthquake. The Foundation for San Francisco's Architectural Heritage operates the home, whose carefully kept rooms provide an intriguing glimpse into late-19th-century life. | 2007 Franklin St., between Washington and Jackson Sts. | 415/441–3004 | www.sfheritage.org/house.html | $5 | Wed. noon–4 (last tour at 3), Sun. 11–5 (last tour at 4). Pacific Heights tours ($5) leave the house Sun. at 12:30.

Japan Center. The noted American architect Minoru Yamasaki created this 5-acre complex, which opened in 1968. The development includes a hotel; a public garage; shops selling Japanese furnishings, clothing, cameras, tapes and records, porcelain, pearls, and paintings; an excellent spa; and a multiplex cinema. Between the Miyako Mall and Kintetsu Building are the five-tier, 100-ft-tall Peace Pagoda and the Peace Plaza. The pagoda was designed by Yoshiro Taniguchi to convey the "friendship and goodwill" of the Japanese people to the people of the United States. | Bordered by Geary Blvd. and Fillmore, Post, and Laguna Sts. | 415/922–6776.

Spreckels Mansion. This estate was built for sugar heir Adolph Spreckels and his wife, Alma. Mrs. Spreckels was so pleased with her house that she commissioned George Applegarth to design another building in a similar vein: the California Palace of the Legion of Honor. | 2080 Washington St., at Octavia St.

Civic Center

The Civic Center—the beaux-arts complex between McAllister and Grove streets and Franklin and Hyde streets that includes City Hall, the War Memorial Opera House, the Veterans Building, and the old Public Library (slated to become the Asian Art Museum and Cultural Center in early 2003)—is a product of the "City Beautiful" movement of the early 20th century. City Hall, completed in 1915 and renovated in 1999, is the centerpiece.

Asian Art Museum. In early 2003 the Asian Art Museum, one of the largest collections of Asian art in the world, opens in its new home. Holdings include more than 12,000 sculptures, paintings, and ceramics from 40 countries, illustrating major periods of Asian art. | 200 Larkin St., between McAllister and Fulton Sts. | 415/668–8921 or 415/379–8801 | www.asianart.org.

City Hall. This masterpiece of granite and marble was modeled after St. Peter's cathedral in Rome. City Hall's bronze and gold-leaf dome, which is even higher than the U.S. Capitol's version, dominates the area. Some noteworthy events that have taken place here include the marriage of Marilyn Monroe and Joe DiMaggio (1954); the hosing—down the central staircase—of civil-rights and freedom-of-speech protesters (1960); the murders of Mayor George Moscone and openly gay supervisor Harvey Milk (1978); and the weddings of scores of gay couples in celebration of the passage of San Francisco's Domestic Partners Act (1991). Free tours are available weekdays at 10, noon, and 2 and weekends at 12:30. | Between Van Ness Ave. and Polk, Grove, and McAllister Sts. | 415/554–6023 | www.ci.sf.ca.us/cityhall.

The Northern Waterfront

For the sights, sounds, and smells of the sea, hop the Powell–Hyde cable car from Union Square and take it to the end of the line. The views as you descend Hyde Street down to the bay are breathtaking—tiny sailboats bob in the whitecaps, Alcatraz hovers in the distance, and the Marin Headlands form a rugged backdrop to the Golden Gate Bridge. When you reach the cable car turnaround, Aquatic Park and the National Maritime Museum are immediately to the west, and Fisherman's Wharf is to the east. Bring good walking shoes and a jacket for the perpetual breezes or foggy mists.

★ **Alcatraz Island.** The boat ride to the island is brief (15 minutes) but affords beautiful views of the city, Marin County, and the East Bay. The audio tour, highly recommended, includes observations of guards and prisoners about life in one of America's most notorious penal colonies. A separate ranger-led tour surveys the island's ecology. Plan your schedule to allow at least three hours for the visit and boat rides combined. Reservations, even in the off-season, are recommended. | Pier 41 | 415/773–1188 boat schedules and information; 415/705–5555; 800/426–8687 credit-card ticket orders; 415/705–1042 park information | www.nps.gov/alcatraz | $13.25, $9.25 without audio ($20.75 evening tours, including audio); add $2.25 per ticket to charge by phone | Ferry departures Sept.–late May, daily 9:30–2:15 (4:20 for evening tour Thurs.–Sun. only); late May–Aug., daily 9:30–4:15 (6:30 and 7:30 for evening tour.

Fisherman's Wharf. You'll see more tourists and souvenir stands than fishing boats along the Wharf, but a rewarding stroll here takes in bustling streets lined with numerous seafood restaurants, among them sidewalk stands where shrimp and crab cocktails are sold in disposable containers. T-shirts and sweats, gold chains galore, redwood furniture, acres of artwork (precious little of it original), and generally amusing street artists also beckon visitors. Everything's overpriced, especially the novelty museums, which can provide a diversion if you're touring with antsy kids. | Jefferson St. between Leavenworth St. and Pier 39.

Ghirardelli Square. Most of the redbrick buildings in this early 20th-century complex were part of the Ghirardelli chocolate factory. Now they house name-brand emporiums, tourist-oriented restaurants, and galleries that sell everything from crafts and knickknacks to sports memorabilia. Placards throughout the square describe the factory's history. | 900 N. Point St. | 415/775–5500.

★ **Hyde Street Pier.** The pier, one of the wharf area's best bargains, always crackles with activity. Depending on the time of day, you might see boatbuilders at work or children manning a ship as though it were still the early 1900s. The highlight of the pier is its collection of historic vessels, all of which can be boarded: the *Balclutha,* an 1886 full-rigged three-masted sailing vessel that sailed around Cape Horn 17 times; the *Eureka,* a side-wheel ferry; the *C. A. Thayer,* a three-masted schooner; and the *Hercules,* a steam-powered tugboat. | Hyde and Jefferson Sts. | 415/556–3002 or 415/556–0859 | www.maritime.org | $6 | Mid-May–mid-Sept., daily 9:30–5:30, mid-Sept.–mid-May, daily 9:30–5.

National Maritime Museum. Part of the San Francisco Maritime National Historical Park, which includes Hyde Street Pier, the museum exhibits ship models, maps, and other artifacts chronicling the development of San Francisco and the West Coast through maritime history. | Aquatic Park at the foot of Polk St. | 415/556–3002 | www.nps.gov | Donation suggested | Daily 10–5.

Pier 39. This is the most popular—and commercial—of San Francisco's waterfront attractions, drawing millions of visitors each year to browse through its dozens of shops. Ongoing free entertainment, a brilliantly colored carousel, accessible validated parking, and nearby public transportation ensure crowds most days. The din on the northwest side of the pier comes courtesy of the hundreds of sea lions that bask on the docks. | Beach St. at the Embarcadero | www.pier39.com.

The Marina, Cow Hollow, and the Presidio

The Marina district was a coveted place to live until the 1989 earthquake, when the area's homes suffered the worst damage in the city—largely because the Marina is built on landfill. Many homeowners and renters fled in search of more solid ground, but young professionals quickly replaced them, changing the tenor of this neighborhood. A bank became a Williams-Sonoma, and the local grocer gave way to a Pottery Barn.

West of the Marina is the sprawling Presidio, a former military base. The Presidio has superb views and the best hiking and biking areas in San Francisco.

★ **Exploratorium.** The curious of all ages flock to this fascinating "museum of science, art, and human perception" within the Palace of Fine Arts. The more than 650 exhibits focus on sea and insect life, computers, electricity, patterns and light, language, the weather, and much more. | 3601 Lyon St., at Marina Blvd. | 415/561–0360 general information | www.exploratorium.edu | $10, free 1st Wed. of month | Late May–early Sept., Sun.–Tues. and Thurs.–Sat. 10–6, Wed. 10–9; early Sept.–late May, Tues. and Thurs.–Sun. 10–5, Wed. 10–9.

Reservations are required to crawl through the pitch-black, touchy-feely **Tactile Dome,** an adventure of 15 minutes. The object is to crawl and climb through the space relying solely on the sense of touch. | Reservations 415/561–0362 | $4 extra.

Fort Point. Fort Point was constructed between 1853 and 1861 to protect San Francisco from sea attack during the Civil War—but it was never used for that purpose. It was, however, used as a coastal defense fortification post during World War II. This National Historic Site is a museum filled with military memorabilia. On days when Fort Point is staffed, guided group tours and cannon drills take place. Take care when walking along the front side of the building, as it's slippery. | Marine Dr. off Lincoln Blvd. | 415/556–1693 | www.nps.gov/fopo | Free | Thurs.–Mon. 10–5.

★ **Golden Gate Bridge.** The suspension bridge that connects San Francisco with Marin County has long wowed sightseers with its rust-color beauty, 750-ft towers, and simple but powerful art deco design. At nearly 2 mi, the Golden Gate, completed in 1937 after four years of construction, was built to withstand winds of more than 100 mph. Though frequently gusty and misty (walkers should wear warm clothing), the bridge offers unparalleled views of the Bay Area. Muni Buses 28 and 29 make stops at the Golden Gate Bridge toll plaza, on the San Francisco side. | Lincoln Blvd. near Doyle Dr. and Fort Point | 415/921–5858 | www.goldengatebridge.org | For pedestrians: Winter daily 6–6; summer daily 5 AM–9 PM.

Palace of Fine Arts. San Francisco's rosy rococo Palace of Fine Arts is at the western end of the Marina. The palace is the sole survivor of the many plaster buildings (a temporary classical city of sorts) built for the 1915 Panama-Pacific International Exposition. Bernard Maybeck designed this faux Roman Classic beauty, which was reconstructed in concrete. The massive columns, great rotunda (dedicated to the glory of Greek culture), and swan-filled lagoon have been used in countless fashion layouts and films. | Baker and Beach Sts. | 415/561–0364 palace tours | www.exploratorium.edu/palace.

Presidio. Part of the Golden Gate National Recreation Area, the Presidio was a military post for more than 200 years. Today, after much controversy, the area is being transformed into a self-sustaining national park with a combination of public, commercial, and residential projects. The more than 1,400 acres of hills, majestic woods, and redbrick army barracks include two beaches, a golf course, a visitor center, and picnic sites, and the views of the bay, the Golden Gate Bridge, and Marin County are sublime. | Between the Marina and Lincoln Park, Presidio | www.nps.gov/prsf.

Golden Gate Park

★ William Hammond Hall conceived one of the nation's great city parks and began in 1870 to put into action his plan for a natural reserve with no reminders of urban life. But it took John McLaren the length of his tenure as park superintendent, from 1890 to 1943, to complete the transformation of 1,000 desolate brush- and sand-covered acres into a landscaped oasis. Urban reality now encroaches on all sides, but the park remains a great getaway. In addition to endless pathways and greenery, the park offers diversions like two windmills at the western edge of the park, a 15-acre grove dedicated to those lost to AIDS, and a lake where you can rent a rowboat. On Sunday John F. Kennedy Drive is closed to cars and comes alive with joggers, cyclists, and in-line skaters. The fog can sweep into the park with amazing speed; always bring a sweatshirt or jacket.

Beach Chalet. This Spanish colonial–style structure, architect Willis Polk's last design, was built in 1925 after his death. A wraparound Federal Works Project mural by Lucien Labaudt depicts San Francisco in the 1930s. A three-dimensional model of Golden Gate Park, artifacts from the 1894 Mid-Winter Exposition and other park events, a visitor center, and a gift shop that sells street signs and other city paraphernalia are on the first floor as well. On a clear day, the brewpub-restaurant upstairs has views past Ocean Beach to the Farallon Islands, about 30 mi offshore. | 1000 Great Hwy., at west end of John F. Kennedy Dr. | www.beachchalet.com.

California Academy of Sciences. A three-in-one attraction, the nationally renowned academy houses an aquarium, numerous science and natural-history exhibits, and a planetarium. | Music Concourse Dr. off South Dr. | 415/750–7145 | www.calacademy.org | $8.50 ($2.50 discount with Muni transfer), free 1st Wed. of month | Late May–early Sept., daily 9–6; early Sept.–late May, daily 10–5; 1st Wed. of month closes at 8:45 PM.

Leopard sharks, silver salmon, sea bass, and other fish loop around the mesmerizing Fish Roundabout, the big draw at **Steinhart Aquarium.** Feeding time is 1:30 PM. Always amusing to watch, the penguins dine at 11:30 AM and 4 PM.

The multimedia earthquake exhibit in the Earth and Space Hall at the **Natural History Museum** simulates quakes, complete with special effects. Videos and displays in the Wild California Hall describe the state's wildlife, and there's a re-creation of the environment of the rocky Farallon Islands.

There is an additional charge ($2.50) for **Morrison Planetarium** shows. Daily multimedia shows present the night sky through the ages under a 55-ft dome, complete with special effects and music.

Conservatory of Flowers. The last remaining wood-frame Victorian conservatory in the country, the Conservatory, which was built in the late 1870s, is a copy of the one in the Royal Botanical Gardens in Kew, England. Heavily damaged during a 1995 storm, the whitewashed facility is closed indefinitely, but its architecture and gardens make it a worthy stop nonetheless. The gardens in front of the Conservatory are planted seasonally, with the flowers often fashioned like billboards—depicting the Golden Gate Bridge or other city sights. | John F. Kennedy Dr. at Conservatory Dr.

Japanese Tea Garden. A serene 4-acre landscape of small ponds, streams, waterfalls, stone bridges, Japanese sculptures, *mumsai* (planted bonsai) trees, perfect miniature pagodas, and some nearly vertical wooden "humpback" bridges, the tea garden was created for the 1894 Mid-Winter Exposition. Go in the spring if you can, when the cherry blossoms are in bloom. | Tea Garden Dr. off John F. Kennedy Dr. | 415/752–4227 or 415/752–1171 | $3.50 | Mar.–Sept., daily 9–6; Oct.–Feb., daily 8:30–5.

Strybing Arboretum & Botanical Gardens. The 55-acre arboretum specializes in plants from areas with climates similar to that of the Bay Area, such as the west coast of Australia, South Africa, and the Mediterranean; more than 8,000 plant and tree varieties bloom in gardens throughout the grounds. Maps are available at the main and Eugene L. Friend entrances. | 9th Ave. at Lincoln Way | 415/661–1316 | www.strybing.org | Free | Weekdays 8–4:30, weekends 10–5.

Lincoln Park and the Western Shoreline

From Land's End in Lincoln Park you'll have some of the best views of the Golden Gate (the name was originally given to the opening of San Francisco Bay, long before the bridge was built) and the Marin Headlands. From the historic Cliff House south to the sprawling San Francisco Zoo, the Great Highway and Ocean Beach run along the western edge of the city. The wind is often strong along the shoreline, summer fog can blanket the ocean beaches, and the water is cold and usually too rough for swimming.

★ **California Palace of the Legion of Honor.** Spectacularly situated on cliffs overlooking the ocean, the Golden Gate Bridge, and the Marin Headlands, this landmark building is a fine repository of European art. The lower-level galleries exhibit prints and drawings, English and European porcelain, and ancient Assyrian, Greek, Roman, and Egyptian art. The 20-plus galleries on the upper level display the permanent collection of European art from the 14th century to the present day. An original cast of Rodin's *The Thinker* is a highlight of the noteworthy Rodin collection. | 34th Ave. at Clement St. | 415/863–3330 information | www.thinker.org | $8 ($2 off with Muni transfer); free 2nd Wed. of month | Tues.–Sun. 9:30–5.

Cliff House. The original Cliff House, built in 1863, hosted several U.S. presidents and wealthy locals who would drive their carriages out to Ocean Beach; it was destroyed by fire on Christmas Day 1894. The second Cliff House, the most resplendent of the three, was built in 1896; it rose eight stories with an observation tower 200 ft above sea level, but it burned down in 1907. The current complex, which includes restaurants, a pub, and a gift shop, remains open while undergoing a gradual renovation to restore its early 20th-century look. | 1090 Point Lobos Ave. | 415/386–3330 | www.cliffhouse.com | Weekdays 8 AM–10:30 PM, weekends 8 AM–11 PM; cocktails served nightly until 2 AM.

San Francisco Zoo. More than 1,000 birds and animals—220 species altogether—reside at the zoo. Among the more than 130 endangered species are the snow leopard, Sumatran tiger, jaguar, and Asian elephant. The children's zoo has a population of about 300 mammals, birds, and reptiles, plus an insect zoo, a meerkat and prairie dog exhibit, a nature trail, a nature theater, and a restored 1921 Dentzel carousel. | Sloat Blvd. and 45th Ave. | 415/753–7080 | www.sfzoo.org | $10 ($1 off with Muni transfer), free 1st Wed. of month | Daily 10–5; children's zoo weekdays 11–4, weekends 10:30–4:30.

Mission District

The sunny Mission District wins out in San Francisco's war of microclimates—it's always the last to succumb to fog. Italian and Irish in the early 20th century, the Mission became heavily Latino in the late 1960s, when immigrants from Mexico and Central America began arriving. In the late 1990s gentrification led to skyrocketing rents, causing clashes between the longtime residents forced out and the wealthy yuppies moving in. The Mission lacks some of the glamour of other neighborhoods, but the colorful murals painted on dozens of its buildings are worth a look, and there's no better neighborhood for hip restaurants and nightlife.

Mission Dolores. Mission Dolores encompasses two churches standing side by side. Completed in 1791, the small adobe building known as Mission San Francisco de Asís is the oldest standing structure in San Francisco and the sixth of the 21 California missions founded by Father Junípero Serra. Its ceiling depicts original Ohlone Indian basket designs, executed in vegetable dyes. The tiny chapel includes frescoes and a hand-painted wooden altar; some artifacts were brought from Mexico by mule in the late 18th century. There is a small museum, and the pretty little mission cemetery (made famous by a scene in Alfred Hitchcock's *Vertigo*) maintains the graves of mid-19th-century European immigrants. (The remains of an estimated 5,000 Native Americans lie in unmarked graves.) | Dolores and 16th Sts. | 415/621–8203 | www.sfmuseum.org/hist5/misdolor.html | Free (donations welcome), audio tour $7 | Daily 9–4.

Precita Eyes Mural Arts and Visitors Center. This nonprofit arts organization sponsors guided walks of the Mission District's murals. Most tours start with a 45-minute slide presentation. The bike and walking trips, which take between one and three hours, pass by several dozen murals. You can pick up a map of 24th Street's murals at the center and buy T-shirts, postcards, and other mural-related items. | 2981 24th St. | 415/285–2287 | www.precitaeyes.org | Center free, tours $8–$12 | Center weekdays 10–5, Sat. 10–4, Sun. noon–4; walks weekends at 11 and 1:30 or by appointment; bike tours 2nd Sun. of month at 11.

The Castro and the Haight

The Castro district—the social, cultural, and political center of the gay and lesbian community in San Francisco—is one of the liveliest and most welcoming neighborhoods in the city, especially on weekends. Come Saturday and Sunday, the streets teem with folks out shopping, pushing political causes, heading to art films, and lingering in bars and cafés.

Once an enclave of middle-class families of European immigrants, the Haight began to change during the late 1950s and early 1960s. Families were fleeing to the suburbs, and the big old Victorians were deteriorating or being chopped up into cheap housing. Young people found the neighborhood an affordable spot in which they could live according to new precepts. By 1966 the Haight had become a hot spot for rock bands like the Grateful Dead and Jefferson Airplane.

★ **Castro Theatre.** The neon marquee is the neighborhood's great landmark, and the 1,500-seat theater, which opened in 1922, is the grandest of San Francisco's few remaining movie palaces. Before many shows the theater's pipe organ rises from the orchestra pit and an organist plays pop and movie tunes, usually ending with the Jeanette McDonald standard "San Francisco." | 429 Castro St. | 415/621–6120.

Haight-Ashbury intersection. On October 6, 1967, hippies took over the intersection of Haight and Ashbury streets to proclaim the "Death of Hip." If they thought hip was dead then, they'd find absolute confirmation of it today, what with the Gap holding court on one quadrant of the famed corner. Among the folks who hung out in or near the Haight during the late 1960s were writers Richard Brautigan, Allen Ginsberg, Ken Kesey, and Gary Snyder; anarchist Abbie Hoffman; rock performers Marty Balin, Jerry Garcia, Janis Joplin, and Grace Slick; LSD champion Timothy Leary; and filmmaker Kenneth Anger.

Dining

South of Market and Embarcadero

LuLu. Mediterranean. Beneath a high barrel-vaulted ceiling, you can feast on mussels roasted in an iron skillet, wood-roasted poultry, meats, and shellfish, plus pizzas and pastas. Each day a different main course prepared on the rotisserie is featured, such as the suckling pig on Friday. Sharing dishes is the custom here. | 816 Folsom St. | 415/495–5775 | $11–$18 | AE, D, DC, MC, V.

Mo's Grill. American/Casual. Within easy walking distance of the Moscone Center and SFMOMA, Mo's dresses up burgers in lots of ways: with Monterey Jack and avocado; with bacon; with cheese and chiles; and more. Salmon, lamb, and turkey burgers are also cooked over the volcanic-rock grill, and sides of fries or onion rings fill out the plates. | 772 Folsom St. | 415/957–3779 | $5–$10 | MC, V.

Financial District

Café Claude. French. This standout French bistro, in an alley near the French consulate, has a true Parisian interior, with a zinc bar, old-fashioned banquettes, and cinema posters that once actually outfitted a bar in the City of Light's 11th arrondissement. | 7 Claude La. | 415/392–3505 | Closed Sun. | $11–$14 | AE, DC, MC, V.

★ **Yank Sing.** Chinese. The city's oldest tea house, Yank Sing prepares 100 varieties of dim sum on a rotating basis, serving some 60 varieties daily. The Spear Street location is large and upmarket, while the older Stevenson Street site is far smaller, a cozy refuge for neighborhood office workers who fuel up on steamed buns and parchment chicken at lunchtime. | 49 Stevenson St., at Market St. | 415/541–4949 | One Rincon Center, 101 Spear St. | 415/957–9300 | No dinner | $3–$8 | AE, DC, MC, V.

Chinatown

Great Eastern. Chinese. Cantonese chefs are known for their expertise with seafood, and the kitchen at Great Eastern continues that venerable tradition. In the busy dining room, tanks are filled with Dungeness crabs, black bass, abalone, catfish, shrimp, and other creatures of the sea, and a wall-hung menu in both Chinese and English specifies the cost of selecting what can be pricey indulgences. | 649 Jackson St. | 415/986–2550 | $7–$24 | AE, MC, V.

North Beach

Helmand. Afghan. Don't be put off by Helmand's location on a rather scruffy block of Broadway—inside you'll find authentic Afghan cooking, elegant surroundings with white table linens and Afghan carpets, and amazingly low prices. Highlights include *aushak* (leek-filled ravioli served with yogurt and ground beef), pumpkin with a yogurt and garlic sauce, and any of the lamb dishes. There's free validated parking at 468 Broadway. | 430 Broadway | 415/362–0641 | Closed Mon. No lunch | $10–$16 | AE, MC, V.

★ **L'Osteria del Forno.** Italian. An Italian-speaking staff, a small and unpretentious dining area, and irresistible aromas drifting from the open kitchen make customers who pass through the door of this modest storefront operation feel as if they've just stumbled into Italy. The kitchen produces small plates of simply cooked vegetables, a few baked pastas, a roast of the day, creamy polenta, and thin-crust pizzas. | 519 Columbus Ave. | 415/982–1124 | Reservations not accepted | Closed Tues. | $8–$13 | No credit cards.

Rose Pistola. Italian. The name honors one of North Beach's most revered barkeeps, and the food celebrates the neighborhood's Ligurian roots. An assortment of antipasti—roasted peppers, house-cured fish, fava beans dusted with pecorino shards—and pizzas from the wood-burning oven are favorites, as are the cioppino and fresh fish of the day. | 532 Columbus Ave. | 415/399–0499 | $11–$26 | AE, DC, MC, V.

Civic Center

Suppenkuche. German. Bratwurst and braised red cabbage accompany a long list of German beers at this lively, hip outpost of simple German cooking. Strangers sit down together at unfinished pine tables when the room gets crowded, which it regularly does. There's also a good Sunday brunch. | 601 Hayes St. | 415/252–9289 | No lunch | $10–$17 | AE, MC, V.

The Marina, Cow Hollow, and the Presidio

Betelnut. Pan-Asian. A pan-Asian menu and an adventurous drinks list draw a steady stream of hip diners to this Union Street landmark. Lacquered walls, bamboo ceiling fans, and period posters create a comfortably exotic mood in keeping with the unusual but accessible food. Among the big and small plates are steamed dumplings, chicken satay, tea-smoked quail, and Korean grilled pork. | 2030 Union St. | 415/929–8855 | $11–$19 | D, DC, MC, V.

Greens. Vegetarian. This beautiful restaurant with expansive bay views is owned and operated by the Green Gulch Zen Buddhist Center of Marin County. Creative meatless dishes are served, such as Thai-style vegetable curries, thin-crust pizzas, house-made pastas, and desserts like apricot and blueberry cobbler with vanilla ice cream. Dinners are à la carte on weeknights, but only a four-course prix-fixe dinner is served on Saturday. | Bldg. A, Fort Mason (enter across Marina Blvd. from Safeway), | 415/771–6222 | No lunch Mon., no dinner Sun. | $13–$18 | D, MC, V.

Mission District

La Taqueria. Mexican. Although there are many taquerias in the Mission, this attractive spot, with its arched exterior and modest interior, is one of the oldest and finest. The tacos are superb: two warm corn tortillas topped with your choice of meat—*carne asada* (grilled steak) and *carnitas* (slowly cooked pork) are favorites—and a spoonful of perfectly fresh salsa. | 2889 Mission St. | 415/285–7117 | $3–$5 | No credit cards.

Luna Park. Contemporary. Anytime after 6:30, it's a tight and noisy fit in this wildly popular bistro serving steamed mussels with french fries, poke salad (Hawaiian raw tuna partnered with wonton chips), and grilled flatiron steak. Though the crowd is mostly twenty- and thirtysomethings here to sip *mojitos,* the deafening roar means no one will hear your kids acting up. Plus, dessert choices include make-your-own s'mores with melted chocolate, marshmallows, and a handful of house-made graham crackers. | 694 Valencia St. | 415/553–8584 | No lunch weekends | $8–$14 | MC, V.

The Castro and the Haight

★ **Indian Oven.** Indian. One of the Lower Haight's most popular restaurants, this cozy Victorian storefront never lacks for customers. Many of them come here to order the tandoori specialties—chicken, lamb, breads—but the *sag paneer* (spinach with Indian cheese) and *aloo gobhi* (potatoes and cauliflower with black mustard seeds and other spices) are also excellent. | 223 Fillmore St. | 415/626–1628 | No lunch | $8–$19 | AE, D, DC, MC, V.

Thep Phanom. Thai. The fine Thai food and the lovely interior at this Lower Haight institution keep local food critics and restaurant goers singing its praises. Duck is deliciously prepared in several ways—in a fragrant curry, minced for salad, resting atop a bed of spinach. Other specialties are seafood in various guises, stuffed chicken wings, fried quail, and addictive Thai curries. | 400 WallerSt. | 415/431–2526 | No lunch | $9–$16 | AE, D, DC, MC, V.

Lodging

Union Square

Golden Gate Hotel. Captain Nemo, a 25-pound cat who must live very well indeed, serves as the unofficial doorman for this homey, family-run B&B. The original "birdcage" elevator lifts you to hallways lined with historical photographs and guest rooms individually decorated with antiques, wicker pieces, and Laura Ashley bedding. Fourteen rooms have private baths, some with clawfoot tubs. Continental breakfast and afternoon tea and cookies are served in the cozy parlor by a fire. Parking (fee); no smoking | 775 Bush St. | 415/392–3702 or 800/835–1118 | fax 415/392–6202 | www.goldengatehotel.com | 25 rooms, 14 with bath | $85–$130 | AE, DC, MC, V.

Chinatown

Grant Plaza Hotel. Amazingly low room rates for this part of town make the Grant Plaza a find for budget travelers wanting to look out their window at the striking architecture and fascinating street life of Chinatown. The small rooms, all with private baths, are very clean and modern. Rooms on the top floor are newer, slightly brighter, and a bit more expensive; for a quieter stay ask for one in the back. Room TVs, some in-room VCRs, concierge, business services, parking (fee); no a/c | 465 Grant Ave. | 415/434–3883 or 800/472–6899 | fax 415/434–3886 | www.grantplaza.com | 71 rooms, 1 suite | $72–$99 | AE, DC, MC, V.

North Beach

★ **San Remo.** This three-story 1906 Italianate Victorian just a few blocks from Fisherman's Wharf was once home to longshoremen and Beats. A narrow stairway from the street leads to the front desk, and labyrinthine hallways to the small but charming rooms with lace curtains, forest-green wooden floors, brass beds, and other antique furnishings. About a third of the rooms have sinks; all rooms, except a charming penthouse cottage, share scrupulously clean black-and-white tile shower and toilet facilities with pull-chain toilets. Laundry facilities, Internet, parking (fee); no room phones, no room TVs, no smoking | 2237 Mason St. | 415/776–8688 or 800/352–7366 | fax 415/776–2811 | www.sanremohotel.com | 62 rooms, 1 suite | $50–$90 | AE, DC, MC, V.

Nob Hill and Russian Hill

San Francisco Residence Club. In contrast to the neighboring showplace hotels, the S. F. Residence Club is a humble guest house with million-dollar views, a money-saving meal plan, and a pleasant garden patio. The building has seen better days, and most of the modest rooms share baths, but many have sweeping bay views. The international clientele ranges from leisure travelers and business professionals to longer-term residents who take advantage of the full American breakfast *and* dinner included in the daily, weekly, or monthly room rate. A $100 advance deposit via check is required. Dining room, some refrigerators, laundry facilities; no TV in some rooms | 851 California St. | 415/421–2220 | fax 415/421–2335 | 84 rooms | $78–$148 | No credit cards.

Civic Center

Abigail Howard Johnson Hotel. This hotel, built in 1926 and a former B&B, retains its art deco–tiled lobby floor, faux-marble front desk, vintage gated elevator, and old-fashioned telephone booth in the lobby. Smallish rooms have hissing steam radiators and antiques. Room 211—the hotel's only suite—is the most elegant and spacious. Complimentary Continental breakfast is served. Restaurant, fans, cable TV, dry cleaning, business services, laundry service, parking (fee); no a/c, no-smoking floors | 246 McAllister St. | 415/626–6500 | fax 415/626–6580 | 60 rooms, 1 suite | $88–$129 | AE, D, DC, MC, V.

The Marina, Cow Hollow, and the Presidio

Bel-Aire Travelodge. Made up of twin white-and-blue buildings built in the mid-1950s, this cute motel is much quieter than many motels on Lombard Street, the Marina's main drag. The rooms have contemporary motel-style blond-wood furniture, with pale mauve walls and blue carpeting. Bathrooms have showers only, and there is a mirrored vanity table in each room. Other amenities are coffeemakers, a daily newspaper, and free local calls. Fans, in-room data ports, cable TV, airport shuttle, free parking; no a/c, no-smoking rooms | 3201 Steiner St. | 415/921–5162 or 800/280–3242 | fax 415/921–3602 | www.the.travelodge.com/sanfrancisco09664 | 32 rooms | $96–$185 | AE, D, DC, MC, V.

Hotel Del Sol. Once a typical '50s-style motor court, the Del Sol is now an anything-but-typical artistic statement. The sunny yellow-and-blue three-story building and courtyard are a riot of stripes. Rooms open onto the courtyard's heated pool and hammock under towering palm trees and evoke a beach-house mood with plantation shutters, tropical-stripe bedspreads, and rattan chairs; some have brick fireplaces. The baths are small with bright-yellow tiling. Family suites have child-friendly furnishings and games for the kids. In-room data ports, in-room safes, some kitchenettes, cable TV, pool, sauna, laundry service, concierge, free parking; no smoking. | 3100 Webster St. | 415/921–5520 or 877/433–5765 | fax 415/931–4137 | www.thehoteldelsol.com | 47 rooms, 10 suites | $150–$180 | AE, D, DC, MC, V.

Pacific Heights Inn. One of the most genteel-looking motels in town, this two-story motor court near the busy intersection of Union and Van Ness is dressed up with wrought-iron railings and benches, hanging plants, and pebbled exterior walkways facing onto the parking lot. Rooms are on the small side; however, most of the units are suites, some with full kitchens, some with extra bedrooms. Morning pastries and coffee are served in the lobby. Room TVs, some kitchens, some kitchenettes, free parking, some pets allowed; no-smoking rooms. | 1555 Union St. | 415/776–3310 or 800/523–1801 | fax 415/776–8176 | www.pacificheightsinn.com | 15 rooms, 25 suites | $95–$115 | AE, D, DC, MC, V.

Presidio Travelodge. After most of the west-bound traffic on Lombard Street veers off onto the Golden Gate Bridge approach, the street continues for two much quieter blocks leading up to the Presidio, a former army base, now woodsy national parkland. It's a terrific location for this three-story motel. Rooms have blond-wood furniture and standard motel amenities such as coffeemakers. One room, the Bear's Den, has a VCR and library of children's videos. Refrigerators, cable TV, free parking; no-smoking rooms | 2755 Lombard St. | 415/931–8581 | fax 415/776–0904 | www.travelodge.com | 27 rooms | $106–$126 | AE, D, DC, MC, V.

Arts and Entertainment

City Box Office. There's a charge-by-phone service for many concerts and lectures. | 180 Redwood St., Suite 100, | 415/392–4400.

Tickets.com. This is the city's charge-by-phone ticket service. | 415/776–1999 or 510/762–2277.

TIX Bay Area. Half-price, same-day tickets to many local and touring stage shows go on sale (cash only) at 11 AM from Tuesday through Saturday at this booth, which is inside the Geary Street entrance of the Union Square Garage, between Stockton and Powell streets. | 415/433–7827.

Dance

San Francisco Ballet. The performances of both classical and contemporary works under artistic director Helgi Tomasson have won admiring reviews. Tickets and information are available at the War Memorial Opera House. | 301 Van Ness Ave. | 415/865–2000.

Music

San Francisco Opera. Founded in 1923, this world-renowned company presents approximately 70 performances of 10 to 12 operas from September through January and June through July. | 301 Van Ness Ave. | 415/864–3330.

San Francisco Symphony. The symphony performs from September through May, with additional summer performances of light classical musical and show tunes. | Davies Symphony Hall, 201 Van Ness Ave. | 415/864–6000.

Theater

★ **American Conservatory Theater (ACT).** The city's major nonprofit theater company was founded in the mid-1960s and quickly became one of the nation's leading regional theaters. | Ticket office, 405 Geary St. | 415/749–2228.

Shopping

Although the big-name stores, both large department stores and world-renowned little boutiques, are clustered around Union Square, better deals can be found in locally owned stores in other areas like the Haight, Castro, and Mission. For out-of-the-ordinary souvenirs consider unusual Chinese food items or inexpensive pottery from Chinatown, funky new or vintage jewelry from the Haight, or a San Francisco– or Beat era–theme book from one of the city's many new- or used-book stores.

Union Square

Serious shoppers head straight to Union Square, San Francisco's main shopping area and the site of most department stores, as well as the Virgin Megastore, F.A.O. Schwarz, and the Disney Store. Nearby are the pricey international boutiques of Alfred Dunhill, Cartier, Emporio Armani, Gucci, Hermès of Paris, Louis Vuitton, and Versace.

South of Market

High San Francisco rents mean that there aren't many discount outlets in the city, but a few do exist in the semi-industrial zone known as South of Market. At the other end of the spectrum is the gift shop of the San Francisco Museum of Modern Art, which sells books, handmade ceramics, art-related games, and other great gift items.

Chinatown

The intersection of Grant Avenue and Bush Street marks the gateway to Chinatown—24 blocks of shops, restaurants, and markets. Dominating the exotic cityscape are the sights and smells of food: crates of bok choy, tanks of live crabs, and hanging whole chickens. Racks of Chinese silks, toy trinkets, colorful pottery, baskets, and carved figurines are displayed chockablock on the sidewalks, alongside fragrant herb shops.

Pacific Heights

Residents seeking fine items for their luxurious homes head straight for Fillmore Street between Post Street and Pacific Avenue, and Sacramento Street between Lyon and Maple streets, where private residences alternate with fine clothing and gift shops and housewares stores.

The Castro

Often called the gay capital of the world, the Castro is also a major shopping destination for nongay travelers, filled with men's clothing boutiques, home accessory stores, and various specialty stores.

Haight Street

Haight Street is a perennial attraction for visitors, if only to see the sign at Haight and Ashbury streets—the geographic center of the Flower Power movement during the 1960s. These days chain stores like the Gap and Ben and Jerry's have taken over large storefronts near the famous intersection, but it's still possible to find high-quality vintage clothing, funky jewelry, folk art from around the world, and used records and CDs galore in this always-busy neighborhood.

Sports and Outdoor Activities

Beaches

Always read posted warnings at beaches. Many San Francisco–area beaches are subject to unsafe conditions, but almost all provide stunning views and perfect picnic spots—provided you're prepared for the often chilly weather.

Aquatic Park. Nestled in a quiet cove between the lush hills adjoining Fort Mason, Ghirardelli Square, and the crowds at Fisherman's Wharf, this park has a tiny, ¼-milong sandy beach with gentle water.

Baker Beach. Though the views of the Golden Gate Bridge and the Marin Headlands are gorgeous, the pounding surf makes swimming a dangerous prospect. Picnic tables, grills, rest rooms, and drinking water are available.

China Beach. One of the city's safest swimming beaches is a 600-ft strip of sand, just south of the Presidio, with gentle waters as well as changing rooms, rest rooms, and showers.

Muir Beach. Tucked in a rocky cove just north of the city in Marin County, this tiny, picturesque beach is usually filled with kids, dogs, families, and cuddling couples.

Ocean Beach. South of the Cliff House, Ocean Beach is certainly not the city's cleanest shore, but its wide, sandy expanse stretches for miles, making it ideal for long walks and runs. Because of extremely dangerous currents, swimming is not recommended.

Bicycling

San Francisco has a number of scenic routes of varied terrain. The *San Francisco Biking / Walking Guide* ($3), sold in select bookstores, indicates street grades and delineates biking routes that avoid major hills and heavy traffic. Golden Gate Park is a beautiful maze of roads and hidden bike paths and, ultimately, a spectacular view of the Pacific Ocean. On Sundays, John F. Kennedy Drive is closed to motor vehicles, making it a popular route for those on bikes.

Golden Gate Cyclery. Bikes can be rented for about $40 per day. | 672 Stanyan St. | 415/379–3870.

Fishing

One-day licenses, good for ocean fishing only, are available for $7 on charters.

Wacky Jacky. Salmon-fishing excursions are in a fast and comfortable 50-ft boat. | Fisherman's Wharf, Pier 45 | 415/586–9800.

In-line Skating

Golden Gate Park is one of the country's best places for in-line skating, with smooth surfaces, manageable hills, and lush scenery. John F. Kennedy Drive, which extends almost to the ocean, is closed to traffic on Sunday.

Skates on Haight. This shop near the Stanyan Street entrance to the park offers free lessons (with rentals) on Sunday morning at 9 AM and rents recreational in-line or roller skates for $6 per hour and $24 overnight. | 1818 Haight St. | 415/752–8375.

Essential Information

When to Go

You can visit San Francisco comfortably any time of year. The climate here is always moderate—though with a foggy, sometimes chilly bite. The temperature rarely drops lower than 40°F, and anything warmer than 80°F is considered a heat wave. Be prepared for rain in winter, especially December and January. Winds off the ocean can add to the chill factor, so pack warm clothing, even if you're visiting in the middle of summer. North, east, and south of the city, summers are warmer. Shirt-sleeves are usually fine for the Wine Country.

FESTIVALS AND SEASONAL EVENTS

WINTER

Whale Watching. Hundreds of gray whales migrate along the coast every winter and can be seen from the coast north and south of the city. Contact the Oceanic Society for information. | 415/441–1104 or 800/326–7491 | www.oceanic-society.org.

Feb.: **Chinese New Year.** North America's largest Chinese community celebrates for two weeks, culminating with the Golden Dragon Parade. | 415/982–3071 | www.chineseparade.com.

SPRING

Apr.: **Cherry Blossom Festival.** This elaborate presentation of Japanese culture and customs winds up with a colorful parade through Japantown. | 415/563–2313.

May: **Carnaval.** A parade and street festival take place in the Mission District over Memorial Day weekend. | 415/826–1401.

SUMMER

June: **North Beach Festival.** Every Father's Day weekend Washington Square Park and Grant Avenue are transformed into an Italian marketplace with food, music, and entertainment. | 415/989–2220.

Lesbian, Gay, Bisexual, and Transgender Pride Parade and Celebration. The parade winds its way from the Embarcadero to the Civic Center on the third or fourth Sunday of the month. | 415/864–3733 or 415/677–7959 | www.sfpride.com.

AUTUMN

Oct.: **Fleet Week.** Beginning the second weekend of the month, the city celebrates the navy's first day in the port of San Francisco with a Blue Angels air show over the bay.

Bargains

Many of San Francisco's favorite attractions are free, including a walk across the Golden Gate Bridge, a visit to the Wells Fargo History Museum, and the view from Coit

Tower. Admission to the San Francisco Cable Car Museum (Washington and Mason streets), where you can examine the winding machinery designed to make the motorless cars navigate the city's streets, is also free (☞ Exploring).

Good areas for inexpensive dining are the Mission District, Chinatown, and Clement Street between 2nd and 14th avenues. Inexpensive souvenirs are available in the Fisherman's Wharf area.

Half-price tickets to many stage shows go on sale at 11 AM Tuesday–Saturday at the TIX booth inside the Geary Street entrance of the Union Square Garage, between Stockton and Powell streets (☞ Arts and Entertainment).

Stern Grove. Free summer concerts take place on summer Sundays in this amphitheater on Sloat Boulevard. | 415/252–6252.

Tours

ORIENTATION TOURS

Gray Line. In addition to bay cruises, Gray Line offers city tours in motor coaches and motorized cable cars ($15–$37). | 415/558–9400 | www.graylinesanfrancisco.com.

Great Pacific Tours. City tours start at $37. | 415/626–4499 | www.greatpacifictour.com.

WALKING TOURS

Javawalk. This tour explores San Francisco's historic ties to coffee while visiting a few of the city's cafés. | 415/673–9255 | www.javawalk.com.

Victorian Home Walk. Learn about the different styles of Victorian buildings while exploring Pacific Heights and Cow Hollow. | 415/252–9485 | www.victorianwalk.com.

HISTORIC TOURS

Chinese Culture Center. A Chinatown heritage walk and a culinary walk are offered for groups of four or more only. | 415/986–1822 | www.c-c-c.org.

Trevor Hailey's "Cruising the Castro." This popular tour focuses on the history and development of the city's gay and lesbian communities. | 415/550–8110 | www.webcastro.com/castrotour.

Visitor Information

San Francisco Convention and Visitors Bureau's Visitor Information Center. | Lower level, Hallidie Plaza | 415/391–2000 or 415/974–6900 | www.sfvisitor.org.

Arriving and Departing

BY AIR

Airports

San Francisco International Airport (SFO). The airport is just south of the city, off U.S. 101. Allow a half hour of driving time from downtown. | 650/761–0800 | www.flysfo.com.

Oakland International Airport (OAK). This is another option in the Bay Area. | 510/577–4000 | www.flyoakland.com.

Airport Transportation

Public Transit: A new BART extension that will connect SFO to downtown San Francisco is scheduled for completion in 2003. Check at airport information kiosks for the latest details.

Shuttle Bus: SFO Airporter. Shuttles ($12) pick up passengers at baggage claim (lower level) and serve selected downtown hotels. | 800/532–8405.

SuperShuttle. This service stops at the upper-level traffic islands and takes you from the airport to anywhere within the city limits of San Francisco. It costs from $12 to $17. | 415/558–8500 or 800/258–3826.

Taxi: A taxi ride from SFO to downtown costs about $30.

BY BUS

Transbay Terminal. Greyhound buses arrive at the Transbay Terminal at 1st and Mission streets. | 425 Mission St.

BY TRAIN

The nearest Amtrak stations are in Emeryville, just over the Bay Bridge, and in Oakland. A free shuttle operates between these two stations and the Ferry Building and CalTrain station in San Francisco.

Getting Around

BY BOAT AND FERRY

Blue & Gold Fleet. Ferries depart daily for Sausalito from Pier 41 at Fisherman's Wharf. | 415/705–5555 | www.telesails.com.

Golden Gate Ferry. Golden Gate crosses the bay to Sausalito from the south wing of the Ferry Building at Market Street and the Embarcadero. The trip to Sausalito takes 30 minutes. | 415/923–2000.

Oakland/Alameda Ferry. The ferries run several times daily between San Francisco's Ferry Building, Alameda, and the Clay Street dock near Jack London Square. Purchase tickets on board. | 510/522–3300 | www.eastbayferry.com.

BY CAR

Driving in San Francisco is a challenge because of the hills, one-way streets, traffic, and limited parking. Use public transportation or a cab whenever possible.

Parking

Remember to curb your wheels when parking on hills. Read signs carefully before parking; illegally parked cars may be towed. Downtown parking lots are often full and most are expensive. Larger hotels often have parking available, but most charge $25–$30 a day for the privilege.

BY PUBLIC TRANSIT

San Francisco is generally well served by public transportation, though traffic snarls mean that traveling by bus can be slow going.

BART

You can use Bay Area Rapid Transit (BART) trains to reach Oakland, Berkeley, and other East Bay cities. | 650/992–2278 | www.bart.gov.

Cable Cars

Don't miss the sensation of moving up and down some of San Francisco's steepest hills in a clattering cable car. As it pauses at a designated stop, jump aboard and wedge yourself into any available space. The fare (for one direction) is $2. You can buy tickets on board (exact change is not necessary).

The heavily traveled Powell-Mason and Powell-Hyde lines begin at Powell and Market streets near Union Square and terminate at Fisherman's Wharf; lines for these routes can be long. The less spectacular California Street line runs east and west from Market and California streets to Van Ness Avenue; there is often no wait to board this route.

Muni

The San Francisco Municipal Railway, or Muni, operates light-rail vehicles, the historic streetcar line along Fisherman's Wharf and Market Street, buses, and the world-famous cable cars. On buses and streetcars, the fare is $1. Exact change is required, and dollar bills are accepted in the fare boxes. For all Muni vehicles other than cable cars, 90-minute transfers are issued free upon request at the time the fare is paid. | 415/673–6864 | www.sfmuni.com.

BY TAXI

Taxi service is notoriously bad in San Francisco, and hailing a cab can be difficult in some parts of the city. In a pinch, hotel taxi stands are an option, as is calling for a pickup. Taxis in San Francisco charge $2.50 for the first ⅙ of a mile, $1.80 for each additional mile, and 40¢ per minute in stalled traffic.

City Wide Cab | 415/920–0700. **DeSoto Cab** | 415/970–1300. **Yellow Cab** | 415/626–2345.

Virginia

Revised and Updated by Kevin Myatt

SHENANDOAH VALLEY AND THE BLUE RIDGE

Into the fertile soils of the Shenandoah Valley and Blue Ridge region were planted the seeds of a nation. German and Scotch-Irish Colonial settlers brought an agrarian lifestyle, practical work ethic, and Protestant beliefs that would eventually become the lifeblood of the American Midwest. From the Blue Ridge foothills came three of the nation's first five presidents, including Thomas Jefferson, who wrote the Declaration of Independence.

The Shenandoah Valley slants southwesterly through western Virginia between two Appalachian mountain ranges—the Blue Ridge to the east and the Alleghenies to the west. Once the route blazed by European settlers from the coastal colonies into Kentucky, the valley was an important corridor for Civil War campaigns and witnessed many battles and skirmishes. Today, the valley is sought out by travelers for its colorful old towns, its early crafts, and its old inns and eating places. Three towns of unusual interest in the valley are Lexington, where Generals Robert E. Lee and Stonewall Jackson lie buried near the educational institutions they served; Winchester, where George Washington embarked in youth on his military career; and Staunton, Woodrow Wilson's birthplace.

Forming Virginia's spine, the Blue Ridge beckons travelers to enjoy expansive vistas from two famous scenic highways: Skyline Drive and the Blue Ridge Parkway. A portion of the Appalachian Trail, a 2,000-mi footpath, also follows the crest of the ridge on its route from Georgia to Maine, traversing Shenandoah National Park, for those who want a more intimate natural experience.

East of the Blue Ridge in the vineyard-dotted foothills along the western Piedmont is Charlottesville, home of Thomas Jefferson's architectural wonders at his estate, Monticello, and the college he founded, the University of Virginia. The homes of Presidents James Madison and James Monroe are also nearby. Much in line with Jefferson's diverse tastes, Charlottesville today attracts writers, artists, scholars, and celebrities from around the world, both to visit and to live.

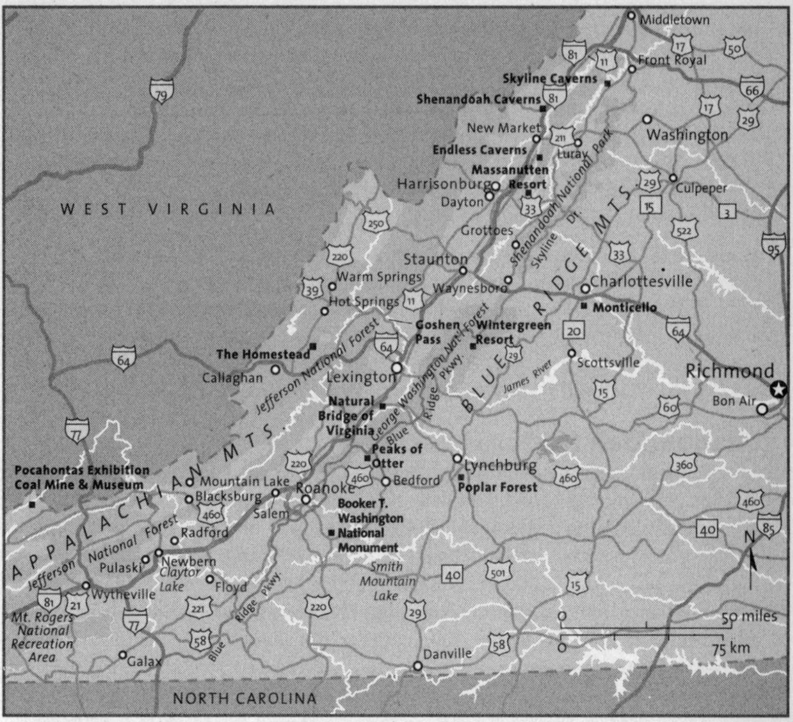

Exploring

I–81, often ranked among the nation's most scenic interstate highways, slices through the middle of the Shenandoah Valley, connecting its principal communities. Using I–81 and Skyline Drive–Blue Ridge Parkway, you can form a loop around the valley, completing the circuit on the north with I–66 at Front Royal and to the south with U.S. 460 at Roanoke. Travel will be much slower on the scenic drives—each has a strictly enforced speed limit (35 mph on Skyline Drive, 45 mph on the Blue Ridge Parkway) and only two lanes. On weekends in good weather, traffic can be abominable, so be warned. From Waynesboro—the south end of Shenandoah National Park and where Skyline Drive and the Blue Ridge Parkway connect—it's only 18 mi east on I–64 to Charlottesville.

Winchester

Settled in the 1730s by Pennsylvania Quakers, Germans, Scots, and Irish, Winchester has played a strategic role in wartime. George Washington used it as a base while fighting for the British during the French and Indian War, and during the Civil War, the town changed hands between the Union and the Confederacy 72 times. Winchester is much more peaceful today, now known for its annual Shenandoah Apple Blossom Festival and a 45-block historic downtown shopping district. It was also the birthplace of country music legend Patsy Cline; thousands visit her grave each year at the Shenandoah Memorial Park cemetery on U.S. 522, where a bell tower memorializes her.

Glen Burnie Manor House and Gardens. Colonel James Wood, Winchester's founder, called his home the "glen of streams." His 1736 Georgian country estate is surrounded by 25 acres of formal gardens. A self-guided tour lets you meander through a maze of rose, pattern, and perennial gardens; a Chinese garden stocked with koi; and even a water garden trickling with waterfalls over mossy rocks. The house features fine antiques, paintings, and decorative objects collected by the last family member to live here, Julian Wood Glass, Jr., who died in 1992. | 100 W. Picadilly St. | 540/662–1473 | $8 | Apr.–Oct., Tues.–Sat. 10–4, Sun. noon–4.

Stonewall Jackson's Headquarters Museum. This restored 1854 home served as Jackson's base of operations during the Valley Campaign in 1861–1862. Among the artifacts on display are his prayer book and camp table. The reproduction wallpaper was a gift from Mary Tyler Moore; it was her great grandfather, Lieutenant Colonel Lewis T. Moore, who loaned Jackson the use of the house. | 415 N. Braddock St. | 540/667–3242 | www.winchesterhistory.org | $3.50 | Apr.–Oct., Mon.–Sat. 10–4, Sun. noon–4.

Shenandoah National Park

Established in 1936, Shenandoah National Park follows the Blue Ridge Mountains for almost 80 mi from Front Royal south to Waynesboro, encompassing 196,466 acres of steep mountain terrain; some peaks top 4,000 ft. Its Native American name has been variously translated as "Daughter of the Stars" and "River of High Mountains." The park is graced with varied species of animal and plant life, trout streams, gorgeous panoramas, campgrounds, and hundreds of miles of hiking trails, including a stretch of the Appalachian Trail. Some 200 species of birds make their home here—from ruffed grouse to barred owl—along with white-tailed deer, woodchuck, gray fox, and black bear. Wildflowers fill the Big Meadows, the park's largest open area in April and May, and hardy hikers can explore waterfall-graced White Oak Canyon nearby. | 540/999–3253 | www.nps.gov/shen | $10 per vehicle; $5 for motorcyclists, bicyclists, or pedestrians; permits good for 7 days | Daily.

Skyline Drive, a 105-mi scenic highway, winds from one end of the national park to the other, offering panoramas of the valley to the west and the rolling country of the Piedmont to the east. The speed limit is 35 mph, and weekend crowds can make traffic even slower; winter storms often shut the road down entirely. Nevertheless, for easily accessible wilderness and exciting views, few routes can compete with this one. Seven picnic areas are scattered along the route. For maps, trail and campground information, or postings of current ranger programs, visit one of the park's two visitor centers at mileposts 4.5 and 51 along the drive.

New Market

New Market was originally known as Cross Roads because it sprang up at the intersection of two Native American trails. The first known settlers arrived from Pennsylvania in 1727 and called their village Massanutten. (It was renamed New Market in 1777.) New Market is famous for a Civil War battle that took place here on May 15, 1864. Reinforcing the Confederate troops in the battle were several hundred cadets recruited from Virginia Military Institute; 5 of the boys were killed and 15 wounded. The battlefield is now a historic park maintained by VMI. Luray, 13 mi east of New Market on the other side of Massanutten Mountain, is a popular entrance to Shenandoah National Park.

New Market Battlefield State Historical Park. This 260-acre battlefield park was the site of the Battle of New Market, which took place on May 15, 1864. Young cadets from the Virginia Military Institute joined the Confederate brigades to defeat Union forces here. At the Hall of Valor, the park's focal point, the courage of those 257 cadets is commemorated in a stained-glass window mosaic. The hall also contains a chronology of the Civil War and a short film that deals with Stonewall Jackson's legendary campaign in the Shenandoah Valley. An 1860 farmhouse that figured in the fighting still stands on the premises. Maps for self-guided walking tours are available at the visitor center. The battle is reenacted at the park each May. | 8895 Collins Dr. | 540/740–3101 | www.vmi.edu/museum/nm | $8 | Daily 9–5.

★ **New Market Battlefield Military Museum.** This museum stands in the area where the New Market battle began. The front of the building is a replica of Arlington House, Robert E. Lee's home near Washington, D.C. More than 3,000 artifacts from all American wars are displayed, beginning with the Revolution and including Desert Storm (though most deal with the Civil War). A 35-minute film covers aspects of the Civil War. | 9500 Collins Dr. | 540/740–8065 | fax 540/740–3663 | $7 | Mid-Mar.–mid-Nov., daily 9–5.

Staunton

Unlike New Market, Staunton was unscathed by the Civil War, preserving many buildings dating to the 1700s. Staunton was briefly the capital of Virginia, when the General Assembly fled here from the British in 1781. President Woodrow Wilson was born in Staunton in 1856, and his birthplace is now a museum. Staunton contains a wealth of Victorian, Greek Revival, and Italianate architecture. Five of the town's neighborhoods are national historic districts.

★ **Blackfriars Playhouse.** Experience Shakespeare's plays the way the Elizabethans did at an internationally acclaimed near-duplicate of the playwright's Globe Theatre. Like those in 17th-century London, the benches have no backs (modern seat backs and cushions are available), and some stools are right on stage. | 10 S. Market St. | 540/885–5588 | www.shenandoahshakespeare.com.

Frontier Culture Museum. This outdoor museum re-creates agrarian life in early America with American, Scotch-Irish, German, and English farmsteads, painstakingly removed from their original sites in the four nations and reassembled on the grounds. Livestock has been back-bred and ancient seeds germinated in order to create an environment accurate in all details. Festivals and programs are held throughout the year, from sheep shearing at Easter to corn husking in the fall. A visitor center has displays and a short film about the museum. | 1250 Richmond Rd. | 540/332–7850 | www.frontiermuseum.org | $8.

Statler Brothers Museum. The Statlers were four country-music brothers who defied Nashville, Tennessee, by cutting their records in their hometown, right here in Staunton. A converted elementary school showcases artifacts from their careers. Tours are given once each weekday at 2; the gift shop remains open 10:30–3:30 each weekday. | 501 Thornrose Ave. | 540/885–7297 | www.statlerbrothers.com | Free | Tours weekdays at 2 PM.

★ **Woodrow Wilson Birthplace and Museum.** This 150-year-old Greek Revival house has been restored to its appearance during Wilson's childhood, with some original furnishings. The 28th U.S. president was born here in 1856, son of the Rev. Joseph R. Wilson, a Presbyterian minister, and his wife, Jesse Woodrow. Some items from Wilson's political career are displayed, including his presidential limousine, a 1919 Pierce-Arrow sedan. | 24 N. Coalter St. | 540/885–0897 or 888/496–6376 | fax 540/886–9874 | www.woodrowwilson.org | $7 | Mon.–Sat. 10–5, Sun. noon–5.

Blue Ridge Parkway

The Blue Ridge Parkway takes off where Skyline Drive leaves off at Waynesboro, extending 469 mi south to Cherokee, North Carolina, connecting Shenandoah and Great Smoky Mountains national parks. Between Waynesboro and Roanoke, the route traces the spine of the Blue Ridge through the George Washington National Forest, providing dramatic views of the Shenandoah Valley to the west and the Piedmont to the east. Its elevation ranges from 659 ft where it crosses the James River to 4,200 ft on Apple Orchard Mountain; it goes even higher, to 6,053 ft, in North Carolina. In the spring, hillsides blaze with blooming rhododendrons, mountain laurels, and azaleas. In October, motorists flock to see the brilliant mountain foliage. Recreation areas, visitor centers, short hiking trails, campgrounds, picnic areas, and wayside overlooks offer pleasant diversions for the traveler. The speed limit, 45 mph, is strictly enforced, and sections of the road close during icy or snowy weather.

Humpback Rocks Visitor Center. This center, near the Rockfish Gap entrance to the Blue Ridge Parkway, has free maps, books for sale, picnic tables, and updates on ranger programs. A short trail leads you to a reconstructed pioneer mountain farm, with a cabin, spring house, chicken coop, and barn. | Milepost 5.8, Blue Ridge Pkwy. | 540/943–4716 | www.blueridgeparkway.org | Free | May–Oct., daily 9–5.

James River Visitor Center. At this wayside visitor center is a footbridge across the James River and a trail leading to the Kanawha Canal Lock exhibit. Before railroads became the favored mode of transport, engineers built locks to move freight along the river. The restored lock was part of a 200-mi canal system running from Richmond across the Blue Ridge to Buchanan. | Milepost 63, Blue Ridge Pkwy. | www.blueridgeparkway.org | Free | May–Oct., daily 9–5.

★ **Peaks of Otter Recreation Area.** The name Peaks of Otter refers to two promontories, Sharp Top and Flat Top. Thomas Jefferson once called Sharp Top the tallest mountain in North America; at 3,875 ft, it is actually not even quite as tall as Flat Top, at 4,004 ft. Nevertheless, a 360-degree view awaits on Sharp Top, either by hiking trail or a bus ride. You can see living-history demonstrations many weekends at the Johnson Farm, a homestead dating from the 1800s. A restaurant and lodge rest beside a 23-acre lake in Sharp Top's shadow. | Milepost 86, Blue Ridge Pkwy. | 540/586–4357 | www.blueridgeparkway.org | Free | Apr.–Nov., daily 9–5.

Lexington

In the early 1730s, Scotch-Irish and German colonists migrated south from Pennsylvania. One of the communities they established was Lexington, which in 1778 became the seat of the newly created Rockbridge County. Wiped out by fire in 1796, it was rebuilt with the proceeds of a lottery. During the Civil War, Federal troops raided it, and many of its buildings were razed again. Today, Lexington is a college town, with Washington and Lee University and Virginia Military Institute sitting side by side. Lexington's heritage and many of its present-day attractions revolve around several great military leaders—George Washington, Confederate generals Robert E. Lee and Thomas J. "Stonewall" Jackson, and World War II hero George C. Marshall, winner of the Nobel Peace Prize. Outstanding natural areas also surround the town, including Goshen Pass on Route 39 west of town, a dramatic gorge gouged by the boulder-strewn Maury River.

Cyrus McCormick Farm. On this 634-acre farm, known as Walnut Grove, McCormick demonstrated the first mechanical grain reaper in 1831. The revolutionary invention, which harvested grain five times faster than a scythe or sickle, transformed agricultural production. You can tour the blacksmith shop, gristmill, and museum, which contains an original reaper. The farm, just off I–81 5 mi north of Lexington, is now a research station operated by Virginia Tech. | Rte. 606, 128 McCormick Farm Cir. | 540/377–2255 | fax 540/377–5850 | Free | Daily 8:30–5.

★ **Natural Bridge.** Over millions of years, this massive limestone arch 20 mi south of Lexington has been carved out of rock by Carver Creek, which rushes 215 ft below. The Mono-can Indians called this geologic formation—23 stories high and 90 ft long—the Bridge of God. Surveying the structure for Lord Halifax, George Washington carved his initials in the stone; Thomas Jefferson bought it (and more than 150 surrounding acres) from George III in 1774. During the Revolutionary War, it was used as a shot tower to manufacture ammunition. Today, this natural wonder is owned by a private corporation and is part of a tourist complex that includes a wax museum and caverns said to be the deepest in the East, at 34 stories underground. There's a sound-and-light show held underneath the bridge each evening at sunset. Natural Bridge also supports U.S. 11, and the Cedar Creek Nature Trail passes nearby. | 15 Appledore La. | 540/291–2121 or 800/533–1410 | fax 540/291–1896 | www.naturalbridgeva.com Bridge | $10, wax museum $7, caverns $7 | May–Aug., daily 8–8; Sept.–Nov. and Mar.–Apr., daily 8–6; Dec.–Feb., Wed.–Sun. 8–5.

Stonewall Jackson House. The Confederate general lived in this brick town house, built in 1801, for two years while teaching physics and military tactics to cadets at the nearby Virginia Military Institute. Furnished with period pieces and some of his belongings, it was the only house he ever owned. The general's grave is marked in a small cemetery named after him on South Main Street. Guided tours are provided every half hour. | 8 E. Washington St., 24450 | 540/463–2552 | fax 540/463–4088 | www.stonewalljackson.org | $5 | Sept.–May, Mon.–Sat. 9–5, Sun. 1–5; June–Aug., Mon.–Sat. 9–6, Sun. 1–6.

Virginia Military Institute. Founded in 1839, VMI is the nation's oldest state-supported military college, often called the West Point of the South. About 1,300 cadets undergo the rigors of a traditional college curriculum combined with a daily regime of military training and discipline. Stonewall Jackson and oceanographer Matthew Fontaine Maury were among its early faculty members; George C. Marshall was perhaps the most famous alumnus. Following court decisions allowing women to enter the Citadel, a similar college in South Carolina, the male-only academy became coeducational in 1997. At Lejeune Hall, cadet guides are available for walking tours of the post. Two museums on campus explore VMI's rich tradition more in-depth. | Jefferson St. (U.S. 11) | 540/464–7232 | fax 540/464–7388 | www.vmi.edu | Tours daily 10–4.

The **Virginia Military Institute Museum** houses displays and memorabilia highlighting VMI's history. Stonewall Jackson's stuffed and mounted horse, Little Sorrel, and the coat Jackson wore that was pierced by the bullet that killed him at Chancellorsville are among the exhibits. | Daily 9–5.

The **George C. Marshall Museum** traces the general's career. Marshall's Nobel Peace Prize is displayed among other medals and awards. | $3 | Daily 9–5.

Washington and Lee University. Founded in 1749 as Augusta Academy, this university was later renamed Washington College in gratitude for a donation from George Washington. After Robert E. Lee served as its president following the Civil War, it received its present name. Lee is entombed in Lee Memorial Chapel and Museum on campus; a statue of the general, sculpted by Edward Valentine to give the general a gentle look, graces the altar of the chapel. Today, with 2,000 students, the university occupies a campus of white-column, neoclassical buildings grouped around a central colonnade. Tours are available at the Admissions Office on the hour weekdays from 10 to 3 and on Saturday mornings during spring and fall. | Jefferson St. (U.S. 11) | 540/463–8768 | fax 540/463–8062 | www.wlu.edu | Free | Campus daily. Chapel Apr.–Oct., Mon.–Sat. 9–5, Sun. 1–5; Nov.–Mar., Mon.–Sat. 9–4, Sun. 1–4.

Charlottesville

Charlottesville is Thomas Jefferson's city—its leading attractions are Monticello, the third president's ridge-top home, and the University of Virginia, the architectural and educational masterwork of his later years. Two other presidents associated with Jefferson—James Monroe and James Madison—had homes nearby as well. Named in 1762 for Queen Charlotte, wife of George III, Charlottesville today is a cosmopolitan college town known for its architectural gems and lush countryside. Several annual festivals have added to the city's fame, among them the Virginia Film Festival in October and the Virginia Festival of the Book each spring.

Ash Lawn-Highland. This modest farmhouse was James Monroe's residence from 1799 to 1826, chosen, in part, so that he could be close to his friend, Thomas Jefferson, who lived a few miles away at Monticello—within sight when leaves are off the trees in winter. The house is crowded with the fifth U.S. president's possessions, including gifts from notable persons and souvenirs from his time as envoy to France; the furniture is mostly original. Sheep and peacocks roam the 535-acre grounds. The outdoor Ash Lawn-Highland Summer Festival draws music aficionados June through August to see some of the country's best opera companies. | 1000 James Monroe Pkwy. | 434/293–9539 | $8 | Apr.–Oct., daily 9–6; Nov.–Mar., daily 10–5.

★ **Monticello.** Thomas Jefferson constructed this mountaintop home over a 40-year period from 1769 and 1809. It is considered a revolutionary structure, typical of no single architectural style. The staircases are narrow and hidden because he considered them unsightly and a waste of space; contrary to plantation tradition, his outbuildings are in the rear, not on the side. Throughout the house are Jefferson's inventions, including a seven-day clock and a "polygraph," a two-pen contraption that allowed him to make a copy of his correspondence as he wrote it. April through October, interpreters give tours of Mulberry Row, the plantation "street" where Jefferson's slaves lived and labored. Jefferson and members of his family are buried in a nearby graveyard. The Monticello Visitors Center, 3 mi away on Rte. 20 just off I–64 (Exit 121), is a good stop either before or after a tour of Monticello itself. The center includes exhibits, personal memorabilia, and a half-hour film. | Rte. 53 | 434/984–9800 for Monticello; 434/977–1783 for visitor center | fax 434/977–6140 | www.monticello.org | $11 | Mar.–Oct., daily 8–5; Nov.–Feb., daily 9–4:30.

Montpelier. The former residence of James Madison (1751–1836), the fourth president of the United States, is 25 mi north of Charlottesville, near Orange. Yet Montpelier has a dual legacy; its present state has more to do with its 20th-century owners, the Du Pont family, who enlarged and redecorated it. The landscape walking tour includes the cemetery where Madison and his wife, Dolley, are buried. | Rte. 20, 4 mi south of Orange | 540/672–2728 | www.montpelier.org | $9 | Nov.–Mar., daily 9:30–4:30; Apr.–Oct., daily 9:30–5:30.

★ **University of Virginia.** Thomas Jefferson founded this university in 1819, drafted its first curriculum, helped select its first faculty, designed the original buildings, and served as the first rector of its board of visitors. Today it ranks among the nation's most distinguished institutions of higher education. The heart of the university is the "academical village," built around a rectangular, terraced green space called the Lawn. Anchoring the north end of the Lawn is the domed Rotunda, a half-scale replica of the Pantheon in Rome. Rows of single-story rooms are accented by large pavilions, each in a different classical style. Behind are public gardens delineated by serpentine brick walls. Maps and other brochures about the university can be picked up at the visitor center (2304 Ivy Rd. about ½ mi from campus). | 434/924–3239 | fax 434/924–3587 | www.virginia.edu | Free | Daily; closed during winter break in Dec.–Jan. and during spring exams 1st 3 wks of May; tours daily at 10, 11, 2, 3, and 4.

Virginia Discovery Museum. Hands-on exhibits are meant to interest kids in science, history, and the humanities. Programs include a computer lab and make-it-and-take-it art studio. | 524 E. Main St. | 434/977–1025 | fax 434/977–9681 | www.vadm.org | $4 | Tues.–Sat. 10–5, Sun. 1–5.

Dining

The ethnic roots of upland Virginia go back not only to England but also to Scotland and Germany, and the fare is apt to have a hearty Germanic flavor. Fresh, homemade rolls and German pancakes are popular, along with sauerkraut, sauerbraten, cottage cheese, and pastries made from local apples, peaches, and berries. The valley is also known for its locally cured hams and bacon. Wineries also abound, especially in Albemarle County, around Charlottesville.

Winchester

Cafe Sofia. Eastern European. This small restaurant serves top Bulgarian cuisine, including a goulash featured in *Bon Appétit* magazine. The waitstaff wear traditional Bulgarian dress, and the dining room is filled with weavings, dolls, and other crafts. | 2900 Valley Ave. | 540/667–2950 | Closed Sun.–Mon. and July | $15–$29 | AE, D, DC, MC, V.

Violino Ristorante Italiano. Italian. Some 20 different kinds of homemade pasta fill the menu in this cheery, yellow-stucco restaurant in the city's Old Town. Lobster pansotti—lobster-filled ravioli in a sauce of white wine and lemon sauce—is a favorite. A strolling violinist entertains diners on the weekends. | 181 N. Loudoun St. | 540/667–800 | www.nvim.com/violino | $14–$28 | Closed Sun. | AE, MC, V.

Shenandoah National Park

Panorama Restaurant. American. Virginia country food, sandwiches and pizza are served at this full-service restaurant. Try the fried catfish or the country ham platter. After the meal, check out the many artifacts on display, and the craft store and fudge kitchen. | Skyline Drive, Mile 31.5 at U.S. 211 | 540/999–2265 | Closed mid-Nov.–Apr. | $6–$9 | AE, D, DC, MC, V.

Luray

Brookside. American. Peacocks are the theme at this family-style restaurant, and you'll see plenty of them roaming the grounds outside. There's a salad bar with 32 homemade items, and entrées include brizola steak, pan-fried chicken, pork barbecue, and broiled rainbow trout. | 2978 U.S. 211 E | 540/743–5698 or 800/299–2655 | Closed mid-Dec.–mid-Jan. | $7–$15 | AE, D, DC, MC, V.

Parkhurst at Rainbow Hill. Contemporary. Housed in what was built as a country inn, this casual spot displays paintings by local artists. Outdoor tables on the covered brick porch have views of the Blue Ridge Mountains. Specialty sandwiches—like turkey Reubens, grilled chicken breast, and artichoke and cream cheese—are favorites here. There's also an ice cream shop on the premises. | 2547 U.S. 211 W | 540/743–6009 | $8–$15 | AE, D, DC, MC, V.

New Market

Southern Kitchen. Southern. Visitors and locals have been coming to this restaurant since 1955. Deer trophies decorate the walls, and each booth has its own individual juke box. The peanut soup is a popular starter, and Lloyd's Virginia Fried Chicken, seasoned right down to the bone, is the house specialty. Country ham is another favorite; hams can also be bought to take home. | 9576 Congress St. | 540/740–3514 | $5–$8 | D, MC, V.

Staunton

L'Italia. Italian. In a downtown brick building, this quiet restaurant has white tablecloths, candles, and local artwork on display. After a meal of homemade pasta, veal saltimbocca, or broiled salmon, you have a dozen desserts to choose from. Kids' menu. | 23 E. Beverly St. | 540/885–0102 | fax 540/885–2217 | Closed Mon. | $10–$21 | AE, D, DC, MC, V.

Mill Street Grill. American. Walls in this basement restaurant in a turn-of-the-20th-century mill are original stone and wood, and there are flour bags, stained-glass windows, and other mill relics on display. The baby back ribs are popular, as is the Cajun chicken fettuccine. Try the raspberry brûlée cheesecake for dessert. Kids' menu. | 1 Mill St. | 540/886–0656 | fax 540/433–5523 | Closed lunch | $7–$22 | AE, D, DC, MC, V.

Mrs. Rowe's. American. A homey restaurant with plenty of booths, Rowe's has been operated by the same family since 1947 and enjoys a rock-solid reputation for inexpensive and delicious southern meals. The fried chicken, skillet-cooked to order, is a standout. A local breakfast favorite is oven-hot biscuits topped with gravy (your choice of sausage, tenderloin, or creamy chipped beef). For dessert, try the mince pie in the fall or the rhubarb cobbler in summer. | 74 Rowe's Rd. | 540/886–1833 | fax 540/885–0910 | $6–$15 | D, MC, V.

The Pullman. American. Rail lovers will no doubt love the Pullman. Sharing the 1902 C&O Train Station with the Depot Grille and other businesses, the Pullman arranges its tables so that you can watch the trains pull in while you eat; a fast-moving locomotive along the curved section of tracks under a bluff will make the table shake. Though the food is generic American, there are notable local dishes, like the pecan-coated baked rainbow trout. | 36 Middlebrook Ave. | 540/885–6612 | www.thepullman.com | $8–$14 | AE, D, DC, MC, V.

Blue Ridge Parkway

Otter Creek. American. This rustic restaurant, a short drive from the James River, has outdoor dining on picnic tables by Otter Creek. Known for buckwheat pancakes, the restaurant serve breakfast is served all day. There's also country dinner fare like fried chicken and fish. | Milepost 60.8, Blue Ridge Pkwy. | 804/299–5862 | Closed late Nov.–mid-Apr. | $7–$10 | MC, V.

Peaks of Otter. American. This rustic pine restaurant has a wall of ceiling-high windows with a view of Sharp Top Mountain and Abbott Lake. There's a Friday-night seafood buffet for $21.95, Sunday country brunch, and an extensive selection of Virginia wines. The baked salmon is the local favorite. | Milepost 86, Blue Ridge Pkwy. | 540/586–1081 or 800/542–5927 | www.peaksofotter.com | $6–$22 | MC, V.

Lexington

Frank's Pizza. Pizza. Enjoy the view of the Blue Ridge Mountains from the patio of Lexington's first pizza joint, or eat inside, a bright space with exposed brick walls. Pasta and sub sandwiches are also available. | 511 E. Nelson St. | 540/463–7575 | $4–$10 | No credit cards.

The Palms. American. Palm trees and a teal and mauve color scheme set the scene at this cheerful dining spot. Steaks are hand-cut on the premises and share the menu with steamed shrimp, baby back ribs, fettuccine Alfredo, burgers, and homemade soups and salads. For dessert, try the coconut cream pie. | 101 W. Nelson St. | 540/463–7911 | www.webfeat-inc.com/thepalms | $6–$15 | AE, D, MC, V.

Southern Inn. Contemporary. Established in 1932, this Lexington landmark uses regionally grown organic produce, locally raised pheasants, and fresh seafood to create the nightly specials. Free-range chicken, shrimp, and scallops are usually on the menu, while lamb, duck, pheasant, bison, and seafood are sometimes offered. Live music on Thursday to Saturday. | 37 S. Main St. | 540/463–3612 | $6–$25 | AE, D, MC, V.

Charlottesville

C.&O. French. A boarded-up storefront hung with an illuminated Pepsi sign conceals one of the best restaurants in town. The French-influenced menu has Pacific Rim and American Southwest touches. A popular entrée is steak *chinois* (flank steak panfried with a kind of soy sauce and fresh ginger cream). The wine list is 300 strong. | 515 E. Water St. | 434/971–7044 | www.candorestaurant.com | No lunch | $14–$26 | AE, MC, V.

Continental Divide. Southwestern. A neon sign in the window of this locals' favorite says "Get in here"—you might miss the small storefront restaurant otherwise. The food is southwestern cuisine, with quesadillas, burritos, spicy pork tacos, and enchiladas. The margaritas are potent. Cactus plants decorate the front window, and the booths have funky lights. It can get crowded and convivial, but customers like it that way. | 811 W. Main St. | 434/984–0143 | Reservations not accepted | No lunch | $7–$12 | MC, V.

Crozet Pizza. Pizza. This out-of-the-way rustic clapboard parlor 12 mi west of Charlottesville is renowned for having some of Virginia's best pizza. You can choose from up to 35 toppings, including seasonal items like snow peas and asparagus spears. On the weekend, takeout must be ordered hours in advance. Add your business card to the collection that covers one wall. | Rte. 240, Crozet | 434/823–2132 | Closed Sun.–Mon. | $6–$14 | No credit cards.

Escafe. Café. This trendy café on the west end of the Downtown Mall delights the taste buds with a pleasant mix of European and Asian flavors. A wall of doors opens in the summer to let the outdoors in, and there's also patio seating, perfect for people-watching while you nibble on such delicacies as roasted vegetable lasagna or beef tenderloin with black vinegar sauce. Upstairs, Eastern Standard, open Wednesday–Saturday, is a more upscale version of Escafe. | 102 Old Preston Ave. | 434/295–8668 | www.escafe.com | No lunch Mon. | $5–$16 | AE, D, DC, MC, V.

Hardware Store. American. Deli sandwiches, burgers, crepes, salads, seafood, and ice cream from the soda fountain are what's on sale today in this former Victorian hardware store. The vintage turn-of-the-20th-century signs, tools, and hardware displayed on the walls retain the flavor of a bygone era; some of the wood paneling and brick walls have been here since 1890. The extensive menu of informal American fare has been updated to include smoothies, wraps, and pannini. | 316 E. Main St. | 434/977–1518 or 800/426–6001 | Closed Sun. | $6–$12 | AE, DC, MC, V.

Martha's Cafe. Vegetarian. This friendly restaurant is in a 1920s house just off the trendy Corner, close to the University of Virginia Lawn. Original artwork by the restaurant owners and by members of the community adorns the inside walls; goldfish swim in the bathtub. Dine inside, out under a cool canopy of trees on a brick patio, or on the wooden front porch. Mediterranean quesadillas, eggs Chesapeake with crab cakes, spinach crab soup, black bean burgers, artichoke pasta, micro pizzas, and herb chicken linguine are all house specialties. | 11 Elliewood Ave. | 434/971–7530 | No dinner Mon.–Tues. | $6–$13 | AE, D, DC, MC, V.

Mono Loco. Cuban. The eclectic menu, inspired by Cuban, Caribbean, and Latin cuisines, includes paella loca, giant burritos, and margaritas. Latin kitsch—giant lizards, dragons, and carved wooden angels—and an unforgettably blue-and-green bar add to the fun. Don't miss dessert: bananas Castro, coconut flan, or lime curd with fresh fruit. | 200 W. Water St. | 434/979–0688 | Reservations not accepted | No lunch Sat. | $7–$15 | MC, V.

Lodging

The scale of hotels in the Shenandoah Valley is small, like the valley towns themselves. Motel chains offering standard amenities have one- or two-story structures close to exits in the towns along I–81, and a few old family-owned hotels and many bed-and-breakfasts survive, especially in college towns like Charlottesville, Staunton, and Lexington.

Bed & Breakfast Association of Virginia | Box 791, Orange, VA 22960 | 888/660–2228.

Blue Ridge Bed & Breakfast Reservation Service | 2458 Castleman Rd., Berryville, VA 22611 | 540/955–1246 or 800/296–1246.

Guesthouses, Bed & Breakfast, Inc. (Charlottesville only) | Box 5737, Charlottesville, VA 22905 | 434/979–7264.

Winchester

Hampton Inn. Easy access to I–81, a regional mall, and Old Town Winchester is an advantage here. Kids can enjoy in-room Nintendo. Complimentary Continental breakfast. In-room data ports, cable TV with video games, pool, business services, free parking. | 1655 Apple Blossom Dr. | 540/667–8011 | fax 540/667–8033 | www.hampton-inn.com | 103 rooms | $69–$77 | AE, D, DC, MC, V.

Shenandoah National Park

Skyland Lodge. At the highest point on Skyline Drive (3,680 ft), with views across the Shenandoah Valley, this is the largest lodging facility in Shenandoah National Park. Its 177 rooms include rustic cabins, motel-style rooms, and suites. Big Meadows Lodge (milepost 51) and Lewis Mountain Cabins (milepost 57.5) offer a total of 107 additional rooms within 10 mi of Skyland. Restaurant, bar, playground, business services; no a/c, no room phones, no TV in some rooms. | Skyline Dr., milepost 41.7 | 540/999–2211 or 800/999–4714 | fax 540/999–2231 | www.nps.gov/shen/pphtml/lodging.html | 177 rooms | $52–$112 | Closed Dec.–mid-Mar. | AE, D, DC, MC, V.

Luray

Days Inn. About 7 mi from the entrance to Shenandoah National Park, this chain hotel offers mountain views in almost all of its rooms. Thirteen of the rooms are decorated with antiques collected by the former owner. Restaurant, picnic area, in-room data ports, some in-room hot tubs, cable TV, miniature golf, pool, wading pool, hiking, horseshoes, bar, some pets allowed (fee). | 138 Whispering Hill Rd. | 540/743–4521 | fax 540/743–6863 | www.daysinn-luray.com | 101 rooms | $49–$75 | AE, D, DC, MC, V.

★ **The Mimslyn.** This reconstructed former girls' school is in the center of downtown Luray. Rooms look out over the town and mountains. Soak in the Blue Ridge scenery while sitting on the column-graced veranda, which has its own bar. Or keep an eye on the gardens from inside the solarium. Restaurant, room service, cable TV, business services, some pets allowed. | 401 W. Main St. | 540/743–5105 or 800/296–5105 | fax 540/743–2632 | www.svta.org/mimslyn | 40 rooms, 9 suites | $80–$110 | AE, D, DC, MC, V.

New Market

Cross Roads Inn. Little touches of the innkeepers' Austrian heritage accent the southern and English country furnishings at this family-friendly bed and breakfast. Guest rooms have four-poster canopy beds, some fireplaces, and a blend of antique and contemporary furniture. You can relax, read, play board games, or just watch TV in three large common rooms. Outside there's a kids' play area and a goldfish pond. Some rooms have private baths. No room phones, no room TVs. | 9222 John Sevier Rd. | 540/740–4157 | fax 540/740–4255 | www.crossroadsinnva.com | 6 rooms | $65–$115 | MC, V.

Shenvalee. This golf resort is 2 mi from the New Market Battlefield. Rooms overlook the golf course or the swimming pool. Restaurant, picnic area, refrigerators, cable TV, driving range, 27-hole golf course, putting green, tennis courts, pool, wading pool, bar, business services. | 9660 Fairway Dr. | 540/740–3181 | fax 540/740–8931 | www.shenvalee.com | 42 rooms | $66–$69 | AE, DC, MC, V.

Staunton

Frederick House. Six restored town houses dating from 1810 make up this inn in the center of the historic district. All rooms are decorated with antiques, and some have fireplaces and private decks. Breakfast is complimentary, and a pub and a restaurant are adjacent. Picnic area, cable TV, meeting rooms; no smoking. | 28 N. New St. | 540/885–4220 or 800/334–5575 | www.frederickhouse.com | 9 rooms, 11 suites, 1 cottage | $75–$150 | AE, D, DC, MC, V.

Holiday Inn Golf and Conference Center. The hotel overlooks rolling hills, 8 mi north of town, next to I–81. Restaurant, room service, in-room data ports, some microwaves, some refrigerators, cable TV, driving range, 18-hole golf course, putting green, tennis court, indoor-outdoor pool, exercise equipment, bar, business services, airport shuttle, free parking. | I–81 and Rte. 275, Exit 225, Woodrow Wilson Pkwy. | 540/248–6020 | fax 540/248–2902 | www.holiday-inn.com | 116 rooms, 4 suites | $85–$115 | AE, D, DC, MC, V.

Blue Ridge Parkway

Peaks of Otter Lodge. This unpretentious, peaceful lodge is so popular that reservations are accepted beginning October 1 for the following year. Every room looks out on Abbott Lake from a private terrace or balcony, and their interiors have a folksy quality. Restaurant, fishing, hiking, bar, business services, meeting rooms; no room phones, no room TVs. | Milepost 86, Blue Ridge Pkwy. | 540/586–1081 or 800/542–5927 | fax 540/586–4420 | www.peaksofotter.com | 63 rooms | $66–$90 | MC, V.

Lexington

★ **Maple Hall.** This former plantation, dating to 1850, is on 56 acres, 6 mi north of Lexington. All rooms have period antiques and modern amenities; most have gas log fireplaces as well. Complimentary Continental breakfast. Restaurant, pool, tennis courts, fishing, hiking, business services, meeting rooms. | 3111 N. Lee Hwy. | 540/463–6693 | fax 540/463–6693 | www.lexingtonhistoricinns.com/maplehall.htm | 17 rooms (9 with shower only), 4 suites | $100–$165 | D, MC, V.

Natural Bridge Inn and Conference Center. This redbrick Colonial-style hotel is next to the Natural Bridge tourist complex. Long porches with rocking chairs allow leisurely appreciation of the Blue Ridge Mountains. Rooms are done in a Colonial Virginia style. Restaurant, snack bar, some microwaves, cable TV with movies and video games, miniature golf, 2 tennis courts, indoor pool, hiking, bar, business services, meeting rooms. | U.S. 11 | 540/291–2121 or 800/533–1410 | fax 540/291–1551 | www.naturalbridgeva.com | 180 rooms in 2 buildings | $69–$89 | AE, D, DC, MC, V.

Charlottesville

Best Western Cavalier Inn. This facility's best feature is its location, directly across the street from the grounds of the University of Virginia and one block from the sports arena. The comfortable lobby has a library with many books to choose from and a large overstuffed chair, and the rooms are just as relaxed. Restaurant, cable TV, pool, business services, airport shuttle, free parking, some pets allowed. | 105 Emmet St. | 434/296–8111 | fax 434/296–3523 | www.bestwestern.com | 118 rooms | $69–$89 | AE, D, DC, MC, V.

English Inn of Charlottesville. This well-apportioned small chain hotel has an English Tudor–style exterior and a three-story atrium lobby with cascading plants and Oriental rugs. Suites have antiques and a wet bar; other rooms have modern furnishings. Complimentary Continental breakfast. Some refrigerators, cable TV, indoor pool, gym, sauna, business services, airport shuttle. | 2000 Morton Dr. | 434/971–9900 or 800/786–5400 | fax 434/977–8008 | www.wytestone.com | 88 rooms, 21 suites | $62–$83 | AE, D, DC, MC, V.

★ **Wintergreen Resort.** Accommodations at this 6,700-acre ski and golf resort 25 mi southwest of Charlottesville include everything from studio apartments to seven-bedroom houses. Most rooms have fireplaces and full kitchens; the housing units' wood exteriors blend into the surrounding forest. 6 restaurants, picnic area, kitchenettes, cable TV, two 18-hole golf courses, one 9-hole golf course, 2 putting greens, 24 tennis courts, 6 pools (1 indoor), wading pool, hot tubs, massage, boating, bicycles, hiking, downhill skiing, children's programs (ages 2½–17), playground, business services, convention center, airport shuttle. | Rte. 664 | 434/325–2200 or 800/266–2444 | fax 434/325–8003 | www.wintergreenresort.com | 305 rooms | $125–$250 | AE, MC, V.

Camping

Inside the Parks

Shenandoah National Park. There are developed campgrounds and backcountry camping opportunities in the park. The former are open on a first-come, first-served basis, except for Big Meadows, which requires reservations from mid-May through November. Most have coin showers, laundry facilities, a dump station, and a camp store. No RV hook-ups are available. In addition to Big Meadows, the park's campsites are at Mathews Arm (milepost 22.1), Lewis Mountain (milepost 57.5), Loft Mountain (milepost 79.5), and Dundo Group Campground (milepost 83.7). All campgrounds have a 14-day limit and allow pets. Back-country camping requires a permit, available free of charge at the park headquarters, entrance stations, and visitor centers. | 540/999–2266.

Across Skyline Drive from a scenic meadow, the high-elevation **Big Meadows Campground** offers solitude and cool summer nights. Flush toilets, dump station, laundry facilities, showers, service station, general store | Milepost 51.3 | 800/365–2267 | 164 RV or tent sites, 53 tent-only sites | $17 | Reservations essential. | Apr.–Oct.

Blue Ridge Parkway. There are campgrounds at Otter Creek (milepost 60.9) and Peaks of Otter (milepost 86); each first-come, first-served primitive sites with flush toilets and dumping stations but no showers or hook-ups. | 540/857–2213.

George Washington and Jefferson National Forests. A total of 37 campgrounds are spread across the western half of Virginia. Facilities range from primitive sites with pit latrines to some with showers and bathrooms; a few have electrical hook-ups. | 540/265–5100 or 888/265–0019.

Located 8 mi south of Natural Bridge, **Cave Mountain Lake Recreation Area** can handle RVs up to 22 ft long. A beach and swimming area are available at the lake, and hiking trails lead upward onto the Blue Ridge. Flush toilets, dump station, showers, picnic tables, swimming (lake) | Rte. 781 | 540/265–5100 or 888/265–0019 | 42 sites, 3 hike-in tent sites | $10 | May–Nov.

Elsewhere in the Shenandoah Valley

Many privately owned campgrounds are also scattered throughout the region. Contact the Virginia Division of Tourism (☞ Visitor Information) for more information.

Yogi Bear's Jellystone Park at Natural Bridge. Just 5 mi from Natural Bridge, this campground is located along the James River. Flush toilets, full hook-ups, showers, picnic tables, swimming. | Rte. 782, Natural Bridge Station | 540/291–2727 | 180 sites | $20–$27 | Mar.–Dec.

Shopping

Antiques shops and farmers' markets are commonplace in the Shenandoah Valley; almost every town has at least one of each.

★ **Dayton Farmers Market.** At this market, near Harrisonburg, just off I–81 between New Market and Staunton, you can buy homemade baked goods, fresh fruit and vegetables, and butter churns and speckleware made by the Mennonites who live in the area. | Rte. 42, south of Dayton | 540/879–9885.

Downtown Mall. Charlottesville's six-block brick pedestrian mall has specialty stores, cinemas, art galleries, restaurants, and coffeehouses in restored 19th- and early 20th-century buildings. It is a particularly attractive area for book lovers, with several independent and used-book stores to browse through. | Main St.

Sports and the Outdoors

Bicycling

All parks and forests in the valley permit biking, with some restrictions as to use on walking trails, and separate biking trails are not usually designated. Steep grades and rough surfaces make mountain bikes desirable.

Boating And Canoeing

The Shenandoah River is popular for canoeing and kayaking. Several local outfitters rent boats and shuttle trips.

Downriver Canoe. At this outfitter near Front Royal day and overnight trips start at $29 per canoe (or $32 per kayak, $14 per tube, and $59 per raft). | Rte. 613, near Front Royal | 540/635–5526 | www.downriver.com.

Front Royal Canoe. Near the north end of Shenandoah National Park, Front Royal offers a $14 tube trip as well as canoe, kayak, and raft trips of one hour up to three days for $30–$116. | U.S. 340, near Front Royal | 540/635–5440 or 800/270–8808 | www.frontroyalcanoe.com.

Shenandoah River Outfitters. Canoes and kayaks start at $20. | 6502 S. Page Valley Rd., Luray | 540/743–4159 | www.shenandoahriver.com.

Fishing

Virginia Fishing License. To take advantage of the trout that abound in some 50 streams of Shenandoah National Park, you will need a license; it's available in season (early April to mid-October) for $5 at concession stands along Skyline Drive.

Hiking

★ **Appalachian Trail.** The 2,000-mi wilderness footpath from Maine to Georgia follows the Blue Ridge from south to north across the region, roughly paralleling and at times crisscrossing Skyline Drive and the Blue Ridge Parkway. The closeness of these scenic drives provides many opportunities for casual walkers to bite off a small section of the famous trail. For the serious backpacker seeking seclusion, the AT also traverses wilderness areas far from the road and connects to hundreds of miles of trail in the George Washington National Forest and Shenandoah National Park.

Horseback Riding

Skyland Stables, Shenandoah National Park. Guided horseback trips follow White Oak Canyon trail, which passes several waterfalls. Book 24 hours in advance (or bring your own horse). | Skyland Lodge, Milepost 41.7, near Luray | 540/999–2210.

★ **Virginia Horse Center.** Competitions—show jumping, hunter trials, multibreed shows—are staged several days a week. An indoor arena seating 4,000 permits year-round operation. Most events are free. | 487 Maury River Rd., Lexington | 540/463–2194 | www.horsecenter.org.

Skiing

★ The Shenandoah Valley and Blue Ridge average 2 to 3 ft of snow a winter, but some years get only a few inches. Four downhill ski resorts utilize snowmaking expertise on cold, crisp nights to augment and sometimes offset unreliable natural snowpack. Wintergreen and Massanutten are centrally located along the Blue Ridge, while Bryce Resort and the Homestead hug the state's western border.

Bryce Resort | Rte. 263, Basye | 540/856–2121 | www.bryceresort.com.

The Homestead | Rte. 220, Hot Springs | 540/839–1766 or 800/838–1766 | www.thehomestead.com.

Massanutten Resort | Rte. 33, Harrisonburg | 540/289–9441 | www.massresort.com.

Wintergreen Resort | Rte. 664, Wintergreen | 434/325–2200 or 800/325–2200 | www.wintergreenresort.com.

Essential Information

When to Visit

Though May through October is best, Virginia's relatively mild climate makes touring the region pleasant almost any time of year. Summer months are usually kind, with temperatures typically rising no higher than the 80s. By mid-September, leaves turn in the highest elevations; the brilliant colors then work their way down the slopes into the valleys through October. May and June are blooming time for mountain laurel and rhododendron, which decorate hills and valleys alike with pink-white blossoms. Except for an infrequent big snowstorm, winters are by no means harsh and make for an excellent time to enjoy the region's four ski resorts or find even the most popular attractions uncrowded.

FESTIVALS AND SEASONAL EVENTS

SPRING

Mar.: **Virginia Festival of the Book.** More than 100 writers attend this Charlottesville literary celebration, which offers dozens of events for book lovers of all ages: storytelling, seminars, book fairs, readings, and book signings. | 434/924–3296.

Apr.–May: **Shenandoah Apple Blossom Festival.** Winchester hosts more than 30 events over five days, including arts-and-crafts shows, live music, and many children's activities. Nationally known celebrities from film, sports, and music make appearances, but none outshine the Apple Blossom Queen, crowned during the festivities. | 540/662–3863 or 800/230–2139 | www.sabf.org.

May, Oct.: **Crozet Arts and Crafts Festival.** This nationally ranked art show on Mother's Day weekend displays the work of more than 120 craftspeople with live music and food 12 mi west of Charlottesville. There's another show in October if you miss this one. | 434/977–0406.

SUMMER

July–Aug.: **Shenandoah Valley Music Festival.** Classical, jazz, and folk music echoes off the Allegheny Mountains on many summer weekends as nationally acclaimed bands perform at the Orkney Springs Hotel, an early 19th-century spa that's now an Episcopal Church retreat on Route 23 near Bryce Resort at the state's northwestern fringe. | 540/459–3396 | www.musicfest.org.

AUTUMN

Oct.: **Virginia Film Festival.** Filmmakers, critics, actors, scholars, and moviegoers gather in downtown Charlottesville and on the nearby University of Virginia grounds to view and discuss several independent films. | 800/882–3378.

Bargains

The biggest bargain in the region is the Blue Ridge Parkway, the Park Service's free mountain drive. Free admittance to grounds and historic buildings is offered by Washington and Lee University, Virginia Military Institute, and the University of Virginia. Another freebie is the Cyrus McCormick Farm and Workshop at Steele's Tavern, where the McCormick reaper was invented.

Tours

Historic Staunton Foundation. Free one-hour walking tours are given Saturday mornings at 10, Memorial Day through October, departing from the Woodrow Wilson Birthplace at 24 North Coalter Street. | 540/885–7676.

Lexington Carriage Company. Tours around town in a horse-drawn carriage are given April to October. | 540/463–5647.

Visitor Information

Blue Ridge Parkway | 400 BB and T Building, 1 Pack Sq., Asheville, NC 28801 | 828/298–0398 or 800/727–5928 | www.blueridgeparkway.org. **Charlottesville/Albemarle Convention and Visitors Bureau** | 600 College Dr., Charlottesville, VA 22902 | 434/977–1783 or 877/386–1102 | www.charlottesvilletourism.org. **Lexington Visitors Bureau** | 106 E. Washington St., Lexington 24450 | 540/463–3777 or 877/453–9822 | www.lexingtonvirginia.com. **Luray-Page Chamber of Commerce** | 46 E. Main St., Luray 22835 | 888/743–3915 | www.luraypage.com. **Shenandoah National Park Headquarters** | 3655 U.S. 211 E, Luray, VA 22835 | 540/999–3500 | www.nps.gov/shen. **Shenandoah Valley Travel Association** | Box 1040, New Market 22844 | 540/740–3132 or 877/847–4878 | www.shenandoah.org **Staunton Convention and Visitors Bureau** | Box 810 Staunton, VA 24401 | 540/332–3865 or 800/342–7982 | www.staunton.va.us. **Virginia Division of Tourism** | 901 E. Byrd St., Richmond, VA 23219 | 804/786–4484 or 800/932–5827 | www.virginia.org. **Winchester–Frederick County Chamber of Commerce** | 1360 S. Pleasant Valley Rd., Winchester, VA 22601 | 540/662–4135 or 800/662–1360 | www.shentel.net/wfcedc.

Arriving and Departing

BY AIR

Airports

Charlottesville-Albemarle Airport (CHO). Eight miles north of Charlottesville at the intersection of Routes 606/649 off Route 29, this airport has regional flights to and from New York, Charlotte, and Washington, D.C. | 434/973–8342.

Airport Transportation

Major national rent-a-car companies are available at the Charlottesville airport, and several taxi companies also serve the airport.

Van on the Go. Shuttles carry guests from the Charlottesville airport to hotels, downtown, and area tourist attractions. Reservations are required. | 434/975–8267 or 877/973–7667.

BY BUS

Greyhound Lines serves Charlottesville (310 W. Main St. | 434/295–5131). Buena Vista (211 W. 21st St. | 800/231–2222), near Lexington, and Staunton (1143 Richmond Rd. | 540/886–2424) have daily service to and from New York City and points south.

BY CAR

Charlottesville is where U.S. 29 (north–south) meets I–64. I–81 and Route 11 run north–south the length of the Shenandoah Valley and continue south into Tennessee. I–66 west from Washington, D.C., which is 90 mi to the east, passes through Front Royal to meet I–81 and Route 11 at the northern end of the valley. I–64 connects the same highways with Charlottesville.

BY TRAIN

Union Station. Charlottesville is a stop on Amtrak's runs between Washington, D.C., and Chicago (three times a week) and between New York City and New Orleans (daily). | 810 W. Main St. | 434/296–4559.

Amtrak also has three stops a day in Staunton (1 Middlebrook Ave.) en route from New York and Chicago.

Getting Around

BY CAR

Public transit is available in Charlottesville; elsewhere, you'll need a car to travel the region. Traffic jams are rare in the mostly rural region, though the interstates (I–81, I–64, I–66) are heavily traveled trucking routes and can sometimes get congested. The biggest traffic problems are usually weather related, as the rugged terrain poses the threats of mountain-shrouding clouds, valley fog banks, gusty ridge-top winds and, in winter, ice and snow conditions that can vary dramatically in a few miles as elevation changes.

BY PUBLIC TRANSIT

Bus

Charlottesville Transit Service. Ten routes operate during the day in the city and adjacent areas and 6 at night. Buses run hourly; fare is 75¢. CTS also offers a free trolley service daily between downtown and the University of Virginia. | 315 4th St. NW | 434/296–7433.

Revised and Updated by Gary McKechnie

WALT DISNEY WORLD® RESORT, UNIVERSAL ORLANDO® RESORT, AND THE ORLANDO AREA

October 1971. That's when the "roadside attractions" (aka *tourist traps*) of Central and Southern Florida saw the rise of Walt Disney World, a 47-square-mi resort that would change the face of the state. Joining old favorites such as the southern belles of Cypress Gardens and mermaids of Weeki Wachee were Disney characters, two resort hotels, a campground, and the Magic Kingdom theme park.

In three decades, Disney's influence gave Central Florida bragging rights to seven of the world's top 10 theme parks. Disney added Epcot, the Disney–MGM Studios, and Disney's Animal Kingdom. Walt Disney World pampers guests with two spas, two water parks, five championship golf courses, hundreds of restaurants, and a multitude of diverse nighttime entertainment complexes.

Disney's success sparked the arrival of nautically themed Sea World, which itself charted new territory with Discovery Cove, a one-day, all-inclusive visit to a soothing beachside paradise complete with dolphin swim. A few miles east, Universal Orlando and its original theme park, Universal Studios, marked their first decade in business by adding three resort hotels, a second theme park (Islands of Adventure), and an entertainment complex (CityWalk).

The end result is that Orlando vacations can be extremely satisfying with the sheer magnitude of entertainment or discouraging due to an overabundance of activities that the ordinary traveler couldn't see in a dozen Disney trips. As you plan your vacation, select the few places that will provide the highest degree of fun for your group, allow a day or two to check out unexpected surprises (or just rest), and know that you can always return for more.

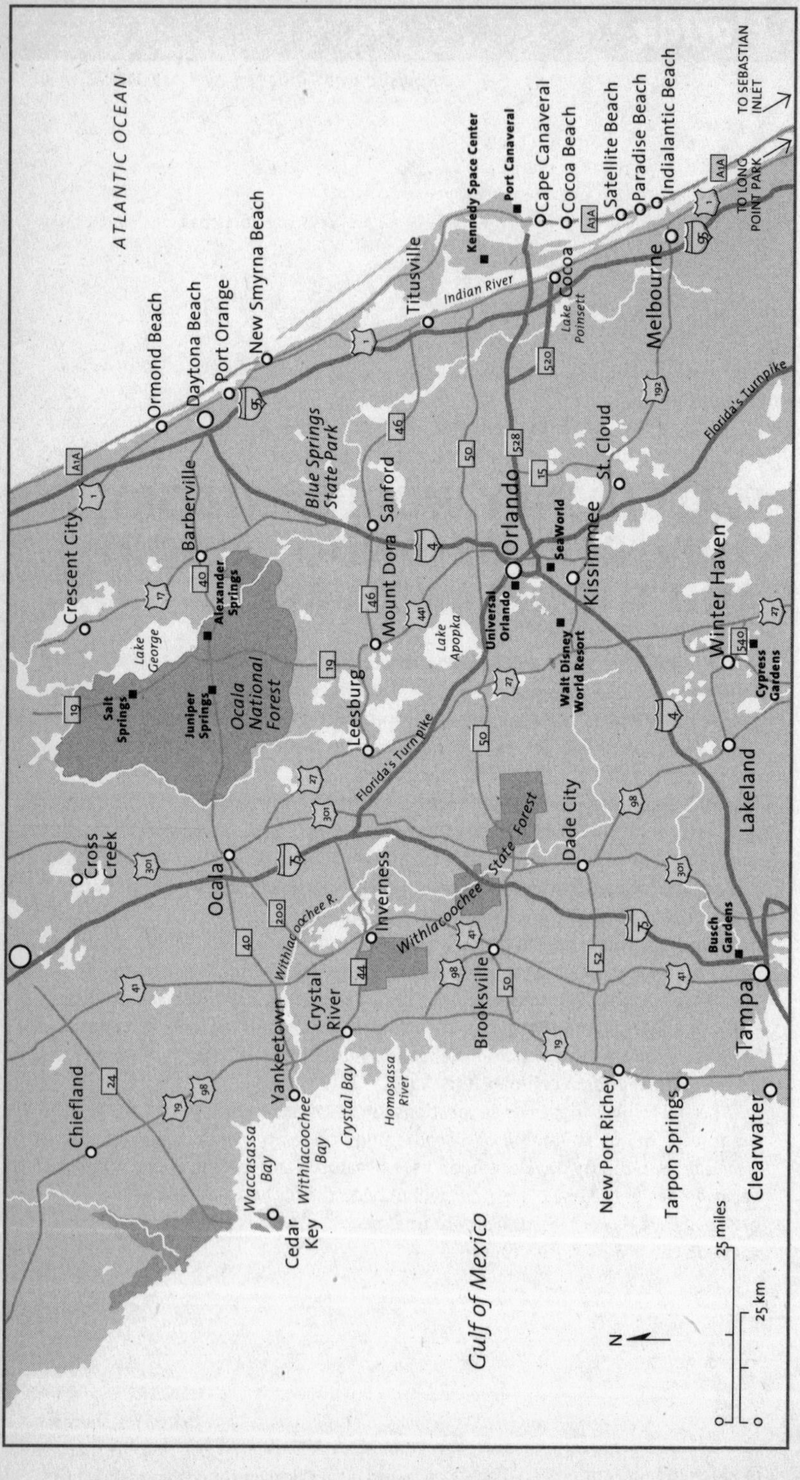
ATLANTIC OCEAN
Gulf of Mexico
Crescent City
Ormond Beach
Daytona Beach
Port Orange
New Smyrna Beach
Barberville
Titusville
Kennedy Space Center
Port Canaveral
Cape Canaveral
Cocoa Beach
Cocoa
Satellite Beach
Paradise Beach
Indialantic Beach
Melbourne
TO SEBASTIAN INLET
TO LONG POINT PARK
Indian River
Lake Poinsett
Blue Springs State Park
Sanford
Orlando
SeaWorld
Kissimmee
St. Cloud
Florida's Turnpike
Lake George
Alexander Springs
Salt Springs
Juniper Springs
Ocala National Forest
Mount Dora
Lake Apopka
Universal Orlando
Walt Disney World Resort
Winter Haven
Cypress Gardens
Leesburg
Lakeland
Dade City
Withlacoochee State Forest
Cross Creek
Ocala
Inverness
Withlacoochee R.
Crystal River
Yankeetown
Brooksville
Busch Gardens
Tampa
Chiefland
Cedar Key
Waccasassa Bay
Withlacoochee Bay
Crystal Bay
Homosassa River
New Port Richey
Tarpon Springs
Clearwater
A1A
1
17
40
19
46
441
27
4
95
520
192
528
50
15
540
98
301
75
200
44
41
52
24
N
0
25 miles
25 km

Exploring

Walt Disney World Resort

MAGIC KINGDOM

★ The Magic Kingdom is the heart and soul of the Disney empire. Wielding worldwide influence, the 98-acre park is packed with nearly 50 attractions within seven lands. Adding to these attractions are themed restaurants, stage shows, fireworks, parades, characters, and, as of late, an annoyingly tacky influx of retail kiosks, shops, and outlets that have squeezed out traditional favorites like the cinema, penny arcade, and magic shop.

Cinderella Castle is the focal point and epicenter of the park, with "spokes" connecting it to every land.

Main Street, U.S.A. With its pastel Victorian-style buildings filled with charming shops, Main Street is where the spell is first cast.

There are few "rides" here, save for the **Walt Disney World Railroad** at the Magic Kingdom's entrance. Authentic and meticulously restored steam locomotives chuff around the 1½-mi perimeter of the Magic Kingdom.

Adventureland. Disney's jungle homage takes a bow to British colonialism.

Highlights include the humorous spiel of the wisecracking skippers at the **Jungle Cruise.** Down mysterious rivers, through jungles, and past cartoonish vignettes, the crew entertains with clever one-liners and bad puns. Kids love the **Magic Carpets of Aladdin,** a new arrival where magic carpets circle a central post. The carpets rise and dip at your command, and the challenge is to avoid the spitting "camels" that encircle the ride. The **Pirates of the Caribbean** is classic Disney, with incredible detailing, catchy music, and fantastic scenes of pirates in battle. The slowly cruising boat drifts past a stone fortress, cannonballs, muskets, a plundered shopping village, and a dungeon. It's festive, fun, cool, and completely entertaining.

Frontierland. Split-rail fences, wooden boardwalks, and the pleasing sight of an old-fashioned paddle-wheeler chugging along the Rivers of America invoke the American frontier.

Big Thunder Mountain Railroad is a roller coaster that seems tame but catches attention with intricate details and stunning scenery along every inch of the 2,780-ft-long wooden track. The **Country Bear Jamboree** is an old favorite, with Audio-Animatronics bears cracking jokes, playing jug band tunes, and leading clap-along songs. Silly, simple, and satisfying. Based on the animated sequences in Disney's 1946 film *Song of the South,* **Splash Mountain** is an incredibly popular log-flume ride.

Liberty Square. It's a seamless transition from weathered Frontierland into the stately oaks, cobblestones, and crisp architecture of Liberty Square's Colonial America.

At the **Hall of Presidents,** a multimedia tribute to the Constitution starts with a film that leads to a roll call of all U.S. presidents and then a lifelike Animatronic Abraham Lincoln speaking on America. A few steps away, the **Haunted Mansion** is great fun for teens and adults but slightly spooky for kids as a "doom buggy" weaves its way through a haunted ball room, hallways, library, and cemetery. Cruising around Tom Sawyer Island, the ***Liberty Belle* Riverboat** is a real old-fashioned steamboat that's slow and not exactly thrilling, but it's certainly relaxing.

Fantasyland. Many of the rides here are for children, but add the parents and the lines grow longer and slower.

The centerpiece for the entire Magic Kingdom is **Cinderella Castle.** With its elongated towers, lacy fretwork, and graceful design, this is a perfect backdrop for photos. In the breezeway, an intricate mosaic tells the story of Cinderella. Visiting the Magic Kingdom and not stopping at **it's a small world** is practically un-American. Dancing, swirling dolls in various national costumes sing the ubiquitous song over and over and over again. The uncommonly popular Pooh is the star of the **Many Adventures of Winnie the Pooh,** where you'll tour the Hundred Acre Wood to meet Piglet, Eeyore, bouncing Tigger, and all honey lover's friends. Don't miss it. **Peter Pan's Flight,** a tame and easy ride, finds magic sailing ships soaring above Victorian London en route to Never Land.

Mickey's Toontown Fair. Disney pays homage to the mouse that started it all, with a toddler-friendly collection of miniature cartoonish houses, rides, and landscaping.

At **Barnstormer at Goofy's Wiseacres Farm,** red barns and farm buildings lead to a kid-size roller coaster aboard a 1920s crop-dusting biplane. In the heart of Toontown Fairgrounds, **Mickey's Country House** seems to have been lifted directly from a cartoon, with Mickey-size appliances, clothes, baby pictures, and a photo of Minnie. At the more cosmopolitan **Minnie's Country House,** you'll see her Martha Stewart–ish quilts, paints, and gardens.

Tomorrowland. A land based on a 1950s sci-fi future has tried to keep pace by changing exteriors and adding new rides themed to recent Disney films.

You board a fast-moving, swirling, twirling vehicle and shoot a laser gun at alien targets on **Buzz Lightyear's Space Ranger Spin.** The movie *Alien* was the inspiration for the **ExtraTERRORestrial Alien Encounter,** which may be the scariest attraction at Disney. An alien gets loose in the darkened space station, and the realistic sound effects and smoke trigger a host of screams and goose bumps. The hands-down, old-time favorite is **Space Mountain,** which lasts just two minutes and 38 seconds but offers devious twists and drops *in the dark* to make it seem twice as long and four times as thrilling.

Entertainment

At Disney, parades are nearly as popular as attractions. At 3 PM, the **Share a Dream Come True** brings floats, cartoon characters, dancers, singers, and much waving and cheering to Frontierland and Main Street. In peak seasons, **SpectroMagic** rolls down Main Street, U.S.A. in a splendidly choreographed surge of electroluminescent, fiber-optic, and prismatic lighting effects. Every evening, the **Fantasy in the Sky** fireworks display explodes behind Cinderella Castle for a memory that will last a lifetime.

EPCOT

Walt Disney believed Epcot would be a utopia, but his accountants realized it would just have to be a collection of gift shops, restaurants, and travelogues. The educational theme park is far more popular with adults and senior citizens than kids. From the entrance, the first half of the park is Future World; then World Showcase surrounds the 40-acre World Showcase Lagoon with 11 international pavilions.

Future World

The core of Future World is the Spaceship Earth geosphere, bracketed by the crescent-shape Innoventions East and West and surrounded by six—soon to be seven—corporate-sponsored pavilions.

Innoventions. This corporate commercial tries to sell you on 21st-century technology with product demonstrations, hands-on displays, and video games.

Imagination! The theme here is the imagination and the fun that can be had when you set it loose.

The most crowd-pleasing attraction is ***Honey, I Shrunk the Audience,*** a 3-D adventure written solely to unleash special effects that alternate between fun and shocking. Don't miss this one.

The Land. Six acres are dedicated to everyone's favorite topic: food.

Rock-and-roll performers in the shape of favorite foods (the Peach Boys, Chubby Cheddar, and Neil Moussaka) sing about the joys of nutrition in **Food Rocks.** The main event is **Living with the Land,** a boat ride through rain forest and desert to see experimental greenhouses and planting techniques.

The Living Seas. The pavilion next door has a 5.7-million-gallon aquarium.

The two-level **Sea Base Alpha** is a typical Epcot playground with six modules dedicated to the history of robotics, ocean exploration, ocean ecosystems, dolphins, porpoises, and sea lions.

Spaceship Earth. The multifaceted silver geosphere of Spaceship Earth is to Epcot what Cinderella Castle is to the Magic Kingdom. However, it only contains a dull and slow presentation on the history of communication.

Test Track. This is like a flat roller coaster where multi-passenger test cars zip around a track at speeds near 65 mph.

Universe of Energy. A large, lopsided pyramid sheathed in thousands of mirrors houses one of the most technologically complex shows at Epcot.

Ellen's Energy Adventure stars Ellen DeGeneres on a quiz show learning about energy with help from Bill Nye the Science Guy.

Wonders of Life. This pavilion takes an amusing but serious and educational look at health, fitness, and modern lifestyles.

The **Body Wars** flight simulator is a thrilling ride through the human circulatory system, while at ***The Making of Me*** Martin Short explains the birds and bees, balancing a touchy subject with gentle humor.

World Showcase

It's a long walk around the 40-acre World Showcase Lagoon (1⅓ mi), but the trek is tempered by pavilions representing 11 countries in Europe, Asia, North Africa, and the Americas. Each includes native food, entertainment, art, and handicrafts and usually a multimedia presentation showcasing the particular culture and people; architecture and landscaping re-create well-known landmarks. Traveling in counterclockwise order, you'll reach Canada first.

Canada. A striking rocky chasm and tumbling waterfall welcome you, and a gift shop and quiet sit-down restaurant are added attractions. Not bad, eh?

The CircleVision film ***O Canada!*** stars the Great White North's stunning natural scenery.

United Kingdom. This pavilion captures multiple eras of England. Beatles soundalikes play in a rose garden, and a village of thatched-roof cottages re-creates the shops of a typical High Street. The Rose and Crown pub becomes the terminus of many a traveler's intended around-the-world walk.

France. Accordion music, a mock Eiffel Tower, a patisserie, sidewalk café, and mimes and artists make up this impression of France.

Impressions de France is a film celebrating the beauty and romance of the nation's vineyards, cities, mountains, and valleys.

Morocco. Through the pointed arches of the Bab Boujouloud gate is the Koutoubia Minaret, a replica of the prayer tower in Marrakesh. There's less here than in most other pavilions, but the marketplace show and winding alleyways are interesting to see.

Japan. Highlights are a mock-up of the Itsukushima Shrine, a Tokyo department store, a rock and water garden, and performances by traditional Japanese drummers.

American Adventure. The park's centerpiece has hosts Mark Twain and Ben Franklin looking at highlights of American history, making this a patriotic favorite.

Italy. Piazza San Marco is the star, along with a re-creation of Venice's Doge's Palace complete with gondolas, Roman columns, and Byzantine mosaics. The antiquated look is part of the fun; the other part is the fancy restaurant, Alfredo's.

Germany. Here you'll see accurate architecture, classy gift shops with German mugs and cuckoo clocks, a glockenspiel tolling the hours, and an oompah band in the Biergarten restaurant. Seeing is Bavarian.

China. A marketplace is all there is to Africa, which is followed by a shimmering red-and-gold three-tier replica of Beijing's Temple of Heaven in China. It towers over a serene Chinese garden, an art gallery displaying treasures from the People's Republic, a spacious emporium devoted to Chinese goods, and two restaurants.

The ***Wonders of China*** is a sensational panorama of the land and people, dramatically portrayed on a 360° CircleVision screen.

Norway. A 14th-century stone fortress mimics Oslo's Akershus, while cobbled streets, rocky waterfalls, and a wood-stave church, modeled after one built in 1250, create an amalgam of Scandinavian culture.

The **Maelstrom** takes a voyage through rough seas and encounters evil trolls, which are more interesting than frightening. Kids love the Age of the Vikings playground area.

Mexico. A spectacular Maya pyramid hosts an exhibit of pre-Columbian art, a restaurant, and shopping plaza. The cool, dark insides of the pyramid can provide a welcome respite from a hot Orlando day.

Entertainment

What Epcot lacks in activities and real attractions it makes up for in entertainment. Show times are in your park map. Above the lagoon every night, about a half hour before closing, don't miss the spectacular **IllumiNations** sound-and-light show, with fireworks, lasers, and lots of special effects to the accompaniment of a terrific score.

DISNEY–MGM STUDIOS

Disney–MGM Studios blends a theme park with fully functioning (but seldom used) movie and television production center. Older visitors appreciate the Silver Screen–era architecture, and kids like the attractions based on movies they have seen in the theaters. Although the park is divided into sections, the delineation is less obvious than at Epcot or the Magic Kingdom. You'll likely just wander from Hollywood Boulevard to New York to the Animation Courtyard without noticing too many changes. At only 110 acres (a quarter the size of Universal Studios) and with 20 major attractions, this a one-day park.

Hollywood Boulevard. This area of the park has the palm trees, neon, and 1930s Tinseltown down pat, but it only has one attraction.

The **Great Movie Ride** is a 22-minute guided tour of great moments in film shown inside a replica of Grauman's Chinese Theater.

Sunset Boulevard. For real thrills, head down Sunset for some must-sees.

Rock 'n' Roller Coaster Starring Aerosmith is WDW's wildest roller coaster, while the **Twilight Zone Tower of Terror** is a deserted and haunted 13-story hotel where you enter a strange universe before your elevator takes several 130-ft free-falls. The antidote may be the **Theater of the Stars** and its presentation ***BEAUTY AND THE BEAST—Live on Stage.***

Animation Courtyard. This is a kid-oriented area with one of the best WDW shows for children.

The stars of several popular Disney Channel shows appear in ***Playhouse Disney—Live on Stage!*** In a self-guided tour through the animation process, the **Magic of Disney Animation** starts with a film starring Walter Cronkite and Robin Williams, who introduce the working animation studios.

Mickey Avenue. Stroll down this street and you'll pass the soundstages that are used to produce some of today's television shows and motion pictures.

Departing from here is the **Disney-MGM Studios Backlot Tour,** a 60-minute exploration of the back-lot building blocks of movies: set design, costumes, props, lighting, and special effects.

New York Street. It's worth touring the sets here on foot so that you can check out the windows of the shops and apartments, the taxicabs, and other details.

New York Street features the splendid **Jim Henson's MuppetVision 3-D,** as well as the ***Honey, I Shrunk the Kids*** **Movie Set Adventure,** an oversize state-of-the-art playground that's quite popular with kids.

Echo Lake. The last "land" in the park, an idealized California, presents two can't-miss attractions.

The **★Indiana Jones Epic Stunt Spectacular!** show is an action-packed, loud, and testosterone-rich blowout, and **Star Tours** is a ride using flight-simulator technology and based on scenes from the classic film *Star Wars.*

Entertainment

The live *Beauty and the Beast* and *Hunchback of Notre Dame* stage shows are winners. And don't miss the **daily parade** that wends its way up Hollywood Boulevard. **Fantasmic!** is the perfect finale to the day; an elaborate laser-and-fireworks show starring Mickey Mouse as he reprises his role as the Sorcerer's Apprentice.

DISNEY'S ANIMAL KINGDOM

Disney's fourth Orlando theme park explores the story of all animals—real, imaginary, and extinct—in a true Disney fashion. Make sure you arrive early, when the animals are at their liveliest, or you may miss out on some of the best reasons to go.

Discovery Island. This is the site of the park's centerpiece, the 14-story-high Tree of Life.

Inside the **Tree of Life** is the extremely entertaining 3-D show ***★It's Tough to Be a Bug!*** Enormous fun for older kids and adults, it may be scary for kids creeped out by bugs.

DinoLand U.S.A. Just as it sounds, this is the place to come into contact with prehistoric creatures.

The **Boneyard** playground gives kids a chance to slide, bounce, and slither around an archaeological dig site, while the **DINOSAUR** ride gives everyone the chance to be scared silly in a race across our prehistoric planet as an asteroid speeds toward earth. A new coaster is **Primeval Whirl,** which spins, twists, and turns in a low-impact coaster ride.

Asia. The beauty of Asia is seen in its exotic rain forest and tiger shrine.

The **Kali River Rapids** is a water-flume ride that races the Chakranadi River through a huge bamboo tunnel and into temple ruins. For great souvenir photos, take the **Maharajah Jungle Trek** for wonderful up-close view of jungle animals, including magnificent tigers, a Komodo dragon, and fascinating fruit bats.

Africa. On the opposite side of the park, Africa reveals itself at Harambe, a coastal "village" spotlighting Swahili architecture, food, and shopping with African themes.

The highlight here is **Kilimanjaro Safaris,** which rolls guests through 100 acres of savanna, forest, rivers, and rocky hills to see herds of African animals, including elephants, rhinos, giraffes, hippos, and cheetahs. A bachelor group of lowland gorillas, hippos (viewed from under the water), meerkats, exotic birds, and even naked mole rats live at the walk-through **Pangani Forest Exploration Trail.**

Camp Minnie-Mickey. Near the entrance, this Adirondack-style land is designed for kids.

The ***Festival of the Lion King,*** however, will please every age with its delightful live tribal celebration of song, dance, and acrobatics starring characters from the film.

THE DISNEY WATER PARKS

Blizzard Beach. Ski resort meets tropical lagoon at Blizzard Beach. A sandy beach features the obligatory wave pool, a lazy river, and play areas for both young children and preteens.

An alpine (!) village sets the stage for **Mt. Gushmore,** a "snowcapped" mountain with toboggan and sled runs to ride. At 55-mph, **Summit Plummet** is billed as the "world's tallest, fastest free-fall speed slide." **Teamboat Springs** sets six-passenger rafts zipping along a twisting series of rushing waterfalls.

Typhoon Lagoon. Disney's second water park boasts of a surf lagoon the size of two football fields, with arrow-straight water slides and white-water rapids.

Shark Reef is a 360,000-gallon tank containing an artificial coral reef and 4,000 real tropical fish. The **Humunga Kowabunga** waterslide offers a drop of more than 50 ft, while in the children's area, **Ketchakiddie Creek** replicates adult rides on a smaller scale.

WALT DISNEY WORLD RESORT A TO Z

Admission Fees

Visitors 10 and over pay adult prices; "children" are ages 3 through 9. No discounted family tickets are available. When it comes to tickets and passes, a "ticket" is a single day's admission to the Magic Kingdom, Epcot, Disney–MGM Studios, or Disney's Animal Kingdom. For stays of three days or longer, consider a **Park Hopper** pass for unlimited visits to the four major parks on any four or five days, depending on the length of the pass, with any combination of parks on a day. The five-, six-, and seven-day **Park-Hopper Plus** passes include unlimited visits to the four theme parks on any five, six or seven days, plus visits to WDW's minor attractions. Disney-resort guests can purchase **Length of Stay Passes** passes, valid from arrival until midnight of the day of departure day. Tickets are available at all park entrances, on-site resorts, and at the Walt Disney World kiosk at Orlando International Airport. With them, you can go anywhere at any time, saving you the trouble of buying more tickets. Remember, this is for resort guests only.

To speed up your visits to the parks, try **FASTPASS,** a free system that reserves a time for you to visit the most popular attractions. All you need to do is look for a FASTPASS kiosk near the ride entrance, punch a few buttons, and receive a card stamped with the time you should return to the attraction. Return at the appointed time and head for the FASTPASS entrance, and proceed to the preshow or boarding area with little or no wait. You'll lose wait fast.

Ticket prices rise rapidly and without warning, and at press time rates (including 6% tax) were as follows: **One-day ticket,** $53 adults, $42.40 children; **Park Hopper,** four days: $210.94 adults, $168.54 children; five days: $242.74 adults, $194.05 children; **Park Hopper Plus,** five days: $274.56 adults, $220.49 children; six days: $306.37 adults, $245.95 children; seven days: $338.17 adults, $271.38 children. **Blizzard Beach** and **Typhoon Lagoon,** $32.86 adults, $26.50 children. Check the WDW website for the latest prices and for online booking discounts.

Getting Around
Walt Disney World Resort has its own transportation system, with boats, buses, and monorails that run from early morning until at least midnight. Allow 45 minutes to an hour to get from one point to your destination.
Opening and Closing Times
In general, summer and holidays offer the longest operating hours, usually from 9 AM until at least 10 PM. However, hours vary greatly, and it pays to call ahead or check the parks' Web-site calendar.
Parking
Disney parking lots cover an area the size of Salt Lake City. Always write down exactly where you've parked your car and take the note with you. The cost is $6 for cars and $7 for RVs and campers, although the fee is waived for WDW resort guests with I.D.
Visitor Information
Walt Disney World Information | 407/824–4321. **WDW Switchboard** | 407/824–2222. **WDW Central Reservations** | 407/934–7639. **WDW Dining Reservations** | 407/939–3463.

Disney–MGM Studios TV-show tapings | 407/560–4651. **KinderCare** | 407/827–5444 for in-room; 407/827–5437 for drop-off. **Water Parks** | 407/560–928.

Universal Orlando Resort

UNIVERSAL STUDIOS

Contained in 444 acres are attractions primarily geared more to teenagers and adults than to the stroller set.

Production Central. Composed of six huge warehouses with working soundstages, this area is adding new attractions based on the Shrek and Jimmy Neutron: Boy Genius films.

New York. Gotham-style streets here play host to performances by the Blues Brothers.

TWISTER . . . Ride It Out makes you an eyewitness to an ominous tornado. Loud and scary. Another new ride, based on the Scorpion King movie, will open here in 2003.

San Francisco/Amity. This land mixes scenes of San Francisco with a New England–y fishing village.

JAWS is a boat ride filled with explosions, noise, shaking, and the gnashing teeth of shark after shark after shark. The live ***Wild, Wild, Wild West Stunt Show!*** is fun and funny but not overly exciting.

World Expo. The far corner of the park features two popular futuristic rides.

BACK TO THE FUTURE . . . The Ride is a jarring, jouncing flight-simulator ride inside a DeLorean. The second favorite is **MEN IN BLACK—Alien Attack,** a ride through New York streets, where you fire at aliens to rack up points.

Woody Woodpecker's KidZone. For the preschool set, the thrill of it all is here.

A Day in the Park with Barney is a stage show filled with syrupy sing-alongs kids will love. **E. T. Adventure** will take you on a bicycle ride across the universe to the alien's quirky home, and ***Animal Planet Live!*** features a menagerie of talented performing critters.

Hollywood. Deco storefronts and a few attractions pay tribute to the Silver Screen.

Don't miss the ***Universal Horror Make-up Show,*** which is exactly what the name implies; and ***TERMINATOR 2 3-D,*** an action-packed stage show based on the movie.
Entertainment
Don't miss Universal's seasonal evening parties—most notably **Mardi Gras** (late February through early March), **Fiesta Caliente** (May), **Rock the Universe** (Christian

music, September), and the wildly popular **Halloween Horror Nights** (October). Except for Halloween and Rock the Universe, these festivals are included with park admission.

UNIVERSAL ISLANDS OF ADVENTURE

Islands of Adventure elevated theme-park attractions to a new level. Five islands encircling a broad lagoon are the foundation of the park, with enough standout rides to make this a must-see.

Seuss Landing. While adults recall why Dr. Seuss was their favorite author, kids are introduced to the Cat, Things One and Two, Horton, and the Lorax.

The **Cat in the Hat: Ride Inside** is a whirling, twirling look inside the book, and the colorful **One Fish, Two Fish, Red Fish, Blue Fish** is a silly, simple, and sometimes wet ride aboard flying fish.

Lost Continent. Ancient myths from around the world inspired this land.

A twin roller coaster, **Dueling Dragons,** is fast, furious, and frightening, while the **Eighth Voyage of Sindbad** is an action-packed stunt show in a cool amphitheater.

Jurassic Park. The Jurassic Park of Steven Spielberg's blockbuster movies is recreated here.

The prehistoric theme reaches its peak at attractions like **Jurassic Park River Adventure,** a boat ride past—and nearly into the clutches of—mighty frightening dinosaurs. If you have kids, don't miss the **Jurassic Park Discovery Center,** which will fill their little heads with even more dinosaur intelligence and trivia than they probably already possess.

Toon Lagoon. This land is geared for children, although adults do enjoy getting soaked on the rides.

Popeye & Bluto's Bilge-Rat Barges is a churning white-water raft ride, while the **Dudley Do-Right's Ripsaw Falls** flume ride is definitely wet and wild.

Marvel Super Hero Island. The facades along Stanley Boulevard (named for Marvel's famed editor and co-creator Stan Lee) put you smack in the middle of the adventures in a Marvel comic book.

The **Incredible Hulk Coaster** will command your attention before it scares the pants off you with its twisted spaghetti loops and rollovers. The best ride in the park—and perhaps in the world—is the ★**Amazing Adventures of Spider-Man,** an unusual and surreal blend of moving vehicles, 3-D film, simulator technology, and special effects. It's as good as the movie.

UNIVERSAL ORLANDO A TO Z

Admission Fees

One day at Universal Studios or Islands of Adventure costs $52.95 for adults and $43.41 for children three to nine, including tax. Two-day **Escape Passes** are $100.65 for adults and $86.87 for children and do not need to be used consecutively.

Discounts

Orlando/Orange County Convention & Visitors Bureau. Discounted tickets are available. You'll save about $4 per adult ticket ($3 on children's prices). | 8723 International Dr. | 407/363–5871.

American Automobile Association. Members get 10% off, sometimes more, at AAA offices. | 888/937–5523.

Parking

It costs $7 for cars, $8 for campers, and $14 for valet parking at Universal Orlando. All but valet is covered parking, which makes returning to your car a cool experience.

Visitor Information

Universal Orlando | 1000 Universal Studios Plaza, Orlando 32819-7610 | 407/363–8000 or 888/331–9108 | www.universalorlando.com.

Other Theme Parks

SEAWORLD ORLANDO

A favorite park for older guests and travelers without kids, SeaWorld combines quiet sanctuaries with action-packed and very funny shows. The entire park has a slower and lazier feel than others, and walking the promenade to shows and exhibits is a casual and comfortable experience. | 7007 Sea Harbor Dr., Orlando 32821 | 407/351–3600 or 800/327–2424 | www.seaworld.com | $55.33 for adults, and $45.74 for children three to nine, including tax; 10% discount for on-line purchase; occasional "2d Day Fun" promotion provides a complimentary pass valid for return within 7 days | Daily 9–7, until as late as 10 summer and holidays; educational programs daily 9–3, every 30 mins.

At the ★**Atlantis Bayside Stadium** some of the world's best skiers do on water what gymnasts have difficulty doing on land. At ★**Shamu Stadium,** another popular show features the star of the park, SeaWorld's orca mascot. Two classics shows at **Sea Lion & Otter Stadium** and **Key West Dolphin Stadium** star extremely talented seals, otters, walruses, bottle-nosed dolphins, and Pseudorca whales (close cousins to the killers) in funny stories for an always entertained audience.

To jazz things up, SeaWorld introduced two roller coasters: **Journey to Atlantis,** a water coaster that races through the world of Greek mythology; and **Kraken,** a high-intensity ride of seven inversions and moments of weightlessness.

Highlighting the park's wildlife are attractions like **Pacific Point Preserve,** where California sea lions and harbor and fur seals relax on a rocky promontory. Drop into a refrigerated re-creation of Antarctica at **Penguin Encounter**; see the lumbering manatees at **Manatees: the Last Generation?**; and view tropical fish and scary sea life at **Tropical Reef** and popular **Terrors of the Deep.**

DISCOVERY COVE

A 32-acre limited-admission park is a re-creation of a tropical beach-side oasis. Cascading waterfalls and white beaches fringed with thatched huts, cabanas, and hammocks brings to mind the Bahamas, Tahiti, and Micronesia. The steep price (at press time, $219; $119 if you don't want to swim with a dolphin) loses its sting when you realize that it includes access to all swim and snorkeling areas and the free-flight aviary; a full meal (drinks not included); use of a mask, snorkel, towel and other amenities; parking; and seven-day admission to SeaWorld. | 877/434–7268 for reservations | www.discoverycove.com | Daily 9–5:30.

CYPRESS GARDENS

A 45-minute drive from Walt Disney World Resort, one of Florida's first tourist attractions is a combination botanical garden, ski show, and soul-soothing sanctuary. As this book went to press, Cypress Gardens closed. Call the park for the latest status updates. | 941/324–2111 or 800/237–4826; 800/282–2123 in FL | www.cypressgardens.com | $37.05 adults, parking $6 regular, $7 preferred | Daily 9:30–5:30, later in peak season.

The **Botanical Gardens Cruise** floats through the cypress-hung canals of the Botanical Gardens, passing flowering shrubs and actresses dressed up as southern belles. In the lovely ★**Wings of Wonder: The Butterfly Conservatory,** more than 1,000 butterflies from 50 species flit about.

Elsewhere in the Area

KISSIMMEE

Flying Tigers Warbird Air Museum. Just outside of Disney's gates, this museum showcases about 30 vintage fighter planes. | 231 Hoagland Blvd. | 407/933–1942 | www.warbirdmuseum.com | $9 | Daily 9–5:30.

Gatorland. Opened 22 years before Walt Disney World, this theme park presents thousands of gators, turtles, and snakes in shows and displays and lazing in the sun. | 14501 S. Orange Blossom Trail, between Orlando and Kissimmee | 407/855–5496 or 800/393–5297 | www.gatorland.com | $17.93 | Daily 9–sunset.

Splendid China. There's live entertainment, a playground, and, primarily, painstakingly re-created versions, both full scale and miniature, of China's greatest landmarks. | 3000 Splendid China Blvd. | 407/397–8800 recording; 407/396–7111 voice | www.floridasplendidchina.com | $28.88 | Daily 9:30–7, later in peak season.

NEAR INTERNATIONAL DRIVE

Between WDW and downtown Orlando, I-Drive is a meandering road crowded with tacky shops and some small but interesting attractions.

WonderWorks. This fascinating playground's hands-on activities are similar to those at a science museum. Experience an earthquake or a hurricane; design and ride a virtual roller coaster. Adults like it as much as the kids. | 9067 International Dr. | 407/352–8655 | $16.95 | Daily 9 AM–midnight.

DOWNTOWN ORLANDO

The downtown corridor waxes and wanes, but nearby neighborhoods like Thornton Park thrive with new shops, galleries, and cafés. Lake Eola has been the focal point of Orlando for ages, and it is best enjoyed by strolling around the shores or pedaling a swan boat by its fountain.

Orange County Regional History Center. This newly renovated museum pays tribute to the past with great Florida-ish displays on Orlando's pre-Disney days. | 65 E. Central Blvd. | 407/836–8500 or 800/965–2030 | www.thehistorycenter.org | $7 | Mon.–Sat. 10–5, Sun. noon–5.

WINTER PARK

A few minutes from downtown, Winter Park is a charming community of upscale shops, chic boutiques, cafés, and museums. Along popular Park Avenue, Central Park borders the old-fashioned shopping district, which is highlighted by a still active railroad station.

Charles Hosmer Morse Museum of American Art. This museum holds the world's largest collection of Louis Comfort Tiffany stained-glass windows, lamps, and watercolors. | 445 Park Ave. N | 407/645–5311 | $3 | Tues.–Sat. 9:30–4, Sun. 1–4.

Rollins College. Take a walk around campus at the southern end of Park Avenue. The circa-1920 Spanish Mediterranean buildings, lakeside setting, and free Cornell Fine Arts Museum make this a nice hidden treasure. | End of Holt Ave. | 407/646–2526 | Museum Tues.–Fri. 10–5, weekends 1–5.

★ **Wekiwa Springs State Park.** Crystal-clear Wekiwa Springs flow into the mysterious Wekiva River within the confines of this state park. The 72°F water is perfect for swimming, pavilions are great for picnicking, and a canoe concession allows you to explore natural Florida. Roughly 12 mi from downtown Orlando (about 30 from the theme parks), it's a pleasant discovery in a city of dense traffic and urban overflow. | 1800 Wekiva Cir., Apopka | 407/884–2009 | $4 per vehicle | Daily 8–sunset.

MOUNT DORA

Roughly 45 minutes from Orlando, this authentic village is known as the New England of Florida for its hilly landscape and northern architecture. It's also known as the Antiques Capital of Florida and Festival City for obvious reasons. With its quaint shops, gift galleries, and natural beauty, Mount Dora makes a nice transition back to the real world.

Dining

Because tourism is king here, casual dress is the rule, and few restaurants require fancier attire.

Walt Disney World Resort

Central Reservations Line. For restaurants within Walt Disney World Resort, reservations are especially easy to make, thanks to this service. | 407/939–3463 or 407/560–7277.

ESPN Sports Club. American/Casual. Sports fan? Not only is the restaurant filled with big-screen TVs showing virtually every important sporting event on the planet, there are also live sports-trivia contests when the bar is not doubling as a broadcast studio. Burgers are big and juicy, and there are slow-cooked, barbecued pork ribs and a 10-ounce sirloin. Open late on Friday and Saturday. | Disney's BoardWalk | 407/939–5100 | $8–$16 | AE, MC, V.

★ **House of Blues.** Cajun/Creole. Although the blues theme suggests adults, kids can eat hearty with catfish, pork chops, and hamburgers. A gospel Sunday brunch is righteous—and so popular you'll need reservations. | Downtown Disney West Side, Downtown Orlando | 407/934–2583 | $8–$25 | AE, D, MC, V.

Official All-Star Café. American/Casual. You have to like sports to dine here, where you'll find celebrity sports memorabilia and a menu ranging from burgers to steaks to pasta. | Disney's Wide World of Sports | 407/827–8326 | $6–$20 | AE, MC, V.

Universal's CityWalk

Hard Rock Cafe Orlando. American/Casual. It's crowded, but kids like the activity and rock memorabilia. Their parents like the selection of basics like burgers, ribs, and meat loaf. | 5800 S. Kirkman Rd. | 407/351–7625 | Reservations not accepted | $10–$20 | AE, D, DC, MC, V.

Jimmy Buffett's Margaritaville. American/Casual. Parrot-heads can probably name the top two menu items before they ever walk in the door. This is the place to order a Cheeseburger in Paradise, as well as quesadillas, chowder, and crab cakes, stone crab claws, steak, and great desserts. | Universal Studios Plaza | 407/224–9255 | Reservations not accepted | $8–$20 | AE, D, DC, MC, V.

NASCAR Café Orlando. American/Casual. Racing fans love the theme here. If the memorabilia on the walls is not enough for you, there are a couple of actual race cars hanging from the ceilings. The menu selections, including popcorn shrimp, the Thunder Road burger, and chicken potpie, are better than you might think. | 6000 Universal Blvd., at Universal Studios Escape's CityWalk | 407/224–9255 | Reservations not accepted | $8–$20 | AE, D, MC, V.

International Drive, Orlando

Bahama Breeze. Caribbean. This Orlando creation serves a great mix of island-style food, and the low-key tropical setting may be perfect for families settling down after a day in the parks. | 8849 International Dr. | 407/248–2499 | Reservations not accepted | $10–$25 | AE, D, DC, MC.

Lodging

There are about 110,000 rooms in Orlando, and prices can range from less than $50 to about $200. Stay at Disney and you have the advantage of free on-site transportation. Make reservations as far in advance as possible, and consult a map to see where your lodging is in relation to what you want to see. Rooms are cheaper between September and mid-December. Orlando lodging prices tend to be a little higher than elsewhere in Florida, but in all but the smallest motels there is little or no charge for children under 18 who share a room with an adult.

WDW: Disney-Owned Properties

WDW Central Reservations. Advance reservations may be booked through this service; for same-day reservations contact the number listed for the individual property. | Box 10100, Lake Buena Vista 32830 | 407/934–7639 or 407/560–7277.

All-Star Sports, All-Star Music, and All-Star Movies Resorts. Disney's economy resorts depict sports, music themes, and movie themes. Each room has two double beds, a closet rod, an armoire, and a desk. The All-Star resorts are as economically priced as most any hotel in Orlando. The food courts sell standard fast food. 3 food courts, cable TV, 6 pools, 3 bars, baby-sitting, playground, laundry facilities, laundry service | 407/939–5000 Sports; 407/939–6000 Music; 407/939–7000 Movies | fax 407/939–7333 Sports; 407/939–7222 Music; 407/939–7111 Movies | 1,920 rooms at each | $77–$124 | AE, D, DC, MC, V.

WDW: Other Hotels

Courtyard by Marriott at WDW Resort. A tranquil 14-story atrium, tropical gardens, and attractive guest rooms with green carpets, rose-colored couches, and floral print bedspreads put you near, not in, Disney. Restaurant, in-room data ports, cable TV, 2 pools, wading pool, hot tub, gym, lobby lounge, playground, laundry facilities, laundry service. | 1805 Hotel Plaza Blvd., 32830 | 407/828–8888 or 800/223–9930 | fax 407/827–4623 | www.courtyard.com | 323 rooms | $89–$139 | AE, DC, MC, V.

Orlando

Fairfield Inn by Marriott. Few frills are found in Marriott's answer to the Motel 6 and Econolodge. It is squeezed between International Drive and Interstate 4, but a few perks like free coffee, tea, and local phone calls make this hotel worth a thought. Cable TV, pool | 8342 Jamaican Ct., 32819 | phone/fax 407/363–1944 | 800/228–2800 | www.fairfieldinn.com | 134 rooms | $59–$89 | AE, D, DC, MC, V.

★ **Holiday Inn SunSpree Resort Lake Buena Vista.** Arcades and play areas attract the kids, while lower-rate rooms and free children's buffets please the parents. The family-friendly focus continues in the guest rooms, many of them Kidsuites, a playhouse-style room within a larger room. Add a refrigerator, microwave, and coffeemaker, and you have a reasonably priced alternative to typical suites that still provides some privacy. Restaurant, grocery, cable TV, pool, wading pool, gym, 2 hot tubs, basketball, Ping-Pong, bar, lobby lounge, theater, children's programs (ages 3–12), playground, laundry facilities, laundry service. | 13351 Rte. 535, Lake Buena Vista 32821 | 407/239–4500 or 800/366–6299 | fax 407/239–7713 | 507 rooms | $69–$209 | AE, D, DC, MC, V.

Sheraton Studio City. With its Hollywood theme and unique circular design, this I-Drive hotel offers a little more pizzazz than the average hotel box. The Wet n' Wild water park is just blocks away. Restaurant, room service, cable TV, pool, wading pool, hair salon, hot tub, bar, lobby lounge, laundry service, concierge, business services | 5905 International Dr., 32819 | 407/351–2100 or 800/327–1366 | fax 407/345–5249 | www.grandthemehotels.com | 302 rooms | $89–$159 | AE, D, DC, MC, V.

Summerfield Suites Hotel. From four to eight people can sleep in the one- and two-bedroom units at the all-suites Summerfield. Popular two-bedroom units have fully equipped kitchens, a living room with TV and VCR, and another TV in one bedroom. Grocery, cable TV, pool, wading pool, hot tub, gym, lobby lounge, laundry facilities, laundry service, business services, meeting rooms | 8480 International Dr., 32819 | 407/352–2400 or 800/830–4964 | fax 407/352–4631 | www.summerfield-orlando.com | 146 suites | $89–$159 | AE, D, DC, MC, V.

Travelodge Orlando South. Comfy, but not spectacular, rooms have two double beds, and children 17 and under stay free in their parents' room (with a maximum of four people per room). The hotel is ¼ mi from SeaWorld. Restaurant, cable TV, 3 pools, bar, laundry facilities, laundry service | 6263 Westwood Blvd., 32821 | 407/345–8000 or 800/346–1551 | fax 407/345–1508 | www.travelodge.com | 144 rooms | $59–$129 | AE, D, DC, MC, V.

Kissimmee

Best Western Kissimmee. Value is above par at this hotel overlooking a 9-hole, par-3 executive golf course. It's a hit with senior citizens and golfers. The pool area offers some shaded spots, and spacious rooms are done in soft pastels, with light-wood furniture and attractive wall hangings. Units with king-size beds and kitchenettes are available. Restaurant, picnic area, cable TV, 2 pools, bar, lobby lounge, playground | 2261 E. Irlo Bronson Memorial Hwy., 34744 | 407/846–2221 or 800/944–0062 | fax 407/846–1095 | 285 rooms | $39–$119 | AE, D, DC, MC, V.

Quality Suites Maingate East. Spacious rooms equipped with microwaves, refrigerators, and dishwashers are designed to sleep between 6 and 10. Suites have two bedrooms with two double beds each and a living room with a double pullout couch. Freebies include breakfasts, plus afternoon beer and wine at the pool-side bar, as well as one admission (per suite) to Cypress Gardens, Water Mania, or Splendid China. Restaurant, cable TV, microwaves, refrigerators, pool, wading pool, hot tub, bar, lobby lounge, playground, laundry service | 5876 W. Irlo Bronson Memorial Hwy., 34746 | 407/396–8040 or 800/848–4148 | fax 407/396–6766 | 225 units | $59–$169 | AE, D, DC, MC, V.

★ **Radisson Resort Parkway.** The Radisson offers an attractive location, good facilities, and competitive prices for generously proportioned rooms decked out in tropical patterns. Rooms with the best view and light face the pool. Restaurant, snack bar, cable TV, tennis courts, 2 pools, wading pool, 2 gyms, 2 hot tubs, sauna, volleyball, 2 lobby lounges, laundry facilities, laundry service | 2900 Parkway Blvd., 34746 | 407/396–7000 or 800/634–4774 | fax 407/396–6792 | 712 rooms, 6 suites | $69–$149 | AE, D, DC, MC, V.

Sevilla Inn. This family-operated motel is one of the best buys in Orlando. Up-to-date rooms have colorful bedspreads, tasteful wall hangings, and cable TV. If you just need a place to rest between theme parks, park it here and enjoy the pool. Cable TV, pool, laundry facilities | 4640 W. Irlo Bronson Memorial Hwy., 34746 | 407/396–4135 or 800/367–1363 | fax 407/396–4942 | 50 rooms | $30–$50 | AE, D, MC, V.

Camping

WDW: Disney-Owned Properties

★ **Fort Wilderness Resort and Campground.** Amid 700 acres of scrubby pine and tiny streams are campsites as well as fully equipped trailer sites. You'll also find two tennis courts, boating, bicycling, basketball, horseback riding, shuffleboard, and volleyball. This is one of the cheapest ways to be on Disney property. Flush toilets, full hook-ups, partial hook-ups (electric and water), dump station, drinking water, laundry facilities, showers, grills, picnic tables, restaurant, snack bar, public telephone, general store, playground, 2 pools | 397 campsites, 386 trailer sites, 408 cabins | On Bay Lake, about 1 mi from Wilderness Lodge | 407/824–2900 | $34–$299 | AE, MC, V.

Arts and Entertainment

Dinner Shows

What these shows lack in substance and depth they make up for in color and enthusiasm; children often love them. At most shows, you'll share a long table with strangers. Always call and make reservations in advance, especially for weekends and shows at Walt Disney World Resort.

WALT DISNEY WORLD RESORT

Hoop-Dee-Doo Revue. This Wild West show serves up corny jokes with barbecued ribs, fried chicken, corn on the cob, and strawberry shortcake. | Fort Wilderness Resort | 407/939–3463 in advance; 407/824–2803 day of show | $46.33 adults, $23.78 children 3–11, includes tax and gratuities | Daily 5, 7:15, and 9:30 PM | No smoking.

Polynesian Luau. Join fire jugglers and hula-drum dancers at a South Pacific picnic of traditional island dishes and tropical fruit. | Polynesian Resort | 407/939–3463 (WDW–DINE) in advance; 407/824–1593 day of show | $47.80 adults, $24.81 children 3–11, including tax and gratuities | Daily 5:15 and 8 PM | No smoking.

ORLANDO

Arabian Nights. The show includes eerie fog, an Arabian princess, and a buffoonish genie, but the real stars are the 54 fabulous horses that perform in acts representing horse-loving cultures from around the world. The three-course dinners are of prime rib or vegetarian lasagna. | 6225 W. Irlo Bronson Memorial Hwy., Kissimmee | 407/239–9223; 800/553–6116; 800/533–3615 in Canada | $44 adults, $27 children 3–11 (plus tax) | Shows nightly; times vary | AE, D, MC, V.

Capone's Dinner and Show. This performance somehow manages to make gangland Chicago seem like a perfect dinner-table topic. The unlimited Italian buffet is heavy on pasta. | 4740 W. Irlo Bronson Memorial Hwy. | 407/397–2378 | $39.95 adults, $23.95 children 4–12 | Daily 7:30 | AE, D, MC, V.

Medieval Times. A cast of 75 knights, nobles, and maidens, not to mention 30 charging horses, performs in a huge, ersatz-medieval manor house. Sword fights and jousting matches complement a bill of fare centered on meat and potatoes. | 4510 W. Irlo Bronson Memorial Hwy., Kissimmee | 407/239–0214 or 800/229–8300 | $42 adults, $26 children 3–11 | Performances usually daily at 8 but call ahead to check | AE, D, MC, V.

Sleuths Mystery Dinner Show. Your four-course meal is served up with a healthy dose of conspiracy. If you haven't got a Clue, then stop here and question the characters in an attempt to solve the mystery. | 7508 Universal Blvd. | 407/363–1985 or 800/393–1985 | $39.95 adults, $23.95 children 3–11 | Weekdays 7:30 PM (and sometimes 8:30); Sat. 6, 7:30, and 9 PM; Sun. 7:30 PM | AE, D, MC, V.

Shopping

Orlando welcomes about 38 million visitors a year, so shopping has to be plentiful and diverse. And it is. Look around and you'll find malls and flea markets and antiques districts and more malls and independent gift shops with cut-rate theme-park merchandise.

Factory Outlets

Belz Factory Outlet World. At the northern tip of I-Drive is the area's largest collection of outlets—more than 180—in two malls and four nearby annexes. | 5401 W. Oak Ridge Rd., Orlando | 407/354–0126 or 407/352–9611 | Mon.–Sat. 10–9, Sun. 10–6.

Orlando Premium Outlets. The 127 upscale shops occupy an open-air layout at the confluence of I–4, Highway 535, and International Drive. It's easy to see but awkward to reach. Call for directions. | 8200 Vineland Rd. | 407/238–7787 | www.orlandopremiumoutlets.com | Mon.–Sat. 10–10, Sun. 10–9.

Flea Markets

Flea World. There are dozens of markets in Orlando, but this is the biggest, open Friday–Sunday 9–6. New merchandise is sold at more than 1,600 booths. | 3 mi east of I–4 Exit 50 on Lake Mary Blvd., then 1 mi south on U.S. 17–92, Sanford | 407/321–1792.

★ **Renninger's Twin Markets.** This flea and antiques market attracts hundreds of dealers to Mount Dora (45 minutes from Orlando) on the weekends. Wintertime Extravaganzas draw nearly 1,500 dealers. | U.S. 441, Mount Dora | 352/383–8393.

Shopping Areas, Malls, and Department Stores

AT THE THEME PARKS

Chances are, you'll want to buy souvenirs while you visit the parks. Both Disney and Universal offer you that option with figuratively thousands of shops in the parks and dozens more in on-site shopping villages. Get those credit cards ready, folks.

Downtown Disney. Two shopping-entertainment areas, Downtown Disney Marketplace and Downtown Disney WestSide, have plenty of just about everything—from the Disney superstore to end all Disney superstores to a Virgin Megastore.

Universal's CityWalk. Great shops, such as Endangered Species and Cigarz, rub shoulders with restaurants and nightclubs.

ORLANDO

Crossroads of Lake Buena Vista. Across from Downtown Disney Marketplace, this is perhaps the most convenient stop for essentials for Disney guests. | Rte. 535 and I–4, Lake Buena Vista.

Florida Mall. More than 200 stores and 1.6 million square ft of retail space guarantee plenty of shopping action. | 8001 S. Orange Blossom Trail.

Outdoor World. At the north end of I-Drive is a 150,000-square-ft western-style lodge carrying every possible piece of outdoor gear ever invented. If you're an outdoor enthusiast, this is a must-see. | 5156 International Dr. | 407/563–5200.

Pointe*Orlando. Seventy specialty shops including a mighty impressive F.A.O. Schwarz are across from the Orange County Convention Center. | 9101 International Dr.

Sports and Outdoor Activities

Bicycling

Orlando has good bike trails that have been created from former railroad lines. The West Orange Trail runs some 19 mi through western Orlando and a neighboring town, Apopka. The best place to access the trail is at Clarcona Horseman's Park (3535 Damon Rd., Apopka).

BICYCLING AT WALT DISNEY WORLD RESORT

The most scenic bike riding in Orlando is on Walt Disney World Resort property, along roads that take you past forests, lakes, golf courses, and Disney's wooded resort villas and campgrounds.

Fort Wilderness Bike Barn. Bicycles rent for about $8 per hour and $21 per day. | 407/824–2742.

Fishing

Central Florida lakes and rivers teem with largemouth black bass, perch, catfish, sunfish, and pike. To fish in most Florida waters—but not at Walt Disney World Resort—anglers over 16 need a fishing license (available at bait-and-tackle shops, fishing camps, and sporting-goods stores). Top fishing waters include Lake Kissimmee, the Butler and Conway chains of lakes, and Lake Tohopekaliga (also known as Lake Toho).

East Lake Fish Camp. On East Lake Tohopekaliga, this fishing camp provides guides. | 3705 Big Bass Rd., Kissimmee | 407/348–2040.

Golf

Golf is extremely popular in Central Florida. Be sure to reserve tee times well in advance. Greens fees at most non-Disney courses fluctuate with the season. A twilight discount applies after 2 in busy seasons and after 3 during the rest of the year; the discount is usually half off the normal rate.

Golfpac. This service packages golf vacations and prearranges tee times at more than 40 courses around Orlando. Contact Golfpac for information on local courses; rates vary based on hotel and course. | Box 162366, Altamonte Springs 32701 | 407/260–2288 or 800/327–0878,

GOLF AT WALT DISNEY WORLD RESORT

Three of Walt Disney World's five championship 18-hole courses are on the PGA Tour route. The three original Disney courses—Lake Buena Vista, Magnolia, and the Palm—have the same fees and discount policies regardless of season and are slightly less expensive than Eagle Pines and Osprey Ridge, whose fees change during the year. All offer a twilight discount rate, $22–$80, which goes into effect at any time from 2 to 4, depending on the season. Call 407/939–4653 for tee times.

Horseback Riding

Horse World Riding Stables. Basic as well as longer, more advanced nature-trail tours wind along beautifully wooded trails near Kissimmee. Pony rides are also available, and the stables area has picnic tables, farm animals you can pet, and a pond to fish in. Trail rides are $32 for basic, $37 for intermediate, and $49 for advanced. Pony rides for children under six are $6. Reservations a day in advance are recommended for the advanced trails. | 3705 S. Poinciana Blvd., Kissimmee | 407/847–4343.

Miniature Golf

Fantasia Gardens Miniature Golf Course. This putt-putt course, heavily themed in imagery from Disney's *Fantasia*, is adjacent to the Swan and Dolphin Resort complex and the Winter Summerland Mini-Golf Course. Games are $9.67 for adults, $7.78 for children ages 3–9. | 407/560–4870.

Water Sports

Marinas at the Caribbean Beach Resort, Contemporary Resort, Dixie Landings Resort, Downtown Disney Marketplace, Fort Wilderness Resort and Campground, Grand Floridian, Polynesian Resort, Port Orleans Resort, Wilderness Lodge, and Yacht and Beach clubs rent Sunfish, catamarans, motor-powered pontoon boats, pedal boats, and tiny two-passenger Water Sprites—a hit with kids—for use on their nearby waters.

Buena Vista Watersports. This first-class operation offers ski boats and personal-watercraft rentals. | 13245 Lake Bryan Dr. | 407/239–6939.

Essential Information

When to Go

The parks can be more pleasing when school's in session and kids are scarce, but parents, by necessity, populate the parks heavily in the summer and during school breaks. Slower seasons mean shorter lines; peak seasons offer more staffing, longer hours, and extra entertainment and parades. Orlando's peak seasons are Christmas, late March, Easter weeks, and mid-June through mid-August. February, May, October, and early December (just before and after school breaks) are pleasingly quiet and often cool.

FESTIVALS AND SEASONAL EVENTS

WINTER

Jan.: **Zora Neale Hurston Festival.** In Eatonville, America's oldest incorporated black community, the local author is honored with a festive and colorful celebration of African-American art, cooking, music, and stories. | 800/972–3310 | www.zoranealehurston.cc.

Feb.: **Florida Film Festival.** Hoping to retain the title of "Hollywood East" for their town, Orlando filmmakers and production people showcase an assortment of independent domestic and foreign films. | 407/629–1088.

SPRING

Mar.: **Winter Park Art Sidewalk Art Festival.** One of the most popular art festivals in the Southeast, this sidewalk show is held along the streets and parks of this charming village. | 407/644–8281.

AUTUMN

Nov.: **Fall Fiesta in the Park.** Under cool skies, more than 550 artists and crafters present and peddle their wares along the picturesque shores of downtown's Lake Eola. | 407/246–2827.

Bargains

Orlando FlexTicket. To compete with Disney, Universal, SeaWorld, and Tampa's Busch Gardens joined forces on this $180.15 (adult) ticket, which covers four parks of your choice, including Universal, Wet 'n Wild, SeaWorld, and Busch Gardens. The $215.46 five-park version buys unlimited admission to all of the above plus a safari through Busch Gardens. Each ticket is good for 14 days.

Tours

Each theme park offers special (sometimes pricey) guided tours for nearly instant access to attractions and a peek behind the scenes. SeaWorld's "Trainer for a Day" tours put you in contact with their aquatic stars; Universal Orlando's personal guided tours cover meals and the privilege to cut in line; Disney theme parks allow you to go "backstage" to see how this seamless production is prepared (☞ Exploring).

Scenic Boat Tour. In the affluent Orlando suburb of Winter Park, this tour cruises a chain of lakes for a look at grand homes and calming beauty. Open daily 10–4; admission is $7 for adults and $3 for children 2–11. | 312 E. Morse Blvd., Winter Park | 407/644–4056.

Visitor Information

Kissimmee/St. Cloud Convention and Visitors Bureau | 1925 E. Irlo Bronson Memorial Hwy., Kissimmee 34744 | 407/847–5000 or 800/327–9159 | www.floridakiss.com. **Orlando/Orange County Convention and Visitors Bureau** | 6700 Forum Dr., Suite 100, Orlando 32821-8087 | 407/363–5800 | www.orlandoinfo.com. **Winter Park Chamber of Commerce** | Box 280, Winter Park 32790 | 407/644–8281.

Arriving and Departing

BY AIR

Airports

Orlando International Airport (MCO). The airport is south of Orlando and northeast of Walt Disney World. | 407/825–2001 | www.orlando-mco.com.

Airport Transportation

Find out in advance whether your hotel offers a free airport shuttle; if not, ask for a recommendation.

Public Transit: Lynx, the city's mass transit system, has a route between the airport and the main terminal downtown and to Disney (via SeaWorld) as well. Although the cost is very low, other options are preferable, since the terminal is far from most hotels used by theme-park vacationers.

Shuttle: Mears Transportation Group. Orlando's main transport service has vans, buses, town cars, and limos. Vans run to and along U.S. 192 every 30 minutes; prices range from $16 one-way for adults ($12 for children 4–11) to $28 round-trip for adults ($20 children 4–11). Limo rates run around $50–$60 for a town car that accommodates three or four and $90 for a stretch limo that seats six. | 407/423–5566.

Town & Country. Depending on the hotel, this service charges $30–$40 one-way for up to seven. | 407/828–3035.

Taxi: Taxis take only a half hour to get from the airport to most hotels used by WDW visitors. They charge about $30 to the International Drive area, about $10 more to the U.S. 192 area.

BY BUS

Greyhound Lines | 555 N. John Young Pkwy. | 407/292–3422.

BY CAR

From Interstate 95, which runs down Florida's east coast, you can turn off onto Interstate 4 just below Daytona; it's about 50 mi from there to Orlando. If you're taking I–75 down through the middle of the state, get off at Wildwood and take Florida's Turnpike for about 50 mi. The scenic Beeline Expressway, a toll road, links Orlando and Cocoa Beach, about an hour away.

BY TRAIN

Amtrak has terminals in Winter Park at 150 West Morse Boulevard, in Orlando at 1400 Sligh Boulevard, and in Kissimmee at 416 Pleasant Street. Thirty miles north of Orlando, the city of Sanford is the southern terminus for the AutoTrain, which carries passengers and their cars between Central Florida and Lorton, Virginia—a 900-mi overnight shortcut.

Getting Around

Pubic transportation is available in Orlando, but the best bet is to rent a car—with one exception: if you are staying at Disney and plan to visit only Disney parks. In that case, as a Disney guest, you have access to an efficient transportation system that will get you where you want to go, and for free.

Away from Disney, most larger hotels and motels will offer (for a few bucks) a shuttle to the parks. And if you are traveling with your family, you may spend more on these shuttles, which charge by the head, than on a rental car. Orlando offers some of the lowest rental-car rates in the United States.

BY CAR

Interstate 4 is Central Florida's main highway, linking the Atlantic in Daytona Beach with Tampa Bay and the Gulf of Mexico. Although referred to as an east–west highway, in Orlando it runs north–south. Other important roads for travelers are International Drive, also known as I-Drive, which is a main tourist corridor of hotels, restaurants, and shops roughly 10 minutes east of Disney. Closer to Disney, U.S. 192 runs between Disney's main gate and the nearby Kissimmee–St. Cloud resort area. The Greeneway, an almost ring road around Central Florida, with stops near the attractions, east Orlando, and Sanford, is nearing completion. Large sections of this toll road are already in use, easing traffic congestion in the area considerably.

BY PUBLIC TRANSIT

Bus

Lynx. If you are staying along International Drive, in Kissimmee, or in Orlando proper, you can ride public buses to get around the immediate area. | 407/841–8240.

Shuttle

Scheduled service and charters link just about every hotel and major attraction, and many hotels run their own shuttles especially for guests. One-way fares are usually $6–$7 per adult, a couple of dollars less for children ages 4–11, between major hotel areas and the WDW parks. Round-trip excursion fares to Cypress Gardens are $27 per person, including admission. Ask hotel staff for schedules.

Gray Line of Orlando | 407/422–0744 **Mears Transportation Group** | 407/423–5566.

TAXI

Taxi fares start at $2 for the first mile and cost $1.50 for each mile thereafter. Sample fares: to WDW's Magic Kingdom, about $22 from International Drive, $12–$16 from U.S. 192. To Universal Studios, $7–$12 from International Drive, $25–$32 from U.S. 192. To Church Street Station, downtown, $20–$26 from International Drive, $34–$42 from U.S. 192.

A-1 Taxi | 407/328–4555, **Checker Cab Company** | 407/699–9999, and **Star Taxi** | 407/857–9999.

District of Columbia

Revised and Updated by Maureen Graney

WASHINGTON, DC

The byzantine workings of the federal government; the sound-bite–ready oratory of the well-groomed politician; the murky foreign policy pronouncements issued from Foggy Bottom: they all cause many Americans to cast a skeptical eye on anything that happens "inside the Beltway." Washingtonians take it all in stride, though, reminding themselves that, after all, those responsible for political hijinks don't come *from* Washington, they come *to* Washington. Besides, such ribbing is a small price to pay for living in a city whose charms extend far beyond the bureaucratic. World-class museums and art galleries (nearly all of them free), tree-shaded and flower-filled parks and gardens, bars and restaurants that benefit from a large and creative immigrant community, and nightlife that seems to get better with every passing year are as much a part of Washington as floor debates or filibusters.

There's no denying that Washington, the world's first planned capital, is also one of its most beautiful. And though the federal government dominates many of the city's activities and buildings, there are places where you can leave politics behind. Washington is a city of vistas—pleasant views that shift and change from block to block, a marriage of geometry and art. Unlike other large cities, Washington isn't dominated by skyscrapers, largely because in 1910 Congress passed a height-restrictions act to prevent federal monuments from being overshadowed by commercial construction. Its buildings stretch out gracefully and are never far from expanses of green. Like its main industry, politics, Washington's design is a constantly changing kaleidoscope that invites contemplation from all angles.

Exploring

The best way to see Washington is by neighborhood. Bear in mind that the Mall itself can take several days to explore. Some neighborhoods, such as Dupont Circle and Georgetown, are good destinations in the evening, when their lively street life and varied restaurants can be best experienced, though museums and historic sites in these areas will have to be visited during the day.

The Mall

Arthur M. Sackler Gallery. The collection includes works from China, Southeast Asia, Korea, Tibet, and Japan. The lower level connects to the Freer Gallery of Art. | 1050 Inde-

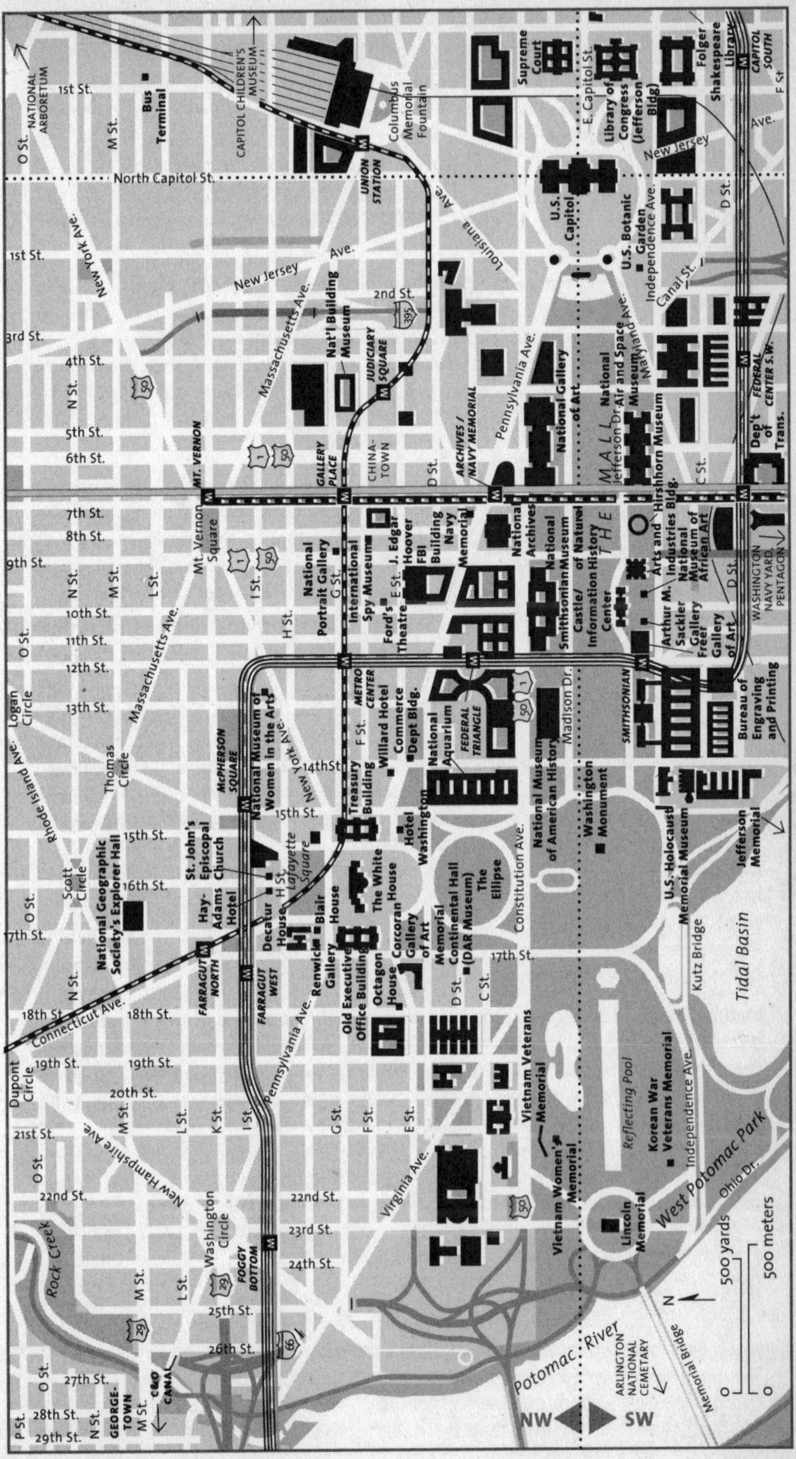

NATIONAL ARBORETUM
CAPITOL CHILDREN'S MUSEUM
Bus Terminal
North Capitol St.
Columbus Memorial Fountain
UNION STATION
Supreme Court
Library of Congress (Jefferson Bldg)
Folger Shakespeare Library
CAPITOL SOUTH
E. Capitol St.
New Jersey Ave.
U.S. Capitol
U.S. Botanic Garden
Independence Ave.
Canal St.
Louisiana Ave.
Massachusetts Ave.
New York Ave.
Nat'l Building Museum
JUDICIARY SQUARE
National Gallery of Art
National Air and Space Museum
Maryland Ave.
FEDERAL CENTER S.W.
Dep't of Trans.
Pennsylvania Ave.
ARCHIVES / NAVY MEMORIAL
Hirshhorn Museum
Jefferson Dr.
THE MALL
GALLERY PLACE
CHINATOWN
MT. VERNON
Mt. Vernon Square
National Archives
Navy Memorial
J. Edgar Hoover FBI Building
National Portrait Gallery
International Spy Museum
Ford's Theatre
National Smithsonian Museum of Natural History
Castle/ Information Center
Arts and Industries Bldg.
National Museum of African Art
Arthur M. Sackler Gallery
Freer Gallery of Art
WASHINGTON NAVY YARD, PENTAGON
SMITHSONIAN
Bureau of Engraving and Printing
METRO CENTER
Willard Hotel
Commerce Dept Bldg.
National Aquarium
FEDERAL TRIANGLE
Madison Dr.
National Museum of Women in the Arts
McPHERSON SQUARE
Logan Circle
Thomas Circle
Rhode Island Ave.
Scott Circle
Treasury Building
Hotel Washington
National Museum of American History
Washington Monument
U.S. Holocaust Memorial Museum
Jefferson Memorial
Tidal Basin
Kutz Bridge
Constitution Ave.
The Ellipse
Continental Hall (DAR Museum)
The White House
Lafayette Square
St. John's Episcopal Church
Hay-Adams Hotel
Decatur House
Blair House
Renwick Gallery
Corcoran Gallery of Art
Memorial Continental Hall
Old Executive Office Building
Octagon House
National Geographic Society's Explorer Hall
FARRAGUT NORTH
FARRAGUT WEST
Connecticut Ave.
Dupont Circle
New Hampshire Ave.
Virginia Ave.
Vietnam Veterans Memorial
Vietnam Women's Memorial
Reflecting Pool
Korean War Veterans Memorial
Independence Ave.
West Potomac Park
Ohio Dr.
Lincoln Memorial
Washington Circle
FOGGY BOTTOM
Rock Creek
C&O CANAL
GEORGETOWN
Potomac River
ARLINGTON NATIONAL CEMETARY
Memorial Bridge
NW
SW
N
500 yards
500 meters

pendence Ave. SW | 202/357–2700; 202/357–1729 TDD | www.asia.si.edu | Free | Daily 10–5:30 | Metro: Smithsonian.

Arts and Industries Building. This building, the second Smithsonian museum to be constructed, was originally called the United States National Museum, the name that's still engraved in stone above the doorway. Today it houses changing exhibits, a museum shop, and the Discovery Theater for children. The Smithsonian carousel is right outside. | 900 Jefferson Dr. SW | 202/357–2700; 202/357–1500 Discovery Theater show times and ticket information; 202/357–1729 TDD | www.si.edu | Free | Daily 10–5:30 | Metro: Smithsonian.

Bureau of Engraving and Printing. Paper money has been printed here since 1914. In addition to all the paper currency in the United States (some $38 million worth of currency a day), stamps, military certificates, and presidential invitations are printed here, too. | 14th and C Sts. SW | 202/874–3188 | www.bep.treas.gov | Free | Sept.–May, weekdays 9–2; June–Aug., weekdays 9–2 and 5–6:30 | Mar.–Sept., same-day timed-entry passes issued starting at 8 AM at Raoul Wallenberg Pl. SW entrance | Metro: Smithsonian.

Freer Gallery of Art. One of the world's finest collections of masterpieces from Asia includes works from the Far and Near East, including Asian porcelains, Japanese screens, Chinese paintings and bronzes, Korean stoneware, and Islamic objects. Detroit industrialist Charles Freer, whose endowment made the museum possible, was introduced to Asian art by his friend James McNeill Whistler. The American painter is represented in the vast collection by paintings and by the blue-and-gold Peacock Room, designed by Whistler as the dining room of a shipping magnate and moved by Freer from London to the United States in 1904. A lower-level exhibition gallery connects the building to the Arthur M. Sackler Gallery. | 12th St. and Jefferson Dr. SW | 202/357–2700; 202/357–1729 TDD | www.asia.si.edu | Free | Daily 10–5:30 | Metro: Smithsonian.

Hirshhorn Museum and Sculpture Garden. A striking round building houses a collection of works by American artists such as Edward Hopper, Willem de Kooning, Andy Warhol, and Richard Diebenkorn. It's also one of the best places in Washington to find exhibitions of contemporary art. The Hirshhorn's impressive sculpture collection is displayed throughout the museum, as well as on the lawns and granite surfaces of the fountain plaza and across Jefferson Drive in the sunken Sculpture Garden. | Independence Ave. and 7th St. SW | 202/357–2700; 202/633–8043 TDD | www.hirshhorn.si.edu | Free | Museum daily 10–5:30, sculpture garden 7:30–dusk | Metro: Smithsonian or L'Enfant Plaza (Maryland Ave. exit).

National Air and Space Museum. Suspended from the ceiling of this museum are dozens of aircraft, including the *Wright 1903 Flyer,* Charles Lindbergh's *Spirit of St. Louis,* the X-1 rocket plane in which Chuck Yeager broke the sound barrier, and a backup model of the Skylab orbital workshop that you can walk through. Upstairs, the Albert Einstein Planetarium is the first in the world to employ all-dome digital technology to create a feeling of movement through space. In December 2003, the National Air and Space Museum Steven F. Udvar-Hazy Center, two additional hangar-size exhibition spaces at Washington Dulles International Airport, is scheduled to open. | Independence Ave. and 6th St. SW | 202/357–1400 | www.nasm.si.edu | Free, IMAX $7.50, planetarium $7.50 | Daily 10–5:30 | Metro: Smithsonian.

National Gallery of Art, East Building. The atrium is dominated by Alexander Calder's mobile *Untitled,* and the galleries display modern and contemporary art, though you'll also find major temporary exhibitions that span many years and artistic styles. Permanent works include Pablo Picasso's *Family of Saltimbanques,* four of Matisse's cutouts, Miró's *The Farm,* and Jackson Pollock's *Lavender Mist*. To reach the East Building from the West Building, take the underground concourse. | Constitution Ave.

between 3rd and 4th Sts. NW | 202/737–4215; 202/842–6176 TDD | www.nga.gov | Free | Mon.–Sat. 10–5, Sun. 11–6 | Metro: Archives/Navy Memorial.

National Gallery of Art, West Building. The West Building's rotunda, with its 24 marble columns surrounding a fountain topped with a statue of Mercury, sets the stage for the masterpieces on display. The western hemisphere's only painting by Leonardo da Vinci, a comprehensive survey of Italian paintings, Flemish and Dutch works, and a self-portrait by Rembrandt are all here. The Chester Dale Collection comprises works by such Impressionists as Edgar Degas, Claude Monet, Auguste Renoir, and Mary Cassatt. | Constitution Ave. between 4th and 7th Sts. NW | 202/737–4215; 202/842–6176 TDD | www.nga.gov | Free | Mon.–Sat. 10–5, Sun. 11–6 | Metro: Archives/Navy Memorial.

National Gallery of Art Sculpture Garden. Sculptures on display from the museum's permanent collection include Roy Lichtenstein's playful *House I.* The huge central fountain, which has plenty of places to sit around it, is a relaxing space where younger kids can run around. It's used as a skating rink during the winter. | Constitution Ave. between 7th and 9th Sts. NW | Free.

National Museum of African Art. This underground building hosts exhibits of African visual arts, including sculpture, textiles, photography, archaeology, and modern art. | 950Independence Ave. SW | 202/357–2700; 202/357–1729 TDD | www.nmafa.si.edu | Free | Daily 10–5:30 | Metro: Smithsonian.

National Museum of American History. The museum explores America's cultural, political, technical, and scientific past. Many exhibits emphasize the history of science and technology and include farm machines, automobiles, and a 280-ton steam locomotive. Still others are devoted to U.S. social and political history; a permanent exhibit on the second floor, "First Ladies: Political Role and Public Image," displays gowns worn by presidential wives. | Constitution Ave. and 14th St. NW | 202/357–2700; 202/357–1729 TDD | americanhistory.si.edu | Free | Daily 10–5:30 | Metro: Smithsonian or Federal Triangle.

National Museum of the American Indian. As of this writing, this new Smithsonian museum was still under construction at a site bounded by 3rd and 4th streets and Independence Avenue and Jefferson Drive SW. It is scheduled to open in 2004. | 202/357–2700; 202/357–1729 TDD | www.nmai.si.edu.

National Museum of Natural History. This is one of the world's great natural history museums, filled with bones, fossils, stuffed animals, and other natural delights—124 million specimens in all. The first-floor rotunda is dominated by a stuffed, 8-ton, 13-ft-tall African bull elephant, one of the largest ever found. Highlights include the popular Dinosaur Hall, the Janet Annenberg Hooker Hall of Geology, Gems and Minerals (home of the Hope Diamond) and the O. Orkin Insect Zoo, where you can pet live insects. | Constitution Ave. and 10th St. NW | 202/357–2700; 202/357–1729 TDD | www.mnh.si.edu | Free; IMAX $7.50 | Museum daily 10–5:30 | Metro: Smithsonian or Federal Triangle.

Smithsonian Institution Building. This red sandstone, Norman-style building, better known as the Castle, houses Smithsonian administrative offices. Also here is the Smithsonian Information Center, which can help you get your bearings and decide which attractions you want to visit. There is overview of the Smithsonian museums and the National Zoo, as well as updates on the day's events. The center opens an hour before the museums on the Mall. | 1000 Jefferson Dr. SW | 202/357–2700; 202/357–1729 TDD | www.si.edu | Free | Daily 9–5:30 | Metro: Smithsonian.

United States Botanic Garden. This glistening, plant-filled oasis, established by Congress in 1820, is the oldest botanic garden in North America. With equal attention paid to science and aesthetics, the Botanic Garden contains plants from all around the world, with an emphasis on tropical and economically useful plants, desert plants, and orchids. On a 3-acre plot immediately to the west, the new National Garden is being constructed and is scheduled to open in 2004. | 1st St. and Maryland Ave. SW | 202/225–8333 | www.usbg.gov | Free | Daily 10–5 | Metro: Federal Center SW.

United States Holocaust Memorial Museum. A permanent exhibition tells the stories of the millions of Jews, Gypsies, Jehovah's Witnesses, homosexuals, political prisoners, mentally ill, and others killed by the Nazis between 1933 and 1945. Like the history it covers, the museum can be profoundly disturbing; it's not recommended for children under 11, although "Daniel's Story," in a ground-floor exhibit not requiring tickets, is designed for children ages 8 and up. Same-day timed-entry passes (distributed on a first-come, first-served basis at the 14th Street entrance starting at 10 AM or available through tickets.com) are necessary for the permanent exhibition. | 100 Raoul Wallenberg Pl. SW (enter from Raoul Wallenberg Pl. or 14th St. SW) | 202/488–0400; 800/400–9373 tickets.com | www.ushmm.org | Free | Daily 10–5:30 | Metro: Smithsonian.

The Monuments

Franklin Delano Roosevelt Memorial. This monument is a 7½-acre landscape-style memorial to the 32nd president employing waterfalls and reflection pools, four outdoor gallery rooms—one for each of his terms as president—and 10 bronze sculptures. | West side of Tidal Basin | 202/426–6841 | www.nps.gov/fdrm | Free | 24 hrs; staffed daily 8 AM–midnight | Metro: Smithsonian.

Jefferson Memorial. The same classical sources inform the plan for this 20th-century memorial as inspired the University of Virginia buildings Jefferson himself designed. It houses a statue of Jefferson, and its walls are lined with inscriptions based on the Declaration of Independence and his other writings. | Tidal Basin, south bank | 202/426–6821 | www.nps.gov/thje | Free | Daily 8 AM–midnight | Metro: Smithsonian.

Korean War Veterans Memorial. This memorial honors the 1.5 million United States men and women who served in the Korean War. The statue group in the triangular Field of Service depicts 19 multiethnic soldiers on patrol in rugged Korean terrain. To the south of the soldiers stands a 164-ft-long granite wall etched with the faces of 2,400 unnamed service men and women. | West end of Mall at Daniel French Dr. and Independence Ave. | 202/619–7222 | www.nps.gov/kwvm | Free | Daily 8 AM–midnight | Metro: Foggy Bottom.

Lincoln Memorial. Daniel Chester French's somber statue of the seated Abraham Lincoln, in the center of this inspiring marble memorial, gazes out over the Reflecting Pool. Inscribed on the south wall is the president's Gettysburg Address, and on the north wall is his second inaugural address. | West end of Mall | 202/426–6895 | www.nps.gov/linc | Free | 24 hrs; staffed daily 8 AM–midnight | Metro: Foggy Bottom.

Vietnam Veterans Memorial. One of the most-visited sites in Washington, the wall's black granite panels reflect the sky, the trees, and the faces of those looking for the names of friends or relatives who died in the war. The names of more than 58,000 Americans are etched on the face of the memorial in the order of their deaths. Directories at the entrance and exit to the wall list the names in alphabetical order. | Constitution Gardens, 23rd St. and Constitution Ave. NW | 202/634–1568 | www.nps.gov/vive | Free | 24 hrs; staffed daily 8 AM–midnight | Metro: Foggy Bottom.

Vietnam Women's Memorial. The Vietnam Women's Memorial depicts two uniformed women caring for a wounded male soldier while a third woman kneels nearby. | Constitution Gardens, southeast of Vietnam Veterans Memorial | Metro: Foggy Bottom.

Washington Monument. The 555-ft, 5-inch Washington Monument is visible from nearly everywhere in the city. To avoid the formerly long lines of people waiting for the minute-long elevator ride up the monument's shaft, the park service now uses a free timed-ticket system. A limited number of tickets are available at the kiosk on 15th Street daily beginning half an hour before the monument opens, though in spring and summer lines start well before then. | Constitution Ave. and 15th St. NW | 202/426–6840; advance tickets (up to 6) 800/967–2283 | www.nps.gov/wamo | Free; advance tickets require a $2 service and handling fee per ticket | Late May–early Sept., daily 8 AM–11:45 PM; early Sept.–late May, daily 9–4:45 | Metro: Smithsonian.

Capitol Hill

Capital Children's Museum. This sprawling, hands-on museum with culture, science, and crafts keeps kids ages 1 through 12 busy. Children can "drive" a Metrobus, stage a puppet show, or enclose themselves in huge soap bubbles. The museum has in-depth exhibitions on the cultures of Mexico and Japan, including a spectacular Mexican plaza re-created in the museum's three-story atrium. | 800 3rd St. NE, | 202/675–4120 | www.ccm.org | $7 | Daily 10–5 | Metro: Union Station.

Capitol. The United States Capitol provides the best example of democracy in action that Washington has to offer. Its attractions aren't only political, though, since the building is also packed with fine art, including Constantino Brumidi's 1865 fresco, *Apotheosis of Washington,* in the center of the Capitol dome. The allegorical figure atop the outside of the dome, often mistaken for Pocahontas, is called *Freedom*. Just below the statue, a light burns whenever Congress is in session. Due to construction of the subterranean Capitol Visitor Center, tours begin on the west front of the Capitol in a special screening facility. Note that there is a strict limit to the personal possessions that can be brought into the building and there are no facilities for checking items. If you're planning a visit, call ahead to check the status of tours and access. | East end of Mall | 202/224–3121 Capitol switchboard; 202/225–6827 guide service | www.aoc.gov | Free | Metro: Capitol South or Union Station.

Library of Congress. One of the world's largest libraries, the Library of Congress contains some 115 million items, including manuscripts, prints, films, photographs, sheet music, and maps in addition to books. The copper-dome Thomas Jefferson Building is the oldest of the three buildings that make up the library and is the one that hosts most exhibitions. You have to be over 18 to do research here, but the galleries are open to all. One of only three perfect Gutenberg Bibles in the world is displayed in its second-floor Southwest Gallery and Pavilion. | Jefferson Bldg., 1st St. and Independence Ave. SE | 202/707–4604, 202/707–5000, or 202/707–6400 | www.loc.gov | Free | Mon.–Sat. 10–5:30. Free tours Mon.–Sat. 10:30, 11:30, 1:30, 2:30, and weekdays 3:30 | Metro: Capitol South.

National Postal Museum. Exhibits include horse-drawn mail coaches, railway mail cars, airmail planes, and a collection of philatelic rarities. The family-oriented museum has more than 40 interactive and touch-screen exhibits. | 2 Massachusetts Ave. NE, | 202/357–2700; 202/357–1729 TDD | www.si.edu/postal | Free | Daily 10–5:30 | Metro: Union Station.

Supreme Court Building. The Supreme Court convenes behind the Corinthian columns of its 1935 white-marble building on the first Monday in October and remains in session until it has heard all of its cases and handed down all of its decisions (usually the end of June). On Monday through Wednesday of two weeks in each month, the justices hear oral arguments in the velvet-swathed court chamber. Stop by for a quick impression or stay for the whole show; for the latter, it's best to be in line by 8:30 AM. | 1 1st St. NE | 202/479–3000 | www.supremecourtus.gov | Free | Weekdays 9–4:30 | Metro: Union Station or Capitol South.

The White House Area

Corcoran Gallery of Art. The gallery's permanent collection includes American paintings by Gilbert Stuart, Rembrandt Peale, John Singer Sargent, and Hudson River School artists as well as Dutch, Flemish, and French Romantic paintings. | 500 17th St. NW |

202/639–1700 | www.corcoran.org | $5, free Mon. and Thurs. after 5 | Mon., Wed., and Fri.–Sun. 10–5; Thurs. 10–9 | Metro: Farragut West or Farragut North.

DAR Museum. The Daughters of the American Revolution collection includes 33 period rooms are decorated in styles representative of various U.S. states. There's an 1850 California adobe parlor and a New Hampshire attic filled with toys from the 18th and 19th centuries. During the "Colonial Adventure" tours, held the first and third Sunday of the month at 1:30 and 3 from September through May, costumed docents teach children ages five to seven about the exhibits and day-to-day life in Colonial America. Make reservations at least 10 days in advance. | 1776 D St. NW | 202/879–3241 | www.dar.org | Free | Weekdays 8:30–4, Sun. 1–5 | Metro: Farragut West.

Renwick Gallery. The collection of the Renwick Gallery of the Smithsonian American Art Museum remains at the forefront of the crafts movement. The Renwick has exquisitely designed and made utilitarian items, as well as objects created out of such traditional crafts media as fiber and glass. | Pennsylvania Ave. at 17th St. NW | 202/357–2531; 202/357–1729 TDD | www.americanart.si.edu | Free | Daily 10–5:30 | Metro: Farragut West.

★ **White House.** This "house" surely has the best-known address in the United States: 1600 Pennsylvania Avenue. Irishman James Hoban's plan, based on the Georgian design of Leinster Hall in Dublin and of other Irish country houses, was selected in a 1792 contest. The building wasn't ready for its first occupant, John Adams, the second U.S. president, until 1800, and so George Washington, who seems to have slept every place else, never slept here. | 1600 Pennsylvania Ave.

The **White House Visitor Center,** which exhibits photographs, artifacts, and videos, is in charge of handing out tickets to see the interior, but at this writing, tours of the White House were available only to certain groups on a very limited basis. Updates on the situation are available by calling the White House Visitor Office's 24-hour information line. | Visitor center address: 1450 Pennsylvania Ave. NW entrance: | Department of Commerce's Baldrige Hall, E St. between 14th and 15th Sts., | 202/208–1631 or 202/456–7041 | www.nps.gov/whho | Free | Daily 7:30–4 | Metro: Federal Triangle.

Old Downtown and Federal Triangle

Chinatown. If you don't notice you're entering Washington's compact Chinatown by the Chinese characters on the street signs, the ornate, 75-ft-wide Friendship Arch spanning H Street might clue you in. This slightly run-down area borders many blocks undergoing revitalization, and it's *the* place to go for Chinese food in the District. | Bounded by G, H, 5th, and 8th Sts. | Metro: Gallery Place/Chinatown.

City Museum. The beautiful beaux arts Carnegie Library building, once Washington's Central Public Library, has undergone a spectacular renovation and is scheduled to open in 2003 as a museum devoted to the nation's capital. The facility will include an archaeology exhibit and galleries for multimedia presentations about Washington's neighborhoods, ethnic groups, and prehistory. It's across the street from Washington's new convention center. | 801 K St. NW | 202/785–2068 | www.hswdc.org | Call for admission fee | Call to confirm opening date and to check hrs | Metro: Gallery Place/Chinatown or Mt. Vernon Square/UDC.

Ford's Theatre. On the night of April 14, 1865, during a performance of *Our American Cousin*, John Wilkes Booth entered the state box and shot Abraham Lincoln. The stricken president was carried across the street to the house of tailor William Petersen, where he died the next morning. The theater, now restored to its 1865 appearance, presents a complete schedule of plays and has a basement museum full of Lincoln artifacts. | 511 10th St. NW, | 202/426–6924 | www.nps.gov/foth | Free | Daily 9–5 | Metro: Metro Center or Gallery Place.

International Spy Museum. Fans of John Le Carré will revel in exhibits about how spies are trained, spying from biblical times through the world wars, Cold War spy techniques, and the latest spy trends. | 800 F Street NW | 202/393–7798 | www.spymuseum.org | $11.

National Aquarium. Incongruously, the National Aquarium is housed in the basement of the Department of Commerce. It's the country's oldest public aquarium, with more than 1,200 fish and other creatures—such as eels, sharks, and alligators. The halls look somewhat dated, but the easy-to-view tanks, accessible touching pool, and low admission fee make this a good, low-key outing. | 14th St. and Constitution Ave. NW | 202/482–2825 | www.nationalaquarium.com | $3 | Daily 9–5 (last admission at 4:30) | Metro: Federal Triangle.

National Archives. The Declaration of Independence, the Constitution, and the Bill of Rights are on display in the National Archives's rotunda. Other objects in the archives' vast collection include veterans and immigration records, treaties, Richard Nixon's resignation letter, and the rifle Lee Harvey Oswald used to assassinate John F. Kennedy. Call at least three weeks in advance to arrange a behind-the-scenes tour. | Constitution Ave. between 7th and 9th Sts. NW | 202/501–5000; 202/501–5205 tours | www.nara.gov | Free | Apr.–early Sept., daily 10–9; early Sept.–Mar., daily 10–5:30; tours weekdays at 10:15 and 1:15 | Metro: Archives/Navy Memorial.

National Building Museum. The open interior of this mammoth redbrick edifice is one of the city's great spaces, as exhilarating for toddlers as for VIPs at inaugural balls. Formerly known as the Pension Building, it was erected between 1882 and 1887 to house workers who processed the pension claims of veterans and their survivors, an activity that intensified after the Civil War. It is now a museum devoted to architecture and the building arts, with some hands-on displays that are great for kids. Family programs are available at 2:30 Saturday and Sunday. | 401 F St. NW, between 4th and 5th Sts. | 202/272–2448 | www.nbm.org | Free | Mon.–Sat. 10–5, Sun. 11–5 | Metro: Judiciary Square.

National Museum of Women in the Arts. Works by female artists from the Renaissance to the present are showcased at this museum, housed in a beautifully restored 1907 Renaissance Revival building; ironically, it was once a Masonic temple, for men only. The museum has a permanent collection that includes paintings, drawings, sculpture, prints, and photographs by Georgia O'Keeffe, Mary Cassatt, Élisabeth Vigée-Lebrun, Frida Kahlo, and Camille Claudel. | 1250 New York Ave. NW | 202/783–5000 | www.nmwa.org | $8 | Mon.–Sat. 10–5, Sun. noon–5 | Metro: Metro Center.

National Portrait Gallery. This museum is in the Old Patent Office Building along with the Smithsonian American Art Museum. Unfortunately, a major renovation of the building set to last through 2005 means that the gallery is temporarily closed. | 8th and F Sts. NW | 202/357–2700; 202/357–1729 TDD | www.npg.si.edu | Closed during renovation | Metro: Gallery Place/Chinatown.

Smithsonian American Art Museum. This museum (formerly the National Museum of American Art) is housed in the Old Patent Office Building, which is under major renovation through 2005. Until then, it continues its public presence through its Web site and a full program at the Renwick Gallery. | 8th and G Sts. NW | 202/357–2700; 202/357–1729 TDD | www.americanart.si.edu | Metro: Gallery Place/Chinatown.

Georgetown

It's a 15-minute walk from the Dupont Circle or Foggy Bottom Metro station to Georgetown–there's no Metro stop here. Alternately, you can take a bus or taxi. (The G2 Georgetown University bus goes from Dupont Circle west along P Street. The 34 and 36 Friendship Heights buses leave from 22nd and Pennsylvania and deposit you at 31st and M.)

Cox's Row. To get a representative taste of the area, walk along the 3300 block of N Street. The group of five Federal-style houses between 3339 and 3327 N Street is known collectively as Cox's Row, after Colonel John Cox, a former mayor of Georgetown, who built them in 1817. The flat-front, redbrick Federal-style house at 3307 N Street was the home of then-Senator John F. Kennedy and his family before the White House beckoned.

Dumbarton Oaks. In 1944 representatives of the United States, Great Britain, China, and the Soviet Union met in the music room at Dumbarton Oaks to lay the groundwork for the United Nations. If you have even a mild interest in flowers, shrubs, trees, and magnificent natural beauty, visit Dumbarton Oaks's 10 acres of formal gardens, one of the loveliest spots in Washington (enter at 31st and R streets). | 1703 32nd St. NW | 202/339–6401 or 202/339–6400 | Art collections Tues.–Sun. 2–5. Gardens Apr.–Oct., daily 2–6; Nov.–Mar., daily 2–5.

Georgetown University. Georgetown is known now as much for its perennially successful basketball team as for its fine programs in law, medicine, foreign service, and the liberal arts. When seen from the Potomac or from Washington's high ground, the Gothic spires of Georgetown's older buildings give the university an almost medieval look. | 37th and O Sts. | 202/687–5055 | www.georgetown.edu.

Dupont Circle

National Geographic Society. Explorers Hall, entered from 17th Street, is the magazine come to life. It invites you to learn about the world in a decidedly interactive way: you can experience everything from a mini tornado to special events in the Earth Station One Interactive Theatre, a 72-seat amphitheater that sends the audience on a journey around the world. | 17th and M Sts. NW | 202/857–7588; 202/857–7689 group tours | Free | Mon.–Sat. 9–5, Sun. 10–5 | Metro: Farragut North.

Phillips Collection. The masterpiece-filled Phillips Collection is a comfortable museum. Works of an artist are often grouped together in "exhibition units," and, unlike most other galleries (where uniformed guards appear uninterested in the masterpieces around them), the Phillips employs students of art, many of whom are artists themselves, to sit by the paintings and answer questions. | 1600 21st St. NW | 202/387–2151 | www.phillipscollection.org | $7.50 | Sept.–May, Tues.–Wed. and Fri.–Sat. 10–5, Thurs. 10–8:30, Sun. noon–7; June–Aug., Tues.–Wed. and Fri.–Sat. 10–5, Thurs. 10–8:30, Sun. noon–5. Tour Wed. and Sat. at 2. Gallery talk 1st and 3rd Thurs. at 12:30 | Metro: Dupont Circle.

Cleveland Park

Washington National Cathedral. Like its 14th-century Gothic counterparts, the stunning 20th-century National Cathedral (officially the Cathedral Church of St. Peter and St. Paul) has a nave, flying buttresses, transepts, and vaults that were built stone by stone. It's adorned with fanciful gargoyles created by skilled stone carvers. The cathedral is Episcopal but has hosted services of many denominations. | Wisconsin and Massachusetts Aves. NW | 202/537–6200; 202/537–6207 tour information | www.cathedral.org | Suggested tour donation $3 | Early May–early Sept., weekdays 10–5, Sat. 10–4:30, Sun. 8–5; early Sept.–early May, daily 10–5. Sun. services at 8, 9, 10, 11, and 4; evening prayer daily at 4:30; tours every 15 mins Mon.–Sat. 10–11:30 and 12:45–3:15, Sun. 12:45–2:30.

National Zoological Park. Part of the Smithsonian Institution, the National Zoo is one of the foremost zoos in the world. Innovative compounds show many animals in naturalistic settings, including the Great Flight Cage (a walk-in aviary), the Reptile Discovery Center, the American Prairie, the Cheetah Conservation Area, and Amazonia, a reproduction of a South American rain-forest ecosystem. Panda fans can observe Tian Tian and Mei Xiang, who arrived from China in 2001. | 3001 Connecticut Ave. NW | 202/673–4800 or 202/673–4717 | www.si.edu/natzoo | Free, parking $5 | May–mid-Sept., daily 6 AM–8 PM; mid-Sept.–Apr., daily 6–6. Zoo buildings open at 10 and close before the zoo closes | Metro: Cleveland Park or Woodley Park/Zoo.

Arlington

Arlington National Cemetery. More than 250,000 American war dead, as well as many notable Americans (among them presidents William Howard Taft and John F. Kennedy, General John Pershing, and Admiral Robert E. Peary), are interred in these 612 acres across the Potomac River from Washington, established on the Custis-Lee estate as the nation's cemetery in 1864. Although not the largest cemetery in the country, Arlington is certainly the best known, a place where you can trace America's history through the aftermath of its battles. Also here are Arlington House (the family home of Robert E. Lee's wife), the Tomb of the Unknowns, the Memorial Amphitheater, and memorials to the astronauts killed in the *Challenger* shuttle explosion. The graves of JFK, Jacqueline Bouvier Kennedy Onassis, and Robert Kennedy are at Sheridan and Weeks drives. | West end of Memorial Bridge | 703/607–8052 to locate a grave | www.arlingtoncemetery.org | Cemetery free; parking $1.50 for first three hrs. Tourmobile $4.50 | Apr.–Sept., daily 8–7; Oct.–Mar., daily 8–5 | Arlington Cemetery.

Pentagon. This office building, the headquarters of the United States Department of Defense, is the largest in the world. Part of the building was reconstructed following the September 11, 2001, crash of hijacked American Airlines Flight 77 into the northwest side of the structure. Tours are given on a very limited basis to educational groups by advance reservation; tours for the general public have been suspended indefinitely. | I–395 at Columbia Pike and Rte. 27 | 703/695–1776 | www.defenselink.mil/pubs/pentagon | Arlington Cemetery.

United States Marine Corps War Memorial. Better known simply as the "Iwo Jima," this memorial is based on Joe Rosenthal's Pulitzer Prize–winning photograph of five marines and a navy corpsman raising a flag atop Mt. Suribachi on the Japanese island of Iwo Jima on February 19, 1945. | Arlington Cemetery.

Dining

The Mall

Cascade Café. Café. For a quick, casual meal, try the Cascade Café in the concourse between the East and West buildings of the National Gallery of Art. It has a selection of sandwiches and salads, as well as espresso and *gelato* (Italian-style ice cream) that's made in-house. | National Gallery of Art, East Building Constitution Ave. between 3rd and 4th Sts. NW | Mon.–Sat. 10–3, Sun. 11:30–4 | Metro: Archives/Navy Memorial.

Sculpture Garden Pavilion Café. Café. Indoor and outdoor seating take in a panoramic view of landscaping in the National Gallery of Art Sculpture Garden. On offer are specialty pizzas and sandwiches. | National Gallery of Art Sculpture Garden Constitution Ave. between 7th and 9th Sts. NW | Sept.–May, Mon.–Sat. 10–5, Sun. 11–6; June–Aug., Mon.–Thurs. and Sat. 10–6, Fri. 10–8, Sun. 11–6 | Metro: Archives/Navy Memorial.

Wright Place. Fast Food. This fast-food-style restaurant is in the eastern end of the National Air and Space Museum. It's operated by McDonald's: though at first glance it looks like the offerings are mostly burgers and fries, you can also find pizza from Donato's, scrambled eggs and roast chicken from Boston Market, and Caesar and green salad. Two ice cream kiosks are set among the tables. | National Air and Space Museum, Independence Ave. and 6th St. SW | Weekdays 7:30–5, weekends 9–5 | Metro: Smithsonian.

Capitol Hill

Dining options are augmented by **Union Station** (☞ Shopping), which contains some decent—if pricey—restaurants. It also has a large food court for quick bites that range from barbecue to sushi.

Tortilla Cafe. Latin. Right across from bustling Eastern Market, this small carry-out restaurant serves the best *pupusas* (rounded cornmeal dough stuffed with meat, cheese, or corn) in town. The menu is a mix of mostly Salvadorian and Mexican fare with favorites such as tamales, Peruvian ceviche, and fried plantains served with sour cream and refried beans. The café is open 10–7 weekdays and 7–7 weekends. | 210 7th St. SE | 202/547–5700 | Reservations not accepted | $4–$10 | AE, D, MC, V | Metro: Eastern Market.

Downtown

Austin Grill. Tex-Mex. This fine, local Tex-Mex chain is decorated in a Texas-funk style and serves some of the best Texas chili and margaritas in town. House specialties include quesadillas with fresh jumbo lump crab or Portobello mushrooms with beef; "Austin special" enchiladas with three sauces; and grilled, chili-rubbed shrimp and scallops. Most locations are open until midnight on weekends. | 750 E St. NW | 202/393–3776 | AE, D, DC, MC, V | Metro: Gallery Place/Chinatown.

Bread Line. Contemporary. Crowded, quirky, sometimes chaotic, this restaurant specializes in breads and bread-based foods and not only makes the city's best baguette but also some of its best sandwiches. Owner Mark Furstenburg makes everything on the premises, from the breakfast bagels and muffins to the ciabatta loaves for the tuna salad sandwich with preserved lemons. It's best to arrive early or late to avoid the noontime rush. Outdoor seating is available in warmer months. | 1751 Pennsylvania Ave. NW | 202/822–8900 | Reservations not accepted | Closed weekends. No dinner | $4–$9 | AE, MC, V | Metro: Farragut West.

Li Ho. Chinese. Head for unassuming Li Ho if you're seeking good Chinese food in satisfying portions. Kitchen specialties like duck soup with mustard greens and Singapore noodles, a rice-noodle dish seasoned with curry and bits of meat, are favorites among the lunchtime crowd. | 501 H St. NW | 202/289–2059 | $5–$13 | MC, V | Metro: Gallery Place/Chinatown.

Oodles Noodles. Pan-Asian. Packed from the day they opened and with long lines waiting for tables and takeout, these attractive Pan-Asian noodle houses have remarkably good Chinese, Japanese, Thai, Indonesian, Malaysian, and Vietnamese dishes; all are served on plates appropriate to the cuisine. Try the Thai drunken noodles, the Chinese clay-pot noodles, or the Vietnamese rice noodles with grilled chicken. | 1120 19th St. NW | 202/293–3138 | Reservations essential | Closed Sun. | $7–$10 | AE, DC, MC, V | Metro: Farragut North.

Teaism. Japanese. A stock of more than 50 teas (black, white, and green) imported from India, Japan, and Africa is the main source of pride for this tranquil tea house. But the tea doesn't outshine the healthy and delicious Japanese, Indian, and Thai food. Diners mix small dishes—tandoori kabobs, tea-cured salmon, Indian flat breads, salads, and various chutneys—to create light meals or snacks. | 400 8th St. NW, Downtown | 202/638–7740 | Breakfast served, closes at 9 PM weekends | AE, MC, V | Metro: Navy/Archives Branch: | 800 Connecticut Ave. NW, Downtown | 202/835–2233 | Breakfast served, closed weekends, no dinner | AE, MC, V | Metro: Farrugut West Branch: | 2009 R St. NW, Dupont Circle | 202/667–3827 | Reservations not accepted | $8–$9 | AE, MC, V | Metro: Dupont Circle.

Georgetown/Glover Park

Clyde's of Georgetown. American/Casual. The flagship restaurant of this popular local chain draws a crowd of both locals and out-out-towers for pub food of unusually high quality. Summertime is a special treat here—Clyde's sends trucks to the country for local produce, which it then incorporates in its daily specials. | Georgetown Park Mall, 3236 M St. NW, between Wisconsin Ave. and Potomac St. | 202/333–9180 | $8–$17 | AE, MC, V | Foggy Bottom–GWU.

Two Amys. Italian. Judging from the long lines here, the best pizza in D.C. may have moved uptown. Simple recipes allow the ingredients to speak for themselves at this Neapolitan pizzeria. It's no surprise that Peter Pastan, owner of fine Italian restaurant Obelisk, is co-owner of this restaurant. You can taste his high standards in every bite. This Glover Park spot is very child-friendly. | 3715 Macomb St. NW | 202/885–5700 | Reservations not accepted | $8–$14 | MC, V.

Dupont Circle

Kramerbooks and Afterwords. American/Casual. A favorite neighborhood breakfast spot, this popular bookstore-cum-café is also a late-night haunt on weekends, when it's open around the clock. There's a simple menu with soups, salads, and sandwiches, but many people drop in just for cappuccino and dessert. Live music, from rock to blues, is performed Wednesday through Sunday 10 PM to midnight. | 1517 Connecticut Ave. NW | 202/387–1462 | Reservations not accepted | $13–$17 | AE, D, MC, V | Metro: Dupont Circle.

Pizzeria Paradiso. Italian. The ever popular Pizzeria Paradiso sticks to crowd-pleasing basics: pizzas, *panini* (sandwiches such as Italian cured ham and sun-dried tomatoes and basil), salads, and desserts. The intensely flavored gelato is a house specialty. A trompe l'oeil ceiling adds space and light to a simple interior. | 2029 P St. NW | 202/223–1245 | Reservations not accepted | $10–$15 | DC, MC, V | Metro: Dupont Circle.

Adams-Morgan/Woodley Park

Lebanese Taverna. Middle Eastern. Arched ceilings, cedar panels etched with leaf patterns, woven rugs, and brass lighting fixtures give the Taverna a warm elegance. Start with an order of Arabic bread, baked in a wood-burning oven. Lamb, beef, chicken, and seafood are either grilled on kabobs, slow-roasted, or smothered with a garlicky yogurt sauce. A group can make a meal of the *mezza* platters—a mix of appetizers and sliced *shawarma* (spit-roasted lamb). | 2641 Connecticut Ave. NW | 202/265–8681 | $12–$17 | AE, D, DC, MC, V | Metro: Woodley Park/Zoo.

Meskerem. African. Ethiopian restaurants abound in Adams-Morgan, but Meskerem is distinctive for its bright dining room and the balcony, where you can eat Ethiopian-style, seated on the floor on leather cushions, with large woven baskets for tables. Entrées are served family-style on a large piece of *injera,* a sourdough flat bread; you scoop up mouthful-size portions of the hearty dishes with extra injera. Specialties include stews made with spicy *berbere* chili sauce and a tangy, green-chili–vinaigrette potato salad. | 2434 18th St. NW | 202/462–4100 | Reservations essential | $9–$13 | AE, DC, MC, V | Metro: Woodley Park/Zoo.

Pasta Mia. Italian. Patrons don't seem to mind waiting their turn to eat in this affordable 40-seat trattoria. Pasta Mia's southern Italian appetizers and entrées all cost a palatable $7 to $10. Large bowls of steaming pasta are served with a generous layer of fresh-grated Parmesan. Some best-sellers are penne *arrabiata* (in spicy marinara sauce with olives) and fusilli with broccoli and whole cloves of roasted garlic. Tiramisu, served in a teacup, is an elegant way to finish your meal. | 1790 Columbia Rd. NW | 202/328–9114 | Reservations not accepted | Closed Sun. No lunch | $9–$10 | MC, V | Metro: Woodley Park/Zoo.

Maryland/Virginia Suburbs

Pines of Rome. Italian. Large, child-friendly, and inexpensive, this is the kind of neighborhood restaurant where you can expect dependable and comfortable food. Pass on the pastas and start with an order of white pizza to share. Then choose from the list of specials—roast meats, including pork and veal, are served in enormous portions. The kitchen fries well; try the soft-shell crabs if they're in season or the calamari. | 4709 Hampton La., Bethesda, MD | 301/657–8775 | $6–$15 | AE, D, MC, V | Metro: Bethesda.

Red Hot & Blue. Barbecue. Ribs are the specialty at this Memphis-style barbecue joint. They come "wet"—with sauce—or, when simply smoked, "dry." The delicious pulled-meat sandwiches and low prices lure hungry crowds. This chain has additional locations in Annapolis, Fairfax, Gaithersburg, and Laurel. | 1600 Wilson Blvd., Arlington, VA | 703/276–7427 | Reservations not accepted | $6–$19 | AE, D, DC, MC, V | Metro: Court House.

Tastee Diner. American/Casual. As 24-hour diners go, Tastee is a classic. Each branch is a sentimental favorite that invokes a sense of old-fashioned community appropriate to its location. Students and others on low budgets (or little sleep) ignore the dust and relish the coffee, which flows endlessly. | 7731 Woodmont Ave., Bethesda, MD | 301/652–3970 | Reservations not accepted | MC, V | Metro: Bethesda Branch: | 8601 Cameron St., Silver Spring, MD | 301/589–8171 | Reservations not accepted | $2–$10 | AE, MC, V | Metro: Silver Spring.

Lodging

Capitol Hill

Holiday Inn Capitol. One block from the National Air and Space Museum, this large hotel is family friendly yet well equipped for business travelers. The downtown sightseeing trolley stops here, and you can buy discount tickets for NASM's IMAX movies at the front desk. Restaurant, food court, room service, in-room data ports, cable TV, pool, gym, hair salon, bar, laundry facilities, business services, meeting rooms, parking (fee); no-smoking floor | 550 C St. SW 20024 | 202/479–4000 | fax 202/488–4627 | 505 rooms, 24 suites | $119–$239 | AE, D, DC, MC, V | Metro: L'Enfant Plaza.

Holiday Inn on the Hill. Expect clean, comfortable rooms and a friendly staff in this hotel, which is convenient to Union Station and the Capitol building. Hotel amenities include a Discovery Zone site for children, with supervised educational games, snacks, and contests. The Senators Sports Grille has a fine collection of D.C. baseball memorabilia, including photographs of various Senators players. Restaurant, room service, in-room data ports, cable TV, pool, exercise equipment, gym, sauna, bar, children's programs (ages 4–14), laundry service, business services, meeting rooms, parking (fee); no-smoking floor | 415 New Jersey Ave. NW 20001 | 202/638–1616 or 800/638–1116 | fax 202/638–0707 | www.holiday-inn.com/hotels/wasch. | 343 rooms | $109–$225 | AE, D, DC, MC, V | Metro: Union Station.

Downtown

Hotel Harrington. One of Washington's oldest continuously operating hotels, the Harrington doesn't offer many frills, but it does have low prices and a location right in the center of everything. It's very popular with springtime high school bus tours and with families who like the two-bedroom, two-bathroom deluxe suites. Restaurant, cafeteria, room service, cable TV, hair salon, bar, pub, laundry facilities, business services, meeting rooms, parking (fee), some pets allowed; no-smoking floor | 436 11th St. NW 20004 | 202/628–8140 or 800/424–8532 | fax 202/347–3924 | www.hotelharrington.com | 246 rooms, 36 suites | $89–$139 | AE, D, DC, MC, V | Metro: Metro Center.

Washington Renaissance Hotel. Opposite the Washington Convention Center and a 10-minute walk from the Smithsonian museums, the Renaissance was designed as a business hotel, with the requisite facilities and central location. Guests here have free access to the 10,000-square-ft fitness center and its lap pool. A food court is just outside the lobby. Restaurant, coffee shop, snack bar, room service, in-room data ports, minibars, refrigerators, cable TV, indoor pool, gym, health club, hot tub, sauna, 2 bars, business services, parking (fee), some pets allowed; no-smoking floor | 999 9th St. NW 20001 | 202/898–9000 or 800/228–9898 | fax 202/289–0947 | www.renaissancehotels.com | 791 rooms, 10 suites | $99–$229 | AE, D, DC, MC, V | Metro: Chinatown.

Adams-Morgan

Jurys Normandy Inn. On a quiet street in the embassy area of Connecticut Avenue stands this small, quaint European-style hotel. The cozy rooms come with coffeemakers and are attractively decorated with Colonial reproduction furniture. Each Tuesday evening a wine-and-cheese reception is held for guests. Complimentary coffee and tea are available in the morning and afternoon. Café, in-room data ports, in-room safes, refrigerators, cable TV, library, laundry facilities, parking (fee) | 2118 Wyoming Ave. NW 20008 | 202/483–1350, 800/424–3729, or 800/842–3729 | fax 202/387–8241 | www.jurysdoyle.com | 75 rooms | $79–$155 | AE, D, DC, MC, V | CP | Metro: Dupont Circle.

Suburban Maryland

American Inn of Bethesda. At the north end of downtown Bethesda, the American Inn is five blocks from the Metro and is within walking distance of restaurants. Rooms at this budget-friendly hotel are clean, well furnished, and bright. Guapo's restaurant, on the premises, serves moderately priced Tex-Mex fare. Restaurant, in-room data ports, refrigerators, cable TV, pool, hair salon, bar, laundry facilities, laundry service, business services, meeting rooms, free parking | 8130 Wisconsin Ave., Bethesda, MD 20814 | 301/656–9300 or 800/323–7081 | fax 301/656–2907 | www.american-inn.com | 75 rooms, 1 suite | $86–$190 | AE, D, DC, MC, V | CP | Metro: Bethesda.

Four Points Sheraton. Adjacent to a Metro stop, this hotel is particularly popular with government employees and business travelers. But its heavily discounted weekend rates attract vacationers who don't mind being just outside of D.C. as well. There is an outdoor Olympic-size swimming pool as well as a microwave on each floor. Chatters Restaurant and Sports Bar has wide-screen TVs, a pool table, a jukebox, and seasonal outdoor dining. Restaurant, in-room data ports, refrigerators, pool, gym, hair salon, laundry facilities, meeting rooms, parking (fee) | 8400 Wisconsin Ave., Bethesda, MD 20814 | 301/654–1000 or 800/272–6232 | fax 301/986–1715 | 164 rooms | $109–$159 | AE, D, DC, MC, V | CP | Metro: Medical Center.

Suburban Virginia

Days Inn Crystal City. On Route 1 between the Pentagon and National Airport, this eight-floor hotel is only four Metro stops from the Smithsonian. There is free shuttle service to nearby shops and Ronald Reagan National Airport. The Crystal City Underground—with its many shops and restaurants and a Metro stop—is a very short walk away. Restaurant, room service, in-room data ports, cable TV, pool, exercise equipment, gym, bar, laundry service, business services, airport shuttle, car rental, free parking | 2000 Jefferson Davis Hwy. (Rte. 1), Arlington, VA 22202 | 703/920–8600 | fax 703/920–2840 | 242 rooms, 3 suites | $139–$154 | AE, D, DC, MC, V | Metro: Crystal City.

Holiday Inn Rosslyn. Comfortable and affordable, this 17-story hotel is just two blocks from the Rosslyn Metro and a leisurely 3/4-mi stroll across Key Bridge to Georgetown with its restaurants and nightclubs. Fort Myer and Arlington National Cemetery are very close. Each rooms has a balcony, but the hotel's best feature may be the view of Washington's monuments from the Vantage Point restaurant's panoramic windows. Restaurants, café, in-room data ports, in-room safes, some refrigerators, cable TV, indoor pool, exercise equipment, health club, hair salon, bar, dry cleaning, laundry facilities, laundry service, business services, meeting rooms, free parking, some pets allowed | 1900 N. Fort Myer Dr., Arlington, VA 22209 | 703/807–2000 or 800/368–3408 | fax 703/522–7480 | 306 rooms, 28 suites | $130–$170 | AE, D, DC, MC, V | Metro: Rosslyn.

Arts and Entertainment

Ticketmaster. You can place phone charges for events at most venues around the city or you can purchase Ticketmaster tickets in person at all Hecht's department stores. No refunds or exchanges are allowed. | 202/432–7328 or 410/481–7328 | www.ticketmaster.com.

TicketPlace. Half-price, day-of-performance tickets are available for select shows. It's closed on Sunday and Monday, but tickets for performances on those days are on sale Saturday. | Old Post Office Pavilion, 1100 Pennsylvania Ave. NW, Downtown | 202/842–5387 | Metro: Federal Triangle.

Tickets.com. Reservations for events at Arena Stage, Center Stage, Ford's Theatre, the Holocaust Museum, the 9:30 Club, and Signature Theater can be made through tickets.com. | 703/218–6500 | www.tickets.com.

Film

Smithsonian Theaters. IMAX films are shown at the Smithsonian's National Air and Space Museum (Lockheed Martin IMAX Theater) and National Museum of Natural History (Johnson IMAX Theater). Call for information on what's playing. | 202/633–4629.

Music

A rich assortment of music—both free and ticketed—is presented at the Smithsonian and other museums, including the National Gallery, the Corcoran, and the Phillips Collection. Check museum Web sites or call in advance.

John F. Kennedy Center for the Performing Arts. The Kennedy Center is five stages under one roof: the Concert Hall; the Eisenhower Theater; the Terrace Theater; and the Theater Lab. There's a free performance every evening at 6 on the Millennium Stage in the center's Grand Foyer. | New Hampshire Ave. and Rock Creek Pkwy. NW | 202/467–4600 or 800/444–1324 | www.kennedy-center.org | Metro: Foggy Bottom/GWU (free shuttle-bus service every 15 min to and from Kennedy Center on performance days).

The **National Symphony Orchestra** performs from September to June. In summer the NSO gives free concerts at the Carter Barron Amphitheatre and, on Memorial Day and Labor Day weekends and July 4, on the West Lawn of the Capitol. The cheapest way to hear the NSO perform in the Kennedy Center Concert Hall is to get $19 second-tier side seats. | 202/416–8100 | www.nationalsymphony.org.

Armed Forces Concert Series. From June to August, service bands from all four military branches perform Monday, Tuesday, Thursday, and Friday evenings on the East Terrace of the Capitol and several nights a week at the Sylvan Theater on the Washington Monument grounds. Concerts usually include marches, patriotic numbers, and some classical music. | 202/767–5658 Air Force; 703/696–3718 Army; 202/433–2525 Navy; 202/433–4011 Marines.

Shopping

The Mall

Washington's many museum shops offer a surprising and original selection of merchandise. Next to the cafeteria in the **National Gallery, East Building** is a shop that sells carefully selected art-related children's toys and kits. The **National Air and Space Museum** displays and sells airplanes and rockets as well as packets of freeze-dried astronaut ice cream. The **National Museum of Natural History** has a selection of science kits and animal-related educational toys in its main store and a specialty selection in its **Tricerashop,** a boutique devoted to dinosaur items.

Capitol Hill

Eastern Market. As the Capitol Hill area has become gentrified, unique shops and boutiques have sprung up, many clustered around this redbrick structure. Inside are produce and meat counters, plus the Market Five art gallery; outside are a farmers' market (on Saturday) and a flea market (on weekends). Along 7th Street you'll find a number of small shops, selling everything from art books to handwoven rugs to antiques and knickknacks. | 7th and C Sts. SE | Metro: Eastern Market, Union Station, or Capitol South.

Union Station. This delightful shopping enclave, resplendent with marble floors and gilded, vaulted ceilings, is inside a working train station. You'll find several familiar retailers, including Jones New York, Aerosole, Swatch, and Ann Taylor, as well as a bookstore and a multiplex cinema. The east hall, reminiscent of London's Covent Garden, is filled with vendors of expensive and ethnic wares in open stalls. Christmas is an especially pleasant time to shop here. | 50 Massachusetts Ave. NE | 202/371–9441 | www.unionstationdc.com | Metro: Union Station.

Downtown

The domain of the city's many office workers, downtown tends to shut down at 5 PM sharp with the exception of the larger department stores. Old downtown is where you'll find Hecht's and sundry specialty stores; established chains such as Ann Taylor and Gap tend to be concentrated near Farragut Square. Avoid the lunch-hour crowds to ensure more leisurely shopping.

Old Post Office Pavilion. This handsome shopping center is hidden inside a historic 19th-century post office building. There are about a dozen food vendors and 17 shops. | 1100 Pennsylvania Ave. | 202/289–4224 | Metro: Federal Triangle.

Shops at National Place. There are many youth-oriented stores, and those in search of presidential souvenirs may find the White House Gift Shop handy. | 13th and F Sts. NW | 202/662–1250 | Metro: Metro Center.

Georgetown

Georgetown remains Washington's favorite shopping area. In addition to hosting tony antiques, elegant crafts, and high-style shoe and clothing boutiques, Georgetown offers wares that attract local college students and young people. Most stores lie to the east and west on M Street and to the north on Wisconsin.

Shops at Georgetown Park. This posh tri-level mall looks like a Victorian ice-cream parlor inside. The pricey clothing and accessory boutiques and the ubiquitous chain stores draw international visitors in droves. | 3222 M St. NW, Georgetown | 202/298–5577 | Metro: Foggy Bottom/GWU.

Dupont Circle

You might call Dupont Circle a younger, hipper version of Georgetown—almost as pricey and not quite as well kept, with more apartment buildings than houses. Its many restaurants, offbeat shops, and specialty book and record stores lend it a distinctive, cosmopolitan air. The street scene here is more urban than Georgetown's, with bike messengers and chess aficionados filling up the park while shoppers frequent the many coffee shops and stores.

Sports and Outdoor Activities

Bicycling

Each day, bicyclists cruise the Mall amid the endless throngs of runners, walkers, and tourists. Rock Creek Park covers an area from the edge of Georgetown to Montgomery County, Maryland. The bike path is asphalt and has a few challenging hills, and the roadway is closed to traffic on weekends. For scenery, you can't beat the **C&O Canal Towpath,** which starts in Georgetown and runs along the C&O Canal into Maryland.

Bicycle Pro Shop Georgetown. Rent a bike for the day at this shop near Georgetown University and Key Bridge by the Potomac River. | 3403 M St. NW | 202/337–0254.

Bike the Sites. Advance reservations are required for three-hour, 8-mi guided tours of downtown Washington. | 202/966–8662.

Boating and Sailing

Canoeing, sailing, and powerboating are all popular in the D.C. area. Several places rent boats along the Potomac River north and south of the city. You can dip your oars just about anywhere along the river—go canoeing in the C&O Canal, sailing in the widening river south of Alexandria, or even kayaking in the raging rapids at Great Falls, a 30-minute drive from the capital.

Thompson's Boat Center. The center, which is near Georgetown and Theodore Roosevelt Island, rents canoes, single kayaks, and rowing sculls. | 2900 Virginia Ave. NW, at the corner of Virginia Ave. and Rock Creek Pkwy. behind Kennedy Center | 202/333–4861.

Tidal Basin. The entrance is on 1501 Maine Avenue SW, on the east side of the Tidal Basin. You can rent paddleboats beginning in April and usually ending in September, depending on how cold the water gets. | 1501 Maine Ave. SW | 202/479–2426.

Essential Information

When to Go

In spring, the city's ornamental fruit trees are budding and its many gardens are in bloom. In autumn, you can again enjoy the sights without extremes of temperature. Summers can be uncomfortably hot and humid, but since that's when school is out, you may want to factor in a day pass on the Tourmobile or Old Town Trolley bus and spend longer intervals at air-conditioned destinations, such as museums.

FESTIVALS AND SEASONAL EVENTS

WINTER

Dec.: **National Christmas Tree Lighting/Pageant of Peace.** In mid-December, the president lights the tree at dusk on the Ellipse. Military bands perform at the People's Christmas Tree Lighting on the west side of the Capitol. | 202/619–7222.

SPRING

Mar. or Apr.: **Cherry Blossom Festival.** A gift from the people of Tokyo, the cherry trees that surround the Tidal Basin are the centerpiece of this celebration held each spring. | www.nationalcherryblossomfestival.org.

May: **Memorial Day Concert.** The National Symphony Orchestra officially welcomes summer to D.C. at 8 PM on the Capitol's West Lawn. | 202/619–7222.

Memorial Day at Arlington National Cemetery. Ceremonies include a wreath-laying ceremony at the Tomb of the Unknowns, services at the Memorial Amphitheatre featuring military bands, and a presidential keynote address. | 703/607–8052.

Memorial Day at the Vietnam Veterans Memorial. There is a wreath-laying ceremony and a concert by the National Symphony at the wall. | 202/619–7222.

SUMMER

June–July: **Folklife Festival.** The Smithsonian celebrates various cultures with this festival of music, arts and crafts, and food on the National Mall. | 202/357–2700 | www.folklife.si.edu.

July: **Independence Day Celebration.** Daytime festivities include a grand parade past many monuments. In the evening, the National Symphony Orchestra gives free performances on the Capitol's West Lawn; this is followed by fireworks over the Washington Monument. | 202/619–7222.

AUTUMN

Sept.: **Labor Day Weekend Concert.** The National Symphony Orchestra gives this free performance on the Capitol's West Lawn. | 202/619–7222 National Park Service; 202/467–4600 Kennedy Center.

National Black Family Reunion Celebration. The festival includes free performances by nationally renowned R&B and gospel singers, exhibits, and food on the Washington Monument grounds. | 202/737–0120.

Bargains

Washington is not cheap; however, many of its best-known sights are free. It's possible to plan a trip here with no other costs besides transportation, food, and lodging.

You can get obstructed-view tickets to National Symphony Orchestra performances in the Kennedy Center Concert Hall for $6.

Tours

BOAT TOURS

D.C. Ducks. Ninety-minute tours are given in converted World War II amphibious vehicles from March through October. | 202/832–9800 | www.historictours.com.

Odyssey III. The long, sleek vessel, specially built to fit under the Potomac's bridges, offers lunch, dinner, and Saturday and Sunday brunch cruises. | 202/488–6010 | www.odysseycruises.com.

ORIENTATION TOURS

Old Town Trolley Tours. Orange-and-green motorized trolleys take in the main downtown sights and also foray into Georgetown and the upper northwest. | 202/832–9800 | www.trolleytours.com.

Tourmobile. Buses, authorized by the National Park Service, make 25 stops at more than 40 historical sites between the Capitol and Arlington National Cemetery. | 202/554–5100 | www.tourmobile.com.

Visitor Information

D.C. Chamber of Commerce Visitor Center | Reagan Bldg., 1300 Pennsylvania Ave. NW, Suite 309, Washington, DC 20004 | 202/328–4748 | www.dcvisit.com. **Washington, D.C.,**

Convention and Tourism Corporation | 1212 New York Ave. NW, Suite 600, Washington, DC 20005 | 202/789–7000 or 800/422–8644 | www.washington.org.

Arriving and Departing

BY AIR

Airports

Ronald Reagan National Airport (DCA). National is 4 mi south of downtown Washington. | 703/417–8000 | www.mwaa.com.

Dulles International Airport (IAD). Dulles is 26 mi west of Washington. | 703/572–2700 | www.mwaa.com.

Baltimore-Washington International Airport (BWI). BWI is in Maryland, about 30 mi northeast of Washington. | 410/859–7100 | www.bwiairport.com.

Airport Transportation

Bus: SuperShuttle. Shuttles, which serve Reagan National, Dulles, and BWI airports, will take you to a specific hotel or residence. Make reservations at the ground transportation desk. | 800/258–3826 or 202/296–6662 | www.supershuttle.com.

Public Transit: At Ronald Reagan National Airport, a Metro station is within walking distance of the baggage claim area.

Washington Flyer. This coach service provides a convenient link between Dulles Airport and the West Falls Church (Virginia) Metro station. The 20-minute ride is $8 one-way or $14 round-trip; buses run every half hour. | 888/WASHFLY or 703/572–8400 | www.washfly.com.

At BWI Airport, there's a free shuttle bus to the Amtrak every day. On weekdays only, the shuttle connects to **Maryland Rail Commuter Service** (MARC; | 800/325–7245 | www.mtamaryland.com) trains that go to Washington's Union Station from around 6 AM to 10 PM.

Taxi: Expect to pay about $14 to get from Ronald Reagan National Airport to downtown, $50–$65 from Dulles, and $58–$65 from BWI. Airport and rush-hour surcharges apply.

BY BUS

Greyhound Bus Station | 1005 1st St. NE | 202/289–5160 or 800/231–2222 | www.greyhound.com.

BY CAR

Interstate 95 skirts D.C. as part of the Beltway, the six- to eight-lane highway that encircles the city. If you are coming from the south, take I–95 to I–395 and cross the 14th Street Bridge to 14th Street in the District. From the north, stay on I–95 south. Take the exit to Washington, which will place you onto the Baltimore–Washington (B-W) Parkway heading south. The B-W Parkway will turn into New York Avenue, taking you into downtown Washington, D.C.

Interstate 66 approaches the city from the southwest. You can get downtown by taking I–66 across the Theodore Roosevelt Bridge to Constitution Avenue.

Interstate 270 approaches Washington from the northwest before hitting I–495. To get downtown, take I–495 east to Connecticut Avenue south, toward Chevy Chase.

BY TRAIN

Union Station. Amtrak serves Washington's Union Station. | 50 Massachusetts Ave. NE | 202/371–9441 | www.unionstationdc.com.

Getting Around

BY CAR

Driving in Washington, D.C., itself is often confusing, with many lanes and some entire streets changing direction suddenly during rush hour. Traffic circles send drivers in unexpected directions and randomly arranged one-way streets surprise even locals.

Parking

The police are quick to ticket, tow, or immobilize with a "boot" any vehicle parked illegally. (If you find you've been towed from a city street, call ☎202/727–5000.) Private parking lots downtown charge around $5 an hour and $20 a day. There's free, three-hour parking around the Mall on Jefferson, Madison, and Ohio drives, though these spots are almost always filled. You can park free—in some spots all day—in parking areas off Ohio Drive near the Jefferson Memorial and south of the Lincoln Memorial.

BY PUBLIC TRANSIT

Bus

Washington Metropolitan Area Transit Authority. All Metrobus bus rides within the District are $1.10. All-day passes are available on the bus for $2.50. | 202/637–7000; 202/638–3780 TDD | www.metroopensdoors.com.

Metro

Washington Metropolitan Area Transit Authority. Farecard machines accept coins and crisp $1, $5, $10, or $20 bills. Insert your Farecard into the turnstile to enter the platform and then hang on to the card—you'll need it to exit at your destination. Some Washingtonians report that the Farecard's magnetic strip interferes with the strips on ATM cards and credit cards, so keep the cards separated in your pocket or wallet. | 202/637–7000; 202/638–3780 TDD | www.metroopensdoors.com.

BY TAXI

Taxis in the District are not metered; they operate instead on a zone system. Before you set off, ask your cab driver how much the fare will be. There are surcharges for additional passengers, for travel during rush hour, for suitcases, and for calling—as opposed to hailing–the cab. Maryland and Virginia taxis are metered but are not allowed to take passengers between points in D.C.

Diamond Cab | 202/332–6200. **Taxi Transportation** is an affiliation of 14 cab companies. | 202/398–0505. **Yellow Cab** | 202/544–1212.

D.C. Taxicab Commission. Unscrupulous cabbies prey on out-of-towners, especially at the airport. If the fare seems astronomical, get the driver's name and cab number and threaten to call the D.C. Taxicab Commission. | 202/645–6018.

Virginia

Revised and Updated by John A. Kelly

WILLIAMSBURG

Of the surviving American Colonial towns, none is more colorful nor historic than Williamsburg. Craftspeople of 16 trades make rifles, wigs, wagon wheels, and other colonial necessities and extravagances. Costumed interpreters bring the Capitol and the Governor's Palace to life, and up and down Duke of Gloucester Street carriages roll as the bell clangs in Bruton Church's tower. Taverns serve 18th-century food, actors and musicians perform, and militiamen drill.

On the peninsula between the York and James rivers in eastern Virginia, Williamsburg was established as Middle Plantation in 1633. After the capitol in Jamestown burned in 1699 Middle Plantation was renamed Williamsburg in honor of King William III and became Virginia's capital. It served as a cultural and political center until 1780, when invading British forced removal to Richmond. Williamsburg faded in significance and fell into general decay in the 19th century.

Rector W. A. R. Goodwin convinced John D. Rockefeller Jr. to fund Williamsburg's restoration. Work began in 1926, and by the 1930s buildings were being opened to the public. Roughly 600 post-Colonial structures were demolished, more than 80 period buildings were restored, and 40 replicas were reconstructed over excavated foundations. The historic district is approximately 1 mi long and ½ mi wide and surrounded by a greenbelt to preserve the illusion of a Colonial city. Even older, the College of William and Mary, America's second-oldest university, adjoins the reconstructed Williamsburg. Outside there are numerous restaurants, lodgings, outlet shops, and amusement parks.

Colonial Parkway connects Williamsburg with Jamestown and Yorktown, site of the conclusive battle of the Revolution. Near Williamsburg lie several of the historic James River plantations.

Exploring

Williamsburg

COLONIAL WILLIAMSBURG

★ The work of archaeologists and historians of the Colonial Williamsburg Foundation continues, and the 173-acre restored area is operated as a living-history museum. There

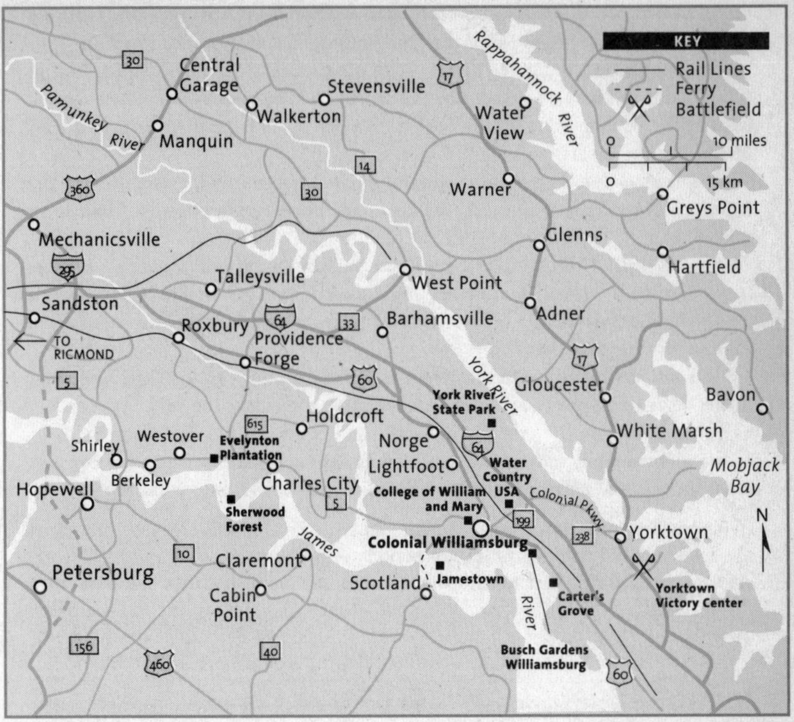

are 88 original 18th-century buildings and another 40 that have been reconstructed on their original sites. In all, 225 rooms have been furnished from the foundation's collection of more than 100,000 pieces of furniture, pottery, china, glass, silver, textiles, and tools. Authenticity also governs the grounds, which include 90 acres of gardens. Costumed interpreters lead house tours and demonstrate historic trades. The restored area can only be toured on foot; all vehicular traffic is prohibited.

Colonial Williamsburg Visitor Center. Here you can purchase tickets for Colonial Williamsburg and pick up a *Visitor's Companion* guide, which lists regular events and special programs and includes a map of the historic area. The center also shows a 35-minute introductory movie, "Williamsburg—The Story of a Patriot." Information about dining and lodging is available (there's a reservation service). Shuttle buses to the historic area run continuously throughout the day. There's also a bookstore. | 100 Visitor's Center Dr. | 757/220–7659 | Free | Summer daily 8:30–7, earlier fall and winter.

Exhibit Sites. In Colonial Williamsburg, you'll feel you have stepped into another century as you stroll the restored area of authentic renovations, reconstructions, gardens and public greens. Elegant homes, government buildings, and merchant shops outfitted in their finest Colonial trappings are staffed by costumed reenactors.

Anchoring the east end of Duke of Gloucester Street is the ★**Capitol,** the center of Virginia politics from 1699 to 1781; it was here that the pre-Revolutionary House of Burgesses challenged the royally appointed council. A tour explains the development of American democracy from its English parliamentary roots. The building is a reproduction with dark-wood wainscoting, pewter chandeliers, and towering ceilings.

The reconstructed ★**Governor's Palace,** originally built in 1720, housed seven royal governors and Virginia's first two state governors, Patrick Henry and Thomas Jefferson. It is furnished as it was just before the Revolution; 800 guns and swords arrayed on the walls and ceilings of several rooms herald the power of the Crown.

The **Magazine** (1715), an octagonal brick warehouse, stored arms and ammunition; it was used for this purpose by the British, then by the Continental Army, and later by the Confederates during the Civil War. Today, 18th-century firearms are on display within the arsenal.

The **Courthouse** of 1770 was used by municipal and county courts until 1932; the exterior has been restored to its original appearance. Stocks, once used to punish misdemeanors, are located outside the building.

Bruton Parish Church, built in 1715, has served continuously as a place of worship; many local eminences, including one royal governor, are interred in the graveyard.

The **Public Hospital** is a reconstructed 1773 asylum that treated the mentally ill in the 18th and 19th centuries.

The ★**DeWitt Wallace Decorative Arts Gallery** contains English and American furniture, textiles, prints, and ceramics spanning the 17th to the early 19th century as well as a full-length portrait of George Washington by Charles Willson Peale.

Nearby, the **Abby Aldrich Rockefeller Folk Art Center** showcases American folk art, from toys and weather vanes to sculptures, doll houses, and paintings.

Living History Programs. The Williamsburg Institute has special weekend programs like seminars and demonstrations of period design, home decorating, needlework, woodworking, and gardening. Costumed interpreters bring a variety of programs to the historic district. Craftspeople such as the silversmith, wheelwright, and wigmaker demonstrate their trades each day. Performers provide 18th-century entertainment; courts convene for trials; and the Continental Army is encamped. | 800/603–0948.

★ **Carter's Grove.** Carter Burwell built the mansion on a bluff above the James River in 1755, on land purchased by his grandfather, Robert "King" Carter, one of Virginia's wealthiest landowners. Remodeled in 1919, the house retains its original wood paneling and elaborate carvings and is furnished in Colonial Revival style. The settlement around Carter's Grove was reconstructed after extensive archaeological investigation and includes slaves' quarters. Exhibits in the Winthrop Rockefeller Archaeology Museum include displays about Wolstenholme Towne, a settlement destroyed by Indians in 1622 that is believed to have been the first planned town in British America. | 8797 Pocahontas Trail | 757/229–1000 | fax 757/220–7173 | www.colonialwilliamsburg.org | $18 (included in Williamsburg Patriot's Pass) | Mid-Mar.–Dec., Tues.–Sun. 9–5.

Colonial Williamsburg Information

| Jct. Rte. 5 and Rte. 31/Jamestown Rd. | 800/603–0948 | fax 757/220–7702 | www.colonialwilliamsburg.org | Freedom Pass $39, valid for admission to all exhibition buildings, daytime programs, and museums throughout Colonial Williamsburg, including Carter's Grove for 1 yr. Day Pass $33, includes admission to all of the above except Carter's Grove. Both include parking at visitor center. Museums $8, annual museums pass $18. | Daily 9–5.

ELSEWHERE IN WILLIAMSBURG

Busch Gardens Williamsburg. This theme park has more than 40 rides and attractions, including five roller coasters and six European hamlets, each with native cuisine. The world's tallest inverted roller coaster, the Alpengeist, and Apollo's Chariot, the coaster with the longest "free-flight" (two minutes and 825 ft), are here. Shows and rides are included in the admission price. Bounce Passes include Water Country, a separate park nearby (which is closed in cool months).| One Busch Place | 800/343–7946 | www.buschgardens.com/buschgardens/va | One-day Bounce Pass $44.99, 2-day $59.99, 3-day $69.99, 4-day $79.99; parking $7–$10 | Late Mar.–late Apr., Fri.–Sun. 10–7; late Apr.–mid-May, Sun.–Thurs. 10–7, Fri. 10–9, Sat. 10–10; mid-May–mid-June, Sun.–Fri. 10–7, Sat. 10–10; mid-June–late Aug., daily 10–10; mid-Aug.–late Aug., weekdays 10–8, weekends 10–10; late Aug.–early Sept., weekdays 10–6, weekends 10–10; early Sept.–late Sept., Fri. 10–6, weekends 10–7.

College of William and Mary. The second-oldest college in the United States (after Harvard University), William and Mary was chartered in 1693 by the reigning king and queen of England, William III and Mary II, for whom it was named. The college severed ties with Britain in 1776. Thomas Jefferson, James Monroe, John Marshall, and John Tyler are among its alumni. | West end of Duke of Gloucester St. | 757/221–4000 | www.wm.edu.

The college's **Earl Gregg Swem Library** has more than 1 million volumes, 3 million manuscripts, and documents from many historical figures, including the papers of U.S. Chief Justice Warren Burger. | 757/221–3050 | www.swem.wm.edu | Free | Mon.–Thurs. 8 AM–midnight, Fri. 8–6, Sat. 9–6, Sun. 1–midnight.

William and Mary's original structure, the **Wren Building,** dates from 1695, predating Williamsburg. Its design is attributed to the celebrated London architect Sir Christopher Wren. The redbrick outer walls are original, but fire gutted the interior several times, and the present quarters are largely 20th-century reconstructions. The oldest academic building in use in America, it includes the chapel where Peyton Randolph, prominent Colonist and revolutionary who served as president of the First Continental Congress, is buried. | Free.

Colonial Parkway. The 23-mi roadway connects three historic sites—Jamestown, Williamsburg, and Yorktown. Created in the 1930s by the National Park Service, the parkway has a number of turnouts with unobstructed views of the James and York rivers; many of these are good spots for a picnic. Commercial traffic is prohibited. | Colonial National Historical Park, Box 210, Yorktown 23690 | 757/898–3400 | fax 757/898–6346 | www.nps.gov.

Water Country USA. More than 30 water rides and attractions, live entertainment, shops, and restaurants pack the park. They include the Nitro Racer speed slide, with a 382-ft drop. The biggest attraction is a 4,500-square-ft heated pool. | Rte. 199 | 800/343–7946 | www.watercountryusa.com | $31.99 (included in Busch Gardens Bounce Passes). | May–mid-June, weekends 10–6; mid-June–Aug., daily 10–8; early Sept.–mid-Sept., Fri.–Sat. 10–6.

York River State Park. This 2,491-acre park, 11 mi northeast in James City County, is an estuarine environment, formed by the York River, Taskinas Creek, and a saltwater marsh. More than 20 mi of hiking, biking, and horseback-riding trails wind through the marsh, river shoreline, and upland forests. The park has fresh- and saltwater fishing, picnic pavilions, a boat launch, and bike and boat rentals. Exhibits at the visitor center highlight the history and preservation efforts. | 5526 Riverview Rd., Croaker | 757/566–3036 | www.dcr.state.va.us | $1 per vehicle, $2 weekends Late May–early Sept. | Daily 8 AM–dusk.

Charles City County

Colonial Virginia was divided into four political units in 1619, and Charles City County is one of the oldest "incorporated" settlements in America. Its early glory days can be glimpsed along Route 5, a scenic road that follows the James River past nine plantations, the oldest dating from 1723. You can tour four of the estates (Berkeley, Evelynton, Sherwood Forest, and Shirley) on one combination ticket for $33. Ironically, there is no city in Charles City County; despite its proximity to Richmond and Williamsburg, the municipality is largely rural, with extensive timberlands and cultivated farmland.

★ **Berkeley.** Benjamin Harrison, a signer of the Declaration of Independence, and William Harrison, the 9th U.S. president, were born in this brick Georgian house. (William's grandson Benjamin Harrison, the 23rd president, was born in Ohio.) Berkeley Hundred—so called because it could support 100 families—now called Berkeley Plantation, was settled by 38 men of Berkeley Parish, England, in 1619 and was the most important plantation in early Virginia. The riverfront mansion is furnished with period antiques; five terraces of boxwoods and flower gardens offering a James River vista have been restored. | 12602 Harrison Landing Rd. | 804/829–6018 | $9.50 | Daily 8–5.

Evelynton Plantation. In 1846, the 2,500-acre working plantation was purchased by the family of Edmund Ruffin, who fired the first shot at Fort Sumter at the beginning of the Civil War. He also revived Virginia agriculture in the 18th century and earned the title "Father of American Agronomy." Ironically, the original house and outbuildings were destroyed during the Civil War's Peninsula Campaign in 1862. The present house, designed in the 1930s by architect Duncan Lee, contains 18th-century English and American antiques and is surrounded by landscaped lawn and gardens. The plantation is still operated by Ruffin descendants. | 6701 John Tyler Memorial Hwy., 23030 | 804/829–5075 or 800/473–5075 | www.evelyntonplantation.org | $9 | Daily 9–5.

★ **Sherwood Forest.** John Tyler, 10th president of the United States, renamed this circa-1720 house to refer to his reputation as a political "outlaw." Tyler lived here from 1845 until his death in 1862. At 301 ft, it is said to be the longest wood-frame house in the country as a result of Tyler's ballroom addition. Sherwood Forest has remained in the Tyler family and contains many heirloom antiques; the surrounding 25 acres include a tobacco barn and other outbuildings. | 14501 John Tyler Memorial Hwy. | 804/282–1441 | www.sherwoodforest.org | $5 | Daily 9–5.

★ **Shirley.** The oldest plantation in Virginia, Shirley has been occupied by a single family, the Carters, for 11 generations. Robert E. Lee's mother, Anne Hill Carter, was born here. The present mansion, a Georgian manor begun in 1723, stands at the end of a drive lined by towering Lombardy poplars; inside, the hall staircase rises three stories with no visible support. The family silver is on display, ancestral portraits are hung throughout, and rare books line the shelves. | 501 Shirley Plantation Rd. | 804/829–5121 | fax 804/829–6322 | www.shirleyplantation.com | $10.50 | Daily 9–5.

Westover. Colonel William Byrd II, an American aristocrat who served in both the upper and lower houses of the Colonial legislature at Williamsburg, built Westover between 1726 and 1730. Educated in England, Byrd founded the cities of Richmond and Petersburg, owned the best library in Virginia, and recorded the life of a classic Colonial gentleman. While the grounds are open to the public daily, the house, a renowned example of Georgian architecture, is open only during Garden Week in late April. | 7000 Westover Rd. | 804/829–2882 | $2 | Grounds daily 9–5:30.

Jamestown

Jamestown Island, separated from the mainland by a narrow isthmus, was the site of the first permanent English settlement in North America. Colonists sent by the Virginia Company of London arrived on May 14, 1607; they called the new enterprise "James Towne" after their king. The colony served as the capital of Virginia until 1699 and was the site of the first American legislative assembly in 1619. Now uninhabited, the island bears only tantalizing traces of that early colony. The ruin of a church tower from the 1640s, brick foundation walls, and other clues help delineate the settlement, together with artists' renderings. Jamestown Island is a historic park, full of archaeological excavations, and historians continue to uncover more evidence about the lifestyle of these early pioneers. During the Civil War, five Confederate earthworks were constructed at Jamestown; two remain accessible to the public.

★ **Jamestown, the Original Site.** Nothing of Jamestown remains above ground except the Old Church Tower. Cooperative archaeological efforts by the National Park Service and the Association for the Preservation of Virginia Antiquities (which owns 22 acres of the island, including the Old Church Tower) have exposed foundations, streets, property ditches, fences, and the James Fort site. The island is part of the Colonial National Historical Park. Jamestown Island Loop Drive winds through the woods and marshes for 5 mi and is posted with historically informative signs and interpretive paintings that show what a building might have looked like where only ruins or foundations now remain. | Jamestown Island | 757/229–1733 | fax 757/898–6025 | www.nps.gov/colo | $5 (includes all sites on the island) | Daily 9–5.

Begin your visit at the **Jamestown Visitor Center,** where, in addition to maps, information, and ranger-led tours, you can watch a 15-minute film about the island's history, see one of the most extensive collections of 17th-century artifacts in the United States, and rent audio tapes for self-guided tours.

At the reconstructed **Glasshouse,** artisans demonstrate glassblowing, an unsuccessful business venture of the early colonists.

A 103-ft obelisk at **First Landing Site** commemorates Jamestown's founding in 1607.

The **Memorial Church,** erected in 1907 for the Jamestown Exposition, contains the foundations of two earlier, 17th-century churches.

Old Church Tower, dating from the 1640s, marks the site of the first permanent English settlement in North America (1607) and is now part of Memorial Church.

New Towne contains the ruins of several early country houses, a part of the old James City, and foundations of several statehouses. A 1-mi self-guided walking tour takes you along the old streets, where markers indicate the sites of former structures.

Dale House holds the laboratories and offices of the Jamestown Rediscovery Project, an ongoing archaeological investigation. Archaeologists have found pieces of armor like those worn by soldiers in Europe in the late 16th and early 17th centuries and animal bones that indicate the early colonists survived on fish and turtles.

★ **Jamestown Settlement.** Adjacent to the original site of Jamestown, Jamestown Settlement is a living-history museum built in 1957 to celebrate the 350th anniversary of Jamestown's founding. The museum, which includes a film and permanent galleries, provides a glimpse of life during the early 1600s. On the grounds, you will also find James Fort, a re-creation of the home of the first settlers; the Powhatan Indian Village, reconstructed Quonset huts like those once inhabited by the Powhatan; and the *Godspeed, Discovery,* and *Susan Constant,* full-scale reproductions of the ships that brought the settlers to Virginia. In all three areas, costumed interpreters ply their trades and describe their lives. | Rte. 31 S, at Colonial Pkwy. | 757/253–4838 or 888/593–4682 | fax 757/253–5299 | www.historyisfun.org | $10.75 (combination ticket with Yorktown $16; Yorktown alone $8.25) | Mid-Aug.–mid-June, daily 9–5; mid-June–mid Aug., daily 9–7.

Yorktown

Settled in 1691, Yorktown had become a thriving tobacco port and a prosperous community of several hundred houses by the time of the Revolution. It was at Yorktown that the combined American and French forces surrounded Lord Cornwallis's British troops in 1781—this was the end to the Revolutionary War. Yorktown remains a living community, albeit a small one. Route 238 leads into town, where along Main Street are preserved 18th-century buildings (some of them open to visitors) on a bluff overlooking the York River.

★ **Yorktown Battlefield.** On this spot, the British surrendered to American and French forces in 1781. The museum in the visitor center has on exhibit part of General George Washington's original field tent. Dioramas, illuminated maps, and a short movie about the battle make the sobering point that Washington's victory was hardly inevitable. Guided by an audio tour ($2) rented from the gift shop, you may explore the battlefield by car, stopping at the site of Washington's headquarters, a couple of crucial redoubts (breastworks dug into the ground), and the field where surrender took place. | Rte. 238 off Colonial Pkwy. | 757/898–2410 | $5 | Visitor center daily 9–5 (extended hrs in summer).

★ **Yorktown Victory Center.** On the western edge of Yorktown Battlefield, the Victory Center has wonderful exhibits and demonstrations that bring to life the American Revolution. The Road to Revolution walkway covers the principal events and personalities. Life-size tableaux show 10 "witnesses," including an African-American patriot, a loyalist, a Native American leader, two Continental army soldiers, and the wife of a Virginia plantation owner. The exhibit galleries contain more than 500 period artifacts, including many recovered during underwater excavations of "Yorktown's Sunken Fleet" (British ships lost during the siege of 1781). Outdoors, in a Continental army encampment, interpreters costumed as soldiers and female auxiliaries reenact and discuss daily camp life. In another outdoor area, interpreters re-create 18th-century farm life. | Rte. 238 off Colonial Pkwy. | 757/253–4838 or 888/593–4682 | $8.25; combination ticket for Yorktown Victory Center and Jamestown Settlement $16 | Daily 9–5.

Dining

Williamsburg offers the spectrum of food and dining, from stand-up to tavern to elegant Colonial. Traditional tidewater cooking shows up in the Smithfield ham, kale, turnip greens, and hot breads served in a few restaurants.

Williamsburg

COLONIAL WILLIAMSBURG

★ **18th-Century Taverns.** There are four authentic taverns with costumed waiters and oversize napkins and cutlery in the historic district. The fare is all hearty early American but differs in each tavern. All offer outdoor dining. These taverns help support the Colonial Williamsburg Foundation. | 800/447–8679 | Reservations essential | $15–$30 | AE, D, MC, V | No smoking.

Chownings, a reconstructed alehouse, serves casual meals including Welsh rarebit, oyster fritters, and sandwiches and heartier fare such as Brunswick stew, duckling, and prime rib.

Christiana Campbell's was George Washington's favorite tavern; its specialty is seafood, and it looks out upon the Capitol just across the street.

King's Arms, the most upscale of the Colonial taverns, catered to the gentry in its day. Today strolling balladeers entertain; specialties include peanut soup and game pie.

Shields Tavern serves 18th-century low-country cuisine in eight dining rooms and the garden.

ELSEWHERE IN WILLIAMSBURG

Berret's. Seafood. Specialties of this popular dining room include a raw bar, seafood platter, Cuban seafood with black beans and rice, and the Virginia crab-meat combination. Dine indoors or out. | 199 S. Boundary St. | 757/253–1847 | Closed Mon. Jan.–Mar. | $18–$25 | AE, D, MC, V.

Giuseppe's. Italian. This eatery highlights northern and coastal Italian cuisines, which don't rely on tomato sauce and cheese but concentrate on beans, olive oil, wine, seafood, and pasta. Seating includes an indoor café, with maroon walls and green tables, and a tiny outside terrace. | 5601 Richmond Rd. | 757/565–1977 | www.giuseppes.com | Closed Sun. | $7–$18 | AE, D, DC, MC, V.

Old Chickahominy House. American. The house specialty in the morning is the plantation breakfast: real Virginia ham with eggs, biscuits, cured country bacon, sausage, grits, and coffee. At lunch, Miss Melinda's special is Brunswick stew, Virginia ham on biscuits, fruit salad, and homemade pie. Adjoining the dining area are rooms that house a charming antiques-gift shop. Beer and wine only. | 1211 Jamestown Rd. | 757/229–4689 | $7–$12 | Closed 2 wks mid-Jan. | MC, V.

Polo Club. American. On the edge of Williamsburg, the Polo Club is the neighborhood place to go for a beer and burger. Eat in a wooden booth while checking out the clutter of polo paraphernalia around you. | 135 Colony Sq., Williamsburg 23185 | 757/220–1122 | $8–$13 | AE, D, DC, MC, V.

★ **The Trellis.** Contemporary. Worth a splurge, the Trellis combines simplicity and elegance. Lunch and dinner menus present the best foods of each season. Don't leave without indulging in the famous Death by Chocolate dessert. | 403 Duke of Gloucester St. | 757/229–8610 | fax 757/221–0450 | www.thetrellis.com | $18–$28 | AE, DC, MC, V.

Yorkshire Steak and Seafood House. Steak. A fixture since 1970, this Colonial redbrick eatery offers a full menu including prime rib and steaks and a wide variety of fresh and delicious seafood, most from Virginia's own local waters. | 700 York St. | 757/229–9790 | fax 757/229–7685 | No lunch | $13–$19 | AE, MC, V.

Charles City County

River's Rest Motel and Marina. American. Enjoy casual dining inside or outside beside the Chickahominy River. Breakfast, lunch, and nightly dinner specials are home-cooked daily. Barbecued chicken, teriyaki chicken, steaks, and lasagna are served. Salad and dessert come with the entrée. Popular with fishermen. | 9100 Wilcox Neck Rd. | 804/829–2753 | $8–$12 | AE, MC, V.

Lodging

The most famous and convenient hostelries—the Williamsburg Inn, the Williamsburg Lodge, Woodlands, and the Governor's Inn—are run by Colonial Williamsburg, which depends upon their income. Though memorable, they are not for the faint of purse. Several very reasonable bed-and-breakfasts and motels are available with less Colonial atmosphere; you'll get even lower prices in Yorktown and Newport News.

Williamsburg

COLONIAL WILLIAMSBURG

Governor's Inn. Least expensive of the Colonial Williamsburg hotels, the Governor's Inn is only three blocks from the visitor center and has shuttle-bus service. Completely renovated and redecorated, the inn gained a new wing as well as an outdoor swimming pool. Rooms are furnished with two double beds. Cable TV with video games, pool, business services, free parking. | 506 N. Henry St., 23185 | 800/447–8679 | fax 757/220–7019 | 200 rooms | $65–$100 | Closed Jan.–mid-Mar. | AE, D, MC, V.

Governor Spottswood Motel. A redbrick motel, it has gradually added onto the main building for 60 years. The decor of Colonial Williamsburg is expressed in reproduction period furniture. Seven cottages sleep up to seven people, and 14 rooms have kitchens. Pool, shuffleboard, 3 playgrounds | 1508 Richmond Rd., 23185 | 757/229–6444 or 800/368–1244 | fax 757/253–2410 | www.govspottswood.com | 78 rooms | $32–$64 | AE, D, DC, MC, V.

ELSEWHERE IN WILLIAMSBURG

Bassett Motel. Dogwood trees and flower beds (azaleas and tulips in the spring, begonias in the fall) surround this well-run, amazingly reasonable single-story brick motel between Colonial Williamsburg and Busch Gardens. Cable TV | 800 York St. (U.S. 60), 23185 | 757/229–5175 | www.williamsburghotel.com | 18 rooms | $34–$55 | Closed Mid-Nov.–mid-Mar. | MC, V.

Heritage Inn. A spacious tree-shaded lawn with fountain welcomes you to this hostelry located 1 mi from Colonial Williamsburg, a short walk to the college of William and Mary, and a few miles from Busch Gardens and outlet shopping centers. Rooms feature fine traditional furnishings. Cable TV, pool, business services, some pets allowed | 1324 Richmond Rd. | 757/229–6220 or 800/782–3800 | fax 757/229–2774 | www.heritageinnwmsb.com | 54 rooms | $42–$84 | AE, D, DC, MC, V.

Howard Johnson's–Historic Area. Not your typical chain hotel, this family-run franchise has washers and dryers on each floor and spacious guest rooms with coffee makers and irons. The friendly staff makes this a particularly good choice for families. Cable TV, pool, gym, laundry facilities, concierge | 7135 Pocahontas Trail, 23185 | 800/841–9100 | fax 757/220–3211 | 86 rooms, 14 suites | $59–$79 | AE, D, DC, MC, V.

Quality Inn Lord Paget. Tall white columns front this modern motel. Eight rooms are accessed via stairs off the spacious lobby with Oriental carpets; others are motel-style with parking at their doors. Some have canopy beds. Refrigerators and microwaves are available for a fee. There is a 2½-acre lake and gardens. Coffee shop, cable TV, pool, putting green, dock, fishing, laundry service, no-smoking rooms | 901 Capitol Landing Rd., 23185 | 757/229–4444 or 800/444–4678 | 94 rooms | $39–$69 | AE, D, DC, MC, V | CP.

War Hill Inn. This two-story redbrick building in a 32-acre operating cattle farm is 4 mi from the Colonial Williamsburg visitor center. | 4560 Long Hill Rd., 23188 | 757/565–0248 | www.warhillinn.com | 4 rooms, 1 suite, 1 cottage | $80–$130 | MC, V.

Williamsburg Hospitality House. The hotel is close to the College of William and Mary. Restaurant, in-room data ports, cable TV, pool, bar, business services. | 415 Richmond Rd. | 757/229–4020 or 800/932–9192 | fax 757/220–1560 | www.williamsburghosphouse.com | 296 rooms | $89–$190 | AE, D, DC, MC, V.

Charles City County

Red Hill Bed and Breakfast. Situated on 50 serene acres in the heart of the James River plantations, this white Williamsburg-style home with dormer windows, built in 1989, is surrounded by pastures, farms, and cornfields. Guests are welcomed with refreshments and are served a full country breakfast featuring homemade breads. Located halfway between Richmond and Williamsburg on historical Route 5. | 7500 John Tyler Memorial Hwy., Charles City County, 23030 | 804/829–6213 | fax 804/829–6213 | 4 rooms, 2 with private bath | $85 | MC, V.

Camping

Most area campgrounds (around Jamestown and along I–64, at least 5 mi from Williamsburg) are open March–mid-November. Advance reservations for June–August are needed at all of them. Contact the Williamsburg Area Convention and Visitors Bureau (☞ Visitor Information) for information.

Williamsburg KOA Resorts. Near a lake, the camp provides free van service to Williamsburg and Busch Gardens and even sells tickets. There are family activities available, as well as Internet access. Flush toilets, full hook-ups, partial hook-ups, dump station, drinking water, picnic table, fire pit, showers, laundry, pool, public telephone | 330 RV sites, 43 cabins | 2 mi west of I–64 Exit 234 | 800/635–2717 | MC, V.

Shopping

Peanuts from nearby farms, Smithfield and country hams, glassware reproductions from the Jamestown Glasshouse, and reproductions of the salt-glaze and brown-glaze pottery of the early settlers are bargain finds in this area.

Nine reconstructed stores and shops in the historic area sell Colonial-style silver tea services, jewelry, pottery, pewter and brass items, ironwork, tobacco and herbs, candles, hats, baskets, books, maps and prints, approved reproductions, and baked goods. Merchants Square, on the west end of Duke of Gloucester Street, has upscale shops like Laura Ashley, Quilts Unlimited, and the Campus Shop with William and Mary gifts and apparel. The tiny nearby town of Lightfoot has many outlet malls. Most outlet shops are open Monday–Saturday 10–9, Sunday 10–6. In January and February, some stores close weekdays at 6.

★ **Williamsburg Pottery Factory.** This is an attraction unto itself, and the parking lot is usually crammed with tour buses. The enormous outlet store sells luggage, clothing, furniture, food and wine, china, crystal, and—its original commodity—pottery. Individual stores such as Pfaltzgraff and Banister Shoes are within the compound. | Richmond Hwy. near Rte. 199 | 757/564–3326.

Sports and Outdoor Activities

Bicycling

The historic district limits auto traffic, favoring pedestrians and bicyclists. The pamphlet *Biking Through America's Historic Triangle*, available at bike shops, maps a 20-mi route along the bike path of the scenic Colonial Parkway, which goes past Williamsburg, Yorktown, and Jamestown. You can rent bicycles at the Williamsburg Lodge or Williamsburg Woodlands.

Bikesmith. This shop also rents bicycles. | 515 York St. | 757/229–9858.

Golf

Colonial. This public course has a spacious range and 3 practice holes. | Forge Rd., Rte. 60 west of town | 757/566–1600.

Golden Horseshoes. The Gold Course, by Robert Trent Jones, covers 6,817 yards with an island green on the 16th hole. The Green Course, by Rees Jones, is set in a wildlife preserve. | Just south of historic district | 757/220–7696.

Kingsmill Resort. Three courses at a resort with golf as the main course. The River Course is home of the Michelob Championship. | East on Rte. 60 to Kingsmill Dr. | 757/253–3906.

Hiking

The 5-mi nature trail on Jamestown Island is an ideal place for getting exercise, with the added possibility of seeing wildlife. York River State Park has many miles of trails. At both the Jamestown and Yorktown ends of the Colonial Parkway, turnoffs lead to waterfront recreation areas, where people walk, picnic, or play volleyball.

Essential Information

When to Visit

Most visitors come in July and August, when the temperature is frequently in the 90s. Spring and fall have better weather and fewer people; from January to the end of March and from mid-September through November the crowds are thinnest. (Many businesses close briefly during January and/or February.) The height of spring bloom comes at the end of April, when Virginia celebrates Historic Garden Week and many old homes open to the public. Many visitors come for Christmas shopping on Merchants Square in town and at the discount outlets on Richmond Road.

FESTIVALS AND SEASONAL EVENTS

WINTER

Dec.: **Traditional Christmas Activities.** There are holiday programs, tours, workshops, and concerts in the historic district during the Christmas season. A highlight is the Grand Illumination, when all the windows in the historic district are lit with candles; the event also includes fireworks, a military tattoo, and twilight entertainment. Separate celebrations are held at the plantations and at Yorktown. | 800/603–0948.

SPRING

Mar–Oct.: **Military Drill.** A fife-and-drum corps and 18th-century soldiers perform afternoons in the historic district. | 800/603–0948.

Apr.: **Historic Garden Week Symposium.** Colonial Williamsburg's longest-running symposium is a part of the Historic Garden Week, a state-wide annual event that raises funds for the restoration of historic gardens and grounds. | 800/603–0948 or 804/644–7776 | fax 804/644–7778 | www.vagardenweek.org.

May: **Jamestown Day.** An encampment, tactical demonstrations, maritime demonstrations, and lectures commemorate the founding of Jamestown in 1607. | 757/898–2410.

SUMMER

July: **Independence Day Celebrations at Berkeley Plantation.** Benjamin Harrison, a signer of the Declaration of Independence, is honored in a living-history program and guided tours of his manor house. | 888/466–6018.

AUTUMN

Oct.: **An Occasion for the Arts.** Held every year at Merchants' Square (usually the first Sunday of October), events include a juried competition of artists, live Dixieland jazz, and rock music. Food is plentiful, and there are things for kids to do, too. | 757/220–1736.

Yorktown Day and Victory Celebration. Revolutionary War reenactors hold a weekend encampment and commemorate the war's end with a parade, demonstrations, and patriotic ceremonies. | 757/220–1736.

The First Thanksgiving Celebration. On Thanksgiving Day, tours, festivities, and a program at Berkeley Plantation commemorate the first American Thanksgiving, which immediately followed the 1619 landing. | 804/829–6018.

Bargains

Free concerts and lectures are held at William and Mary (804/221–2630). The Yorktown Visitor Center and the battlefields are free. The Jamestown–Scotland Wharf toll ferry (fee charged) makes a beautiful 2½-mi crossing of the James River.

Tours

Williamsburg Limousines, Inc. Guided tours to Jamestown and Yorktown are available. It also runs buses from Williamsburg hotels and motels to Jamestown, Yorktown, Busch Gardens, and Carter's Grove plantation. | 804/877–0279.

Visitor Information

Colonial Williamsburg Foundation | Box 1776, Williamsburg 23187-1776 | 800/603-0948 | www.history.org. **Colonial National Historical Park** | Box 210, Yorktown 23690 | 757/898-2410 or 757/229-1733 | www.nps.gov/colo. **Williamsburg Area Convention and Visitors Bureau** | 421 N. Boundary St., Williamsburg 23185 | 800/368-6511 | www.visitwilliamsburg.com.

Arriving and Departing

BY AIR

Airports

Newport News–Williamsburg International Airport (PHF). The airport is 20 mi away. | 804/877-0924 | www.nnwairport.com.

Norfolk International (ORF). Norfolk is 46 mi away. | 804/857-3351 | www.norfolkairport.com.

Richmond International (RIC). Richmond is also 46 mi away. | 804/226-3052 | www.flyrichmond.com.

Airport Transportation

At Newport News–Williamsburg International Airport, you can rent a car from Avis, Budget, Hertz, and National. Norfolk offers car rentals from Avis, Budget, Dollar, Enterprise, Hertz, National, Payless, and Thrifty. Richmond International Airport has Avis, Budget, Enterprise, Hertz, and National car rental services.

BY BUS

Greyhound Lines | 468 N. Boundary St. | 800/231-2222.

BY CAR

Most visitors arrive by car on I–64. Those coming from Richmond may want to take slower-paced Route 5, the John Tyler Highway, past the James River plantations.

BY TRAIN

Amtrak has train service from Washington, D.C. | 468 N. Boundary St.

Getting Around

BY CAR

Most of the historic area of Williamsburg is not open to driving. Otherwise traffic and roads are not difficult. You will want a car to visit Charles City Country, Jamestown, and Yorktown sights.

Parking

Free parking is available at the visitor center in the historic area.

BY PUBLIC TRANSIT

Bus: Historic district shuttle buses (free for ticket holders) make nine stops on a constant circuit of the area before returning to the visitor center. Williamsburg is best seen on foot and by bus.

Wyoming

Revised and Updated by Candy Moulton

YELLOWSTONE NATIONAL PARK

A "window on the earth's interior" is how one geophysicist described Yellowstone National Park, and it's true that few places in the world can match Yellowstone's collection of accessible wonders, from rainbow-color hot springs to thundering geysers. As you visit the park's hydrothermal areas, you'll be walking on top of the Yellowstone Caldera—a 28- by 47-mi collapsed volcanic cone, which last erupted about 600,000 years ago. The park's geyser basins, hot mud pots, fumaroles (steam vents), and hot springs are kept bubbling by an underground pressure cooker filled with magma.

Yellowstone is a high plateau, ringed by even higher mountains; the park lies mostly in northwestern Wyoming and extends into Montana and Idaho. Roadside elevations range from 5,314 ft at the North Entrance to 8,859 ft at Dunraven Pass. The Gallatin Range to the west and north, the Absaroka and Beartooth ranges to the north and east, and the Tetons to the south all have peaks higher than 10,000 ft. Scenery in the park ranges from near-high desert around the North Entrance to lodgepole pine forests around the South Entrance, and otherworldly landscapes of stunted pine and shrub around thermal areas.

Yellowstone's appeal is as strong today as it was in 1872, when the region became the country's first national park. The lure for the more than 3 million people who visit annually is the park's diversity of wildlife. Long known for its elk and buffalo herds, Yellowstone has once again became home to North American wolves thanks to an experimental repopulation program.

Exploring

Yellowstone National Park

For any trip to Yellowstone plan to do this at the minimum: Take a hike on one of the park's trails (they range from a short distance of less than ½ mi to many miles in length and from nearly flat and easy to steep and difficult, so choose one that fits your mood and ability); explore at least one of the geyser basins (Norris is the most active; Old Faithful is busiest); learn about Yellowstone history at one of the park's museums or visitor centers; and spend some time just sitting quietly and watching the wildlife or the incredible scenery.

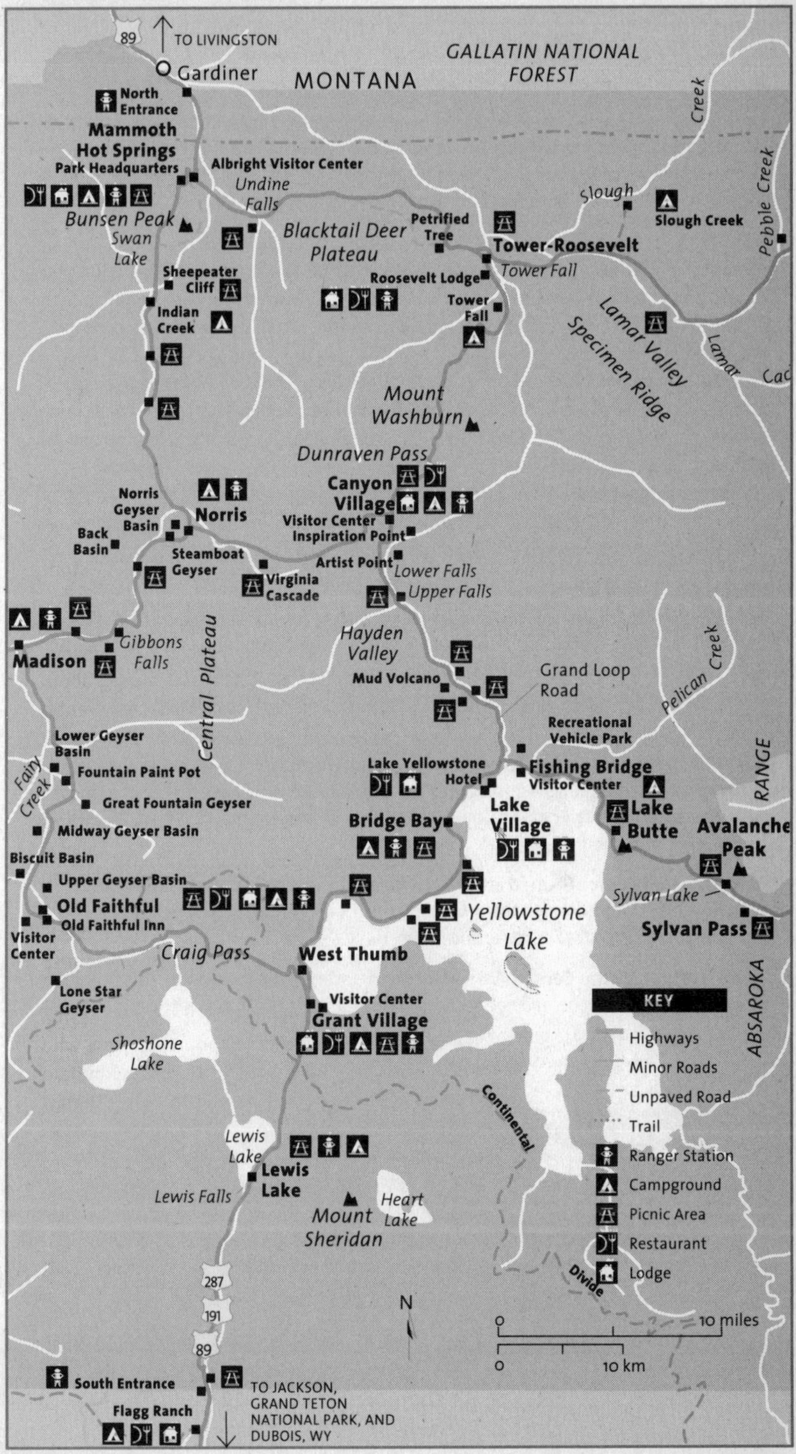
TO LIVINGSTON
Gardiner
MONTANA
GALLATIN NATIONAL FOREST
North Entrance
Mammoth Hot Springs
Park Headquarters
Albright Visitor Center
Undine Falls
Bunsen Peak
Swan Lake
Blacktail Deer Plateau
Petrified Tree
Tower-Roosevelt
Slough
Slough Creek
Pebble Creek
Creek
Sheepeater Cliff
Roosevelt Lodge
Tower Fall
Indian Creek
Tower Fall
Lamar Valley
Specimen Ridge
Lamar
Mount Washburn
Dunraven Pass
Canyon Village
Norris Geyser Basin
Norris
Visitor Center
Inspiration Point
Back Basin
Steamboat Geyser
Artist Point
Lower Falls
Virginia Cascade
Upper Falls
Gibbons Falls
Madison
Central Plateau
Hayden Valley
Mud Volcano
Grand Loop Road
Pelican Creek
Recreational Vehicle Park
Lower Geyser Basin
Fountain Paint Pot
Fairy Creek
Lake Yellowstone Hotel
Fishing Bridge
Visitor Center
RANGE
Great Fountain Geyser
Lake Village
Lake Butte
Bridge Bay
Midway Geyser Basin
Avalanche Peak
Biscuit Basin
Upper Geyser Basin
Sylvan Lake
Old Faithful
Old Faithful Inn
Yellowstone Lake
Sylvan Pass
Visitor Center
Craig Pass
West Thumb
Lone Star Geyser
Visitor Center
Grant Village
KEY
Highways
Minor Roads
Unpaved Road
Trail
Ranger Station
Campground
Picnic Area
Restaurant
Lodge
ABSAROKA
Shoshone Lake
Continental Divide
Lewis Lake
Lewis Lake
Lewis Falls
Mount Sheridan
Heart Lake
287
191
89
N
0
10 miles
0
10 km
South Entrance
Flagg Ranch
TO JACKSON, GRAND TETON NATIONAL PARK, AND DUBOIS, WY

Fees: Entrance fees of $20 per car and $15 per visitor arriving on a bus, motorcycle, or snowmobile entitle visitors to seven days in both Yellowstone and Grand Teton. An annual pass to the two parks costs $40.

Hours: Depending on the weather, Yellowstone is generally open late April to October and mid-December to February. From mid-October to late April only one road—from the Northeast Entrance at Cooke City to the North Entrance at Gardiner—is open to wheeled vehicles; other roads are used by over-snow vehicles.

SCENIC DRIVES

Firehole Lake Drive. About 8 mi north of Old Faithful Village, the 3-mi road takes you past Great Fountain Geyser, which shoots out jets of water that occasionally reach as high as 200 ft. If you're touring the park in winter, watch for bison along this one-way road.

South Entrance Road. The sheer black lava walls of the Lewis River Canyon make this a memorable drive. Turn into the parking area at the highway bridge for a close-up view of the spectacular Lewis River Falls, one of the park's often-photographed sights.

Upper Terrace Loop Drive. Limber pines as old as 500 years line this 1½-mi loop near Mammoth Hot Springs. You'll also spot a variety of mosses growing through white travertine, composed of lime deposited here by the area's hot springs.

SIGHTS TO SEE

Albright Visitor Center. Serving as bachelor quarters for calvary officers from 1886 to 1918, this red-roofed building now holds a museum with exhibits on the early inhabitants of the region and a theater showing films about the history of the park. | Mammoth Hot Springs | 307/344–2263 | June–Aug., daily 8–7; Sept., daily 9–6; Oct.–May, daily 9–5.

Back Basin. There are several geysers in this area, the most famous being the Steamboat Geyser. Although it performs only periodically, when it does it shoots a stream of water nearly 400 ft. Echinus Geyser erupts roughly every hour. | Grand Loop Rd. at Norris.

Canyon Visitor Center. Located in Canyon Village, the center has an exhibit about bison dealing with the history of the animals and their current status in Yellowstone. | Canyon Village | 307/242–2550 | June–Sept., daily 8–7.

Fishing Bridge Visitor Center. With a distinctive stone-and-log design, this building, dating from 1931, has been designated a National Historic Landmark. It has exhibits

YELLOWSTONE SCENERY AND WILDLIFE

Yellowstone's scenery is awesome any time of day, though the play of light and shadow makes the park most appealing in early morning and late afternoon. That is exactly when you should be out looking for wildlife, as most are active around dawn and dusk. May and June are the best months for seeing baby bison, moose, and other new arrivals. Spring and early summer find the park covered with wildflowers, while autumn is a great time to visit because of the vivid reds and golds of the changing foliage. Winters visitors are the ones who see the park at its most magical, with steam billowing from geyser basins to wreath trees in ice, and elk foraging close to roads transformed into ski trails.

on birds and other wildlife found in Yellowstone. | East Entrance Rd., 1 mi from Grand Loop Rd. | 307/242–2450 | June–Aug., daily 8–7; Sept., daily 9–6.

★ **Grand Canyon of the Yellowstone.** A cascading waterfall and rushing river carved this 24-mi-long canyon. The red and ochre canyon walls are topped with emerald-green forest. The best view of the falls is from Artist Point. | Great Loop Rd. at Canyon Village.

Lower Geyser Basin. Shooting more than 150 ft, the Great Fountain Geyser is the most spectacular sight at this basin. Less impressive but more regular is White Dome Geyser, which shoots from a 20-ft-tall cone. You'll also find pink mud pots and blue pools at Fountain Paint Pots. | Midway between Madison and Old Faithful Village on Grand Loop Rd.

Mammoth Hot Springs. Multicolored travertine terraces formed by slowly escaping hot water mark this unusual geological formation. Elk are frequent visitors, as they graze nearby. | Mammoth Hot Springs.

Midway Geyser Basin. Called "Hell's Half Acre" by writer Rudyard Kipling, Midway Geyser Basin is actually an extension of the Lower Geyser Basin. Here you'll find the richly colored pools of Grand Prismatic Spring and Excelsior Geyser, two of the largest hot springs in the world. | Midway between Madison and Old Faithful Village on Grand Loop Rd.

★ **Norris Geyser Basin.** The oldest such basin in Yellowstone, Norris is constantly changing and one of the most fun to explore as a result. Some geysers might suddenly stop flowing, but others soon blow and hiss to life. Here you'll discover colorfully named features such as Whirligig Geyser, Whale's Mouth, Emerald Spring, and Arch Steam Vent. | Grand Loop Rd. at Norris.

★ **Old Faithful.** The mysterious plumbing of Yellowstone has lengthened Old Faithful's cycle somewhat in recent years, but the geyser still spouts the same amount of water—sometimes reaching to 140 ft—every 88 minutes or so. Sometimes it doesn't shoot so high, but in those cases the eruption usually lasts longer. To find out when Old Faithful is next expected to erupt, check at any of the visitor centers or lodging property reception areas. Marked trails in the Upper Geyser Basin lead to Geyser Hill, and you can visit sights such as Castle Geyser and Morning Glory Pool as well as Giantess Geyser and Giant Geyser. Be on the lookout for elk and buffalo. In winter, cross-country ski trails converge at Old Faithful. | Old Faithful Bypass Rd.

Petrified Tree. This ancient redwood is reached by a short walk from a parking area. | Grand Loop Rd., 1 mi west of Tower-Roosevelt.

Yellowstone Lake. North America's largest mountain lake, Yellowstone Lake was formed when glaciers that once covered the region receded. Many head here for the excellent fishing, but others simply like to sit along the shore. In winter you can sometimes see otters and coyotes stepping gingerly on the ice at the lake's edge. | Grand Loop Rd. between Fishing Bridge and Grant Village.

Attractions Nearby

For additional attractions nearby, *see* Grand Teton National Park chapter.

★ **Buffalo Bill Historical Center.** Five museums rolled into one, this sprawling complex includes the Whitney Gallery of Western Art, the Plains Indian Museum, the Cody Firearms Museum, the Buffalo Bill Museum, and the Draper Natural History Museum. The real star, of course, is William F. "Buffalo Bill" Cody. Plan to spend at least four hours, or even more if you're really interested in the Old West. There are lots of interactive things for kids in both the Plains Indian and Draper museums. | 720 Sheridan Ave., Cody, WY | 307/587–4771 | www.bbhc.org | $10 for two-day entrance | Apr., daily 10–5; May, daily 8–8; June–Sept., daily 7–8; Oct., daily 8–5; Nov.–Mar., Tues.–Sun. 10–3.

Grizzly Discovery Center. This nonprofit center is devoted to protecting the natural habitat of grizzlies and other endangered species. Get up close to the bears and gray wolves that live here. | 201 S. Canyon, West Yellowstone, MT | 406/646–7001 or 800/257–2570 | www.grizzlydiscoveryctr.com | $8.50 | Oct.–Apr., daily 8:30–dusk; May–Sept., daily 8:30–8:30.

Dining

You will find beef on nearly every menu in every restaurant in the Northern Rockies, but you'll almost always also find fish, pasta, and in places, vegetarian selections. Expect less formality than you'd find elsewhere, even in the fanciest restaurants. Along with the informality come better prices.

In Yellowstone

Canyon Lodge Cafeteria. American. The park's busiest lunch spot serves traditional American fare. For early risers, it also has a full breakfast menu. There is a nearby deli where you can get quick sandwiches or chicken to go for a picnic. | Canyon Village | 307/344–7311 | Closed mid-Sept.–early June | $6–$13 | AE, D, DC, MC, V.

Old Faithful Inn Dining Room. American. Lodgepole walls and ceiling beams, a giant volcanic rock fireplace graced with a painting of Old Faithful, and green-tinted windows etched with scenes from the 1920s set the mood here. Soaked in history, the restaurant has always been a friendly place where servers find time amid the bustle to chat with diners. Don't pass up the grilled chicken breast glazed with honey-lemon butter. | Old Faithful Village | 307/344–7311 | Reservations essential | Closed mid-Oct.–mid-May | $11–$23 | AE, D, DC, MC, V.

Old Faithful Lodge Cafeteria. American/Casual. You'll have a view of the famous geyser as you select from traditional American fare or sandwiches and pasta. There is a nearby bake shop that sells cookies, muffins and soft pretzels, a snack shop that has ice cream products, and an espresso cart. | South end of Old Faithful Bypass Rd. | 307/344–7311 | Closed mid-Sept.– late May | $5.50–$13 | AE, D, DC, MC, V.

Roosevelt Lodge Dining Room. American. At this rustic log cabin set in a pine forest, the menu ranges from barbecued ribs and Roosevelt beans to hamburgers and French fries. For a real western adventure, call ahead to join a chuck-wagon cookout that includes an hour-long trail ride or a stagecoach ride. | Tower-Roosevelt | 307/344–7311 | Closed early Sept.–early June | $12–$17; cookout $22 | AE, D, DC, MC, V.

Terrace Grill. American/Casual. Although the exterior looks rather elegant, this restaurant in Mammoth Hot Springs only serves fast food for breakfast, lunch, or dinner. | Mammoth Hot Springs | 307/344–7311 | Closed early Oct.–early May | $6–$8.25 | AE, D, DC, MC, V.

Picnic Areas. There are 49 picnic areas in the park, ranging from secluded spots with a couple of tables to more popular stops with a dozen or more tables and more amenities. Only nine—Snake River, Grant Village, Spring Creek, Nez Perce, Old Faithful East, Bridge Bay, Cascade Lake Trail, Norris Meadows, and Yellowstone River—have fire grates. Only gas stoves may be used in the other areas. None have running water; all but a few have pit toilets. You can purchase box lunches from most Yellowstone restaurants, snack shops, and delis, or supplies at park stores in each of the main activity areas.

At the **Firehole River** area, you might see elk grazing along the banks of the river. | Grand Loop Rd., 3 mi south of Madison.

Fishing Bridge has 11 tables within the busy Fishing Bridge area. It's walking distance to the amphitheater, store, and visitor center. | East Entrance Road, 1 mi from Grand Loop Rd.

You are likely to see elk or buffalo along the Gibbon River from one of nine tables at **Gibbon Meadows,** which has a handicapped-accessible pit toilet. | Grand Loop Rd., 3 mi south of Norris.

Near the Park

For more dining options (in Jackson and Dubois), *see* Grand Teton National Park chapter.

The Irma. Contemporary. Hearty breakfasts, sandwiches, and meat-and-potatoes dinners with a salad-bar option are offered in this historic hotel named for Buffalo Bill Cody's daughter. | 1192 Sheridan Ave., Cody, WY | 307/587–4221 | $9–$15 | D, MC, V.

Old Piney Dell. Steak. A favorite among locals, this small restaurant on the banks of Rock Creek has good steak and Wiener schnitzel as well as daily pasta specials. It's part of the Rock Creek Resort. | Rock Creek Rd., Red Lodge, MT | 406/446–1196 | No lunch Mon.–Sat. | $16–$23 | AE, D, DC, MC, V.

Trapper's Inn. American. This popular restaurant recalls the days of the mountain men with massive breakfasts featuring sourdough pancakes, biscuits, and rolls. Trout with eggs will fortify you for a day exploring Yellowstone. Lunch standouts include buffalo burgers on sourdough bread, while there are plenty of hearty steaks for dinner. | 315 Madison Ave., West Yellowstone, MT | 406/646–9375 | $12–$18 | AE, MC, V.

Yellowstone Mine. American. Decorated with mining equipment such as picks and shovels, this is a place for casual family-style dining. Town residents come in for the steaks and seafood. | U.S. 89, Gardiner, MT | 406/848–7336 | No lunch | $10–$20 | AE, D, MC, V.

Lodging

In Yellowstone

Park lodgings range from two of the National Park Service's magnificent old hotels to simple cabins to modern motels. Make reservations at least two months in advance for July and August for all park lodgings. Old Faithful Snow Lodge and Mammoth Hot Springs Hotel are the only accommodations open in winter; rates are the same as in summer.

Cascade Lodge. Pine wainscoting and brown carpets set the tone in this motel-style facility in the trees above the Grand Canyon of the Yellowstone. The lodge, among the newest in the park, is at the farthest edge of the Canyon Village, which means it's quite a hike to the nearest dining facilities. 3 restaurants, horseback riding, bar, shops; no room TVs | North Rim Dr. at Grand Loop Rd. North Rim Dr. | 307/344–7311 | fax 307/344–7456 | www.travelyellowstone.com | 40 rooms | $129 | Closed early Sept.–early June | AE, D, DC, MC, V.

Grant Village Motel. The six lodge buildings that make up this sprawling motel have rough pine exteriors painted gray and rust. These rooms are basic, with few features beyond a bed and night stand. 2 restaurants, boating, bar, shops; no room TVs | Grant Village | 307/344–7311 | fax 307/344–7456 | www.travelyellowstone.com | 300 rooms | $95–$106 | Closed late Sept.–late May | AE, D, DC, MC, V.

★ **Lake Yellowstone Hotel, Lodge and Cabins.** This distinguished hotel, dating from 1891, attracts mainly older visitors who gather in the sun room each afternoon to gaze at the lake while a string quartet plays. Rooms have brass beds and solid pine furniture. Set unobtrusively in the trees behind the Lake Yellowstone Hotel are pine-paneled cabins that provide more basic accommodations and the motel-style lodge, both of which are less expensive than the hotel. 3 restaurants, bar, shops; no room TVs | At far end of Lake

Village Rd. | 307/344–7311 | fax 307/344–7456 | www.travelyellowstone.com | 1 suite, 158 rooms, 102 cabins | $412 suite, $165–$175 hotel rooms, $112 lodge, $54–$87 cabins | Closed early Oct.–mid-May | AE, D, DC, MC, V.

Mammoth Hot Springs Hotel and Cabins. Built in 1937, this hotel has a spacious art-deco lobby. The rooms are smaller and less elegant than those at the park's other two historic hotels, but the hotel is less expensive and usually less crowded. The cabins, set amid lush lawns, are the nicest inside the park. This is one of only two lodging facilities open in winter. 2 restaurants, horseback riding, bar, shops; no room TVs | Mammoth Hot Springs | 307/344–7311 | fax 307/344–7456 | www.travelyellowstone.com | 97 rooms, 67 with bath; 2 suites; 115 cabins, 76 with bath | $274 suites, $68–$95 hotel rooms, $57–$90 cabins | Closed mid-Sept.–mid-Dec. and mid-Mar.–late May | AE, D, DC, MC, V.

★ **Old Faithful Inn.** When you breeze through the iron-latched front door, you enter a log-pillared lobby of one of the most distinctive national park lodgings. From the main building, where many gables dot the wood-shingled roof, you can watch Old Faithful erupt. Rooms in the 1904 "Old House" have brass beds, and some have deep claw-foot tubs. Premium rooms have views of Old Faithful. The less expensive rooms share a bathroom down the hall. 2 restaurants, some room phones, bar, shops; no room TVs | Old Faithful Village | 307/344–7311 | fax 307/344–7456 | www.travelyellowstone.com | 327 rooms, 6 suites | $351 suites, $72–$172 rooms | Closed mid-Oct.–early May | AE, D, DC, MC, V.

Old Faithful Lodge Cabins. Not to be confused with the Old Faithful Snow Lodge, these small, plain cabins are a good budget option. Some do not have bathrooms. Restaurant, shops; no room TVs | At far end of Old Faithful Bypass Rd. | 307/344–7311 | fax 307/344–7456 | www.travelyellowstone.com | 99 cabins | $42–$68 | Closed mid-Sept.–mid-May | AE, D, DC, MC, V.

★ **Old Faithful Snow Lodge.** Built in 1998, this massive structure brings back the grand tradition of park lodges by making good use of heavy timber beams and wrought-iron accents in the distinctive facade. Inside you'll find soaring ceilings, natural lighting, and a stone fireplace in the spacious lobby. This is one of only two lodging facilities open in winter, when the only way to get here is over-snow vehicles. Restaurant, cross-country skiing, snowmobiling, bar, shops; no room TVs | At far end of Old Faithful Bypass Rd. | 307/344–7311 | fax 307/344–7456 | www.travelyellowstone.com | 100 rooms | $141 | Closed mid-Oct.–mid-Dec. and mid-Mar.–May | AE, D, DC, MC, V.

Roosevelt Lodge. Near the beautiful Lamar Valley in the park's northeast corner, this simple lodge dating from the 1920s surpasses some of the more expensive options. The rustic accommodations (some have baths, some don't), in nearby cabins set around a pine forest, mean you need to bring your own bedding. You can arrange for horseback or stagecoach rides. Restaurant, horseback riding, bar, shops; no room TVs | Tower–Roosevelt Junction on Grand Loop Rd. | 307/344–7311 | fax 307/344–7456 | www.travelyellowstone.com | 80 cabins, 8 with bath | $50–$90 | Closed early Sept.–early June | AE, D, DC, MC, V.

Near the Park

For more lodging options (in Jackson and Dubois), *see* Grand Teton National Park chapter.

Pahaska Teepee Resort. Buffalo Bill's original hideaway in the mountains is 2 mi east of Yellowstone. Most of the small, basic cabins are scattered through a pine forest. In winter, the lodge grooms a network of cross-country ski trails and rents skis and snowmobiles. Restaurant, horseback riding, cross-country skiing, snowmobiling, bar; no a/c, no room phones, no room TVs | 183 Yellowstone Hwy., Cody, WY | 307/527–7701 or 800/628–7791 | fax 307/527–4019 | www.pahaska.com | 48 cabins | $90–$135 | D, MC, V.

Camping

In Yellowstone

Yellowstone has a dozen campgrounds scattered around the park. Most campgrounds have flush toilets, and some campgrounds have coin-operated showers and laundry facilities. Most campgrounds are operated by the National Parks Service and are available on a first-come, first-served basis. Those campgrounds run by Xanterra—Bridge Bay, Canyon, Fishing Bridge, Grant Village, and Madison—accept bookings in advance. To reserve, call 307/344–7311. Larger groups can reserve space in Bridge Bay, Grant, and Madison from late May through September.

Camping outside designated areas is strictly prohibited, but there are about 300 backcountry sites available all over the park. Permits are $20, regardless of the length of time spent in the park or the number of people in the group. These sites may be reserved in advance by visiting any ranger station or by mail at Backcountry Office, Box 168, Yellowstone National Park, WY 82190.

Bridge Bay. The park's largest campground, Bridge Bay rests in a wooded grove. You can rent boats at the nearby marina, take guided walks, or listen to rangers lecture about the history of the park. Don't expect solitude, as there are more than 400 campsites. Hot showers and laundry are 4 mi north at Fishing Bridge. Flush toilets, dump station, drinking water, showers, fire pits, public telephone, ranger station | 430 sites | 3 mi southwest of Lake Village on Grand Loop Rd. | 307/344–7311 | fax 307/344–7456 | www.travelyellowstone.com | $15 | AE, D, DC, MC, V | Late-May–mid-Sept.

Fishing Bridge RV Park. Although Fishing Bridge is on Yellowstone Lake, there's no boat access here. Near Bridge Bay Marina, this is the only facility in the park that caters exclusively to recreational vehicles. Because of bear activity in the area, only hard-sided campers are allowed. Liquid propane is available. Flush toilets, full hook-ups, dump station, drinking water, showers, public telephone, ranger station | 344 full hook-ups | East Entrance Rd. at Grand Loop Rd. | 307/344–7311 | fax 307/344–7456 | www.travelyellowstone.com | $29 | AE, D, DC, MC, V | Mid-May–mid-Sept.

Slough Creek. Reached by a little-used spur road, this creekside campground is about as far from the beaten path as you can get without actually camping in the backcountry. It's popular among fishing aficionados, who come here for the trout. Pit toilets, drinking water, fire pits | 29 sites | Northeast Entrance Rd., 10 mi east of Tower–Roosevelt Junction | 307/344–2017 | $10 | AE, D, DC, MC, V | Late May–late Oct.

Near the Park

For additional camping nearby, *see* Grand Teton National Park chapter.

Flagg Ranch Village. In a wooded area near the Snake River, this sprawling complex is 2 mi from the South Entrance of Yellowstone. It has a main lodge with dining room, bar, convenience store, and gas station. Flush toilets, full hook-ups, drinking water, laundry facilities, showers, fire pits, restaurant, public telephone | 150 full hook-ups | Moran, WY 83013 | 307/733–8761 or 800/443–2311 | $17–$25 | D, MC, V | Mid-May–mid-Oct.

Wagon Wheel Campground and Cabins. Located within West Yellowstone and a few blocks west of Yellowstone, this campground has tent and RV sites along with cozy one-, two-, and three-bedroom cabins. Flush toilets, full hook-ups, drinking water, laundry facilities, showers, public telephone | 40 full hook-ups, 8 tent sites; 9 cabins | 408 Gibbon Ave., West Yellowstone, MT 59758 | 406/646–7872 | $22–$32 | D, MC, V | May 25–Oct. 1.

Shopping

Some of Yellowstone's stores are interesting destinations themselves. The Old Faithful Lower Store, for example, has a knotty-pine porch with benches that beckon tired hikers, as well as an inexpensive and very busy lunch counter. All stores sell souvenirs ranging from the tacky (cowboy kitsch and rubber tom-toms) to the authentic ($60 buffalo-hide moccasins and $200 cowboy coats). From May to September, most stores are open 7:45 AM to 9:45 PM; Mammoth Hot Springs is open year-round. All the stores accept credit cards.

Sports and Outdoor Activities

Bicycling

More and more people tour Yellowstone by bicycle every year, despite the heavy traffic, large vehicles, and rough, narrow, shoulderless roads that make it somewhat hazardous. To be on the safe side, ride single-file and wear a helmet and reflective clothing. Remember that some routes, such as those over Craig Pass, Sylvan Pass, and Dunraven Pass, are especially challenging because of their steep climbs. Bikes are prohibited on most hiking trails and in the backcountry.

Fountain Freight Road. Fountain Flats Drive departs the Grand Loop Road south of the Nez Perce picnic area and follows the Firehole River to a trailhead 1½ mi away. From there, the Fountain Freight Road continues along the old roadbed, giving bikers access to the Sentinel Meadows Trail and the Fairy Falls Trail. The total length of the route is 5½ mi. Mountain bikes are recommended; you'll share Fountain Flats Drive with one-way automobile traffic and the Freight Road with hikers.

Old Faithful to Morning Glory Pool. This paved 2-mi trail starts at the Hamilton Store at Old Faithful Village, loops near Old Faithful Geyser, and ends at Morning Glory Pool. The entire route is through a geyser basin, so stay on the trail. Watch for elk and buffalo.

FreeHeel and Wheel. Bicycle sales, service, and rentals are all available here. | 40 Yellowstone Dr., West Yellowstone | 406/646–7744 | fax 406/646–7788 | www.freeheelandwheel.com.

Boating

Yellowstone Lake attracts the most attention, but the park is filled with pristine waters waiting to be explored. Most of its 175 lakes, except for Sylvan Lake, Eleanor Lake, and Twin Lakes, are open for boating. You must purchase a $5 permit at Bridge Bay Marina, Grant Village visitor center, Lewis Lake Campground, or Mammoth Hot Springs visitor center.

Xanterra Parks & Resorts. Watercraft from rowboats to powerboats are available at Bridge Bay Marina by the hour or by the day for trips on Yellowstone Lake. You can even rent 22- and 34-ft cabin cruisers. | Grand Loop Rd., 2 mi south of Lake Village | 307/344–7311 | www.TravelYellowstone.com | Mid-June–mid-Sept., daily 8 AM–9:30 PM | $7.50–$30 per hr.

Fishing

Anglers flock to Yellowstone on Memorial Day weekend, when fishing season begins. By the time the season ends in November, thousands have found a favorite spot along the park's rivers and streams. Many varieties of trout—cutthroat, brook, lake, and rainbow—along with grayling and mountain whitefish inhabit Yellowstone's waters. Popular sport-fishing opportunities include the Gardner and Yellowstone rivers as well as Soda Butte Creek, but the top fishing area in the region is Madison River, known to fly fishermen throughout the country. Catch and release is the general policy. Get a copy of the fishing regulations at any visitor center. Fishing supplies are at all Hamilton stores; the biggest selection is at Bridge Bay.

Hiking

There are 1,210 mi of trails and 85 trailheads in Yellowstone. Trails are occasionally closed due to weather conditions or bear activity. Park rangers can provide accurate information about trail conditions.

Back Basin Trail. A 1½-mi loop passes Emerald Spring, Steamboat Geyser, Cistern Spring (which drains when Steamboat erupts), and Echinus Geyser. | Grand Loop Rd. at Norris.

Fountain Paint Pot Nature Trail. An easy ½-mi loop boardwalk passes hot springs, colorful mud pots, and dry fumaroles at its highest point. | Grand Loop Rd. at Firehole Lake Dr.

★ **North and South Rim Trails.** Offering great views of the Grand Canyon of the Yellowstone, the 1¾-mi North Rim Trail runs from Inspiration Point to Chittenden Bridge, while the 2-mi South Rim Trail starts at Chittenden Bridge and makes its way to Artist Point. You can wander along small sections of these trails, or combine them into a three-hour trek through one of the park's most breathtaking areas. Especially scenic is the ½-mi section of the North Rim Trail from the Brink of the Upper Falls parking area to Chittenden Bridge that hugs the rushing Yellowstone River as it approaches the canyon. Both trails are partly paved and fairly level. | 1 mi south of Canyon Village.

★ **Storm Point Trail.** Well marked and mostly flat, this 1½-mi loop leaves the south side of the road for a perfect beginner's hike out to Yellowstone Lake. | 3 mi east of Lake Junction on East Entrance Rd.

Uncle Tom's Trail. Spectacular and very strenuous, this 700-step trail descends 500 ft from the parking area to the roaring base of the Lower Falls of the Yellowstone. Much of this walk is on steel sheeting, which can have a film of ice in early morning or in spring and fall. | Artist Point Dr., about ½ mi east of Chittenden Bridge.

Horseback Riding

About 50 area outfitters lead horse-packing trips and trail rides into Yellowstone. Expect to pay about $1,200 for a four-night backcountry trip, including meals, accommodations, and guides. A guide must accompany all horseback-riding trips.

Rimrock Dude Ranch. Outfitter Gary Fales has been leading multiday pack trips into Yellowstone for decades, operating out of his dude ranch west of Cody. Trips last a week and include backcountry camping, fishing, hiking, and horseback activities. | 2728 Northfork Route, Cody, WY 82414 | 307/587–3970 | fax 307/527–5014 | www.rimrockranch.com | $1,600 per wk | May–Sept.

Xanterra Parks & Resorts. One- and two-hour horseback trail rides leave from three sites in the park: Mammoth Hot Springs, Roosevelt Lodge, and Canyon Village. Children must be at least 8 years old and 48 inches tall; kids 8–11 must be accompanied by someone age 16 or older. | Box 165, Mammoth Hot Springs, Yellowstone, WY 82190 | 307/344–7311 | www.TravelYellowstone.com | $25–$37 | May–Sept.

Skiing and Snowshoeing

Even those who have visited Yellowstone many times in summer would never recognize it after the first snow. Rocky outcroppings are smoothed over by snow. Waterfalls that tumbled over the sides of canyons have been transformed into jagged sheets of ice. Canyon Village, West Thumb, and Madison have warming huts that are intermittently staffed; huts at Indian Creek, Fishing Bridge, and Old Faithful Village are unstaffed. All are open 24 hours.

Lone Star Geyser Trail. This easy trail, which leads 2.3 mi to the Lone Star Geyser, starts south of Keppler Cascades. You can ski back to the Old Faithful area. | Shuttle at Old Faithful Snow Lodge; trailhead 3½ mi west of Old Faithful Village.

Madison River Bridge Trails. Five ski trails begin at the Madison River Bridge trailhead. The shortest is 4 mi and the longest is 14 mi. | West Entrance Rd., 6 mi west of Madison.

Xanterra Parks & Resorts. At Mammoth Hot Springs Hotel and Old Faithful Snow Lodge you can rent skis and snowshoes. Skier shuttles run from Mammoth Hotel to Mammoth Terraces and to Tower and from Old Faithful Snow Lodge to Fairy Falls. | Mammoth Hot Springs Hotel or Old Faithful Snow Lodge | 307/344–7901 | www.TravelYellowstone.com | $10–$13 | Dec.–Mar.

Snowmobiling

Snowmobiling is one of the most exhilarating ways to experience Yellowstone, and there is an ongoing debate about how long and how much snowmobiling should be allowed in the park due to concerns over both noise and pollution. For now it's still an option, and many outfitters are using newer snowmobiles with four-stroke engines that are more environmentally acceptable because they have fewer emissions and are quieter.

Pahaska Teepee. Just outside the East Entrance, this full-service resort rents four-stroke snowmobiles and leads guided treks into Yellowstone. | 183 Yellowstone Hwy., Cody, WY | 307/527–7701 or 800/628–7791 | www.pahaska.com | $110 for machine rentals, $250 per day for guide service | Year-round, ski equipment Dec.–Mar.

Essential Information

When to Go

Most people visit Yellowstone in summer, when warm days give way to brisk evenings. You'll find the biggest crowds—*really* big crowds—from mid-July to mid-August. There are fewer people in the park the month or two before and after this peak season, but there are also fewer dining and lodging facilities open. Except for holiday weekends, there are few visitors in winter. Remember that snow is possible the entire year at high elevations such as Mt. Washburn.

FESTIVALS AND SEASONAL EVENTS

SPRING

Mar.: **Winter Carnival.** A traditional parade downtown kicks off this snowy celebration in Red Lodge. Other events include a costume contest, a fire-hose race, and a treasure hunt for the kids. | 406/446–1718.

World Snowmobile Expo. Top-notch racing is combined with a sneak peek at next year's hot models. The SnowWest SnoCross attracts racers to West Yellowstone from throughout the snowbelt. | 406/646–7701.

Apr.: **Cowboy Songs and Range Ballads.** Music in the style of the cattle-driving cowboys is the focus of this weekend event, which includes concerts, informal music jam sessions, and instruction about the music style. | 307/587–4771.

SUMMER

June–Aug.: **Cody Nite Rodeo.** Some western towns host a rodeo now and then, but come summer Cody has one every night. The action includes bronco busting and bull riding. | 307/587–5155.

Aug.: **Burnt Hole Rendezvous.** At a primitive camp near West Yellowstone you can learn about pre-1840s crafts, try your hand at tomahawk and knife throwing, and enjoy Native American dancers. | 406/646–7110.

Bargains

Free and varied ranger-led activities inside the park, usually held during the summer months and listed daily at visitor centers, range from photography workshops to bird and wildlife watching or natural history talks. For the best high-season lodging deals, if you're willing to stay in a cabin without many amenities you can find one at Mammoth, Old Faithful, Lake, Roosevelt, and Canyon. Prices for the most basic cabins (some without a bath, so be sure to ask), range from $42 to $87. Travel early in the season (May) or late in the season (late September or early October) and you can get reduced rates (as much as 40%) at some Yellowstone lodging properties. To find the best deals during that early or late season, book online at www.travelyellowstone.com. Another good way to control costs is to carry a cooler in your vehicle so you can have snacks and picnic lunches; you can buy supplies in the park and surrounding communities and box lunches from most restaurants. Besides the cost consideration, having a picnic in Yellowstone will give you a chance to enjoy the natural surroundings while you eat, and if you have younger children, they can burn off some energy exploring during your meal breaks.

Nearby Towns

Wyoming has three gateways into Yellowstone: Cody to the east and Jackson and Dubois to the south. Named for William F. "Buffalo Bill" Cody, the town of **Cody** sits near the park's East Entrance. Situated at the mouth of the Shoshone Canyon (where the north and south forks of the Shoshone River join), Cody is a good base for hiking trips, horseback-riding excursions, and white-water rafting on the North Fork of the Shoshone or the Clarks Fork of the Yellowstone. Because of its proximity to two national parks, Grand Teton and Yellowstone, **Jackson** is the busiest community in the region in summer. It has the widest selection of dining and lodging options. The least well-known gateway to the national parks, the little town of **Dubois** is a great base if you want to stay away from the madding crowds. Both Jackson and Dubois lead to the park's South Entrance.

The most popular gateway from Montana—particularly in winter—is **West Yellowstone,** near the park's West Entrance. This is where the open plains of southwestern Montana and northeastern Idaho come together along the Madison River valley. Affectionately known among winter recreationists as the "snowmobile capital of the world," this town of 1,000 is also a good place to go for fishing, horseback riding, and downhill skiing. At the only entrance to Yellowstone that's open the entire year, **Gardiner** is always bustling. The town's Roosevelt Arch has marked the park's North Entrance since 1903, when President Theodore Roosevelt dedicated it. The Yellowstone River slices through town, beckoning fishermen and rafters. The small town has quaint shops and good restaurants. With both Yellowstone and the Absaroka-Beartooth Wilderness at its back door, the village of **Cooke City** is a good place for hiking, horseback riding, mountain climbing, and other outdoor activities. Some 50 mi to the east, **Red Lodge** provides ample dining and lodging options. These communities guard the Northeast Entrance, least used of all entry points to the park. But it's by far the most spectacular entrance. Driving along the Beartooth Scenic Byway between Red Lodge and Cooke City, you'll cross the southern tip of the Beartooth range, in the ramparts of the Rockies.

Tours

Yellowstone offers a busy schedule of guided hikes, evening talks, and campfire programs. Check *Discover Yellowstone*, the newsletter available at all entrances and visitor centers, for dates and times.

Campfire Programs. Gather around to hear tales about Yellowstone's fascinating history, with hour-long programs on topics ranging from the return of the bison to 19th-century photographers. Events are held nightly, June–August, at campgrounds in Bridge Bay, Canyon, Madison, and Mammoth Hot Springs.

Grub Steak Expeditions and Tours. These tours, ranging from half a day to several days in length, focus on photography, geology, history, wildlife, and other topics. They're led by a former Yellowstone park ranger, professional photographer, and retired teacher. | 307/527–6316 or 800/527–6316 | www.grubsteaktours.com.

Xanterra Parks & Resorts. The company that runs most of the concessions in the park offers bus, boat, horseback, fishing, photography, and stagecoach tours of Yellowstone in summer and skiing, snowcoach, snowmobiling, and snowshoeing or cross-country skiing treks in winter. | 307/344–7311 | fax 307/344–7456 | www.TravelYellowstone.com.

Visitor Information

Yellowstone Association | Box 117, Yellowstone National Park, WY 82190 | 307/344–2293. **Yellowstone National Park** | Box 168, Mammoth, WY 82190 | 307/344–7381; 307/344–2386 TDD | fax 307/344–2005 | www.nps.gov/yell.

Cody Country Chamber of Commerce | 836 Sheridan Ave., WY 82414 | 307/587–2777 | fax 307/527–6228 | www.codychamber.org. **Cooke City Chamber of Commerce** | Box 1071, Cooke City, MT 59020 | 406/838–2495 | www.lewisclark.org/c/cookeccc.htm. **Dubois Chamber of Commerce** | 616 West Ramshorn, Dubois, WY 82513 | 307/455–2556 | www.duboiswyoming.org. **Gardiner Chamber of Commerce** | 222 Park St. (Box 81), Gardiner, MT 59030 | 406/848–7971 | www.gardinerchamber.com. **Jackson Chamber of Commerce** | 990 W. Broadway, Jackson, WY 83001 | 307/733–3316 | fax 307/733–5585 | www.jacksonholechamber.com. **Park County Travel Council** | 836 Sheridan Ave. (Box 2777), Cody, WY 82414 | 307/587–2297 | www.pctc.org. **Red Lodge Chamber of Commerce** | 601 N. Broadway, Red Lodge, MT 59068 | 406/446–1718 | www.redlodge.com. **West Yellowstone Chamber of Commerce** | 30 Yellowstone Ave., West Yellowstone, MT 59758 | 406/646–7701 | www.westyellowstonechamber.com.

Arriving and Departing

BY AIR

Airports

Gallatin Field (BZN). Gallatin, in Bozeman, Montana, 90 mi from the West Entrance, has daily flights connecting to Minneapolis, Seattle, Salt Lake, or Denver. | 406/388–8321 | www.gallatinfield.com.

Jackson Hole Airport (JAC). Fifty miles from the South Entrance, Jackson Hole is served by daily flights connecting to Denver or Salt Lake City on several national and commuter airlines | 307/733–7682.

Yellowstone Regional Airport (YRA). The airport in Cody also has connections to Denver or Salt Lake. | 307/587–5096 | www.flyyra.com.

Airport Transportation
For Jackson Hole Airport transportation, *see* Grand Teton National Park chapter.

Car: At Gallatin Field rental cars are available from Avis, Budget, Hertz, and National car rentals. Rental cars are available at the Yellowstone Regional Airport in Cody from Budget, Hertz, and Thrifty Rentals.

Taxi: Phidippides Services. Shuttles serve the Cody area. One-way fare from the airport to any location in Cody is $10 for one person and $5 for each additional person; outside of Cody city limits a base fee is charged plus $1 per mile. | 307/527–6789 or 866/527–6789.

BY BUS

Cody Bus Lines. There is daily service from Billings. | 800/733–2304.

Greyhound Lines. Greyhound connects Bozeman, Montana, to points nationwide. | 800/231–2222.

BY CAR

All five park entrances join the Grand Loop Road. The most spectacular entry is from the northeast on U.S. 212, the Beartooth Highway. The 69 mi from Red Lodge, Montana, traverse the 11,000-ft-high Beartooth Pass, the nation's highest mountain highway pass, with dizzying switchbacks. The northern approach on U.S. 89 is a straight shot through Paradise Valley, flanked by the Absaroka Range on the east and Gallatin Range on the west, to the original stone entry arch in the funky old tourist town of Gardiner, Montana. The South Entrance (U.S. 89), which is ideal for anyone also stopping at Grand Teton Park, the West Entrance on U.S. 20 through West Yellowstone, and the East Entrance on U.S. 14–16–20 from Cody are the most heavily trafficked.

Getting Around

BY CAR

The best way to keep your bearings in Yellowstone is to remember that the major roads form a figure-eight. It doesn't matter at which point you begin, as you can hit most of the major sights if you follow the entire route. The 370 mi of public roads in the park provide easy access to extraordinary sights, but that means you'll encounter many motor homes pulled over on narrow shoulders so that the occupants can photograph grazing elk or buffalo cows with their calves. There is always road construction in Yellowstone, and details are included in the park newspaper or at park visitor centers. At press time, improvements were under way between Madison and Norris junctions and between Canyon and Fishing Bridge, with periodic closures. The road between Tower Fall and Canyon Village over Dunraven Pass will be closed for construction in 2003. Check with park rangers for information on road repairs.

All roads except between Mammoth Hot Springs and the North Entrance and Cooke City and the Northeast Entrance are closed to wheeled vehicles from mid-October to early late April; they are only open to over-snow vehicles from mid-December to mid-March. Remember that all roads don't open at the same time. The road from Mammoth Hot Springs to Norris generally opens mid-April. The West Entrance opens in mid-April, while the East and South entrances open early May. These openings can be affected by late-spring snowstorms.

California

Revised and Updated by John Vlahides

YOSEMITE NATIONAL PARK

You can lose your perspective in Yosemite. This is a land where everything is big. Really big. There are big rocks, big trees, and big waterfalls. The park has been so extravagantly praised and so beautifully photographed that some people wonder if the reality can possibly measure up. For almost everyone it does. With 1,169 square mi of park land, 94.5% of it undeveloped wilderness accessible only to the backpacker and horseback rider, Yosemite is a nature lover's wonderland. The western boundary dips as low as 2,000 ft in the chaparral-covered foothills; the eastern boundary rises to 13,000 ft at points along the Sierra crest. Yosemite Valley has many of the park's most famous sites and is easy to reach, but take the time to explore the high country above the Valley and you'll see a different side of Yosemite. The high country's fragile and unique alpine terrain is arresting. Wander through this world of gnarled trees, scurrying animals, and bighorn sheep buffeted by the wind, and you'll come away with a distinct sense of peace and solitude.

Abraham Lincoln established Yosemite Valley and the Mariposa Grove of Giant Sequoias as public land in 1864. The high country above the Valley, however, was not protected. John Muir, concerned about the destructive effects of overgrazing on subalpine meadows, rallied together a team of dedicated supporters and lobbied for expanded protection of lands surrounding Yosemite Valley. As a result of their efforts, Yosemite National Park was established by Congress on October 1, 1890.

Exploring

Yosemite National Park

Fees: The vehicle admission fee is $20 and is valid for seven days. Individuals arriving by bus, or on foot, bicycle, motorcycle, or horseback pay $10 for a seven-day pass.

Hours: The park is open 24 hours a day, every day, year-round.

SCENIC DRIVES

Route 41. Curvy Route 41 from the South Entrance station provides great views and stopover points en route to the Valley. Just past the gate, an offshoot to the right leads to the Mariposa Grove of Big Trees (it's closed once there's snow on the ground). A few miles farther north on Route 41 is Wawona, where you can stop for lunch. Drive

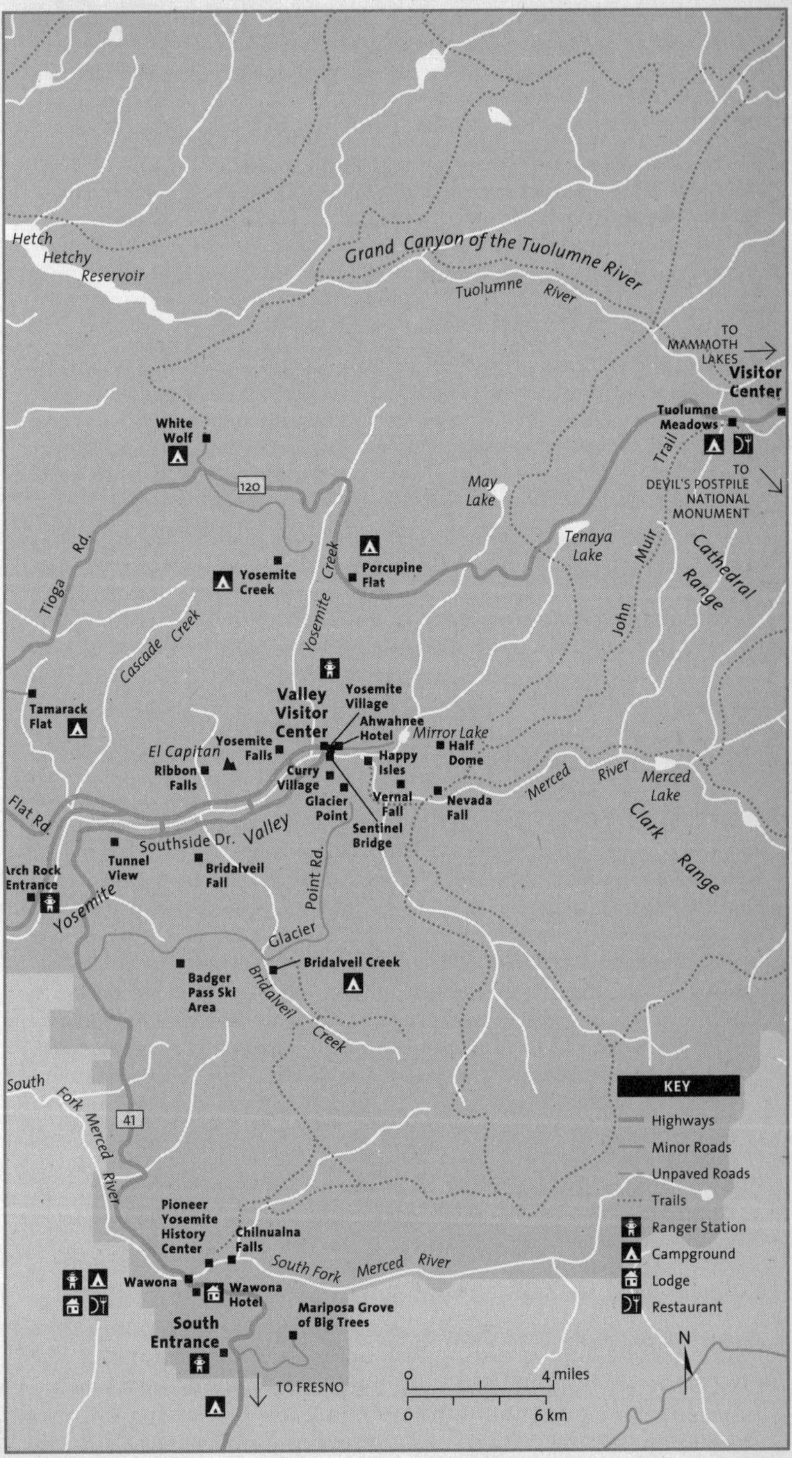
Hetch Hetchy Reservoir
Grand Canyon of the Tuolumne River
Tuolumne River
TO MAMMOTH LAKES
Visitor Center
Tuolumne Meadows
TO DEVIL'S POSTPILE NATIONAL MONUMENT
White Wolf
120
May Lake
Tenaya Lake
John Muir Trail
Cathedral Range
Tioga Rd.
Yosemite Creek
Porcupine Flat
Yosemite Creek
Cascade Creek
Tamarack Flat
Valley Visitor Center
Yosemite Village
Ahwahnee Hotel
Mirror Lake
Half Dome
El Capitan
Yosemite Falls
Ribbon Falls
Happy Isles
Curry Village
Glacier Point
Vernal Fall
Nevada Fall
Sentinel Bridge
Merced River
Merced Lake
Clark Range
Flat Rd.
Southside Dr.
Valley
Tunnel View
Bridalveil Fall
Arch Rock Entrance
Yosemite
Glacier Point Rd.
Bridalveil Creek
Badger Pass Ski Area
South Fork Merced River
41
Pioneer Yosemite History Center
Chilnualna Falls
South Fork Merced River
Wawona
Wawona Hotel
Mariposa Grove of Big Trees
South Entrance
TO FRESNO
KEY
Highways
Minor Roads
Unpaved Roads
Trails
Ranger Station
Campground
Lodge
Restaurant
N
0
4 miles
0
6 km

another 15 mi, and you come to the turnoff for Glacier Point. Farther along on Route 41, you pass through a tunnel, where you can pull off the road and park. "Tunnel View" is one of the most famous views of Yosemite Valley, with El Capitan on the left, Bridalveil Fall on the right, and Half Dome as a backdrop. Continue another 5 mi on Route 41, and you reach Yosemite Valley. The one-way route takes about 1½ hours.

Route 120. In summer, take a drive up to the high country toward Tioga Pass on Tioga Road (Rte. 120) to the alpine scenery of Tuolumne Meadows. Highlights include crystal-blue lakes, grassy meadows, and rounded granite peaks. Keep a sharp eye out for the neon colors of rock climbers, who seem to defy gravity on the cliffs. Wildflowers peak in July and August. The one-way trip to Tioga Pass takes approximately 1½ hours.

SIGHTS TO SEE

★ **Ahwahnee Hotel.** Built in 1927, this stately lodge of granite and concrete beams, stained to look like redwood, is a perfect man-made complement to Yosemite's natural majesty. Even if you aren't a guest, take time to visit the immense parlors with their walk-in hearths and priceless, antique Native American rugs and baskets. The dining room, its high ceiling interlaced with massive sugar-pine beams, is extraordinary. Dinner is formal, breakfast and lunch more casual. | Yosemite Valley, shuttle stop 4 | 209/372–1489.

Ahwahneechee Village. Tucked behind the Valley visitor center, a short loop trail of about 100 yards circles through a re-creation of an Ahwahneechee Native American village as it might have appeared in 1872, 20 years after the Native Americans' first contact with Europeans. Markers explain the lifestyle of Yosemite's first residents. Allow 30 minutes to see it all. | Yosemite Village, shuttle stop 6 | Daily sunrise–sunset | Free.

YOSEMITE SCENERY AND WILDLIFE

Dense stands of incense cedar, Douglas fir, and assorted pines cover much of the park, but the stellar stand-out, quite literally, is the *Sequoia sempervirens*, the giant sequoia. Sequoias grow only along the west slope of the Sierra Nevada between 4,500 and 7,000 ft in elevation. Starting from a seed the size of a rolled oat flake, each of these ancient monuments assumed remarkable proportions in adulthood. In late May the valley's dogwood trees bloom with white, starlike flowers. Wildflowers, such as black-eyed Susan, bull thistle, cow parsnip, lupine, and meadow goldenrod, peak in June in the valley and in July at higher elevations. Yosemite's waterfalls are at their most spectacular in May and June. By summer's end, some falls will have dried up. They begin flowing again in late fall, and in winter they may be hung dramatically with ice. Visit the park during the period of the full moon, and you can stroll in the evening without a flashlight and still make out the silhouettes of the giant granite monoliths and ribbons of falling water. Regardless of the season, sunset casts a brilliant orange light onto Half Dome, a stunning sight.

The most visible animals are the mule deer, the only kind of deer in Yosemite. Though sightings of bighorn sheep are infrequent in the park itself, you can see them on the eastern side of the Sierra Crest, just off Route 120 in Lee Vining Canyon. The American black bear, which often has a brown, cinnamon, or blond coat, is the only species of bear in Yosemite (the California grizzlies were hunted to extinction in the 1920s), though few people ever see them. Watch for the blue Steller's jay along trails, in campgrounds, and around public buildings. The golden eagle is sometimes seen soaring above the valley.

Curry Village. Opened in 1899 by David and Jenny Curry, Curry Village offers tented lodgings for a modest price. This is also where you should come to rent rafts or bicycles. There are several stores, an evening campfire program in summer, and an ice-skating rink in winter. | Yosemite Valley, shuttle stop 1.

★ **El Capitan.** Rising 3,593 ft—more than 350 stories—above the Valley, El Capitan is the largest exposed-granite monolith in the world. It's almost twice the height of the Rock of Gibraltar. Look for climbers scaling the vertical face. | Off Northside Dr., about 4 mi west of the Valley visitor center.

★ **Glacier Point.** A Yosemite hot spot for its sweeping, bird's-eye views, Glacier Point looms 3,214 ft above the Valley. From the parking area, walk a few hundred yards and you'll see waterfalls, Half Dome, and other mountain peaks. Glacier Point is a popular hiking destination. You can hike up, or take a bus ($15) to the top and hike down. The bus runs June through October, weather permitting. | Glacier Point Rd., 16 mi northeast of Rte. 41.

★ **Half Dome.** Though you may have seen it on countless postcards and calendars, it's still a shock to see Half Dome, the Valley's most recognizable formation, which tops out at an elevation of 8,842 ft. The afternoon sun lights its face with orange and yellow shades that are reflected in the Merced River. Stand on the Sentinel Bridge at sunset for the best view.

Hetch Hetchy Reservoir. The Hetch Hetchy Reservoir, which supplies water and hydroelectric power to San Francisco, is about 40 mi from Yosemite Valley. Some say John Muir died of heartbreak when this grand valley was dammed and flooded beneath 300 ft of water in 1913. | Hetch Hetchy Rd., about 15 mi north of the Big Oak Flat entrance station.

★ **High Country.** The above-tree-line, high-alpine region east of the Valley—land of alpenglow and top-of-the-world vistas—is often missed by those only focusing on the Valley's more publicized splendors. If you've never seen Sierra high country, go. If you've already been there, you know why it's not to be missed. Summer wildflowers, which usually spring up mid-July through August, carpet the meadows and mountainsides with pink, purple, blue, red, yellow, and orange. On foot or on horseback are the best ways to get there. For information on trails and backcountry permits, go to the visitor center.

Indian Cultural Museum. With demonstrations in beadwork, basket-weaving, and other traditional activities, the museum displays the cultural history of Yosemite's Miwok and Paiute people. | Yosemite Village, next to the Visitor Center | 209/372–0299 | Daily 9–4:30 | Free.

Le Conte Memorial Lodge. The Valley's first visitor center is now operated by the Sierra Club, featuring a small children's library, environmental exhibits, and evening programs. It's across from Housekeeping Camp. | Southside Dr., at shuttle stop 12 | Late May–early Sept., Wed.–Sun. 10–4.

Mariposa Grove of Big Trees. Mariposa is Yosemite's largest grove of giant sequoias. The Grizzly Giant, the oldest tree here, is estimated to be 2,700 years old. You can visit the trees on foot or, in summer, on a one-hour tram tour. If the road to the grove is closed in summer, which happens when Yosemite is crowded, park in Wawona and take the free shuttle (9 AM to 4:30 PM) to the parking lot. The access road to the grove may also be closed by snow for extended periods from November to mid-May. You can still usually walk, snowshoe, or ski in. | Rte. 41, 2 mi north of the South Entrance station.

Pioneer Yosemite History Center. Yosemite's first log buildings, relocated here from around the park, make up this historic collection near the Wawona Hotel. Enter on the covered bridge that welcomed the park's first tourists. There's also a homesteader's cabin, a blacksmith's shop, a bakery, and a U.S. Cavalry headquarters, all from the late-19th or early 20th centuries. In summer, costumed docents play the roles of the pioneers. Ranger-led walks leave from the covered bridge, Saturdays at 10 in summer. | Rte. 41, Wawona | 209/379–2646 | Free | Building interiors mid-June–early Sept., Wed.–Sun. 9–1, Mon.–Tues. 2–5.

Sentinel Dome. The view from here is similar to that from Glacier Point, except you can't see the Valley floor. A 1$^1/_{10}$-mi path climbs to the viewpoint from the parking lot. The trail is long and steep enough to keep the crowds away, but it's not overly rugged. | Glacier Point Rd., off Rte. 41.

★ **Tuolumne Meadows.** The largest subalpine meadow in the Sierra, at 8,575 ft, is a popular way station for backpack trips along the Sierra-scribing Pacific Crest and John Muir trails. The colorful wildflowers peak in mid-July and August. Tioga Road provides easy access to the high country, but the highway closes when snow piles up, usually in mid-October. | Tioga Rd. (Rte. 120), about 8 mi west of the Tioga Pass entrance station.

Valley Visitor Center. For maps, guides, and information from park rangers, be sure to stop here. There's a Sierra visitor bureau and exhibits on the history of Yosemite Valley. | Yosemite Village, shuttle stop 6 | 209/372–0299 | www.yosemitepark.com | Free | Late May–early Sept., daily 9–6; early Sept.–late May, daily 9–5.

★ **Waterfalls.** When the snow starts to melt (usually peaking in May), almost every rocky lip or narrow gorge becomes a sluiceway for streaming snowmelt churning down to meet the Merced River. But even in drier months, the waterfalls can take your breath away. If you choose to hike any of the trails to or up the falls, be sure to wear shoes with good, no-slip soles; rocks can be extremely slippery. Stay on trails at all times.

Bridalveil Fall, a filmy fall of 620 ft that is often diverted as much as 20 ft one way or the other by the breeze, is the first marvelous view of Yosemite Valley you will see if you come in via Route 41.

Climb Mist Trail from Happy Isles for an up-close view of 594-ft **Nevada Fall,** the first major fall as the Merced River plunges out of the high country toward the eastern end of Yosemite Valley.

At 1,612 ft, **Ribbon Fall** is the highest single fall in North America. It's also the first Valley waterfall to dry up in summer; the rainwater and melted snow that create the slender fall evaporate quickly at this height. Look just west of El Capitan from the Valley floor.

Fern-covered black rocks frame 317-ft **Vernal Fall,** and rainbows play in the spray at its base. Take Mist Trail from Happy Isles to see it.

Yosemite Falls—which form the highest waterfall in North America and the fifth-highest in the world—are actually three falls, one on top of another. The water from the top descends all of 2,425 ft. To view it up close, head to its base on the trail from Camp 4.

Wawona Hotel. In the southern tip of Yosemite, this was the park's first lodge, built in 1879. With a whitewashed exterior and wraparound verandas, this is a fine example of Victorian resort architecture—a blend of rusticity and elegance—and is now a National Historic Landmark. The hotel annexes on this estate were built by 1918. The Wawona is an excellent place to stay or stop for lunch when making the drive from the South Entrance to the Valley; the dining room is open weekends only from January through March. | Rte. 41, Wawona | 209/375–1425.

Yosemite Museum. With demonstrations in beadwork, basket-weaving, and other traditional activities, the museum elucidates the cultural history of Yosemite's Miwok and Paiute people. | Yosemite Village, shuttle stop 6 | 209/372–0299 | Daily 9–4:30 | Free.

Near the Park

★ **Bodie Ghost Town.** Old shacks and shops, abandoned mine shafts, a Methodist church, the mining village of Rattlesnake Gulch, and the remains of a small Chinatown are among the sights at this fascinating ghost town. At an elevation of 8,200 ft, the town boomed from about 1878 to 1881, but by the late 1940s, all its residents had departed. Evidence of Bodie's wild past survives at an excellent museum, and you can tour an old stamp mill (where ore was stamped into fine powder to extract gold and silver) and a ridge that contains many mine sites. No food, drink, or lodging is available in Bodie. The town is 23 mi from Lee Vining, north on U.S. 395, east on Route 270. The last 3 mi are unpaved. Snow may close Route 270 late fall through early spring, but you can snowshoe in. | Main and Green Sts., Bodie | 760/647–6445 | www.parks.ca.gov | $1 | Park late May–early Sept., daily 8–7; early Sept.–late May, daily 8–4. Museum late May–early Sept., daily 9–6; early Sept.–late May, hrs vary.

Devils Postpile National Monument. East of Mammoth Lakes lies a rock formation of smooth, vertical basalt columns sculpted by volcanic and glacial forces. A short, steep trail winds to the top of the 60-ft cliff for a bird's-eye view of the columns. Follow Route 203 13 mi west from Mammoth Lakes. | Minaret Rd., Mammoth Lakes | 760/934–2289, 760/934–0606 shuttle | www.nps.gov/depo | Free | Late June–late Oct., daily.

A 2-mi hike past the Postpile leads to the monument's second scenic wonder, **Rainbow Falls,** where a branch of the San Joaquin River plunges more than 100 ft over a lava ledge. When the water hits the pool below, sunlight turns the resulting mist into a spray of color. In summer, the area is accessible only by shuttle bus. Scenic picnic spots dot the banks of the river. | 760/934–0606 | $9 | June–Nov., daily.

Hot Creek Geologic Site. Forged by an ancient volcanic eruption, the Hot Creek Geologic Site is a landscape of boiling hot springs, fumaroles, and occasional geysers about 10 mi southeast of the town of Mammoth Lakes. You can soak (at your own risk) in hot springs or walk along boardwalks through the canyon to view the steaming volcanic features. | Off U.S. 395, Mammoth Lakes | 760/924–5500 | Daily sunrise–sunset.

★ **Mono Lake.** Since the 1940s the city of Los Angeles has diverted water from the streams that feed the lake, lowering its water level and exposing striking towers of tufa, or calcium carbonate. Court victories by environmentalists have forced a reduction of the diversions, and the lake is again rising. Millions of migratory birds nest in and around Mono Lake. | South of Lee Vining on U.S. 395.

If you join the naturalist-guided **South Tufa Walk,** bring your binoculars for close-up views of Mono Lake's wildlife and calcified tufa towers. Tours depart the South Tufa parking lot 5 mi east of U.S. 395 on Route 120 and last about 1½ hours. | 760/647–3044 | www.monolake.org/main/natact.htm | $3 | Weekends 1 PM.

Yosemite Mountain–Sugar Pine Railroad. This 4-mi, narrow-gauge, steam-powered railroad excursion takes you along the rails near Yosemite's south gate. Travel back to a time when powerful locomotives once hauled massive log trains through the Sierra. There's also a moonlight special, with dinner and entertainment. Take Route 41 south from Yosemite about 8 mi. | 56001 Rte. 41, Fish Camp | 559/683–7273 | www.ymsprr.com | $9–$36 | Mar.–Oct., daily.

Dining

In Yosemite

Food Court at Yosemite Lodge. American/Casual. Fast and convenient, the food court serves simple fare, ranging from hamburgers and pizzas to pastas and salads at lunch and dinner. At breakfast, there are pancakes and eggs made any way you like. There's also a selection of beer and wine. | Yosemite Valley, about $^3/_4$ mi west of visitor center | 209/372–1265 | $3–$12 | AE, D, DC, MC, V.

Tuolumne Meadows Grill. Fast Food. Serving continuously throughout the day, this fast-food grill cooks up breakfast, lunch, and dinner. Stop in for a quick meal before exploring the Meadows. | Tioga Rd. (Rte. 120) | 209/372–8426 | Closed Oct.–mid-June | $3–$7 | AE, D, DC, MC, V.

Picnic Areas. Ready-made picnic lunches are available through Yosemite hotels with advance notice. Otherwise, stop at the grocery stores in the Village to pick up supplies. Many picnickers prefer to hike along one of the many scenic trails and choose an impromptu spot or vista to enjoy their meal. Otherwise, there are 13 designated picnic areas around the park. Rest rooms and grills or fire grates are available at those in the Valley only.

Tucked behind the Ahwahnee Hotel, **Church Bowl** nearly abuts the granite walls below the Royal Arches. If you're walking from the Village with your supplies, this is the shortest trek to a picnic area. No drinking water.

At the western end of the Valley on Northside Drive, the **El Capitan** picnic area has great views straight up the giant granite wall above. No drinking water.

Near the Park

Banny's Café. Contemporary. Its calm, pleasant environment and hearty yet refined dishes make Banny's an attractive alternative to Sonora's noisier eateries. Try the grilled salmon fillet with scallion rice and ginger wasabi aioli. | 83 S. Stewart St., Sonora | 209/533–4709 | No lunch | $12–$15 | D, MC, V.

Coffee Express. American/Casual. If you're coming into Yosemite via Route 120, you'll pass this cozy diner. Try the chicken salad with apples and alfalfa sprouts and at least one sliver of irresistible fruit pie. The Iron Door Saloon, one of the oldest operating saloons in California, is across the street. | 18744 Rte. 120, Groveland | 209/962–7393 | No dinner | $4–$6.50 | No credit cards.

Nicely's. American. Pictures of local attractions decorate this eatery, which has been around since 1965. Try the blueberry pancakes and homemade sausages at breakfast. For lunch or dinner, try the chicken-fried steak or the fiesta salad. Kids' menu. | U.S. 395 and 4th St., Lee Vining | 760/647–6477 | $9–$15 | MC, V.

Red Fox Restaurant American. You'll find everything from homemade soups, stews, sandwiches, and salads at lunch to pastas, meat loaf, fresh seafood, and hand-cut steaks at dinner at this moderately priced family restaurant near downtown Mariposa. The breakfasts are also delicious. | 5114 Hwy. 140 (at 12th St.), Mariposa | 209/966–7900 | $9–$20 | AE, D, MC, V.

Schat's Bakery &Café Vermeer. American/Casual. Part restaurant, part bakery, this family-run business serves everything from huge, perfectly cooked omelets to monster pancakes and awesome French toast. The pastries and breads are fresh and delicious. You can also get great sandwiches to go. | Main St., Mammoth Lakes | 760/934–6055 or 760/934–4203 | No dinner. | $5–$10 | MC, V.

Lodging

In Yosemite

Reserve your room or cabin in Yosemite as far in advance as possible. You can make a reservation up to a year before your arrival. The Yosemite Lodge is often sold out on weekends, holiday periods, and all days between May and September. All reservations for lodging in Yosemite are made through Yosemite Concession Services

Corporation. | 5410 E. Home Ave., Fresno, CA | 559/252–4848 | fax 559/456–0542 | www.yosemitepark.com.

Curry Village. This is a large community of basic hotel rooms, cabins, and tent cabins in a wooded area on the eastern end of Yosemite Valley, in the shadow of Glacier Point. The one-room cabins, spartan but adequately furnished, are less expensive than Yosemite's hotels. Tent cabins have wood frames and canvas walls and roof. Those without bath share campground-style community showers and toilets. Linen service is provided, but cooking is not allowed in the cabin area. Restaurant, pool; no a/c, no room phones, no room TVs | Yosemite Valley | 559/252–4848 | 22 rooms, 100 cabins, 400 tent cabins | $112, $92 cabin with bath, $77 cabin without bath, $59 tent cabin | AE, D, DC, MC, V.

White Wolf Lodge. Set in the high country in a subalpine meadow, this tiny lodge offers rustic accommodations in tent cabins without baths or in cabins with baths. If you want to hike the backcountry, this is an excellent base camp. Book as far in advance as possible to ensure availability. Restaurant; no a/c, no room phones, no room TVs | Off Tioga Rd. (Rte. 120), 45 mins west of Tuolumne Meadows | 24 tent cabins, 4 cabins | $49–$83 | Mid-June–early Sept. | AE, D, DC, MC, V.

Yosemite Lodge. This lodge is so near Yosemite Falls that you can hear the water roar. The typical motel-style rooms have two double beds, while the larger "lodge rooms" also have dressing areas and balconies. 2 restaurants, pool, bar; no a/c, no room TVs | Yosemite Valley, about 3/4 mi west of visitor center | 239 rooms | $103–$130 | AE, D, DC, MC, V.

Near the Park

Best Western Sonora Oaks. The standard-issue motel rooms at this East Sonora establishment are roomy, with some outside sitting areas. Suites have fireplaces, whirlpool tubs, and hillside views. Because the motel is right on Route 108, the front rooms can be noisy. Restaurant, bar | 19551 Hess Ave., Sonora | 209/533–4400 or 800/532–1944 | fax 209/532–1964 | 96 rooms, 4 suites | $84–$129 | AE, D, DC, MC, V.

Little Valley Inn. Pine paneling, historical photos, and old mining tools recall Mariposa's heritage at this modern B&B with three attractive guest bungalows. One suite sleeps five people and includes a kitchen. Refrigerators, cable TV; no room phones | 3483 Brooks Rd., off Rte. 49, Mariposa | 209/742–6204 or 800/889–5444 | fax 209/742–5099 | www.littlevalley.com | 4 rooms, 1 suite, 1 cabin | $99–$125 | AE, MC, V.

Swiss Chalet. One of the most reasonably priced motels in the town of Mammoth Lakes, the Swiss Chalet has great views of the mountains and simple, comfortable rooms. There's a fish-cleaning area and a freezer to keep your summer catch fresh. Kitchenettes, hot tub, sauna, cable TV | 3776 Viewpoint Rd., Mammoth Lakes | 760/934–2403 or 800/937–9477 | fax 760/934–2403 | www.mammoth-swisschalet.com | 21 rooms | $55–$110 | AE, D, MC, V.

Tioga Lodge. Just 2½ mi north of Yosemite's eastern gateway, this 19th-century building has been by turns a store, a saloon, a tollbooth, and a boarding house. Now restored and expanded, it's a popular lodge that's close to local ski areas and fishing spots. No room phones | U.S. 395, Lee Vining | 760/647–6423 or 888/647–6423 | fax 760/647–6074 | www.tiogalodge.com | 13 rooms | $95–$105 | AE, D, MC, V.

Camping

In Yosemite

There are lots of camping sites in Yosemite (nearly 2,000 in summer, 400 year-round). The most popular are listed here; for a complete list, contact the park. Though none of the campgrounds have RV hook-ups, they fill up quickly, especially in the Valley. Reservations are required at many of Yosemite's campgrounds, especially in summer. You can reserve a site up to five months in advance; bookings made more than 21 days in advance require pre-payment. Unless otherwise noted, book your site through the central **National Park Reservation Service.** | Box 1600, Cumberland, MD 21502 | 800/436–7275 | reservations.nps.gov | D, MC, V.

Housekeeping Camp. These concrete three-wall cabins with canvas roofs, set on a beach along the Merced River, are difficult to come by; reserving a year in advance is advised. You can cook on gas stoves rented from the front desk. Toilets and showers are in a central building, and there's a camp store for provisions. Flush toilets, drinking water, laundry facilities, showers, bear boxes, fire pits, electricity | 226 units | ½ mi west of Curry Village, Southside Dr. | $56 | Reservations essential | May–Oct.

Lower Pines Campground. This campground on the Merced River is a short walk away from the Mirror Lake and Mist trails. Expect small sites and crowds. Flush toilets, drinking water, bear boxes, fire grates, picnic tables, public telephone, ranger station, swimming (river) | 60 sites | East Yosemite Valley | $18 | Reservations essential | Mar.–Oct.

Tuolumne Meadows Campground. This large, high-country campground affords easy access to high peaks with spectacular views. You can use the hot showers at the Tuolumne Meadows Lodge at certain times of the day. Half the sites are first-come, first-serve, but arrive very early if you hope to get one. The beautiful scenery makes this one of the most sought-after campgrounds in Yosemite. Flush toilets, dump station, drinking water, bear boxes, fire grates, picnic tables, public telephone, general store, ranger station | 314 sites | Tioga Rd. (Rte. 120), 46 mi east of the Big Oak Flat entrance station | $18 | Reservation required for half of all sites. | June–Sept.

Wawona Campground. Near the Mariposa Grove, sites here are less closely packed than those in the Valley, but it's an hour's drive to the Valley's major attractions. Reservations are essential May through September. Flush toilets, drinking water, bear boxes, fire grates, picnic tables, ranger station, swimming (river) | 93 sites | Rte. 41, 1 mi north of Wawona | $18 May–Sept.; $12 Oct.–Apr. | Reservations required May–Sept.

Near the Park

Dimond O Campground. Set at 4,400 ft, the camp is 2 mi from Yosemite's western border. When the park's campgrounds are sold out and you want to be within an hour's drive of the Valley, this is a good bet. From Route 120, take Evergreen Road (2 mi west of the Big Oak Flat entrance station) north and continue 6 mi. Pit toilets, drinking water, bear boxes, grills, picnic tables | 38 sites | Evergreen Rd. | 209/962–7825 | $13 | Reservations not accepted | No credit cards | Apr.–Oct.

Ellery Lake Campground. High in the Inyo National Forest at 9,600 ft, you'll find fishing and camping near a high country lake. There are several other campgrounds in the vicinity if this one is full. Flush toilets, drinking water, bear boxes, grills, picnic tables | 12 sites | Off Rte. 120, south side, 4 mi east of Yosemite's Tioga Pass entrance | 760/873–2408 or 760/647–3044 | $11 | Reservations not accepted | No credit cards | June–Sept.

Shopping

You can pick up basic provisions at a general store in Wawona, Tuolumne Meadows, or Crane Flat. You'll find a full selection of groceries, fast food, camping supplies, and a few unusual souvenirs in Yosemite Village, at the east end of the Valley, the primary shopping destination for most park visitors. Many of the park's major tourist destinations also have souvenir stores. Check the *Yosemite Guide* and *Yosemite Today* for seasonal hours and opening dates.

Ansel Adams Gallery. At the Valley's most elegant gift shop, you'll find original prints, Native American crafts, photography supplies, and camera rentals. | Yosemite Village | 209/372–4413 | AE, D, MC, V | Daily 9–5.

Sports and Outdoor Activities

Bicycling

The eastern Valley has 12 mi of paved bike paths, or you can ride—with traffic—on 196 mi of paved park roads. Kids under 18 must wear a helmet. Bikes are not allowed on hiking trails or in the backcountry. Stick to the Valley floor for the safest, easiest terrain.

Yosemite Bike Rentals. You can rent bikes by the hour ($5.50) or by the day ($21) from either Yosemite Lodge or Curry Village bike stands. Helmets are always included. Bikes with child trailers, baby-jogger strollers, and wheelchairs are also available. | Yosemite Lodge, shuttle stop 8; Curry Village, shuttle stop 1 | 209/372–1208 | www.yosemitepark.com | Apr.–Oct.

Bird-Watching

More than 200 bird species have been spotted in the park, including the sage sparrow, pygmy owl, blue grouse, and mountain bluebird. Park rangers lead free bird-watching walks in Yosemite Valley in summer, one day each week, when staff members are available. Binoculars are sometimes available for loan.

Birding Seminars. The Yosemite Association sponsors two- to four-day seminars for beginning and intermediate birders. Meeting points vary, and prices range from $190 to $225. | 209/379–1906 | www.yosemite.org | Apr.–Aug.

Fishing

The waters in Yosemite are not stocked. Trout, mostly brown and rainbow, live here but are not plentiful. Yosemite's fishing season begins on the last Saturday in April and ends on November 15. Some waterways are off-limits at certain times; be sure to inquire at the visitor center about regulations, especially in wilderness areas.

Department of Fish and Game. The required license costs $11.05 for two days or $30.45 for 10 days. A full-season license costs $35 for in-state and $81 for out-of-state residents. Buy your license in season at Yosemite Village Sport Shop (209/372–1286), between the Village Store and the Old Bank Building, or at the Wawona Store (209/375–6574). Or buy it any time of year by writing the License and Revenue Branch. License and Revenue Branch, Department of Fish and Game | 3211 S St., Sacramento 95816 | 916/653–7664 | www.dfg.ca.gov.

Hiking and Backpacking

From paved rambles to multiday scrambles, Yosemite's 840 mi of trails have a hike for you. Be sure to purchase a detailed guide, compass, and topographic map, on sale in park stores and visitor centers.

Yosemite Valley Wilderness Center. The helpful staff provides trail-use reservations (recommended for popular trailheads on weekends and between May and September) as well as permits, maps, and advice on backcountry treks. It's in Yosemite Valley next to the post office.

Overnight stays in the backcountry require a free **wilderness permit,** available at permit stations throughout the park. During high season, from May through September, permit reservations are highly recommended. Permit reservations cost $5. Phone reservations are accepted from 24 weeks to two days in advance, or you can request reservations online or in writing 24 weeks to two weeks in advance. | Wilderness Reservations, Box 545, Yosemite, CA 95389 | 209/372–0740 | www.nps.gov/yose.

John Muir Trail. Ardent and courageous trekkers can continue on from the top of Nevada Fall, off Mist Trail, to the top of Half Dome. Some hikers attempt this entire 10- to 12-hour, 16¾-mi round-trip trek from Happy Isles in one day. If you're planning to do this, remember that the 4,800-ft elevation gain and the altitude of 8,842 ft will cause shortness of breath. Backpackers can hike to a campground in Little Yosemite Valley near the top of Nevada Fall the first day, then climb to the top of Half Dome and hike out the next day. It's highly recommended that you get your wilderness permit reservations at least a month in advance. Wear hiking boots and bring gloves. The last pitch up the back of Half Dome is very steep. The only way to climb this sheer rock face is to pull yourself up using the steel cable handrails, which are in place only from late spring to early fall. Those who brave the ascent will be rewarded with an unbeatable view of Yosemite Valley below and the high country beyond. | Happy Isles.

★ **Mist Trail.** You'll walk through rainbows when you visit 317-ft Vernal Fall. The hike to the bridge at the base of the fall is only moderately strenuous and less than 1 mi long. It's another steep (and often wet) ¾-mi grind up to the top. From there, you can continue 2 mi more to the top of Nevada Fall, a 594-ft cascade, as the Merced River plunges out of the high country. The trail is open late spring to early fall, depending on snowmelt. | Happy Isles.

★ **Yosemite Falls Trail.** This is the highest waterfall in North America. The upper fall (1,430 ft), the middle cascades (675 ft), and the lower fall (320 ft) combine for a total of 2,425 ft and, when viewed from the Valley, appear as a single waterfall. The ¼-mi trail leads from the parking lot to the base of the falls. Upper Yosemite Fall Trail, a strenuous 3½-mi climb rising 2,700 ft, takes you above the top of the falls. | Northside Dr. at Camp 4.

Horseback Riding

Reservations must be made in advance at the hotel tour desks or by phone. For any of the overnight saddle trips, which use mules, call on or after September 15 to request a lottery application for the following year. Scenic trail rides range from two hours to full days. Four- to six-day High Sierra saddle trips are also available.

Tuolumne Meadow Stables | Tioga Rd. | 209/372–8427 | www.yosemitepark.com | $40–$80 | Late May–early Sept. | Reservations essential.

Rafting

Rafting is permitted only on designated areas of the Middle and South forks of the Merced River. Check with the visitor center for closures and other restrictions.

Curry Village Raft Stand. The $13.50 rental fee is per person and covers the raft, paddles, and life jackets, plus a shuttle to the launch point on Sentinel Beach. You raft 3 mi down the Merced River, and a tram takes you back to Curry Village. | 209/372–8319 | www.yosemitepark.com | May–July.

Rock Climbing

The granite canyon walls of Yosemite Valley are world-renowned for rock climbing. El Capitan, with its 3,593-ft vertical face, is the most famous and difficult of all, but there are many other options for all skill levels.

Yosemite Mountaineering School and Guide Service. The one-day basic lesson includes some bouldering and rappelling, and three or four 60-ft climbs. If you're already an experienced climber, ask at the mountain shop what areas are best for your skill level. | Curry Village Mountain Shop | 209/372–8344 | www.yosemitepark.com | $70–$220 | Mid-Apr.–early Oct.

Skiing and Snowshoeing

Badger Pass. A free, 40-minute shuttle ride takes you from Yosemite Valley to Badger Pass, where you can ski downhill and cross-country. Badger Pass opened in 1934 and is the oldest operating ski area in California (and the only one in the park). It's a compact area with gentle terrain, ideal for families and beginners. Four chairlifts and one surface lift access 10 runs. Winter ski packages are available in conjunction with Yosemite's hotels; inquire when you book. Ski and snowshoe lessons and rentals are available. | Glacier Point Rd. | 209/372–8444 or 209/372–1000 | www.yosemitepark.com | $25–$28, rentals $20 | Mid-Dec.–early Apr.

Essential Information

When to Go

With summer come the crowds. During extremely busy periods, like July 4, you may experience delays at the entrance gates. If you can only make it here in the warmest months, try to visit midweek. In winter, heavy snows occasionally cause road closures, and tire chains may be required on roads that remain open. Tioga Road is closed from late October through the end of May. The road to Glacier Point beyond the turnoff for Badger Pass is closed after the first major snowfall, usually in late October, through May. Mariposa Grove Road is typically closed for a shorter period in winter. The ideal time to visit is from mid-April through Memorial Day and from mid-September through October, when the park is only moderately busy and the days are usually sunny and clear.

FESTIVALS AND SEASONAL EVENTS

SPRING

May: **Fireman's Muster.** North of Sonora in the old mining town of Columbia, history springs to life at this festival of antique fire engines, with hose-spraying contests and a parade of the old pumpers the major highlights. | 209/536–1672.

Mother Lode Roundup Parade and Rodeo. On Mother's Day weekend the town of Sonora celebrates its gold-mining, agricultural, and lumbering history with a parade, rodeo, entertainment, and food. | 209/532–7428 or 800/446–1333.

SUMMER

July: **Mammoth Lakes Jazz Jubilee.** This festival, founded in 1989, is hosted by the local group Temple of Folly Jazz Band and takes place in 10 venues, most with dance floors. | 760/934–2478 or 800/367–6572 | www.mammothjazz.org.

Bargains

Photo enthusiasts will delight in the free camera walks given each morning year-round by professional photographers. From early April through October, professional artists offer free workshops in watercolor, etching, drawing, and other mediums.

Bring your own materials or purchase them at the Art Center. Rangers lead free discovery walks throughout the year and free snowshoe walks in winter. Children can participate in the free Junior Ranger naturalist activities. Free evening activities include films and slide shows on Yosemite.

In winter, you can find discounts on lodging and bargain ski packages, especially midweek. And if you plan to visit more than one or two national parks on your trip, consider buying an annual parks pass for $50.

Nearby Towns

Marking the southern end of the Sierra's gold-bearing Mother Lode, **Mariposa** is the last moderately sized town before you enter Yosemite from the west. In addition to a mining museum, Mariposa has a number of shops, restaurants, and service stations. Motels and restaurants dot both sides of Route 41 as it cuts through the town of **Oakhurst,** once a boomtown during the gold rush. Oakhurst has a population of about 14,000 and sits at the southern edge of Yosemite National Park. The gracious city of **Sonora** retains evidence of its own vibrant gold-rush history. Stroll Washington Street and see western-style storefronts, second-story porches, and 19th-century hotels. Sonora is the seat of Tuolumne County, 70 mi west of Yosemite Village. The tiny town of **Lee Vining** is home to eerily beautiful Mono Lake, where millions of migratory birds nest. You'll pass through Lee Vining if you're coming to Yosemite through the eastern entrance. Visit **Mammoth Lakes,** about 40 mi southeast of Yosemite's Tioga Pass entrance, for some of California's best skiing and snowboarding in winter, with fishing, mountain biking, hiking, and horseback riding in summer. Nine deep-blue lakes form the Mammoth Lakes Basin, and another hundred dot the surrounding countryside. At the base of Mammoth Mountain sits Devils Postpile National Monument, a geological formation of smooth, vertical basaltic columns formed by volcanic and glacial forces.

Tours

Most of the guided tours in the park are conducted by Yosemite Concession Services Corporation. It's a good idea to call two days to a week in advance to verify schedules and to make reservations, if they're required. For a complete listing, check the *Yosemite Guide* or log onto yosemitepark.com.

★ **Camera Walks.** Photography enthusiasts shouldn't miss the 1½-hour guided camera walks offered by professional photographers. Some walks are hosted by the Ansel Adams Gallery, some by Yosemite Concession Services, and the meeting points vary. All are free. Participation is limited, so call in advance, or visit the gallery or tour desks at the hotels. | 209/372–0299 or 209/372–4413 | www.yosemitepark.com | Free | Reservations essential.

Children's Programs. From June through August, children 3–13 can participate in the informal, self-guided Little Cub and Junior Ranger programs. Stop at the Valley visitor center or Happy Isles to pick up a handbook ($3–$5), which children take with them around the park to complete activities. Once they're done, rangers perform a small ceremony, presenting kids with certification and a badge. | 209/372–0299.

Discover Yosemite Family Program. The Yosemite Institute, the park's non-profit educational division, offers three-hour, hands-on summer learning tours geared for families with children of all ages. Specific activities depend on the group's dynamic, but they usually include games, stories, and nature hikes. At least one parent must accompany participating children. Reserve in advance. | 209/372–1240 | www.yosemitepark.com | Children $10; first two adults free, each additional $10 | Jun.–Aug.

★ **Evening Programs.** Lectures by rangers, slide shows, and documentary films present unusual perspectives on Yosemite. On summer weekends, Camp Curry and Tuolumne

Meadows campgrounds both host sing-along campfires. Programs vary according to season, but there's usually at least one ranger-led activity per night in the Valley; schedules and locations are published in *Yosemite Today* and the *Yosemite Guide*. | 209/372–0299 | www.yosemiteparktours.com | Free.

Tuolumne Meadows Tour. If you want a full day's outing to the high country, opt for this ride up Tioga Road to Tuolumne Meadows. You stop at several overlooks, and you can connect with another shuttle at Tuolumne Lodge. This is mostly for hikers and backpackers who want to reach high-country trailheads, but anyone can ride. | 209/372–1240 | www.yosemiteparktours.com | $22 | Reservations essential | July–early Sept.

Visitor Information

Yosemite National Park | Information Office, Box 577, Yosemite National Park 95389 | 209/372–0200 or 209/372–0264 | www.nps.gov/yose. **Yosemite Concession Services** | 5410 E. Home Ave., Fresno 93727 | 559/252–4848; 209/372–1240 tours | www.yosemitepark.com.

Lee Vining Office and Information Center | Box 29, Lee Vining, CA 93541 | 760/647–6595 | www.monolake.org. **Mammoth Lakes Visitors Bureau** | Box 48; along Rte. 203 (Main St.), near Sawmill Cutoff Rd., Mammoth Lakes, CA 93546 | 760/934–2712 or 888/466–2666 | www.visitmammoth.com. **Mariposa County Visitors Bureau** | Box 784, 5158 Hwy. 140, Mariposa, CA 95338 | 209/966–7082 or 888/554–9013 | www.homeofyosemite.com. **Tuolumne County Visitors Bureau** | Box 4020, Sonora, CA 95370 | 209/533–4420 or 800/446–1333 | www.thegreatunfenced.com. **Yosemite Sierra Visitors Bureau** | 40637 Hwy. 41, Oakhurst, CA 93644 | 559/683–4636 | www.yosemite-sierra.org.

Arriving and Departing

BY AIR

Airports

Fresno Yosemite International Airport (FYI). The nearest major airport is served by major domestic and several regional carriers. | 559/498–4095 | www.flyfresno.org.

Oakland International Airport (OAK) | 510/577–4000 | www.flyoakland.com.

San Francisco International Airport (SFO) | 650/821–8211 | www.flysfo.com.

Sacramento International Airport (SMF) | 916/874–0700 | airports.co.sacramento.ca.us.

Airport Transportation

Major rental car companies have desks at all of the airports listed; the drive from Fresno will take 1–1½ hours, while the drives from Oakland, San Francisco, and Sacramento average 3–4 hours.

BY BUS

Greyhound offers frequent service to Merced.

Yosemite VIA. Buses run to Yosemite from Merced ($20 round-trip, 2½ hours one-way); the company also offers single-day or overnight tours to the park, as well as combination service with Amtrak. The Greyhound and Amtrak stations are regular stops, but call ahead to let the bus company know when you plan to arrive so that you can ensure your connection. | 209/384–2576 | www.via-adventures.com.

BY CAR

Yosemite is a four-hour drive from San Francisco and a six-hour drive from Los Angeles. From the west, three highways come to Yosemite; all intersect with Highway 99, which runs north–south through the Central Valley. Highway 120 is the northernmost and most direct route from San Francisco, but it rises higher into the mountains, which can be snowy in winter; chains or snow tires may be mandatory. Highway 140 from Merced is the recommended route in winter. It is the least mountainous, and chains are not usually required. Highway 41 from Fresno is the shortest route from Los Angeles and offers the most dramatic first look at Yosemite Valley.

Coming from the east, Highway 120, the Tioga Road, climbs over the highest point a car can drive in the state, then past Tuolumne Meadows, and down into the Valley. It's scenic, but the mountain driving may be stressful and the road is closed for much of the year due to snow.

BY TRAIN

Amtrak has train service to Merced, where you can connect with bus transportation.

Getting Around

BY CAR

Note that there are few gas stations within Yosemite, so fuel up before you reach the park. From late fall until early spring, the weather is unpredictable and driving can be treacherous. You should carry chains no matter what route you take. They are often mandatory on Sierra roads in snowstorms. If you have to buy chains in the Valley, you'll pay twice the normal price. For information about road conditions, call 800/427–7623 from within California or 209/372–0200, or go to www.dot.ca.gov. Once in the Valley, the primary destination for most visitors, follow signs for parking, and take the free shuttle bus around the Valley. Avoid driving unless you want to travel outside the shuttle area.

BY PUBLIC TRANSIT

Yosemite Valley Shuttle Bus. Although you can visit the Yosemite Valley sites in your car, doing so is discouraged in summer, since traffic congestion and exhaust are serious problems in the park. When it's especially crowded, some roads are closed to private vehicles. You can avoid traffic jams by leaving your car at any of the designated lots and taking the free shuttle bus, which serves eastern Yosemite Valley year-round, every day. From May to September, shuttles run from 7 AM to 10 PM; the rest of the year, shuttles run from 9 AM to 10 PM. | 209/372–1240 | www.nps.gov/yose/trip/shuttle.htm.

Index

A. Lincoln's Place, Gettysburg, PA, 72
Abby Aldrich Rockefeller Folk Art Center, Colonial Williamsburg, VA, 360
Abe's Buggy Rides, Bird-in-Hand, PA, 251
Abraham Lincoln Birthplace National Historic Site, Lincoln Trail, KY, 144
Academy of Natural Sciences, Philadelphia, PA, 245
Adler Planetarium & Astronomy Museum, Chicago, IL, 54
Ahwahnee Hotel, Yosemite National Park, CA, 386
Ahwahneechee Village, Yosemite National Park, CA, 386
Aladdin Hotel and Casino, Las Vegas, NV, 131
Albright Visitor Center, Yellowstone National Park, WY, 372
Alcatraz Island, San Francisco, CA, 285
American Cave Museum/Hidden River Cave, Horse Cave, KY, 180–181
American Museum of Natural History, New York, NY, 210–211
Amish Experience, Bird-in-Hand, PA, 251
Anne Rice's House, New Orleans, LA, 192
Antelope Flats Road, Grand Teton National Park, WY, 92, 94
Appalachian Trail, Great Smoky Mountains National Park, NC/TN, 106–107
Aquarium of Niagara, Niagara Falls, NY, 227
Aquarium of the Americas, New Orleans, LA, 187, 189
Arkansas Alligator Farm and Petting Zoo, Hot Springs, AR, 118
Arlington National Cemetery, Arlington, VA, 347
Art Institute of Chicago, Chicago, IL, 51
Arthur M. Sackler Gallery, Washington, D.C., 338, 340
Arthur M. Sackler Museum, Boston, MA, 20
Artpark, Niagara Falls, NY, 227
Arts and Industries Building, Washington, D.C., 340
Ash Lawn-Highland, Charlottesville, VA, 306
Asian Art Museum, San Francisco, CA, 284
Audubon Park and Zoo, New Orleans, LA, 193
Autry Museum of Western Heritage, Los Angeles, CA, 157

Back Basin, Yellowstone National Park, WY, 372
Badlands National Park, SD, 1–13
Badlands Wilderness Area, Badlands National Park, SD, 3
Barren River Dam and Lake State Resort Park, Glasgow, KY, 180
Bass Hole Boardwalk, Yarmouth Port, MA, 36
Battery Park, New York, NY, 204, 206
Battleship New Jersey, Philadelphia, PA, 244
Bayside Trail, San Diego, CA, 264
Beach Chalet, San Francisco, CA, 287
Bear Country U.S.A., Rapid City, SD, 5
Beauregard-Keyes House, New Orleans, LA, 189
Belvedere Castle, New York, NY, 210
Ben Reifel Visitor Center, Badlands National Park, SD, 3–4
Berkeley, Charles City County, VA, 361–362
Betsy Ross House, Philadelphia, PA, 241
Big Pig Dig, Badlands National Park, SD, 4
Black Heritage Trail, Boston, MA, 14
Black Hills, SD, 1–13
Black Hills Central Railroad, Southern Hills, SD, 5
Black Hills National Forest, Rapid City, SD, 5
Black Hills Wild Horse Sanctuary, Hot Springs, SD, 6
Blackfriars Playhouse, Staunton, VA, 303
Blackstone Block, Boston, MA, 17
Blaine Kern's Mardi Gras World, New Orleans, LA, 194
Blue Ridge, VA, 300–316
Boathouse Row, Philadelphia, PA, 248
Bodie Ghost Town, Yosemite National Park, CA, 389
Boston, MA, 14–32
Boston Common, Boston, MA, 14, 16
Boston Public Garden, Boston, MA, 16–17
Boston Tea Party Ship and Museum, Boston, MA, 19
Botanical Museum, Boston, MA, 21
Brewster Store, Brewster, MA, 36
Bridalveil Fall, Yosemite National Park, CA, 388
Bright Angel Point, Grand Canyon National Park, AZ, 82
Broken Boat Gold Mine, Deadwood, SC, 5
Brooklyn Bridge, New York, NY, 206
Bruton Parish Church, Colonial Williamsburg, VA, 360
Buckingham Fountain, Chicago, IL, 54
Buckstaff Bathhouse, Hot Springs National Park, AR, 118
Buffalo Bill Historical Center, Yellowstone National Park, WY, 373
Bunker Hill Monument, Boston, MA, 18
Bureau of Engraving and Printing, Washington, D.C., 340
Busch Gardens Williamsburg, Williamsburg, VA, 360–361
Busch-Reisinger Museum, Boston, MA, 21

Cable Car Museum, San Francisco, CA, 283
Cabrillo National Monument, San Diego, CA, 264
Cades Cove, Great Smoky Mountains National Park, NC/TN, 107
Caesars Palace, Las Vegas, NV, 131
California Academy of Sciences, San Francisco, CA, 287
California African-American Museum, Los Angeles, CA, 158
California Palace of the Legion of Honor, San Francisco, CA, 288
California Science Center, Los Angeles, CA, 158
Canal Street, New Orleans, LA, 189
Canyon View Information Plaza, Grand Canyon National Park, AZ, 81
Canyon Visitor Center, Yellowstone National Park, WY, 372
Cape Cod, MA, 33–49
Cape Cod Museum of Natural History, Brewster, MA, 36
Cape Cod National Seashore, Eastham, MA, 37
Cape Museum of Fine Arts, Dennis, MA, 36
Cape Royal, Grand Canyon National Park, AZ, 83
Capital Children's Museum, Washington, D.C., 343
Capitol, Colonial Williamsburg, VA, 359
Capitol, Washington, D.C., 343
Carousel Gardens, New Orleans, LA, 193
Carpenters' Hall, Philadelphia, PA, 241–242
Carson Pirie Scott, Chicago, IL, 51

Carter's Grove, Colonial Williamsburg, VA, 360
Cartoon Art Museum, San Francisco, CA, 280
Casino Niagara, Niagara Falls, Ontario, 228
Castro Theatre, San Francisco, CA, 289
Cathedral of Our Lady of the Angels, Los Angeles, CA, 158
Cave of the Winds Trip, Niagara Falls, NY, 228
Central Park Wildlife Center, New York, NY, 210
Chapel of the Transfiguration, Grand Teton National Park, WY, 94
Charles Hosmer Morse Museum of American Art, Winter Park, FL, 328
Charles Street, Boston, MA, 16
Chatham Light, Chatham, MA, 37
Chicago, IL, 50–69
Chicago Children's Museum, Chicago, IL, 55–56
Chicago Cultural Center, Chicago, IL, 51
Chicago Historical Society, Chicago, IL, 56
Chicago Office of Tourism Visitor Information Center, Chicago, IL, 51
Chicago Shakespeare Theatre, Chicago, IL, 56
Children's Museum, Boston, MA, 19
Children's Pool, San Diego, CA, 265
Chinatown, Boston, MA, 19
Chinatown, Los Angeles, CA, 159
Chinatown Gate, San Francisco, CA, 282
Chinese-American National Museum and Learning Center, San Francisco, CA, 282
Chinese Six Companies, San Francisco, CA, 282
Choo-Choo Barn, Traintown, USA, Strasburg, PA, 251
Christ Church, Philadelphia, PA, 242
Christ Church Cathedral, New Orleans, LA, 192
Circus Circus, Las Vegas, NV, 132–133
City Hall, San Francisco, CA, 285
City Lights Bookstore, San Francisco, CA, 283
City Museum, Washington, D.C., 344
City Park, New Orleans, LA, 193
CityWalk, Los Angeles, CA, 159
Cliff House, San Francisco, CA, 288
Clifton House, Niagara Falls, Ontario, 228
Clingmans Dome, Great Smoky Mountains National Park, NC/TN, 107
Coit Tower, San Francisco, CA, 283
College of William and Mary, Williamsburg, VA, 361
Colonial Parkway, Williamsburg, VA, 361
Colonial Williamsburg Visitor Center, Colonial Williamsburg, VA, 359
Colter Bay Visitor Center, Grand Teton National Park, WY, 94
Conservatory of Flowers, San Francisco, CA, 287–238
Conservatory Water, New York, NY, 210
Constitution Museum, Boston, MA, 18
Contemporary Arts Center, New Orleans, LA, 191
Copley Square, Boston, MA, 17
Copp's Hill Burying Ground, Boston, MA, 17
Corcoran Gallery of Art, Washington, D.C., 343–344
Cosmic Cavern, Eureka Springs, AR, 120
Courthouse, Colonial Williamsburg, VA, 360
Cox's Row, Washington, D.C., 346
Crater of Diamonds State Park, Hot Springs, AR, 118
Crazy Horse Memorial, Southern Hills, SD, 5
Crystal Onyx Cave and Campgrounds, Cave City, KY, 180
Cunningham Cabin Historic Site, Grand Teton National Park, WY, 94
Curry Village, Yosemite National Park, CA, 387
Custer State Park, Southern Hills, SD, 6
Cyrus McCormick Farm, Lexington, VA, 304

Dale House, Jamestown, VA, 363
Daley Center, Chicago, IL, 51
DAR Museum, Washington, D.C., 344
Declaration House, Philadelphia, PA, 242
Desert View and Watchtower, Grand Canyon National Park, AZ, 81
Devil's Hole State Park, Niagara Falls, NY, 227
Devils Postpile National Monument, Yosemite National Park, CA, 389
DeWitt Wallace Decorative Arts Gallery, Colonial Williamsburg, VA, 360
Diamond Caverns, Cave City, KY, 180
Discovery Cove, FL, 327
Disneyland, Los Angeles, CA, 160–161
Disney's California Adventure, Los Angeles, CA, 161
Dollywood, Gatlinburg, TN, 108
Downtown Disney, Los Angeles, CA, 161
Dumbarton Oaks, Washington, D.C., 346
Dutch Wonderland, Lancaster, PA, 250

Earl Gregg Swem Library, Williamsburg, VA, 361
Eastern State Penitentiary Historic Site, Philadelphia, PA, 245
Effreth's Alley, Philadelphia, PA, 242
Eisenhower National Historic Site, Gettysburg, PA, 72
El Capitan, Yosemite National Park, CA, 387
Ellen Browning Scripps Park, San Diego, CA, 265
Ellis Island, New York, NY, 206
Embarcadero, San Diego, CA, 262–263
Empire State Building, New York, NY, 208
Esplanade, Boston, MA, 16
Eureka Springs Gardens, Eureka Springs, AR, 119
Eureka Springs Historical Museum, Eureka Springs, AR, 119
Eureka Springs Model Railroad Co., Eureka Springs, AR, 119
Evans Plunge, Hot Springs, SD, 6
Evelynton Plantation, Charles City County, VA, 362
Excalibur Hotel and Casino, Las Vegas, NV, 128
Exploratorium, San Francisco, CA, 286

Fair Grounds Race Course, New Orleans, LA, 194
Faneuil Hall Marketplace, Boston, MA, 17–18
Farmers Market, Los Angeles, CA, 156
Fenway Park, Boston, MA, 20
Field Museum, Chicago, IL, 54–55
Fireman's Hall Museum, Philadelphia, PA, 242
First Church of Christ, Scientist, Boston, MA, 17
First Landing Site, Jamestown, VA, 363
First Union Science Park, Philadelphia, PA, 246
Fisherman's Wharf, San Francisco, CA, 285
Fishing Bridge Visitor Center, Yellowstone National Park, WY, 372–373
Floral Clock, Niagara Falls, Ontario, 228
Flying Tigers Warbird Air Museum, Kissimmee, FL, 328
Fogg Art Museum, Boston, MA, 21
Ford's Theatre, Washington, D.C., 344
Fordyce Bathhouse, Hot Sprigs National Park, AR, 118

Fort Niagara State Park, Niagara Falls, NY, 227
Fort Point, San Francisco, CA, 286
Franklin Court, Philadelphia, PA, 242
Franklin Delano Roosevelt Memorial, Washington, D.C., 342
Franklin Institute Science Museum, Philadelphia, PA, 246
Free Library of Philadelphia, Philadelphia, PA, 246
Freer Gallery of Art, Washington, D.C., 340
Fremont Street Experience, Las Vegas, NV, 134
French Market, New Orleans, LA, 189
Friedsam Memorial Carousel, New York, NY, 210
Frontier Culture Museum, Staunton, VA, 303

Gallier House, New Orleans, LA, 189
Garvan Woodland Gardens, Hot Springs, AR, 118
Gaslamp Quarter Association, San Diego, CA, 263
Gatlinburg Sky Lift, Gatlinburg, TN, 108
Gatorland, Kissimmee, FL, 328
GE Building, New York, NY, 208
General Lee's Headquarters, Gettysburg, PA, 72
George C. Marshall Museum, Lexington, VA, 305
Georgetown University, Washington, D.C., 346
Getty Center, Los Angeles, CA, 153
Gettysburg, PA, 70–78
Gettysburg College, Gettysburg, PA, 72
Gettysburg National Cemetery, Gettysburg, PA, 72
Ghirardelli Square, San Francisco, CA, 285
Glacier Point, Yosemite National Park, CA, 387
Glasshouse, Jamestown, VA, 363
Glen Burnie Manor House and Gardens, Winchester, VA, 302
Glen Canyon National Recreational Area, Grand Canyon National Park, AZ, 83
Goat Island, Niagara Falls, NY, 228
Golden Gate Bridge, San Francisco, CA, 286
Golden Gate Fortune Cookies Co., San Francisco, CA, 282
Governor's Palace, Colonial Williamsburg, VA, 359–360
Grace Cathedral, San Francisco, CA, 283
Granary Burying Ground, Boston, MA, 16
Grand Canyon National Park, AZ, 79–91
Grand Canyon of the Yellowstone, Yellowstone National Park, WY, 373
Grand Canyon Railway, Grand Canyon National Park, AZ, 84
Grand Central Terminal, New York, NY, 208–209
Grand Teton National Park, WY, 92–104
Grant Park, Chicago, IL, 54
Great Canadian Midway, Niagara Falls, Ontario, 228
Great Gorge Adventure, Niagara Falls, Ontario, 228
Great Smoky Mountains National Park, NC/TN, 105–115
Great Smoky Mountains National Park Headquarters, Great Smoky Mountains National Park, NC/TN, 108
Griffith Observatory and Planetarium, Los Angeles, CA, 157
Griffith Park, Los Angeles, CA, 157
Grizzly Discovery Center, Yellowstone National Park, WY, 374
Guggenheim-Hermitage Museum, Las Vegas, NV, 132
Guinness Museum of World Records, Niagara Falls, Ontario, 228

Haas-Lilienthal House, San Francisco, CA, 284
Haight-Ashbury Intersection, San Francisco, CA, 289
Half Dome, Yosemite National Park, CA, 387
Hallet's, Yarmouth Port, MA, 36
Hard Rock Hotel and Casino, Las Vegas, NV, 130
Harvard Museum of Natural History, Boston, MA, 21
Harvard University, Boston, MA, 21
Heritage Center Museum, Lancaster, PA, 250
Heritage Plantation, Sandwich, MA, 33
Hermann-Grima House, New Orleans, LA, 189
Hermits Rest, Grand Canyon National Park, AZ, 81
Hetch Hetchy Reservoir, Yosemite National Park, CA, 387
High Country, Yosemite National Park, CA, 387
Hirshhorn Museum and Sculpture Garden, Washington, D.C., 340
Historic Round Barn and Farm Market, Gettysburg, PA, 72
Hollywood & Highland, Los Angeles, CA, 157
Hollywood Entertainment Museum, Los Angeles, CA, 157
Hollywood Walk of Fame, Los Angeles, CA, 157–158
Holocaust Memorial, Boston, MA, 18
Hoover Dam, Las Vegas, NV, 134
Hornblower Dining Yachts, Los Angeles, CA, 153
Horse Cave Theatre, Horse Cave, KY, 181
Hot Creek Geologic Site, Yosemite National Park, CA, 389
Hot Springs Mountain Tower, Hot Springs, AR, 118
Hot Springs National Park, AR, 116–127
Hotel Del Coronado, San Diego, CA, 263
Humpback Rocks Visitor Center, Blue Ridge Parkway, VA, 304
Huntington Library, Art Collection, and Botanical Gardens, Los Angeles, CA, 160
Hyde Street Pier, San Francisco, CA, 285

Imperial Palace Hotel and Casino, Las Vegas, NV, 131
Ina Coolbrith Park, San Francisco, CA, 283
Independence Hall, Philadelphia, PA, 242–243
Independence Seaport Museum, Philadelphia, PA, 244
Independence Visitor Center, Philadelphia, PA, 243
Indian Arts Museum, Grand Teton National Park, WY, 94
Indian Cultural Museum, Yosemite National Park, CA, 387
Indian Museum of North America, Southern Hills, SD, 5
International Spy Museum, Washington, D.C., 345
Intrepid Sea-Air-Space Museum, New York, NY, 209
Isabella Stewart Gardner Museum, Boston, MA, 20

Jackson Lake, Grand Teton National Park, WY, 95
Jackson Square, New Orleans, LA, 189
Jackson Square, San Francisco, CA, 281
James River Visitor Center, Blue Ridge Parkway, VA, 304
Jamestown Settlement, Jamestown, VA, 363
Jamestown Visitor Center, Jamestown, VA, 363
Japan Center, San Francisco, CA, 284
Japanese House, Philadelphia, PA, 248
Japanese Tea Garden, San Francisco, CA, 288
Jean Lafitte National Park Visitor Center, New Orleans, LA, 189
Jefferson Memorial, Washington, D.C., 342
Jennie Wade House, Gettysburg, PA, 72–73

Jenny Lake, Grand Teton National Park, WY, 95
John F. Kennedy Hyannis Museum, Hyannis, MA, 35
John G. Shedd Aquarium, Chicago, IL, 55
John Hancock Center, Chicago, IL, 55
Journey Behind the Falls, Niagara Falls, Ontario, 228–229
Julia Street, New Orleans, LA, 191
Julius Sturgis Pretzel House, Lititz, PA, 252

Kennedy Compound, Hyannis, MA, 35
Kentucky Down Under/Mammoth Onyx Cave, Horse Cave, KY, 181
Kentucky Railway Museum, Lincoln Trail, KY, 145
King's Chapel, Boston, MA, 19
Knott's Berry Farm, Los Angeles, CA, 161
Kolb Studio, Grand Canyon National Park, AZ, 81
Korean War Veterans Memorial, Washington, D.C., 342
Kraft Education Center, Chicago, IL, 51

La Brea Tar Pits, Los Angeles, CA, 156
La Jolla Cove, San Diego, CA, 265
La Petit Théâtre, New Orleans, LA, 189
Lake Catherine State Park, Hot Springs, AR, 118
Lake Ouachita State Park, Hot Springs, AR, 119
Lake Pontchartrain, New Orleans, LA, 194
Land of Little Horses, Gettysburg, PA, 73
Landis Valley Museum, Lancaster, PA, 250
Las Vegas, NV, 128–142
Las Vegas Hilton, Las Vegas, NV, 133
Las Vegas National History Museum, Las Vegas, NV, 133
Le Conte Memorial Lodge, Yosemite National Park, CA, 387
Lees Ferry, Grand Canyon National Park, AZ, 84
Legoland California, San Diego, CA, 265
Liberty Bell, Philadelphia, PA, 243
Library of Congress, Washington, D.C., 343
Lied Discovery Children's Museum, Las Vegas, NV, 133
Lights of Liberty, Philadelphia, PA, 243
Lincoln Boyhood National Memorial, Lincoln Trail, IN, 145
Lincoln-Herndon Law Office Building, Lincoln Trail, IL, 146
Lincoln Home National Historic Site, Lincoln Trail, IL, 146
Lincoln Jamboree, Lincoln Trail, KY, 145
Lincoln Memorial, Washington, D.C., 342
Lincoln Memorial Garden and Nature Center, Lincoln Trail, IL, 146
Lincoln Museum, Lincoln Trail, KY, 145
Lincoln Park Zoo, Chicago, IL, 56–57
Lincoln State Park, Lincoln Trail, IN, 145
Lincoln Tomb State Historic Site, Lincoln Trail, IL, 146
The Lincoln Trail, KY/IN/IL, 143–151
Lincoln Train Museum, Gettysburg, PA, 73
Lincoln's Boyhood Home, Lincoln Trail, KY, 145
Lincoln's New Salem State Historic Site, Lincoln Trail, IL, 146
Linear Parkway, New Orleans, LA, 194
Lipan Point, Grand Canyon National Park, AZ, 81
Logan Circle, Philadelphia, PA, 246
Lombard Street, San Francisco, CA, 284
Long Beach Aquarium of the Pacific, Los Angeles, CA, 160
Longfellow National Site, Boston, MA, 21
Longue Vue House and Gardens, New Orleans, LA, 194
Looff carousel, San Francisco, CA, 281
Lookout Studio, Grand Canyon National Park, AZ, 82
Los Angeles, CA, 152–176
Los Angeles County Museum of Art (LACMA), Los Angeles, CA, 156–157
Los Angeles Zoo, Los Angeles, CA, 157
Louis Armstrong Park, New Orleans, LA, 191
Louisiana Children's Museum, New Orleans, LA, 192
Lower East Side Tenement Museum, New York, NY, 207
Lower Geyser Basin, Yellowstone National Park, WY, 373
Lundy's Lane Historical Museum, Niagara Falls, Ontario, 229
Lutheran Theological Seminary, Gettysburg, PA, 73
Luxor Hotel-Casino, Las Vegas, NV, 130

M&M's World, Las Vegas, NV, 131
Magazine, Colonial Williamsburg, VA, 359
Magic Springs and Crystal Falls, Hot Springs, AR, 118
Maid of the Mist Boat Tour, Niagara Falls, NY/Ontario, 227
Maiden Lane, San Francisco, CA, 280
Mammoth Cave Chair Lift and Guntown Mountain, Cave City, KY, 180
Mammoth Cave National Park, KY, 177–186
Mammoth Hot Springs, Yellowstone National Park, WY, 373
Mammoth Site, Hot Springs, SD, 6
Mandalay Bay Resort and Casino, Las Vegas, NV, 130
Mann's Chinese Theatre, Los Angeles, CA, 158
Marina del Ray, Los Angeles, CA, 153
Marineland, Niagara Falls, Ontario, 229
Mariposa Grove of Big Trees, Yosemite National Park, CA, 387
Marshall Field's, Chicago, IL, 51, 54
Massachusetts Audubon Wellfleet Bay Sanctuary, Wellfleet, MA, 38
Mather Point, Grand Canyon National Park, AZ, 82
Memorial Church, Jamestown, VA, 363
Memor's Ferry Historic Area, Grand Teton National Park, WY, 95
Metreon, San Francisco, CA, 280
Metropolitan Museum of Art, New York, NY, 209–210
MGM Grand, Las Vegas, NV, 130
Mid-America Science Museum, Hot Springs, AR, 118
Midway Geyser Basin, Yellowstone National Park, WY, 373
Millennium Park, Chicago, IL, 54
Mineralogical and Geological Museum, Boston, MA, 21
Mingus Mill, Great Smoky Mountains National Park, NC/TN, 108
Mirage Hotel and Casino, Las Vegas, NV, 132
Mission Dolores, San Francisco, CA, 289
Mono Lake, Yosemite National Park, CA, 389
Monomoy National Wildlife Refuge, Chatham, MA, 37
Monticello, Charlottesville, VA, 306
Montpelier, Charlottesville, VA, 306
Moose Visitor Center, Grand Teton National Park, WY, 95
Morrison Planetarium, San Francisco, CA, 287

Mosiaculture Garden and Niagara Parks Greenhouse, Niagara Falls, Ontario, 229
Mount Dora, FL, 329
Mount Moriah Cemetery, Deadwood, SD, 5
Mount Rushmore National Memorial, SD, 1–13
Mountasia Family Fun Center, Las Vegas, NV, 133
Movieland Wax Museum, Niagara Falls, Ontario, 228
Musée Conti Wax Museum, New Orleans, LA, 190
Museum of Afro-American History, Boston, MA, 16
Museum of Broadcast Communications, Chicago, IL, 51
Museum of Comparative Zoology, Boston, MA, 21
Museum of Contemporary Art, Chicago, IL, 55
Museum of Fine Arts, Boston, MA, 20
Museum of Science, Boston, MA, 16
Museum of Science and Industry, Chicago, IL, 57
Museum of Television & Radio, Los Angeles, CA, 156
Museum of the Cherokee Indian, Cherokee, NC, 108
Museum of Tolerance, Los Angeles, CA, 156

National Air and Space Museum, Washington, D.C., 340
National Archive, Washington, D.C., 345
National Bighorn Sheep Interpretive Center, Grand Teton National Park, WY, 95
National Building Museum, Washington, D.C., 345
National Civil War Wax Museum, Gettysburg, PA, 73
National Constitution Center, Philadelphia, PA, 243
National D-Day Museum, New Orleans, LA, 192
National Elk Refuge, Grand Teton National Park, WY, 95
National Gallery of Art, Washington, D.C., 340–341
National Gallery of Art Sculpture Garden, Washington, D.C., 341
National Geographic Society, Washington, D.C., 346
National Liberty Museum, Philadelphia, PA, 243–244
National Maritime Museum, San Francisco, CA, 286
National Museum of African Art, Washington, D.C., 341
National Museum of American Art, Washington, D.C., 341
National Museum of Natural History, Washington, D.C., 341
National Museum of the American Indian, Washington, D.C., 341
National Museum of Women in the Arts, Washington, D.C., 345
National Portrait Gallery, Washington, D.C., 345
National Postal Museum, Washington, D.C., 343
National Toy Train Museum, Strasburg, PA, 251
National Zoological Park, Washington, D.C., 346–347
Natural Bridge, Lexington, VA, 304–305
Natural History Museum, San Francisco, CA, 287
Natural History Museum of Los Angeles County, Los Angeles, CA, 159
Navajo Point, Grand Canyon National Park, AZ, 82
Navy Pier, Chicago, IL, 55
NBC Studios, New York, NY, 208
Nevada Fall, Yosemite National Park, CA, 388
New England Aquarium, Boston, MA, 19
New Market Battlefield State Historic Park, New Market, VA, 303
New Orleans, LA, 187–203
New Orleans Botanical Garden, New Orleans, LA, 193
New Orleans Center for Creative Arts (NOCCA), New Orleans, LA, 190
New Orleans Historic Voodoo Museum, New Orleans, LA, 190
New Orleans Museum of Art (NOMA), New Orleans, LA, 193
New Orleans School of Glassworks and Printmaking Studio, New Orleans, LA, 192
New Towne, Jamestown, VA, 363
New York, NY, 204–224
New York-New York Hotel and Casino, Las Vegas, NV, 130
Newfound Gap, Great Smoky Mountains National Park, NC/TN, 107
Niagara Falls, NY/Ontario, 225–238
Niagara Falls Botanical Gardens and School of Horticulture, Niagara Falls, Ontario, 229
Niagara Falls IMAX Theatre/The Daredevil Adventure Gallery, Niagara Falls, Ontario, 229
Niagara Parks Butterfly Conservatory, Niagara Falls, Ontario, 229
Niagara Power Project Visitor Center, Niagara Falls, NY, 227
Niagara Reservation State Park, Niagara Falls, NY, 227
Niagara Spanish Aero Car, Niagara Falls, Ontario, 229
Norris Geyser Basin, Yellowstone National Park, WY, 373
North Avenue Beach, Chicago, IL, 57
North Rim, Grand Canyon National Park, AZ, 82
Norton Simon Museum, Los Angeles, CA, 160

Ober Gatlinburg Tramway, Gatlinburg, TN, 108–109
Oconalufee Indian Village, Cherokee, NC, 108
Oconalufee Visitor Center, Great Smoky Mountains National Park, NC/TN, 107–108
Ogden Museum of Southern Art, New Orleans, LA, 192
Old Church Tower, Jamestown, VA, 363
Old Faithful, Yellowstone National Park, WY, 373
Old Fort Niagara, Niagara Falls, NY, 227
Old North Church, Boston, MA, 18
Old Point Loma Lighthouse, San Diego, CA, 264
Old South Meeting House, Boston, MA, 19
Old State Capitol State Historic Site, Lincoln Trail, IL, 146
Old State House, Boston, MA, 19
Old Town Pasadena, Los Angeles, CA, 160
Old Town San Diego State Historic Park, San Diego, CA, 265
Old Ursuline Convent, New Orleans, LA, 190
Olde Dutch Candy and Antiques, Boston, MA, 20
Olvera Street Visitors Center, Los Angeles, CA, 159
Ontario, Canada, 225–238
Orange Avenue, San Diego, CA, 263
Orange County Regional History Center, Orlando, FL, 328
Orlando, FL, 317–337
Ouachita National Forest, Hot Springs, AR, 119
Oxbow Bend, Grand Teton National Park, WY, 95
The Ozarks, AR, 116–127

Page Museum of the La Brea Tar Pits, Los Angeles, CA, 156
Palace of Fine Arts, San Francisco, CA, 286–237
Paris Las Vegas, Las Vegas, NV, 132
Park House Information, Philadelphia, PA, 248
Paul Revere House, Boston, MA, 18
Pea Ridge National Military Park, Eureka Springs, AR, 120

Peabody Museum of Archaeology and Ethnography, Boston, MA, 21
Peaks of Otter Recreation Area, Blue Ridge Parkway, VA, 304
Peggy Notebaert Nature Museum, Chicago, IL, 57
Pennsylvania Academy of the Fine Arts, Philadelphia, PA, 246
Pennsylvania Dutch Country, PA, 239–259
Pentagon, Arlington, VA, 347
People's Place, Intercourse, PA, 250
Petersen Automotive Museum, Los Angeles, CA, 157
Petrified Tree, Yellowstone National Park, WY, 373
Philadelphia, PA, 239–259
Philadelphia Museum of Art, Philadelphia, PA, 246–247
Philadelphia Zoo, Philadelphia, PA, 248
Phillips Collection, Washington, D.C., 346
Pier 16, New York, NY, 206
Pier 39, San Francisco, CA, 286
Pilgrim Monument, Provincetown, MA, 38
Pioneer Yosemite History Center, Yosemite National Park, CA, 387–388
Pima Point, Grand Canyon National Park, AZ, 83
Pipe Spring National Monument, Grand Canyon National Park, AZ, 84
Please Touch Museum, Philadelphia, PA, 247
Point Imperial, Grand Canyon National Park, AZ, 83
Precita Eyes Mural Arts and Visitors Center, San Francisco, CA, 289
Presidio, San Francisco, CA, 287
Prospect Point Observation Tower, Niagara Falls, NY, 228
Province Lands, Provincetown, MA, 38
Public Hospital, Colonial Williamsburg, VA, 360
Prudential Center Skywalk, Boston, MA, 17
Pumping Station, Chicago, IL, 56

Queen Mary, Los Angeles, CA, 160
Quigley's Castle, Eureka Springs, AR, 119

Railroad Museum of Pennsylvania, Strasburg, PA, 251
Rainbow Falls, Yosemite National Park, CA, 389
Reading Terminal Market, Philadelphia, PA, 247
Renwick Gallery, Washington, D.C., 344
Reuben H. Fleet Science Center, San Diego, CA, 262
Ribbon Fall, Yosemite National Park, CA, 388
The Rink, New Orleans, LA, 192
Ripley's Believe It or Not Museum and the New Ripley's Moving Theatre, Niagara Falls, Ontario, 228
Rittenhouse Square, Philadelphia, PA, 247
RiverLink Ferry, Philadelphia, PA, 244
Riverwalk Marketplace, New Orleans, LA, 192
Roaring Fork Motor Nature Trail, Great Smoky Mountains National Park, NC/TN, 106
Roberts Prairie Dog Town and Overlook, Badlands National Park, SD, 4
Robinson-Rose House, San Diego, CA, 265
Rodeo Drive, Los Angeles, CA, 156
Rollins College, Winter Park, FL, 328
Rooftop@Yerba Buena Gardens, San Francisco, CA, 280

Sahara Hotel and Casino, Las Vegas, NV, 134
St. Louis Cathedral, New Orleans, LA, 190
St. Louis Cemeteries, New Orleans, LA, 191
St. Patrick's Church, New Orleans, LA, 192
St. Paul's Chapel, New York, NY, 206
Salt Pond Visitor Center, Eastham, MA, 37
San Diego, CA, 260–277
San Diego Harbor Excursion, San Diego, CA, 263
San Diego Natural History Museum, San Diego, CA, 262
San Diego Wild Animal Park, San Diego, CA, 265
San Diego Zoo, San Diego, CA, 262
San Francisco, CA, 278–299
San Francisco Museum of Modern Art (SFMOMA), San Francisco, CA, 281
San Francisco Zoo, San Francisco, CA, 288
Sandwich Boardwalk, Sandwich, MA, 35
Santa Monica Pier, Los Angeles, CA, 153
Scenic Highway 7, Hot Springs, AR, 119
Schriver House, Gettysburg, PA, 73
Scott Street, San Diego, CA, 264
Seaport Village, San Diego, CA, 263
Sears Tower, Chicago, IL, 54
SeaWorld of California, San Diego, CA, 264
Second City, Chicago, IL, 57
Sentinel Dome, Yosemite National Park, CA, 388
Sert Gallery, Boston, MA, 21
Shenandoah Valley, VA, 300–316
Sherwood Forest, Charles City County, VA, 362
Shirley, Charles City County, VA, 362
Shooting of Wild Bill Hickok, Deadwood, SD, 5
Showcase Mall, Las Vegas, NV, 130
Signal Mountain Road, Grand Teton National Park, WY, 94
Six Flags Magic Mountain, Los Angeles, CA, 159
Skydeck, Chicago, IL, 54
Skyline Drive, Shenandoah National Park, VA, 302
Skyline Stage, Chicago, IL, 56
Skylon Tower, Niagara Falls, Ontario, 229
Smithsonian American Art Museum, Washington, D.C., 345
Smithsonian Institute Building, Washington, D.C., 341
Smoky Mountain Gold and Ruby Mine, Cherokee, NC, 108
Soldiers' National Museum, Gettysburg, PA, 73
South Street Seaport Museum, New York, NY, 206
South Tufa Walk, Yosemite National Park, CA, 389
Spanish Plaza, New Orleans, LA, 192
Splendid China, Kisimmee, FL, 328
Spreckels Mansion, San Francisco, CA, 284
Springfield Children's Museum, Lincoln Trail, IL, 146
State House, Boston, MA, 16
Statler Brothers Museum, Staunton, VA, 303
Statue of Liberty, New York, NY, 206–207
Steinhart Aquarium, San Francisco, CA, 287
Stonewall Jackson House, Lexington, VA, 305
Stonewall Jackson's Headquarters Museum, Winchester, VA, 302
Storybook Island, Rapid City, SD, 5
Storyland, New Orleans, LA, 194
Strasburg Rail Road, Strasburg, PA, 251
Stratosphere Hotel Tower and Casino, Las Vegas, NV, 134
Strybing Arboretum & Botanical Gardens, San Francisco, CA, 288
Studio Inferno Glassworks, New Orleans, LA, 190
Sugarlands Visitor Center, Great Smoky Mountains National Park, NC/TN, 108

Supreme Court Building, Washington, D.C., 343

Tactile Dome, San Francisco, CA, 286
Telegraph Hill, San Francisco, CA, 283
Third Street Promenade, Los Angeles, CA, 153
Thorncrown Chapel, Eureka Springs, AR, 119
Times Square, New York, NY, 209
Tin How Temple, San Francisco, CA, 282
Trailview Overlook, Grand Canyon National Park, AZ, 83
Transamerica Pyramid, San Francisco, CA, 281
Travel Town, Los Angeles, CA, 157
Treasure Island Las Vegas, Las Vegas, NV, 132
Treasure Island Pirate Show, Las Vegas, NV, 132
Tribune Tower, Chicago, IL, 56
Trinity Church, Boston, MA, 17
Tuolumne Meadows, Yosemite National Park, CA, 388
Turpentine Creek Wildlife Refuge, Eureka Springs, AR, 119–120
Tusayan Ruin and Museum, Grand Canyon National Park, AZ, 83
20Q, Intercourse, PA, 250

UCLA Fowler Museum of Cultural History, Los Angeles, CA, 153
UCLA Hammer Museum, Los Angeles, CA, 153
Under the Prairie, Lincoln Trail, IL, 146
Union Square, San Francisco, CA, 280
United Nations Headquarters, New York, NY, 209
United States Botanic Garden, Washington, D.C., 341–342
United States Holocaust Memorial Museum, Washington, D.C., 342
United States Marine Corps War Memorial, Arlington, VA, 347
Universal Orlando Resort, FL, 317–337
Universal Studios Hollywood, Los Angeles, CA, 159
University Museum of Archaeology and Anthropology, Philadelphia, PA, 249
University of California, Los Angeles (UCLA), Los Angeles, CA, 153
University of Chicago, Chicago, IL, 57–58
University of Virginia, Charlottesville, VA, 306
USS *Becuna*, Philadelphia, PA, 244
USS *Constitution*, Boston, MA, 18
USS *Olympia*, Philadelphia, PA, 244–245

Valley Forge National Historical Park, Philadelphia, PA, 249
Valley Visitor Center, Yosemite National Park, CA, 388
Venetian Resort-Hotel-Casino, Las Vegas, NV, 132
Venice Boardwalk, Los Angeles, CA, 153
Vernal Falls, Yosemite National Park, CA, 388
Vietnam Veterans Memorial, Washington, D.C., 342
Virginia Discovery Museum, Charlottesville, VA, 306
Virginia Military Institute Museum, Lexington, VA, 305

Wall Drug, Badlands National Park, SD, 4
Walt Disney World Resort, FL, 317–337
Warner Bros. Studios, Los Angeles, CA, 159
Washington, D.C., 338–357
Washington and Lee University, Lexington, VA, 305
Washington Monument, Washington, D.C., 342–343
Washington National Cathedral, Washington, D.C., 346
Washington Square Park, New Orleans, LA, 190
Washington State Park, New York, NY, 208
Water Country USA, Williamsburg, VA, 361
Water Tower, Chicago, IL, 56
Wawona Hotel, Yosemite National Park, CA, 388
Wekiwa Springs State Park, Winter Park, FL, 328
Wells Fargo Bank History Museum, San Francisco, CA, 281–282
Westin St. Francis Hotel, San Francisco, CA, 280
Westover, Charles City County, VA, 362
Whirlpool Jet Boat Tours, Niagara Falls, Ontario, 229–230
Whirlpool State Park, Niagara Falls, NY, 228
White House, Washington, D.C., 344
Wilbur Chocolate Company's Candy Americana Museum and Factory Candy Outlet, Lititz, PA, 252
Williamsburg, VA, 358–369
Wissahickon, Philadelphia, PA, 248–249
WonderWorks, International Drive, FL, 328
Woodrow Wilson Birthplace and Museum, Staunton, VA, 303
Woods Hole Oceanographic Institute (WHOI), Woods Hole, MA, 35
World Trade Center site, New York, NY, 207
Wren Building, Williamsburg, VA, 361

Yaki Point, Grand Canyon National Park, AZ, 83
Yellowstone Lake, Yellowstone National Park, WY, 373
Yellowstone National Park, WY, 370–383
Yerba Buena Gardens, San Francisco, CA, 281
York River State Park, Williamsburg, VA, 361
Yorktown Battlefield, Yorktown, VA, 363–364
Yorktown Victory Center, Yorktown, VA, 364
Yosemite Mountain–Sugar Pine Railroad, Yosemite National Park, CA, 389
Yosemite Museum, Yosemite National Park, CA, 388
Yosemite National Park, CA, 384–399

Zeum, San Francisco, CA, 281
Zoological-Botanical Park, Las Vegas, NV, 133